Systems Analysis and Design:

Hoffer/George/Valacich, *Modern Systems Analysis and Design 3/e*

Marakas, *Systems Analysis and Design: An Active Approach*

Valacich/George/Hoffer, *Essentials of Systems Analysis & Design*

Kendall & Kendall, *Systems Analysis and Design 5/e*

Stamper/Case, *Business Data Communications 6/e*

Stamper, *Local Area Networks 3/e*

Decision Support Systems:

Marakas, *Decision Support Systems in the 21st Century 2/e*

Turban & Aronson, *Decision Support Systems and Intelligent Systems 6/e*

Telecommunications, Networking and Business Data Communications:

Panko, *Business Data Networks and Telecommunications 4/e*

Data Mining:

Marakas, *Modern Data Warehousing, Mining, and Visualization: Core Concepts*

Request desk copies for evaluation through your local Prentice Hall representative or by email at CIS Service@prenhall.com

DECISION SUPPORT SYSTEMS IN THE 21st CENTURY

SECOND EDITION

DECISION SUPPORT SYSTEMS
IN THE 21st CENTURY

George M. Marakas

Kelley School of Business
Indiana University

Prentice
Hall

Upper Saddle River, NJ 07458

Library of Congress Cataloging-in-Publication Data

Marakas, George M.
  Decision support systems / George M. Marakas.—2nd ed.
    p. cm.
  Includes index.
  ISBN 0-13-092206-4
  1. Decision support systems. 2. Database management. 3. Data mining. I. Title.

HD30.213.M36 2002
658.4′038′0285574-dc21   2002021821

Executive Editor: Robert Horan
Publisher: Natalie Anderson
Project Manager: Kyle Hannon
Editorial Assistant: Maat Van Uitert
Media Project Manager: Joan Waxman
Senior Marketing Manager: Sharon Turkovich
Marketing Assistant: Scott Patterson
Managing Editor (Production): John Roberts
Production Editor: Kelly Warsak
Permissions Coordinator: Suzanne Grappi
Associate Director, Manufacturing: Vincent Scelta
Production Manager: Arnold Vila
Manufacturing Buyer: Michelle Klein
Cover Design: Kiwi Design
Cover Illustration/Photo: Getty Images, Inc./PhotoDisc, Inc.
Composition: BookMasters, Inc.
Full-Service Project Management: BookMasters, Inc.
Printer/Binder: Courier
Cover Printer: Phoenix Color Corp.

Pearson Education LTD.
Pearson Education Australia PTY, Limited
Pearson Education Singapore, Pte. Ltd
Pearson Education North Asia Ltd
Pearson Education, Canada, Ltd
Pearson Educación de Mexico, S.A. de C.V.
Pearson Education–Japan
Pearson Education Malaysia, Pte. Ltd

10 9 8 7 6 5 4 3 2
ISBN 0-13-092206-4

This book is dedicated to Marti, Jim, and Bernie.
Thank you for your love and friendship.

BRIEF CONTENTS

CONTENTS

PREFACE

We face decisions every day. The really good news about making decisions is that most of the ones encountered in our daily lives are both routine and relatively clear-cut. What clothes to wear, what to have for breakfast, what movie to watch on television, or what food to buy at the grocery are all typical of the day-to-day decisions that confront us. The bad news is that, although important, these decisions do not resemble the type that we must face in the course of pursuing our chosen occupation. We will not get paid for being able to decide what to wear to work. As managers, we establish our worth with our organizations by being able to cope with decisions such as whether to invest in an emerging technology that could create significant competitive advantage for the firm, or how we can best deploy the limited human resources available for a given project, or what mix of products is best for the current and future market conditions. In other words, the really important decisions are often difficult to make and require both a great deal of information and an increased level of decision support, which brings us to what this book is all about: making and supporting managerial decisions.

CONCEPT AND PURPOSE

This text provides a foundation for teaching the subject of decision support systems (DSSs) from a cognitive processes and decision-making perspective. The contents emphasize managerial applications and the implication of decision support technologies on those issues.

Gorry and Scott Morton (1989) are often credited for the classic definition of a DSS:

> Decision support systems couple the intellectual resources of individuals with the capabilities of the computer to improve the quality of decisions. [They comprise] a computer-based support system for management decision makers who deal with semi-structured problems. (p. 60)

I find it somewhat counterintuitive that the definition of the subject is written from a user's perspective, yet the texts available to teach the subject to students in business schools tend to be written from a designer's perspective. In response, this text places strong emphasis on helping the student thoroughly understand the "support" aspect of a DSS. The content focuses on a distinctly "real-world" orientation that emphasizes application and implementation over design and development in all topic areas. The manager of tomorrow does not need to understand DSS design, which is the domain of the computer scientist and the systems analyst. Rather, the skills necessary relate to the effective and strategic application of decision support technologies to advance the quality of problem identification and the associated solutions. Taking a multidisciplinary user/manager approach, this text looks at decisions and technologies necessary to support those decisions in the twenty-first century. The coverage of decision making and cognitive processes includes such topics as models of decision making, biases and heuristics, creativity enhancement, decision strategies, simulation, and discovery. This book reflects an incorporation of the best components of the leading texts on decision support while additionally providing coverage of topics not previously broached (most notably, data visualization and mining).

In short, this book was motivated by my belief in the need to integrate our knowledge of decision making with the application of decision support technology. Application and understanding of use are, and will continue to be, more important to our managers of today and tomorrow than design.

WHO SHOULD USE THIS BOOK

This book is directed to business school students who aspire to a career in management with a firm that is a significant user of technology or is a member of a technology-driven industry—in others words, all students in business school. The primary course targets for this text are upper-level undergraduate or graduate DSS electives. These types of courses are regularly offered at 4-year universities as well as many community colleges. Ideally, students should have completed an introductory MIS program and possibly a semester of systems analysis and design before moving on to a focus on DSSs. In addition, the further students are in their business curriculum, the more relevant the decision-making perspective of the text becomes. In addition to being directed to students, many of the chapters in this text offer a good reference for practitioners in the course of their daily decision-making activities.

ELEMENTS OF PEDAGOGY

The text makes appropriate use of many traditional pedagogical features commonly found in top business school curricula. The writing style is intended to strike a useful balance between a professional and conversational approach. The text uses graphics and examples of each concept introduced extensively throughout. Each chapter contains an introductory minicase highlighting the concepts introduced in that chapter. The end-of-chapter structure contains a summary of the key concepts introduced, review questions and problems, and additional support readings. A brief description of each of the pedagogical features of the text is listed here.

Chapter Learning Objectives
A statement of learning objectives for each chapter is presented in both performance and behavioral terms. In other words, the objectives state what the student should be capable of doing and understanding as a result of reading the chapter.

Chapter Minicase
The minicases are all derived from actual situations and were selected to allow the student a point of reference for the material about to be presented in the chapter. In addition, each minicase makes specific reference to each of the key players in the sce-

nario so that additional investigation using a variety of research tools could be conducted by either an individual student or a student team to further explore the situation presented.

Figures and Tables

Clear, carefully designed figures and tables can aid in the student's understanding of the material. Wherever possible, the diagrams contained in each chapter are not only referenced in the body of the text but are positioned in such a way that they serve as a repeated visual reference for the textual discussion.

Narrative Vignettes

To further the explanation of some of the concepts associated with the process of making a decision, the technique of narrative vignette is employed. Here, a situation using a fictitious cast of characters is presented to allow the student not only to see how the particular technique under discussion is applied but also to relate it to a set of circumstances or a context in which it might be considered relevant or applicable.

Data Mining and Data Visualization Exercises

New to this edition is the bundling of Megaputer's PolyAnalyst and TextAnalyst software. Tutorials found on the supplied CD focus on the component algorithms contained within the applications. Several chapters of the text incorporate exercises that use actual large-scale data sets supplied by Megaputer specifically for this text. In working through these exercises, students receive hands-on experience with actual data mining and data visualization applications.

Key Concepts

Immediately following each chapter summary is an outline of the key concepts presented in the chapter in order of their appearance. This section can aid the student in reviewing the material contained in the chapter in preparation for class discussion or examination.

Questions for Review

Each chapter contains a list of 10 to 20 questions intended to support student retention and understanding of the material contained in the chapter. Each question is phrased in such a manner that a detailed and precise answer can be readily found in the chapter. Sample responses to each question are available in the instructor sections of the World Wide Web (WWW) site for the text.

Further Discussion

Several questions at the end of each chapter expand upon the material presented to allow the student to engage in a richer thought process and discussion than would occur using the review questions. Each of the discussion questions can be used to engage students in an open class discussion, and many of them can be easily expanded into individual or team miniprojects.

Companion Web Site

The companion Web site for this text is located at www.prenhall.com/marakas. This extensive resource contains direct links to DSS-related Internet sites. To further enhance the learning process, the links are organized in the same manner as the text and are categorized according to their direct relevance to a particular section within each chapter. As such, each section of each chapter can be expanded as necessary by using the Internet resources associated with that section to allow for exploration or greater focus on a particular subject.

NEW IN THE SECOND EDITION

Several significant changes have been made in this second edition of the text. Most notable is the inclusion of three completely new chapters covering topics related to intelligent software agents, DSS system development, and building data warehouses. In addition, many of the chapters from the first edition were revised to reflect the state-of-the-art in DSS design and implementation.

The second major change to this new edition is the inclusion of Megaputer's PolyAnalyst and TextAnalyst data mining and visualization software applications. This software suite represents the leading edge in data mining and visualization applications and is being distributed exclusively with this textbook. To purchase a commercial version of this software would cost more than $10,000. The version included with the text is fully enabled but has a time element built into it such that the software will only be available for use by students during the semester in which they are studying with this text. Included with the Megaputer applications is access to several actual data sets to be used in both the tutorials for the application and for many of the Megaputer exercises included at the end of relevant chapters.

IMPORTANT NOTE: The software bundled with this text is intended for use only in conjunction with adoption or purchase of this text. Following the installation and registration process, the software will be fully functional for a period of 6 months from the date of the installation. The software cannot be copied to another machine or re-installed without purchasing an additional software license.

NOTE TO THE INSTRUCTOR

Companion Web Site (www.prenhall.com/marakas)

The instructor-accessible sections of the Web site contain a number of useful support elements and materials. PowerPoint slide files intended for use in preparing class lectures are provided for each chapter.

The review questions found in the text are also posted online so students can conveniently e-mail their answers directly to their professors. In addition, several data sets and sample software packages are either stored or linked to in the instructor section of the site. These resources can be used to create projects of any length or complexity as well as in-class demonstrations of actual DSS-related software applications.

Access to the instructor section of the Web site requires a valid user ID and password to enter. You simply need to register yourself as the instructor of the course by going to the Web site and completing the initial instructor registration process. Upon completion of the process, your registration request will be forwarded to your sales representative for validation. If you have any problem with your authorization, please contact your Prentice Hall sales representative.

INSTRUCTOR'S RESOURCE CD-ROM

The Instructor's Manual, Test Item File, and PowerPoint slides are conveniently found on the Instructor's Resource CD-ROM. The Instructor's Manual and PowerPoint slides are also available for download from the secure faculty section of the Marakas Web site.

MEGAPUTER POLYANALYST AND TEXTANALYST SOFTWARE

Also note that the Megaputer software bundled with this text is designed to be installed on one machine only and, upon completion of the installation and registration process, will operate for a period of 6 months from the date of installation. Sample copies of the software for review can be obtained from your Prentice Hall representative.

CHAPTER DESCRIPTIONS

Chapter 1—Introduction to Decision Support Systems

The first chapter introduces the concept of a DSS and explains each of the commonly associated component elements. Also included is a brief history of the evolution of the DSS to the present day. Additionally, the chapter includes a discussion of the various types and categories of DSSs that are currently available and in use.

Chapter 2—Decisions and Decision Makers

This chapter focuses attention on the decision makers and positions them as an integral part of the DSS environment. Issues such as decision styles, effectiveness of decisions, and the types of support that can be provided by a DSS are discussed. We also focus on the concept of a decision and the process by which it is made. Basic decision theory is introduced and related issues including bounded rationality, biases and heuristics, and fundamental cognitive processes are discussed. In addition, the student is introduced to the concepts of effectiveness and efficiency with a discussion that focuses on comparing and contrasting these often confusing characteristics of a decision.

Chapter 3—Decisions in the Organization

The third chapter focuses on the organization. Because it is in this environment and context that most managerial decisions will be made, it is important to understand the basic concept of an organization and to explore many of its facets including culture, power and politics, and the types of "organizational level" decisions that might be encountered.

Chapter 4—Modeling Decision Processes

The various common techniques employed in the modeling of decision processes are presented along with several examples of common decision model structures. Also in this chapter is a discussion of probability and methods for forecasting probabilistic events that may be associated with a complex managerial decision.

Chapter 5—Group Decision Support and Groupware Technologies

This chapter begins a series of chapters that each focuses on a particular aspect of decision support technologies. We begin with a thorough exploration of the process of group decision making and conclude with identification and explanation of various types of multiparticipant decision-making (MDM) technologies.

Chapter 6—Executive Information Systems

Continuing the focus on specific DSS technologies, this chapter looks at the domain of the executive and the application of DSS technology to the development and application of an executive information system (EIS). Coverage includes a definition of EIS technology, a brief history of its evolution, and the unique characteristics of executive-level decisions and decision makers, as well as issues related to the successful introduction of an EIS into an organizational environment.

Chapter 7—Expert Systems and Artificial Intelligence

A brief overview of the concept of expertise begins this chapter. A thorough discussion of the elements of artificial intelligence and expert systems follows. The chapter concludes with a look at the issues associated with designing, building, and evaluating an expert system. Appended to Chapter 7 is a chronological synopsis of expert system technologies.

Chapter 8—Knowledge Engineering and Acquisition

Chapter 8 extends the discussion of expert systems by focusing on the concept of knowledge and the methods by which it is acquired and codified in an expert system's knowledge base.

Chapter 9—Machines That Can Learn

The newest members of the world of artificial intelligence and decision support systems are the focus of this chapter. The concepts of fuzzy logic and linguistic ambiguity are introduced in detail as a precursor to a discussion of artificial neural networks and genetic algorithms. Appended to Chapter 9 is an overview of a popular software application within this realm. Following this, a mathematical derivation of the most popular artificial neural network learning algorithm is provided.

Chapter 10—The Data Warehouse

This chapter and the next introduce the hottest topics in decision support systems today: the data warehouse and data mining. Chapter 10 thoroughly covers the basic concepts of data warehousing and discusses several commercial data warehousing products.

Chapter 11—Data Mining and Data Visualization

Extending the concepts introduced in Chapter 10, this chapter looks at the realm of data mining and complex pattern extraction. The concept of online analytical processing (OLAP) and its variations are introduced. In addition, the chapter contains a discussion of the techniques used to mine data, their current limitations, and their application in data visualization contexts.

New to this edition is the inclusion of several examples and student problem sets that make use of the bundled PolyAnalyst and TextAnalyst software application from Megaputer. Although optional on the part of the instructor, these exercises and tutorials provide a rich, interactive learning environment for students to actually experience data mining and data visualization techniques using real data sets from real-world problem settings.

This book is the only DSS text available that includes a real commercially available data mining and data visualization software package and integrates it into the content and pedagogy.

Chapter 12—Designing and Building the Data Warehouse

Chapter 12, also new to this edition, delves deeper into the processes, procedures, tools, and techniques commonly found in conjunction with the development of an organizational data warehouse. This material allows students to better understand the unique challenges associated with this new and powerful approach to data storage.

Chapter 13—The Systems Perspective of a DSS

Still another new addition to this text, Chapter 13 presents a variety of issues associated with the predevelopment activities of a modern DSS. In this chapter, we explore the concept of a systems perspective, the DSS information system architecture, and the role of the Internet in DSS design. In keeping with the needs of our adopters, this chapter brings a greater balance between the design and development aspects of a modern DSS and the processes associated with managerial application of the software.

Chapter 14—Designing and Building Decision Support Systems

The topic of decision support, even in its most applied sense, would not be complete without a discussion of the strategies and tools necessary to bring the system to life. This chapter is the first of a two-part focus on the issues associated with the design and development of a modern DSS.

Chapter 15—Implementing and Integrating Decision Support Systems

Chapter 15 concludes our focus on DSS development issues by looking at the activities necessary to effectively implement, integrate, and evaluate an organizational DSS.

Chapter 16—Creative Decision Making and Problem Solving

As we begin to close our in-depth focus on decision making and problem solving, it becomes necessary to include a discussion of one of the most elusive yet critical elements to successful managerial decision making: creativity. This chapter, greatly expanded from the first edition, looks at the concept of creativity and the various methods of enhancing it. Following it is a discussion of a related topic, intelligent agents.

Chapter 17—Intelligent Software Agents, Bots, Delegation, and Agency

Also in this edition, we greatly expanded our coverage and discussion of the new world of delegation and the role that it will play in the DSS of tomorrow. A thorough overview of the various types of intelligent software agents, their design, construction, and applications is presented.

It is the only currently available DSS text to present this material at this level of detail.

Chapter 18—Decision Support in the Twenty-First Century

This capstone chapter looks at the DSS of tomorrow. By reviewing where we have been to date, the chapter guides us into a brief glimpse of what the future holds for DSSs, expert systems and artificial intelligence, and executive information systems.

ACKNOWLEDGMENTS

Having lived through my first and second effort at writing a textbook, and now experiencing my first revision, I am still learning a great deal and am still stumbling on occasion. Without the constant help of a number of people correcting my mistakes, answering my questions, contributing to the vast amount of required labor, and reassuring me in times of self-doubt, I do not believe this book would exist, let alone a second edition of it.

What follows is a brief, but nonetheless heartfelt, expression of my deepest gratitude and dedication to those people who were instrumental in the development of this project.

First and foremost, I wish to thank my biggest supporters, my parents, George and Joan Marakas. Thank you; I am forever in your debt.

To my daughter, Stephanie, who throughout her entire life always insisted that her dad can fix anything, even his own mistakes. Stephanie, thank you for never being shy about expressing your pride in me. Now that you are about to embark on your career as an educator, don't forget to surround yourself with people who care about you.

To my best everything, Debra Herbenick, who quite literally found herself constantly having a stack of papers thrust under her nose accompanied by the request that she provide her editing talents and her constructive suggestions during the creation of the first edition of this text. Without her help, I would not have been able to create a readable manuscript and my message would not have been as clearly delivered. Even though you were spared the agony of reading every word of this revision, I am constantly reminded of the lasting contribution you have made to this work. Thank you, LB, for touching feet, hands, and heart. Your devotion to me is forever embedded in this book.

To my army of assistants—Yu-Ting "Caisy" Hung, Ji-Tsung "Ben" Wu, Han-Chieh "Harry" Jiang, Yu-Lin "Emily" Lin—who invested endless hours in the final compilation of this text and its supporting Web site. You will be a part of this book, and whatever contribution it makes, forever.

To my mentors, Dan Robey and Joyce Elam. In giving of yourself to teach me, you taught me how to teach others. Without your wisdom and guidance I would be lost.

To Bob Horan, David Alexander, Kyle Hannon, Sharon Turkovich, Beth Spencer, JoAnn DeLuca, and the rest of the gang from Prentice Hall: Your combined contagious energy and excitement gave me the courage to write the first edition and to successfully execute its first of, hopefully, many revisions.

To the newest members of this family, Sergei Ananyan and Brian Moore from Megaputer Corporation: Your enthusiasm and hard work made this text better and made the learning experience for all students who experience it much richer indeed.

I am also indebted to a number of people who reviewed the manuscript, offering their praise and suggestions for improvement. Although many of them I have never met, I hope to change that in the near future: William R. Bruyn, DeVry Institute of Technology; Ranjit Bose, University of New Mexico; Fatemeh Zahedi, University of Wisconsin; Jerry Fjermestad, New Jersey Institute of Technology; Madjid Tavana, LaSalle University; B. S. Vijayaraman, The University of Akron; Bradley C. Wheeler, Indiana University; Russell K. H. Ching, California State University, Sacramento; Tom Wichser, DeVry Institute of Technology; Gustav Lundberg, Duquesne University; Ta Tao Chuang, Wichita State University; Fave Teer, James Madison University; Jennifer Williams, University of Southern Indiana; Jim Hightower, California State University Fullerton; and Jung P. Shim, Mississippi State University.

In closing this rather lengthy, but quite necessary, acknowledgment, I would be remiss if I failed to thank my good friends and colleagues Brad Wheeler, Steven Hornik, Richard Johnson, and Deric Rush. Each of you, in your own unique way, gave me energy with your friendship and comfort with your faith.

Finally, my sincere appreciation and thanks go out to all my students who attended my classes and assisted me in my development of ideas, examples, explanations, and content. You are my true motivation and I will always remember you.

ABOUT THE AUTHOR

George M. Marakas is an associate professor of information systems and the BAT Faculty Fellow in Global IT Strategy at the Kelley School of Business at Indiana University in Bloomington. His teaching expertise includes systems analysis and design, technology-assisted decision making, managing IS resources, behavioral IS research methods, and data visualization and decision support. In addition, Marakas is an active researcher in the area of systems analysis methods, data mining and visualization, creativity enhancement, conceptual data modeling, and computer self-efficacy.

Marakas received his doctorate in information systems from Florida International University in Miami and his MBA from Colorado State University. Prior to his academic career, he enjoyed a highly successful career in the banking and real estate industries. His corporate experience includes senior management positions with Continental Illinois National Bank and the FDIC. In addition, Marakas served as president and CEO for CMC Group, Inc., a major RTC management contractor in Miami, for 3 years.

During his tenure at the University of Maryland and now at Indiana University, Marakas distinguished himself both through his research and in the classroom. He received numerous national teaching awards, and his research has appeared in the top journals in his field.

Beyond his academic endeavors, Marakas is also an active consultant and serves as an advisor to a number of organizations including the Central Intelligence Agency, the Department of the Treasury, the Department of Defense, British-American Tobacco, Xavier University, Citibank Asia-Pacific, Nokia Corporation, Eli Lilly Corporation, and United Information Systems, among many others. His consulting activities are concentrated primarily on e-commerce strategy, workflow reengineering, CASE tool integration, and global IT strategy formation. He is a Novell Certified Network Engineer and has been involved in the corporate beta testing program for Microsoft Corporation since 1990. Marakas is also an active member of a number of professional IS organizations, an avid golfer, a PADI-certified divemaster, and a member of Pi Kappa Alpha fraternity.

DECISION SUPPORT SYSTEMS
IN THE 21st CENTURY

1
INTRODUCTION TO DECISION SUPPORT SYSTEMS

Learning Objectives

◆ Understand the definition of a decision support system (DSS) based on three common themes: problem structure, decision outcome, and managerial control

◆ Understand the benefits and limitations of DSS use

◆ Be familiar with the history of DSSs

◆ Grasp the five basic components of a DSS

◆ Learn the roles of data and model management systems

◆ Understand the functions of a DSS knowledge base

◆ Learn the importance of the user interface in a DSS

◆ Learn the user roles and patterns of DSS use

◆ Gain an understanding of the categories and classes of DSSs that are essential in designing or implementing a new system

MERVYN'S DEPARTMENT STORES

Faced with increasing competition from discounters, department stores must reconsider the best way to secure and maintain a competitive advantage. Mervyn's, a leading clothing retailer with more than 280 stores in the United States, uses a sophisticated decision support system (DSS) to help its analysts to identify trend-right products and facilitate quick decisions.

Although existing systems at Mervyn's provided large amounts of data, the challenge was to construct a system that would effectively integrate and distill that data into mission-critical information for decision making. Inadequate data access and analysis capabilities in their earlier systems prevented managers from exploiting the wealth of information buried in Mervyn's transaction data.

Mervyn's need for quick access to 300 to 700 gigabytes of data compounded this problem. Performing sophisticated analyses within a reasonable time frame on a data set of this size was beyond the scope of most existing decision support technologies. The solution required query performance optimization and various parallel software schemes new to decision support.

Mervyn's also needed to standardize business analyses for more meaningful comparisons. Sue Little, manager of Merchandising Planning and Logistics Systems at Mervyn's, says, "We've never had data where units and dollars matched. Buyers looked at everything from a dollar perspective and Inventory Management saw everything from a unit perspective. There was never anything that tied the two kinds of numbers together easily."

To solve these problems, MicroStrategy, a manufacturer of DSS development software, and Mervyn's used DSS Agent (a development application manufactured and sold by Micro-Strategy) to develop the Decision Maker's Workbench (DMW). This DSS application allows for trend, performance, and inventory stock analyses. Analysts can see, by ad zone, how product sales peak and valley over seasons, or how they vary from region to region. These data help them decide when and where to peak or deplete inventory. Through its use of symmetric multiprocessing hardware and parallel query processing technology, DMW reduced the time required to perform this task from an hour to less than a minute, helping Mervyn's realize its strategic aim of securing a competitive advantage through timely decision making.

Sue Little comments, "DMW let us look at different types of merchandise together, online, at the atomic level, in either dollars or units. We're finally comparing apples with apples, and we're now spending only 10 percent of our time gathering data and 90 percent acting upon it, rather than the other way around."

The DMW application incorporates features such as data surfing, drill down, intelligent agents, and alerts. Mervyn's application includes maps that display geography-based exception reporting and executive views that summarize business trends and exceptions in a newspaper-like interface. DMW includes forecasting capabilities, enabling end users to develop what-if scenarios by performing ad hoc analyses on query results.

The study of decision support systems (DSSs for short) is not about computers. Although they play an integral role in the DSS world, computers are just one part of the picture. The study of DSSs is really about people—about how people think and make decisions, as well as how they act on and react to those decisions. The DSS field is one of the few information systems (IS) fields that can claim both identifiable roots and a clear focus. Decision support systems are designed, built, and used to assist in the activity that they are named for: supporting the decision-making process. They are not, however, intended to make the decisions themselves, although we will see examples of DSSs that do almost exactly that. The real purpose of a DSS is to provide support to the decision maker during the process of making a decision. Therefore, when you study DSSs, you study people, decisions, and how those decisions are made.

1-1: DSS DEFINED

COMMON CHARACTERISTICS

This section offers a definition of decision support system, but first we need to look at some characteristics common to most, if not all, DSS applications. Table 1-1 contains a list of those attributes.

As you can see, the typical DSS serves many functions, which makes arriving at a simple but comprehensive definition of a DSS more difficult than it may first appear. In fact, you can probably find as many definitions as you can find books on the subject. The good news is that the various definitions address some common themes, and a focus on those themes should yield a good working definition of the concept.

The first of those themes is problem structure. This dimension focuses on the degree to which a decision or decision-making situation displays certain structural characteristics. For example, in the traditional view of this dimension, a highly structured decision situation includes easily determined objectives that are not subject to conflict, clearly defined or select alternative courses of action, and ascertainable outcomes. Conversely, in a highly unstructured decision the objectives of the situation often conflict, the alternatives available to the decision maker are difficult to isolate, and the effect of a particular course of action or selection of an alternative carries with it a high degree of uncertainty. The role of the DSS is to provide support to the decision maker on the "structurable" portions of the decision. With this support, the decision maker is free to focus his or her cognitive resources on the truly unstructured portions of the problem—those portions that, given the limits of technology to execute the complex problem-solving strategies contained in human memory, are better left for resolution by human decision makers. The decision processes employed in addressing the unstructured portions of a decision situation can be thought of as the human processes we do not yet understand well enough to effectively simulate via automation. More on that will be discussed later.

A second theme found in most definitions of a DSS centers around the decision outcome. The information-rich environment of today's organization is where the DSS

TABLE 1-1   Common DSS Characteristics

- Employed in semistructured or unstructured decision contexts
- Intended to support decision makers rather than replace them
- Supports all phases of the decision-making process
- Focuses on the effectiveness of the decision-making process rather than its efficiency
- Is under control of the DSS user
- Uses underlying data and models
- Facilitates learning on the part of the decision maker
- Is interactive and user-friendly
- Is generally developed using an evolutionary, iterative process
- Provides support for all levels of management from top executives to line managers
- Can provide support for multiple independent or interdependent decisions
- Provides support for individual, group, and team-based decision-making contexts

---

is commonly found and where it performs much of its work. A key element of a technology that is intended to support the process associated with making a decision is the decision itself. We will spend a great deal of our time considering exactly what decisions are and why we need technology to support us in making them. The effectiveness of a given decision, or the degree to which the decision succeeds in reaching its objectives, is an essential element in the decision-making process. Therefore, our definition of a DSS must take into account the role the system plays in supporting decision effectiveness.

A third theme present in definitions of a DSS concerns managerial control. The ultimate responsibility for the outcomes associated with decisions lies with the manager. When you stop to think about it, the decision can be argued to be the manager's most powerful tool. Through decision implementation, all the organization's resources are deployed or structured at any given moment. The decision acts as the primary mechanism to reach the organization's strategic objectives and to fuel its successes. Whether the decision is thought of as a choice, a course of action, or a strategy, decision activity results in the selection of and commitment to one of multiple alternatives. The control of this final selection lies with the decision maker(s). To that end, the DSS must provide support to the selection process but, ultimately, must be positioned to allow the final selection to be made by those managers directly responsible and accountable for the outcomes.

Based on these three common themes, we can devise a formal definition of a DSS that will serve as a foundation upon which a more detailed understanding of the construction, application, and use of DSSs can be built. *A decision support system is a system under the control of one or more decision makers that assists in the activity of decision making by providing an organized set of tools intended to impose structure on portions of the decision-making situation and to improve the ultimate effectiveness of the decision outcome.*

WHAT IT CAN AND CANNOT DO

The DSS clearly offers management a powerful tool and is rapidly becoming an integral component of managerial work. The speed with which today's information becomes yesterday's news continues to increase at a staggering rate. Tomorrow's manager will confront an ever-narrowing window of opportunity within which effective decisions will need to be made. Deadlines will be measured in days, hours, and minutes rather than in quarters, months, and years. The leveraging of technology that will allow tomorrow's manager to be effective in such a high-speed environment is what decision support is all about. To meet the demands of managerial work, a DSS must be able to provide the decision maker with certain key elements vital to his or her success. A DSS cannot offer benefits in all decision situations or by all decision makers, however. Its effectiveness depends on the degree of fit between the decision maker, the context of the decision, and the DSS itself. Assuming the fit is there, however, we can, in general, expect several potential benefits from using a DSS. In addition, we must acknowledge and understand the limitations of using a DSS. Table 1-2 contains a list of such potential benefits and limitations.

As you can see, the DSS is expected to extend the decision maker's capacity in processing the mountain of information involved in making a decision. Further, many components of a decision situation, although structured, are nonetheless highly com-

TABLE 1-2 Benefits and Limitations of DSS Use

Benefits
- Extend the decision maker's ability to process information and knowledge
- Extend the decision maker's ability to tackle large-scale, time-consuming, complex problems
- Shorten the time associated with making a decision
- Improve the reliability of a decision process or outcome
- Encourage exploration and discovery on the part of the decision maker
- Reveal new approaches to thinking about a problem space or decision context
- Generate new evidence in support of a decision or confirmation of existing assumptions
- Create a strategic or competitive advantage over competing organizations

Limitations
- DSSs cannot yet be designed to contain distinctly human decision-making talents such as creativity, imagination, or intuition
- The power of a DSS is limited by the computer system upon which it is running, its design, and the knowledge it possesses at the time of its use
- Language and command interfaces are not yet sophisticated enough to allow for natural language processing of user directives and inquiries
- DSSs are normally designed to be narrow in scope of application, thus inhibiting their generalizability to multiple decision-making contexts

plex and time-consuming. The DSS can solve those portions of the problem, and save on cognitive resources and, more importantly, large blocks of precious time for the decision maker. As a result, using a DSS can be expected to decrease the overall time involved in reaching a complex, unstructured decision.

Additional benefits can be found in the areas of innovation and creativity. Simply using the DSS can provide the decision maker with potential alternatives that might otherwise go unnoticed or appear too complex and difficult to pursue. The tools within the DSS can stimulate the problem solver to reach innovative insights regarding solutions and their associated outcomes. In addition, the output of the DSS may often justify the position of the decision maker(s), thus facilitating consensus among stakeholders. Finally, given the shrinking window of opportunity associated with the pace of business, the DSS may provide competitive advantage to organizations. To achieve some or all of these potential benefits, however, the manager must understand not only the appropriate application of a particular decision support tool but also its limits.

No matter how well a DSS is designed, its value is constrained by certain limitations. To begin with, the DSS, like any other computer-based system, contains only the "knowledge" given to it by its designers, and it possesses only the specific "skills" associated with its tool set. Although we will explore the concept of a DSS that can "think" in Chapter 7, and of one that can "learn" in Chapter 9, the DSS is still limited by its design and its designers.

Other drawbacks of the DSS include limits on its ability to perform reasoning processes that require distinctly human characteristics such as creativity, intuition, or imagination. Such cognitive activities still belong to human experience and do not lend themselves well to automation or machine simulation. Further, the DSS must be designed to communicate its information to its user in an understandable manner that is useful within the context of the decision situation. Although humans can adapt their methods of communication readily to a given situation, computer systems such as DSSs cannot. Therefore, the methods by which we communicate with a DSS and those by which it responds may limit its effective use. We will explore these issues of interface and interaction in Chapter 15.

Finally, and maybe most important, is the understanding that a "universal DSS" does not exist and probably never will. A typical DSS is designed to be useful within a relatively narrow scope of problem-solving scenarios. Thus, to effectively solve a complex problem or reach a decision of significant magnitude may require the use of several DSSs. In that case, the decision maker must coordinate multiple systems that may require output from one as input to another. The integration of multiple DSSs then becomes, in and of itself, a complex and uncertain decision scenario.

In summary, decision support systems can make the decision process more effective for the human decision maker. They cannot, however, overcome or prevent the actions of a poor decision maker. The user ultimately controls the process and must understand when to use a DSS, what DSS(s) to use, and, most importantly, to what degree to depend on the output and information obtained from the DSS. The manager must see the DSS as a valuable tool in the decision process rather than as a mechanism that makes the decision.

1-2: HISTORY OF DECISION SUPPORT SYSTEMS

THE EVOLUTION OF THE DSS

The roots of the DSS grew out of the application of quantitative models to the daily problems and decisions managers faced in an organizational environment. The concept was born in the early 1970s and is generally attributed to two articles written during that time. The first, written by J. D. Little (1970), was entitled "Models and Managers: The Concept of a Decision Calculus." Little observed that the biggest problem with management science models was that managers rarely used them. He described the concept of a decision calculus as a "model-based set of procedures for processing data and judgments to assist a manager in his decision making" (p. B470). Little suggested that for such a system to succeed, it must be simple, robust, easy to control, complete on issues of importance, adaptive to the needs of its user, and easy to communicate with.

The second article, "A Framework for Management Information Systems," was written by Gorry and Scott Morton (1989). In that article, they coined the term *decision support system* and developed a two-dimensional framework for computer support of managerial activities (see Table 1-3). Each of these dimensions within the framework is assumed to be continuous rather than composed of discrete components. The vertical dimension represents a classification of decision structure as originally proposed by Simon (1960). Simon suggested that decisions be categorized according to the degree to which they are *programmed* (repetitive, routine, and commonplace) or *nonprogrammed* (novel, unique, and consequential). The horizontal dimension of the framework represents the levels of managerial activity proposed by Anthony (1965).

TABLE 1-3 Gorry and Scott Morton's Framework for Decision Support

| | Management Activity | | | |
Type of Decision	Operational Control	Management Control	Strategic Planning	Support Needed
Structured	Inventory control	Load balancing for production lines	Physical plant location	MIS, quantitative models
Semistructured	Securities trading	Establishing marketing budgets for new products	Analysis of acquisition of capital assets	DSS
Unstructured	Determining the cover photo for a monthly magazine	Hiring of new managerial personnel	Determination of research and development projects	Human reasoning and intuition

Here, all managerial activities can be categorized into three unique classes: (1) strategic planning, where decisions related to the objectives of the organization are made; (2) management control, where decisions related to the effective and efficient procurement and deployment of the organization's assets are made; and (3) operational control, where decisions relating to the day-to-day tasks and activities of the organization are made. Combining the approaches of Simon and Anthony produces a framework to guide the allocation of IS resources to where the greatest payoff, or return on investment, may be found. From this framework, the concept of the decision support system was born.

The evolution of the DSS from its conception in the 1970s to the present day includes numerous extensions of the original notion. The modern-day study of DSSs must include a focus on conventional model-based systems, knowledge-based systems, artificial intelligence, expert systems, executive information systems, group support systems, data visualization systems, and organizational decision support systems. Each of these areas will be explored in depth in later chapters.

A BRIEF GLIMPSE OF THE FUTURE

If the number and types of DSSs and associated applications are any indication, then the DSS may well be the most successful of all computer-based information systems. Today's organizations recognize the need for embracing information technology as an integral tool in implementing their strategic plans. Tomorrow's organization will employ computer-based IS in virtually every aspect of its operation—from the development and marketing of its product or service to the coordination of its employees, processes, and activities worldwide. The role of the DSS in tomorrow's organization cannot be overstated. Managers will rely on the availability of more powerful and useful DSS applications in conducting their daily activities. The DSS of the twenty-first century will serve as the primary vehicle for keeping up with the seemingly exponential growth in the size, complexity, and speed of business activities. In Chapters 17 and 18, we will explore the various applications and uses for DSS technologies in the global marketplace of the future.

1-3: INGREDIENTS OF A DSS

BASIC DSS COMPONENTS

It should be clear to you by now that a DSS is not a simple system with common, identifiable characteristics and a singular or common purpose. As we have seen, simply defining a DSS requires consideration of numerous factors including its intended purpose, the context within which it will be used, and its outcome objectives. Describing or classifying a DSS in terms of its components poses an equally challenging task. Once again, before we can construct a generalized component structure for a DSS we need to look at the various methods of classifying DSSs by their component parts.

An early classification by Alter (1980) divided the DSS components into seven categories, depending upon the degree of direct influence each component part could have on a given decision. Figure 1-1 shows the classification scheme proposed by Alter along with a mapping of the various components to common problem-solving and decision-making tasks. Originally, Alter's classification assumed that each category could be thought of as a separate and distinct system rather than as a functional component within a larger system. As Figure 1-1 shows, however, the seven separate components can be logically grouped into a simpler classification scheme of either model-oriented or data-oriented systems. We will soon see that this simple dichotomy reflects the more modern classification methods for DSSs.

Another approach to isolating and defining individual components of a DSS focuses on the nature of the language provided by the DSS to manipulate data or models and the degree to which the language used is procedural or nonprocedural. The concept of language procedurality is relatively simple and is unique to the design and application of DSSs. Basically, the user of a DSS should be able to specify the information he or she wants from that DSS, as well as whether that information exists in a database, must be derived or computed by one or more models contained within the DSS, or must be computed by a model constructed by the DSS from other models stored specifically for that purpose. Languages that are highly procedural require the user to be specific with regard to how the data are to be obtained, from where they are to be

FIGURE 1-1 Alter's Classification of DSS Components

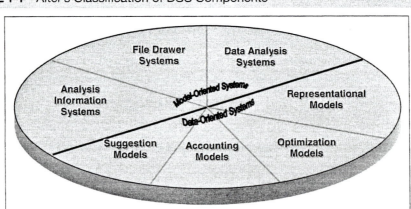

obtained, and exactly how a particular model or set of models is to process that data. Nonprocedural languages simply require the user to specify the necessary information, and the DSS takes care of the rest. Somewhere between these two extremes we find a degree of procedurality that allows users a means of providing parameters to prespecified data retrieval operations or a predetermined set of models. As you can see, the degree of procedurality of the language system allows for a wide variety of configurations and designs.

Building upon the two classification methods discussed, the components of a DSS can generally be classified into five distinct parts:

1. The data management system
2. The model management system
3. The knowledge engine
4. The user interface
5. The user(s)

THE DATA MANAGEMENT SYSTEM

The data management component of a DSS retrieves, stores, and organizes the relevant data for the particular decision context. Additionally, the data management system provides for the various security functions, data integrity procedures, and general data administration duties associated with using the DSS. These tasks are carried out within the data management component by several subsystems. Among these subsystems are the database(s), database management system, data repository, and data query facility. Each of these elements is discussed in greater detail in Section 1–4.

THE MODEL MANAGEMENT SYSTEM

Similar to the role of the data management system, the model management component performs the retrieval, storage, and organizational activities associated with the various quantitative models that provide the analytical capabilities for the DSS. Within this component are the model base, model base management system, model repository, model execution processor, and model synthesis processor. A detailed review and comparison of this component to the data management system is performed in Section 1–4.

THE KNOWLEDGE ENGINE

The knowledge engine performs activities related to problem recognition and generation of interim or final solutions, as well as other functions related to the management of the problem-solving process. The knowledge engine supplies the "brains" of the system. The data and the models come together here to provide the user with a useful application that supports the decision context. We will look at the knowledge engine in greater detail in Section 1–5.

THE USER INTERFACE

As in any other computer-based information system, the design and implementation of the user interface is a key element in DSS functionality. The data, model, and processing components of the DSS must be easily accessed and manipulated if the DSS is to provide the necessary support to the decision context without getting in the way of the task at hand. Furthermore, the ease with which the user can communicate with the DSS, whether for specifying parameters or investigating the problem space, is crucial to the effectiveness of a DSS. These responsibilities, among many others, fall to the user interface and will be discussed in Section 1–6.

THE DSS USER

The design, implementation, and use of a DSS cannot be effective without considering the role of the user. User skill set, motivations, knowledge domain, patterns of use, and role(s) within the organization constitute the essential elements in the successful application of a DSS to a decision context. Remember, one of the primary characteristics of a DSS is user control. Without considering the user as a part of the system, we are left with a set of computer-based components that, by themselves, provide no useful function at all. We look at the user more closely in Section 1–7 and again in Chapter 2.

1-4: DATA AND MODEL MANAGEMENT

THE DATABASE

As more and more organizations realize the importance of data as a corporate asset that must be managed, the processes by which data are collected, stored, and disseminated continue to improve. This increased focus on the value of data to the organization is particularly relevant to the study of decision support systems because the quality and structure of the DSS database component largely determine the success of the modern DSS.

A database is an integrated collection of data, organized and stored in a manner that facilitates its easy retrieval. The structure of a database should correspond to the needs of the organization and should allow for access by multiple users and, when appropriate, for use by more than one application. A database organizes data into a logical hierarchy based on the degree of aggregation or granularity of that data. This hierarchy consists of four elements:

1. Database
2. Files
3. Records
4. Data elements

Figure 1-2 shows how the various elements of the hierarchy are logically integrated in a typical database.

Just as the database is a collection of integrated data organized into files, the file serves as a collection of data organized into records that all relate to a particular information focus. For example, a particular data file may contain information regarding sales transactions during a specific period, say for an organization's last fiscal year—or a similar data file may contain historical sales volume information for an entire industry over the last 5 years. Regardless of the nature of the data, it must all be related to a common subject and must be organized so that various useful aggregations of the data within that file can be created and compared.

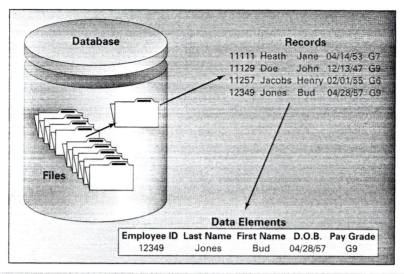

FIGURE 1-2 Hierarchy of Data

Although data within files are organized into a common structure, the sources of the data contained within the files may be quite diverse. The files may include data generated from internal transactions, external sources, and individual users of the DSS.

Internal data normally come from an organization's daily transaction processing systems. Payroll and salary data, sales transactions, production level and throughput, as well as other transactions generated by the various business units of the organization, are all examples of internal data sources that may appropriately contribute one or more files to a typical DSS database. Transaction-level data are a major source of information regarding the operations of an organization or business unit. Depending on the problem context in which the DSS is operating, these data may be all that is necessary for the DSS to provide the necessary level of decision support. Oftentimes, however, an internal data source is only one contributor of information to the DSS database.

External data sources are as broad as the imagination allows. They may include targeted collections of data for a particular industry, market research data, employment information for a particular geographic region, rate schedules or cost tables for particular products or product classes, geopolitical economic or census data, or a historical list of all court cases within a particular legal jurisdiction, such as the Supreme Court. The list is literally endless. It is a safe bet that if a source of data generation exists, then a database containing that data also exists. The good news for DSS designers and users is that most of the imaginable external data can be obtained with relative ease and at little or no cost. The bad news is that, with all of the data out there and with more being made available each day, just figuring out where to look can be a monumental task. Fortunately, however, developments such as the Internet and World Wide Web make access to external data much easier than in the past. In addition, data delivery services such as Mead Data Central's LEXIS-NEXIS, Dow Jones News Retrieval, CompuServe, and a myriad of others aid the downloading, integration, and analysis of external data for use in the corporate DSS environment.

Regardless of their source, the data contained within the files in the DSS database can be organized into homogenous structures, or subunits, called records. In turn, the data contained within each record are organized into a series of data elements, or fields. The data element is the smallest unit of decomposition within the logical hierarchy and cannot normally be broken down further. Each record is constructed so that it contains a set of data elements related to a specific instance of the type of information contained within the file. An example might begin with a file containing data about the sales of various items in an organization's product line. Information such as product code, product name, date and time of sale, quantity or amount of sale, location of sale, and other specific pieces of data concerning the transaction may be organized and stored within a data record. Once these records are stored, they can be retrieved individually based on a unique piece of data, such as invoice number, or they can be retrieved as a unique subset, such as all records containing a particular product code. More importantly, they can be combined with other sources of organized data within the DSS database to allow for extensive analysis of relationships that might otherwise go unnoticed by the DSS user. Through its ability to combine data records from multiple sources, the DSS increases the value of the data within the decision-making process.

One additional source of data that may be contained within the typical DSS database is referred to as individual-level or private data. Each instance of use of a DSS generates data about the decisions made, the questions asked, and the various combinations of data constructed for that particular problem context. In addition, individual heuristics, or rules of thumb, used by various DSS users may also be stored in the DSS database. These individual-level data elements and records often create a unique personality for the DSS, thus tailoring the system to the needs of a specific user or group of users within its defined problem context. Information such as an individual's personal assessment of specific data or past situations, a heuristic stating that "during December, sales of Product A can be expected to be 37 percent of the sales of Product B," or simply a library of past queries or data source integrations may all be stored as individual-level data in the DSS database.

THE DATABASE MANAGEMENT SYSTEM

The multitude of data that can be organized into files and databases must be managed, and this important role falls to the database management system (DBMS). The DBMS has two main responsibilities:

1. The coordination of all tasks related to storing and accessing information in the database and disseminating information to the community of DSS users
2. The maintenance of logical independence between the data contained in the DSS database and the DSS application

Modern DBMSs possess a wide variety of capabilities and are generally managed by a skilled database administrator assigned specifically to that task. Commercial DBMS packages from Sybase, Oracle, IBM, and others provide powerful foundational applications from which the DSS database can be managed. Recent DBMS developments include facilitating the integration of a large number of unrelated, or disparate, data sources into a single, accessible database known as a data warehouse. Data warehouses provide large amounts of data to the DSS in a form and manner that is more conducive to DSS use. They will be discussed in greater detail in Chapters 10, 11, and 12.

The first responsibility of the DBMS—the coordination of tasks related to the storage, access, and dissemination of database information—involves several activities and functions. These functions include updating (in the form of adds, deletes, edits, or changes) data records and elements as transactions occur, facilitating the integration of data from various sources, and retrieving data from the database for queries or report generation. In addition, the DBMS performs many administrative functions related to DSS operation such as data security (control of unauthorized access, database error recovery, data integrity, and concurrency issues), the creation of personal or temporary databases for individual user experimentation and analysis, and the tracking of DSS usage and data acquisition, among others. Many of these activities are performed in the background and are intended to be invisible to the DSS user. Nonetheless, they are essential to the successful use of a DSS in a problem-solving context.

The second main responsibility of the DBMS, that of maintaining logical independence between the data and the DSS application, is also crucial to the success of a DSS. The typical DSS scenario involves one or more users making decisions that are largely based upon information taken from a large pool of constantly evolving data. The DBMS must manage the physical organization and structuring of this data within the database and its associated files without constraining the logical arrangement of the data to either the DSS application or the DSS user(s). The same data may need to be presented in one form, such as a graph or table, under one set of circumstances and in a completely different manner, such as input to an analytical model, in another situation. In addition, as new sources of data are made available to the DSS, the DBMS must manage the integration of these disparate sources so that they appear to be all neatly organized in a common structure and location even when they are not. By maintaining independence between physical data structure and DSS applications, the DBMS allows for a much broader use of a single database, either by multiple DSS applications, multiple user groups, multiple problem contexts, or any combination thereof. Table 1-4 describes the various functions of a typical DBMS.

THE MODEL BASE

A model is a simplification of some event or process constructed for the purpose of studying that event and thus developing a better understanding of it. As a simplified form of reality, a model is intended to resemble the actual process or event as closely as possible but normally does not contain the same level or kind of detail as the phenomenon itself. In many cases, we can ascertain from the model many characteristics of a process or event. Moreover, we can often predict the nature or outcome of that event under certain conditions without having to actually experience or re-create the event under study. The value of this capability can be found in the reduced cost, effort, and time derived from studying a model rather than the event itself. Imagine the effort (and risk) necessary to remain inside a hurricane for its duration in order to predict its path or its strengthening. Imagine the costs associated with having to build an airplane to see how fast it will fly, or if it will fly at all. Imagine the time it would take to determine how popular a new product or service is going to be if you had to ask everybody's opinion about it before you began selling it. In each of these cases, modeling can be an

TABLE 1-4 General Functions of the DBMS

Data Definition
- Provides a data definition language (DDL) that allows users to describe the data entities and their associated attributes and relationships
- Allows for the interrelation of data from multiple sources

Data Manipulation
- Provides the user with a query language to interact with the database
- Allows for capture and extraction of data
- Provides rapid retrieval of data for ad hoc queries and reports
- Allows for the construction of complex queries for retrieval and data manipulation

Data Integrity
- Allows the user to describe rules (integrity constraints) to maintain the integrity of the database
- Assists in the control of erroneous data entry based on the defined integrity constraints

Access Control
- Allows identification of authorized users
- Controls access to various data elements and data manipulation activities within the database
- Tracks usage and access to data by authorized users

Concurrency Control
- Provides procedures for controlling simultaneous access to the same data by more than one user

Transaction Recovery
- Provides a mechanism for restart and reconciliation of the database in the event of hardware failure
- Records information on all transactions at certain points to enable satisfactory database restart

effective source of information for the decision process. Although the underlying models contained within a DSS are the essence of the concept of decision support, the degree to which these models are designed and constructed to resemble the real thing normally depends on the needs of the decision maker using them. Nonetheless, the lack of one or more models associated with the problem context under investigation limits a DSS's contribution. We will focus on the various types of models and their construction in detail in Chapter 4.

The model base in a DSS is the modeling counterpart to the database. Just as the DSS database stores the data used by the DSS, the model base contains the various statistical, financial, mathematical, and other quantitative models the DSS uses to perform a variety of analyses. Its model base differentiates a DSS from other computer-based information systems. The ability to run individual or combined models or to construct new models makes the DSS a powerful support tool in the problem-solving environment.

MANAGING THE MODELS

The underlying models in a typical DSS can range in number, size, and complexity much like the data stored in a DSS database. To manage numerous analytical tools, the DSS uses a model base management system (MBMS). Table 1-5 contains a list of the basic functions of the MBMS.

Two important responsibilities of the MBMS are the execution and integration of the models available to the DSS and the modeling of user preferences. The user is normally required to provide data as input to a model or to provide certain parameters that may affect the model's execution. The MBMS takes care of this process by providing the user with easy access to the various models as well as facilitating entry of important parameters and data to the models.

Often to execute one or more models, the user must provide specialized syntax or commands to initiate the process. The MBMS generates the necessary command structure and locates the models for the DSS. The specific formatting requirements for data or parameter entry are also handled by the MBMS subsystem. Finally, the need to combine or integrate several individual models into a more complex one occurs regularly in DSS use. The MBMS facilitates this integration by providing the necessary links between the models as well as controlling the order of model sequencing and execution.

The modeling of user preferences is the process of collecting, organizing, and integrating the preferences, judgments, and intuitions of the individual DSS user into the modeling operation. Decision makers and decision contexts both exhibit constantly changing and conflicting preferences. The MBMS, where appropriate, provides a mechanism to incorporate the individual user or problem context preferences into the analytical process so that the outcomes represent not only the quantitative, or stochastic, results but also the more qualitative, or context-specific, conditions and constraints. In short, the MBMS plays an important role in facilitating the decision support process through a DSS application. We explore this issue of user characteristics and preferences in Chapter 2.

TABLE 1-5   General Functions of the MBMS

Modeling Language
- Allows for the creation of decision models from scratch or from existing modules
- Provides a mechanism for the linking or chaining of multiple models to allow for sequential processing and data exchange
- Allows the user to modify models to reflect specific preferences

Model Library
- Stores and manages all models and solver algorithms for easy access and manipulation
- Provides a catalog and organizational schema of stored models along with brief descriptions of their individual functions or applications

Model Manipulation
- Allows for management and maintenance of the model base with functions similar to those found in a DBMS (i.e., run, store, query, delete, link, etc.)

1-5: DSS KNOWLEDGE BASE

All decision or problem-solving contexts require reasoning. A decision that can be made without reasoning is really not a decision at all. Admittedly, the more structured a decision context is, the less reasoning is necessary for a successful outcome. It follows that we can envision a point at which the reduction in required reasoning converges with the increase in problem structure. At this intersection we find those decisions that are so structured that no reasoning is required to make them. By default then, it must be the point where no decisions exist.

At this stage, it is critical that we clearly express what reasoning is. *Reasoning* is the process by which new information is derived from a combination or combinations of existing, or previously derived, information. In its simplest form, reasoning allows us to rely on information as facts, even though we haven't specifically verified that information personally. For example, if we know for a fact that a particular company has a current ratio (current assets to current liabilities) of 2.6 and a quick ratio (liquid assets to current liabilities) of 1.7, we know two isolated facts about this company. Through the process of reasoning, however, we also can "know" that the liquidity of the company is generally sound. No one told us this piece of information, nor did we personally verify it, but we know it nonetheless. Many forms of reasoning are used in problem solving and decision making, and we will explore them in greater detail in Chapters 7, 8, and 9. At this point, however, our definition is sufficient to aid in our understanding of yet another component of a DSS: the knowledge base.

The knowledge base is where the "knowledge" of the DSS is stored. By *knowledge,* we mean the rules, heuristics, boundaries, constraints, previous outcomes, and any other information that may have been programmed into the DSS by its designers or acquired by the DSS through repeated use.

The information contained within the knowledge base component of a DSS bears unique characteristics that differentiate it from information contained in either the database or the model base components. First, the knowledge base contains information that is generally problem domain-specific; that is to say, it is knowledge that is applicable or relevant within only a narrow problem-solving context. Conversely, the database and model base components store a wide range of domain-related elements. The database or databases associated with a DSS are not limited to a particular problem-solving domain. The models contained within the model base are likewise not constrained by the defined problem-solving context within which the DSS resides. The knowledge base, however, generally does not contain anything that is not directly relevant to, or directly derived from, the problem-solving context. Think of it this way: Knowledge is a domain-specific construct whereas data and models are useful across several domains or tasks.

So what exactly is contained in the DSS knowledge base? All kinds of knowledge that might be used by a domain expert reside within a knowledge base: descriptions of various objects or entities and their relationships; descriptions of various problem-solving strategies or behaviors; domain-related constraints, uncertainties, and probabilities; and so on. The knowledge contained in the knowledge base can be categorized into two simple groups: facts and hypotheses. The *facts* represent what we know to be true at a given time. The *hypotheses* represent the rules or relationships that we believe exist between the facts.

Let's assume that we have a simple knowledge base that contains a select number of variables deemed by experts to be most important in evaluating a potential borrower's creditworthiness:

1. Number of years of credit history (a numerical fact)
2. Quality of the credit history (a ranking fact: perfect, almost perfect, very good, good, not good, awful)
3. Job description of the borrower (a category fact: doctor, lawyer, computer operator, college professor)
4. Number of years of employment in this job area (a numerical fact)
5. Total income of the borrower (a numerical fact)
6. Total debt obligations of the borrower (a numerical fact)
7. Amount of money the borrower wants to borrow (a numerical fact)

Now, in addition to these facts, our knowledge base also contains the relationships among them. In other words, we have also stored the manner in which one or more facts are related to each other. Figure 1-3 graphically illustrates the relationships between the facts contained within our knowledge base.

In this case, our objective is to make a decision regarding whether we should lend money to a specific person. Notice, however, that the relationships between the facts

FIGURE 1-3   Examples of Credit Rule Combinations

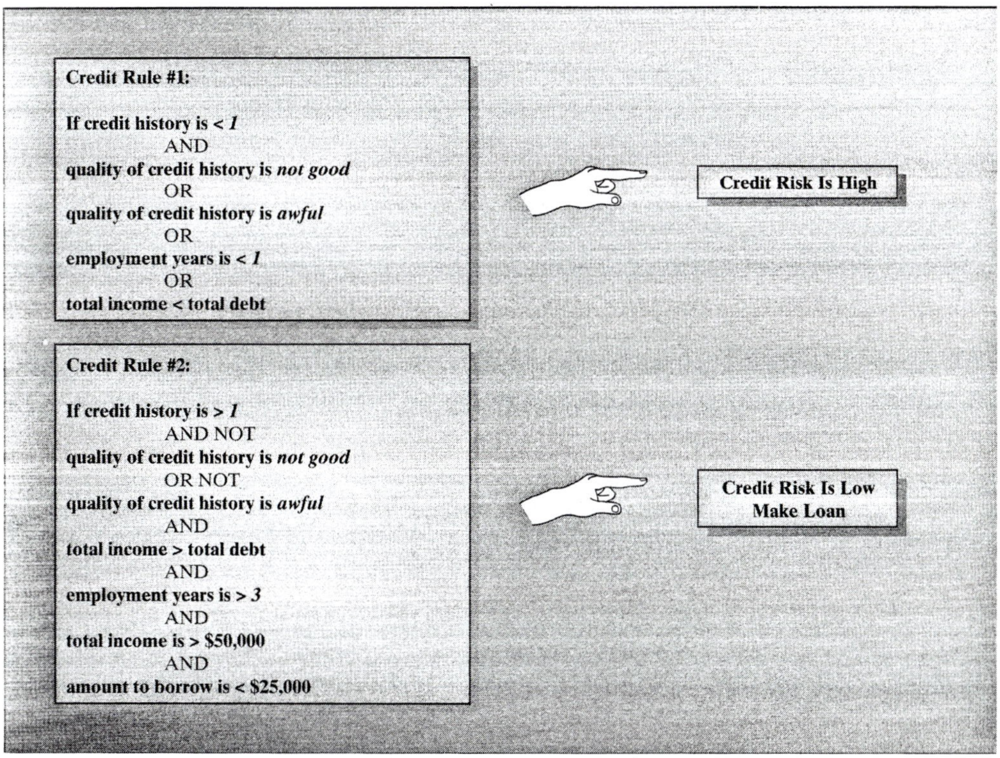

Credit Rule #1:

If credit history is < *1*
      AND
quality of credit history is *not good*
      OR
quality of credit history is *awful*
      OR
employment years is < *1*
      OR
total income < total debt

Credit Risk Is High

Credit Rule #2:

If credit history is > *1*
      AND NOT
quality of credit history is *not good*
      OR NOT
quality of credit history is *awful*
      AND
total income > total debt
      AND
employment years is > *3*
      AND
total income is > $50,000
      AND
amount to borrow is < $25,000

**Credit Risk Is Low
Make Loan**

are not focused on any particular person but rather are simply stated in the form of rules. One rule may state the relationship between fact 1 and fact 2, another rule may state the relationship between fact 5 and fact 6, and so on. Although these rules can be thought of as a series of models, they are unique in that they can be combined in any manner and in any order to produce a decision outcome. Figure 1-3 shows two such combinations. For example, let's say the borrower has a short credit history (high risk), but the history that exists is perfect (extremely low risk). She has a good job and has been employed in this job area for a long time (both low risk). However, her debt is extremely high compared to her income (high risk) and the amount of money she wants to borrow is also extremely large (high risk). In this case, the knowledge base combines the facts we have presented with the relationships among those facts (relationships, by the way, that we programmed into the DSS) and might help us conclude that we should decide against making the loan to the borrower. Bear in mind that this example is a simple one and, when compared to the types and sizes of typical knowledge bases, a somewhat trivial one as well. It demonstrates, however, just how the knowledge base contributes to the DSS as a whole.

KNOWLEDGE ACQUISITION

By now, you should be wondering where all this knowledge and all these rules come from. If the user of the DSS already knows this stuff then why do we need a DSS? Well, that's the point! The typical user of a DSS does not know this stuff. The DSS user relies on the integrity of the data in the database, the quality and accuracy of the models in the model base, and the merit and reliability of the facts and relationships in the knowledge base when using the DSS during a decision-making activity. So how does all that knowledge get into the DSS?

One or more people called *knowledge engineers* (KEs) interview the domain experts and gather the information necessary for the knowledge base. Knowledge engineers are specially trained to interact with domain experts for the purposes of acquiring all of the expert's knowledge in a particular domain and all of the relationships among that knowledge. A variety of knowledge acquisition techniques such as interviewing, protocol analysis (thinking out loud), and modeling, among many others, are used to get the information out of the experts' minds and into the knowledge base. The process of knowledge acquisition is a daunting task, indeed. We will focus on the different techniques associated with acquiring and organizing the knowledge of experts in Chapters 7 and 8.

KNOWLEDGE RETRIEVAL

Once the facts and relationships are collected and inserted into the knowledge base, we need a method of getting them back out in an organized and useful fashion. The inference engine (IE) is that part of the knowledge base component that facilitates this process. The IE is a program module that activates all the gathered domain knowledge and performs inferencing, or basic reasoning, to work toward a solution or conclusion based upon the values for the facts given and the relationships or rules associated with them. The inference engine must be supplied with rules on how to apply the rules, with strategies for conflict resolution in the event that two rules oppose each other, and in many cases, with methods of determining the probability that a conclusion derived from a set of facts and rules is reliable. We will discuss IEs in depth in Chapter 7.

It should be clear that the knowledge base component of a DSS, when combined with the capabilities of modern DBMS and MBMS facilities, creates a potent tool for supporting the complex decisions managers must make. These three components by themselves, however, can accomplish little. They need to be accessible to the DSS user in a manner that truly supports the decision-making process and facilitates their individual and combined use with a minimum of effort. What we need is an interface.

1-6: USER INTERFACES

An interface is simply a component of a system specifically intended to allow the user to access the internal components of that system in a relatively easy fashion and without having to know specifically how everything is put together or how it works together. The easier it is for a user to access the system, the better the interface. Also, the more common the interface, the less effort and training it takes for a user to move from one system to another. For example, programs such as Microsoft Windows and the software applications written for it rely on a common interface. Saving and retrieving files in one Windows program is the same basic process as in all other Windows-based applications. The concept of the common interface is not limited to computer-based systems, however. Modern automobiles achieve an almost universal set of characteristics in their interface, which is why you don't have to get a license to drive a particular car or type of car. Unless you try to drive something radically different in its interface, such as a semitrailer or school bus, you need just one license to drive. The interfaces are so similar that if you know how to drive one car, you know how to drive them all.

As you might expect, however, the world of DSSs does not yet enjoy the benefits of a universal or common interface. Even though it is a desirable goal, it is just not so easily accomplished. Remember, DSSs are not generic applications intended to be used by a variety of users in a variety of settings. On the contrary, a DSS is a domain-specific application that is normally designed for use by a small group. As such, the design and implementation of a common user interface is not easily attained. Typically, however, the limited user base for a particular DSS makes a common interface less important. Because the system is essentially "custom designed" for the user(s), the interface is also designed for the specific user or users of the system.

INTERFACE COMPONENTS

The DSS interface is responsible for all interaction and communication with the user(s). Given this level of responsibility, the interface must not only include software components (such as menus and command languages) and hardware components (such as multiple monitoring or input facilities), it must also deal with factors relating to human interaction, accessibility, ease of use, user skill level, error capture and reporting, and issues relating to documentation, among many others. Because of this breadth and depth of responsibility, DSS experts generally regard the interface as the single most important component in the system. Without a good user interface, the power and functionality of the DSS remain inaccessible. Think of it this way: As far as the user is concerned, the interface and the DSS are one and the same. Poor interface equals poor system. In the past, lack of support for many DSS implementations has been linked to a poor user interface that served only to discourage use rather than facilitate it. Table 1-6 contains the basic components of a DSS interface and lists the factors that must be considered in its design.

Throughout this book we will explore the details of interface design as it relates to a specific DSS application context such as executive information systems, expert systems, or group decision support systems. For now, you can think of the DSS interface as having two components: the communication language and the presentation language.

The Communication Language

The communication language, or action language, component deals with activities associated with the user's direct dialog with the DSS. The various modes of data entry are included in this component. Data can be entered into the DSS by conventional methods such as keyboard, mouse, trackball, or touchpad. More recently, however, expanded communication capabilities allow for a variety of not-so-common data entry mechanisms. Virtual reality devices such as biophysical input gloves, retinal scanners, and head position monitors are becoming common input methods. In addition, DSS applications using joysticks, voice recognition, and optical scanning devices are also being developed. Essentially, anything that can serve as potential input and can be captured as input is fair game for the communication language component of the interface. Figure 1-4 contains examples of common input devices that could be used with a typical DSS.

Probably the most common aspect of the communication language is the menu. Menus provide the user with an organized and intuitive method of selecting among the many functions, alternatives, commands, or outcomes available through the DSS. Properly organized and logically designed, menus can serve as guides for the inexperienced DSS user and as efficient vehicles of navigation for the DSS expert. Poorly designed menus, however, can render an otherwise powerful DSS unusable. As stated

---

TABLE 1-6 General Functions of the DSS Interface

Communication Language
- Allows for interaction with the DSS in a variety of dialog styles
- Identifies the form of input to enter requests into the DSS
- Provides support for communication among multiple DSS users
- Can be effected in a variety of formats including menu driven, question/answer, procedural command language, or natural command language
- Can capture and analyze previous dialogs so that future interactions can be improved

Presentation Language
- Provides for the presentation of data in a variety of formats
- Allows for detailed report definition and generation by the DSS user
- Allows for the creation of forms, tables, and graphics for data output
- Can provide for multiple "windows," or views, of the data to be available simultaneously

---

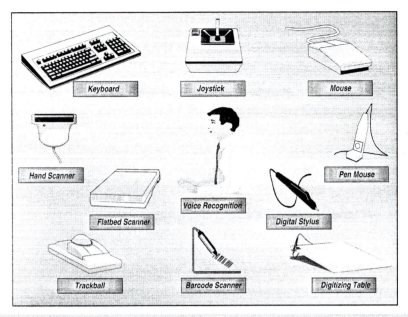

FIGURE 1-4   Common Input Devices

previously, we will explore the details of good interface design throughout the course of the book.

The Presentation Language

The presentation language component of the DSS interface is where all the action is. It is what the user actually sees, hears, or experiences during DSS use. Output devices such as printers, plotters, display monitors, audio monitors, and voice synthesizers are all part of this component. On-screen methods such as multiple windows, graphs, tables, charts, icons, messages, and audio triggers or alerts are also part of the presentation language. Just as the communication language component allows the user to transmit information and commands to the DSS, the presentation language component serves as the vehicle for the DSS to communicate with the user. These two components must be designed to work smoothly together if the DSS is to be considered user-friendly.

Research shows that the method by which information is presented to a user can dramatically affect its perceived value and how accurately it is interpreted. The presentation language component must be designed so that a wide variety of presentation methods can be either preselected as a preference or selected "on the fly" by the DSS user while viewing various stages of output. Various graphs, tables, charts, and combinations must be easily selectable by the user so that the output can be viewed from as many perspectives as possible. This flexibility ensures that the output is appropriate for the many different users of the DSS as well as for the range of problem contexts and decisions to be supported by the system. As with the communication language component, we will discuss issues of presentation in greater detail throughout the book within the context of specific DSS applications.

1-7: THE DSS USER

No DSS can be considered functional or complete without the user. Unlike many other computer-based information systems, in the DSS the user is as much a part of the system as is the hardware or software. The user is commonly defined as the person, or persons, responsible for providing a solution to the problem at hand or for making a decision within the context the DSS was designed to support. The DSS user is central to the entire life cycle of the system. Users may be involved in the conception of a DSS, in its logical and physical design, in its testing and implementation, and, of course, in its use.

USER ROLES

The user as defined in the previous paragraph, however, may not actually ever "use" the DSS. Alter (1980) classifies DSS users into one of five basic roles. He further classifies the various user roles into one of four basic patterns of use. Figure 1-5 shows the relationship between the defined user roles and their patterns of use.

   In Alter's classification, the user is defined as the person who communicates directly with the DSS regardless of method or intention. The decision maker is the person who ultimately makes the decision based, in whole or in part, upon the output from the DSS. An intermediary is a particular type of user who serves as a filter or interpreter of the output from a DSS. The intermediary may work closely with the decision maker to assist in interpreting the DSS output during the various stages of the decision-making process. The maintainer, or operator, is responsible for the daily operational aspects of the DSS,

FIGURE 1-5   Alter's Decision Maker Patterns of Usage

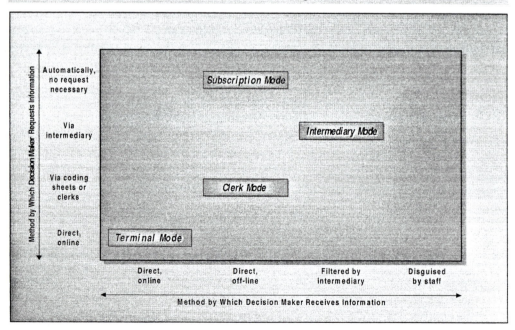

such as keeping the system and its data up-to-date and in operational condition. Finally, the feeder provides data to the DSS but might not ever directly use the DSS as a decision support tool. The role of feeder may be filled by one or several people or groups that regularly generate data relevant to the problem context the DSS was designed to support. In some cases, all the user roles may be simultaneously occupied by a single person; in other cases, those roles may be managed by several different people or groups. Alter suggests that the fewer people involved in the various user roles, the simpler the DSS becomes to implement and use. As you can see, however, the realm of the DSS consists of many users who may never actually "use" the system to make a decision.

PATTERNS OF DSS USE

The patterns of use described by Alter help in understanding how various users may interact with the DSS. In the subscription mode the decision maker typically receives scheduled reports. Such reporting is generally preformatted and generated on a regularly scheduled basis. The reports are often generated automatically by the DSS and require no inquiry (other than the original one) on the part of the user. Moreover, these reports are often generated through consolidation of existing information submitted from several sources throughout the organization and are received either through off-line methods such as hard copy or, increasingly, through asynchronous electronic methods such as e-mail or file transfer. An example of subscription mode usage would be the periodic receipt of a budget variance report.

In the terminal mode, the decision maker interacts directly with the DSS in an online manner. In this mode, the user determines and provides the input, manipulates the models in the model base, and directly receives and interprets the output. The terminal mode user may use the received output to either make the final decision or determine the need for additional or more refined interaction with the DSS. An example of a typical terminal mode access would be the analysis of optimum stock portfolio combinations for a particular brokerage client.

A DSS can also be used in a clerk mode. Here, the decision maker uses the system directly but does not interact with the DSS in an online, real-time manner. Instead, the inputs, parameters, and requests are formed off-line and submitted via input coding forms or other electronic batch submission processes. While the decision maker awaits a response from the system, he or she can work on other activities. Situations in which a large number of users need access to a DSS but do not need online interactions are most compatible with clerk mode usage. Such systems can handle a large number of requests efficiently and can perform many complex analyses before returning the answers to the various clerk mode users. A common example of this type of system usage would be a DSS used to determine renewal rates for insurance customers or custom quotations for highly specialized service industries.

The fourth DSS usage category is the intermediary mode. Here the decision maker interacts with the DSS through one or more intermediary users. In this mode, the intermediaries are necessary due to the complex nature of either the analysis or parameter input process. In an extreme case, the DSS functions as the intermediary's tool in the preparation of his or her final report to a decision maker. This mode of usage frees the decision maker from having to interact with the "automated beast" or to even know how the system works. A common example of this mode of use might be an organizational pricing structure that is predicated on multiple analyses by several divisions but ultimately must be consolidated by a human decision maker. The days of the intermediary usage mode are numbered, however. The windows of opportunity normally associated with typical managerial decisions are becoming ever smaller and more temporally demanding. For this reason, the time spent "interacting" with the technology through intermediaries may be prohibitive for many decisions. Tomorrow's decision maker must have direct access to the support technology and must be skilled in its use. Furthermore, the designers of tomorrow's decision support technologies must keep in mind the speed with which these technologies must be employed and how quickly answers must be obtained. For now, however, each of the four patterns of use has its place and, when properly applied, provides the necessary utility for the particular problem-solving context at hand.

1-8: CATEGORIES AND CLASSES OF DSSs

A variety of methods attempt to classify and categorize decision support systems. Methods based on the type of support offered by the DSS; decision situation; degree of user guidance or procedurality; orientation toward data, text, rules, or models; and focus on individual versus multiple decision makers are all used in classifying the myriad of DSSs in existence or under development. For the moment, however, it is enough to understand that the unique characteristics of a particular DSS classification may be important in determining the best approach to the design or implementation of a new system. We will explore these issues in greater depth in Chapters 14 and 15.

DATA-CENTRIC AND MODEL-CENTRIC DSSs

Building upon Figure 1-1 (page 8), Figure 1-6 contains a classification scheme for DSSs suggested by Alter. In this method, two primary support orientations for a DSS are used. The data-centric orientation focuses primarily on data retrieval and analysis sup-

FIGURE 1-6 Alter's Collapsed DSS Classification Scheme

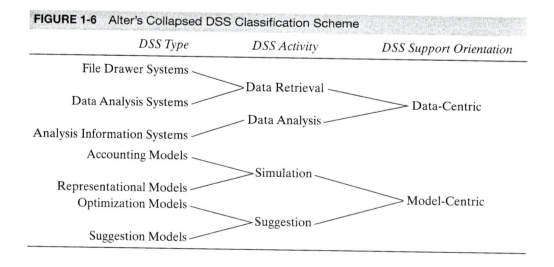

port activities. The model-centric orientation includes activities such as simulation, maximizing or optimizing scenarios, and those DSS outputs that generate suggested actions based upon embedded rules or models. Within these two basic categories, a broad spectrum of DSS types can be positioned.

FORMAL AND AD HOC SYSTEMS

Donovan and Madnick (1977) proposed a method of DSS classification based upon the attributes of the problem-solving context. The formal, or institutional, DSS is designed to focus on periodic or recurring decisions within an organization. Such decision contexts require regular interaction with a DSS to ensure consistent and effective decision outcomes. Examples of this kind of system are found in periodic pricing scenarios typical of the petroleum industry or in dynamic decision contexts such as portfolio management or seasonal inventory control. The formal DSS tends to be stable in its design and evolves over a period of years into a highly refined, reliable support mechanism.

In contrast, the ad hoc DSS is designed to focus on a narrow problem context or set of decisions that is usually not recurring or easily anticipated. In these DSSs, the nature and immediacy of the decision situation drive the design and implementation considerations. A typical scenario for an ad hoc DSS might be the need to make decisions regarding a pending hostile takeover or corporate merger. Historically, the prohibitively high cost of developing ad hoc DSSs limited their availability and usefulness. However, the advent of DSS generators (generalizable software development environments that provide basic DSS components such as DBMS, MBMS, and knowledge management) made the ad hoc DSS a feasible, cost-effective method of providing high-quality decision support to "custom" application?

DIRECTED VERSUS NONDIRECTED DSSs

Silver (1991) proposed a method of classifying DSSs by the degree to which the system provides decisional guidance — that is, the manner in which a DSS guides its users in constructing and executing decision-making processes by providing assistance in choosing and using its operators. Silver defines operators as those elements of the DSS (menus, buttons, models, algorithms, tools) that can or must be manipulated by the user in the course of the decision-making process. This method of classification suggests that users may benefit from such guidance "imposed" upon the process by the DSS. Figure 1-7 illustrates a two-dimensional matrix of decisional guidance used to classify various decision support methods.

Silver's classification initially categorizes a DSS by the type of guidance provided: mechanical versus decisional. Mechanical guidance is the more common form within a DSS and generally consists of assisting users with the "mechanics" of the operating system's features such as menus, buttons, and commands. In contrast, decisional guidance assists the users in dealing with the various decision-making concepts relevant to the problem context. This category can be broken down further into guidance intended to assist in the structuring or execution of the decision-making processes. Finally, each decisional guidance subcategory can be classified by the form the guidance takes: suggestive or informational. The former proposes courses of action to the user. Examples of suggestive guidance would be a suggestion from the DSS regarding which operator to invoke in the next step or a recommended starting value as input to a

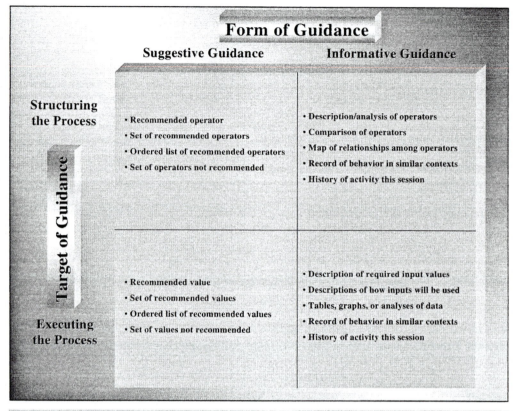

FIGURE 1-7   Silver's Classification of Decisional Guidance

Source: Reprinted by special permission from *MIS Quarterly*, Volume 15, Number 1, March 1991. Copyright 1991 by the Society for Information Management and the Management Information Systems Research Center at the University of Minnesota.

chosen algorithm. The latter provides users with information relevant to the situation at hand but does not indicate how the user should proceed based on that information. Silver contends that the type of guidance is likely to affect how the system is used as well as the decision outcomes made with the system.

PROCEDURAL AND NONPROCEDURAL SYSTEMS

As discussed in Section 1–3, procedurality refers to the degree to which a user of a DSS can specify whatever information he or she wants from that DSS in whatever form he or she wants it. In a method of classification similar to Silver's approach, the various DSSs can be positioned on a continuum according to their degree of procedurality. For example, a DSS using a highly procedural data retrieval language such as COBOL would require the user to provide detailed specifications regarding how the data are to be retrieved and precisely how each of the necessary computational subroutines is to be performed. The slightest deviation from a set of rigid syntactical rules such as a missing parenthesis or comma or a particular variable out of order would result in an unrecognizable command to the DSS, or worse, a command that, although recognizable, may produce some highly unpredictable results. This system would be positioned at the extreme procedurality end of the spectrum.

Systems using less procedural languages—written in typical fourth-generation languages such as Oracle or Smalltalk that employ a structured query language (SQL)—allow the user to use less of a procedural approach to the construction of commands or requests for information. These systems tend to fall near the middle of the procedurality spectrum. The nonprocedural command structure, though easier to understand and construct, nonetheless requires the user to follow a set of rules regarding sequence and syntax that is somewhat foreign to the way one naturally thinks and converses. The bottom line is that the user needs to learn a new vocabulary and grammar to use a command-oriented DSS effectively.

Recently, in an emerging trend toward natural language command languages, systems written in modern development environments such as Lotus Notes provide the user with a command syntax that closely resembles natural English language sentences. An extension of the concept of nonprocedurality, the natural language command processor accepts commands and instructions in the form of commonly structured English sentences that are sequenced and constructed at the convenience of the user rather than at the convenience of the command language. When we speak or write to each other, our sequence of words, punctuation, spelling, and grammar all convey meaning, and we can live with some fairly significant deviations from the rules without losing the essence of the meaning. In written form, if a comma is missing or a word is misspelled, we can usually still understand the message being conveyed. In a command-oriented language, regardless of procedurality, a missing comma or a command parameter out of order can render the message undecipherable by the command processor. The natural language DSS is more tolerant of these issues and can actually be designed to "learn" the user's intentions over time. That is, the command processor can interpret the meaning of a new command within the context of the previous commands or requests made by the user. Additionally, natural language systems can be easily adapted to alternative forms of input, such as voice recognition or even visual pattern matching, that allow commands to be given to the DSS by simply speaking them or by making a specific motion or expression to a camera connected to the system. Despite the obvious advantages of a natural language command processor, however, this type of DSS is in its infancy. Technology is still a long way from providing users with machines they can interact with in a natural, humanlike manner. We will explore some of these issues in Chapters 9, 17, and 18.

HYPERTEXT SYSTEMS

Yet another method for classifying DSSs focuses on the technique used by the system to provide the necessary knowledge management for the problem context. One such technique is the document-centric hypertext system. Such systems support the decision process by keeping track of a large and often disparate knowledge base that is primarily document or text based. Activities including document creation, revision, searching, grouping, merging, indexing, and forwarding, among others, are typically found in a text-based DSS. Using the concept of hypertext, the text-based DSS can facilitate the user's exploration of a particular flow of ideas through a group of documents. Various pieces of text within a document can be linked to related pieces of text in other documents so that a particular thread or train of thought can be explored. The most common example of this concept is found on the World Wide Web.

A user can begin at one Web site and by using hypertext links travel through literally millions of documents, or Web pages (see Figure 1-8), investigating a particular flow of ideas. At any time, the user can restructure the investigation to explore a new twist or turn or simply abandon the search and start over. This natural journey through related documents and pieces of text is driven entirely by the user and closely resembles the way human beings think and make associations among numerous concepts. Hypertext systems support the decision process by relating and remembering things for the user. Computers are far superior to humans at those tasks. The user is thus free to perform the decision process activities related to thinking and evaluating. These activities are still best performed by a human problem solver for most unstructured problem-solving contexts.

SPREADSHEET SYSTEMS

Another technique DSSs use for knowledge representation is the spreadsheet system. This simple, yet powerful, method of representing relationships through the use of a matrix of rows and columns allows the user not only to create and represent relationships in the form of mathematical or locational links but also to directly manipulate those linkages and see the end result. Application packages such as Microsoft Excel or Lotus 1–2–3 are powerful spreadsheet environments that can serve as a foundation for sophisticated and complex decision support systems. More recently, common develop-

FIGURE 1-8   Example of World Wide Web Page with Hypertext Links

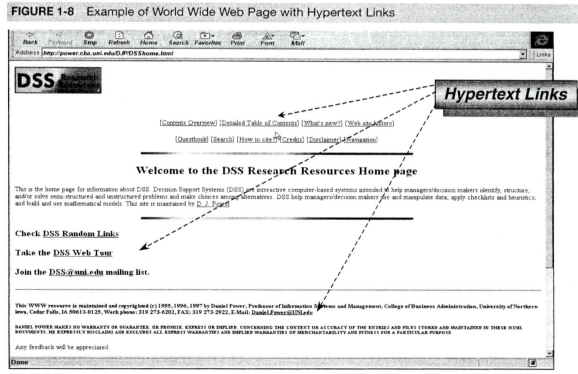

Source: DSS Research Resources Home Page, © 1997. Used by permission of Daniel Power.

ment environments such as Lotus Notes simply integrate these concepts of hypertext representation and spreadsheet systems. Using this approach, the DSS designer can incorporate spreadsheet representation of knowledge within a hypertext-constructed document so that the user can manipulate the data using a combination of the techniques as he or she sees fit.

INDIVIDUAL AND GROUP DSSs

Probably the most widely used method of classifying a DSS is based on its ability to provide support to a single decision maker or to a group of decision makers. In the modern business world, it is unrealistic to assume that decisions of consequence will be made by a lone decision maker. Rather, they are made by a collective or through the consensus of multiple decision makers. As such, the concept of a group decision support system (GDSS) suggests that the design, implementation, and use of such systems differ from that of DSSs intended for use by a single decision maker or problem solver. We will explore the similarities and differences between these two types of systems in Chapters 5 and 6.

1-9: CHAPTER SUMMARY

This chapter introduces you to the world of decision support and DSSs. By using the basic definitions and classification frameworks covered here you will be able to focus on the complexities and details of each type of DSS presented in the remaining chapters, and, in addition, you will be able to relate the use of a particular DSS to its appropriate problem context.

A DSS is truly a dynamic system that requires knowledge beyond that of the typical IS professional. The decision makers of tomorrow will rely on this technology to support their daily activities and to assist them in managing the ever-growing knowledge base necessary to make informed and effective decisions. Although this book cannot possibly serve as a single source of knowledge for computer-based decision support, it can and will provide you with a solid foundation for understanding, interacting with, and effectively using the decision support technologies of tomorrow.

Key Concepts

- Definition

  A decision support system (DSS) is a system under the control of one or more decision makers that assists in the activity of decision making by providing an organized set of tools intended to impose structure on portions of the decision-making situation and to improve the ultimate effectiveness of the decision outcome.

- Benefits/limitations of the DSS

  The manager should see the DSS as a valuable tool in the decision-making process rather than as a mechanism for the making of the decision itself.

- The components of a DSS

  The data management system

  The model management system

The knowledge engine

The user interface

The user(s)

- Categories and classes of DSSs

Data-centric DSS versus model-centric DSS

Formal DSS versus ad hoc DSS

Directed DSS versus nondirected DSS

Procedurality

Hypertext management systems

Spreadsheet systems

Individual versus group DSS

Questions for Review

1. What common characteristics of a decision support system relate to the decision-making process?
2. Why is a DSS a powerful tool for decision makers?
3. Is a "universal DSS" possible? Why or why not?
4. Why is the concept of procedurality important to the design and implementation of a DSS?
5. List and briefly describe the five basic components of a DSS.
6. What is a database? What are the possible sources of data collected in a database? Why is the ability to combine data records from multiple sources so important to DSS users?
7. What is a DBMS? Explain its two main responsibilities and how they contribute to the functionality of a DSS.
8. What is a model? How can a model base support decision makers in the problem-solving process?
9. Describe the two main responsibilities of the MBMS and the role of an MBMS in a decision support system.
10. What is reasoning? Why is reasoning important to the decision-making process?
11. What is a knowledge base? What is its role in a DSS?
12. How does knowledge get into the DSS? How can it be retrieved and organized into useful information?
13. What must be present in order for the user to be able to communicate well with the DSS?
14. Explain the roles of the various types of users of a DSS.
15. Describe and give an example of each pattern of DSS use.
16. Compare and contrast data-centric versus model-centric systems, formal versus ad hoc systems, and directed versus nondirected systems. What are the advantages and disadvantages of each type?
17. Compare the benefits and limitations of highly procedural languages and less or nonprocedural languages.

For Further Discussion

1. Analyze a DSS application in the market. Describe its main components and summarize its functionalities.
2. Observe the decision-making processes in an organization with which you are familiar. Discuss how a decision support system can help in the process. Decide which category of DSS can fit with the characteristics of those decision-making processes.
3. Compare a DBMS and an MBMS. What is common to both? What are the differences between them?
4. The admissions office at the University of Maryland needs a decision support system for evaluating applications. They need to build a database for the DSS. Specify the data sources and data that could be found for the admissions office to use.
5. Interview a member of an organization that is using a DSS. Specify the roles of the users and find their patterns of use.
6. DSS experts generally agree that the interface represents the single most important component in the system. Why is the user interface such an important component in a decision support system? Which kinds of interfaces are considered user-friendly?

2
DECISIONS AND DECISION MAKERS

Learning Objectives

◆ Understand the elements and framework of the decision-making process

◆ Be familiar with the classification of decision makers

◆ Based on decision makers' cognitive complexity and value orientation, understand the classification of decision styles and the three related factors: problem context, perception, and personal values

◆ Understand the interactions between problem context and decision styles in order to design systems that provide appropriate support

◆ Comprehend the definition of a good decision and the forces acting upon the decision makers during the decision process

◆ Learn the common types of support that can be provided by decision support systems

◆ Understand the difficulties of decision making from different angles such as problem structure, cognitive limitations, uncertainty of decision outcomes, and alternatives and multiple objectives

◆ Learn the classification of decisions and understand the role of these typologies in the design of decision support systems

◆ Understand Simon's model of problem solving

◆ Learn the theory of rational decision making

◆ Gain an understanding of Simon's "satisficing" strategy and bounded rationality

◆ Clarify the difference between a symptom and a problem

◆ Become familiar with the process of choice

◆ Understand the decision maker's cognitive process and its effects on decision making

◆ Learn four of the most common heuristic biases and their effects on decision making

◆ Distinguish between effectiveness and efficiency

DISASTER AT TENERIFE

Experts in cockpit resource management study the worst tragedy in aviation history for its many lessons. After a bomb rocked the Las Palmas airport, located in the Canary Islands' capital, early in the afternoon of March 27, 1977, inbound traffic was diverted to Los Rodeos on the island of Tenerife. The airport on Tenerife did not have the capacity of Las Palmas, so aircraft were squeezed in on its ramp. Among those diverted to Los Rodeos that day were Pan Am Flight 1736 and KLM (Royal Dutch Airlines) Flight 4805, both Boeing 747s laden with passengers. Arriving after the KLM flight, the Pam Am jet was parked behind it on the apron, just short of the departure end of runway 12.

On the flight deck of the KLM aircraft, Captain Jacob van Zanten, a highly regarded training captain, was anxious to get back in the air because the duty hours for his crew were running low. When the tower radioed that Las Palmas had reopened, van Zanten decided that, instead of refueling at Las Palmas, which would undoubtedly be busy with the reopening, he would refuel while waiting on the ramp at Los Rodeos. It was now Pan Am 1736's turn to depart, but the only way to reach the departure end of the active runway, runway 30, was to enter runway 12 and backtrack. Unfortunately, KLM 4805 had only just begun refueling, leaving no way for the Pan Am airliner to taxi around it with the limited space at Los Rodeos. Pan Am's First Officer Bragg called the KLM crew, asking how long it would take to refuel, to which they replied, "About 35 minutes." The crew of flight 1736 could do nothing but wait. While flight 4805 was refueling, fog moved in at the airport, and by the time the refueling was completed, visibility had decreased to as little as 900 feet in some areas. The KLM crew finally started their engines and prepared to take off. As they taxied to the beginning of runway 12, the tower instructed flight 4805 to "taxi straight ahead . . . ah . . . for the runway . . . make . . . ah . . . backtrack." At this point, Pan Am 1736

had also started its engines and was holding short of the runway. The visibility now prevented the tower from seeing either the runway or the two aircraft. Bragg then called the tower for instructions and flight 1736 was told to "taxi into the runway and . . . ah . . . leave the runway third . . . third to your left."

Apparently the pronunciation was unclear to Pan Am's Captain Grubbs who said, "I think he said first," to which Bragg replied, "I'll ask him again." Meanwhile the tower called flight 4805, instructing the crew, "at the end of the runway make one eighty and report . . . ah . . . ready for ATC clearance." After this communication, Bragg called back and said, "Would . . . you confirm that you want us to turn left at the third intersection?" The tower replied, "The third one, sir . . . one two three . . . third one." The crew of flight 1736 was still having difficulty sorting out the taxiways as they rolled down the runway. At this point, flight 4805 had reached the end of the runway and was making its 180-degree turn. As the aircraft finished the turn, van Zanten opened the throttle and the plane began to move forward. First Officer Meurs said, "Wait a minute . . . we don't have an ATC clearance," to which van Zanten said, "No, I know that. Go ahead and ask," as he held the brakes. Meurs called for the clearance and as he was reading it back, van Zanten again opened the throttles, saying, "Let's go, check thrust." After repeating the clearance, Meurs, in an attempt to let the controller know what was happening, said, "We are now at takeoff." The tower controller apparently took this to mean they were ready for takeoff, saying, "OK . . . stand by for takeoff . . . I will call you." On the flight deck of the Pan Am aircraft, the crew was obviously anxious about the implications of the transmission from flight 4805, Bragg saying, "We are still taxiing down the runway!" to which the tower replied, "Roger, Pan Am 1736, report the runway clear." Unfortunately, this first transmission blocked the tower's transmission to flight 4805 so all the KLM crew heard

(continued)

(*continued*)

was "OK." The transmission from flight 1736 troubled flight 4805's Flight Engineer Schreuder, prompting him to say, "Did he not clear the runway then?" Van Zanten, now focusing on the takeoff, replied with only "What did you say?" Schreuder repeated himself, saying, "Did he not clear the runway then, that Pan American?" to which both van Zanten and Meurs replied, "Yes, he did." Flight 1736 was still creeping down the runway, trying to find the proper turnoff, but obviously now concerned about KLM 4805's transmissions. Grubbs said, "Let's get the hell right out of here," to which Bragg replied, "Yeah . . . he's anxious, isn't he?" A few seconds later, Grubbs spotted the lights of flight 4805 coming at them through the fog and said, "There he is . . . look at him! Goddamn . . . that son-of-a-bitch is coming!" He opened all four throttles in an attempt to swing the aircraft off the runway as Bragg yelled, "Get off! Get off! Get off!" Van Zanten saw flight 1736 still in the runway and pulled back, attempting to climb off the runway before impacting the aircraft. The nose gear managed to clear flight 1736, but the rest of the aircraft slammed into the Pan Am plane's starboard side. Flight 4805 remained airborne for a few more seconds before slamming into the ground and exploding. Pan Am 1736 was crushed and quickly caught fire as well. Everyone on board KLM 4805 was killed. The flight crew of Pan Am 1736 all survived uninjured, having just missed being hit by flight 4805's engine. Amazingly, 66 others survived from the Pan Am aircraft. Unfortunately, 583 people died that day on Tenerife in what is still today the worst aviation accident in history.

The biggest question on the minds of investigators was why van Zanten, a highly experienced training captain, would make the decision to begin a takeoff without a takeoff clearance from the tower. Meurs was still copying the en route clearance when van Zanten began advancing the throttles. It seems clear that van Zanten was aware that the clearance hadn't been received when Meurs checked him and he replied, "No, I know that. Go ahead and ask." It is likely that van Zanten was in a rush to get to Las Palmas because of the delay on the ground and his crew's lack of extra duty hours. However, even after the en route clearance was given, the tower instructed KLM 4805 to "stand by for takeoff," which the crew failed to hear as well as the clear indications that Pan Am 1763 was still on the runway. In addition, Meurs did nothing to enlighten van Zanten that they were not cleared for takeoff after his initial comment. It is possible that Meurs was not comfortable challenging van Zanten due to his experience level. To exacerbate the situation further, the efforts of the crew of flight 1736 were hampered by the low visibility. They had only a small diagram of the airport and the third taxiway led backwards from their intended taxi direction—a turn of 135 degrees, which would be extremely challenging in a 747. They apparently believed that the fourth taxiway, which was at a 45-degree angle in the proper direction, was the one the tower intended for them to use, so they proceeded past taxiway 3. None of the taxiways at Los Rodeos were marked. A final consideration was the difficulty with English of the tower controller and the KLM (Dutch) crew. With the weather as bad as it was, relying solely on radio communications was already a dangerous practice, but the nonstandard communications of both parties led to a breakdown of situational awareness. The Dutch investigation team placed the blame firmly on the controllers at Los Rodeos, while the American investigation team found the actions of Captain van Zanten to be the primary cause of the accident.

Can you decide?

2-1: DECISION MAKERS: WHO ARE THEY?

In Chapter 1, we explored the component parts and essential elements of a DSS from the inside out. We began with the DBMS, MBMS, and knowledge base and proceeded to weave our way out of the mechanical insides of the system to the user interface, and finally to the user. The purpose of that inside-out investigation was to lay the groundwork for understanding what a DSS is and what it is not. This discussion of what a DSS is and is not will begin with you—the decision maker.

The objective, or purpose, regarding the design and use of a DSS is really quite simple: We know we need to make decisions but we don't know exactly how to make them. In this context, "how" does not always mean procedure or method, although a DSS can be extremely valuable in that part of the decision-making realm. Rather, we are referring to the "how" part of decision making that deals with processing large volumes of seemingly disparate data and managing a myriad of models of reality that "predict" certain key outcomes. This chapter begins by focusing on the reason why we have decision support systems at all: the decision maker. Were it not for the needs of human problem solvers to be supported in certain phases of the often lengthy and complex process of semistructured decision making, we would not have DSSs and, as such, we would not need to talk about them. Happily, for us at least, decision makers need support and a DSS is just the ticket. We begin, therefore, by exploring just who these decision makers are and what makes each of them unique.

PROFILE OF A DECISION

One last point of order remains before focusing directly on the decision maker. We need a working model of what the decision maker, in the generic sense at least, is trying to accomplish during the making of a decision.

The literature on the subject contains many theories about how decisions are made, the steps within the decision-making process, the motivations for making the decision, the steps within the steps, and on and on and on. All of this attention is not bad, but it is too much for a manager to absorb and understand. Here we focus on one or two theoretical frameworks for the decision process and use them to guide our investigation of both the process and the people involved in it.

Figure 2-1 profiles one of the many ways that a decision is made. Describing the process in this way takes into account that in the real world of decision making, a decision is rarely, if ever, made in exactly the order suggested by the model or even by using all of the steps contained in the model. Moreover, the process depicted offers only a static representation of a distinctly dynamic operation. The specific conditions and circumstances of the problem to be solved will ultimately dictate the way in which the decision is made. Nonetheless, we can use the model in Figure 2-1 as a basis for understanding what should be going on in a typical decision context.

The decision maker plays a somewhat schizophrenic role in the process of making a decision. Not only is he or she considered an element, or step, in the process (as shown in Figure 2-1), but the decision maker is also a participant, in varying degrees, in all of the steps in the process. In Chapter 3, we examine how this dual role complicates the process of decision making and further adds complexity to the management of the

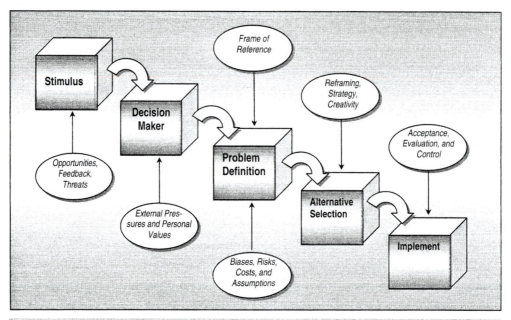

FIGURE 2-1 Example of a Decision-Making Process

Source: Adapted from Rowe, A. J. and Boulgarides, J. D., (1994), *Managerial Decision Making*, Upper Saddle River, NJ: Prentice Hall. Used by permission, © 1985, all rights reserved.

process. For now, however, let's simply look at each element in the process and see how they all fit together.

Stimulus

The first step in the process occurs when the presence of some externality or force causes the decision maker to perceive that one or more problems exist that require one or more decisions to be made. A problem is defined simply as the perception of a difference between the current state of affairs and a desired state of affairs. A variety of stimuli can cause this perception of a problem context. These stimuli may take many forms and can be perceived differently by different decision makers. In other words, what is perceived by one decision maker as a problem may not be viewed as a problem by another member of the same organization. This disparity of perception may occur because a problem really does not exist and the decision maker is misinterpreting existing facts or information or because a problem really does exist and one or more members of the organization fail to recognize it.

The forms the stimuli take can affect the perception of a problem. Often, a problem doesn't manifest itself as a problem per se. It manifests itself as a series of symptoms that indicate the presence of an underlying problem. Either way, the situation triggers the decision-making process.

The Decision Maker

The example in Figure 2-1 shows the decision maker as one part of the process. Throughout our discussion, however, the decision maker functions as a participant in the process. We will focus on the participant role in the next few chapters. Here the decision maker is defined as simply the next step or event following the onset of a stimulus.

The decision maker is truly a "black box" in every sense of the word. We don't know nearly as much as we want to about the DSS user, but perhaps this area of research will contribute significant advances for the manager of tomorrow.

Problem Definition

As already stated, problems often manifest themselves as a series of symptoms that all relate to the real problem or are the results of it. In either situation, however, the problem solver must define the problem before any effective investigation of alternative solutions can be conducted. This phase is crucial to the successful outcome of the decision-making process. If the right problem definition is formulated, then the right problem will be solved. If, however, the problem definition is flawed by an incorrect assessment of the true nature of the problem at hand, then a potentially great solution to the wrong problem may be offered. Worse yet, it may also be implemented. Hopefully, the DSS will guide potential problem identification and result in the definition of the correct one.

Alternative Selection

At the heart of the decision-making process, and where a DSS is often most useful, lies the task of selecting an effective solution from a set of feasible alternatives. It is the essence of decision making—the decision itself. The DSS can be used to provide quantitative approaches to the analysis of the set of feasible alternatives and to assist the manager in choosing the best available solution to the problem at hand. We will see later in this chapter, however, that this selection process is the part we are least naturally equipped to perform and, thus, the one for which we must rely most heavily on the DSS to assist us.

Implementation

Once the user settles on the most effective solution from the set of alternatives the work has really just begun. The decision process triggers actions and events within the organization that are focused on implementing the solution and, thus, solving the problem. These actions include creating consensus and acceptance, negotiation, strategizing, politicking, and intense planning. The greatest solution in the world is worthless if it is not effectively implemented. A DSS can be of limited support in assisting with decisions directly related to issues of implementation; at this phase, the decision maker him- or herself becomes the most important player. The success or failure of implementing a solution ultimately rests with the decision maker. We will explore this aspect of the process in greater detail in Chapter 4.

CLASSES OF DECISION MAKERS

Now that we have a model of the decision process to help us understand what is going on, we need to focus our attention on the decision maker. Many different types of decision makers must be supported in the many different types of problem contexts, which is why so many different types of DSSs exist. Figure 2-2 provides a model of the different decision-maker classifications.

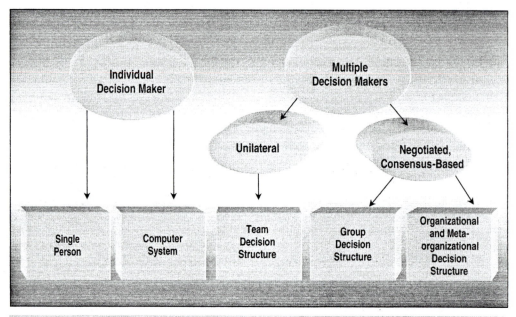

FIGURE 2-2 Decision Maker Classifications

Individual Decision Makers

The individual decision maker, as the name implies, stands alone in the final decision process. This class of users essentially works alone during the decision process in the sense that the analysis of information and the ultimate generation of a final decision rests solely in their hands. Because an individual decision maker is, by definition, an individual, his or her unique characteristics with regard to knowledge, skill set, experience, personality, cognitive style, and individual biases come to bear in the decision-making process. Each of these traits both directly and interactively affects how the decision maker ultimately decides and what types of support are needed during the process. This factor, among others, also contributes to the complexity of many DSS designs. To be truly effective, a DSS intended for use by an individual problem solver must be designed to account for his or her unique characteristics and needs. If more than one individual decision maker is to use the DSS, then the design must reflect the unique characteristics and support needs of each of the intended users. The combinatorial nature of this problem should be readily apparent. Designing a DSS for individual use is a complex and difficult activity. We will see just how these complexities and difficulties manifest themselves and how they are addressed in Chapters 13 and 14.

Multiple Decision Makers

This class of decision makers consists of multiple individuals interacting to reach a decision. We differentiate between multiple decision makers and group or team decision makers in the next section. Here, the multiple decision makers involved have a stake in a particular decision outcome and thus are motivated to reach eventual agreement and common commitment to a course of action. Each member of this class may come with unique motivations or goals and may approach the decision process from a different angle. Furthermore, each may use a common DSS or a variety of systems as support for his or her contribution to the decision-making process. Finally, multiple decision makers seldom possess equal authority to make a particular decision, nor do any of them possess enough authority to make the decision alone. In these problem contexts, multiple decision makers do not necessarily meet in a formalized manner or conduct open forums or discussions as a unit. Instead, the institutionalized patterns of communication—and the various levels of authority within the organization—structure the interaction among the participants in such a way that eventually a "decision" is reached and implementation begins. The best way to conceptualize this class of users is as a dynamic union of users who act individually to bring a decision or solution to a particular problem context and to the point it can be implemented.

Group Decision Makers

In contrast to multiple decision makers, a group decision maker is characterized by membership in a more formal structure where members of the group share a similar vested interest in the decision outcome and an equal say in its formation. Group decision makers generally work in a formal environment that consists of regular meetings devoted to working through the decision process, formal schedules and agendas focusing on specific portions of the process, and often deadlines by which the decision must be finalized and implemented. Common examples of group decision makers are those who make up organizational committees and juries. Each participant is involved in the making of a decision based on consensus of the group, but none possesses any more input or authority to make the decision than any other. The formalization of the decision process differentiates the group decision maker from the multiple decision maker. Therefore, the unique nature of the group process must be understood if support is to be provided by a DSS. We explore these issues in depth in Chapters 6 and 7.

Team Decision Makers

Yet another class of decision maker is called the team decision maker. This class can be thought of as a combination of the individual and group classes. Often, an organization's structure is such that even though the authority to make a particular decision rests with an individual manager, he or she is supported by several assistants working toward the same goal(s). In the team context, decision support may come from several individuals empowered by the key individual decision maker to collect information and/or make certain determinations regarding a portion of the intended decision outcome. Also, support may come from one or more DSSs being used by any combination of team members. In this context, the team produces or "manufactures" the final decision, but the formalization of that decision and authority to make it rest with the individual decision maker. Figure 2-3 illustrates the differences between the individual, multiple, group, and team classes of decision makers.

One unique difference between decisions made by a group and those made by a team is the type of decisions made. In the group class, decision outcomes are often negotiated outcomes. Generally, external forces determine the need for the formation of a group in the first place and, in such scenarios, the choices facing the group are often controversial. The group decision makers, therefore, tend to seek alternatives that permit the attainment of the group's original objectives while serving as a compromise among the concerned parties. In the team class, however, decisions are normally unilateral in nature. Only one decision maker has the authority and responsibility to make

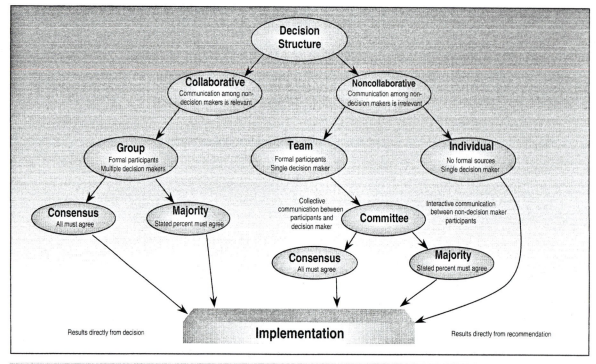

FIGURE 2-3 Classification of Decision Structures

a unilateral decision, even though many people can be said to have influenced that decision's final form. This type of decision is the most basic and generally possesses many characteristics similar to those decisions made by the individual decision-making class.

Organizational and Metaorganizational Decision Makers

More than 50 years ago, Chester Barnard, a noted expert on management as a science, offered a definition of an organization as "a system of consciously coordinated activities of two or more persons" (Barnard, 1938, p. 73). Although a lot has changed since Barnard's definition was first printed, it remains viable today. The glue holding the organization together is the purposes and goals shared by its members. Using this definition, we can easily conceive of organizations within organizations: groups and teams that consciously coordinate their activities for the purpose of reaching a commonly held objective or goal. Decision makers at the organizational level are those who are empowered with the authority and charged with the responsibility of making decisions on behalf of the entire organization. The characteristics of those decisions and the processes used in arriving at them, by definition, bear strong similarities to those made by individual, team, and group class decision makers. If their purposes are so similar, why do we need to identify a unique class of decision makers at the organizational level?

One reason is the breadth and depth of information needed by the organizational decision maker. This class of users is embodied by the most senior level of management: the CEO. As we will see in Chapters 6 and 7, a special type of DSS has been developed for use at this level. We call these special DSSs executive information systems (EIS).

Another reason why we differentiate between the team or group classes and the organizational class is that the decisions made by this class of users generally require support from the entire organization for successful implementation. A classic example of this type of decision making is found in most Japanese organizations. The concept, called *nemawashi*, uses a central decision maker following a prescribed set of consensus-building conventions at all levels of the organization until a global agreement is reached concerning what the final decision should be. Organizational decision makers generally do not have the resources to implement large-scale decision outcomes without support from the vast majority of their subordinates. As such, the special support needs of these decision makers differ from those at the individual, group, or team levels and are appropriately categorized separately.

Yet another class of decision maker exists beyond the organizational level. All of the world's organizations together make up the system of enterprise. Decisions made by users operating at this level tend to be oriented toward social welfare, quality of life, allocation of controlled or limited resources, social order, or civil justice. In other words, decision makers in this class are not principally oriented by economics as are the decision makers within the system of enterprise. They are, rather, focused on decisions that affect the establishment of social order. Because organizations exist within the overall socioeconomic system, all decision makers and their respective decisions must account for the decisions made at the metaorganizational level. More importantly, as with all other classes of decision makers, metaorganizational decision makers require special support and, thus, special systems of support.

2-2: DECISION STYLES

To further our understanding of the decision maker, we need to better understand those things that directly affect his or her behavior. One such area of focus is decision style. *Decision style* is a term used to describe the manner in which a manager makes decisions. The manager's design style is reflected in the way he or she reacts to a given decision-making context—what is believed to be of value or importance, how the information is interpreted, how the externalities and forces are dealt with. The ultimate effect of a particular individual's decision style on a decision outcome depends on factors such as problem context, the perceptions of the decision maker, and the personal set of values that he or she brings to the situation. The mechanisms used to measure and categorize decision styles and the results obtained from these measures provide the input for the design and implementation of a DSS.

CONTEXT, PERCEPTION, AND VALUES

The three interwoven factors of context, perception, and values contribute to decision style. The problem context involves factors relating to the forces acting on the decision maker in the course of making the decision. Organizational and environmental forces such as government regulation, new technologies, market competition, and internal power struggles all affect the problem context. Forces of a more individual nature such as skill set, energy, motivation, and perceived abilities, among others, can also shape the problem context. The decision maker must balance and manage the totality of these forces during the problem-solving process.

Another factor affecting decision style is perception. Decision makers bring personal biases into the problem context, which often serve to "convert" the facts so that they better match their own reality. Various studies demonstrate that managers tend to perceive a problem situation and its potential solutions in relation to their personal goals rather than a strict set of realities. As a result, perceptual biases interact with the problem context to determine a particular decision maker's approach to solving a problem and whether that approach is effective. We focus in depth on the effects of individual biases on decision outcomes in the next chapter.

Last, but not least, the personal values of the decision maker are important in determining his or her decision style. Values consist of those world views or global beliefs that guide individual actions, judgments, and desired outcomes. An individual's values are not tied to any particular object or situation and can be generalized across all modes of conduct. Moreover, values are acquired at an early age and tend to remain strong throughout a person's lifetime. An individual's values, therefore, form a permanent framework that influences a person's behavior and the manner in which he or she makes decisions.

The complexity with which these three factors intertwine in the formation of decision style is significant. Established measures of decision style provide a basis on which to build a classification scheme for decision styles to use when designing DSSs intended for specific problem contexts and users possessing certain decision style characteristics. Let's begin by looking at the basic classes of decision style and their associated characteristics.

Figure 2-4 shows a decision style classification scheme derived from the work of noted psychiatrist Carl Jung. The classification scheme provides the basis for many measures of decision style including the popular Myers-Briggs Type Indicator test (Myers 1962) and the Decision Style Inventory developed by Alan Rowe. As can be seen in the figure, decision style is classified using two component parts: cognitive complexity and value orientation. These two dimensions can be used further to identify four distinct categories of decision style.

DIRECTIVE

The directive decision style combines a high need for structure in the problem context with a relatively low tolerance for context ambiguity. Decision makers possessing these characteristics tend to focus on decisions of a technical nature and often do not require large amounts of information or consider multiple alternatives. They are generally considered efficient managers but require visible levels of both security and status. Finally, directive-style decision makers tend to function best when they communicate verbally rather than through writing or other multichannel media.

ANALYTICAL

This style demonstrates a much greater tolerance for context ambiguity and tends toward the need for greater volumes of information and the consideration of large sets of alternatives. Analytical-style decision makers are best at coping with new, often

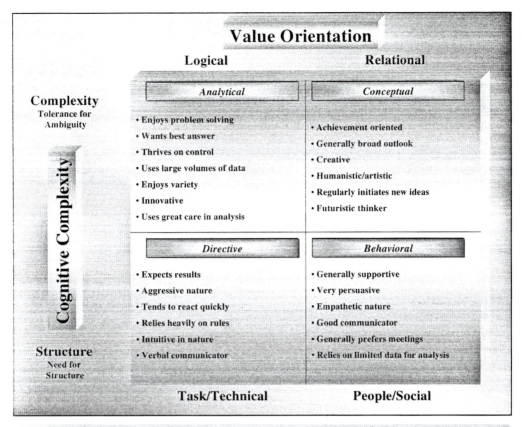

FIGURE 2-4 Decision Style Model

unexpected, situations and problem contexts. They simply enjoy solving problems. In contrast to the directive style, analyticals prefer written communication and are not quick to reach a decision or solution. Their orientation toward detail often results in protracted investigations of the problem context before a final decision is made.

CONCEPTUAL

Much like the analytical decision maker, the conceptual manager demonstrates a high tolerance for ambiguity but tends to be much more of a "people person." Conceptuals display an openness with their subordinates and tend to be driven by an idealistic emphasis on values and ethics. This type of decision maker is a long-term thinker and generally strongly committed to the organization. In addition, conceptual decision makers tend to be achievement oriented and value accolades and organizational recognition. Their management style commonly focuses on participation and exhibits loose control. As implied by their name, conceptuals are thinkers rather than doers.

BEHAVIORAL

The fourth category of decision style falls low on the cognitive complexity scale. Nonetheless, behavioral types display a deep commitment to the organization as well as an employee orientation. This style requires a relatively low amount of data input and, as such, generally demonstrates a relatively short-range vision. Behaviorals are conflict-averse by nature and tend to rely on meetings and consensus for communicating to and organizing subordinates.

DECISION STYLE IN DSS DESIGN

The four classifications of decision style in the Rowe typology provide us with a method of categorizing decision makers according to the characteristics of their particular style, but we need a method of incorporating this knowledge into the design process for a DSS. Effectively using these classifications in DSS design requires that a few key points be addressed.

To begin with, one must recognize that human beings are complex and no simple method of classification, such as the Decision Style Inventory, will reflect completely this complexity. Therefore, we cannot expect managers to fit neatly into a single category. Typically, a manager's responses indicate the presence of a dominant decision style with one or possibly two backup styles. Thus it is better for us to think of a manager's decision style in terms of style patterns rather than a distinct and highly predictable set of rigid behaviors. Knowing an individual's dominant and backup decision patterns can yield a great deal of information useful in the design of interfaces and levels of procedurality or directiveness.

CONTEXT/DECISION STYLE INTERACTION

Table 2-1 lists a number of style-situation comparisons and behavior outcomes regarding the four classifications that can serve to inform the design of a DSS for a particular type of decision maker.

The key issues in our focus on decision style as it relates to DSS design and use are the decision maker's specific reactions to stress and the method in which problems are generally solved. If we use our knowledge of these characteristics in the design of a DSS intended for use by a known decision style we may be able to provide support compatible with the user's preferred approach. Conversely, if we ignore decision style

TABLE 2-1 Common Characteristics of Decision Style Behaviors

Basic Style	Behavior under Stress	Motivations	Problem-Solving Strategy	Nature of Thought
Directive	Explosive, volatile	Power and status	Policies and procedures	Focused
Analytical	Focuses on rules	Challenge	Analysis and insight	Logical
Conceptual	Erratic, unpredictable	Recognition	Intuition and judgment	Creative
Behavioral	Avoidance	Peer acceptance	Feelings and instincts	Emotional

Source: Adapted from Rowe, A. J. and Boulgarides, J. D., (1994), *Managerial Decision Making*, Upper Saddle River, NJ: Prentice Hall. Used by permission, © 1985, all rights reserved.

or fail to provide appropriate support for a particular style, the DSS may actually inhibit the success of the process and reinforce certain biases or weaknesses in the decision maker's approach to solving the problem. Some simple examples may better illustrate this point.

Let's say we know the primary user of a proposed DSS possesses a dominant decision style in the analytical category. We know this style displays a high tolerance for ambiguity, uses considerable data in reaching a conclusion, strives toward optimization of the solution, is creative, and prefers a structured, rule-oriented environment. This type of user would be able to function effectively in a procedural DSS environment and would require access to a wide variety of data sources and models during the course of using the DSS. Systems that are designed to allow for innovative and counterintuitive analyses and model combining would be most useful to the analytical-style manager.

Consider, on the other hand, a system that is highly procedural and directive being used by a manager whose dominant decision style is highly directive. The directive type has a low tolerance for ambiguity and is not good at coping with stressful situations. The user's need for control and power would require an interface that allows for such control to be exercised in the operation of the system. The tedious nature of constructing an exact and semantically accurate query or command to the DSS would soon wear thin on a directive decision maker. Also, recall that the directive type is primarily a verbal communicator, which would suggest that output requiring visual analysis for interpretation would not be utilized as well by a directive as would a simple, concise table or narrative response from the DSS. In sum, designing the system to complement the user's decision style can provide additional support to the decision-making process and failing to do so can inhibit the success of the process.

2-3: DECISION EFFECTIVENESS

WHAT MAKES A GOOD DECISION A GOOD DECISION?

An old adage in the used car business says that a "good deal" is the deal you just agreed to. This approach makes the assumption that the buyer would never knowingly agree to a "bad deal" and therefore, if he or she agreed to it, it must be good. We can think of agreement to a deal as a decision and can assume that the decision to agree is viewed by the buyer as a good decision. But how do we really know whether a decision is a good one?

Given the fact that decision making is at the heart of managerial activities and that good decisions are significantly related to the long-term success of an organization, one would expect to find a wealth of knowledge regarding the profile of a good decision and the determinants of successful decision outcomes. Unfortunately, such knowledge remains elusive. Even though a number of studies investigated the factors relating to successful decisions, few if any offered useful prescriptions for improving the chances of decision success. We are faced, then, with defining a good decision and then using that definition to judge whether a good decision has been made.

The following definition of a "good" decision is offered: *A good decision results in the attainment of the objective or objectives that gave rise to the need for a decision within the boundaries and constraints imposed by the problem's context.* In other words, if we reach our goal given the limitations of our situation, then we have made a "good" decision. Another way of looking at it is that if by our decision we solved the problem at hand without causing any new problems, then our decision must have been a good one. The problem is that we really do not know whether a decision is a good one until after it is made. We are, therefore, faced with analyzing our intended decision in terms of the intended ends that will be accomplished by the means available to us, which partly explains why decisions are often hard to make. We will explore this issue more in the next chapter when we look at the various theories associated with decision making. In the meantime, we need to better understand the various forces that shape the problem context and, thus, both the decision process and its outcome.

DECISION FORCES

Several models attempt to explain the variety of potential forces and constraints that can act on a problem context, and thus on a decision maker, during the course of making a decision. Each of these models suggests that the decision maker must balance the forces acting upon the process and must contend with the dynamics of the forces in formulating and implementing a final decision. Figure 2-5 illustrates these forces. Although each problem context is unique, it may exhibit the majority, if not all, of the forces listed in one form or another during a typical decision-making process. Let's briefly review each of the major categories of forces and constraints found in a typical decision process.

FIGURE 2-5 Forces Acting upon a Typical Decision Maker

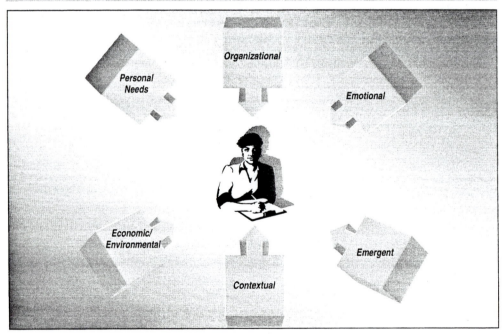

Personal and Emotional Forces

The decision maker does not live in a vacuum and is not without typical human needs. As such, the conditions that relate to his or her feelings, health, security, rewards, frustrations, anxieties, and maybe most important, cognitive limitations can all be of consequence during the process of selecting the appropriate alternative. Each of these personal forces can serve to either reinforce or debilitate the manager's ability to make a sound decision. As a result, the personal forces acting upon the decision process must be given careful consideration by the decision maker during the formulation of a decision strategy.

The human mind has often been referred to as infinite in its capacity and power. However, the practical nature of our understanding of human cognitive processes suggests we are limited in our present ability to store and process knowledge. Compared to the rate at which knowledge is advancing, we possess only a modest amount of knowledge relative to all that is known. Moreover, studies show that we are limited in our capacity for processing the knowledge we do possess. Miller (1956) suggested the concept of "the magic number seven, plus or minus two." We typically are not capable of processing more than five to nine distinct pieces of knowledge at a time. We will see in Chapter 3 that the use of certain strategies for decision making can overcome this and other cognitive limitations, but cognitive limits still act as a significant force in the decision-making process.

Economic/Environmental Forces

This category includes limits on resources, governmental regulation, societal values such as views on the moral or ethical nature of the decision being considered, competitive pressures of the marketplace, the demands of the consumer, the needs and demands of the individual stakeholders potentially affected by the decision outcome, and the emergence of new technology. Individually or in combination, these forces require the decision maker to respond in a manner that may alter the final decision itself in order to account for, or control for, their effects.

In 1994, Intel discovered a bug in its new Pentium processor that caused inaccuracies in certain calculations (see Figure 2-6). The basic problem affected simple division requiring accuracy to sixteen significant digits. Intel executives decided to inform their consumers about the problem but maintained that it was so minor in nature that it would occur only once every 25,000 years for the typical user and that it required no recall by the manufacturer or action on the part of the consumer. Intel failed to consider certain market forces, however, in the making of this decision. IBM, a major consumer of Intel processors, had a significant inventory of 486-class machines in its warehouses. A market excited about the new Pentium processor had stopped buying 486 machines in anticipation of the Pentium. When IBM heard of the Pentium bug, it began a public campaign to discredit Intel's claims. IBM claimed that the problem was much larger than Intel was suggesting, arguing that it could occur once every 24 days and that the typical user would most surely be affected. Although neither side was able to provide substantive evidence to support its claims, the public began to lose their enthusiasm for the Pentium and reverted to purchasing 486-class machines—something that certainly pleased IBM. Intel's failure to simply replace the processors when the original announcement was made magnified the effects of IBM's counterattack on the consumer. Because Intel neglected to account for the environmental forces associated with its competition and with the introduction of new technologies, it

```
FROM: Dr. Thomas R. Nicely
Professor of Mathematics Lynchburg College
1501 Lakeside Drive Lynchburg, Virginia 24501-3199
Phone: 804-522-8374 Fax: 804-522-8499
Internet: nicely@acavax.lynchburg.edu

TO: Whom it may concern
RE: Bug in the Pentium FPU
DATE: 30 October 1994

It appears that there is a bug in the floating point unit (numeric coprocessor) of many, and perhaps all,
Pentium processors. In short, the Pentium FPU is returning erroneous values for certain division
operations.

For example, 1/824633702441.0 is calculated incorrectly (all digits beyond the eighth significant digit are
in error). This can be verified in compiled code, an ordinary spreadsheet such as Quattro Pro or Excel, or
even the Windows calculator (use the scientific mode), by computing

               (824633702441.0)*(1/824663702441.0),

which should equal 1 exactly (within some extremely small rounding error; in general, coprocessor results
should contain 19 significant decimal digits). However, the Pentiums tested return 0.999999996274709702 for
this calculation. A similar erroneous value is obtained for x*(1/x) for most values of x in the interval
824633702418 <= x <= 824633702449, and throughout any interval obtained by multiplying or dividing the
above interval by an integer power of 2 (there are yet other intervals which also produce division
errors). The bug can also be observed by calculating 1/(1/x) for the above values of x. The Pentium FPU
will fail to return the original x (in fact, it will often return a value exactly 3072 = 6*0x200 larger).

The bug has been observed on all Pentiums I have tested or had tested to date, including a Dell P90, a
Gateway P90, a Micron P60, an Insight P60, and a Packard-Bell P60. It has not been observed on any 486 or
earlier system, even those with a PCI bus. if the FPU is locked out (not always possible), the error
disappears; but then the Pentium becomes a "586SX", and floating point must run in emulation, slowing down
computations by a factor of roughly ten. I encountered erroneous results which were related to this bug as
long ago as June, 1994, but it was not until 19 October 1994 that I felt I had eliminated all other likely
sources of error (software logic, compiler, chipset, etc.). I contacted Intel Tech Support regarding this
bug on Monday 24 October (call reference number 51270). The contact person later reported that the bug was
observed on a 66-MHz system at Intel, but had no further information or explanation, other that the fact
that no such bug had been previously reported or observed...
```

FIGURE 2-6 Excerpt of E-mail Posting of First Observed Intel Pentium Division Problem

Source: Courtesy of Dr. Thomas R. Nicely and Lynchburg College.

lost the momentum created by the hype over the new Pentium processor in addition to suffering a $475 million fourth-quarter loss. The dust of course settled, and Intel more than recovered from their "bad" decision. Nonetheless, this example serves as notice of the need to account for economic/environmental forces.

Organizational Forces

Within the manager's own organization, forces and constraints exist that must be accounted for in the process of making a decision. Policies and procedures, issues of group conformity, organizational culture, and coordination of staffing and other resources can affect the nature of the decision process. The degree to which the manager interacts with superiors and subordinates combined with the overall policy structure of the organization can significantly alter a decision process and, thus, its outcome. Consider an organizational climate that tends to discourage new or innovative thinking and prefers to reward conformance to existing policy and procedures. A decision maker in this organization will soon become frustrated with constantly being turned down when suggesting new or innovative decision outcomes. Over time, the omission of creativity from the organization's decision process will become institutionalized, and the decisions made by its managers that remain will be constrained by an organizational culture characterized by lack of vision and foresight.

Contextual and Emergent Forces

A significant source of constraint and consequence to the decision process is the problem context itself. This category faces issues relating to skill inventory, time requirements, motivation to reach a decision, and the perception of importance by the decision maker. Probably the most important and noticeable of these is time requirements. Even if all other forces acting upon the situation are effectively dealt with, time limits can create severe pressure and stress on the decision maker and, if left unattended or ignored, can significantly increase the probability of error or poor-quality decision outcomes. Cognitively demanding activities are often classified as such not because the activity itself is demanding but because the time limitations associated with each decision in the activity make it so. Consider the multitude of decisions an airline pilot must make. Activities associated with deciding to ascend or descend, turn left or right, or increase or decrease power are in and of themselves not necessarily cognitively demanding or stressful. But when those decisions must be made by a pilot traveling at 350 miles per hour while approaching another aircraft traveling at a similar speed, the time limitations completely change the nature of the decision process. The 2 or 3 seconds allowed for these decisions may preclude the consideration of all relevant information or the consideration of multiple decision strategies. Bear in mind that this type of situation is not out of context for a discussion of managerial decision making. The pilot's office is the cockpit and his job is to make these types of decisions on behalf of his organization. In a relative sense, many of the decisions faced by managers on the ground have a time limitation that can induce the same levels of stress found by the airline pilot facing a collision situation.

2-4: HOW CAN A DSS HELP?

This entire book is devoted to answering the question of how a DSS can help, but it is appropriate at least to begin to list the ways in which a DSS can assist in the decision process with respect to the various forces we just discussed.

Recall from Chapter 1 that a DSS, while useful, is not a universal solution with regard to supporting all that needs to be addressed in the course of making a decision. The DSS is not intended to replace the decision maker. Rather, it is intended to provide him or her with focused support for one or more activities within the decision process. Because of this limitation, we must become aware of the nature of available support a DSS can offer. Then we can see the need to incorporate DSS technology in those problem contexts where it is appropriate. Table 2-2 lists the basic types of support that a DSS can provide.

The types of support listed are not always mutually exclusive nor are they always appropriate for a particular problem context. These distinctions make the design,

---

TABLE 2-2 Common Types of Support Provided by a DSS

- Explores multiple perspectives of a decision context
- Generates multiple and higher quality alternatives for consideration
- Explores and tests multiple problem-solving strategies
- Facilitates brainstorming and other creative problem-solving techniques
- Explores multiple analysis scenarios for a given decision context
- Provides guidance and reduction of debilitating biases and inappropriate heuristics
- Increases decision maker's ability to tackle complex problems
- Improves response time of decision maker
- Discourages premature decision making and alternative selection
- Provides control over multiple and disparate sources of data

---

implementation, and application of a DSS challenging and unique from all other information systems. Properly applied, however, a DSS can become an essential element in the creation of a "good" decision.

2-5: WHY ARE DECISIONS SO HARD?

How is it that we often seem to know in advance that a decision is going to be hard to make? When you think about it, our ability to size up many decision situations rather quickly in terms of classifying them as easy or hard is quite spectacular. Faced with the responsibility of deciding whether to spend the day at the beach with friends or stay at home and mow the grass, almost immediately we sense that this decision will not be a difficult one to make. Conversely, if we bear the responsibility of adopting a new technology into our organization that will decrease operational costs while simultaneously improving product quality, but will mean the layoff of as many as 1,000 employees, we also seem to know intuitively that this decision will be no day at the beach. The real question is how do we know whether a decision will be easy or hard before we even begin to gather information about it or to make it?

The answer depends on a variety of structural, psychological, physical, and environmental factors. The difficulties (or lack thereof) associated with making a decision can be the result of innumerable combinations of complexity, uncertainty, organizational and environmental pressures, and individual decision-maker limitations. In this chapter, we will explore four key areas that can individually or collectively determine the relative difficulty of a pending decision: (1) structure, (2) cognitive limitations, (3) uncertainty, and (4) alternatives and multiple objectives.

STRUCTURE

Recall from Chapter 1 that Simon (1960) proposed to classify problems on a continuum from completely structured to completely unstructured. Figure 2-7 illustrates this classification and contains examples of decision structures that would exist at each end of the continuum.

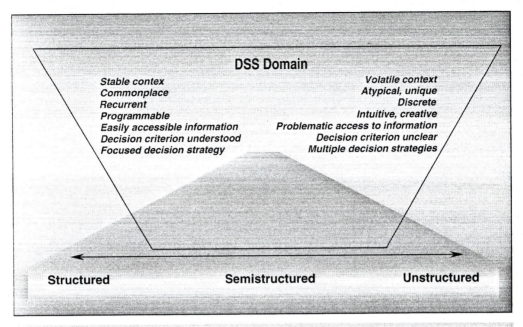

FIGURE 2-7　Continuum of Decision Structures

Simon distinguished between the two ends of the spectrum by discussing the degree to which a decision is programmed:

> Decisions are programmed to the extent that they are repetitive and routine, to the extent that a definite procedure has been worked out for handling them so that they don't have to be treated de novo each time they occur. Decisions are non-programmed to the extent that they are novel, unstructured, and consequential. There is no cut-and-dried method of handling the problem because it hasn't arisen before, or because its precise nature and structure are elusive or complex, or because it is so important that it deserves a custom-tailored treatment. . . . By non-programmed I mean a response where the system has no specific procedure to deal with the situations like the one at hand, but must fall back on whatever general capacity it has for intelligent, adaptive, problem-oriented action. (pp. 5–6)

In other words, programmed decisions are easy because all the parts necessary to make the decision are immediately available to us; we have a "program" to make the decision. Nonprogrammed decisions are hard because, in addition to gathering the necessary information and making the decision, we must also "write the program," or design the process by which the decision is made. In applying Simon's classification method to the realm of the DSS, Keen and Scott Morton (1978) chose to refer to the ends of the continuum as structured and unstructured, and we will adopt this convention as well.

As can be seen in Figure 2-7, the degree of structure of a decision is determined by a variety of factors. Decisions made repeatedly during the normal course of activity tend to be (or become) structured. An airline pilot frequently makes decisions about takeoffs and landings, routing, and passenger comfort such as whether to turn off the seat belt sign. Such decisions, due to their commonplace and repetitive nature, are relatively structured. If, however, the pilot is faced with deciding to land an aircraft with one engine out at an unfamiliar airfield for which no maps are available, the decision becomes much more unstructured.

COGNITIVE LIMITATIONS

We cannot know everything. Sometimes we cannot even handle all that we have to know for the situation at hand. Even worse, occasionally we cannot even summon forth into our conscious mind information we have previously encountered and stored. Worse yet, when we do successfully retrieve previously stored information, it is often not completely accurate. Although the human mind is a marvelous (and theoretically infinite) reasoning, computational, and storage mechanism, our present understanding of it suggests that we are indeed limited in our ability to process and store information and knowledge.

One of the most famous and oft-cited investigations into cognitive limitations is the work of Miller (1956). His research has long stood as an example of the cognitive limits of the human mind. Through a series of experiments using a large sample of human subjects, Miller determined that the immediate field of awareness of the human mind is limited to the manipulation of five to nine distinct pieces of information. In other words, at any given moment, we can only consciously keep track of "the magic number seven plus or minus two" active items of knowledge during the processing of a decision. Miller introduced the term *chunk* to describe an "organized unit of information" stored in the working memory. In essence, Miller's conclusions suggest that the brain's capacity to handle information is constrained by the number of chunks in the receiving stimulus. He also demonstrated that humans tend to develop ways of organizing information into larger chunks according to past experience, with experts being more proficient at chunking information than novices in a given knowledge domain. Although we have developed many methods of aggregating information in an attempt to mitigate this limitation, the basic conclusion of Miller's work remains true. Because decision making is a cognitive exercise, the cognitive limitations of the individual decision maker can substantially increase the degree of difficulty of making a particular decision. We will explore the issue of cognitive limits in more detail later in this chapter.

UNCERTAINTY

The concept of "20/20 hindsight" is a good way to develop an understanding of uncertainty. When one looks back at the outcome of a decision and the process by which it was made, one can see with complete certainty what the outcome of that decision process was. If we could predict the outcome of a particular decision with the same degree of certainty, all decisions would be easy to make.

Total certainty implies complete and accurate knowledge regarding the outcome of a pending decision. Genuine uncertainty suggests that the outcome of a pending decision cannot be determined even within the confines of a probabilistic framework. The bad news is that we are generally faced with some degree of uncertainty in a decision-making situation and that total certainty seldom exists. The good news is that genuine uncertainty is almost equally as uncommon. Usually, the decision maker can assign some subjective probability to the expected decision outcome so that some degree of certainty is assumed. In most cases, the accuracy of such subjective probabilities is based upon the degree of completeness and accuracy of the information used to assign them. Implicit in this assessment is that most decision outcomes contain an element of risk on the part of the decision maker. In Chapter 4, we will look at a variety of methods developed to assist the decision maker in assigning high-quality subjective probabilities to decision outcomes as well as techniques that can be used to reduce the degree of uncertainty in a given decision context. For now, let's assume the axiom that the more uncertain a decision outcome is to the decision maker, the more difficult the decision becomes to make.

ALTERNATIVES AND MULTIPLE OBJECTIVES

Regardless of the context in which a decision is being made, the objective of the exercise is to produce a desired outcome. We can characterize an outcome or a result as the product manufactured during the decision process. In fact, whether the decision is made by an individual, a team of individuals, or at the level of the organization, the objective remains the same: to choose from a selected set of alternatives the one that will produce the greatest number of desirable outcomes with the least number of undesirable consequences. Because we do not know with certainty that any of our outcomes will actually occur we must carefully consider each of the possible outcomes associated with a given decision strategy to determine whether the desired effect will be achieved.

At this point, the complexity or difficulty of a given decision can be significantly increased by the presence of multiple alternatives or objectives. Each new alternative needs to be thoroughly analyzed and compared to the other alternatives. Including additional alternatives in the selection set increases the difficulty of the decision. To further exacerbate this problem, the decision maker may have more than one objective or goal at any given time. As such, the selection of one alternative that, by itself, satisfies the criteria of the decision objective may also impede the progress of another related goal. Now the process is compounded by the shared values and goals of the decision maker in addition to the issues of multiple alternatives.

One method commonly used by managers to cope with this situation is to discard the marginally acceptable alternatives early in the choice process. By doing so, the decision maker can devote energy to concentrating on those remaining alternatives that appear to be better suited to produce the desired outcome. Although this process of elimination appears to assist in making the correct choice, we will see later in this chapter that it may not be a correct assumption. In fact, this very method may actually eliminate the best alternative in light of the objectives and constraints.

2-6: A TYPOLOGY OF DECISIONS

Decisions, decisions, decisions. No two are completely alike. The myriad of decisions facing a manager in his or her lifetime is staggering. In fact, the typical day of a manager can be jam-packed with decisions. The kind of support needed for one decision may be entirely different from the support required for the next decision. We need a method of reducing the vast number of possible decision contexts into a more manageable set of categories.

Many different methods can be used to classify decisions. We could classify them according to managerial level, for instance: line-level decisions versus middle manager decisions versus senior management decisions. Or we could classify them according to their focus, say strategic versus administrative decisions. What about classifying them according to the strategy used to make the decision: computational versus judgmental? You can see that decisions can be logically categorized by a variety of notions. Regardless of the method employed, however, if we are to design and successfully implement a support technology for a given decision context, we must be able to classify (or better yet, isolate) those decisions for which the DSS can be expected to be useful and those for which it cannot. We need a typology. Figure 2-8 illustrates one example of a typology of decisions based on a combination of several methods found in decision-making and DSS literature. Let's focus for a moment on the classification schemes contained in the figure.

NEGOTIATION-BASED DECISIONS

Delbecq (1967) proposed a three-point classification scheme based on the notion of negotiation:

1. **Routine decisions.** The decision maker or makers are clear on the desired goal or objective and the policies, procedures, and technologies that exist to achieve the goal. Routine decisions can be thought of as analogous to Simon's programmed decisions.
2. **Creative decisions.** Novel approaches are needed to handle the complexity of these decisions. An agreed-upon strategy or method is lacking and the outcome is uncer-

FIGURE 2-8 Typology of Decisions

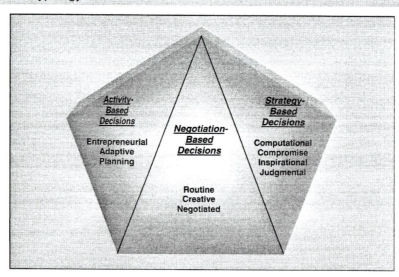

tain due to incomplete knowledge or absence of a known strategy. These decisions can be thought of as analogous to a nonprogrammed or semistructured decision.

3. **Negotiated decisions.** Conflict exists in either goals or approaches to the decision at hand. Therefore, the various opposing factions must confront each other in an effort to resolve the differences. In these decisions the manager may not be the decision maker at all but rather a participant in the decision-making process.

ACTIVITY-BASED DECISIONS

Mintzberg (1973) proposed a typology of decisions that focuses attention on the activity with which the decision is most associated:

1. **Entrepreneurial activities.** This type of decision is generally characterized by high levels of uncertainty. The selection of alternatives is motivated primarily by proactive considerations and is typically focused on near-term growth over long-term issues.
2. **Adaptive activities.** Also characterized by high levels of uncertainty, these types of decisions are typically motivated by reactive considerations and are focused more on the short-term issues at hand.
3. **Planning activities.** This decision environment is characterized by high risk and the decisions made are motivated by both proactive and reactive considerations. The focus here is more on growth and efficiency over the long term.

As can be seen from Mintzberg's approach, the support necessary for decisions classified in this manner would be determined primarily by the environment in which the decision was being made rather than by the actual structure of the decision itself. In this regard, Mintzberg's classification suggests a differentiation based on decision strategy rather than decision structure as with Simon's or Delbecq's approaches.

STRATEGY-BASED DECISIONS

Yet another division in our typology of decisions is represented by the approach taken by Thompson (1967). His classification scheme differentiates decisions based upon the primary strategy used in making the final choice:

1. **Computational strategies.** Considerable certainty exists with regard to outcomes and cause/effect relationships. Strong preferences exist for possible outcomes.
2. **Judgmental strategies.** Preferences for possible outcomes are quite strong but outcomes and cause/effect relationships are highly uncertain.
3. **Compromise strategies.** High certainty exists regarding the outcomes and cause/effect relationships, but the preferences for possible outcomes or alternatives are weak or unclear.
4. **Inspirational strategies.** Preferences for possible alternatives or outcomes are weak or unclear and a high degree of uncertainty exists regarding cause/effect relationships.

In Thompson's approach we find two dimensions in which the strategy is formed: certainty and outcome preference. In this case, necessary support would be determined based upon which strategy would appear most effective given the decision being undertaken.

Despite the method of classification employed, all methods share certain characteristics. As shown in Figure 2-7, they can all be further classified into one of two categories—those of a routine, recurring nature with high certainty and those of a nonroutine, nonrecurring nature with high uncertainty. Using this metaclassification approach we can reduce the complexity of determining what type of support may be warranted given the basic characteristics of the decision type. In other words, by gaining a better understanding of the classification of the decisions to be made in a given context we might be better able to determine what specific features of a DSS would be useful in support of that context.

2-7: DECISION THEORY AND SIMON'S MODEL OF PROBLEM SOLVING

If we are to understand what is actually going on in the "black box" world of the decision maker, we need some point of reference or "lens" through which to view the various behaviors and begin to explain their relationships. This lens is usually found in the form of a theory of the process. Numerous theories attempt to explain the process of decision making. Keen and Scott Morton (1978) proposed a categorization of decision-making theory that organizes the myriad of decision theories into five main perspectives. Table 2-3 contains their taxonomy of decision-making perspectives and provides a brief description of each.

Regardless of which theoretical approach we embrace, it is important to realize that the development of a good prescriptive approach to decision making—such as the design and implementation of a DSS—is rooted in the development of a workable and sound descriptive theory. For our purposes, we will explore and build upon the work of Simon and his colleagues by investigating the decision-making process as a process of rational behavior.

Figure 2-9 illustrates Simon's (1960) three-phase model of problem solving. Though elegantly simple in construction, Simon's model continues to withstand the test of time and, even today, serves as the basis for most models of management decision making. Notice that the model depicts the problem-solving process as a flow of events that can proceed in either a linear or iterative fashion. That is, at any point in the process, the problem solver may choose to return to the previous step(s) for additional refinement. Let's look at each phase of the process in more detail.

Intelligence

The process begins with the intelligence phase. During this phase the decision maker is "on the lookout" for information or knowledge suggesting the presence of a problem or the need for a decision. This scanning activity may be either periodic or continuous in nature. Problems tend to manifest themselves as a noticeable (real or perceived) difference between a desired state and the present state. Implicit in the "activation" of the problem-solving process is the detection of a problem that can be "owned" by the problem solver. If the decision maker or his or her organization cannot solve the problem, then it cannot be owned and therefore does not trigger the next phase of the process. Instead, such conditions tend to be classified as constraints or conditions that may be necessary to consider when solving problems that can be owned. An example

TABLE 2-3   Keen and Scott Morton Classification of Decision-Making Perspectives

Rational Manager Perspective
- Classic conception of decision making
- Assumes rational, completely informed, individual decision maker
- Favored by proponents of cost-benefit analysis
- Requires analytic definition of decision variables
- Requires precise, objective criterion for choice

Process-Oriented Perspective
- Focuses on how decision maker can effectively function with limited knowledge and skills
- Emphasizes heuristics and search for solutions that are "good enough"
- DSS design goal is to assist in improving existing solution, not to seek the optimum

Organizational Procedures Perspective
- Seeks to understand decisions as output of standard operating procedures
- Design goal is to determine which of these procedures might be supported or improved
- Stresses identification of organizational roles
- Includes focus on communication channels and relationships

Political Perspective
- Decision making is viewed as a personalized bargaining process between business units
- Assumes that power and influence determine the outcome of any decision
- Design goal focuses upon the decision-making process rather than the decision itself

Individual Differences Perspective
- Focuses on individual problem-solving behaviors
- Design is contingent on the decision-making style, background, and personality of intended user

FIGURE 2-9   Simon's Model of Problem Solving

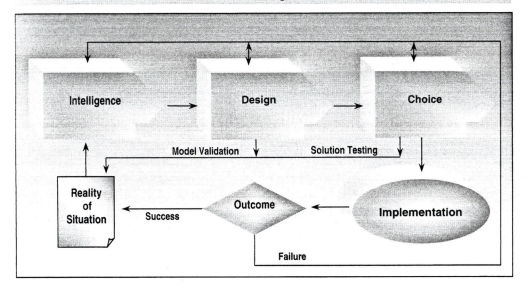

can be found with environmental conditions such as taxes or interest rates. A decision maker may perceive the tax rate imposed on his imports or exports to be excessive. Nonetheless, this perceived difference between the current state and the desired state is beyond the decision maker's direct control. As such, the "problem" must be classified as a constraint or externality that must be considered when solving other "ownable" problems.

Problems within the scope of the decision maker generally manifest themselves during the scanning activity. For example, a daily review of a production log may reveal a need for maintenance. Another example can be found in the cockpit of a commercial airliner. An old adage among pilots describes flying as "hours of boredom occasionally interrupted by stark, raving terror." Most activity in the cockpit of an aircraft consists of scanning the multitude of instruments that provide the pilot with feedback about the aircraft and the environment in which the aircraft is flying. The pilot develops an expectation of the value of each of these bits of information under a variety of conditions. When one or more of the instruments does not conform to this expected range of values, the pilot detects a problem and must move on to the next phase of the problem-solving process.

Design

After identifying the problem and formally defining it, the decision maker must begin activities related to the formation and analysis of alternatives intended to serve as potential solutions to the problem. This phase is critical in the process. The host of potential solutions to the problem must be explored and reduced to a workable subset. Each potential solution must be carefully analyzed and compared to all others with regard to expected outcome, cost, probability of success, and any other criteria deemed critical by the decision maker.

Another critical activity performed during this phase is the analysis and selection of a problem-solving strategy. Determining the range of feasible solutions is one thing, but determining how to go about actually selecting an acceptable solution and implementing it is quite another. As you can see, the process of problem solving sometimes involves decisions within decisions and problems within problems. It is one reason why making decisions is often difficult and fraught with risk and error. The decision maker must decide on the best approach to modeling the problem, identifying the key factors or variables to be contained within the model, and discerning the relationships among those variables. Finally, decisions must be made regarding what analytical tools are most appropriate for testing the integrity of the chosen model and its possible outcomes. During this phase, the decision maker may find that he or she needs more information regarding the problem at hand and may return to the intelligence phase in an attempt to satisfy that need before returning to design further phase activities and proceeding to the third phase of the process.

Choice

Intuitively this phase should be the most clear-cut of the three in terms of associated activities; however, we will soon see that it is exactly the opposite. It is also where the concept of decision making as a rational behavior will be explored in detail.

In this phase, the decision maker selects one of the available solution alternatives generated and analyzed in the previous phase. Once again, we find complexity as a result of decisions within decisions. For instance, before the decision maker can select a feasible solution to the problem, a secondary scanning of the internal and external environments must be conducted to ensure that the solution about to be implemented is still the best choice given the constraints at hand. Although many decisions can be made in environments of reasonable stability and expectation, in some cases the dynamics of a decision-making environment are so fluid that solutions cannot be selected based upon conditions that exist at the moment but must be based upon the expected or estimated conditions at the time the solution will be physically implemented. The petroleum industry is a perfect example of this issue. Consider the problems facing a typical global petroleum producer. The decisions regarding the price of oil and refined petroleum products must be made in an environment of constant flux. An error of a single penny per gallon can cost the company millions of dollars in future revenues. In addition, the decision as to pricing (the solution) must be made for a future period, thus requiring an estimation of the market conditions some time in the future.

This dichotomy of environmental conditions (stable versus fluid) often requires a return to the previous design phase for further refinement of the selection strategy and definition of the feasible solution subset. In addition, a decision maker must consider what constitutes an acceptable solution. Does the situation require an "optimal" solution or will an "acceptable" one suffice? What level of risk are we willing to assume in the selection of a solution alternative? The stability or fluidity of the decision context can serve to determine the answers to these questions and thus the selection of a decision-making strategy. Table 2-4 identifies several modeling and analysis strategies associated with our decision either to optimize or to satisfy.

2-8: RATIONAL DECISION MAKING

Before we go any further, let's take a closer look at our two strategic alternatives. The concept of optimization suggests that the decision maker will choose the alternative that is clearly the best possible one providing the best overall value and outcome. Such an optimal solution may manifest itself as the lowest cost, the highest goal attainment, or the highest ratio of goal attainment to cost. Regardless of the structure of the outcome, the optimal solution is the "best of all possible solutions." The problem is, how do we know what "all the possible solutions" are? We will address that question shortly.

TABLE 2-4 Modeling and Analysis Strategies

Satisficing Strategies	*Optimizing Strategies*
Simulation	Linear programming
Forecasting	Goal programming
"What-if" analysis	Simple queuing models
Markov analysis	Investment models
Complex queuing models	Inventory models
Environmental impact analysis	Transportation models

Note: Techniques such as Markov analysis and queuing are advanced methods of determining probabilities of events. For a detailed explanation of such methods the reader is referred to any good management science text.

In many circles, particularly the disciplines of economics and management science, optimization is considered rational behavior. In other words, it is rational to make a decision that, after review of all possible alternatives, brings the maximum satisfaction or utility to the decision maker. "The end of rational behavior, according to economic theory, is the maximization of profits in the case of business firms and the maximization of utility in the case of people in general" (Katona, 1953, p. 313). Most normative economic theory, such as laws of market equilibrium or supply and demand, is built upon the assumption that man is distinctly rational in behavior and will always seek the optimal solution to a problem.

Despite the attractiveness of optimization as a decision-making strategy, its practical application in managerial decision-making contexts is problematic. A number of conditions exist in the realm of management decisions that make optimization difficult, if not impossible, to operationalize. First, many decisions managers face are distinctly qualitative in nature and thus do not lend themselves to the quantitative approaches associated with optimization. For example, the decision faced by General Motors in 1984 regarding the location for its new 4 million-square-foot Saturn manufacturing facility was one of a complex, qualitative nature. Admittedly, issues of a quantitative nature such as cost of land, cost of labor, transportation and shipping issues, availability of necessary resources, and taxes were relevant to the final decision. However, other issues such as quality of life afforded for the employees, quality of available education, and other life-sustaining services were equally relevant. Although the quantitative issues could be accurately measured, the relevant qualitative issues could not. As such, optimization is of little value in this scenario. Simon (1960) identified a second problem with optimization as a viable solution strategy. He made the point that it is just not feasible to attempt to search for every possible alternative for a given decision. The cost of doing so is easily enormous. Furthermore, the ability of humans to keep track of all possible alternatives and to effectively compare them to one another is limited by our cognitive capacity (remember, seven plus or minus two). In the next section, we will look at a more narrowly defined and more realistic approach to rational decision making that does not suffer from these impracticalities and offers a more accurate model of what is occurring in that "black box" between our ears.

2-9: BOUNDED RATIONALITY

Once again, we must look to Nobel Prize–winning scholar Herbert A. Simon for a more practical theory of problem-solving behavior than the rational model. Simon can be credited for his "demolition" of the rational, economic man. In his early work, he questioned the concepts of maximization and optimization as they were applied to normative economic models. Simon suggested that were the concept of man as a profit-optimizing entity tenable, price tags would not exist. Think about it: If man truly wanted to maximize profit, then each transaction would be a negotiation for the highest possible price. Although some buyers would obtain the product at a lower price than the last buyer, others might be willing to pay much higher prices. This practice would, over time, theoretically result in optimized profits. So why doesn't the "economic" man do this?

It's much too hard, that's why! Simon argued that the cognitive limitations of humans make it impractical to consider all possible alternatives to a particular problem. And even if we could review all relevant alternatives, we would not be able to assimilate all the information so that we could make an appropriate decision. Instead, Simon suggested that we tend to "simplify reality" by focusing our energy on finding a solution that meets our preconceived notion of what an acceptable solution looks like. When we find such a solution, we immediately adopt it and stop looking for a better one. In the case of our price tag example, we decide upon an acceptable margin of profit and then we openly price our product to reflect that margin. Although this procedure may not result in optimal profits, it does satisfy our criterion of profiting from our sales, and it is much easier than negotiating each sale to a quantifiable end. Simon used the term *satisficing* to refer to this search-limiting strategy. Further, because decision makers are bounded by the cognitive limitations of all human decision makers, they actually do make rational decisions that are bounded by often uncontrollable constraints, which Simon referred to as *bounded rationality*.

PROBLEM SPACE

Simon's concept of bounded rationality can best be understood by an example. Figure 2-10 contains a graphical representation of a typical problem space.

Assume that the graphic on the left represents the boundary of the identified problem at hand and all possible solutions to that problem: good ones, bad ones, great ones, OK ones, and so on. In addition, the problem space contains the "best" or optimal solution to the identified problem. The rational model of decision making suggests that the problem solver would seek out and test each of the solutions found in the problem space until all solutions were tested and compared. At that point, the best solution would be known and identifiable.

FIGURE 2-10 Problem Space and Search Space

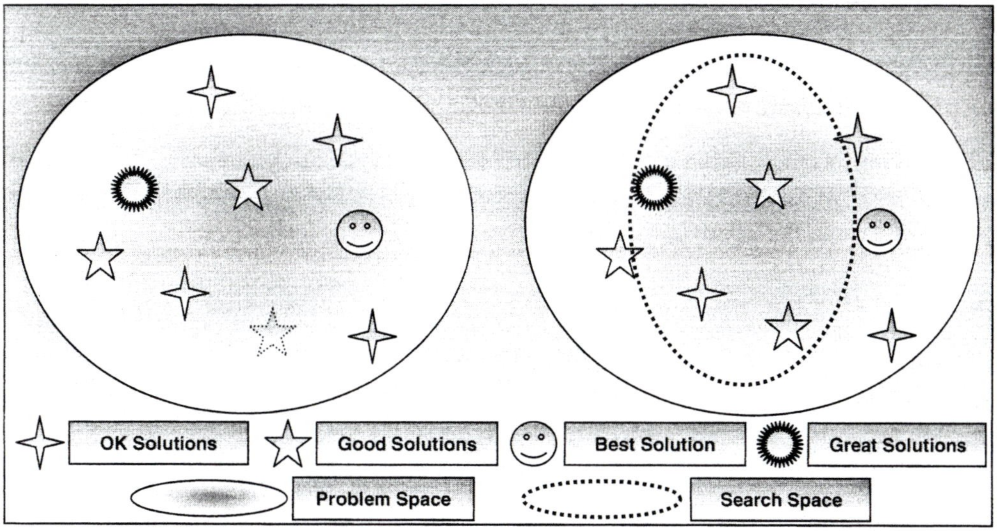

Simon argued that what really happens in a typical decision-making scenario is illustrated by the graphic on the right. The decision maker actually develops a model of what an acceptable solution to the problem looks like. Then he or she searches the problem space for a sufficient match to that preconceived solution model. When such a match is found, the search ends and the solution is implemented. Thus, the decision maker will most likely not choose the optimal solution because the narrowed search of the problem space makes it improbable that the best solution will ever be encountered. Using this approach, the decision maker settles for a satisfactory solution to the given problem rather than searching for the best possible solution.

So how does bounded rationality relate to the design and use of a DSS? To begin with, we can see that a human decision maker is not likely to expend the energy necessary to gather all relevant information available regarding a particular decision. Next, we can assume that even if all information were available, the decision maker probably could not assimilate it and thus would not use it. Finally, given the concept of bounded rationality, it appears that left alone the typical decision maker preconceives the structure of a desired solution before the search for a solution even begins. All these factors suggest the need for guidance and structure in the identification of a problem and the selection of a satisfactory alternative—thus, the need for a DSS.

A secondary issue of some importance to this discussion is the strategy used by the decision maker in exploring the problem space and selecting the final alternative. A method is needed to "measure" each alternative encountered against the preconceived model. Simon suggested that decision makers tend to develop a set of heuristics, or "rules of thumb," to manage their search. These heuristics arise from experience, perception, opinion, intuition, bias, and training. These search rules, while intended to improve the efficiency of the search process, often reduce the decision maker's effectiveness rather than improve it. We will explore this issue in detail in the last section of this chapter.

PROBLEMS VERSUS SYMPTOMS

One aspect of bounded rationality that can have a debilitating effect on the decision-making process is the typical decision maker's confusion between a symptom and a problem. Not understanding or consciously distinguishing between the two can lead to disastrous results.

As defined previously, a problem represents the difference between a perceived condition and a desired condition. If you have a headache (the perceived condition) and you really don't want one (the desired condition) then you believe you have a problem. So, then, what exactly is a symptom?

The notion of symptom is rooted in the concepts of cause and effect. Let's go back to the headache example as a rather simple but effective method of understanding the differences. The headache is perceived as undesirable and therefore is classified as a problem. We determine the situation to be undesirable and wish to "solve the problem" by taking action to eliminate the headache. This action results in a trip to the doctor. Here is where the difference between symptoms and problems becomes clearer.

If the doctor chooses to classify the headache as a problem then he will prescribe some medication, let's say aspirin, and before long the headache goes away. Everything seems okay until we sit down the next day in class and begin taking notes on the material being presented on the blackboard. Suddenly, the headache returns. We learned about a desirable relationship between the headache and aspirin so we take some and the headache, once again, goes away. Unfortunately, the next day it comes back. So what is the problem?

The "problem" is that our bounded rationality is allowing us to become temporarily satisfied with "treating the symptom" rather than "treating the disease." The headache is simply a manifest condition of a more deeply rooted phenomenon: We need eyeglasses! Therein lies the distinction between symptoms and problems. *A symptom is evidence of a problem but not necessarily the problem itself.* Think of a symptom as simply a deviation from the norm. Defined this way, a symptom does not necessarily have to be bad to be a symptom. If during the review of a periodic budget versus actual report the reviewer notices that costs for a particular item exceeded estimates, then a perception of a problem immediately manifests itself. Further review shows that sales for the product manufactured with that high-cost item are way up in a certain region. That sounds good. Would that "favorable variance" trigger the perception of a potential problem? Probably not, but it should. In both cases, the variance was a deviation from the expected norm. At the very least, these deviations should result in a more detailed review. Although they may seem unrelated or rooted in completely different areas, they may in fact be highly related and point to a deeper problem. Suppose the higher-than-expected sales in a particular region were due to an overzealous marketing manager reducing the price of the product severely below market simply to increase sales. Without a reasonable short-term strategy for increasing market share or competing with a local vendor, this price reduction is unacceptable. Moreover, this sudden increase in sales also accounts for the sudden increase in costs associated with the material necessary to make the product. If each variance were treated as a core problem then the real problem would not be solved. Moreover, depending on the method used to treat the symptoms, they may simply disappear, thus masking the problem from further investigation.

It should be clear that distinguishing between a problem and its related symptoms is critical to successful decision making. We can define a symptom as a manifest effect of an underlying cause. The real difference lies in the results associated with the symptom's elimination. The treatment of a symptom normally results in the elimination of the symptom (effect) but does not result in the removal of the associated problem (cause). The reverse, however, is not true. If we take the time and energy to fully identify and define the root problem, we will be able to craft a solution that will result in not only the elimination of the problem but of its associated symptoms as well. We will explore how a DSS can assist in sorting through the symptoms to get to the problems in Chapter 5. For now, just remember that if we get eyeglasses, we see better and we don't have a headache. If we simply take aspirin, we get rid of the headache for a little while, but we never will be able to see clearly.

2-10: THE PROCESS OF CHOICE

In a sense, the choice phase of the problem-solving model represents the climax of the decision-making process. Simon suggests:

> The decision itself is the culmination of the process. Regardless of the problem, the alternatives, the decision aids, or the consequences to follow,

once a decision is made, things begin to happen. Decisions trigger action, movement, and change. . . . All of these images have a significant point in common. In them, the decision-maker is . . . at a moment of choice, ready to plant a foot on one or another of the routes that lead from the crossroads. All of the images falsify decision by focusing on its final moment. All of them ignore the lengthy, complex process of alerting, exploring, and analyzing that precede that final moment. (1960, p. 1)

In other words, if we expend all of our energies focusing on the choice phase as our goal, we will not do justice to the entire process and will, most likely, not make a good decision. The key is, as Simon points out, to identify the problem before trying to solve it.

The choice phase focuses principally on those decisions of the semistructured to unstructured type. Again, if a decision is highly structured, it is not much of a decision at all. Where there is true choice, there is uncertainty. The decision maker is faced with the selection of an alternative derived from a primarily judgmental decision strategy. Quantitative models can be used to compare and evaluate the alternatives and, in some cases, can reduce the level of uncertainty facing the decision maker. Nonetheless, in the end, the uncertainty is always present and the decision maker must make a choice in the face of it.

NORMATIVE VERSUS DESCRIPTIVE CHOICE

It is important to understand the difference between the normative and descriptive, or behavioral, approaches to decision making. In the normative approach, choice is a theory in and of itself, whereas in the behavioral approach, choice is simply a step within a process. This distinction is crucial to the successful design and use of a DSS. Theories of choice make the assumption that future consequences are predictable to a degree of certainty and that the decision maker has to make a guess concerning the future preference of one of those consequences. Theories of choice address uncertainty simply by assigning a probability distribution to each of the future consequences. What these theories do not address, however, are the activities associated with framing, developing alternatives, determining goals and objectives, and implementing the decision once it has been made. Despite this seemingly narrow focus on the process, we must have a thorough understanding of the tools developed to assist in a normative decision-making approach because the use of a computer decision aid implicitly follows a normative perspective. This statement does not suggest that a DSS cannot support a behavioral decision process, because it most certainly can. What it means is that the majority of the support within the capabilities of a modern DSS is distinctively normative in nature. Many of the other activities associated with a behavioral approach must often be supported by means other than the DSS itself. We will explore the advantages and limitations of these normative support approaches in greater detail in Chapter 4.

MEASURABLE CONSTRAINTS

Another aspect of the choice phase that we must consider in the design of a DSS is that choice challenges the decision maker with a number of measurable constraints. Table 2-5 lists a number of characteristics generally associated with models of choice.

TABLE 2-5 Common Characteristics of Models of Choice

• *Unfamiliarity*	Degree to which decision task is foreign to decision maker
• *Ambiguity*	Degree to which decision task is unclear to decision maker
• *Complexity*	Number of different components to decision task
• *Instability*	Degree to which decision components change during or after choice
• *Reversibility*	Degree to which choice can be reversed if outcome appears undesirable
• *Significance*	Importance of choice to both decision maker and the organization
• *Accountability*	Degree to which decision maker is culpable for choice outcome
• *Time/Money*	Constraints on decision process and solution set
• *Knowledge*	Amount of relevant knowledge possessed by decision maker
• *Ability*	Degree of intelligence and competence of decision maker
• *Motivation*	Desire of decision maker to make a successful decision

Source: Adapted from Beach and Mitchell (1978).

Obstacles such as cognitive limitations, incomplete or inaccurate information, time limitations, and cost restrictions all place boundaries on the possible solution set during the choice phase. In addition, the decision maker is further constrained by his or her own psychological makeup. Stress, perceived commitment to a course of action, fear of failure or reprisal, and personal biases further intensify the constraints of the choice process. "There can be little doubt that human frailty pervades the act of choice and renders the entire decision-making process amenable to scrutiny and question at virtually every point" (Harrison, 1995, p. 58).

2-11: COGNITIVE PROCESSES

We touched on many cognitive processes so far but need to focus a bit more on several of them. Remember, one of the primary reasons a decision maker needs a DSS in the first place is because the cognitive processes of human decision makers are limited in many ways. The successful design and implementation of a DSS depends to a great extent on our complete understanding of the cognitive processes in place during decision-making activities.

COGNITIVE LIMITATIONS

Table 2-6 contains a list—based on research—of many of the psychological factors that contribute to the cognitive limits of the human decision maker.

As the list indicates, the decision maker faces a formidable task if he or she is to overcome, or at least compensate for, these cognitive limitations. It appears that the typical decision maker uses many techniques that do not fall within the normative concept of choosing an ideal alternative. Probably the most important technique associated with attempting to overcome cognitive complexity is the natural tendency toward simplification.

Any constraint on an activity, no matter what the context, serves to increase the complexity of the activity and can normally be expected to increase the effort necessary to complete it successfully. Cutting a large tree down in the middle of a forest or a

TABLE 2-6 Factors Contributing to Cognitive Limitations

- Humans can retain only a few bits of information in short-term memory.
- Decision makers display different types and degrees of intelligence.
- Decision makers that embrace closed belief systems tend to inordinately restrict information search.
- Decision makers that employ a concrete thinking approach tend to be limited information processors.
- Propensity for risk varies among decision makers. Risk takers require less information than risk avoiders.
- Decision maker's level of aspiration is positively correlated with desire for information.
- In general, older decision makers appear to be more limited than younger ones.

Source: Harrison (1995).

pasture is significantly easier than cutting the same tree down next to a house. The very existence of the house constrains how one might go about cutting down the tree. If knowledge and analysis prevail, then the tree will come down only if a feasible method of preventing any damage to the house is found. Otherwise, the tree stays put. In most cases, a method can be designed to reach the objective within the confines of the situation, but that method may radically depart from the normal, and probably easier, method. If knowledge and analysis do not prevail, however, the tree may still come down, but the chances of damage to the house are great. In this case, the decision maker may attempt to relieve some of the cognitive pressure associated with the problem by simplifying the situation. In essence, he or she may simply "wish" the house away.

The previous example is not as far-fetched as it may seem. Cognitive limitations can often cause a decision maker to simplify a decision context to a more manageable level of complexity. One method for reducing complexity is to create a simplified model of reality. Once this model of reality is constructed, the decision maker can focus attention on solving the problem represented by the model rather than the one represented by reality. If the simplified model accurately represents the salient characteristics of the problem then this strategy should result in an acceptable decision. If, however, as is often the case, the construction of this simplified model of reality omits several subtle, yet salient, factors, then the probability of a successful outcome markedly decreases. At this point, one might wonder how any rational person could ignore a house that stands in the way of a falling tree. In Section 2-12, we will see exactly how this seemingly irrational behavior occurs. For the moment, believe that it can, and does, happen.

PERCEPTION

Perception is a special kind of cognitive limitation. Decision makers tend to act upon what they can "see." This form of "selective discrimination" applied to the structure of a particular decision context may effectively limit the decision-making process. It is, however, through perception that the degree of constraint or limitation imposed by an internal or external force gains its significance.

Perception is key to the decision-making process because it is the "filter" through which all facts must pass. Once the facts pass through the perception filter, they emerge as much more aligned with the decision maker's version of reality. In other words, reality is what one perceives it to be. This filtering of facts can result in a decision that is

TABLE 2-7   Common Perceptual Blocks

- Difficulty in isolating the problem
- Delimiting the problem space too closely
- Inability to see the problem from various perspectives
- Stereotyping
- Cognitive saturation or overload

Source: Clemen (1991).

based on the perceived reality of a problem context rather than its true structure. Depending upon the degree to which the decision maker "filters" reality, the perception of a given problem-solving context may be significantly distorted. When a distortion happens, successful decision outcomes become questionable.

Several factors make up a decision maker's perceptual filter. The most common factor is simply the uniqueness of the decision maker him- or herself. Perception is the cumulative result of experience, personal frame of reference, goals, values, beliefs, motivations, and instinctive biases. In addition, a person's cognitive limitations often extend to his or her inability to accurately perceive a situation at all. These perceptual blocks may even filter out the facts. Table 2-7 lists several perceptual blocks.

One of the most common perceptual blocks is the inability of the decision maker to isolate the problem at hand. Often the complexity of the symptoms makes it difficult to identify the underlying problem. Without a structured approach to the collection and organization of symptoms, the problem may go undetected. If we cannot isolate the problem, we cannot solve it.

Bounded rationality is another form of perceptual block. In attempting to make the problem conform to a preconceived notion of reality, decision makers can blind themselves to potential solutions to the problem that deviate from the expected solution. This perceptual block is often referred to as "thinking inside the box." Adams's (1979) classic nine-dot puzzle serves as an excellent vehicle for demonstrating this concept. Figure 2-11 shows the initial layout of the puzzle.

FIGURE 2-11   Nine-Dot Puzzle

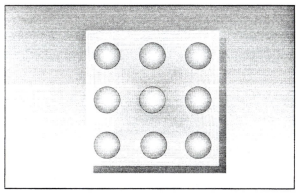

Source: J. Adams, *Conceptual Blockbusting* (pp. 2–25). © 1986 by James L. Adams. Reprinted by permission of Addison Wesley Longman.

Note: Answers appear at the end of this chapter.

The problem is to find a solution in which, without lifting your pencil from the page, you draw no more than four straight lines that connect all nine dots. At the end of this chapter you will find the "standard" solution to this problem as well as a number of extremely creative solutions collected by Adams over the years.

So what does this puzzle have to do with perceptual blocks and DSS design? Decision makers often impose constraints or rules on a problem that do not exist in reality. In doing so, they create artificial boundaries on the solution set that limit the range of potential solutions. As you can see by the common solution offered to this problem, one must be sure not to create tacit or unspoken constraints if the problem is to be solved effectively. DSS design must acknowledge the common tendency of the user to impose artificial constraints and must be designed so that real constraints are recognized and artificial or self-imposed constraints are questioned. Chapter 14 will focus more on this topic.

Yet another perceptual block is the practice of stereotyping. We all do it to some degree, and it acts as a barrier to seeing the true facts of any situation. Suppose, for instance, that you are a passenger in the first-class cabin of a commercial aircraft. You are sitting quietly reading a magazine, enjoying a beverage, and occasionally gazing out the window at the serenity of the clouds and sky above and below you. You haven't a care in the world and you feel quite safe knowing the pilot is a professional and highly trained individual. In fact, you recall being impressed with how smooth the takeoff and climb to cruising altitude were compared to other flights you have taken.

Suddenly, you look up and notice the cabin attendant speaking with a man chewing on a toothpick dressed in blue jeans and a tee shirt. His hair is shoulder length and he is wearing two hoop earrings on one earlobe. The attendant appears to be focused on his every word and smiles respectfully as he opens the door to the flight deck and disappears. Your curiosity takes over. You immediately motion to the flight attendant and inquire as to the man's identity. "Why that's Captain Conway," replies the flight attendant. "He is one of our most experienced pilots. It's always a delight to be assigned to his crew," he continues. Just what are you thinking and feeling at that moment?

The true facts of the situation are that Captain Conway is an experienced pilot and his demonstration of that ability up to that moment was truly exemplary. So what is the problem? The problem is that the persona of Captain Conway is not what you expected it to be and, because of this single incident you begin to question all of the facts associated with the pilot. Granted, a commercial airline pilot is expected to be in uniform and well groomed, but the fact that he isn't doesn't change the reality of the situation; you are under the care of a highly skilled, professional aviator. Stereotyping is simply a self-imposed perceptual barrier to reality.

JUDGMENT

Although numerous strategies exist with regard to the comparison and evaluation of solution alternatives, judgment often appears to be the most favorable. Using judgment, the decision maker makes a choice based upon experience, values, perception, and intuition. One reason judgment is often preferred is that, when compared to detailed analysis, judgment is much faster, more convenient, and less stressful. When properly applied in harmony with other selection strategies, judgment is a meaningful and useful tool in the choice process and can contribute significantly to decision quality. When applied in isolation, however, judgment is nothing more than a guess.

One of the primary reasons judgment cannot be used exclusively in the choice process is that it relies heavily on the decision maker's recollection and recognition of events. If the situation allows for accurate recall of experiences and a factual identification of the current set of events with those experienced in the past, then judgment will be effective in determining the appropriate choice. If, as is more often the case, recollection is "blurred" by cognitive limitations, then judgment becomes flawed and other analytic strategies must be employed to confirm or deny the decision maker's judgment. Table 2-8 lists several ways that cognitive limitations can affect judgment.

In the next section, we will explore various biases and heuristics that are often inherent in a decision maker's strategies and that can contribute to "errors" in perception or judgment.

2-12: BIASES AND HEURISTICS IN DECISION MAKING

HEURISTIC SEARCH AND THE "RULE OF THUMB" APPROACH

No matter what the situation, no matter who we are, no matter how well trained we become in decision making and problem solving, we have certain "rules of thumb" that we rely on in making decisions. "It never rains here on the Fourth of July," or "Only buy stocks with a price/earnings ratio of less than 9," or "Professors never cover anything important on the first day of class" are all examples of rules of thumb that we use when making decisions. Another term for such "rules" is *heuristics*. The word *heuristic* comes from the Greek word for "discovery." This derivation is appropriate because heuristics are often developed through trial-and-error experience that, over time, is subjected to a wide variety of analysis and experimentation. If a heuristic is well tested and thought out it can serve as a reliable tool for reducing the search process to more manageable levels. This approach is referred to as heuristic search or heuristic programming. This type of search process tends to follow a series of steps based on the "rules" known to the decision maker until a satisfactory solution is found. Such searches are often less costly and more efficient than a completely blind search where all alternatives are tested in the order of discovery. Moreover, several researchers, such as Zanakis and Evans (1981), showed that heuristic searches can provide solutions very close to those produced by a comprehensive blind search. Table 2-9 lists the major advantages associated with the use of heuristics as well as situations where the use of heuristics may be more appropriate than an optimization strategy.

TABLE 2-8 Ways in Which Cognitive Limitations Can Affect Judgment

- Judgment is more dependent on preconceptions and bias than relevant new information.
- Intuitive judgments are often misleading.
- Availability is an intuitive judgment about the frequency of events or proportion of objects (see Section 2-12).
- Representation attempts to classify concepts and is often illusory.
- Judgmental fixation describes the anchoring of an individual regarding consequences.

Source: Clough (1984).

TABLE 2-9 Advantages and Appropriate Uses of Heuristics in Problem Solving

Advantages of Heuristic Use
- Simple to understand.
- Easy to implement.
- Requires less conception time.
- Requires less cognitive effort (human) or less CPU time (computer).
- Can produce multiple solutions.

Appropriate Uses of Heuristics
- The input data are inexact or limited.
- The computation time for an optimal solution is excessive.
- Problems are being solved frequently and repeatedly and consume unnecessary time.
- Symbolic rather than numerical processing is involved.
- Simulation models are oversimplified when compared to problem complexity.
- A reliable, exact method is not readily available.
- The efficiency of an optimization process can be improved by good starting solutions.
- The optimization is not economically feasible.

Source: Zanakis and Evans (1981).

A common problem used to demonstrate combinatorial complexity also serves as an excellent example of a heuristic solution strategy: the problem of the traveling salesperson.

The nature of the problem is rather simple. A traveling salesperson must visit customers in several cities across the country. Because of policies relating to efficiency and cost restriction for travel, the salesperson can only visit each city once during the trip and must visit all the cities along the route before returning to home base. Because the salesperson's costs are primarily associated with the total distance traveled, the solution should be one where the policies of the company are followed and the route taken is the shortest possible route. Sounds simple enough, doesn't it?

Figure 2-12 depicts the cities in which the salesperson visits customers and the distances between each city.

The complexity of the problem increases as the number of cities increases. If we assume a route to go only in a single direction (because of the rule of not visiting the same city twice) then the total number of unique routes can be determined by the following formula:

$$\text{number of unique routes} = 0.5 \, (\text{number of cities} - 1)$$

If the number of cities is 9, as shown in the figure, then the total number of routes is 20,160. If we increase the number of cities by 1 for a total of 10 cities, the number of routes jumps to 181,440. Adding only one additional city raises the total to more than 1.8 million, and with 12 cities the number jumps to just under 20 million possible routes. Even with a computer the solution to this problem becomes time consuming and difficult. One method of finding the solution is a quantitatively based method known as branch and bound. This method, although effective, is not necessarily effi-

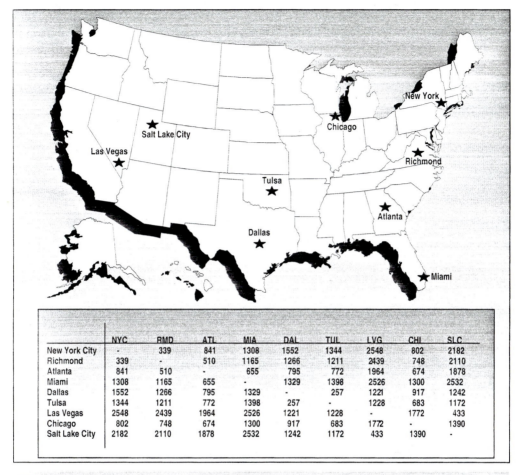

FIGURE 2-12   Traveling Salesperson Problem—Cities to Visit

	NYC	RMD	ATL	MIA	DAL	TUL	LVG	CHI	SLC
New York City	-	339	841	1308	1552	1344	2548	802	2182
Richmond	339	-	510	1165	1266	1211	2439	748	2110
Atlanta	841	510	-	655	795	772	1964	674	1878
Miami	1308	1165	655	-	1329	1398	2526	1300	2532
Dallas	1552	1266	795	1329	-	257	1221	917	1242
Tulsa	1344	1211	772	1398	257	-	1228	683	1172
Las Vegas	2548	2439	1964	2526	1221	1228	-	1772	433
Chicago	802	748	674	1300	917	683	1772	-	1390
Salt Lake City	2182	2110	1878	2532	1242	1172	433	1390	-

cient for combinations of any significant magnitude. This problem can be satisfactorily solved by following a heuristic. One heuristic might be the following: "Starting from your home base, go to the closest city. Continue going to the closest city until the last city is visited. Then return to your home base." Figure 2-13 shows the solution derived from following this heuristic.

As you can see, the solution seems to be relatively reasonable and acceptable although we do seem to "pass by" cities we have already visited (see the routes from Miami to Chicago or Salt Lake City to New York City, for instance). What if we modify our heuristic to the following: "Always follow an exterior route so that a connection between two cities is never crossed and no backtracking is performed." Figure 2-14 shows the derived solution based on this modification.

With a single modification we improved upon our first solution by 575 miles. More importantly, we didn't have to test all 20,160 solutions to find an acceptable one. This scenario is but one example of how, when employed properly, heuristics offer a valuable problem-solving tool.

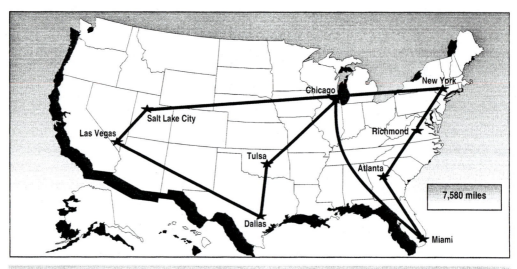

FIGURE 2-13 Initial Heuristic Solution

HEURISTIC BIAS

In some situations, however, the use of heuristics can be detrimental to finding an effective solution. Geoffrion and Van Roy (1979) explain:

> Common sense approaches and heuristics can fail because they are often arbitrary. They are arbitrary in the choice of a starting point, in the sequence in which assignments or other decision choices are made, in the resolution of ties, in the choice of criteria for specifying the procedure, in the level of effort expended to demonstrate that the final solution is in fact best or nearly so.

FIGURE 2-14 Modified Heuristic Solution

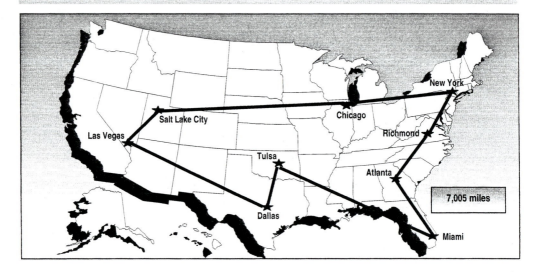

The result is erratic and unpredictable behavior—good performance in some specific applications and bad in others. (p. 117)

The typical decision maker develops a set of simplified models of reality in the form of decision heuristics and then relies upon that set of rules to make the decisions at hand. If the rules are arbitrarily developed, as suggested by Geoffrion and Van Roy, then less than stellar solutions will result.

In the early 1970s, Tversky and Kahneman published a series of papers focusing on the various biases they observed with regard to the use of arbitrarily developed heuristics. Their results show that decision makers tend to rely on a limited set of heuristic principles that often lead to severe and systematic errors in their thinking. Table 2-10 contains a description of common biases demonstrated by individual decision makers.

Of the extensive list of biases and heuristics developed by Tversky and Kahneman four of the most common categories are (1) availability, (2) adjustment and anchoring, (3) representativeness, and (4) motivational. Each of these categories is relevant to the design and use of an effective DSS.

Availability

The availability bias is the result of the typical individual's inability to accurately assess the probability of a particular event occurring. Individuals tend to assess an event's probability based upon past experience, which may not be representative. In other words, we tend to judge the probability of an event occurring according to the ease with which we can recall the last time it occurred. Before Hurricane Andrew hit in August of 1992 (see Figure 2-15), most individuals (including myself), and even most insurance companies, grossly underestimated the probability of total devastation of the magnitude that Andrew produced. I would have estimated that the probability of losing everything I owned was very small—and it very well might have been. Despite my low probability estimate I insured my house and belongings to their fullest value. The day after Andrew struck I realized that the chances of losing everything had suddenly risen to 100 percent! The insurance companies suddenly realized it too, much to their dismay. The point is that all of the estimates were based upon the recollection of the last time a storm of that magnitude occurred. In my case, it was never. Even in the case of most native Floridians it was never. Nonetheless, it did happen and only a few were well prepared.

TABLE 2-10   Common Biases of Individual Decision Makers

- They tend to overestimate low probabilities and underestimate high probabilities.
- They appear to be insensitive to the true sample size of their observations.
- They adjust their first estimate incrementally based on additional evidence.
- They tend toward overconfidence in their ability to estimate probabilities.
- They tend to overestimate the ability of others to estimate probabilities.
- They tend to compare pairs of alternatives rather than a whole list.
- They tend to minimize reliance on explicit trade-offs or other numerical computations.
- They often exhibit choices that are inconsistent.
- They tend toward viewing mutually exclusive events.

Source: Adapted from Harrison (1995).

FIGURE 2-15 Damage Caused by Hurricane Andrew in August 1992

This same bias resulted in the general decline in security at U.S. airports, which materially contributed to the tragic events of September 11, 2001. What were the odds of four commercial aircraft being simultaneously hijacked with two from the same airport? Obviously not zero, and someone figured it out.

A subset of the availability bias is the bias of illusory correlation. In this case, an individual decision maker inappropriately assumes that because two events appear to have occurred frequently in relation to each other, then they must be strongly correlated. During late 1996 and early 1997 a large number of black churches were the sites of apparent arson. It seemed obvious that these fires were all related, yet after a thorough investigation no evidence of relationship could be established. Several individuals were apprehended and found guilty of the crime of arson, yet no relationship among them could be demonstrated. In fact, several of the fires were later determined not to be the result of arson at all. In other words, the evidence suggested that the fires were not correlated, at least not in the sense that they were set by the same person or group of people. Illusory correlation can serve to bias a search process for an appropriate solution.

A structured review and analysis of objective data can reduce the effects of the availability bias. In the absence of such data, a decision maker can at least attempt to honestly assess the potential bias in his or her recollections and then adjust the estimate up or down accordingly. In any event, support for a decision process must include provisions for the identification and control of availability and illusory correlation wherever reasonable.

Adjustment and Anchoring

People often make estimates by choosing an initial starting value and then adjusting this starting point up or down until they arrive at a final estimate. Unfortunately, people have a tendency to underestimate the need for adjustments and to remain biased, or anchored, to their original starting estimate. For example, an individual might estimate the number of people in attendance at an event to be 22,000. This starting value may be based upon observation or logic such as knowing how many seats exist at the location and then estimating the percentage of empty seats. Or it may be based on a number that appeared to the decision maker to be representative of the number of people in attendance. In either case, any change in the estimate will be made in the form of an increase or decrease from that initial starting point of 22,000, and will tend to be biased toward it. Because of this tendency to underadjust, most subjectively derived probability distributions are too narrow and fail to estimate the true variance of the event.

One method a DSS might employ to minimize error from this bias is to require the user to assess the intervals associated with more than one point. Instead of assessing the variability from a single point, say the mean, a DSS asks the user to assess an interval from the 0.05 fractile to the 0.95 fractile. Implicit in this single estimate is the fact that the true value may lie outside the ends of the interval. Then the DSS asks the user to estimate the quartiles (0.25 to 0.75). The combination of these estimates is then used to determine a midpoint of final estimate. Accuracy can be improved in this manner by assisting the user to avoid anchoring on a central value where possible.

Representativeness

A third common heuristic bias, representativeness, is quite similar to the bias of illusory correlation. Decision makers often attempt to ascertain the probability that a person or object belongs to a particular group or class by the degree to which characteristics of the person or object conform to a stereotypical perception of members of that group or class. The closer the similarity between the two, the higher is the estimated probability of association. Tversky and Kahneman offer a simple problem as evidence of the effect of representativeness. Consider the following:

> Tom W. is of high intelligence, although lacking in true creativity. He has a need for order and clarity, and for neat and tidy systems in which every detail finds its appropriate place. His writing is rather dull and mechanical, occasionally enlivened by somewhat corny puns and by flashes of imagination of the sci-fi type. He has a strong drive for competence. He seems to have little feeling and little sympathy for other people and does not enjoy interacting with others. Self-centered, he nonetheless has a deep moral sense.

The preceding personality sketch of Tom W. was written during his senior year in high school by a psychologist on the basis of projective tests. Tom W. is now a graduate student. Please rank order the following nine fields of graduate specialization by the likelihood that Tom W. is now a graduate student in each of these fields (adapted from Tversky and Kahneman, 1973):

1. Business Administration
2. Computer Science
3. Engineering
4. Humanities and Education
5. Law
6. Library Science
7. Medicine
8. Physical and Life Sciences
9. Social Science

The usual classification for Tom W. is based on the subjective assessment that he is a "nerd." As such, most people tend to classify him either in computer science or engineering. If, however, we use a different method of determination, say the base rates of graduate students in a particular discipline, we might come to a completely different conclusion. The fact is, despite the popularity of the two fields mentioned, many more graduate students can be found in humanities and education or social science programs than in either computer science or engineering. Simply stated, the probability of Tom W. being in either field 4 or 9 is greater than for fields 2 or 3. Failing to consider base rates in favor of representativeness can negatively affect a decision outcome.

Another form of this bias is commonly referred to as gambler's fallacy or insensitivity to sample size. In this case, individuals draw conclusions of probability from highly representative small samples despite their extreme sensitivity to statistical error. Take the case of the man standing next to the roulette wheel at a casino. You approach the table and the man turns to you and whispers, "Put everything on black!" You ask why you should, and the man replies, "Listen friend, I have been standing here for the last half hour and red has come up fifteen times in a row. C'mon man, black is due!"

His mistake is twofold. First, your friend failed to realize that the spin of a roulette wheel (assuming it is fair) is an event independent from either the previous or subsequent spins; the number of times red comes up in a row has nothing to do with the probability of either red or black occurring again. Second, he based a probability estimate on a small sample size. We know from the laws of probability that if the roulette wheel is spun a large number of times the true probabilities of each occurrence will be manifest. Small samples can be highly biased above or below their true mean.

Yet another form of representativeness bias is failure to recognize regression to the mean. Tversky and Kahneman related an anecdote to illustrate this bias. A flight instructor always made it a point to praise a student for a good landing and to reprimand a student for a poor landing. The instructor began to notice that when a student was praised, the next landing was not as good. When, however, a student was reprimanded the next landing was much improved. The instructor concluded that a reprimand was an effective form of feedback whereas a compliment was not.

The instructor's conclusion was clearly in error. When a phenomenon is random, then extreme examples tend to be followed by less extreme ones, because the true mean lies somewhere between the two examples. The laws of probability suggest that given enough trials the true mean will be realized. So an extremely good landing will probably be followed by one that is not so good and an extremely bad landing (not too bad, we hope) will tend to be followed by a better one.

Motivational

So far, the biases discussed are related to each other by their cognitive roots and based on the way an individual processes information received during the course of problem solving. A person, however, may be subject to a noncognitive bias that can dramatically affect solution outcomes. Incentives, either real or perceived, often lead the decision maker to estimate probabilities that do not accurately reflect his or her true beliefs. These incentives are referred to as motivational biases. The estimates derived under the conditions of a motivational bias often reflect the personal interests of the decision maker who is providing them. Such estimates can also come from an information provider who is thought to be an expert in a particular field. In that case, the decision maker must be aware of the potential for motivational bias and must decide how much credence to give the expert's estimates.

Motivational biases can manifest themselves in a number of scenarios. For example, a salesperson may be required to provide a monthly sales forecast indicating expected sales productivity. A motivational bias may cause the salesperson's estimate to be lower than reality so that exceeding a forecast helps the salesperson's performance look exceptionally good. In another example, evidence suggests that weather forecasters tend to report chances of rain slightly higher than the true probability. This bias apparently exists primarily at the subconscious level. It is thought that weather forecasters subconsciously prepare people for bad weather and have them be pleasantly surprised by the sunshine rather than have them expect good weather and be disappointed.

This type of bias may be the most difficult to address through the design of a DSS. One possible method would be to have the DSS solicit a number of estimates from similar sources both related to and unrelated to the problem context. Given enough information, the user may be able to detect motivational bias in a trend associated with estimates obtained from related parties that does not exist from unrelated sources. Although this approach is not foolproof, it may heighten the awareness of the decision maker to the potential of motivational biases.

2-13: EFFECTIVENESS AND EFFICIENCY

In Chapter 1, we learned that a major goal of a DSS is to improve the effectiveness of decision outcomes. It is probably the most important claim in the entire body of DSS literature. A close second is the desire to improve the efficiency of the decision-making process for a given context. These two concepts, although complementary in nature, are nonetheless distinct and often are in conflict with each other in the design and implementation of a DSS. Distinguishing between the two concepts is necessary to fully understand their impact on the usefulness of a DSS.

Effectiveness in decision making is focused on what should be done, whereas efficiency is focused on how we should do it. To be effective requires careful consideration of the various criteria influencing the decision at hand. If we are to design a DSS that can assist in increasing the decision maker's effectiveness, we must uncover his or her perception of the decision context. In contrast, improving efficiency implies focusing only on issues that will minimize completion time, cost, or effort. Often a tension exists between the two goals because an increased focus on one can result in a reduction of the other. Keen and Scott Morton provide a good example of the distinction between effectiveness and efficiency:

> A company's computer center . . . proudly boasts of its efficiency: it generates more output—management reports—than almost any other center in the country. The computer downtime is low and the machine is fully utilized, with minimal idle time. Inputs are quickly processed and outputs are delivered promptly. Unfortunately, the reports produced are not seen as useful by their recipients. Managers instruct their secretaries either to file the hundred-page summary of last month's operations unread or to throw it in the wastebasket. The center is efficient in its pursuit of an ineffective goal. (Keen and Scott Morton, 1978, p. 7)

Table 2-11 lists some outcomes from the use of a DSS categorized by their contribution to efficiency and effectiveness.

The primary difference between the two goals is that effectiveness requires constant adaptation, learning, and rethinking, often at the risk of slow progress and many false starts, whereas efficiency simply focuses on more economical ways of doing the same thing. A good example of the tension between the two can often be seen in the research

---

TABLE 2-11 Contributions to Effectiveness and Efficiency from DSS Use

Effectiveness
- Easier access to relevant information
- Faster and more efficient problem recognition and identification
- Easier access to computing tools and proven models to compute choice criteria
- Greater ability to generate and evaluate large choice sets

Efficiency
- Reduction in decision costs
- Reduction in decision time for same level of detail in the analysis
- Better quality in feedback supplied to the decision maker

---

and development (R&D) function in an organization. R&D can be argued to be a grossly inefficient expenditure of resources for the purpose of providing future effectiveness. R&D could be eliminated because it is not needed to perform any current operational tasks, and its elimination would have a significantly favorable impact on the current year's profits. If the scale is tipped in favor of efficiency then this argument is virtually irrefutable. If, however, effectiveness is the goal, then the elimination of R&D could be the death of the organization. In the interest of effectiveness, efficiency must often be sacrificed. It becomes a significant task for the DSS designer to create the appropriate balance between these two, often conflicting, goals. Heuristically speaking, the more unstable the environment, the more the focus is on effectiveness. If the environment is stable, then a company can focus its attention on performing next year's operation more efficiently than it did this year's. In the years to come managers' focus will more likely favor effectiveness over efficiency. And the DSS will become a primary tool in support of that focus.

2-14: CHAPTER SUMMARY

This chapter demonstrated that even though all people may be created equal, all decision makers are not. Decision makers come in many different forms. Some are individuals, others come in groups, yet others are part of teams or organizations. Each type faces unique problem contexts, and each requires unique sources and kinds of support to reach a particular decision. The unique characteristics associated with different types of decision makers combined with the unique nature of the problem contexts faced by each type reinforce the reasoning behind the statement that a generic DSS does not, and probably never will, exist. In the next chapter we begin to examine the process of making a decision and various models of decision making in use.

We also discussed the processes involved in making a decision. The difficulty in programming a decision bears a relationship to its structure. Easy (structured) decisions involve repetitive and routine procedures. On the other hand, a decision is difficult, or unstructured, when cognitive limitations and relative uncertainty cloud the decision-making process. When random factors affect an outcome in ways that cannot be determined, the accuracy of the pending decision is equally uncertain.

Decisions can be classified by type: activity-based, negotiation-based, or strategy-based. Activity-based decisions focus attention on the activity with which the decision is most associated. Negotiation-based decisions are classified into three types based on the notion of negotiation. Finally, strategy-based decisions are differentiated based on the primary strategy used in making the final choice.

The process of making a decision is complex and often unclear to even the most proficient decision makers. Being aware of the natural barriers to effective decision making can help to improve both the process and its associated outcomes.

Key Concepts

- Profile of a decision (2-1)
  Stimulus
  The decision maker
  Problem definition

Alternative selection

Implementation

- Classes of decision makers (2-1)

Individual

Multiple

Group

Team

Organizational

Metaorganizational

- Factors intertwine in the formation of decision styles (2-2)

Problem context

Perception

Personal values

- Decision styles (2-2)

Directive

Analytical

Conceptual

Behavioral

Context/decision style interaction

- Definition of a good decision (2-3)

A good decision results in the attainment of the objective or objectives that gave rise to the need for a decision within the boundaries and constraints imposed by the problem's context.

- Decision forces (2-3)

Personal and emotional

Economic/environmental

Organizational

Contextual and emergent

- Difficulties of decision making (2-5)

The difficulties associated with making a decision lie in a variety of structural, psychological, physical, and environmental areas:

Problem structure

Cognitive limitations

Uncertainty of decision outcomes

Alternatives and multiple objectives

- A typology of decisions (2-6)

By gaining a better understanding of the classification of the decisions in a given context, we can better determine what specific features of a DSS would be useful in support.

Negotiation-based decisions:

Routine decisions

Creative decisions

Negotiated decisions

Activity-based decisions:

Entrepreneurial activities

Adaptive activities

Planning activities

Strategy-based decisions:

Computational strategies

Judgmental strategies

Compromise strategies

Inspirational strategies

Metaclassification:

Decisions of a routine, recurring nature with high certainty

Decisions of a nonroutine, nonrecurring nature with high uncertainty

- The design and implementation of a DSS is rooted in the development of a workable and sound descriptive theory. (2-7)

  Simon's problem-solving model (2-7)

  Intelligence

  Problem perception and definition process

  Design

  Alternatives formation and analysis

  Problem strategy selection and analysis

  Choice

  Alternatives selection process

- Optimization is considered a rational decision-making behavior in which the decision maker will choose the alternative that is clearly the best in providing overall value and outcome. (2-8)

- Satisficing strategy (2-9)

  Decision makers tend to find the first acceptable solution that meets their preconceived notion instead of looking for the optimal one.

- Bounded rationality (2-9)

  Bounded by their cognitive limitations, decision makers make rational decisions subject to uncontrollable constraints.

  The confusion between a symptom and a problem, one issue of bounded rationality, can have a debilitating effect on the decision-making process. The difference between a problem and its related symptoms lies in the results associated with its elimination. (2-9)

  The treatment of a symptom results in the elimination of the symptom but does not result in the removal of the problem.

  The elimination of the root problem results in not only the removal of the problem but the removal of its associated symptoms as well.

- One of the primary reasons for a DSS is the many limitations of the cognitive processes of human decision makers. (2-11)

Perception is the cumulative result of experience, personal frame of reference, goals, values, beliefs, motivations, and instinctive biases. Common perceptual blocks include difficulty in isolating the problem, bounded rationality, and stereotyping.

Using judgment, decision makers make a choice selection based upon experience, values, perception, and intuition. When judgment is applied in isolation, it is nothing more than a guess with often little basis in reality.

- Decision makers tend to rely on a limited set of heuristic principles when making decisions. Biases will be introduced if these rules of commonsense approaches and heuristics are arbitrarily developed. Four of the most common heuristic biases are availability, adjustment and anchoring, representativeness, and motivational. (2-12)

- It is a significant task for DSS designers to create a balance between the two, often conflicting, goals of a DSS. (2-12)

Effectiveness

With constant adaptation, learning, and rethinking, decision makers focus on the improvement of decision outcome.

Efficiency

By using more economical ways, decision makers focus on the improvement of the decision-making process for a given context.

Questions for Review

1. List the major components of the decision-making process.
2. Define *stimulus* and describe its place in the decision-making process.
3. Depict the dual roles of a decision maker in the decision-making process.
4. In which portion of the decision-making process is a DSS most helpful for decision makers? Why?
5. List and briefly describe the classes of decision makers.
6. Define individual decision makers and describe the various traits that affect the way they make decisions.
7. Specify the unique differences between decisions made in a group environment and a team environment.
8. Identify the characteristics of decision makers at the organizational level. What is the special type of DSS developed for them?
9. Describe the three forces that affect a particular individual's decision style.
10. Briefly describe the classifications of decision styles based on the nature of problem context, cognitive complexity, and value orientation.
11. Why is the understanding of decision makers' decision styles important to the design and implementation of a DSS?
12. What makes a good decision a good decision?
13. List and briefly describe the forces that can act on a problem context and on a decision maker during the course of making a decision.
14. How do personal and emotional forces act upon the decision process?
15. How do organizational forces and constraints influence the decision process?
16. What is the role of a DSS in relation to a decision maker?
17. State the difficulties of decision making from the perspective of problem structure.
18. Why is the understanding of a decision typology so important to the design of a DSS?
19. Describe the activity-based typology of decisions. Give an example of each class.

20. Briefly describe the components of Simon's problem-solving model.
21. Is it possible to make an optimal decision? Why or why not?
22. What is *satisficing?*
23. Why is the concept of bounded rationality important to the decision process?
24. What is the difference between a problem and a symptom?
25. What is the impact of confusing a problem and a symptom during the decision-making process?
26. What are the dangers associated with simplifying a decision context?
27. Describe the effect of a decision maker's perception on the decision-making process.
28. What is the effect of a decision maker's judgment on decision making?
29. What are the benefits of using a heuristic search (heuristic programming) approach?
30. Define *heuristic bias.*
31. List and briefly describe the four most common heuristic biases.
32. Compare and contrast the concepts of effectiveness and efficiency.

For Further Discussion

1. In the decision-making process, which element do you think is most important? Please state your reasons.
2. Discuss the nature of multiple and group decision makers. Give an example for each of them. What are the differences between them?
3. Observe a decision maker in an organization that you are familiar with. Based on the nature of the problem context, and personal perception and values of the decision maker, specify his or her decision style(s).
4. We all understand that designing the system to complement the user's decision style can provide additional support to the decision process and failing to do so can inhibit the success of the process. Find a case that can support this point.
5. Analyze a good decision made by an organization. Discuss the reasons why you think it was a good decision. How did the decision maker(s) make it?
6. You are about to buy a car. Using Simon's problem-solving model, list your activities in each phase.
7. Assume that you are going to make a decision about the price of a new product. Use the typologies described in this chapter to classify this decision. State any assumptions needed.
8. Give an example of the concept of bounded rationality from your own experience.
9. Analyze a problem you encountered recently. List the symptoms and classify the cause(s) of these symptoms. What exactly was the problem?
10. Analyze the cognitive limitations you experience during your decision making. Can a DSS help? If yes, how can it help?
11. Make a list of heuristics that are used regularly by someone in your family, school, or company.
12. Analyze a bad decision made by an organization. Discuss the reasons why it failed. Was the failure related to the cognitive limitations or heuristic biases of the decision maker?

Answers to the Nine-Dot Problem

The common solution to the puzzle is shown in the figure on the left. The figure on the right shows an alternate three-line solution. Other solutions that have been collected by Adams include the following:

- Fold the paper so that the dots line up in a row. Then a single straight line can be drawn through the dots.
- Roll up the paper and tape the ends together so that a spiral can be drawn through all the dots.
- Cut the paper into strips and tape them together so that the dots are in a single row.
- Draw very small dots close together in a square pattern and then draw a single fat line through all of them at once. (This solution was provided by a 10-year-old girl.)

Source: J. Adams, *Conceptual Blockbusting* (pp. 24–25). © 1986 by James L. Adams. Reprinted by permission of Addison Wesley Longman.

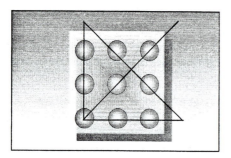
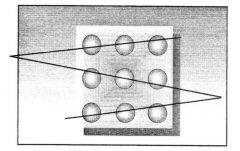

3
DECISIONS IN THE ORGANIZATION

Learning Objectives

◆ Learn the definition of an organization and the decision-making activities within an organization

◆ Be familiar with the five dimensions of organizational decisions: group structure, group roles, group process, group style, and group norm

◆ Understand the need for different types of support systems at different organizational decision levels

◆ Comprehend the meaning of organizational culture and its influence over decision-making activities within an organization

◆ Understand the relationship between organizational culture and the organization's ability to change

◆ Discern the influence of power and politics on decision-making activities within an organization and comprehend their impact on the design and implementation of DSSs

◆ Be familiar with the functionality of organizational decision support systems (ODSSs)

⟨ **DSS MINICASE** ⟩

THE CUBAN MISSILE CRISIS

On October 16, 1962, American aerial photo-reconnaissance revealed Soviet construction of missile bases and placement of both medium-range (1,000 miles) and intermediate-range (2,000 miles) missiles on the island of Cuba, some 90 miles from the border of the United States. President John Kennedy—still smarting from his administration's foreign policy fiasco at Cuba's Bay of Pigs, and fearing that unchecked Soviet interference in the Western Hemisphere would demolish American credibility worldwide—resolved to respond strongly. After a week of intense secret discussions with his most trusted advisers, Kennedy issued an ultimatum to the Kremlin in Moscow. The missiles, he demanded, must be removed immediately or the United States would impose a naval blockade to prevent the delivery of more missiles. Furthermore, the United States would dismantle the existing missiles in Cuba by force. This announcement alarmed both the nation and world. Never before had two superpowers appeared to be on such a direct course toward a nuclear war. U.S. Secretary of State Dean Rusk reported, "We're eyeball to eyeball." The U.S. military advanced plans for the invasion of Cuba; however, the decision was made to resolve the crisis peacefully.

According to Soviet Premier Nikita Khrushchev's memoirs, in May 1962 he conceived the idea of placing intermediate-range nuclear missiles in Cuba as a means of countering the United States' emerging lead in developing and deploying strategic missiles. He also presented the scheme as a means of protecting Cuba from another U.S.-sponsored invasion, such as the failed attempt at the Bay of Pigs in 1961.

The Soviet Union obtained Fidel Castro's approval and then worked quickly and secretly to build missile installations in Cuba. Reconnaissance photographs of these missile installations,

shown to President Kennedy on October 16, prompted 7 days of guarded and intense debate in the U.S. administration. During that time, Soviet diplomats denied that installations for offensive missiles were being built in Cuba. Kennedy, however, in a televised address on October 22, announced the discovery of the installations and proclaimed that any nuclear missile attack from Cuba would be regarded as an attack by the Soviet Union and would be responded to accordingly. He also imposed a naval quarantine on Cuba to prevent further Soviet shipments of offensive military weapons.

During the crisis, the two sides exchanged many letters and other communications, both formal and "back channel." Khrushchev sent letters to Kennedy on October 23 and 24 indicating the deterrent nature of the missiles in Cuba and the peaceful intentions of the Soviet Union. On October 26, Khrushchev sent Kennedy a long, rambling letter seemingly proposing that the missile installations would be dismantled and personnel removed in exchange for U.S. assurances that it or its proxies would not invade Cuba. On October 27, another letter arrived from Khrushchev, suggesting that missile installations in Cuba would be dismantled if the United States dismantled its missile installations in Turkey. The U.S. administration decided to ignore this second letter and to accept the offer outlined in the letter of October 26. Khrushchev then announced on October 28 that he would dismantle the installations and return them to the Soviet Union, expressing his trust that the United States would not invade Cuba. Further negotiations were held to implement the October 28 agreement, including a U.S. demand that Soviet light bombers also be removed from Cuba, and to specify the exact form and conditions of U.S. assurances not to invade Cuba.

(*continued*)

Following is Khrushchev's letter of October 24 to President Kennedy:

His Excellency
Mr. John F. Kennedy President of the United States of America
Washington

Dear Mr. President,

Imagine, Mr. President, what if we were to present to you such an ultimatum as you have presented to us by your actions. How would you react to it? I think you would be outraged at such a move on our part. And this we would understand.

Having presented these conditions to us, Mr. President, you have thrown down the gauntlet. Who asked you to do this? By what right have you done this? Our ties with the Republic of Cuba, as well as our relations with other nations, regardless of their political system, concern only the two countries between which these relations exist. And, if it were a matter of quarantine as mentioned in your letter, then, as is customary in international practice, it can be established only by states agreeing between themselves, and not by some third party. Quarantines exist, for example, on agricultural goods and products. However, in this case we are not talking about quarantines, but rather about much more serious matters, and you yourself understand this.

You, Mr. President, are not declaring a quarantine, but rather issuing an ultimatum, and you are threatening that if we do not obey your orders, you will then use force. Think about what you are saying! And you want to persuade me to agree to this! What does it mean to agree to these demands? It would mean for us to conduct our relations with other countries not by reason, but by yielding to tyranny. You are not appealing to reason; you want to intimidate us.

No, Mr. President, I cannot agree to this, and I think that deep inside, you will admit that I am right. I am convinced that if you were in my place you would do the same.

. . . This Organization [of American States] has no authority or grounds whatsoever to pass resolutions like those of which you speak in your letter. Therefore, we do not accept these resolutions. International law exists, generally accepted standards of conduct exist. We firmly adhere to the principles of international law and strictly observe the standards regulating navigation on the open sea, in international waters. We observe these standards and enjoy the rights recognized by all nations.

You want to force us to renounce the rights enjoyed by every sovereign state; you are attempting to legislate questions of international law; you are violating the generally accepted standards of this law. All this is due not only to hatred for the Cuban people and their government, but also for reasons having to do with the election campaign in the USA. What morals, what laws can justify such an approach by the American government to international affairs? Such morals and laws are not to be found, because the actions of the USA in relation to Cuba are outright piracy. This, if you will, is the madness of a degenerating imperialism. Unfortunately, people of all nations, and not least the American people themselves, could suffer heavily from madness such as this, since with the appearance of modern types of weapons, the USA has completely lost its former inaccessibility.

Therefore, Mr. President, if you weigh the present situation with a cool head without giving way to passion, you will understand that the Soviet Union cannot afford not to decline the despotic demands of the USA. When you lay conditions such as these before us, try to put yourself in our situation and consider how the USA would react to such conditions. I have no doubt that if anyone attempted to dictate similar conditions to you— the USA, you would reject such an attempt. And we likewise say—no.

The Soviet government considers the violation of the freedom of navigation in international waters and air space to constitute an act of aggression propelling humankind into the abyss of a world nuclear-missile war. Therefore, the Soviet government cannot instruct captains of Soviet ships bound for Cuba to observe orders of American naval forces blockading this island. Our instructions to Soviet sailors are to observe strictly the generally accepted standards of navigation in international waters and not retreat one step from them. And, if the American side violates these rights, it must be aware of the responsibility it will bear for this act. To be sure, we will not remain mere observers of pirate actions by American ships in the open sea. We will then be forced on our part to take those measures we deem necessary and sufficient to defend our rights. To this end we have all that is necessary.

Respectfully, /s/ N. Khrushchev
N. KHRUSHCHEV
Moscow 24 October 1962

3-1: UNDERSTANDING THE ORGANIZATION

The previous chapters focused on two fairly microlevel concepts: the decision and the individual decision maker. Without a thorough understanding of these building blocks, no useful macrolevel perspective can be derived. In this chapter, the emphasis shifts from the micro to the macro perspective of decision making: the organization. Looking at the process from the top down allows us to see distinctly different aspects of the activities and characteristics of decision making and problem solving.

Textbooks on organizations abound with a variety of definitions for the term *organization*. Most formulations include some mention of systematic patterns of interaction among various social entities with the intention of achieving some common purpose or goal. The definition used in this text includes these common characteristics but also more broadly includes issues of structure, resources, politics, and the environment. For our purposes, *an organization can be thought of as a unified system of resources defined and structured by a collective of functional and political subsystems bound by a set of stated goals and functioning within a set of loosely defined environments.* Implicit in this definition is the assumption that the whole of an organization is greater than the sum of its parts; it thus allows its members collectively to pursue and achieve greater goals than they could by acting individually. Using this definition, we will look at the various aspects of decision making and decision support necessary for the operationalization of this implied synergy.

A "NEXUS OF DECISIONS"

Stohr and Konsynski (1992) suggest that it is useful to view an organization as a "nexus of decisions." The organization's purpose is to make decisions within a business environment; it is defined by its decision opportunities, authorities, and responsibilities. In this perspective, decisions and decision making are the true essence of the organization and identify its boundaries, policies, procedures, customs, and theater of operations. Note, however, that this view is independent of the physical manifestation of the individual decision makers who make up the organization. Here, the organization can be made up of a complex network of individuals, teams, groups, and computerized decision support systems. How they all fit together is the subject of this chapter.

DIMENSIONS OF ORGANIZATIONAL DECISIONS

If we dissect the definition of organization as previously stated, several factors can be identified. Figure 3-1 depicts five dimensions that can affect both the kinds of decisions made in the organization and the methods necessary to make them effectively.

Group Structure

We discussed briefly in Chapter 2 the concept of decision-making structure. Here, we focus on the relationships between the point of decision (the person or persons who ultimately make the decision) and the participants in the decision-making process. If the decision maker acts alone and does not work with any formal participants other than independent or third-party information sources, then the structure can be thought of as individual. If the decision maker retains sole responsibility and authority to make the decision at hand but employs a formal group of people with defined roles who

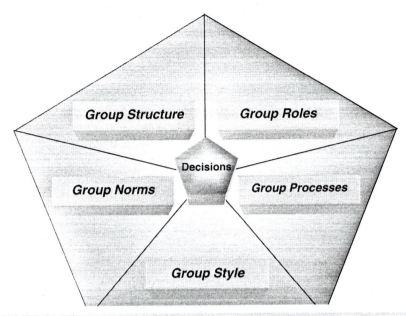

FIGURE 3-1   Factors Affecting Organizational Decisions

together provide information or services to the decision maker, then the structure is more representative of the team approach. Finally, if a formal group of individuals is charged with the responsibility and authority to make a decision, but no single member of the assemblage has any more or less decision-making authority than any other, the structure is most representative of a true group structure. Given the unique nature of these three decision structures, we can see how the types of decisions made, as well as the methods employed, can vary significantly. Chapter 8 will focus on these various structures as they relate to specific DSS design requirements.

Group Roles
Each member of a decision-making body takes one or more specified roles. In the individual structure, all necessary roles are assigned to the sole decision maker: information gatherer, analyzer, DSS user, and so on. As the structure evolves toward a team or group structure, however, the necessary roles spread outward among the various members so that each participant becomes a more active component of the process. Depending upon how the organization defines these roles (and who is assigned to them), the nature of the decision strategy employed as well as the scope of decision types assigned can be materially changed.

Group Processes
Using a kind of "chicken and egg" analogy, the process employed by a decision-making body can dramatically affect the type of decisions that can be effectively made by that body, which in turn affects the method or process that must be used to make those types of decisions. Implicit in this seemingly circular problem is that the concepts of decision process and decision type must mesh with the decision-making body's perspectives. If a particular multiparticipant structure is employed, then certain decision processes are no longer relevant or effective for that group. For example, in the United

States the final decision to go to war rests with a single person: the president. Although the president must formally request that Congress grant a declaration of war, the decision to enter a war, nonetheless, lies with a single decision maker. The framers of the Constitution realized that this type of decision would not be best made by assemblage. The need for multiple sources of informed advice and knowledge is clear but the need for consensus seeking, which is typically associated with a group, is clearly not. If the time ever comes to make such a decision, it is best left to a decision process employed by one person.

Group Style

In Chapter 2, we also visited the concept of decision style. In any decision-making context, the various interpersonal relations, consequences of outcome, power and politics, and like-mindedness can determine both the method and type of decision best assigned to a particular decision-making body. The decision maker's style can affect the process, his or her behavior under specified conditions, and the quality of outcome. For example, a decision-making context such as whether to declare war on a foreign country would not be best suited for a diverse group of individuals with equally diverse views on the concept of war. Such a decision is better placed in the hands of a group of individuals who share similar beliefs regarding the salient concepts and can make the necessary decision based only on the information presented rather than on personal beliefs or political stances. Organizations must be aware of these components and must work to create decision-making bodies that possess the best combination of ingredients for the given decision situation.

Group Norms

This final dimension is probably the most important. The social psychology of decision making is a powerful force affecting the activities of any decision-making "body" from individual to metaorganizational. Issues relating to shared meaning among the constituents, individual and collective social pressures, genres and prescriptions regarding behavior, personal beliefs, and potential sanctions, among others, all serve to shape the decision-making environment within an organization.

Viewing all five of these factors in relation to each other, we can see decision making within the organization as a continuous process. That is, the factors are "fluid elements that change based on their independent dynamics . . . constantly out of adjustment and seeking equilibrium, yet never quite in balance with each other in spite of a leader's best efforts" (Gore, 1964, pp. 26–27). This statement underscores the futility of optimization and the reality of satisficing with respect to the set of decisions being made within a particular organization. To complicate this discussion further, we must also recognize that this balancing act occurs in not two but three dimensions: (1) number of participants, (2) structure of the group and roles of the participants, and (3) positioning of the participants within the organizational hierarchy.

Organizational Decision Levels

An organization, when viewed from a decision-making perspective, can be thought of as a hierarchy of three discrete levels: (1) operations, (2) tactical, and (3) strategic (see Figure 3-2). All organizational decisions can be positioned within one of these three levels.

The decision makers in an organization are a large and diverse population of individuals. At the foundational or operations level, the line personnel make decisions regarding day-to-day activities relating to production or services while the line supervisors deploy available resources and make decisions necessary to meet assigned quo-

FIGURE 3-2 Hierarchy of Organizational Decision Levels

tas or schedules. The tactical (or planning) level implements decisions made at the highest level of the organization as well as decisions to acquire the resources necessary to maintain desired capacities and output at the operations level. Most decisions relating to the internal administration of the organization are made at this level as well.

The members of the strategic decision-making hierarchy of an organization include the senior executives of the largest industrial and service firms in the world, the top administrators of the largest government agencies, and the generals and senior officers in the military. This elite group of decision makers, though the smallest of the three in number, consists of the principal decision makers in our society. Their decisions are usually the most far-reaching of any made across the three levels.

The level at which a decision is made within the organization must be considered when designing and implementing a DSS. Different types of systems are generally associated with different levels of the organization. One problem facing the designer of a DSS for a particular organizational level is the fluidity and diversity of skills and competencies found at each level. As workers in one level are promoted to a higher one, they must change many of their decision-making perspectives and strategies and assimilate new roles and assignments. Old habits sometimes persist, however, and necessary changes do not occur. Here the DSS designer must account for a phenomenon referred to as the Peter Principle, which suggests that an individual will eventually be promoted to his or her level of incompetence (Peter and Hull, 1969). When this occurs, the skill set and competency expected by the DSS designer may not exist, and thus the effectiveness of the applied decision aid becomes questionable. We will focus on this issue in greater detail in Chapters 15 and 16.

3-2: ORGANIZATIONAL CULTURE

SO WHAT IS THIS CULTURE THING, ANYWAY?

The term *organizational culture* is widespread in the literature on organizational behavior, theory, structure, and management, as are the various definitions of it. A brief perusal of the literature reveals examples such as dominant values espoused by an organization (Deal and Kennedy, 1982); the philosophy that guides organizational policy toward employee and customers (Pascale and Athos, 1981); the basic assumptions and beliefs that are shared by the members of an organization (Bowers and Seashore, 1966); or "just the way things are done around here." Regardless of the sources of the definitions, however, they all seem to have a common denominator: shared meaning. For our purposes, we will adopt the definition offered by Edgar Schein (1985), a noted organizational theorist, who defines organizational culture as *a system of shared meaning consisting of beliefs, symbols, rituals, myths, and practices that have evolved over time.* Through his definition we will explore the cultural facet of the organization and its relationships to the decisions being made within.

Organizational culture is not an abstract environment with no well-defined elements. Research shows that organizational culture exerts an extremely powerful influence over the activities, including decision making, of an organization. Robbins (1990) identified 10 elements that, when mixed together, define a particular organization's culture. Table 3-1 lists these 10 characteristics of organizational culture.

Note that the characteristics are not limited to strictly structural issues. They also include several dimensions of behavior. It is important to note that an organization's culture is an evolutionary product of both the historical structure and the various courses of action of its members.

RELATIONSHIP OF CULTURE TO PERFORMANCE AND CHANGE

Performance

In Chapter 2 we said that individual decision style affects decision strategy and quality of outcome. Decision style can also influence the way individuals act within an organizational environment. In some environments individuals are supportive of others; others

---

TABLE 3-1   Ten Characteristics of Organizational Culture

1. *Individual initiative*   The degree of responsibility, freedom, and independence that individuals have
2. *Risk tolerance*   The degree to which employees are encouraged to be aggressive, innovative, and risk seeking
3. *Direction*   The degree to which the organization creates clear objectives and performance expectations
4. *Integration*   The degree to which units within the organization are encouraged to operate in a coordinated manner
5. *Management support*   The degree to which managers provide clear communication, assistance, and support to their subordinates
6. *Control*   The number of rules and regulations and the amount of direct supervision that are used to oversee and control employee behavior
7. *Identity*   The degree to which members identify with the organization as a whole rather than with their particular work group or field of professional expertise
8. *Reward system*   The degree to which reward allocations (i.e., salary increases, promotions) are based on employee performance criteria in contrast to seniority, favoritism, and so on
9. *Conflict tolerance*   The degree to which employees are encouraged to air conflicts and criticisms openly
10. *Communication patterns*   The degree to which organizational communications are restricted to the formal hierarchy of authority

---

Source: Organization Theory, 3rd ed. by Robbins, S. P., © 1990. Reprinted by permission of Prentice-Hall, Inc., Upper Saddle River, NJ.

experience a pervasive struggle for control. Some organizations appear to be rigid and inflexible with regard to novelty or change while others encourage innovative thinking and approaches to problems. Because of these issues, the DSS designer must become aware of the influence of organizational culture on the types of decisions made and the appropriateness of various strategies employed within a particular cultural climate.

One method of viewing the relationship between organizational culture and decision making is to focus on the concept of cultural fit. Successful organizations tend to display a "good fit" between their culture and their external and internal environments. A good external fit suggests a culture that is shaped to both the organization's strategy and its marketplace. For instance, market-driven strategies tend to be more successful in environments that are fluid and dynamic. Such climates emphasize conflict tolerance, individual initiative, risk taking, high departmental integration, and horizontal communication channels. The types of decisions and their associated strategies made in this culture will tend to be unstructured with a focus on effectiveness, novelty, and creativity, and will require a broad range of information sources. As such, certain DSS functions that tend to support these types of decisions and strategies will need to be emphasized and available in the firm's support technologies. In contrast, organizations that tend toward a product-driven approach to the marketplace often focus on high efficiencies, function best in more stable climates, and tend to promote a culture high in control and low in conflict and risk propensity. The decisions made in this environment clearly fall toward the structured end of the continuum, and the decision support technologies employed in such an organization need to be highly structured in their underlying model base and analytical tools. It is important to note, however, that one approach is neither right nor better than another. If the culture fits with the external climate, then the organization has a better chance of succeeding.

Internal fit is another key element in organizational success. It refers to the match between an organization's culture and its primary technologies. Cultures that tend to minimize individual initiative and risk taking, such as those of a product-driven orientation, also tend to adopt more routine technologies that provide additional stability to the organization. Such technologies take the form of well-developed control mechanisms, automated assembly machinery, and common back-office processing mechanisms. In addition, because these types of technologies are generally well developed and require little individual intervention, they also tend to support a more centralized decision-making emphasis in which operating procedures, policies, schedules, and the like are all prescribed from a central authority. In cultures where initiative, creativity, and risk taking are supported or rewarded, nonroutine technologies that require adaptability are more prevalent. In these climates DSS technologies are likely to be found as an integral part of the problem-solving activities. Putting DSS technology in the wrong organizational culture is the technological equivalent of trying to fit a square peg into a round hole—it may fit, but it won't work very well.

Change

Another important aspect of organizational culture is that it often determines a firm's ability to change or adapt to changes in environmental conditions. Axiomatically speaking, survival equals ability to change. Organizations with cultures that do not allow for flexibility and change will fail to maintain their market position and will often fail to survive altogether. Cultures that promote the status quo and demonstrate

---

TABLE 3-2 Characteristics of Excellent Companies

- The have a bias for action.
- They stay close to and understand the customers.
- They provide autonomy and encourage entrepreneurship.
- They recognize that productivity is based on people.
- They are hands-on and value driven.
- They "stick to their knitting."
- They display a simple form and a lean staff.
- They maintain simultaneous loose-tight controls.

---

a passion for stability will find it difficult, if not impossible, to respond to flux in the environment. In their book *In Search of Excellence*, Peters and Waterman (1982) identify eight characteristics of excellent companies. Table 3-2 contains a list of these hallmarks of excellence.

Note that each of the characteristics identified by Peters and Waterman is action oriented. Decisions made and strategies employed under these conditions tend to be highly diverse and depend upon a wide variety of support technologies and methods. In contrast, the more bureaucratic-type organization tends to use the "boardroom decision strategy," where a centralized control system is operationalized and managed, thus eliminating the need for individual or group DSS technology within the organization. Culture is important!

3-3: POWER AND POLITICS

It is a fact of life in most organizations: Power and politics are integral parts of the myriad of decisions made on a daily basis. Although the term *power* is often thought of in a pejorative sense, Zaleznick (1970) recognized it as an important, positive element in effective decision making:

> Whatever else organizations may be, problem-solving instruments, sociotechnical systems, reward systems, and so on, they are political structures. This means that organizations operate by distributing authority and setting a stage for the exercise of power. It is no wonder, therefore, that individuals who are highly motivated to secure and use power find a familiar and hospitable environment in business. (p. 47)

As with many of the other concepts of organizations discussed so far, a variety of definitions exists for *organizational power*. Given our focus on decision making and support, we can identify power as composed of five basic factors. Table 3-3 contains an outline of these five factors.

We can think of power as it relates to decision making as a multifaceted capacity of one person or group within an organization to prevent another from reaching a desired goal. In addition, it includes the potential of one person or group to influence another to act or change in a particular direction. Authority, informal power, influence, and politics all contribute to the effect of power on decision making in organizations.

TABLE 3-3   Five Factors of Power

1. *Power sharing*   Determines how a manager exercises authority and whether he or she wishes to exercise the power available to them
2. *Authority*   The legitimacy a manager has for activities that come under his or her domain and direct supervision
3. *Informal power*   The set of relationships that permit the accomplishment of interdependent tasks and coordinated activities
4. *Influence*   The result of direct or indirect intervention in which the manager's preferences are the basis for arriving at a decision
5. *Politics*   Related to negotiation, consensus formation, assertion of influence, or devious practices employed toward achieving a specific objective

Source: Adapted from Rowe and Boulgarides (1994).

Managerial decision-making power within an organization can manifest itself in a multitude of scenarios. Such power is broad in scope and its support must often come in the form of control or constraints to such power. Harrison (1995) identified 12 significant elements of managerial decision-making power:

1. The power to decide the kind and quantity of jobs made available
2. The power to decide (within legal limits) where, when, and how the operations of the organization will be conducted
3. The power to decide what services, supplies, or raw materials to buy from other firms or subcontractors, and the power to decide (within legal limits) how, where, and when to purchase them
4. The power to decide the service to be provided or the product to be produced
5. The power (within legal limits) to set and administer prices
6. The power to decide the amount of new investment and how, where, and when to invest it
7. The power to shape and temper the value systems of the nation's population through sponsorship of the mass media
8. The power to influence the administration of existing legislation and the preparation and passage of new legislation by supporting candidates for political offices and lobbying
9. The power to influence the general health and welfare of entire communities and of the general population through the use of technology and processes that produce noxious and irritating emissions
10. The power to pay or withhold dividends
11. The power to decide the amount of resources (if any) to be given to educational and philanthropic institutions and how, where, and when to make such gifts
12. The power to withhold power

As indicated by the preceding list, decision making and power go hand in hand. Each of the 12 power elements would require a type of decision support mechanism completely different from the others. Furthermore, within each of the 12 categories a multitude of subcategories of decisions can be found. For example, within the power to decide the amount of new investment lies a variety of problem-solving contexts and needs for decision support. Different investments require different analyses using different models and different heuristics. Each of these subcategories of decisions would require a DSS designed specifically to meet the needs of its decision maker(s). The point is that even though the design and implementation of a DSS are primarily dependent on the context in which it is to be used, the bigger picture of the organization and its power centers must also be considered if effective support is to be provided.

Politics

Although they exist in a somewhat symbiotic relationship, power and politics can be thought of as distinct and thus can permeate the decision-making processes within an organization in different manners. More important, politics is an essential element in the formation of decision-making strategies.

Patz and Rowe (1977) described politics as a process that "increases certainty in an organization, based on reducing the effect of factors contributing to uncertainty." In this sense, politics is related to decision-making through negotiation, formation of consensus, and influence. Each of these forces can materially affect a decision strategy or outcome, and the need for political competence in any given problem-solving context is clear. Skill and competence in the political aspects of decision-making can result in measurable benefits to an organization that might otherwise go unrealized.

Mintzberg (1985) observed that organizational politics in decision making are not automatically dysfunctional to the organization but can instead be beneficial:

1. Politics may correct deficiencies in other more legitimate systems of influence and provide for certain forms of flexibility not otherwise available.
2. Politics can act in a Darwinian sense to bring the strongest members of an organization into the most critical decision-making roles.
3. Politics can often serve to ensure an objective hearing of all sides of an issue when no other reasonable means are available.
4. Politics can often promote necessary organizational change blocked by more traditional means.
5. Politics can facilitate the decision-making process, particularly the effective implementation of choices to serve particular interests.

In the design, implementation, and use of a DSS in an organization, the political environment in general and the direct political influences on the decision context in particular merit careful consideration. The politics of a given decision require the decision maker to be fully aware of the various relationships among the stakeholders involved in the choice outcome. Such political factors can include the probability of a stakeholder group supporting or rejecting a particular choice strategy, or it might include information about constraints imposed by one political unit on another that impede the implementation of a certain choice set. For example, a decision involving the merging of two previously autonomous organizational units into one for the purpose of reducing common costs may involve political issues, such as conflicting authority over certain organizational resources or processes, differing or opposing policies of conduct, or even lack of a shared vision of the mission for the new, combined departments. Regardless of the level at which the decision is made—individual, team, group, or organization—power and politics shape and mold the decision context and thus the type of decision support required.

3-4: SUPPORTING ORGANIZATIONAL DECISION MAKING

Although organizational decision support systems (ODSSs) will be covered in greater detail later in the text, it is important to our discussion of organizational decision making to briefly introduce the concept here. This section describes the boundaries of this level of decision support.

An ODSS can be thought of as support technology that focuses on decisions involving many people. This conceptualization enlarges the notion of group decision support (GDSSs will be covered in detail in Chapter 5), where a small group of individuals is provided support in making decisions of mutual interest and importance. The characteristic that sets an ODSS apart from a GDSS is managerial control. In an ODSS environment, the support technology is designed and deployed so that the organization's division of labor with regard to decision making is defined and controlled to a certain extent by the technology. Although traditional decision-making structures tend toward a conventional hierarchical arrangement and often resemble the organization's formal authority configurations, the more modern organization acknowledges that many decisions cut across conventional lines of authority. When this situation occurs (and it does with great frequency), temporary or virtual decision-making functions become necessary. In these contexts, the need for a decision may actually manifest itself as a set of related decisions distributed across a set of decision makers in such a manner that not all decisions are the province of an individual or a group. Despite this distribution, however, these decisions are assumed to be related and need to be coordinated. Such distributed decision scenarios call for an ODSS design to support them. Culnan and Gutek (1989) suggest four fundamental activities that create the need for organizations to gather, store, and use information through an ODSS. Table 3-4 contains these four activities along with a listing of several types of ODSS functions that may be relevant in support of the activities.

Swanson and Zmud (1989) provide us with yet another taxonomy of strategies for organizational decision support:

1. **Decision ordering.** Decisions may be ranked or ordered such that the higher-ordered decisions reflect those of a higher priority to the organization.
2. **Information sharing.** Decisions are made independently, but all participating organizational decision makers share relevant information. Such information sharing may be directed by management or may exist in a more bottom-up, ad hoc manner.
3. **Negotiated choice.** Because distributed decision making can often involve conflict, some decisions may be made through negotiation among the conflicting parties. A negotiated decision is, in effect, made jointly among the negotiating factions.

As we will see in the remainder of this text, it is not the technology itself that will enhance the decision making within an organization but rather the degree to which the support technology, decision strategies, and organizational power and politics work together. At this point, you may still feel a certain lack of clarity between the concepts of groups and teams and between organizations and groups. This fuzziness exists in academic research of organizational processes as well and is an area of constant

---

TABLE 3-4   ODSS Application Contexts and Functions

- *Specific task problem solving.* These contexts include new product development, R&D, and improved manufacturing processes.
- *Information gathering.* Information is not necessarily gathered in response to a specific need or crisis but rather as a form of "stock on hand." As such, gathering and use are asynchronous.
- *Communication across subunits.* This entails the use of information for ongoing coordination of activities and implementation of decisions.
- *Political behavior.* Competing interests, scarcity of resources, and/or equivocality may give rise to symbolic or strategic use of information.

---

debate. Regardless of this blurring, however, the real benefits of ODSSs may manifest themselves in an interorganizational sense. As designers of decision support technologies, you will need a platform for managing the wide variety of decisions among related, yet disparate, decision makers as companies begin to interconnect directly with their customers, suppliers, government agencies, and even their competitors. The ODSS may serve as such a platform, which is discussed further in Chapter 6.

3-5: CHAPTER SUMMARY

In Chapter 3, we focused on the concept of individual decision style and its effects on decision strategy and quality of outcome. Furthermore, we saw that decision style can also influence the way individuals act within an organizational environment.

This chapter introduced the definition of an organization and the decision-making activities within an organization. The decision makers in an organization comprise a large and diverse population of individuals. Managers should be familiar with the influence of power and politics on decision-making activities within an organization as well as understand the need for different types of support systems at different organizational decision levels.

Key Concepts

- The definition of an organization (3-1)

  Assuming that the whole of an organization is greater than the sum of its parts and that it thus allows its members collectively to pursue and achieve greater goals than they could by acting individually, an organization can be thought of as a unified system of resources defined and structured by a collective of functional and political subsystems bound by a set of stated goals and functioning within a set of loosely defined environments.

- Five dimensions of organizational decisions (3-1)

  Group structure

  Given the nature of the three decision structures of individual, team, and group, it can easily be seen how the type of decisions made as well as the methods employed can vary significantly.

  Group roles

  Each member of a decision-making body will have one or more specified roles. Depending upon how the organization defines these roles and to whom it assigns them, the nature of the decision strategy employed as well as the scope of decision types assigned can be materially changed.

Group processes and style

The concepts of decision process and decision type must be in harmony with the decision-making body's perspective. Organizations must be aware of the components and must try to create decision-making bodies that possess the best combination of ingredients for the given decision situation.

Group norm

The social psychology of decision making is a powerful force affecting the activities of any decision-making body from individual to metaorganizational.

- Organization decision levels (3-1)

Operations

Most decisions made at this level concern day-to-day activities relating to production or service by deploying available resources.

Planning

Most decisions made at this level relate to the internal administration of the organization.

Strategic

Decisions made at this level are usually the most far-reaching of all decisions made across the three levels.

- The level at which a decision is made within the organization must be taken into consideration when designing and implementing a DSS. (3-1)

- Organizational culture (3-2)

Organizational culture is a system of shared meaning consisting of beliefs, symbols, rituals, myths, and practices that have evolved over time. It exerts an extremely powerful influence over the various activities, including decision making, occurring within an organization.

DSS designers must be aware of the influence of organizational culture on the types of decisions made and the appropriateness of various strategies employed within a particular cultural climate. By understanding the concept of cultural fit, the fit between the culture and both the internal and external environment, DSS designers are able to design and deploy supportive systems and technologies.

Organizational culture often determines a firm's ability to change or adapt to changes in environmental conditions. Organizations with cultures that do not allow for flexibility and change may fail to maintain their market position and may fail to survive altogether.

- In most organizations, power and politics are integral parts of the myriad of decisions made on a daily basis. Regardless of the level at which the decision is being made—individual, team, group, or organization—they shape and mold the decision context and thus the type of decision support required. (3-3)

- An organizational decision support system is a support technology that focuses on decisions involving many people. An ODSS can gather, store, and use information within an organization through four fundamental activities. (3-4)

Specific task problem solving

Information sharing

Communication across subunits

Political behavior

- The ODSS may serve as the platform for managing the wide variety of decisions among related, yet disparate, decision makers as companies begin to interconnect directly with their customers, suppliers, government agencies, and even their competitors. (3-4)

Questions for Review

1. Define *organization.*
2. List and briefly describe the five dimensions of organizational decisions.
3. What are the three decision levels in an organization?
4. Define *organizational culture.*
5. What are the influences of organizational culture on performance?
6. What is the relationship between organizational culture and change?
7. Identify the five basic factors that define power in an organization.
8. Describe the influences of power within organizations on decision making.
9. What are politics? Why are they important to DSS design?
10. What is the relationship between politics and decision making?
11. Describe the class of support technology that focuses on decisions involving many people.
12. What are the major distinguishing features of ODSSs and GDSSs?
13. List the activities that can be supported by an ODSS.

For Further Discussion

1. Study and observe an organization. Try to describe its organizational culture. Feel free to explain your observations by examples. What cultural influences in this environment will have the greatest effect on the performance of the organization and its ability to change?
2. Discuss the major characteristics of each organizational decision level. Give an example of each.
3. How can the organizational environment influence the design and implementation of decision support systems?
4. Find an article describing a successful or unsuccessful implementation of a DSS in an organization. Identify the influences of organizational culture, power, and politics.
5. Analyze an ODSS application in the market. Describe its functionalities and how it supports organizational decisions.

4

MODELING DECISION PROCESSES

Learning Objectives

◆ Learn how a fully formed problem statement is developed using three key components: the current state of affairs, the desired state of affairs, and the objective(s)

◆ Identify the problem scope

◆ Understand the three fundamental components of problem structuring: choice, uncertainty, and objective

◆ Be familiar with two decision-modeling tools: influence diagram and decision tree

◆ Based on an understanding of the problem structure components and tools, learn the common decision structures and their variations

◆ Describe various types of decision models, either abstract or conceptual, which will be the foundations for the decision maker's analysis and subsequent forecasts and prediction

◆ Understand the three requirements of probability

◆ Explain the different types of probabilities: long-run frequency, subjective probability, and logical probability

◆ Use direct probability forecasting, odds forecasting, or comparison forecasting to estimate and forecast probabilities of the identified uncertainties

◆ Recognize the techniques of estimating measurable liability (calibration), analyzing sensitivity (sensitivity analysis), and evaluating information costs (value analysis)

WHAT WERE THE ODDS?
THE *EXXON VALDEZ*

At 4 minutes past midnight, on March 24, 1989, the *Exxon Valdez,* loaded with 1,264,155 barrels of North Slope crude oil, ran aground on Bligh Reef in the northeastern portion of Prince William Sound, Alaska. About one-fifth of the total cargo, 11.2 million gallons, spilled into the sea. After 3 days of calm weather and smooth seas, strong northeasterly winds arose and spread the oil beyond any hope of containment. Driving winds mixed much of the oil with seawater into an emulsion known as mousse, which will not burn and is difficult to remove from the surface of the sea or from shore. The spilled oil, now in the form of thin sheets and thick mousse, continued to spread to the southwest. The oil came ashore along 750 kilometers (470 miles) of coast that ran from Prince William Sound to the southern Kodiak Archipelago and Alaska Peninsula. Scientists estimated that 35 percent of the spilled oil evaporated, 40 percent was deposited on beaches within Prince William Sound, and 25 percent entered the Gulf of Alaska where it either became beached or was lost at sea. Field surveys conducted in the summer of 1989 identified 790 miles of shoreline within Prince William Sound that had been oiled, more than 200 miles of which were classified as heavily oiled. In the Kenai Peninsula–Kodiak region, more than 2,400 miles of shoreline were found to be oiled.

The response effort involved unloading the unspilled cargo, vessel salvage, booming of sensitive areas, beach surveys and assessments, overflights to track the floating oil, skimming of floating oil, cleanup of oiled beaches, wildlife rescue, waste management, logistics support, and public relations. Major cleanup operations were conducted each spring and summer from 1989 to 1992. More than 11,000 workers and 1,400 marine vessels were involved in the cleanup and logistics support operations that also included hundreds of aircraft and a substantial land-based infrastructure in 1989. The multiyear cleanup cost more than $2 billion. Techniques used to remove or clean oil included burning, chemical dispersants, high-pressure hot water washing, cold-water washing, fertilizer-enhanced bioremediation, and manual and mechanical removal of oil and oil-laden sediments. Some interesting statistics include the following:

- The oil recovered by skimming operations in 1989 accounted for only about 8.5 percent of the original spill volume.

- Cleanup operations on the beaches during the first four summers led to the recovery and disposal of approximately 31,000 tons of solid oily wastes, which were estimated to account for 5 to 8 percent of the original spill volume.

- About 90 percent of the oil in surface (25 centimeters) beach sediments was removed by natural processes (storm erosion and biodegradation) during the winter of 1989–1990, whereas only about 40 percent of the deeper oil was removed.

- By 1992, the combination of natural processes and cleanup activities had eliminated nearly all of the surface oil, though small amounts persisted along many shoreline segments in the Sound.

The federal on-scene coordinator, Admiral Ciancaglini, released a letter officially concluding the shoreline cleanup on June 10, 1992. The cleanup for the *Exxon Valdez* oil spill took 3 years and exceeded $2.1 billion in costs. Subsequent investigations determined that Aleyeska, the consortium of oil companies responsible for constructing and maintaining the Alaska pipeline, had adopted an oil spill contingency plan that was totally inadequate to protect against a spill of such magnitude. Investigators found evidence of a gross underestimation of probabilities of risk associated with various oil spill scenarios, including one such as the *Exxon Valdez.* It was further determined that had the plan been more realistic regarding the probability of disaster, more resources would have likely been appropriated and would have been on hand when disaster struck.

4-1: DEFINING THE PROBLEM AND ITS STRUCTURE

Recall that the key to the many functions of a DSS and the variety of modern computer-based DSSs comes in the form of one or more underlying models that can be used to study the problem at hand and to derive specific information about it. In this chapter, we will focus on the various problem definition and decision models available to the DSS designer.

PROBLEM DEFINITION

No matter how hard you try, you cannot possibly know how to get where you are going unless you know where you are. This adage acts as a virtual law in the world of problem solving and decision making. As much as you desire to solve the problem and arrive at a choice decision, you cannot be successful if you don't take the time first to identify and define the problem fully. This prescription may sound simplistic or trivial but the typical decision maker, more often than one might imagine, fails to identify the problem formally and concisely before beginning the process of solving it. Remember the headache problem from Chapter 3? Failing to identify and define the problem fully results in a solution that may look like a great idea but does not solve the problem.

In Chapter 2, a problem was defined as the perception of a difference between the current state of affairs and a desired state of affairs. If we can identify and describe the current state of affairs and the desired state of affairs, we can develop a fully formed problem statement. This statement should contain three key components: (1) the current state of affairs, (2) the desired state of affairs, and (3) a statement of the central objective(s) that distinguishes the two. The value of these components can be better understood by looking at a typical problem statement and analyzing its content.

A common error in the formation of a problem statement is a premature focus on the choice set of solutions for the problem rather than the problem itself. When this shortcut thinking happens, bounded rationality "kicks in" and the problem space becomes limited to those alternatives that appear to match the preconceived one embedded in the problem statement. The decision maker is left not with a fully formed problem statement but rather a statement of a solution looking for a problem to solve. For example, let's analyze the following statement using the three components of a fully formed problem statement:

> Should convicted murderers be subject to a death penalty?

The statement actually represents a solution looking for a problem. To begin with, the problem statement isn't a statement at all—it is a question. When the statement is formed this way, the answer becomes either an affirmation or denial of the solution provided in the question. If the answer is yes, then the problem is solved by invoking a death penalty. If the answer is no, then the problem is solved by abolishing the death penalty. In neither case, however, is any real problem being stated—thus no real problem will be solved. One way to determine what the real underlying problem might be is to explore the reasons why a particular choice alternative is under consideration:

> Why should convicted murderers be put to death?

Exploring this perspective refocuses our attention on a reason for the choice rather than the choice itself. The answer to this question moves us closer to a statement containing the three necessary components:

> Many convicted murderers are being released back into society and are committing murders again. A determination must be made regarding how to prevent convicted murderers from killing again.

By stating the problem in terms of the current situation, desired situation, and objective, a clear definition is provided and a path toward a solution is discovered.

PROBLEM SCOPE

Once a problem statement is fully formed and stated, the decision maker must examine the scope of the problem. Upon examination, it may be determined that the problem is definitely worth solving but that the scope of it, as stated, is beyond the available resources, cognitive limitations, or time constraints. In such cases, the scope of the problem must be reduced to a focus that allows for successful deployment of the available resources toward a solution set. Generally speaking, the scope of the problem will be determined by the priorities of the decision maker.

To limit the scope of a problem one must first identify its breadth. One method is to identify details about the problem through a series of questions. How many people are affected? How much does it currently cost? When did this issue first begin? What has been tried before? Who else knows of this problem? Who else is working on a solution to this problem? What is the true magnitude of this problem? These and similar questions can help the decision maker determine the breadth of the problem and thus determine a reasonable scope to focus on.

PROBLEM STRUCTURE

The design of a problem structure is similar to the design of any other structural entity, such as a car, a building, a landscape, or even a work of art. In each case, the basic approach remains the same: Detailed thought and analysis must occur simultaneously with regard to (1) final appearance, (2) elemental details, and (3) the relationships between those elements. This type of design process is often iterative and can, at times, become quite complex. Many times the designer must revise a decision made at one point in the process to account for a change made at another. This constant movement continues until the designer is satisfied with the equilibrium created among the three dimensions.

Regardless of the decision context, a problem structure can be described in terms of three fundamental components: (1) choices, (2) uncertainties, and (3) objectives. Using these three components, we explore the basic problem-structuring tools, common structural configurations, and issues of model selection based on the problem at hand.

Choices

Implicit in the concept of choice is the existence of multiple alternatives. If only one alternative exists then choice is eliminated and, thus, no decision required. One way of thinking about this need for at least two alternatives is to assume that for all decisions one alternative is to simply "do nothing." Although this approach will not solve the problem, it is nonetheless a viable alternative that can and often should be considered. We will assume that all problems and decisions offer this alternative of inaction and will not include it in the models we construct. Just remember that it exists and should at least be given early consideration in any problem analysis.

One of the most common methods of modeling a problem structure is the influence diagram. Using this approach, the three components of a problem structure are represented by specific shapes that are combined and connected to represent the problem being modeled. Another common approach is the decision tree, which focuses on the choice set and the expected outcomes. We will cover these modeling techniques in greater detail later in this section but will begin using them now to illustrate the three components. Figure 4-1 illustrates the shapes used for each structural element in both techniques and an example of a decision tree with four alternatives.

Uncertainties

If one were able to determine all events in a problem context with certainty (meaning a 100 percent probability of occurrence), then making complex decisions would be simple. Also, the process of decision making would be far less interesting and would not need to be studied. Fortunately for teachers of problem-solving techniques and students (such as yourself) who are interested in the subject, certainty is seldom the case. All problem structures contain uncertainties that must be accounted for by the decision maker. It is important to note that the primary difference between choices and uncertainties is the probability of occurrence. With a choice, the probability is 100 percent that at least one alternative is selected with an equal probability of any particular one being selected. This supposition is true because by the time a set of viable alternatives is identified, each has already been placed in the set after identifying and accounting for its various uncertainties. Thus, the selection of an alternative "branch" on the structural tree is under the complete control of the decision maker. With regard to uncertainties, however, the same is not true. By definition, uncertainties are situations beyond the direct control of the decision maker, and their individual probability of occurrence is only estimable within a certain range of possibilities. Therefore, the occurrence of one uncertain event may

FIGURE 4-1   Components of Influence Diagrams and Decision Trees

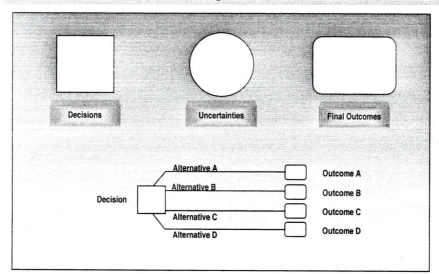

require a complete restructuring of all future events, which is where the real complexity of problem solving begins and where the real value of problem structuring can be found. By diagramming each of the uncertainties and including the expected probability of each one occurring, the decision maker can visualize the various paths of future events and can more easily compare one possible scenario to another. This basic approach is used to create complex computer-based simulations. We will look at these types of models in Section 4-2. Figure 4-2 illustrates the modeling of an uncertainty with three possible outcomes and their associated probabilities.

Objectives

Once the last of the uncertainties has been resolved and the myriad of choices analyzed and selected, the destiny of the decision is set: An outcome will occur. At this point, we need to model how that outcome, whatever it may be, is to be evaluated with respect to its desirability or degree of success. Objectives provide us with a method of establishing the criteria that can be used to measure the value or desirability of a particular outcome. The closer the outcome matches the criteria, the more desirable it is. Examples of objectives include specific reductions in disease, specific percentage increases in market share, and specific increases in revenues or decreases in costs, among many others. Note that a well-formed objective must allow for a quantifiable comparison. An objective such as "to increase profits" is difficult to evaluate. Have we met our objective if profits are $1 more this year than last? According to the way the objective is stated, we have. Most likely, however, this outcome was not the intention of the decision-making activity. A more fully formed objective, such as "to increase profits by 10 percent over last year" or "to improve profits by $50,000 over the prior period," would better reflect the original intent. Decisions can have multiple objectives to evaluate outcomes, but to be a fully modeled decision at least one measurable objective must be identified.

STRUCTURING TOOLS

Influence Diagrams

An influence diagram is a simple method of graphically modeling a decision. The three components of a decision (as illustrated in Figure 4-1) are included, as appropriate, and are linked with rules to model the relationships between them. Figure 4-3 contains sev-

FIGURE 4-2 Uncertainty Model with Outcomes

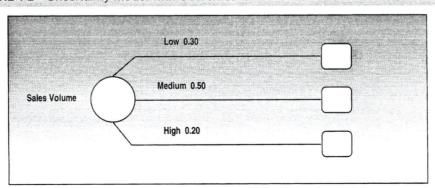

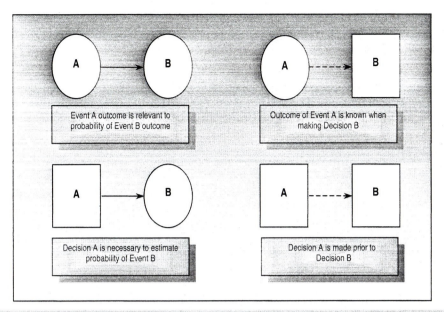

FIGURE 4-3   Relevance Arrows in Influence Diagrams

eral simple influence diagrams along with an explanation for the various shapes and line types used in their construction.

As shown in the figure, two types of arrows (referred to as *arcs*) are used to connect the nodes (the component elements of the decision model). The solid arrows point to uncertainties and objectives and represent a relationship of relevance. In other words, the use of a solid arrow indicates that the predecessor is relevant for assessing the value of the succeeding component. In the lower left of the figure, notice that Decision A is related to Event B using a solid arrow, which indicates that Decision A (the predecessor) is relevant in the determination of the probability of Event B occurring. For instance, the chance of a student receiving an A for a particular exam is dependent to some extent on whether he or she chose to study. Also notice that Event A is related to Event B by a solid arrow (upper left of the figure). In this case, the probability of Event A occurring is relevant to the probability of Event B occurring. For example, the probability of getting caught in a rainstorm and getting wet partly depends on the probability of rain occurring.

Dashed arrows only point to decisions and indicate that a decision was made with knowledge of the outcome of the predecessor node. Thus, the relationship between Event A and Decision B suggests that the decision maker made Decision B already knowing the outcome of Event A (upper right in the figure). If a dashed arrow is used to connect one decision event to another (lower right), it means that the first decision was made before the second decision was made. In this way, we can depict the sequential ordering of decisions in the diagram by the path through the various nodes.

One additional characteristic of an influence diagram is that, when properly constructed, it has no cycles; regardless of where you start in the diagram, no path will lead you back to the starting point. The arrows form a one-way path. Leaving a node eliminates any potential path that will allow a return to it. This rule for construction is faithful to the reality of decision making and problem solving. Once a decision is made, it is made. We cannot go back to a decision at a later time and "unmake" it.

Decision Trees

Although the influence diagram is an excellent tool for modeling the structure of a particular decision context, it does not allow for the depiction of many of the details associated with the decision at hand. Another structuring tool that can be used to complement the influence diagram is the decision tree. In this diagram, only choices and uncertainties are modeled. Lines, referred to as branches, connect the two components. The branches extending from a choice node represent the items contained in a choice set available to the decision maker. The branches radiating from an uncertainty node represent the possible outcomes from a particular event. The value of each outcome is attached to the end of each outcome branch. Figure 4-4 contains an example of a simple decision tree.

A decision tree is typically constructed to be read beginning on the left and continuing to the right until an outcome is reached. In addition, several "rules" must be followed in its construction to assure that the diagram clearly represents the details of the decision context.

First, the branches extending from a choice node must be constructed so that the decision maker can choose only one option. No branch can be modeled as a combination of choice options. Second, the branches radiating from an uncertainty node must represent a set of outcomes that are both mutually exclusive and collectively exhaustive. The first condition, mutually exclusive, means that only one of the possible outcomes can occur. For example, an uncertainty node's two branches represent success or failure. In this case, the rule is followed because a project can either succeed or fail but not both. The second condition, collectively exhaustive, means that the branches represent all possible outcomes; no other possibilities exist. Together these two conditions require that when the uncertainty is resolved, one and only one outcome will prevail.

The third rule of decision tree construction is that all possible paths available to a decision maker are fully mapped in the tree, including all possible choices and uncertainty outcomes. This rule affects a decision tree's size. As a decision context becomes more complicated, the size of the decision tree will increase exponentially. For example, a choice node with three branches, each with two outcomes, results in a total of six possible outcomes. If, however, we add one additional choice node with three alternatives

FIGURE 4-4 Simple Decision Tree

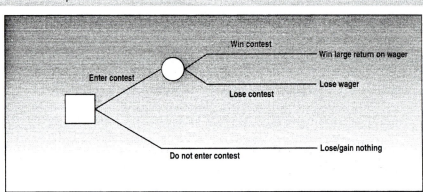

after each uncertainty in the model, we increase the total number of possible outcomes from 6 to 18. This exponential growth is often referred to as "the tree getting bushy."

Finally, the decision tree must be constructed to depict an accurate chronology of events over time. Strictly adhering to the left-to-right construction of the tree provides the best way to accomplish this requirement. From left to right, a typical decision tree begins with a choice node, followed by subsequent choice nodes or uncertainties that must be resolved until the decision tree accounts for all possible paths.

COMMON DECISION STRUCTURES

No debate is needed concerning whether all decision contexts are unique; they are. Nonetheless, as with many other situations in our lives, decision contexts share certain common characteristics and patterns. In this section, we examine decision structures that occur quite frequently during the course of daily managerial activities. By understanding these common structures, a decision maker can more quickly identify the probable structure of a new decision context.

Basic Risky Decision

Many problems faced by a decision maker require a choice selection in the face of some uncertainty. In the basic risky decision structure, a successful decision is a function of both the correct selection from the choice set and the outcome of an uncertainty. See Figure 4-5 for an example of how this decision structure could be used to model a decision to buy stock. Here is another example:

> Product manager Stephanie Essington is considering a sales promotion for her company's new soft drink, Blaster. She would like to focus on consumers who regularly go to the beaches during the summer. The campaign would be called "Blaster's Fun in the Summer Sun" and would promote the new soft drink with mini concerts, giveaways, beach volleyball, and other such events. The rationale for the beach setting is that when people play in the sun they often enjoy a cool, refreshing drink to quench their thirst. If this summer proves to be a particularly hot one, Blaster and Stephanie could both become quite successful. If, however, it rains a great deal this summer in the beach areas, then both Blaster and Essington will be "all wet."

FIGURE 4-5 Basic Risky Decision

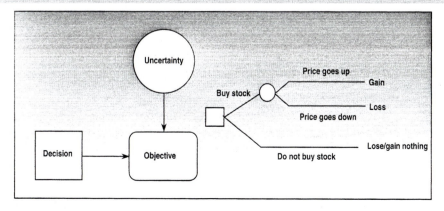

In the preceding example, the decision context is modeled with three components: (1) choice—whether or not to run the promotional campaign; (2) uncertainty—whether it will be sunny or rainy; and (3) objective—to make Blaster successful. The objective of making Blaster successful is a function of both the choice to run the campaign and the amount of rain at the beaches. The basic risky decision structure can be used to describe a variety of common managerial decision situations. The two most common variations of this structure are the basic risky policy and the basic risky decision with multiple objectives.

In Figure 4-6, the basic risky policy variation describes a problem context in which the choice—made from the set of alternatives—directly influences the probabilities of an uncertainty as well as the objective. Consider this example:

> Stephanie Essington's summer beach campaign for Blaster was a remarkable success, and the new product is off and running. Essington is still the product manager but her bonus check allowed her to buy a new Corvette. Now she is working on a new campaign intended to increase sales even further while still building on the beach theme established during the product's initial roll-out. Stephanie believes that the packaging for Blaster could be redesigned to be more "outdoor friendly." She is proposing a package with a built-in, resealable spout and one that is more heavily insulated than a typical soft drink container. Introducing this new packaging could serve to greatly increase market share. However, the new packaging would be more expensive than conventional methods and would also decrease profits to a certain degree.

FIGURE 4-6   Variations of Basic Risky Decision Model

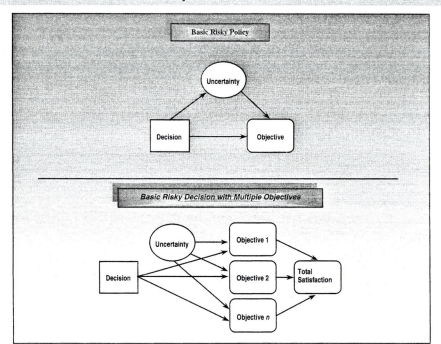

This problem is still modeled with three components but their relationships differ slightly from the basic risky decision structure. Here, both the choice (whether to repackage the product) and the uncertainty (market share) directly influence the objective (profits). In addition, however, the uncertainty associated with the probability of a given increase in market share is also directly affected by the choice. If Stephanie doesn't repackage the product then the probability of increased market share as a result of repackaging will be reduced to zero.

In the second variation, the basic risky decision with multiple objectives, the decision maker is faced with making a trade-off between objectives in order to manage the uncertainty present in the decision context. The best solution will be the one that results in the greatest measured success. Our soft drink example demonstrates this variation:

> Blaster, now the number one soft drink at all of America's beaches, is fast becoming a big seller throughout the country, no small thanks to "Super Steph" as she is now affectionately referred to by her colleagues. The company has given her carte blanche to move Blaster into the international arena. Because of this increased responsibility, Essington needs to increase the size of the product management team. She has considered several different configurations for her team that mainly differ by the number and location of the new team members. More new team members means greater market coverage for Blaster, but they also increase the overall cost of managing the product.

Here, the choice (which team configuration to select) is directly related to more than one objective (market coverage and management cost). The uncertainty (sales) is also directly related to the multiple objectives. In addition, the choice will also affect the probability distribution of the uncertainty. If one objective is maximized then the other will suffer. The decision maker must strike a suitable balance between the multiple objectives by selecting the appropriate alternative from the choice set.

Certainty

A second common decision structure involves those situations in which the trade-off among the various objectives and risk is not a significant consideration. In this structure, the multiple-objective, no-risk decision, the degree of measured success or satisfaction with the final choice is based on an appropriate trade-off among the objectives of the various stakeholders. A variation of this structure is the multiple-objective/multiple-approach, no-risk decision, as shown in Figure 4-7. This structure arises in situations that are so broad and so complex that a single approach would not resolve the problem completely. It represents the structure of issues of public policy such as drug abuse, crime, unemployment, or homelessness. In business, managers face this situation with new product development, low employee morale, and issues of improved efficiency or effectiveness. In most cases, these situations are so complex that designing a single decision-structure model is untenable. To accomplish the analysis, the decision maker must decompose the problem context into more manageable submodels. At this point, the decision maker must determine the degree of emphasis to be placed on each submodel and then select the alternative available from the choice component of each one. Let's get back to Stephanie and see how Blaster is doing:

> The new Blaster product management team, in place for quite some time now, continues to enjoy overwhelming success. Senior management promoted

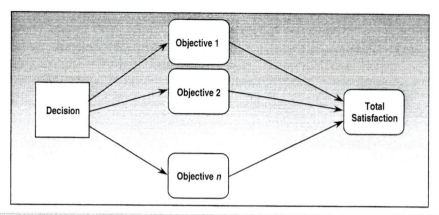

FIGURE 4-7 Multiple-Objective, No-Risk Decision

and rewarded Stephanie with numerous raises based on the successes of her team, and she did the same for her team members. Now, however, the company wants Stephanie and her team to "do it again," so to speak, with a new product introduction. Because Team Blaster is so well respected by senior management, they offered Stephanie the authority to design as well as market the new product. To begin this process, she must assign the various team members to new roles based on their individual strengths and weaknesses; she must determine which market niche to target based on recent consumer survey data; she must schedule the testing and rollout for the new product; and she must create an initial budget for the research and development effort. Each of these decisions, while somewhat affected by the others, is essentially individual in nature and fairly complex in total.

Here the element of risk, while arguably present to some degree in each of the choice scenarios, is not of major importance. The focus is on combining the individual objectives so that the largest measurable degree of success can be expected.

Sequential

Decision processes do not always present themselves in a way that allows a clear beginning and clear ending as part of the structure. More often, conditions change over time and a choice made earlier may no longer be appropriate or deemed useful. Furthermore, an alternative that was not viable at a particular time in the past may now appear more desirable based on the new set of conditions. The sequential decision structure represents a series of basic risky decisions in successive time periods with arrows to indicate the relationships between each temporal choice set. Figure 4-8 illustrates this type of decision structure.

As you can see, a decision made in one time period affects the degree of total measured success across all time periods in addition to the measured success of that individual time period. Decisions in the following time periods (and possibly the prevailing conditions) are affected to varying degrees by the decision(s) made previously. Using a sequential structure model, the decision maker explicitly acknowledges the links between decisions with a common objective made over time. The opportunity to change course at some point in the future leaves open the possibility that a somewhat riskier

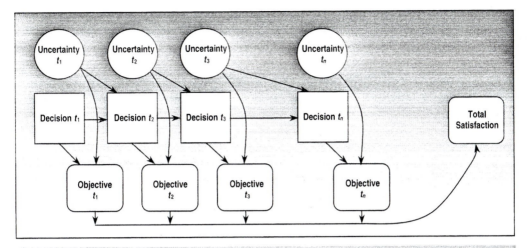

FIGURE 4-8   Multiple-Period Sequential Decision

strategy could be pursued in one time period and, if not successful, could be followed by a more conservative approach to mitigate the damage from the prior period. Also, this modeling structure provides information to the decision maker that may make a decision to defer action until a period sometime in the future the appropriate choice.

4-2: DECISION MODELS

The arsenal of analytical models contained within the model base of a typical DSS and used to solve a particular problem or problem type is only one aspect of any problem situation. The decision maker must also be concerned with the structure of the problem context. In this sense, a problem can be thought of as a set of subsystems that are functionally decomposable at the desire of the decision maker. Each of these subsystems can be modeled to form an accurate representation of that part of the problem context. Once this simplified representation of reality is in place, decision makers can use it with the models as a foundation for their analysis and subsequent forecasts and predictions. In this section, we look at the various classes and types of decision models and their applications to specific problem types.

Decision models can be classified in a number of ways. One common high-level classification divides the models in terms of their explicit inclusion of time as an element. Models that do not explicitly acknowledge time are called static models and those that do are referred to as dynamic models. Another widespread method of classification is by the technique's mathematical or logical focus.

ABSTRACT MODEL TYPES

An abstract decision model focuses on the mathematical precision with which various outcomes can be predicted. This type of model can, theoretically, determine which alternative should result in the most favorable outcome. Based on this prediction, a decision maker then develops a strategy for implementing the proposed alternative and thus solves the problem. This process sounds good; however, as each subsystem of a problem context is modeled and further decomposed, some detail of the information is lost to the decision maker. This loss of information is built into the modeling process as it attempts to create a simplified representation of reality. To achieve this simplification we eliminate certain pieces of information from the abstraction. The decision maker must create a balance between models that capture the complexity of the problem and models that are simple enough to analyze and solve. This balance is never completely attainable and thus the decision maker must always be aware of the "credo of humility" for mathematical modeling: All models are wrong; some models are useful (Golub, 1997). This caveat notwithstanding, mathematical abstractions are useful when their limitations are known and acknowledged by the decision maker.

In keeping with the concept of functional decomposition, abstract models can be divided into four subsystems, each displaying unique characteristics (see Table 4-1).

Deterministic Models

In a deterministic model, no variable can take more than one value at any given time. The same output values will always result from any given set of input variables. Most of the traditional models of normative economic theory are deterministic as are many of the common models used in financial analysis. These model types are particularly useful when a problem structure contains a large number of elements and complex relationships. Common deterministic models include linear programming, nonlinear programming, and differential equations.

Stochastic Models

In a stochastic model, at least one of the variables is uncertain and must be described by some probability function. These model types are often referred to as probabilistic models because they explicitly incorporate uncertainty into their structure. When constructing a stochastic model, the decision maker distributes the input value of one or more variables around some mean value and the output variables take the form of a frequency distribution rather than a discrete set of values. In general, a stochastic model with the same number of elements as a deterministic model is more difficult to manage and becomes more complicated to solve, ceteris paribus.[1] Common stochastic modeling techniques include game theory, queuing theory, linear regression, time series analysis, path analysis, and logistical regression or logit analysis.

TABLE 4-1   Decision Model Classification

Deterministic	Optimization, linear programming, financial planning, production planning, convex programming
Stochastic	Queuing theory, linear regression, logit analysis, path analysis, time series
Simulation	Production modeling, transportation and logistics analysis, econometrics
Domain-specific	Normative economic models, economic-order-quantity, constraint modeling, behavior modeling, technology diffusion, meteorological models

---

[1]*Ceteris paribus* is a Latin phrase that means "all things being equal."

Simulation Models

Unfortunately for most decision makers, problem structures do not often readily fall into either a strictly deterministic or probabilistic realm. More often, some of the subsystems of a problem context are deterministic, some are stochastic, and some are a combination of both. One technique developed to allow for this combined complexity in problem structures is the simulation model. A simulation tests various outcomes that result from combining modeled subsystems in a dynamic environment. Simulation is intended to imitate reality rather than simply model it. Simulation modeling is commonly applied in areas where the cost of a full-scale experiment to determine the best alternative is prohibitive. Other areas where simulation has proven to be valuable include proof of concept testing—where new ideas are tested using a minimum of resources or time—and the study of current processes and operations in order to gain a better understanding and to explore methods of improvement. The following scenario illustrates a situation in which simulation modeling would be an appropriate problem-solving technique:

> Postmaster Steve Hornik arrived at his new location a little more than a year ago, and during that year, he corrected many of the operational deficiencies that existed. The customers of the postal facility seem to be generally pleased with the level of service provided by the employees and business shows an increase. The new postmaster continues to be troubled, however, by the regular occurrence of long lines at the only two service windows at various times of the day. Although the clerks appear to be serving each of their customers as effectively and efficiently as possible, Steve wonders whether more windows and a defined procedure for staffing the windows would improve service even more and reduce the waiting times associated with the long lines. After much thought, Postmaster Hornik narrows his focus to four possible strategies:
>
> **1.** Add one window for parcel pickup and delivery only. Staff this window full-time with one employee to handle both drop-offs and pickups.
> **2.** Use the same strategy as in strategy 1 except use two employees: one for drop-offs only and one for retrieving customer parcel pickups.
> **3.** Add two windows and staff them with clerks who can handle any type of service request including parcel pickup. These windows would be open during all regular business hours.
> **4.** Use the same basic strategy as in strategy 3, but only open the additional windows during peak business hours.
>
> Hornik believes that one of the four strategies will solve the problem effectively. The problem is that he doesn't know how to determine which one to choose, and he cannot tear up the post office to build new windows to find out.

In this situation, the problem cannot be analyzed effectively with static, abstract models. Many of the variables in the model are not only dynamic but vary in relation to the time of day, the day of the week, and probably the season. Furthermore, physically investigating each of the scenarios would not only be expensive and time consuming but would negatively disrupt the current environment at the post office. Using simulation modeling, however, these various scenarios can be compared against each other and can be tested over days, weeks, or even years in a matter of a few hours. The decision maker can easily design a series of simulations that account for the time of day, the expected frequency of various service requests (parcel pickup, drop-off, postage purchase, etc.), the distribution of arrivals and departures, number of windows, speed of execution of each service request, and so on. Based on the comparative results of the various simulation runs, the decision maker can then determine the most desirable alternative and the best balance among the stated objectives.

Despite its attractiveness, simulation modeling is not without disadvantages. First, an optimal solution is not guaranteed by a simulation model. The model will only inform the decision maker of the probabilistic outcome and allow for a comparison of modeled scenarios (remember bounded rationality?). Second, the construction of a simulation model, although often the most cost-effective solution to a problem analysis, is nonetheless time consuming and costly. Third, the results obtained from a simulation model are distinctly context specific and are not generalizable to other problem domains. Finally, simulation is an attractive and entertaining method to managers. Because of simulation's "glitz," other analytical solutions that could yield equal or even better or more accurate results are often overlooked. When its limitations are understood and acknowledged, however, simulation offers a powerful abstract analytical modeling technique that can provide positive results when properly applied.

The construction of a simulation model for discrete events is a relatively straightforward exercise. The following steps outline the process and sequence for its creation:

1. **State the objective of the model:** Every simulation model must have a defined objective. Questions such as "What is the decision we need to make?" "What must be optimized in order to make the decision?" and "What information must be supplied by the simulation in order to make the decision?" can be used to assist in stating the objective of the model.

2. **Define the scope and boundary of the system:** What are the component elements of the system? What elements are inside the system boundary; which are not? Which elements are controllable, and what are the appropriate parameters?

3. **Define the state of the system:** Consider each of the component elements in the system and determine their state. Some elements are not relevant to the outcome of the simulation and can be ignored. For example, in our post office example, where the patrons park before entering the post office is irrelevant to our simulation. Conversely, how many and what type of packages they are carrying are relevant issues.

4. **Define all events that can affect the system state and their individual impact on each state variable:** Certain events can be classified as *endogenous* in that they originate inside the system boundary. Their occurrence depends on the state of the system. Other events are referred to as *exogenous*. These events originate outside the system boundary, and their occurrence is not affected by the state of the system. Customers arriving at the post office is an exogenous event while patrons being served at a postal window is an endogenous event.

5. **Define the unit of time used by the system:** The rate at which the process under study occurs and the defined objective of the model will assist in determining the appropriate unit of time. A fine time unit can assist in generating highly accurate output but the objective of the model may not warrant such precision. Conversely,

a coarse time unit can dramatically reduce simulation time and required processing power but the results may prove limited in their usefulness.

6. **Create a statistical definition for each event in the model:** Each processing step must be defined in statistical terms. For example, customer arrival is generally modeled using a gamma distribution while other events may be modeled using a normal distribution.

7. **Determine, *a priori*, the metrics desired from the model:** Each output of the model must be defined so that the desired information can be generated. For example, if we wish to know the distribution of waiting times for each customer at the package window, we need to define a table for each time interval so that the appropriate entry can be made at the end of the simulation run.

8. **Define the starting state of the model:** The state of all events as the simulation begins must be determined. Is the post office closed? Are customers waiting at the door or already in line?

Once these eight decisions are made, the simulation can be constructed in the form of a computer program using simulation program generators. Some graphical simulation packages can even create animations of the events as they are processed thus allowing the user to see the simulation as it happens. Figure 4-9 contains a screen shot from a graphical simulation package.

Domain-Specific Models

The fourth type of common abstract model is the domain-specific model. The advances in the science disciplines prompt the need for highly specific types of decision-making techniques and contexts. In these cases, each discipline develops its own set of abstract mathematical modeling techniques to serve its needs. Models of supply and demand are unique to the toolbox of economists. Other well-known domains such as operations research, sociology, ecology, medicine, and meteorology each rely on its own unique abstract modeling techniques. In the design of a DSS for a specific problem domain, the designer must become aware of any domain-specific models available for inclusion in the model base.

CONCEPTUAL MODEL TYPES

Despite the variety of abstract mathematical models to choose from and their individual and combined power to assist in problem structuring, a formal mathematical approach to a problem may not always be the most appropriate strategy. Examples include problem contexts in which abstract models oversimplify the structure or the mathematical modeling process may be too time consuming or too costly. Another example occurs when the decision maker is so familiar with the problem context that an abstract representation would yield no gains. In these cases, a conceptual model becomes the more appropriate method of forecasting the outcomes associated with various choice alternatives.

Conceptual models can be thought of as analogies to the problem context. Implicit in this perspective is the notion that even though all problems are unique, no problem is completely new. Experience from a past problem context can be used to assist in forecasting events and outcomes in the new context. Using this method, decision makers can recall and combine a variety of past experiences and contexts to create an

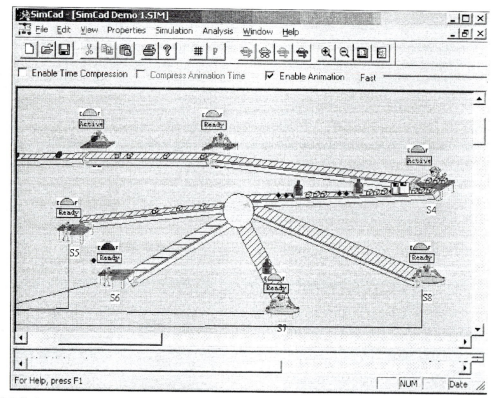

FIGURE 4-9 Example of Simulation Graphics

accurate conceptual model of the current situation and to assign probabilities to those event components that remain uncertain.

Conceptual modeling is often criticized as overly subjective and individually biased toward the beliefs of the decision maker. Although this argument certainly shows some merit, we must also recognize that the choice of a particular abstract modeling approach is also a subjective decision and is dependent on the decision maker's expertise in the chosen technique. Furthermore, abstract models are based on equally subjective mathematical assumptions of how things are related. Suffice it to say that both methods allow individual biases and assumptions to creep into their construction and use. Both the designer and user of a DSS must be fully aware of the appropriateness (or lack thereof) of a particular technique when applying it in a given problem context. The use of conceptual modeling and analogical reasoning will be explored in greater detail in Chapter 9 as it applies to artificial intelligence and knowledge engineering. Returning to our post office problem, we can see an example of conceptual modeling in action:

Postmaster Steve Hornik completed his simulation of the four customer service scenarios, and the results proved to be effective in improving the long lines. Because of Hornik's demonstrated success with the redesign of the mail lobby, the postmaster general selected him to design and test a drive-up mail window. Five different locations received resources to test this new concept and were told to be creative and to experiment where applicable. Steve is excited about this opportunity but is struggling with exactly how to implement it. Because the post office serves a relatively small community, the bulk of the customer traffic arrives on foot. Those who arrive by automobile usually park down the street at the main parking garage for the business district and then walk to their desired destinations. Hornik wonders whether this behavior is a result of the convenience associated with the central parking facility or because no previous alternative such as the drive-up facility existed. He creates three scenarios to identify the uncertainties:

1. **Strong acceptance.** Postal customers will use the new drive-up facility extensively because it will be easier than hand-carrying large packages and bulky mail in addition to other parcels the customer may have.
2. **Poor acceptance.** Postal customers will avoid using the new facility because it will require them to "schedule" their trip to the post office either before parking for shopping or after completing their shopping.
3. **Moderate acceptance.** Some of the elderly customers will find the availability of the new facility to be beneficial. Overall, the drive-up window will fill a void in the range of services provided and will prove to be moderately useful.

Hornik reasons that, of the three possible scenarios, the strong acceptance scenario is the least compelling, and the moderate acceptance outcome is the most compelling. He therefore assigns the following probabilities to the three outcomes: $P[\text{Strong}] = 10$ percent, $P[\text{Moderate}] = 60$ percent, $P[\text{Poor}] = 30$ percent.

HOWARD'S TEST OF CLARITY

Whether a decision maker chooses to employ abstract techniques, conceptual approaches, or a combination of both, the final step in the structuring process is ensuring that all components of the context model are clearly defined. Howard (1988) proposed a useful method for determining when the conceptualizations of variables and outcomes have been identified and defined sufficiently:

> Imagine a clairvoyant who has access to all future information. . . . Would the clairvoyant be able to determine unequivocally what the outcome would be for any event in the structure diagram? No interpretation or judgment should be required of the clairvoyant. (quoted in Clemen, 1991, 55)

Given the preceding scenario, could the events at every node of the model be fully determined without interpretation? The decision model passes the clarity test when this question can be answered affirmatively. It should allow no room for interpretation or misunderstanding regarding the basic components of the decision structure. Applying the clarity test to a structuring model is an iterative approach to the refinement of each individual component. Only after ensuring that all elements are fully refined should the decision maker move on to considering selection of a solution strategy.

4-3: TYPES OF PROBABILITY

It should be clear by now that a decision is not much of a decision unless some uncertainty is present. If all things are crystal clear then the decision becomes mostly a mechanical process in which logic and common sense are the primary tools. The important point here is that virtually all decisions contain elements of uncertainty and for a decision to be made with any degree of success, those uncertainties must be quantified in some manner. At this point, the importance of understanding the concept of probability enters the picture.

A central tenet of modern decision analysis is that we can symbolize any kind of uncertainty through an appropriate application of basic probability. Despite the obvious appropriateness of probability theory for describing uncertainties it is probably the most misused and misunderstood tool of decision making. Properly applied, probability theory can be invaluable in the structuring, resolution, and choice selection of a given problem context. Improperly applied, however, it can lead to decisions that are perfect in all respects except for their outcome. In the next few sections, we will explore the fundamentals of probability theory and will focus on various methods of estimating and forecasting the probabilities of uncertain events.

THREE REQUIREMENTS OF PROBABILITY

No matter what the scenario, the proper application of probability theory requires that three conditions be met. Table 4-2 contains a list of these requirements.

The first requirement implies that all probabilities are positive and that no event can have less than a 0 percent chance of occurring. Conversely, it makes perfect sense that no event can have greater than a 100 percent chance of occurring either.

The second requirement imposes a mathematical constraint on the probability of multiple outcomes to a particular event. Assuming that the outcomes are mutually exclusive—that is, if one can happen, then the other cannot—then the probability that one of them occurs must be equal to the sum of their respective probabilities. If the probability that a new policy in a company will boost employee morale is 25 percent and the probability that morale will stay the same despite the implementation of the new policy is 35 percent, then the probability that morale will either increase or stay the same is 60 percent. (What might the probability be of morale going down?)

The third requirement is probably the most important to successful decision making. If we know the complete set of outcomes for a given event, at least we know what cannot happen: An outcome that is not contained within the set of all possible outcomes cannot happen. If a baseball game is played, we do not know who will win, but

---

TABLE 4-2   The Three Requirements of Probabilities

1. All probabilities must lie within the range of 0 to 1.
2. The probabilities of all individual outcomes of an event must add up to the probability of their union.
3. The total probability of a complete set of outcomes must be equal to 1.

---

we do know that the only possible outcomes are that one of the two teams playing will win and one will lose. Because the rules do not allow for a tie, we know that the probability of a tie occurring is 0 percent. Once we know the set of mutually exclusive outcomes for an event, we are said to have a set that is collectively exhaustive. The sum of probabilities for this set of all possible outcomes must equal 1. In other words, if we know all possible outcomes for an event that must occur then the probability that one of them will occur is 100 percent. If the uncertainties contained within a decision context are modeled within these three qualifying factors, then the probabilities will be appropriate. Once we establish the appropriateness of our probabilities we can focus our attention on the degree of accuracy of the various estimations. We will cover the accuracy issue in detail in the following sections.

TYPES OF PROBABILITY

Regardless of whether a problem context is modeled via an abstract approach or a more conceptual method, we eventually must estimate the probabilities of the identified uncertainties. Probability in this context can be expressed in three different ways: (1) long-run frequency, (2) subjective, and (3) logical.

Long-Run Frequency

Most introductory texts in statistics and probability begin their presentation with probability viewed as a measure of long-run frequency. This approach relies on the so-called "law of large numbers," which states that if an event or an experiment is repeated a large number of times, the observed frequency of a particular outcome of that event will be a good estimate of the true probability of that outcome. The most common example used to demonstrate the long-run frequency approach is the flip of a coin:

> Take a coin from your pocket or purse and flip it into the air. Let the coin fall to the ground and lay flat. What is the probability that the coin will land heads up?

The answer to this question should be easily determined and irrefutable. The two possible outcomes to the event are heads or tails. We assume the coin is fair and that the two possible outcomes are mutually exclusive. Given these conditions, the probability of each possible outcome occurring is 50 percent. Note that this simple analysis also satisfies the three requirements for probabilities. If we repeat this "experiment" a large number of times we will find that each outcome occurs approximately 50 percent of the time.

Advocates of a long-run frequency approach are often referred to as frequentists. The frequentist approach advocates the estimation of probability through experimentation and repetition. At times, however, thinking about probabilities in terms of long-run frequencies is either impractical or untenable. Consider the need to estimate the probability of a major nuclear accident at a power plant nearing completion. Let's narrow the scope of the problem to the probability of a nuclear accident within the next 15 years. It would be impractical to run a repetitive set of experiments to estimate the probability (nor would we want to even if it were practical). Nonetheless, we must make such estimates all the time and we must have a reasonable sense that we can rely on such estimates. To accomplish this type of estimation we have to think of probability in another way.

Subjective Probability

Consider the following questions:

- What is the probability that the coin flipped at the beginning of the 1986 Super Bowl game between the Chicago Bears and the New England Patriots came up heads?
- What is the probability that James Knox Polk was the president of the United States in 1843?
- What is the probability that Button Gwinnett, Caesar Rodney, William Whipple, and William Williams were all signers of the U.S. Declaration of Independence?

If the answers to the preceding questions do not come readily to mind, don't worry. In every case, the true probability of the event is known because it already occurred. Nonetheless, if you do not know the answer, you are uncertain. Let's go back to our coin flip example:

> Using the same coin you used in the previous example, flip the coin into the air. This time, however, catch the coin before it lands and slap it onto the back of your other hand. Do not look at the coin. What is the probability that the coin is heads up?

If you are like most people your initial reaction is to argue that the probability of heads in this experiment is exactly the same as the last one: 50 percent. You reason that knowing that the coin was flipped did not provide you with any new information regarding the outcome and that slapping it on your other hand does not change the probability of the outcome. Thus, the probability remains at 50 percent. Your initial reaction fails, however, to correctly identify the probability in question. In this experiment, your uncertainty lies not with the randomness of the coin but, rather, with your uncertainty of the outcome. Your probability estimation was made after the fact. The uncertainty is completely within your own mind. In this case, the probability estimation is not a measure of the outcome itself, but is a measure of your uncertainty of the outcome. From a frequentist perspective, the answer to the question is either 100 percent or 0 percent; you just don't know which.

Situations like these require a perspective different from the classical long-run frequency approach. The subjective probability approach views probability as an individual's "degree of belief" that a particular outcome will occur. To adopt this approach is more than just allowing for probability estimations that are "acts of faith." Implicit in its acceptance is a set of underlying assumptions that, if satisfied, infer a set of numbers that can describe our degree of belief and, more importantly, conform to the requirements for probabilities such that they can be combined to infer the probabilities of other related uncertainties. Several researchers developed and formalized such assumptions (e.g., de Finetti, 1964; Savage, 1954). Table 4-3 contains these axioms for probability that allow us to estimate probabilities subjectively.

Shared Meaning and the Need for Numbers While on the subject of subjective probability estimation, we need to briefly revisit the concept of shared meaning introduced in Chapter 3. If I use a particular term or phrase to describe something and you understand it in the same way as I do, we are said to have a shared meaning with regard to that phrase. If you don't understand my meaning, then I need to rephrase or restate myself. When it comes to probability estimation, the concept of shared meaning takes

TABLE 4-3 Axioms for Subjective Probability Estimation

- For any two uncertainties, A is more likely than B, or B is more likely than A, or A and B are equally likely.
- If A_1 and A_2 are any two mutually exclusive events, and B_1 and B_2 are any other mutually exclusive events; and if A_1 is not more likely than B_1, and A_2 is not more likely than B_2; then (A_1 and A_2) is not more likely than (B_1 and B_2). Further, if either A_1 is less likely than B_1, or A_2 is less likely than B_2, then (A_1 and A_2) is less likely than (B_1 and B_2).
- A possible event cannot be less likely than an impossible event.
- Suppose $A_1, A_2, \ldots A_n$ is an infinite decreasing sequence of events; that is, if A_n occurs, then A_1 occurs, for any n. Suppose further that each A_n is not less likely than some other event B, again for any n. Then the occurrence of all of the infinite set of events:

$$A * n = 1, \ldots, \infty, \text{ is not less likely than } B.$$

- There is an experiment with a numerical outcome such that each possible value of that outcome, in a given range, is equally likely.
- If an individual is able to, or wishes to, express his or her judgments of likelihood according to these axioms, then numbers must exist that describe his or her perceptions of the uncertainty of any event that satisfy the rules of the probability calculus. Conformity to these rules is our definition of what it means to be rational in evaluating uncertainty.

Source: Watson, S. R. and Buede, D. M., *Decision Synthesis: The Principles and Practice of Decision Analysis.* Cambridge University Press, © 1987.

on great importance. We can describe the probability of an event with words such as *common, rare, infrequent, regular,* and *typical,* among many others. The problem with using this approach, however, is that it requires a shared meaning between us if we are truly to communicate. Research in the field of cognitive psychology suggests that different adjectives or phrases can mean different things to different people in different contexts. Beyth-Marom (1982) studied the relationship between certain descriptive phrases and the specific probability estimations associated with them. Subjects given the phrase "There is a nonnegligible chance . . ." provided specific probability estimations ranging from below 0.36 to more than 0.77. In addition, we can change our subjective estimations based upon the context in which we are estimating them. Consider this: The statement "There is a slight chance of rain later this evening" arguably carries with it a completely different subjective probability estimation (and a different connotation) than the statement "There is a slight chance of a category five hurricane later this evening." Shared meaning is important in probability estimation, and numbers make it happen. Section 4-4 contains several methods for eliciting numerical estimations of subjective probability.

Logical Probability

Use of the third type of probability is most often confined to those situations in which accuracy is tantamount to success and the probability of a probability is involved. The concept of logical probability suggests that even though a probability may be derivable, its accuracy may not be acceptable under any circumstances. The following example serves to illustrate the concept:

Betty Boggess just received some distressing news from her doctor. A recent set of chest X-rays revealed a small tumor in one of her lungs. The doctor explained to her that the tumor is either benign or malignant. If it is benign, it poses no danger to her health and need not be removed. If, however, the tumor is cancerous then it must be removed immediately or it will prove fatal. Ninety percent of the time, tumors of this type are not malignant. The doctor then picked up the telephone and scheduled Betty for immediate surgery. Why?

The doctor's decision to schedule immediate surgery may, at first glance, appear to be both counterintuitive and hasty. Surely a biopsy procedure would be able to determine the nature of the tumor and would clearly be less intrusive to the body than major surgery. So why wouldn't the doctor perform a biopsy before performing surgery?

The answer to this question lies with the concept of logical probability. Although the biopsy procedure could determine the condition of the tumor, the accuracy of the procedure is not 100 percent. If the pathologist extracts lung tissue directly from the tumor and the results indicate malignancy, then immediate surgery will be indicated. If, however, the pathologist extracts lung tissue that is not a part of the tumor (even one cell outside the actual tumor boundary) then the test for malignancy will be negative and the need for surgery will appear moot. The problem lies not with the accuracy of the test itself but with the logical probability of performing it correctly. The location of the tumor is such that the slightest margin of error is intolerable. Because the doctor cannot be 100 percent certain that the tissue tested was from the actual tumor he has no logical choice but to perform surgery. Situations in which a probability estimation of less than 100 percent is the same as zero call for the application of logical probability.

4-4: TECHNIQUES FOR FORECASTING PROBABILITIES

If we accept the notion that all probabilities, regardless of their type, must be represented by numbers, then we must develop a set of acceptable methods to determine them. Techniques for forecasting probabilities using a long-run approach, such as statistical regression, time series analysis, or network optimization, are numerous, and discussion of them is beyond the scope of this text. Instead, this section will concentrate on techniques for eliciting numerical subjective probability estimations that can then be combined with other estimates using the laws of probability. Three such approaches are (1) direct forecasting, (2) odds forecasting, and (3) comparison forecasting.

DIRECT PROBABILITY FORECASTING

The direct method is the simplest of all techniques for eliciting subjective probabilities. It is as straightforward as its name implies: The decision maker or expert is simply asked to estimate the probability of an outcome for a particular event. If the source is highly skilled and experienced at providing quantitative forecasts, such as a professional meteorologist, then the potential for obtaining an accurate estimation is high. If, however, the source is not sufficiently experienced then the accuracy of the estimate is suspect and its usefulness limited. Nevertheless, properly obtained direct estimates can be both useful and efficient methods of assigning numerical values to subjective probabilities.

ODDS FORECASTING

The second common method for eliciting subjective probability estimations focuses on a gambling perspective. The goal of odds forecasting is to find specific amounts of money to win or lose such that the decision maker is willing to accept either side of the bet. Once these amounts are determined, they can be transformed into odds and from there into estimates of probabilities. Oddsmakers use this basic concept when setting odds for such things as sporting events.

Odds are simply another method of expressing a subjective probability. An odds-maker who sets the odds for a particular sporting event at 2 to 1 believes the favored team's chance of winning to be twice as great as the other team's chance. Given this scenario, the oddsmaker is indifferent to which team you bet on. If you take the favorite and they win, you win even money. If they lose, you lose your bet. If, however, you take the underdog and they win, you win double your money; if they lose you simply lose your bet. In either case, the expected value of the bet is the same regardless of which side is taken. Consider the following:

The Miami Heat had their best season ever. They played so well that they advanced to the second round of the NBA playoffs. Now, they face the four-time champion Chicago Bulls in a best of seven series. Even though, in previous playoff series, the team never beat the Bulls, the Heat was the only team to beat the Bulls twice in the regular season, once on the Bulls' home court. The decision maker is faced with two possible bets:

- Win $X if the Bulls win the series.
- Lose $Y if the Bulls lose the series.
- Lose $X if the Bulls win the series.
- Win $Y if the Bulls lose the series.

The amounts for X and Y can be thought of as amounts of money placed into a pool. The winner gets all the money in the pool and the loser gets nothing. The two bets can be referred to as symmetrical because they are simply mirror images of each other. Figure 4-10 contains the decision tree for this example.

If the amounts for X and Y are set so that the decision maker is indifferent to which side of the bet to take, we can represent them in the following mathematical form:

$$X * P(Bulls\_Win) - Y * [1 - P(Bulls\_Win)] =$$
$$Y * [1 - P(Bulls\_Win)] - X * P(Bulls\_Win)$$

From this equation, we can derive the following:

$$2\{X * P(Bulls\_Win) - Y[1 - P(Bulls\_Win)]\} = 0$$

If we divide both sides through by 2 and expand the left side of the equation we get the following:

$$X * P(Bulls\_Win) - Y + Y * P(Bulls\_Win) = 0$$

Now, by collecting terms:

$$(X + Y) * P(Bulls\_Win) - Y = 0$$

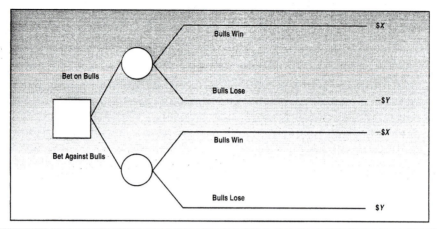

FIGURE 4-10 Decision Tree for Odds Forecasting Method

we can reduce it to the following equation:

$$P(Bulls\_Win) = Y / (Y + X)$$

All we need to do now is determine the values of X and Y and we can calculate a subjective probability estimate. Assume the decision maker is willing to win $100 if the Bulls win and lose $225 if the Bulls lose. His subjective probability estimate can be calculated as follows:

$$P(Bulls\_Win) = 225 / (100 + 225) = 225 / 325$$
$$= 0.6923, \; or \; approximately \; 0.70$$

Based on this estimate, the odds for the bet are 7 to 3 in favor of the Bulls.

Procedure for Establishing the Indifference Bet

Finding the amounts for which the decision maker is indifferent to the bet involves a simple iterative process known as bracketing. Begin establishing values that are highly favorable to one of the two bets and ask which side of the bet is preferred. Depending upon the response, vary the amounts so that the opposite bet becomes favorable. Continue this process of gradual adjustment until no particular bet appears more favorable than the other to the decision maker. At this point, the indifference amounts are established and a subjective probability estimation can be calculated.

COMPARISON FORECASTING

Similar to the odds forecasting method, the comparison approach (sometimes referred to as the lottery forecast) presents the decision maker with a choice between participating in one of two lottery-like games. The two games are constructed in such a way that one is an uncertain event and the other is a reference game with a known probability of winning. The idea is to determine a probability of winning so that the decision maker is indifferent as to whether the uncertain game is played or the reference game is played. The uncertain event is usually constructed in the form of winning a big prize or losing a small amount of money, such as winning an all-expense-paid European vacation or losing $100. The reference game is often structured in the form of a partially shaded wheel of fortune where the shaded area represents a winner and the unshaded area represents a loser. Figure 4-11 illustrates the decision tree for this method and the structure of the two lotteries.

As with the odds forecasting method, the probability of winning the reference lottery is repeatedly adjusted slightly upward or downward until the decision maker is indifferent as to which game to play. The assumption is that the decision maker's subjective probability estimation of winning the uncertain game creates his or her indifference.

DECOMPOSING COMPLEX PROBABILITIES

The example problem contexts examined so far were fairly straightforward and did not contain uncertainties that were dependent on other uncertainties. In practice, however, the difficulty in estimating a probability lies in its dependency on one or more other uncertain events. Probability estimation for various situations can also depend on a sequence of prior events. Under these conditions, the phrase "That depends . . ." often prefaces a request for a subjective probability estimation.

When faced with a complex decision structure containing conditional probabilities, the decision maker must use a technique known as decomposition. In this approach, we rely on the rules of probability to determine the probabilities of each possible outcome in the problem structure and then determine the probability of the event in question using a formula for calculating total probability. The following example illustrates this approach:

> LB Industries, a regional New England–based firm, manufactures a heat recovery unit called HeaTrap for use on both electric and gas forced-air residential furnaces. HeaTrap uses a patented method of recycling lost heat and can result in energy savings up to 30 percent annually. Vice President of Sales Debra Herbenick is trying to determine the probability that sales for HeaTrap will exceed 25,000 units for the forthcoming winter sales period. She

FIGURE 4-11   Decision Tree for Comparison Forecasting Method

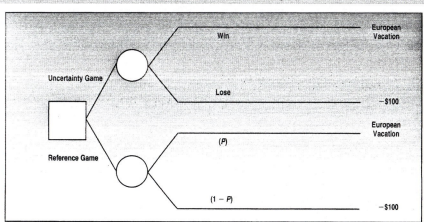

needs to notify the production division of her estimates so that they can plan for the necessary production schedules. She knows from past years that sales of HeaTrap depend to a large extent on the winter conditions in their regional market area. She estimates the probability that sales will exceed 25,000 units to be 0.80 if winter conditions prove to be severe and 0.50 if conditions are moderate. Currently, the probability of severe winter conditions is forecast to be 0.70 and for moderate conditions, 0.30. Herbenick has to make a decision fast.

In order to determine the probability of an event conditioned by one or more other outcomes we need to determine the probabilities along each branch of the decision tree. In this example, to determine the probability of sales exceeding 25,000 units, ($P[A]$), three additional probabilities must be identified: (1) the probability of severe winter conditions ($P[B]$), (2) the probability of sales exceeding 25,000 units if conditions are severe ($P[A|B]$), and (3) the probability of sales exceeding 25,000 units if conditions are moderate ($P[A|B']$).

Debra has set up the decision tree (Figure 4-12) necessary to solve the problem and determine the answer to her question. She uses the following formula for total probability to solve for the probability of sales exceeding 25,000 units:

$$P[A] = \{P[A \mid B] * P[B]\} + \{P[A \mid B] * P[B]\}$$

By using the probability estimations known to her, she calculates the probability that sales will exceed 25,000 units for the forthcoming winter sales period and contacts production with her estimate:

$$P[A] = (0.80 * 0.70) + (0.50 * 0.30) = 0.71$$

FIGURE 4-12   Decision Tree for LB Industries Decomposition Problem

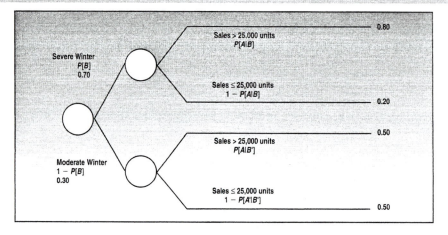

INCORPORATING FORECASTING TECHNIQUES INTO A DSS

The majority of probability forecasting techniques, either objective or subjective, can be easily included in the model base of a typical DSS. The real question facing the designer is which ones to include and under what circumstances to offer them to the user.

In practice, no set of rules or "absolute truths" governs the selection and application of an appropriate forecasting technique. Research shows that the set of tools selected by a decision maker is not necessarily based on any particular unique insight but is rather a function of which tools and techniques he or she is most comfortable with. Given this generality, the burden of educating the user as to the appropriateness and limitations of each of the available techniques falls to the DSS designer. Although the choice is not always clear-cut, several factors can influence the selection of one technique over another. Table 4-4 contains a list of these elements affecting the choice of method.

Although each of the factors listed in the table can affect the selection of a forecasting technique, the application of the most appropriate technique for the problem context solves only half of the problem. Even if the correct technique is being used, the source of the estimation must be skilled enough to provide an estimate of measurable reliability. Reliability becomes most important when a technique such as direct estimation is deemed appropriate. The last section in this chapter addresses this problem.

4-5: CALIBRATION AND SENSITIVITY

BEING WELL CALIBRATED

In most situations we don't really need to know the exact probability for a particular outcome or event. In fact, even if we could know the exact probability of an event occurring, it is still just a probability. A probability is just a specialized way of specifying an average, and an average simply means that given enough time the event will occur this often. Although averages are useful descriptors they can also be misleading. Take, for example, the man who places his left hand in a vat of boiling oil (497.2°F) and his right hand in vat of liquid nitrogen (−300° F). On the "average," he should be quite comfortable (98.6°F). Although this situation is exaggerated, you still see the point. We need more information than simply a probability estimation to make an informed decision.

Despite the skill of the estimator and the accuracy of the estimate, accidents do happen and things do not always go as smoothly as we would like. Rather than using a single probability estimation, we might benefit from an estimation of the worst-case scenario and the best-case scenario. Properly constructed, we can say that the actual

TABLE 4-4   Factors Affecting the Selection of a Forecasting Technique

Problem structure	Complexity	Problem size
Precision	Availability	DSS designer preference

Source: Davis (1988).

probability estimate lies somewhere between these two values. This range of values is referred to as a confidence interval. A decision maker might indicate with 90 percent confidence that the probability of the event outcome will fall between the values estimated for best-case and worst-case scenarios. With this additional information, we can more reliably move forward in making our decision. Or can we?

Simply having a stated confidence interval does not necessarily make the estimate reliable. The ability of the decision maker or expert to make such an estimate will significantly affect reliability. To test this point, we might have the decision maker make 10 independent estimates for the same subjective probability. Assuming 90 percent confidence, 9 out of the 10 estimates should contain the true value for the probability. If they do, the decision maker is said to be well calibrated with regard to that type of estimation and we can assume that the estimator is well aware of his or her predictive abilities. If, on the other hand, the number of correct estimates is less than 9 out of 10, the decision maker is overconfident in his or her knowledge and ability to provide useful estimates in this domain.

A well-calibrated source requires years of experience and feedback to develop. It is one reason why (despite evidence to the contrary on any given weekend) professional meteorologists have been found to be generally well calibrated. They make the same set of estimations day after day and year after year. Each of their estimations gets direct feedback in the form of what weather actually occurred. Over time, they become highly skilled at making such estimations and their confidence interval becomes narrower.

Most decision makers, however, are not well calibrated even in areas of general knowledge. The confidence intervals we assume in making our general knowledge estimations are often too narrow, suggesting we are generally overconfident in our basic knowledge of the world around us (recall the biases of anchoring and adjustment discussed in Chapter 3). Try your hand at the list of questions in Table 4-5 to see how well calibrated you are in general knowledge.

TABLE 4-5 Calibration Test for General Knowledge

For each question, provide a 90 percent confidence interval for your answer. The answers to some questions may be quite familiar to you, whereas others may not. Vary your confidence interval accordingly.

1. What percentage of U.S. citizens over 15 years of age is considered literate?
2. What is the present life expectancy for the total U.S. population?
3. How many stripes are on the American flag?
4. How many televisions were owned in the United States in 1993?
5. How many airports are there in the United States?
6. How many terms of office did Theodore Roosevelt serve as U.S. president?
7. What NBA team set a record in the 1980s for the most consecutive losses to start a regular season?
8. What is considered to be the most popular activity in the Catholic Church besides Mass?
9. Who quit as PTL chairman on October 8, 1987?
10. What state was former White House Chief of Staff John Sununu governor of for three terms of office?

Note: Answers appear at the end of this chapter.

SENSITIVITY ANALYSIS

After making the estimations, the decision maker can begin the process of selecting the most desirable alternative given the information at hand. Assuming the models are accurate reflections of reality and their underlying assumptions are valid and appropriately modeled, the decision maker should be in a reasonable position to make an informed choice. The problem remaining is that the "assumptions about the assumptions" must be valid or the success of the entire process becomes questionable.

Simply because a model suggests a particular direction or course of action does not necessarily make it the only choice. Even if the underlying assumptions in the model appear reasonable, other sets of assumptions might be equally as reasonable. Sensitivity analysis provides a method for testing the degree to which the alteration of an underlying assumption affects the results obtained from the model. Another common name for this method is what-if analysis because the decision maker is interested in the change in the various outcomes "if" this changes or that changes.

Performing sensitivity analysis on a model or model set can accomplish a number of useful objectives. Models that have large swings in output values based on minor changes in inputs can be identified and adjusted if necessary. Variables known to be sensitive to minor change can be tested for range of stability. Models can be adjusted to reflect the real-world sensitivity to change within the problem context. Regardless of the objective, the sensitivity of a model to change is as important to the success of a decision scenario as the accuracy of the model's construction.

Although many methods exist to guide the decision maker in performing sensitivity analysis, all follow the same basic process. The first step is to set all variables within the model to their nominal or expected state. Then choose a variable to study and vary it within, and external to, its assigned range of values while recording the associated outcomes. If a small change in the variable of interest causes a measurable change in the outcome then that variable is said to be highly sensitive or significant and its inclusion in the model is both necessary and appropriate. If, on the other hand, varying a particular variable over its expected range produces only a minor change in the outcome, it is said to be relatively insensitive or insignificant and it can either be removed from the model entirely or fixed at a nominal value, thus removing one variable from affecting the set of possible outcomes:

> A state variable may become fixated either because it has an important influence on the worth per unit of its range, but an extremely small range, or because it has little influence on the worth per unit of its range, even though it has a broad range. (Howard and Matheson, 1968, p. 719)

You can easily see that as the model contains more variables, the combinations of potentially sensitive interactions become quite large. In this area, as in the others already mentioned, automated decision support can be invaluable to the decision maker. Chapter 6 will cover the most common type of what-if analysis tool, the spreadsheet, in greater detail.

VALUE ANALYSIS

One final consideration precedes the decision selection: the determination of whether enough information of sufficient reliability is available to make a successful decision. Because many of our daily decisions must be made in the face of uncertainty, we often think about whether we could improve our knowledge of an uncertain event. If the outcome of an uncertainty could be known with certainty, then we could say we possess perfect information about that event. If, however, we possess information that allows us to estimate the probability of an uncertain event and we could get additional information that would allow us to better refine that estimate but not reach certainty, we still possess only imperfect information. The question becomes how much we can afford in time or money (essentially the same thing) to acquire additional imperfect information and further our chances of success.

One method of answering this question uses the concept of expected value to determine the relative costs of various pieces of information. An approach known as the expected value of perfect information (EVPI) can be employed to determine whether to spend additional resources to acquire additional imperfect information.

Assume we could consult a clairvoyant (remember Howard's Test of Clarity?) regarding the true outcomes of each uncertain event in our decision tree. In that case, the decision maker would know exactly what was going to happen before it happened and could, therefore, make a decision with 100 percent success. The expected value of making a decision would then be equal to its true value. In other words, if the expected value of a decision is $1 million and we can make it with 100 percent certainty of success, then the true realizable value is also $1 million, and thus the two values are equal. Because we know we cannot make such a decision with 100 percent confidence, we must calculate an expected value based on the various probabilities for each possible outcome contained within our model. Consider the following example:

> Councilman John Bradley Freeman is still a little uncomfortable about voting to commit the city to a consortium of other city governments formed to negotiate the forthcoming cable television franchise with Televiz Cable Corporation (TCC). He still isn't sure whether the consortium's $50,000 membership fee will result in a significant gain over negotiating the franchise agreement with TCC independently of the consortium. He decides to do an EVPI calculation to identify how much it is worth.

Assuming perfect information, the expected payoff associated with the consortium is $375,000. The expected value of the uncertain scenario is $200,000. Thus, the EVPI cost becomes $175,000. Since the cost of joining the consortium is significantly less than the EVPI, the correct decision is to vote in favor of joining.

4-6: CHAPTER SUMMARY

Decision and problem modeling is a fundamental skill for effectively studying a problem context, and more importantly, for deriving and organizing the necessary information about it. Models need to be clearly defined and formulated to solve a problem successfully. This chapter focused on identifying and explaining the numerous problem modeling and definition techniques available to the DSS designer to refine the DSS model base.

In addition to understanding how to formulate the problem, a DSS designer must also understand the available pathways the problem could follow. The modern computer-based DSS is capable of taking many forms, but its essence is always the presence of an underlying model base. No underlying model, no DSS.

Key Concepts

- Failing to fully identify and define the problem results in a solution that may look like a great idea but doesn't solve the problem. By developing a fully formed problem statement—a statement stating the problem in terms of the current situation, the desired situation, and the objective—decision makers can get a clear definition of a problem. (4-1)

- Once a problem statement is fully formed and stated, the decision maker must examine the scope of the problem, which must be reduced or limited to a focus that allows for successful deployment of the available resources toward a solution set.

- Regardless of the decision context, problem structure can be described in terms of three fundamental components: (4-1)

Choices

Implicit in the concept of choice is the existence of multiple alternatives. Influence diagram and decision tree are two common methods of modeling a problem structure of multiple alternatives.

Uncertainties

All problem structures contain uncertainties that must be accounted for by the decision maker. By diagramming each of the uncertainties and including the expected probability of each one occurring, the decision maker can visualize the various paths of future events and can more easily compare one possible scenario to another.

Objectives

A well-formed objective that allows quantifiable comparison provides decision makers the criteria to measure the value or desirability of a particular outcome. The closer the outcome matches the criteria, the more desirable the outcome is.

- Structuring tools (4-1)

Influence diagram

An influence diagram provides a simple method of graphically modeling a decision. The relationship between the three components (choice, uncertainty, and objective) can be modeled by linking them with solid and dashed arrows.

Decision tree

In this diagram, only choices and uncertainties are included in the model. They are connected by lines that are referred to as branches. By following the construction rules, the details of the decision context can be represented clearly.

- By understanding the common decision structures, a decision maker can more quickly identify the probable structure of a new decision context. Common decision structures include the following: (4-1)

Basic risky decision

In this structure, a successful decision is a function of both the correct selection from the choice set and the outcome of an uncertainty. The two variations of this common structure are basic risky policy and basic risky policy with multiple objectives.

Basic risky policy

The basic risky policy variation describes a problem context in which the choice made from the set of alternatives directly influences the probabilities of an uncertainty as well as the objective.

Basic risky decision with multiple objectives

In this variation, the decision maker must make a trade-off between objectives in order to manage the uncertainty present in the decision context. The best solution will be the one that results in the greatest measured success.

Multiple-objective, no-risk decision/certainty decision

This decision structure involves those situations in which the focus is on the trade-off among the various objectives and risk is not a significant consideration. The degree of measured success or the satisfaction with the final choice is based on an appropriate trade-off among the objectives of the various stakeholders. A variation, multiple-objective/multiple-approach, no-risk decision, describes a situation in which the problem context is so broad and complex that a single approach would not resolve the problem completely. The focus is on combining the individual objectives of the decomposed submodels in such a way that the largest measurable degree of success can be expected.

Sequential decisions

The sequential decision structure is a series of basic risky decisions in successive time periods with arrows used to indicate the relationships between each temporal choice set. A decision made in one time period affects the degree of total measured success across all time periods as well as the measured success in that same time period. In addition, the decisions in the following time periods are affected to a degree by the decision(s) made previously.

- Decision makers can use decision models, the simplified representation of reality, as a foundation for their analysis and subsequent forecasts and predictions. (4-2)

Abstract decision model

An abstract decision model focuses on the mathematical precision with which various outcomes can be predicted. This type of model can assist in determining which alternative should result in the most favorable outcome. When using abstract models, decision makers should create a balance between models that capture the complexity of the problem and models that are simple enough to analyze and solve.

- Abstract decision model types

Abstract decision models can be divided into four subsystems, each displaying certain unique, identifiable characteristics:

Deterministic models

A deterministic model is one in which no variable can take more than one value at any given time. That is, the same output values will always result from any given set of input variables.

Stocabilistic models

In a stochastic model, at least one of the variables in the model is uncertain and must be described by some probability function.

Simulation models

Simulation is a technique used to test various outcomes resulting from the combining of modeled subsystems in a dynamic environment. Based on the comparative results obtained from the various simulation runs, the decision maker can then determine the most desirable alternative and the best balance among the stated objectives.

Domain-specific models

In some special domains, each discipline develops its own set of abstract mathematical modeling techniques to serve its needs. In the design of a DSS for a specific problem domain, the designer should be aware of any domain-specific models available for inclusion in the model base.

- Conceptual decision model (4-2)

Conceptual modeling can be thought of as an analogy of problem context. Experience from a past problem context can be used to assist in forecasting events and outcomes in the new context. Using this method, decision makers can recall and combine a variety of past experiences and contexts to create an accurate conceptual model of the current situation and to assign probabilities to those event components that remain uncertain.

- Howard's Test of Clarity (4-2)

  Ensuring that all components of the context model are clearly defined is the final step in the problem-structuring process. The model should leave no room for interpretation or misunderstanding regarding the basic components of the decision structure. Only after all elements have been fully refined should the decision maker move on to considering selection of a solution strategy.

- We can symbolize uncertainty of any nature through an appropriate application of basic probability. Properly applied, probability theory can be invaluable in assisting a decision maker in the structuring, resolution, and choice selection of a given problem context. Improperly applied, however, it can lead to decisions that are perfect in all respects except for their outcome. (4-3)

- The three requirements of probability (4-3)

  All probabilities must lie within the range of 0 to 1.

  The probabilities of all individual outcomes of an event must add up to the probability of their union.

  The total probability of a complete set of outcomes must be equal to 1.

- Type of probabilities (4-3)

  Long-run frequency

  Based on the "law of large numbers," the observed frequency of a particular outcome of an event will be a good estimate of the true probability of the outcomes if that event or experiment is repeated a large number of times.

  Subjective probability

  The subjective probability approach views probability as an individual's "degree of belief" that a particular outcome will occur. Implicit in its acceptance are underlying assumptions that, if satisfied, infer a set of numbers that can describe the degree of belief and, more important, conform to the requirements for probability such that they can be combined to infer the probabilities of other related uncertainties.

  Logical probability

  The concept of logical probability suggests that even though a probability may be derivable, its accuracy may not be acceptable under any circumstance. Situations in which a probability estimation of less than 100 percent is the same as zero call for the application of logical probability.

- Techniques for forecasting probabilities (4-4)

  Direct probability forecasting

  The decision maker or expert is simply asked to estimate the probability of an outcome for a particular event.

  Odds forecasting

  The goal is to find the specific amount of money to win or lose such that the decision maker is willing to accept either side of the bet. Once these amounts are determined, they can be transformed into odds and from there into estimates of probabilities.

  Comparison forecasting

  When faced with a complex decision structure containing conditional probabilities, the decision maker must use the technique of decomposition. In this approach, the probabilities of each possible outcome in the problem structure are determined by relying on the rules of probability. Then, the probability of the event in question can be determined using a formula for calculating total probability.

Research shows that the set of forecasting techniques selected by a decision maker is not necessarily based on any particular unique insight but is rather a function of which tools and techniques are most comfortable to the decision maker.

- In addition to the proper selection and application of forecasting techniques, well-calibrated sources of estimation provide measurable reliability with a narrow confidence interval. (4-5)
- Sensitivity analysis (4-5)

  Sensitivity analysis can determine the degree to which the alteration of an underlying assumption materially affects the results obtained from the model.

- Value analysis (4-5)

  One final consideration precedes the decision selection: the determination of whether enough information of sufficient reliability is available to make a successful decision. By using the concept of expected value, the relative costs of various pieces of information can be determined.

Questions for Review

1. What are the three key components of a fully formed problem statement?
2. List and briefly describe the three fundamental components of a problem structure.
3. Is it true that all decisions have at least two alternatives? Please explain.
4. Compare the two common methods of modeling a problem structure: influence diagram and decision tree. What are the focuses of each?
5. What is the primary difference between choices and uncertainties?
6. What is the purpose of setting up objectives when modeling a decision?
7. Explain why an influence diagram should have no cycles.
8. List and briefly describe the rules that must be followed in the construction of decision tree diagrams in order to assure that the details of the decision context are clearly represented.
9. Describe the basic risky decision structure and its variations.
10. Briefly describe the multiple-objective, no-risk decision structure and its variation.
11. What is the sequential decision structure? State the possible relationships among prior, current, and future decisions.
12. Explain the concept of abstract models.
13. List and briefly describe the types of abstract models.
14. Briefly describe the disadvantages of simulation modeling.
15. What is the purpose of Howard's Test of Clarity?
16. State the three rules of probability.
17. List and briefly describe the various types of probabilities.
18. Explain how shared meaning and the need for numbers are important to subjective probabilities estimation.
19. Compare the main concepts of odds forecasting and comparison forecasting.
20. Define sensitivity analysis and state its value to the decision maker.
21. What is the main purpose of value analysis?

For Further Discussion

1. Tiberon Foods, a $5.4-billion beef, seafood, and frozen foods producer, relies on timely and accurate reports to develop sales and operational plans. However, physically mailing reports to their field sales force was not an efficient process. By the time the reports were in the hands of decision makers, they were often more than a week old. Therefore, Tiberon management decided to adopt a platform that would support more timely collaborative analysis and remote access to leverage their current data warehouse. Based on this description, describe the problem using a fully formed problem statement.

2. Assume that you are the chief information officer (CIO) of Tiberon Foods. Identify the problem scope based on the resources available. Make assumptions if needed.

3. Alice is a senior student at Indiana University. She has decided to pursue her master's degree after graduation. Now she must decide which schools to apply to. Model her decision using either an influence diagram or a decision tree. Specify the choice, uncertainty, and objective(s) in the model. Make assumptions if needed.

4. Discuss the benefits and limitations of using decision models.

5. Study a decision made in an organization you are familiar with. Describe the decision using decision models. What type of model did you choose and why?

6. Try to predict the probability of your favorite sports team winning in an upcoming game using the techniques of direct, odds, or comparison forecasting. Explain your forecasting results.

7. *Hamlet*, Act III, Scene 1

   To be, or not to be, that is the question:
   Whether 'tis nobler in the mind to suffer
   The slings and arrows of outrageous fortune
   Or to take arms against a sea of troubles,
   And by opposing end them. To die—to sleep—
   No more; and by a sleep to say we end
   The heartache, and the thousand natural shocks
   That flesh is heir to. 'Tis a consummation
   Devoutly to be wished. To die—to sleep.
   To sleep—perchance to dream: ay, there's the rub!
   For in that sleep of death what dreams may come
   When we have shuffled off this mortal coil,
   Must give us pause. There's the respect
   That makes calamity of so long life.
   For who would bear the whips and scorns of time,
   The oppressor's wrong, the proud man's contumely,
   The pangs of despised love, the law's delay,
   The insolence of office, and the spurns
   That patient merit of the unworthy takes,
   When he himself might his quietus make
   With a bare bodkin? Who would these fardels bear,

To grunt and sweat under a weary life,
But that the dread of something after death—
The undiscovered country, from whose bourn
No traveller returns—puzzles the will,
And makes us rather bear those ills we have
Than fly to others that we know not of?

Hamlet is faced with a major decision. Had he had some of the decision modeling tools outlined in this chapter he may have been better equipped to make the decision. Identify Hamlet's choices and his perceptions of risk and use a decision tree and influence diagram to model his decision.

Answers to General Knowledge Calibration Test

1. 97 percent
2. 75.9 years
3. 13 stripes
4. 218 million television sets
5. 13,363 airports
6. 2
7. Miami Heat
8. Bingo
9. Jerry Falwell
10. New Hampshire

5

GROUP DECISION SUPPORT AND GROUPWARE TECHNOLOGIES

Learning Objectives

◆ Understand the concept of multiparticipant decision maker (MDM), the basic MDM structures, and the basic types of communication networks

◆ Understand the different types of problems with groups

◆ Be familiar with the basic concepts and definitions of MDM support technologies

◆ Learn two different classes and types of MDM support technology classifications by features and by technology

◆ Be familiar with the six types of groupware

◆ Understand the common MDM coordination methods

◆ Comprehend the meaning of the virtual workplace

PLANO POLICE DEPARTMENT

With criminals using every resource at their disposal to evade the law, police departments are always looking for ways to upgrade their own technology to share information in better ways. The round-the-clock efforts of law enforcement—involving multiple shifts in different departments and interaction with agencies in other jurisdictions—can make trying to share information a near-impossible task.

The Plano, Texas, police department is now better organized to bring in lawbreakers—and is breaking down day-to-day communications barriers within its ranks—thanks to some powerful tools created with Lotus Notes. And the results are particularly satisfying to the developer behind the project—a man who once wore a badge.

"A couple of years ago I saw an article about the Boston Police Department using Lotus Notes to track gang activity," says Randy Rogers, an ex-cop who now runs Technology Helps Company (THC), a company specializing in the development and sale of software applications for law enforcement.

"As a district sales manager for Lotus, and also as a former deputy sheriff, I was interested to see if Notes could have the same impact on law enforcement as it had on the corporate world by organizing information and improving communications. So I got the code that was codeveloped by Lotus and the Boston Police Department and put in the public domain, started developing applications, then gave them to police departments."

Rogers, who lives in Plano, decided his hometown police department would be a good place to use Lotus Notes to develop additional networked applications that could provide an integrated tracking tool for all areas of police work.

He began with a database for gang activities that let officers track details of gang members with physical descriptions, method and areas of operations, and even photos. Soon, gang-activity databases were also installed in neighboring cities in north Texas. The early results were rewarding, and within a few months the database proved its usefulness by helping officers identify drive-by shooting and burglary suspects. But Rogers knew he needed to offer more applications than just tracking gang activities.

"I expanded the system to include a wide range of activities, such as robbery, burglary, forgery, auto theft, sex crimes, and internal affairs complaint tracking," Rogers said. "It gives the department a much more integrated approach to cross-checking files and data. It also streamlines internal administrative tasks. For example, a captain can now review a complaint against an officer electronically and act on it almost immediately, instead of waiting for a piece of paper to make its way through the department."

Rogers said an additional benefit of using Notes in a police department setting was the easy replication and sharing of information by other municipal law enforcement agencies. Currently Plano is linked with four other police departments via direct dial-up connection, but that is expected to expand to a dozen or more in the near future.

"We're extremely pleased with the results," said Bruce Glasscock, chief of police of Plano, which has a population of about 190,000. "One of the most important features of the Notes system is it lets us network all of our investigative units, so investigators can quickly identify if other units are working on the same individual."

Glasscock added that Notes is very easy to use for officers, who only need to "pick up a mouse and click." He said the flexibility of Notes paid off recently when a new law affected how certain materials in personnel files needed to be filed. A standards unit in the police department was able to create a database with

(*continued*)

parameters to meet the new regulations within a couple of hours.

Rogers, who also used Notes to develop a national case tracking system for the National Network of Children's Advocacy Centers, agreed with Glasscock's assessment. "It's a great platform for creating applications, databases, workflow platforms, and messaging systems, including communicating over the Internet," he said.

"Law enforcement had been working much the same way for 200 years," Rogers noted. "Investigators would get on the phone and say, 'Have you ever heard of this guy?' It was like dialing for dollars—you try to get lucky. With our Notes database, this changes everything. The communications barriers aren't there anymore. It's going to make police work a lot more effective."

Source: askibm@vnet.ibm.com.
Reproduced by permission from IBM. Copyright 1997 by International Business Machines Corporation.

5-1: GROUP DECISION MAKING

In previous chapters, we focused on the processes associated with decision making from an individual perspective. Although a large proportion of the daily decisions faced by a typical manager must be made by an individual, many of the decisions in today's workplace are made by groups of individuals. Groups bring several advantages to the choice process: the addition of multiple sources of knowledge and experience, a wider variety of perspectives, and the potential synergy associated with collaborative activity. They also bring with them several disadvantages that, when ignored, can result in decision outcomes ranging from problematic to catastrophic.

A common cliché used to describe groups is the description of a camel as "a racehorse designed and assembled by committee." Despite the improbability of this statement the point is nonetheless clear: Too many decision makers result in either a bad decision or no decision at all. Many senior executives have become so jaded with the concept of group meetings that they condemn and avoid them. The problem, in most cases, lies not with the use of multiple decision makers or participants, but rather with the inappropriate marriage of the problem context and the structure of the assembled participants. In this chapter we explore the structures and problem contexts of group decision making, the advantages and disadvantages associated with groups, and the decision support technologies that exist in support of the group effort.

WHAT MAKES A GROUP A GROUP?

Let's begin with some definitions. Until recently, the literature on group processes and decision making lacked clear definitions of various collections of individuals brought together in a problem-solving context. Groups were defined as simply a collective entity that is independent of the properties of its members. In other cases, the group was characterized as a set of individuals the combined properties of which serve to define the properties of the group. In still other cases, the structure of the problem context served to define the group. As you can imagine, this lack of attention to just what constitutes a group led to some confusion and much debate.

Holsapple (1991) took a giant step toward reducing the confusion by suggesting the term *group decision maker* be replaced with the term *multiparticipant decision maker* (MDM). This approach eliminated the confusion associated with the term *group* and allowed for classification of various MDM structures. As these various structures were established, the unique characteristics of each emerged. Research now focuses on the various interactions among the participants as well as on the conditions under which a particular structure is appropriate.

For our purposes, we will build upon the work of Holsapple and others to provide a definition of multiparticipant decision making. Here, we define multiparticipant decision making to be an activity conducted by a collective entity composed of two or more individuals and characterized in terms of both the properties of the collective entity and of its individual members. Using this definition, we can construct a taxonomy of MDMs based upon structure and decision context. Figure 5-1 contains a hierarchical approach to MDM classification (introduced briefly in Chapter 2) proposed by Marakas and Wu (1997).

As shown in the figure, the differences among the various structures are significant and clearly defined. Using this taxonomy, the structure of a particular MDM can be readily identified and a determination as to its appropriateness for a given problem context can begin. Each of the MDM types exhibits a specific structure of interaction

FIGURE 5-1 Hierarchical Classification of MDM Structures

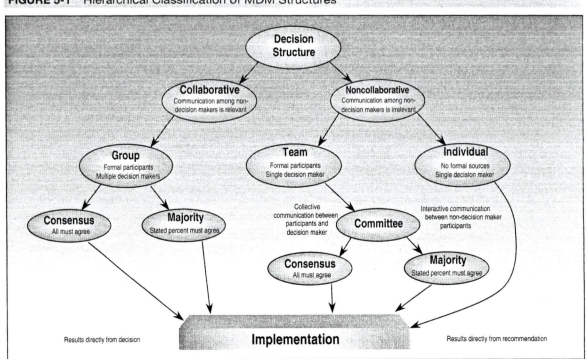

between the decision maker and the participants. Figure 5-2 illustrates each of the basic MDM structures contained in the taxonomy.

Using the taxonomy from Figure 5-1 we can identify the unique characteristics of each of the three main MDM structures. The group structure is classified as a collaborative structure, whereas both the team and committee structures are classified as noncollaborative. These classifications are based on the degree of relevance of nondecision maker interaction to the final product. The differences between the team and the committee structures are also based on participant interaction. Using this approach, we can associate a specific set of criteria with a specific MDM structure.

COMMUNICATION NETWORKS

The structure of an MDM is primarily based on the interaction and flow of communication among the various members. In this sense, communication can be thought of as any means by which information is transmitted to one or more members of the MDM. Implicit here is the establishment of two dimensions of communication: (1) the direction of the information stream, and (2) the structure of the information stream. Figure 5-2 offers evidence of both dimensions in each of the classifications.

Early research into group interactions (Bavelas, 1948; Leavitt, 1951) established four basic types of communication networks: (1) the wheel, (2) the chain, (3) the circle, and (4) the completely connected network. As shown in Figure 5-3, each classification of MDM can be mapped onto one of these four basic types of networks. By mapping the MDMs, we can classify them in terms of the degree of centralization exhibited by each of the four network structures.

The Wheel Network
This communication network is considered to be the most structured and hierarchical of the four types. In our MDM taxonomy, it is best represented by the team structure. In a wheel network, each participant can communicate with the decision maker at the center but cannot interact with any of the other participants. The decision maker can communicate with any or all participants depending upon his or her specific needs.

FIGURE 5-2 Basic MDM Structures

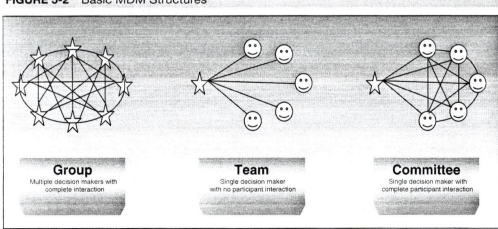

Group
Multiple decision makers with complete interaction

Team
Single decision maker with no participant interaction

Committee
Single decision maker with complete participant interaction

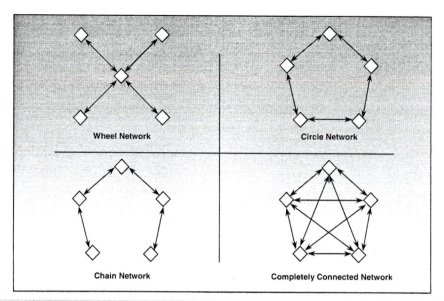

Wheel Network

Circle Network

Chain Network

Completely Connected Network

FIGURE 5-3 Basic Communication Network Structures

Any communication between two or more participants is the result of the decision maker "passing along" information from one to the other. In general, wheel networks are most appropriate when routine or recurring decisions are being made and tend to result in high-quality decisions in contexts where time and cost are priorities. These networks, however, are generally dissatisfying to all participants other than the decision maker given the limitation of interaction built into the structure.

The Chain Network
The chain network is similar to the wheel in terms of focus on the decision maker and lack of free interaction among the participants. This type of network can be thought of as a formalized relay system where each participant receives information from one participant and sends it to another. The end participants provide their information to the middle participants who combine the information with their own and communicate the result to the decision maker. The decision maker makes a decision and sends it back through the relay participants to the end members. Given a five-person chain, the decision maker is, directly or indirectly, in contact with all participants, whereas the middle members communicate with two persons and the end members with only one. As such, the chain network is generally less satisfying to the end members than the middle ones and is most satisfying to the decision maker. Like the wheel, the chain displays a high degree of centrality and is appropriate for routine or recurring decisions with high-probability outcomes.

The Circle Network
In contrast to the previous two communication networks, the circle network provides all members an equal opportunity for communication. In this structure each participant receives the sum of all prior information and serves as a decision maker. Research shows that this structure provides higher satisfaction to its members regarding their roles than the wheel approach offers to its peripheral members. This network serves

as the model for the group and committee MDM structures and is often employed in situations where negotiation or consensus must be the basis for the final decision.

The Completely Connected Network

This network structure offers a complete lack of restriction on communication and interaction among the members. Because it inherently offers such freedom it is generally the most satisfying to the members in terms of their roles. On the other hand, because of the greater potential for interactions in the completely connected network, conveying information takes longer and the possibility of error and message distortion is much higher than in other network forms. This communication network is the basis for the true group structure. Table 5-1 lists the four network structures and classifies them according to their degree of centrality.

GROUP BEHAVIORS AND NORMS

According to our definition of an MDM, the collective entity bears the characteristics of each of its individual members and of the unit as a whole. Therefore, MDMs establish certain norms, or standards of behavior, that guide the decision-making process and represent "the price of continued membership" (Harrison, 1995). Homans (1950) characterized group norms in this way:

> A norm, then, is an idea in the minds of the members of a group, an idea
> that can be put in the form of a statement specifying what the members
> should do, ought to do, are expected to do, under given circumstances. (p. 123)

In most cases, the "social standing" of MDM participants is measured largely by their adherence to the established norms of the group. The behavior of the MDM members and the processes under which the MDM operates are continually guided by a comparison against the desired behavior as dictated by one or more norms. Here, the importance of norm sending increases. Through this process, the participants in an MDM structure let each other know whether a given behavior is considered acceptable. Norm sending can be accomplished through such activities as definition by example (the leader sets an example of appropriate behavior), peer review (periodic assessment of each member's past actions and behaviors), or sanctioning (reward or punishment as a result of conformity or nonconformity). Regardless of the method, once the norms are established and sent, education and enforcement must drive internalization of those

---

TABLE 5-1   Principal Characteristics of Network Structures

Highly Centralized—Wheel, Chain
- They are efficient for routine and recurring decisions.
- They tend to strengthen the leadership position of the central members.
- They tend to result in a stable set of interactions among the participants.
- They tend to produce lower average levels of satisfaction among the participants.

Highly Decentralized—Circle, Completely Connected
- They tend to produce higher average levels of satisfaction among the participants.
- They facilitate nonroutine or nonrecurring decisions.
- They promote innovative and creative solutions.

TABLE 5-2 Factors Used in Determining Decision Structure

- The importance of the quality of the decision
- The extent to which the decision maker possesses the knowledge and expertise to make the decision
- The extent to which potential participants have the necessary information
- The degree of structuredness of the problem context
- The degree to which acceptance or commitment is critical to successful implementation
- The probability of acceptance of an autocratic decision
- The degree of motivation among the participants to achieve organizational goals
- The degree of potential conflict among the participants over a preferred solution

---

Source: Adapted from Vroom & Yetton, 1973.

norms to ensure constant adherence to the standards of behavior. The success of the MDM depends on the fit between the structure, norms, and problem context. In designing a support mechanism for a particular MDM-based scenario, the DSS designer, once again, must maintain a delicate balance among several salient forces. We focus on these forces in greater detail in Section 5-2.

DECIDING HOW TO DECIDE

As discussed previously, each MDM structure carries certain advantages and disadvantages and, when properly employed, can result in decision outcomes with high probabilities of success. The choice of which method to use must be based upon several factors associated with the decision context. Vroom and Yetton (1973) identified the various factors that must be considered when determining an appropriate decision structure (see Table 5-2).

Using these factors, a set of heuristics can be derived to guide the manager in marrying the appropriate MDM structure to the decision context. Table 5-3 contains a matrix composed of the Vroom and Yetton factors and the various MDM structures proposed by Marakas and Wu.

Let's look at a couple of examples. Selection of the individual structure suggests that the following conditions apply to the decision to be made: It is relatively unimportant and highly structured; the information necessary is directly available to the decision maker without any need for formalization of the information source(s); and the expertise of the decision maker is critical. These types of decisions typically deal with

---

TABLE 5-3 Matrix for MDM Structure Selection

Factors	*Individual*	*Team*	*Committee*	*Group*
High importance		✓	✓	
Decision-maker expertise	✓			✓
Participant expertise		✓	✓	✓
High structuredness	✓	✓	✓	
Acceptance critical			✓	✓
Acceptance probable	✓	✓		
Participant motivation				✓
Potential for conflict			✓	

issues such as subordinate hiring, routine task assignments, or decisions involving individual purchases. In these cases, the manager can make the decision quickly and effectively without the need for consultation or formal division of decision-making labor.

Conversely, the selection of the committee structure implies the need for some degree of consensus. It assumes that the decision maker does not possess sufficient information, expertise, or possibly time to make the decision alone. He or she requires subordinate expertise along with acceptance and commitment by various organizational members or constituencies. Problems addressed by this approach would include independent intraorganizational investigations involving issues of conduct or impropriety (such as a Senate hearing to determine misconduct in campaign spending), the potential adoption of an infrastructure support technology (such as the decision to adopt a particular e-mail package or database platform), or decisions requiring the need for widespread commitment and support (such as the appointment of a new department head or division president). As can be seen from these examples, a successful decision outcome hinges on the marriage of structure and context. Before we look at various types of DSS technologies that can be provided to the MDM structures in our taxonomy (in Section 5-3), we must look at the problems faced by the DSS designer when providing support to an MDM environment.

5-2: THE PROBLEM WITH GROUPS

The one thing we know for sure about groups is that some unique processes occur when a group of individuals gets together; however, we just don't know what all those processes are. Despite widespread research into MDM and various group processes, less than widespread agreement can be found regarding the relative effectiveness and benefits associated with managers making decisions as individuals versus as members of an MDM. Much of the literature praises the relative virtues of consensus and collective decision making. On the other hand, literature criticizing the significant disadvantages associated with the MDM approach also can be found. In this next section, we focus on these issues as additional preparation for our discussion of specific methods of support for MDM contexts.

SIZE

The number of members of a particular MDM structure is probably the most widely studied and consequential component of group decision making. Compared to individual decision making where the number of participants is fixed at one, MDM structures can involve from two to an indeterminable large number (consider the size of the MDM structure that elects the president of the United States every 4 years).

MDM size strongly relates to a number of behavioral phenomena. Studies show that as the size of the group increases, individual satisfaction tends to decrease. One reason is that the size of an MDM is tied to the relative amount of participation available to its members. As the size increases, the less active members tend to become noticeably less productive. Further, logic suggests that the management of an MDM requiring consensus or majority is easier when the size is small (five to seven participants) as opposed to large (25 or more participants).

Another reason that size plays such a significant role in MDM success is that member cohesiveness decreases as MDM size increases. Studies indicate that when membership is high, subgroups and internal coalitions tend to form that serve to redirect the focus of the participants away from the common goal of the collective and toward the local interests of the coalition. In some cases, the power of a subgroup within a larger MDM can become significant and must, therefore, be recognized and accounted for when decisions are being made. Boards of directors for large corporations often face this issue when several members of the board band together to form a minority coalition. Political parties also regularly face issues surrounding subgroups within the context of a large MDM. Shull et al. (1970) found that the ability of each individual member to view the other participants as individuals tends to fall off fairly rapidly after the size reaches six or seven, and the identification of the group goals becomes progressively more difficult.

Another issue related to MDM size is the increased likelihood for certain members of large MDMs to feel threatened or reluctant to participate because the size magnifies the impersonal nature of the problem context. Generally speaking, the larger the membership, the more likely a particular member is to receive negative feedback. This situation tends to contribute to the likelihood of coalitions forming and of members becoming dissatisfied. Table 5-4 contains a comparative synopsis of the primary effects associated with MDM size.

Despite the apparent drawbacks, sometimes a large MDM structure provides benefits specific to the unique nature of the problem context. For example, in situations where quantitative judgments must be made, the larger the membership of the MDM, the more likely it is that the results of the judgment will reflect the position of the general population. We draw this conclusion from our understanding of statistics. Consider the need for the Internal Revenue Service to estimate the impact of a new regulation involving a particular tax write-off. It would be beneficial to assemble a large MDM comprising a wide variety of IRS personnel experienced in this particular area of taxation.

Regardless of a specific MDM's structure, the number of its participants is a factor that must be given careful consideration in its formation and that can significantly influence both the design and degree of effectiveness of any decision support mechanisms employed.

GROUPTHINK

Irving Janis, a noted social psychologist, was one of the first to identify a phenomenon uniquely associated with multiparticipant decision making. He coined the term *groupthink* to refer to "a mode of thinking that people engage in when they are deeply involved in a cohesive ingroup, when the members' striving for unanimity overrides their motivation to realistically appraise alternative courses of action" (Janis, 1982, p. 9). Groupthink results in a deterioration of the collective mental efficiency, the propensity to test reality, and the overall moral judgment of an MDM. Harrison (1986) expanded upon Janis's definition of groupthink by suggesting that "the more friendly

---

TABLE 5-4 Effects Related to MDM Size

- Participant interaction tends to decrease as size increases.
- Affective or emotional relationships tend to decrease as size increases.
- Central, dominant leadership tends to increase as size increases.
- Conflict is resolved with political rather than analytical solutions as size increases.

and cooperative the members of a group, the greater the likelihood that independent critical thinking will be suspended in deference to group norms and in observance of group cohesiveness" (p. 184). Groupthink results in a relative ineffectiveness of the MDM at best, and a generally unfavorable set of outcomes at worst. Table 5-5 summarizes the unfavorable outcomes associated with groupthink.

The "agreement-at-any-cost" mentality one finds in groupthink catches the blame for a wide variety of unfavorable decision outcomes, most notably in the public sector. For example, many researchers and historians agree that groupthink was evident in the Nixon cabinet and was a contributing factor to the Watergate scandal and the resulting resignation of a U.S. president in 1974. The debacle associated with the Iran hostage rescue attempt in 1980 has also been attributed to groupthink. More recently, several researchers suggested that groupthink was evident in decisions made just prior to the *Challenger* space shuttle disaster in 1986. It is clear that the design of any tool intended to support decision making in an MDM structure must be able to address and mitigate the problems associated with groupthink.

OTHER SOCIOLOGICAL ISSUES

Conflict

Several additional issues related to MDM structures and member behavior bear mention. The quest for consensual support often brings with it a number of social liabilities. For example, as with groupthink, the desire to be viewed as a "good" member and to be accepted by the other participants often leads to conflict avoidance. Conflict is inherent in most human endeavors (and managerial decision making is certainly no exception), but avoidance of conflict is generally associated with a withdrawal from the source of the confrontation. If that source becomes a salient issue to the decision outcome or even the MDM structure itself, the effectiveness of the MDM is inevitably weakened. The principal problem with conflict avoidance or suppression is that such actions only conceal the basic issues of disagreement rather than resolve them. Natural group dynamics such as the struggle for power, individual role dissatisfaction, personality attributes, and divergence in goals can all result in some form of conflict (or conflict avoidance) and a reduced effectiveness of MDM choice outcomes.

Anonymity

One common method used to control sources of potential conflict and to support other MDM processes is participant anonymity. Most group support technologies provide for individuals to express their opinions, offer analyses, and vote — all anonymously.

TABLE 5-5   Potential Consequences of Groupthink

- Tends to preclude a complete and open-minded analysis of opportunities in the development of objectives
- Inhibits a meaningful search for information and tends to bias any searches toward a self-fulfilling selectivity
- Limits the participants' ability to appraise alternatives impartially
- Often results in a complete failure to consider possibilities associated with cost of failure, which, in turn, tends to result in choice selections that are more risky than is warranted by the payoff
- Tends to eliminate the formation of contingency or fallback positions

---

When the identity of an individual is separated from his or her proposal, then the proposal can be evaluated without regard to the status of its author. Moreover, the "safety" associated with being able to express oneself without fear of retribution or conflict can result in more equal participation among MDM members and allow for more open contributions. In many cases, anonymity results in the generation of more and better information and, thus, better decision outcomes.

Gender Differences and Similarities

During the early stages of the industrial revolution women were not commonly involved in managerial decision making. Women filled their assigned social roles that essentially precluded them from any meaningful participation in the day-to-day managerial functions of an organization. At the dawning of the digital revolution, however, the role of women changed dramatically. Today, women constitute more than 40 percent of the U.S. workforce and their enrollment worldwide in MBA programs continues to rise astronomically. This rise in the number of women in positions of consequential managerial authority resulted in more extensive research into issues related to gender. Most notably, much of the research focuses on issues related not to how men and women may actually differ but rather to how people think they differ. The perceived differences associated with gender appear to affect issues related to decision making in both the individual and MDM realms.

Numerous writings address perceived gender differences in a variety of social settings. Studies show that men tend to accept risk more readily than women. In general, studies indicate that females tend to be more participative than males in MDM decision-making contexts and to demonstrate significantly different values from males. (Values are an important component in all decision-making contexts as discussed in Chapter 2.)

Several studies revealed gender-related value differences such as females placing a higher value on issues of ability, ambition, skill, cooperation, and flexibility. Females generally place the highest value on ability, whereas males tend to consider achievement as most important. Contrary to common stereotypes, women are generally found to be more career-oriented than men. In other studies, females were more apt to award financial assistance based on merit, whereas males favored the awarding of financial aid based on need. Regardless of the situation, however, two important issues need to be noted:

1. Differences in decision making related to gender must be categorized as either inferential or actual. The two categories differ distinctly in their effect on decision outcomes.
2. Differences in decision making related to gender are more often than not a source of strength rather than weakness in an MDM setting.

The point here is not to rank the differences related to gender but simply to note them because of their potential effects on decision processes and outcomes. It is important to note that most studies focusing on measuring the success of decision outcomes found little difference in actual performance across genders but significant differences in perceived or expected performance across genders. This evidence suggests the so-called "gender effect" may be more of a socially constructed, rather than physiologically or psychologically mandated, phenomenon in decision making.

NEGOTIATING AND DECIDING

When more than one person is involved in the role of decision maker, the probability of negotiation increases. The very presence of more than one person responsible for a given decision implies that leaving the specific decision in the hands of a single decision maker would be inappropriate. The decision most likely involves multiple viewpoints that are not in harmony with each other, thus the need to negotiate. In a negotiated decision, opposing perspectives or factions enter into a series of confrontations focusing on issues of ends, means, or both. A common scenario for negotiation can be found in contract talks between management and labor unions. Neither side really wants to go without a decision but both sides have an obligation to ensure the best possible deal for their constituents. Think of negotiation as a tug of war between multiple players. Each player pulls on a rope connected to all other ropes, trying to pull the end of the other ropes nearer to his or her position. When the negotiation is complete, the center has changed but each player has agreed to the new position.

Most important to the design of a support mechanism for MDM contexts is the need to accommodate the inevitable activities of negotiation. Issues such as organization and control of conflicting criteria and preferences, creation of equitable access to all relevant information, and support for the wide variety of possible communication structures must be addressed when deciding on an MDM support technology. Sections 5-3 and 5-4 will explore the current MDM support technologies and their characteristics.

VARIABLES IN MULTIPARTICIPANT DECISION MAKING

By now it should be clear that when two or more individuals come together for the common objective of making a decision, a series of processes unique to the MDM setting are set in motion and a complex set of variables is present. Fellers (1987) suggested that when multiple participants get together to make a decision we know "something" is going on—we just don't always know exactly what that something is. The good news is that we are beginning to get a clear picture of many of the variables and their primary relationships and, through this lens, we gain understanding into that "something"—at least from the perspective of designing and implementing effective support technologies. Figure 5-4 contains a categorization of the variables and their relationships that must be accounted for when designing and implementing an MDM support technology.

5-3: MDM SUPPORT TECHNOLOGIES

Before we focus on the various technologies available to support multiparticipant decision making, it is important to pause briefly and consider the maturity level of this technology and its rate of growth.

In most business organizations today, when groups of executives meet, they gather in a room that is little different from the one in which their predecessors met a hundred or more years ago. Technology is evident only in the electric light, the air conditioning, and perhaps a telephone. The information

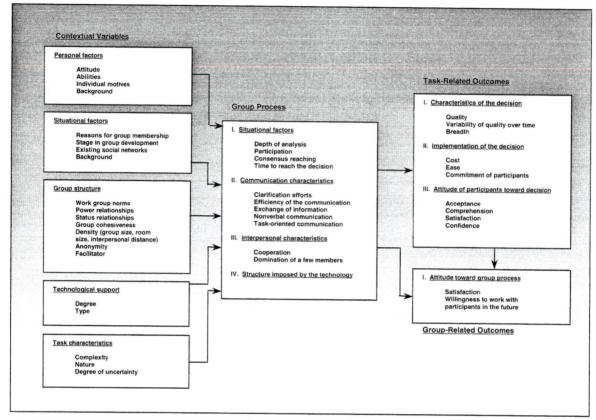

FIGURE 5-4 MDM Support Technology Variables

Source: Reprinted from *European Journal of Operational Research*, Vol. 46, Pinsonneault, A. & Kraemer, K. L., "The Effects of Electronic Meetings on Group Process and Outcomes: An Assessment of Empirical Research," pp. 143–162. © 1990, with permission from Elsevier Science.

available during the deliberations is combined in a few memoranda or a notebook or financial and other reports. They may receive verbal briefings made with the aid of charts or slides. However, as discussion proceeds around the table and various alternatives are considered, the decision-makers have to rely principally on what is in their heads and what has been told to them. (Gray, 1981, p. 123)

Gray's description of group meetings appeared in one of the first papers on group decision support systems. Consider two important issues here: (1) A great number of changes occurred with regard to available technology, knowledge, and understanding of MDM processes; and (2) the preceding quotation is still quite an accurate description of a large majority of the world's organizations. The rate of maturity of multi-participant decision making is curving upward exponentially, but the maturity level measured in terms of widespread use of support technologies is still in its infancy. In this section we focus on the past and present state of MDM support technologies and lay the foundation for development of an understanding and vision of the next generation of MDM technologies.

BASIC CONCEPTS AND DEFINITIONS

During the last two decades a variety of new terms and acronyms evolved with regard to MDM support technologies. One problem, however, is the variety of definitions that developed along with those new terms. Many researchers express differing views on what these definitions should be and what components they should include. Even in areas of emerging consensus, the definitions tend to be stated quite broadly in an effort to apply them to the myriad of situations present within an MDM context. In this text, we adopt a simple categorization method based on a series of concentric circles for the various types of MDM support in order to include various perspectives. Over time, researchers and practitioners may converge on these various definitions and use this convergence to further the maturity of multiparticipant decision making as a field. Figure 5-5 contains this author's basic categorization scheme for MDM support technologies.

The four basic levels of MDM technology in Figure 5-5 are congruent to the taxonomy of MDM structures outlined in Section 5-1. Using this simple approach, the majority (if not all) of the present applications of MDM support technologies can be positioned. No categorization scheme is worth its salt, however, if it does not provide explicit definitions for its categories. To that end, in this text we adopt the following definitions for the four basic levels:

Organizational Decision Support System (ODSS). A complex system of computer-based technologies—including those that facilitate communication—that provides support for decision makers spanning the range of organizational roles and functional levels and accommodates decision contexts that cut across organizational units (George, 1991).

Group Support System and Groupware (GSS). A collective of computer-based technologies used to aid multiparticipant efforts in identifying and addressing problems, opportunities, and issues (Huber, Valacich, and Jessup, 1993).

FIGURE 5-5 MDM Support Technology Categorization

Group Decision Support System (GDSS). A collective of computer-based technologies specifically designed to support the activities and processes related to multi-participant decision making.

Decision Support System (DSS). A system under the control of one or more decision makers that assists in the activity of decision making by providing an organized set of tools intended to impart structure to portions of the decision-making situation and to improve the ultimate effectiveness of the decision outcome.

With the aid of these definitions, we can begin to study and position the various types and structures of decision support technologies.

A BIT OF HISTORY

The existence of specific support mechanisms for MDM activities far predates the modern terminology used to describe them. Winston Churchill's cabinet war room serves as an early example. The design of the room was notably austere, consisting of a rectangle of tables at which the principals in the British war effort sat and made their individual and collective decisions. The primary support technology consisted of the variety of maps on the walls with tacks placed at specific locations to depict the war fronts and troop deployments. New information was continually fed into this environment by staff members who worked in the outer areas surrounding the war room.

By the 1960s and 1970s, many organizations were introducing new media technologies into their "war rooms." Slide projectors, overheads, and graphic depiction technologies enhanced the decision-making processes through standardized presentation of information and the ability to refer back to common information sources for further investigation.

The introduction of the computer during the late 1970s and early 1980s was the next logical step in the progress of MDM support. In 1971, the EMISARI system was deployed at the U.S. Office of Emergency Procedures to support the decision-making activities of close to 200 people scattered all over the United States during periods of national emergency. Stafford Beer and a team of British programmers implemented a computer-based room in Chile during the early 1970s as well. The objective of the room was to monitor the Chilean economy in real time using a system of armchair-mounted monitors. Unfortunately, just prior to its completion, Salvador Allende, the Chilean president, was overthrown and the effort was never officially brought online.

Today, a number of facilities throughout the world support group activities and MDM contexts. Many university-based facilities, such as those at the University of Arizona and the Claremont Graduate School in Claremont, California, provide a wide range of technology support and are configured to accommodate a broad range of group-related and MDM activities. Figures 5-6 and 5-7 show the physical layout of two typical facilities.

OBJECTIVES OF MDM SUPPORT TECHNOLOGIES

We know from our prior discussion that a collective of individuals brings with it several advantages and disadvantages associated with successful decision outcomes. We can think of these advantages and disadvantages as gains and losses associated with the

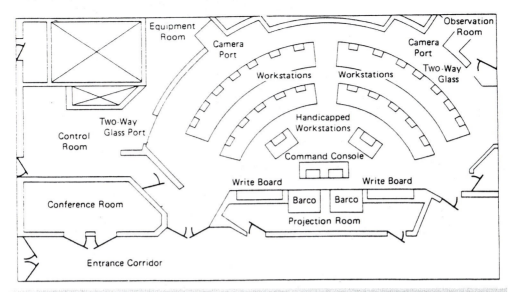

FIGURE 5-6   University of Arizona Large GDSS Facility

Source: "Group Decision Support Systems" by Gray/Nunamaker in *Decision Support Systems* 3rd ed., edited by Sprague/Watson, © 1982. Reprinted by permission of Prentice-Hall, Inc., Upper Saddle River, NJ.

MDM process (Nunamaker et al., 1993). Table 5-6 summarizes the various sources of gains and losses associated with MDM activities.

The primary objective of any support technology in this realm is to apply process-related approaches in such a way that the gains are maximized and the losses minimized. Although that goal sounds simple enough, we know that the complexity of the MDM process and the multitude of variables contained in decision contexts suggest otherwise.

MDM support can be provided through four basic approaches as identified by Nunamaker et al.: (1) process support, (2) process structure, (3) task support, and (4) task structure (1993). The approaches can be used either singularly or in combination depending on the specific characteristics of the problem context.

Process support involves various mechanisms focused on facilitating participant interaction, communication, knowledge gathering, and memory. These mechanisms are integral in current deployments of GSS and groupware applications.

Process structure focuses on mechanisms that govern the various communication activities among participants including the pattern of interaction, the timing, and sometimes even the content. The primary benefit of process structuring approaches is their ability to coordinate MDM activities.

Task support applies mechanisms that can select, organize, or even derive information and knowledge specifically relevant to the task or decision at hand. Task support enhances MDM activities through greater access to knowledge, an increase in participant synergies, and a reduction in losses associated with failure to fully analyze either the task itself or the knowledge necessary to effectively solve the problem.

Lastly, task structure mechanisms provide access to various techniques that assist the participants in filtering, organizing, combining, and analyzing knowledge relevant to the task or problem context—as well as in controlling when that knowledge is

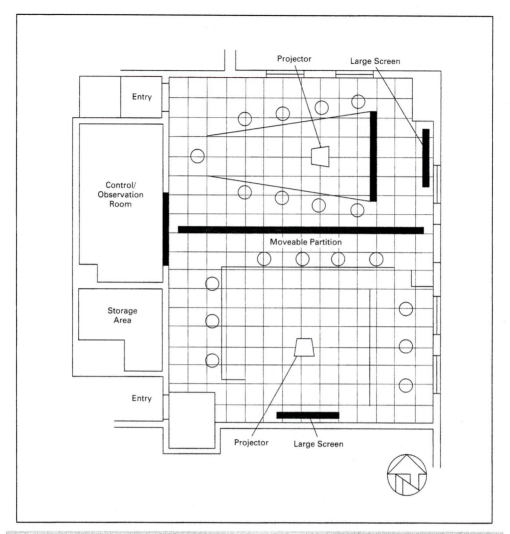

FIGURE 5-7 Claremont Facility

Source: "Group Decision Support Systems" by Gray/Nunamaker in *Decision Support Systems* 3rd ed., edited by Sprague/Watson, © 1982. Reprinted by permission of Prentice-Hall, Inc., Upper Saddle River, NJ.

generated. Similar to task support, task structuring reduces the losses associated with partial problem analysis while simultaneously increasing the gains associated with improved evaluation associated with MDM processes.

CLASSE. AND TYPES OF MDM SUPPORT TECHNOLOGIES

Just as we discussed in earlier chapters focusing on DSSs, the design and implementation of MDM systems must begin with a thorough understanding of the context in which the system will be used and, therefore, of the specific features necessary to support that context. As such, various classes of MDM technologies can be identified

TABLE 5-6   Sources of Gains and Losses in MDM Activities

Gains

- Collective has greater knowledge than any single participant
- Allows for synergistic results otherwise not obtainable
- Interaction stimulates the generation of knowledge or information otherwise unavailable
- Participants can improve individual performance through learning from others
- Improved evaluation over individual decision-making structure

Losses

- Relative allocation of speaking time is reduced with MDM size
- Can block the production of ideas
- Can produce information overload much faster
- Participants may not be able to remember all the contributions of others
- Pressures resulting in conformity can be exacerbated
- Can increase evaluation apprehension in participants
- Allows for "free riding" or social loafing of lazy or nonparticipative individuals
- Can promote cognitive inertia or groupthink
- Increases opportunity for socialization over goal focus
- Increases decision context coordination activities
- Can allow for partial task or knowledge analysis

based on their intrinsic features, characteristics, and technologies or on the specifically identified needs of the MDM structure itself.

Classification by Features

Table 5-7 contains a three-level classification scheme for MDM systems proposed by DeSanctis and Gallupe (1987), which is based on the features offered in support of the multi-participant decision-making activities. Each level contains the features associated with the previous level in addition to features specific to that level. The table shows how the features available in each of the three levels correspond to specific MDM participant needs.

The Level 1 system is primarily intended to facilitate communication among the participants. Its main objective is to speed up and stimulate the exchange of messages and to reduce or remove the barriers to communication associated with MDM activities.

Level 2 systems are designed to reduce the uncertainty that can evolve from an MDM problem-solving activity. Both process and task structuring mechanisms are typically found in this class of MDM support. As shown in Table 5-7, the Level 2 system contains features that focus more on analysis activities than do those contained in Level 1.

The Level 3 system contains all of the features from the previous two levels and expands the support mechanisms through an increase in process structuring techniques intended to control participant interaction. The Level 3 system adds a sense of rigor to the MDM activities not found in the prior two levels.

Classification by Technology

Another method of MDM system classification was proposed by Kraemer and King (1988). This approach focuses on the technologies applied in a particular MDM context. Table 5-8 contains six types of MDM support systems that can be identified using this method of classification.

TABLE 5-7 DeSanctis and Gallupe MDM System Classification

MDM Level	Participant Needs	System Features
1. Reduce Communication Barriers	• Message passing among participants • Access to data files during meeting • Simultaneous display of ideas, graphs, votes, etc. to all participants • Relaxation of inhibitions to contribute • Control for free-riders • Organization and analysis of ideas and votes • Preference quantification • Agenda planning • Schedule coordination	• Electronic messaging • Computer networking • Large shared viewing screen or public display window • Anonymous contribution • Active solicitation of ideas • Summarization and tabulation • Rating/ranking scales • Agenda templates • Continuous display of progress
2. Reduce Uncertainty and Noise	• Problem structuring and solution scheduling • Uncertainty analysis • Analysis of resource allocation problems • Data analysis • Preference analysis • Structured guidance of deliberations	• Automated planning methods (PERT, etc.) • Decision tables, trees, etc. • LP and optimization modeling • Statistical tools • Subjective probability methods • MDM coordination methods (nominal, etc.)
3. Regulate Decision Processes	• Enforcement of formal decision procedures • Increased clarity of options for decision procedures • Structuring and filtering of messages to adhere to rules • Development of deliberation governance rules	• Automated procedure mechanisms • Automated advisor for providing advice regarding various approaches • Structuring and filter agents • Rule set construction and inference mechanisms

Source: Adapted from *Management Science*, "A Foundation for the Study of Group Decision Support Systems," by DeSantis, G. and Gallupe, R. B. Vol. 33, no. 5, pp. 589–609. Copyright © 1987.

In this classification the increasing use and complexity of the technologies employed establishes the boundaries for each system type. The simplest type of MDM support system using this approach is the electronic boardroom in which the primary technology is used in support of audiovisual and multimedia activities. The highest level of system is the decision room in which sophisticated computer technologies provide support for virtually all MDM activities and needs. These systems provide tools to support such activities as brainstorming, analysis of issues, commentary, and consensus

TABLE 5-8 Kraemer and King MDM Classification by Technology

MDM Type	Facility and Hardware	Software	Specific Considerations
Electronic Boardroom	Conference room with computer-controlled audio-visual wide-screen projection capabilities	Application for storage and retrieval of previously prepared presentations	Same time–same place synchronous interaction. Requires audio-visual technician to be present
Teleconference Room	Conference room with computer-controlled audio-visual transmission between locations	Application to control digital transmission of audio, video, and data	Same time–different place synchronous interaction. Requires tele-conferencing technician to be present
Group Network	Separate office facilities connected via a computer network	Applications to allow for either real-time or asynchronous desktop conferencing and exchange of video, audio, and data	Same or different time–different place interaction with one participant serving as coordinator or chair
Information Center	Conference room with video projector for wide-screen viewing. Individual computers with display terminals	Applications for database management, statistical analysis, graphics generation, and word processing	Same time–same place interaction. Requires specialists in modeling and specific application software to be present
Collaboration Laboratory	Conference room with electronic white-board and networked computers	Applications for collaborative interaction and information exchange	Same or different time–same place interaction. Requires MDM process facilitator to be present
Decision Room	Conference room with video projector for wide-screen viewing and networked computers	Applications to support brainstorming, topic commentary, voting, modeling, decision analysis, collaborative interaction, and data exchange	Same or different time–same place interaction. Requires MDM process facilitator to be present

Source: Adapted from *ACM Computing Surveys 20*, No. 2, "Computer-Based Systems for Cooperative Work and Group Decision Making" by Kraemer, K. F., and King, J. L. Copyright © 1988.

TABLE 5-9 Decision Room MDM Support Functions

- Electronic brainstorming
- Topic commentary
- Issue analysis
- Voting and preference indication
- Policy formation
- Stakeholder analysis
- Organization of ideas
- Evaluation of alternatives

- Survey and questionnaire creation and administration
- Multiple-format file readers
- Participant dictionary
- Enterprise analysis of decision outcome on organization
- MDM session management

Source: Adapted from Vogel et al. (1989).

assessment or voting. Table 5-9 lists the various decision support processing mechanisms commonly found in a modern decision room MDM system.

COLLABORATIVE SUPPORT TECHNOLOGIES

The trend toward collaboration in the modern organization accelerates daily, fueled by a number of sources, including the proliferation of networks that facilitate widespread connectivity. Another source is found in the increased global competition facing the world's organizations. The economic pressures common in the operation of a firm in a competitive setting is yet a third force moving the workplace into a collaborative posture. Finally, as organizations strive to take advantage of new technologies that offer greater efficiency and effectiveness, they find that their mainstay hierarchical infrastructures are no longer adequate. As such, the businesses of tomorrow are reinventing themselves through the use of groupware.

Groupware

The term *groupware* refers to a particular type of MDM support technology specifically focused on issues related to collaborative processes among people. In one sense, groupware is people. It is a tool that, when deployed and used appropriately, positively affects the way people communicate with each other, resulting in improvements in the way people work and the decisions people make.

The concept of groupware is really a simple computer-based extension of the traditional tools of the workplace. One of the key elements of success in any organization is the development and preservation of organizational memory. The knowledge gained in the process of conducting business must somehow be captured and stored in a manner that affords easy access for present and future decisions. The tools and stores of organizational memory can be seen throughout the workplace: people, policy and procedure manuals, bulletin boards, newsletters, filing cabinets, in and out boxes, planning boards, and computers.

Currently, the competition among groupware developers is strong with only a handful of major players gaining measurable ground. The current market leaders include

- Lotus Notes and Domino—Lotus Development Corporation
- Microsoft Exchange—Microsoft Corporation

- GroupWise—Novell Corporation
- Oracle Office—Oracle Corporation
- Team Office—ILC, Inc.
- Collabra—Netscape Corporation

Figure 5-8 shows a typical desktop view in the groupware application Lotus Notes, and Figure 5-9 shows the various components and functions contained within the Notes groupware messaging system.

The various features and components of the major groupware applications remain in a constant state of flux. In addition, the manufacturers jockey to create alliances with one or more members of the competition in an effort to "freeze out" the remainder. For instance, in late 1997 Microsoft entered into an agreement with Lotus to package the Microsoft Internet product Internet Explorer 4.0 with all future versions of Notes. With this move, Microsoft may have reduced its effectiveness in the groupware wars (Lotus had significantly more market share in this area than Microsoft) but improved its position as the leading vendor in Internet browsing (Microsoft and Netscape were in direct competition in this area).

Groupware products continue to evolve in response to the ever-increasing speed with which decisions must be made and business must be conducted. This speed

FIGURE 5-8   Lotus Notes Groupware Typical Desktop Layout

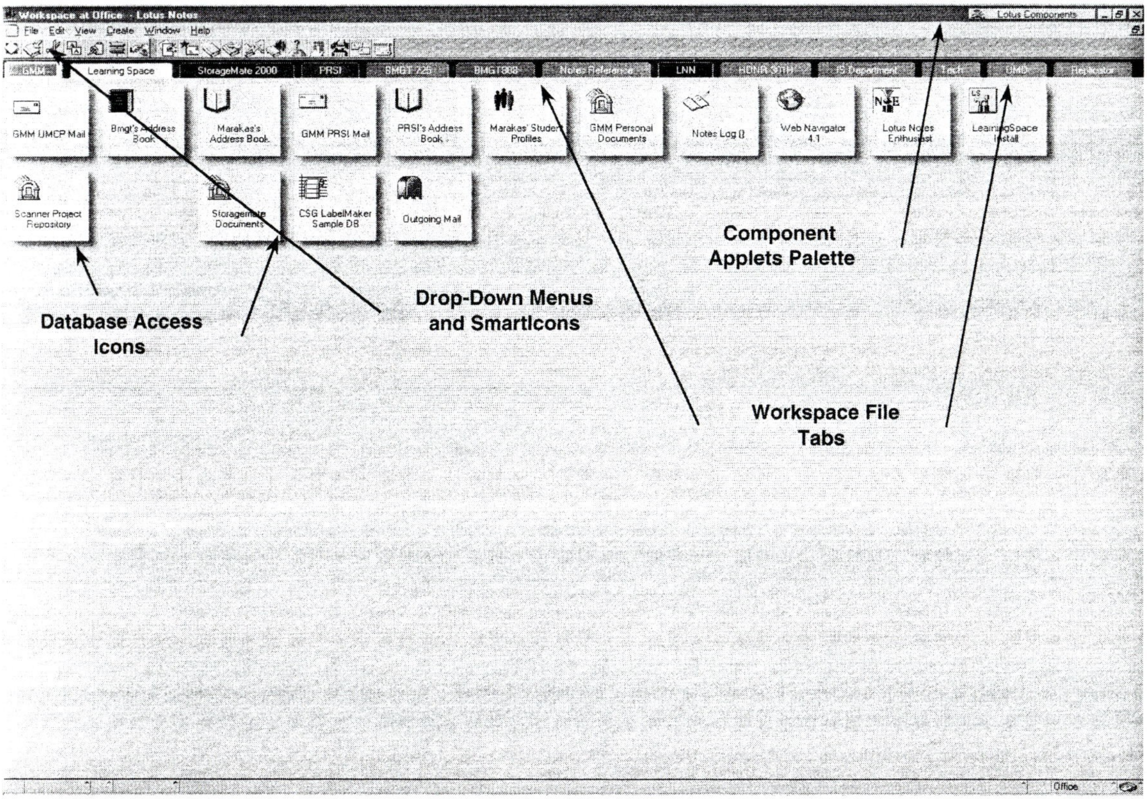

FIGURE 5-9 Typical Lotus Notes Messaging Database Screen Layout

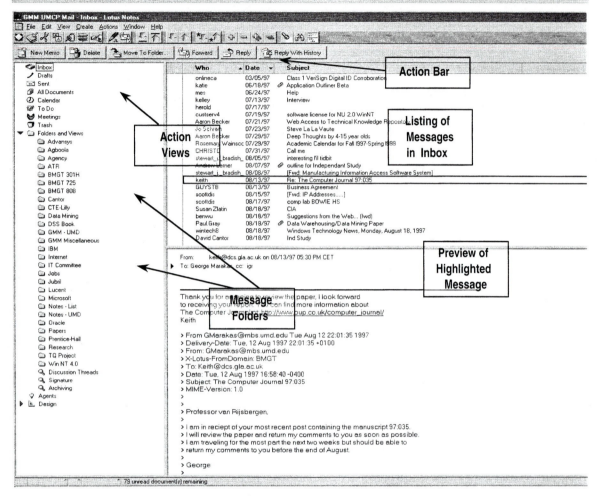

requires immediate, simultaneous, and complete access to the organizational memory by workers at all levels of the organization. The many functions and classes of groupware products are specifically designed to facilitate access to organizational memory using a variety of approaches. Ellis, Gibbs, and Rein (1991) proposed a six-part classification scheme for groupware based on the type of directed support provided to the organization. Table 5-10 shows this method of classification.

Messaging Systems The first level of classification focuses on groupware technologies that facilitate the movement of messages. The most common example of this class is electronic mail, or e-mail. A text-based message along with any attachments (file or graphical inclusions) can be composed and routed to any number of recipients anywhere in the world in a matter of seconds. Unlike the traditional paper-based mail

TABLE 5-10   Groupware Classification

• Messaging systems	• Group decision support systems
• Conferencing systems	• Coordination systems
• Collaborative authoring systems	• Intelligent agent systems

(now referred to as "snail mail"), geophysical location of the recipients is no longer an important factor for delivery. Just as e-mail can be composed and sent from anywhere in the world, it can also be received from anywhere access to an Internet-connected computer can be found. The informality, speed, availability, and ease of use associated with e-mail make it ideal for the questioning and advice-seeking activities associated with decision making. E-mail allows an individual within an organization to cast a wide net in search of specific elements of organizational memory.

This class of groupware supports only asynchronous communication. Therefore, the sending of a message is not in any way associated, or synchronized, with the receiving of that message. The asynchronous nature of this communication system necessarily limits its application to certain problem-solving contexts, but it is nonetheless quite useful in the early stages of decision support by helping multiple individuals become aware of the need for a decision and by facilitating the early acquisition of information and knowledge necessary to make that decision.

Conferencing Systems   The second class of groupware overcomes the asynchronous limitation of messaging systems by facilitating an electronic version of the typical face-to-face meeting. They provide a great advantage through their elimination of the requirement for same-place communication during multiple real-time interactions. Each participant using a conferencing system can be in a convenient location while communicating with others in a synchronous manner. The media available for such conferences can be audio, video, or both. In addition, the environments in which this communication can take place range from a specially equipped meeting room to an individual's private workspace. The advent of desktop teleconferencing technology allows participants to both see and hear each other while simultaneously allowing computer presentation of graphics, deployment of analysis tools, or sharing of data or applications.

Collaborative Authoring Systems   This level of groupware allows multiple participants to collaborate either synchronously or asynchronously on the creation and revision of a common document or set of documents. Activities such as segment revision, commenting, formatting, and development of tables and graphics can be conducted by a group of individuals, and the outcome can be seen immediately by all other participants. In addition, each individual's activities can be recorded for later review and deadlines associated with forthcoming events can be transmitted to the proper individuals, thus facilitating the management of the decision-making process.

Group Decision Support Systems   The key characteristic defining this level of groupware technology is its focus on directly assisting multiparticipant decision making. As previously discussed, a GDSS can facilitate the generation of ideas, commentary, analysis, and consensus.

Coordination Systems   Coordination systems facilitate the integration of participant activities associated with achieving the objective(s) of the collective. For instance, a coordination system may inform one participant of the degree of completion of other activities and suggest that completion is sufficient for commencement of the next stage. Likewise, it may be used to inform a participant that his or her work is due or overdue. A common activity associated with coordination systems is referred to as workflow management. The facilitation of document routing, approvals, multilevel data collection, and information transfer are all activities associated with workflow management.

Intelligent Agent Systems   The final class of groupware technology employs some form of artificial intelligence to carry out a series of steps associated with a particular task. Functions available through intelligent agent systems range from a simple filter that determines the appropriate electronic filing folder for a new e-mail message to more complex "personal assistants" that can schedule meetings, forward messages, or perform background tasks associated with MDM processes. This area of groupware is still in its early stages of development but it nonetheless promises to be a significant factor in MDM support environments. We will explore the technology of intelligent agents in greater detail in Chapter 15.

FORCES DRIVING GROUPWARE DEVELOPMENT

The groupware marketplace has grown into a multibillion-dollar industry. A series of forces and motivations drive the migration toward groupware technologies. Table 5-11 lists a number of factors relevant to the mass adoption of groupware application environments.

One important observation concerning the forces listed in Table 5-11 is that none of them are directly driven by decision-making activities. They are more focused on generalizable organizational processes and activities. This assessment suggests that groupware exists more as infrastructure than as targeted decision support systems,

---

TABLE 5-11   Forces in Favor of Groupware Adoption

- Increased cost control
- Increased productivity
- Improved customer service
- Support for total quality management (TQM) activities
- Reduced number of meetings
- Increased automation of routine workflow processes
- Desire to extend the organization to include both supplier and customer
- Need to integrate geophysically dislocated teams
- Increased competitive advantage through faster time to market
- Need for better global coordination
- Creation of services that differentiate the organization
- Leveraging of professional expertise and knowledge
- Availability of widespread network infrastructures (i.e., Internet, WWW)
- Improved price/performance ratios of both hardware and software necessary
- Increased use of ad hoc teams

Source: Adapted from Coleman and Khanna (1995).

which indicates the need for organization-wide decision support and for infrastructure to support these initiatives.

5-4: MANAGING MDM ACTIVITIES

There are leaders and there are followers. Those who wish to lead can come forward and accept the responsibilities of leadership. Those who prefer to be led, on the other hand, assemble before the leader and await the orders of the day. The problem with this evolutionary approach to coordination is its ad hoc nature, which is often inappropriate for the situation. When multiple individuals come together for the purposes of making a decision, the nature of that decision often guides the structuring of the collective and, thus, guides the selection of an appropriate coordination method. Table 5-12 lists several common MDM coordination methods.

The list of approaches in the table is by no means comprehensive, and variations of variations are constantly being tested, refined, and deployed. The more common approaches are those found to be effective over multiple trials and refined within the contexts deemed most appropriate.

NOMINAL GROUP TECHNIQUE

Developed by Van de Ven and Delbecq (1971), the nominal group technique works best in a consensus context such as group or committee structures. The approach requires each participant to perform his or her activities using the following procedure:

1. Each participant writes down his or her opinions and ideas relating to what the decision or choice should be.
2. Using a round-robin approach, each participant presents the ideas on his or her list. Each idea is recorded in a summary list using a flip chart or whiteboard so that all participants can view the list as it develops. At this point, no discussion regarding the desirability of the idea presented is conducted.
3. After all ideas are presented and listed, the participants ask questions of each other for clarification of any of the alternatives on the list.
4. Each participant votes on each idea in the list using a predetermined scale or ranking system. The votes are tallied and the collective's choice is revealed.

The nominal group technique can be performed in a nonautomated fashion as described in the list of steps or it can be easily computerized so that the entire process is managed and conducted electronically.

TABLE 5-12 Common MDM Coordination Methods

• Nominal group technique	• Issue-based information systems
• Delphi technique	• Nemawashi
• Arbitration	

DELPHI TECHNIQUE

The Delphi technique (Lindstone and Turoff, 1975) is similar to the nominal group technique with the primary difference being that the participants using Delphi never actually meet. The steps associated with the Delphi approach are as follows:

1. Assemble MDM members based upon expertise in the problem context.
2. Send a survey instrument to all members to collect their views regarding the decision at hand.
3. Organize and analyze the survey results.
4. Send a second survey instrument to each member along with a summary of the results obtained from the first questionnaire. Ask the members to consider the summary results and to fill out the second survey instrument after this activity. Should a particular member's view still be significantly different than the majority, he or she should include an explanation of the rationale behind the different position. This explanation should be forwarded to all other MDM members.
5. Repeat steps 2 through 5 until a consensus is reached among the members. Should no consensus emerge within an established time limit, the most preferred choice becomes the final decision.

We will explore nominal group technique and Delphi again in Chapter 15 when we focus attention on methods of fostering creative thinking in an MDM setting.

ARBITRATION

Arbitration is most appropriate where the members of the MDM are in conflict or represent opposing factions. The process begins with a series of bargaining interactions in which the participants attempt to find some mutually agreeable alternative. All participants previously agreed that should such a solution not be reached within a specified time period, the formal arbitration process will begin and they will abide by its outcome. If arbitration becomes necessary, an outside party serves as the arbitrator and selects an alternative that he or she deems most appropriate. This selection is not limited to those alternatives under debate but can come from the set of all possible alternatives. The arbitrator can use whatever method or criteria for selection are deemed appropriate. A modified form of this approach allows for each participant to submit a final offer to the arbitrator. The arbitrator is then limited to the selection of one of the submitted offers.

ISSUE-BASED INFORMATION SYSTEM

The issue-based information system approach (IBIS) is a structured argumentation method that dictates the pattern of arguments and counterarguments among the MDM members (Kunz and Rittel, 1970). An IBIS is represented as a graph containing nodes and links to depict the various issues, positions, and arguments. The creation of an IBIS begins with the selection of a root issue node. Then, the various position nodes corresponding to the alternative solutions available to solve the problem are linked to the root issue. Each position node is evaluated based on the validity and strength of the argument nodes linked to it. The degree of acceptance for the strength of one of these arguments is used as the basis for selection of a final alternative.

The IBIS approach lends itself to electronic implementation through the concept of hypertext linking. The issue net could be constructed so that the various argument nodes are linked by hypertext to their respective position nodes; clicking on a position node then reveals the argument in support of it. Using this approach, the various arguments could be electronically categorized based on content, and their strength and validity could be rated using a predetermined scale or ranking system for easy tabulation and selection.

NEMAWASHI

Introduced briefly in Chapter 2, the nemawashi approach is widely used in Japanese organizations as a method for managing the MDM process. Using nemawashi, the participants perform the following steps:

1. Once a problem context has been identified, one or more members of the MDM are designated as coordinator(s). The coordinator(s) selects the remaining participants in the MDM process and begins soliciting their views regarding the decision at hand. The number of participants can range from a select few to literally dozens.
2. Based upon the solicited views of the members, the coordinator(s) constructs a choice set. Experts are then asked to specify criteria for evaluating the items contained in the choice set and to rate each of the alternatives with respect to their chosen criteria.
3. The coordinator(s) selects a candidate alternative based on the results obtained in step 2.
4. The selected alternative is presented in an informal document that is circulated to all of the MDM members. Using both persuasion and negotiation, the coordinator(s) seeks consensus among the members. This consensus seeking may require substantial alterations to the document or even a return to step 3 to select another candidate choice.
5. Once consensus or possibly impasse is reached, the coordinator(s) prepares a formal document containing the details of the selected alternative and begins circulating the document among the members. The document is first presented to the member at the lowest level in the organization and continues through the members until it is presented to the senior participant. Each member, upon being presented with the document, affixes a personal seal indicating that it has been examined and is supported. Should a member have a strong objection to the document, the personal seal is affixed upside down. The decision is approved if a sufficient number of properly oriented seals is affixed to it. Sufficiency, in this case, differs from organization to organization or even from one project to the next.

Nemawashi techniques are not particularly well suited to MDM structures such as groups or hierarchical teams because of the diverse levels of organizational authority among the members. Nonetheless, under the proper conditions, the nemawashi approach can result in a high degree of buy in and support for decisions that affect multiple levels of organizational members.

5-5: THE VIRTUAL WORKPLACE

In closing our discussion of MDM activities and support technologies, we extend our vision to include the changes taking place within the organization as a result of the introduction of these technologies. The most prevalent change is that of the virtual office. Consider the following:

> With its dimpled aluminum facade and TV-screen-shaped windows, Pittsburgh's Alcoa Building once exemplified the power and pizzazz of the classic corporate skyscraper. When it went up in the 1950s, 2,000 company employees streamed into this 31-story tower every morning, each to work in a private 12-foot by 15-foot office.
>
> But go looking for Aluminum Company of America Chief Executive Paul H. O'Neill in his office these days and you discover that he doesn't exactly have one. The executive suite has no permanent walls or doors. All of Alcoa's senior executives work in open cubicles and gather around a "communications center" with televisions, fax machines, newspapers, and tables to encourage impromptu meetings. O'Neill's own favorite hangout is the kitchen, where he and his staff nuke food, huddle, and talk work. "It's like being at home in your kitchen and sitting around the table," he says happily. . . . Privacy is being replaced with productivity, hierarchy with teamwork, and status with mobility. . . . Work anywhere, anytime is the new paradigm. . . . The need for speed makes it imperative for employees to team up and share information. (Hamilton, Baker, and Vlasic, 1996)

Numerous worldwide organizations are trading in their real estate for collaborative technologies. The ability to coordinate the activities of a large body of participants engaged in a complex web of activities from anywhere in the world is driving the rapid shift in paradigm. In short, work is becoming a thing you do rather than a place you go to. Implicit in this new structure is the need to understand the effects of this change on the nature of individual and MDM decision processes. The near-term results, however, indicate significant increases in employee productivity over the traditional work environment. Procter & Gamble's new $280 million, 1.3 million-square-foot facility in Cincinnati, Ohio, was entirely designed and constructed to serve as a collaborative product development environment. Major architectural changes such as conversation-promoting escalators instead of conversation-inhibiting elevators were used throughout. Corridors were made significantly wider and equipped with strategically placed sofas to allow workers to stop for a quick chat. The traditional office approach was completely replaced with open cubicles, huddle rooms, and central whiteboards that can convert scribblings into e-mail. Early results suggest that the building configuration contributed to productivity increases of 20 to 30 percent by facilitating immediate data sharing and thus allowing higher-quality decisions to be made in less time.

Many unknowns and probably more than a few rough spots associated with this shift to the virtual workplace remain. Most notably, the biggest changes brought about by the virtual workplace may manifest themselves more culturally and sociologically rather than technologically. Furthermore, given the speed at which our technology is changing, what makes sense today could be eclipsed by a more effective approach tomorrow. Nonetheless, the era of the "corporate edifice complex" is ending and the advent of collaborative and MDM support technologies enables its replacement with a new era of work spaces that work.

5-6: CHAPTER SUMMARY

This chapter explains the concept of group decision support. Many of the decisions faced in today's workplace are being made more and more by multiple individuals rather than by a single person. Although the multiparticipant approach carries with it several advantages, it also brings several disadvantages and problems to the decision process.

   Using the variety of available MDM support technologies, managers can carefully manage the multiparticipant decision maker activities throughout the organization and can be more aware of the potential problems of MDMs so that the benefits from support of the group effort can be realized.

Key Concepts

- The definition of multiparticipant decision making (5-1)

   Multiparticipant decision making is an activity conducted by a collective entity composed of two or more individuals and characterized in terms of both the properties of the collective entity and of its individual members.

- Collaborative structure versus noncollaborative structure (5-1)

   Collaborative structure

   Group: Multiple decision makers with complete interaction

   Noncollaborative structure

   Team: Single decision maker with no participant interaction

   Committee: Single decision maker with complete participant interaction

- Four basic types of communication networks (5-1)

   Highly centralized:

   1. Wheel network

   2. Chain network

   Highly decentralized:

   3. Circle network

   4. Completely connected network

- The problem with groups (5-2)

   Size: As the MDM size increases, the individual satisfaction decreases.

   Groupthink: Groupthink results in the relative ineffectiveness of the MDM at best.

   Other sociological issues

   Conflict: Conflict can result in the reduced effectiveness of MDM choice outcomes.

   Participant anonymity: Participant anonymity is used to control sources of potential conflict and in support of other MDM processes.

   Gender differences and similarities: Most studies that measure the success of decision outcomes find significant differences in perceived or expected performance across genders.

- Negotiating and deciding: A negotiated decision is one in which opposing perspectives or factions enter into a series of confrontations focusing on issues of ends, means, or both. (5-2)
- Variables in multiparticipant decision making: (5-3)

  Four basic levels of MDM support technologies

  Organizational decision support system (ODSS)

  Group support system and groupware (GSS)

  Group decision support system (GDSS)

  Decision support system (DSS)
- MDM classification by features (5-3)

  Level 1—to reduce communication barriers

  Level 2—to reduce uncertainty and noise

  Level 3—to regulate decision processes
- MDM classification by technology (5-3)

  Electronic boardroom

  Teleconference room

  Group network

  Information center

  Collaboration laboratory

  Decision room
- The definition of groupware (5-3)

  Groupware is a particular type of MDM support technology specifically focused on issues related to collaborative processes among people.
- The six-part classification scheme for groupware (5-3)

  Messaging systems

  Conferencing systems

  Collaborative authoring systems

  Group decision support systems

  Coordination systems

  Intelligent agent systems
- Common MDM coordination methods (5-4)

  Nominal group technique

  Delphi technique

  Arbitration

  Issue-based information system (IBIS)

  Nemawashi
- The *virtual workplace* is the term applied to an office with open cubicles, huddle rooms, and central whiteboards that can convert scribblings into e-mail. (5-5)

Questions for Review

1. Define the term *multiparticipant decision maker* (MDM).
2. List and briefly describe four basic types of communication networks in group interactions.

3. What are some of the effects associated with MDM size?
4. What is *groupthink?* Provide an example of a groupthink situation.
5. What is a negotiated decision? Briefly describe it.
6. Describe the support functions of a typical MDM decision room.
7. Define *groupware.* Where is it applicable?
8. List and briefly describe the various classifications of groupware.
9. List and briefly describe the common MDM coordination methods.
10. What are some of the differences between the traditional office and virtual office?

For Further Discussion

1. Analyze the leading groupware systems in the market. Describe their main components and compare their functionality.
2. List some methods to control sources of potential conflict in MDM support processes.
3. Compare the group, team, and committee decision structures. What are the similarities and differences among them? Where might each structure be appropriate or inappropriate?
4. Interview someone from an organization that is using a groupware technology. Identify the various costs and benefits associated with its use.
5. Which MDM coordination methods do you use most often? Why?

EXECUTIVE INFORMATION SYSTEMS

Learning Objectives

- ◆ Understand the definition of an executive information system (EIS)
- ◆ Realize the two design requirements of an EIS and its fluidity
- ◆ Understand the drill down capability of an EIS
- ◆ Learn the history of the EIS
- ◆ Be familiar with executive activities and their basic categories
- ◆ Learn the various types of information needed by top executives
- ◆ Be familiar with executive information determination methods
- ◆ Gain an understanding of EIS hardware and software components
- ◆ Become familiar with the categories of the current EIS technologies
- ◆ Comprehend a development framework for the EIS
- ◆ Understand some limitations and pitfalls of the EIS
- ◆ Learn the conditions of transformation in executive decision making
- ◆ Gain an understanding of the potential features of current and future EISs

DSS MINICASE

ALLIEDSIGNAL

The president of AlliedSignal's aerospace sector, along with the more than 500 other AlliedSignal employees, can now access all their desired business information in just seconds. Less than 2 years ago, however, they waited for days to get many of the business reports they needed—if they could get them at all.

AlliedSignal is a $12 billion worldwide manufacturer of aerospace and automotive components and specialty materials such as fibers, chemicals, plastics, and circuit board laminates. With Dan Burnham, president of Allied's aerospace division, as the catalyst, AlliedSignal recently implemented an enterprise-wide EIS that completely changed the way its employees use information.

Burnham wanted to access information such as the top 10 customers by business unit, net sales and income by customer or product line, and unit sales by foreign versus domestic or military versus commercial. All these data were available at the unit level, but had never been collected at the sector level. The units did not even generate other information Burnham wanted. "To compute a cost of quality," Burnham says, "we had to call each unit, ask what their rework dollars were, and then merge it with other data."

The biggest hurdle in getting information to Burnham's desktop in Torrance, California, was distribution. Dozens of division executives at remote sites needed to contribute information that could be collated quickly into a single system.

Allied adopted Comshare Corporation's Commander OLAP to develop a system prototype of the information Burnham requested. In just 30 days, the system was ready to be demonstrated to Allied's financial executives. Three months later, Allied developers installed the first EIS on Dan Burnham's desktop. Then, after a month of training sessions and fine-tuning based on user reactions, they rolled out the system to the desktops of more than 150 people at 15 different sites.

Many of the initial users were executives responsible for providing information to the president's EIS. At least one person from each site, however, was assigned to be a technical support specialist. After the initial installation, emphasis was placed on refining the system to be useful to everybody, not just the president. Initially, the division directors saw the system simply as a mechanism for sending information to Burnham, but the members of the development team knew the EIS wouldn't flourish unless it helped all involved do their jobs.

PROTOTYPING WAS THE KEY

A wary Allied development team hesitated to expand the system through conventional development methods that required defining up-front system specifications. They decided that the most productive way to get value to the end users required building a number of things fast, getting the system into users' hands, then soliciting feedback and making the changes requested. In that way, the system would be based on practical feedback rather than theoretical specifications. They were able to adopt this flexible development model in part because Commander could accommodate such rapid application updates. Commander's reliability was also critical to the rapid prototyping development process. With this development approach, usage of the EIS grew dramatically. In 18 months, the aerospace sector's 150-user EIS became a 500-user system spanning all three AlliedSignal sectors.

One of the first applications developed within the EIS was an aircraft delivery forecast application using Comshare's Windows-based Prism. "We track information on every aircraft that will be built in the world for the next 10 years," explains Burnham. "We know all the manufacturers, the engine builders and the

(continued)

⬡ **DSS MINICASE**

(*continued*)

suppliers, and we can slice and dice the information a thousand different ways."

Since the initial rollout of the system, users inundated the EIS development team with new ideas for applications. The team literally implemented every one of them. The development group can be this flexible because it uses similarly flexible tools. Commander provides the group with a broad range of capabilities that allows flexibility in fulfilling customer needs.

When all the initial EIS functions are complete, more than 750 AlliedSignal employees will be using the system in all three company sectors as well as at corporate headquarters. Despite this phenomenal growth, the development team at Allied still considers the EIS to be in its infancy. People are just beginning to see the possibilities of the system.

The CEO of today's organization is not so far removed from his or her predecessors of decades before. Now, as then, information is the mainstay of the executive suite; the majority of an organization's resources allocated to the

executive branch is deployed in an effort to gather and maintain that information. The character of the information needed by the CEO has not changed that much either. Top executives generally need much broader information than that required by middle or line management. What has changed, however, is the speed with which this vital information is being generated and the speed with which the CEO needs access to it. The typical DSS designed to focus on providing support for a particular problem or decision context, that works so effectively at the line and middle management levels of the firm, cannot provide the diversity of information access and decision support needed by top management. To address the unique information needs of the CEO, a particular class of decision support technologies emerged. This chapter will focus on the information needs of the top executive and the architecture of the executive information system (EIS) used to address those needs.

6-1: WHAT EXACTLY IS AN EIS?

In basic terms, an EIS is a special type of DSS uniquely designed to facilitate the analysis of information critical to the overall operation of an organization and to provide tools that can support the strategic decision-making processes conducted by top executives. More specifically, an EIS can help a CEO get an accurate and almost immediate picture not only of the operations and performance of the organization but of the activities of its competitors, customers, and suppliers as well. An EIS performs these functions by constantly monitoring both internal and external events and trends and then making this information available to the top executive in a manner that best suits the needs of the moment. An EIS can provide a wide range of summarization or detail at the convenience of the executive. For example, a CEO can use the EIS to quickly view sales activity categorized by product, region, subregion, month, local market, or any number of other methods of organization. Simultaneously, the CEO can also monitor the sales activity of the firm's competitors in much the same way. This high degree of summarization provides a quick, comparative snapshot of what's going on in the company and/or the market. Should this snapshot reveal some discrepancy, unusual variance, or anomaly, the executive can drill down into the data to display a greater level of detail. This process of decomposition can continue until the individual transaction level is reached, if necessary, to provide the CEO with the information that explains the variance and helps decide a course of action. The design of an EIS combines access to a wide variety of information sources with a mechanism for relating and summarizing those sources. It also provides the user with the tools necessary to examine and analyze the gathered information so that a swift, yet well-informed, decision can be made.

Regardless of the context in which the EIS is deployed, all have certain characteristics in common. Table 6-1 contains a summary of common characteristics associated with all EIS technologies.

Building upon the common EIS characteristics and the various definitions offered in the literature on EISs, we adopt the following definition in this text: *An EIS is a computer-based system intended to facilitate and support the information and decision-making needs of senior executives by providing easy access to both internal and external information relevant to meeting the stated goals of the organization.* Throughout the literature on this subject, the terms executive information system and electronic support system (ESS) are used interchangeably, though often ESS connotes a system of much broader capabilities than an EIS. With the advent of distributed groupware technologies and improvements in existing decision-making and information-gathering technologies, this distinction is rapidly becoming blurred. For our purposes, we use the term *EIS* to refer to all executive support systems regardless of content or specific target.

At this stage of our discussion it is not particularly important to position various EIS structures within a taxonomy or categorization scheme (although we will ultimately do just that). What is important, however, is to realize that EISs differ considerably in both scope and purpose and, therefore, like DSSs, must be designed and implemented for a particular executive environment and must be based on a particular executive's information needs. Because both of these design requirements are extremely fluid, the EIS must be considered an evolutionary tool in an organization and therefore requires a significant commitment to its ongoing support and development.

A TYPICAL EIS SESSION

To better understand the unique nature of an EIS, let's walk through the activities in a typical EIS session. The session might begin with a report of the organization's financial and business situation. This report would contain several graphics of sales revenues

---

TABLE 6-1   Common Executive Information System Characteristics

- Used directly by top-level executives
- Tailored to individual executive users
- Designed to be easy to operate and require little or no training to use
- Focused on supporting upper-level management decisions
- Can present information in graphical, tabular, and/or textual formats
- Provides access to information from a broad range of internal and external sources
- Provides tools to select, extract, filter, and track critical information
- Provides a wide range of reports including status reporting, exception reporting, trend analysis, drill down investigation, and ad hoc queries

---

by region or categorical costs of goods sold, but it would also have a section displaying the value of key performance indicators ranging from typical financial ratios such as assets–to–liabilities, to more targeted indicators such as the average waiting time for customers accessing telephone support services. The body of the report may use arrows or color to highlight those measures that are going up, staying steady, or declining. Other colors or graphics may be used to indicate those measures that have transcended some predetermined operating range or threshold. At a quick glance, the executive can form an overall assessment of the organization's state.

After reviewing the summary information, the executive may notice a color-coded trend indicator that appears troublesome. Let's say the current ratio appears to be declining unusually fast. The executive will use the drill down capabilities of the EIS to explore the underlying data used to compile the current ratio. In this case, the drill down feature would bring up screens listing asset and liability categories separately. If this level of disaggregation does not give the executive the answer, additional drilling down may be warranted. Drilling down further on assets may reveal itemized dollar figures for cash, inventories, receivables, and other specific assets. This process can occur until the level of detail is sufficient to reveal the root of the change in the ratio.

The drill down capability of an EIS is one of its most important characteristics. This process of decomposition can be selected and controlled by the executive and can be different for every situation. The executive merely selects the level of detail deemed necessary for the situation at hand using a keystroke or mouse click on the interface to bring forth the story behind the information displayed. By going down one layer from a summary of company-wide sales to regional sales, for instance, an executive might learn that a slump in a product category can be attributed to a specific area of the country. Continuing to drill down in the specific region may reveal a lack of promotion. Drilling down in the other regions where sales are good may indicate that sales expectations were actually exceeded wherever distributors advertised the product properly.

Drilling down through the data allows the executive to seek solutions to problems by employing a "top-down" analysis. The EIS summary highlights potential problem areas and the drill down feature allows for further structured investigation. This process leads to better decisions, more successful solutions, and better management performance.

WHAT AN EIS IS NOT

One additional issue of importance is the acknowledgment of what an EIS is not. The organizational EIS is not a panacea or substitute for other forms of information technologies and computer-based systems. Transaction-processing systems (TPS), the core management information systems (MIS), and the individual DSS and MDM support systems are all still vital elements in bringing relevant information to the various levels of a modern organization. The EIS actually feeds off the various information systems within an organization for its internal information needs and then attaches itself to external information sources as necessary to fill in the bigger picture.

Along these same lines, an EIS does not (and above all, should not) turn the executive suite into a haven for computer techies and geeks. The well-designed EIS should offer an interface that is intuitive, flexible, and easily managed by the nontechnical user. In this regard, the EIS should be positioned and viewed by senior management as more of a trusted confidant or assistant who can be easily called upon and relied upon when and where necessary.

6-2: SOME EIS HISTORY

The term *executive information system* was coined at the Massachusetts Institute of Technology (MIT) in the late 1970s. The first EISs were developed by a few organizations in private industry that were willing to take rather large risks in return for the significant competitive advantage perceived to be associated with the use of an EIS. The "coming out" party for the EIS is historically associated with the publishing of a *Harvard Business Review* article by Rockart and Treacy (1982) entitled "The CEO Goes On-Line." This article vividly describes the emergence of the computer in the executive suite—often assumed to be the last bastion of successful resistance to the computing technology monster. Although many were skeptical of the widespread acceptance of this new organizational tool, the skeptics were soon silenced. By the mid-1980s, several vendors such as Pilot Software (Command Center) and Comshare (Commander EIS) were making huge inroads into large corporations by providing relatively easy application environments for EIS development that included easy screen design, flexible interface design, preprogrammed access to electronic news sources, mechanisms to facilitate widespread data importation, and a wide variety of easy-to-use analytical tools. One of the major driving forces behind the adoption of enterprise resource planning (ERP) systems in the next decade will be the ability to easily feed real-time data to an organizational EIS. It is becoming almost axiomatic that where you find an ERP, you will also find a mission critical EIS.

As excitement and support for EIS technology grew throughout the 1980s and early 1990s, new vendors and emerging products increased the scope of available information sources and analytical techniques that allowed the EIS to be used at other levels of the organization. Modern EISs contain a wide variety of data including mission-critical business processes, research and development efforts, customer-related information, financial activity, and, of course, external data to support the necessary environmental scanning activities. The current generation of EISs addresses a much broader audience, and the available applications transcend the boundaries of typical corporate hierarchies. The adoption of an EIS is not without risk, but the number of success stories associated with EIS development and use suggests that the risks are well worth the benefits.

To fully understand and appreciate the value and power of an EIS, we must first understand and appreciate the unique information needs of its users. Section 6-3 focuses on the issues surrounding the information needs of the CEO.

6-3: WHY ARE TOP EXECUTIVES SO DIFFERENT?

To help answer this question we must begin by defining who top executives are and what constitutes their realm of activities. No generalizable definition captures the full meaning of the term *executive,* and its application varies from organization to organization.

As with other such constructs that lack a focused definition, executives tend to be defined by their common characteristics. Table 6-2 lists several commonalities associated with the executive branch of management.

EXECUTIVE INFORMATION NEEDS

To fully appreciate the information needs of any decision support system user, we begin with the nature of the work and the various tasks associated with the process. In the design of an EIS, the unique nature of the target user makes this understanding essential for success.

From your first management class, you learned that all managers perform five basic functions: planning, organizing, staffing, directing, and controlling. You may also recall that even though all managers may perform tasks within each of these functions, they do not spend equal time in all areas. One method of differentiating the various managerial roles within the hierarchy of an organization is to categorize them by frequency of function. The nature of work at the top executive level suggests that executives spend more time focusing on planning and controlling than managers at other levels of the firm. Specific tasks at the executive level include management and operational control, strategic planning, negotiation, and disturbance management. Studies by Rockart (1979) and Jones and McLeod (1986) focused on the identification of the specific tasks performed by top executives and the frequency of their occurrence. In these studies, executives were asked to keep careful track of every activity they performed during the course of their work over an extended period. In addition, they were asked to indicate the sources of information they used during the conduct of each activity and the relative importance of that activity. The results suggested that executive activities can be divided into five basic categories. Figure 6-1 shows these activities and their relative frequency of occurrence.

Disturbance Management

The word *disturbance* may belie the real nature of tasks contained in this area. When something unexpected occurs, particularly something that could materially and negatively affect the financial health of the organization, the immediate attention of executives and the deployment of resources are usually warranted. In times of disturbance, all other executive activities are usually subordinated to those directly related to the crisis. Furthermore, disturbance management activities may require around-the-clock atten-

---

TABLE 6-2   Common Characteristics of Executives

- They manage entire organizations or autonomous subunits.
- They are enterprise-oriented in their thinking.
- They possess the broadest span of control in the organization.
- They are future-oriented and focus on strategic horizons rather than day-to-day activities.
- They are responsible for establishing policies.
- They represent the organization and its interactions with the external environment.
- Their actions can have considerable financial, human, and business consequences.
- They must concern themselves with a wide range of internal and external issues.

Source: Adapted from Watson, Houdeshel, and Rainer (1997).

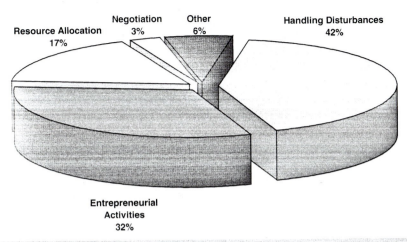

FIGURE 6-1 Frequency of Executive Activities

tion during the early stages of the crisis and may continue for weeks or months before the disturbance is fully managed and under control. As you can see by the figure, the majority of executive time is spent in some form of disturbance management activity.

The events following the May 11, 1996, crash of ValuJet Flight 592 are a vivid example of disturbance management activities. ValuJet President Lewis Jordan was immediately thrust to the forefront of media attention and was charged with the responsibility of representing ValuJet in press conferences, internal and external investigations, and public relations activities, as well as the preparation for the inevitable mire of legal proceedings to come. FAA scrutiny caused so many disruptions in ValuJet's schedule that Jordan faced the decision to cut the number of ValuJet's flights in half so its planes could be inspected in a more orderly fashion. What Jordan called "unprecedented regulatory and media scrutiny" was immediately focused on the airline. Jordan said ValuJet was subjected to 4 years' worth of inspection in 4 weeks.

Jordan then decided to add a "safety czar" and began upping quarterly bonuses to employees despite a less-than-stellar first quarter. "It's clear we're going to forgo a significant amount of revenue," Jordan said. "And we're going to forgo the opportunity to carry a number of people, but we have said we're putting safety first." In the end, Jordan predicted that "we will weather this just fine." In fact, these actions were serious efforts to reclaim public confidence and build employee morale.

Even more recently, the events following the tragic loss of life on September 11, 2001, also emphasize the importance of disturbance management activities. New York City Mayor Rudolph Giuliani, New York Governor George Pataki, and President of the United States George W. Bush all faced a nation in turmoil. Their actions became immediately and simultaneously focused on rescue efforts, expectation management, economic stability, national security, and military action. All consummate executives, these men, and many others, faced their greatest challenge with resolve, clarity, and skill. The ability to conduct successful disturbance management activities was never more valuable to a nation and the world than on September 11, 2001, and the days and weeks that followed.

Entrepreneurial Activities

These activities fall under the general heading of strategic planning tasks. Executives spend a significant portion of their time focusing on the selection, design, and implementation of projects to improve performance and initiate controlled change within the organization. In most cases, the entrepreneurial activities of an executive are triggered by real or perceived changes in the external environment. Executives must focus their attention on understanding the dynamic forces in their markets and the global environment and must use the information gathered to predict changes that can be viewed as opportunities to the firm. Because of the risk associated with making such predictions and the subsequent commitment of present and future resources to projects intended to take advantage of environmental changes, executives must spend a large percentage of their time in this area.

Allocation of Resources

In one form or another and regardless of where in the organizational hierarchy the actual deployment occurs, top executives completely control resource allocation. Typically, managers at various levels are given authority to manage and deploy resources from a predetermined allocation and based upon a control mechanism such as a budget or operational plan. The authority to deploy those resources and the various behind-the-scenes activities to obtain them is normally performed by top executives. Organizational resources include more than just dollars, however. They also include people, equipment, plant and warehouse space, and all other entities associated with reaching the strategic goals of the firm. In general, the demand for resources is greater than their availability and, as such, top executives must decide where and to whom the limited cache of organizational resources will be allocated.

Negotiation

Executives represent the organization in both internal and external disputes. Typically, this role involves responsibility for the resolution of disputes and conflicts and, thus, involves a significant amount of negotiation among the parties. Internal disputes can occur when functional areas within the organization disagree on an issue of procedure or span of authority. In such cases, top executives must facilitate the resolution of the dispute through negotiation among the principal members of the firm who are directly affected by the conflict. External disputes occur when the perspectives of one or more constituencies outside the organization are in conflict with the actions of the firm. Such situations include hostile acquisitions, strikes and labor disputes, shareholder relations issues, and government investigations. Despite the relatively small amount of time spent by executives on these activities (only 3 percent as shown in Figure 6-1), the need for rapid information and decision support may be as critical here as it is during times of disturbance or crisis. Further, situations can occur that require an almost simultaneous conduct of the primary areas of executive actions.

In late 1997, United Parcel Service (UPS) truck drivers went on strike after a vote by the members of the Teamsters Union. The 15-day standoff cost UPS more than $500 million and was characterized by periods of literally around-the-clock negotiations by both sides. During this time, the need for rapid and accurate information was vital to the successful resolution of the dispute. In addition, the UPS executives had to divide their time between activities of negotiation and activities related to disturbance management. Every minute they spent in attempting to resolve the strike was also a minute spent in managing the crippled operations of the organization. Because of the nature of the dispute, the consequences of the various outcome scenarios had to be analyzed with regard to their impact on the availability of present and anticipated resources, the overall strategic plan, and, thus, the future of the company.

TYPES AND SOURCES OF EXECUTIVE INFORMATION

Executive Information Types

We know from past discussion that decisions come in many forms, and the information necessary to make a particular decision carries with it certain attributes relevant to the problem context. In addition to the variance in attributes associated with certain types of information, the relative importance of those attributes varies with regard to management level. Table 6-3 lists the various common attributes of information and compares their relative importance to lower- and higher-level managers.

Given the relevance of the various information attributes, it seems reasonable to expect that the kinds of information sought by executives and their sources may also be uniquely identifiable. Rockart (1979) made several observations concerning the various types of information needed by top executives:

1. Cost accounting systems that relate revenues and expenses to specific functions and operational areas are more useful to top executives for tracking critical success factors than the more traditional financial accounting systems.
2. Externally obtained information about markets, customers, suppliers, and competitors is extremely valuable in determining strategy.
3. Top executives require information that is typically spread across several computer systems and is located throughout the organization.
4. Top executives rely on both objective and subjective assessments of issues internal and external to the organization.
5. High-level executives use information focused on current results and short-run performance levels.
6. Top executives require information that is often both short-term and extremely volatile.

TABLE 6-3   Differences in Information Attributes Between Management Levels

Information Attribute	Lower-Level Management	Top Executive Management
Accuracy	High	Low
Timeliness	High	Low
Scope	Narrow	Broad
Time horizon	Past and present	Future
Relevance	High	Low
Level of detail	High	Low
Summarization	Low	High
Orientation	Internal	Internal and external
Source	Written	Verbal and graphical
Quantifiability	High	Low

Source: Adapted from Watson, Houdeshel, and Rainer (1997).

Executive Information Determination and Sources

Given the unique characteristics of executive information needs, mechanisms for determining and satisfying those needs in a given situation are required. Rockart (1979) identified five basic methods for such determination. Table 6-4 lists these methods in order of increasing formality and level of detail.

By-Product   The by-product method expends the least amount of effort of any of the identified approaches to determining the information needs of top executives. The primary level of support comes from traditional TPSs and other MISs that summarize and aggregate the various informational by-products of the current operations of the organization. Using this method, exception highlighting is limited to those areas with predefined ranges of values or easily summarized historical data. The delivery mechanism for this method is primarily through a collection of online or hard copy reports and summaries.

Null   Using the null approach, no formal effort is made to supply the executive with desired information. The reasoning is that the information needs of executives are so dynamic and fluid that the predefined reports generated by typical information systems are not especially useful. In contrast to the by-product method, the null approach involves the constant, but informal, collection of mostly subjective information from trusted sources via "word of mouth." This method was made famous by Peters and Waterman (1982) in their classic book *In Search of Excellence*, in which they discussed the philosophy of Hewlett-Packard executives using the term *management by walking around*. The null method relies on the spontaneous exchanges and discoveries that take place during informal tours of an organization. Although this method recognizes the value of subjective information, it ignores the value of more objective information such as that obtained through computer-based information systems.

Key Indicator   This method for determining executive information needs is based on three basic notions:

1. The health of an organization can be determined by comparison to a set of key financial indicators.
2. Organizations can be managed based on exception reporting where only those areas operating outside of a preestablished set of norms are of interest.
3. Technology is available to allow for flexible display of key indicator information in graphical form.

TABLE 6-4   Methods for Determining Executive Information Needs

- By-product method
- Null method
- Key indicator method
- Total study method
- Critical success factors method

The first notion requires the identification of relevant financial indicators such as internal financial ratios, production levels, revenues and expenses, and market share. Once these indicators are identified, information about each of them is collected on a continual basis and used to make adjustments or decisions critical to the ongoing success of the organization.

The second notion suggests that a range of operational values and norms can be accurately established in such a way that the concept of "no news is good news" becomes operational. Top executives monitor only that information that reflects an out-of-nominal condition and gather additional information as a basis for making decisions intended to correct the condition.

The third notion requires the information to be made available in graphical rather than tabular form. Using this approach, the executive can more easily "see" the exceptional condition and respond to it more rapidly than would be expected through analysis of tabular data.

Total Study   The total study approach gathers information from a sample of top executives in the organization concerning the totality of their information needs. Following these interviews, system developers make a comparison between the stated needs of the executives and the present information capabilities of the organization's computer systems. Where voids can be identified, the developers create new subsystems to supply the missing information. This method—while more comprehensive than its predecessors—is nonetheless both expensive and somewhat problematic with regard to its ability to meet the needs of any single executive well. As such, this method, while intuitively attractive, has not manifested itself as a practical approach to EIS design.

Critical Success Factors   The fifth and most comprehensive of the approaches identified by Rockart seeks to overcome the various weaknesses associated with the other methods. Regardless of the nature of the organization, certain areas of activity, called critical success factors (CSF), exist in which satisfactory results will ensure the health and competitiveness of that organization. According to Rockart, CSFs are those things that simply must be done right if the organization is to be successful. Similar to the key indicators approach, this method requires information on the identified CSFs to be constantly gathered and supplied to top executives. This information is used as the basis for making decisions that affect the organization.

The primary method for establishing the CSFs of an organization is through structured interviewing of the top executives of the firm. Following this step, CSFs are further refined through a series of facilitated collaborative sessions in which executives discuss the goals and objectives of the firm, the CSFs related to those goals, and just how they might be measured. Given your knowledge of MDM structures from Chapter 5, what might be an appropriate structure for such collaborative sessions?

Of the five approaches identified and discussed, any or all of the last three methods could easily serve as the basis for the design of a computer-based EIS. In the next section, we look at the various components of a typical EIS and explore several available application environments used in their design and implementation.

6-4: EIS COMPONENTS

Many organizations are still evolving from their "big iron" days of the mainframe to the more flexible and functional client/server environment. In many cases, this evolution enables easier development and implementation of computer-based decision support technologies (as well as many other organizational information systems). Several companies already completed this transition in their environments with deployment of their first EIS.

The client/server architecture allows rapid additions and modifications to business applications and facilitates the widespread access and dissemination of databases located throughout the globe. Several of the early EIS products were originally developed for use in a high-powered computing environment, but all of the currently marketed products target the client/server platform, designed to be deployed in a variety of settings (local, mobile, Internet access, etc.). Several of the specific benefits of the client/server architecture are as follows:

1. Multiple views of geographically dispersed data residing on corporate computer platforms ranging from mainframes to personal computers (PCs) regardless of data format
2. Reduction of investment costs in new computer hardware and physical plant
3. Establishment of a flexible platform that can change and adapt to the dynamic needs of the organization
4. Facilitates management use of real-time data, which results in faster, more informed decisions and provides a competitive advantage based on the reduced decision time
5. Facilitates the use of information as a competitive weapon through the easy creation of "strategic" applications that can reveal the "hidden treasures" within an organization's data

Figure 6-2 illustrates a typical EIS implementation within an organization's client/server environment.

HARDWARE COMPONENTS

The EIS does not require any unique computing hardware or peripherals other than those typically found in a modern client/server environment. The important considerations regarding sufficient RAM memory, hard drive space, removable storage, high-speed graphics, data access, large display terminals, and multimedia capabilities relevant to any client-side setup are equally relevant in an EIS environment. A key issue, however, is to be sure that the components of the EIS optimize and conform to the organizational computing resources as well as adapt to the legacy, or existing system, data. The executive user, in many cases, will require the most support in terms of both training in the early stages and modifications in the later ones. The system must be configured so that the organization's resources and capabilities with regard to providing such support are well matched. Otherwise, a disgruntled executive will result, and the benefits surrounding the EIS will never be realized.

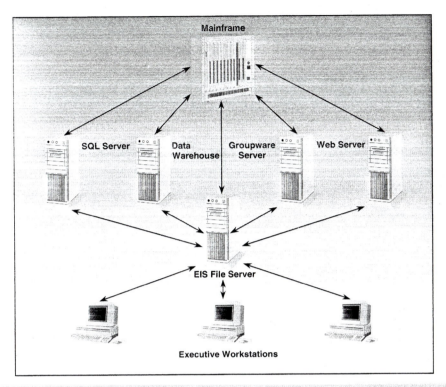

FIGURE 6-2   Typical Client/Server Architecture for EIS Implementation

SOFTWARE COMPONENTS

In contrast to the rather "generic" nature of the hardware components of an EIS, the software components are normally highly specialized and designed to meet the specific needs of specific users. The trend toward open, modular development environments, however, makes the concept of an "off-the-shelf" EIS a reality. Many vendors offer general-purpose EIS application environments that contain the features and capabilities most often required in a typical EIS. These general-purpose environments permit the addition and integration of a wide variety of add-on packages from third-party vendors through which the EIS designer can easily customize the application to meet the specific needs of the executive user group. More recently, EIS applications built around groupware packages provide collaborative features in addition to the standard EIS functions. Two such examples are GroupSystems from Ventana Corporation and Lotus Notes from Lotus Development. GroupSystems can facilitate the complete design and ongoing maintenance associated with an EIS, and Notes can be used as either a partial integration to an existing EIS system or as a total EIS software development platform.

The essential individuality in an EIS, then, comes from the software component rather than from the hardware. Regardless of the specific needs of the executive, all EIS systems tend to possess many commonly requested features and functions. Table 6-5 lists the various common features and functions of a modern client/server-based EIS.

TABLE 6-5 Common Features and Functions of Modern EIS Applications

- Status access, drill down, exception reporting, trend analysis, and ad hoc queries/reports
- Multiple user interfaces
- Multiple search engines and algorithms
- Graphical user interface (GUI) navigation (pull-down menus, pop-up lists, etc.)
- Multiple output channels (screen, hard copy, transparency, etc.)
- Seamless integration with commercial office suites
- Integrated DSS
- Widespread access to external databases and information repositories
- Data management capabilities
- Multidimensional data mining and visualization
- Electronic messaging
- Calendaring and scheduling
- Open architecture
- Online, context-sensitive help mechanisms
- Screen design templates and wizards
- Application design shells
- Multilevel access control security
- Backup and recovery functions
- Usage monitoring

CURRENT EIS TECHNOLOGIES

The EIS marketplace contains various offerings that provide EIS designers with application environments ranging from off-the-shelf solutions to highly customizable and proprietary systems. When considering the various EIS offerings, the components previously discussed render them all relatively similar. To assist in categorizing the current offerings, Dobrzeniecki (1994) proposed a three-tiered functional categorization:

- Category 1: EIS products that include a full set of applications developed by the same vendor
- Category 2: EIS products that are implemented on top of DSS products previously developed by the same vendor
- Category 3: Applications that serve to bind together any number of products currently owned by the client organization into a cohesive, integrated EIS

To be considered an EIS, the software application product(s) should address the needs of the executive in the following areas:

- Office support
  Provide e-mail services and access to intracompany and external industry news services
  Support common office automation functions including word processing, calendaring and scheduling, address book, and to-do list
- Analytical support
  Provide unstructured system query support
  Provide DSS assistance and capabilities

Provide graphic output of trends, key indicators, summary documents, and exception reporting

Provide key word searching, drill down capability, and text-based explanations or help systems

- Customization
  Allow flexible modification to report formats, graphic style and type, and menu content
- Graphics
  Provide a full range of graphic generation and display options
- Planning
  Provide project management and scheduling functions
- Interface
  Provide a user-friendly environment, be easy to learn, and use data navigation modes
- Implementation
  Provide cost-effective integration with organizational computing resources
  Provide training and long-range technical support
  Allow for remote access capability
  Provide data security features

The EIS commercial marketplace is constantly changing with new vendors and applications emerging on an almost daily basis. A section at the end of this chapter contains a fairly comprehensive listing of the major EIS products currently available and provides a short description of each along with sample screenshots of several of the more popular offerings.

6-5: MAKING THE EIS WORK

In one sense, building an EIS is much like building any other type of modern information system. A structured development approach needs to be followed, requirements gathered, prototypes developed, logical models revised, cost analyses performed, and the final system implemented. In another sense, the unique character of an EIS indicates that we still have much to learn about successfully building one. For some developers, their next EIS project will also be their first. They will be thrust into the realm of executives: A world where success has often been realized without a computer, time and patience may be both precious and limited, the problems are often unstructured, and computer literacy and acumen may vary considerably. Furthermore, the physical considerations associated with building an EIS, such as determining the hardware, finding and accessing the necessary data, and integrating the system into the existing computing infrastructure, also contribute to the uniqueness of the challenge. Top these issues off with political issues such as middle management's fear that "Big Brother will be watching," and it becomes easy to see why building a successful EIS may be one of the most formidable development efforts analysts and developers will ever face. This section focuses on many of the issues surrounding these challenges.

AN EIS DEVELOPMENT FRAMEWORK

Numerous researchers and practitioners focused their efforts on studying and refining our understanding of the processes associated with building and implementing a successful EIS. Watson, Rainer, and Koh (1991) provide a touchstone to this ongoing investigation with their EIS development framework. A development framework provides the terminology, concepts, and guidelines necessary for building a system; it is somewhat analogous to a generic instruction manual or road map. Their framework is divided into three major components: (1) the structural perspective, where the key elements that are critical to EIS development and their relationships are delineated; (2) the development process, where the dynamics and interactions of the necessary activities are identified; and (3) the user-system dialog, the interface that directs the system's actions, presents the output, and provides the user with the tools to use the system effectively. A detailed discussion of this framework is beyond the scope of this text; however, we will briefly discuss the three components and their importance to a successful EIS. Figure 6-3 illustrates the elements contained in the structural perspective and their relationships to the EIS.

Structural Perspective

In this component, the focus is on people and data as they relate to the EIS. Key players such as the sponsors or advocates of the system, the user group, the developers and designers, personnel from the various functional areas within the organization, and any vendors and consultants associated with the system are identified and positioned. In

FIGURE 6-3 Structural Perspective of EIS Development Framework

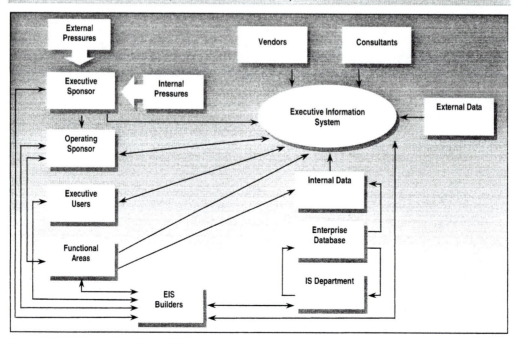

Source: Watson, Rainer, and Koh (1991).

addition, the various sources of internal and external data are identified and positioned. Finally, an acknowledgment of the various forces and pressures either driving or affecting the successful development of the system is included. The structural perspective provides a model for understanding the relationships among the various elements and their potential interaction during the various phases of development of the EIS.

EIS Development Process

The development process builds upon the elements and their relationships contained within the structural model and adds a time dimension to the framework. In this component, the various activities and sequences of events are delineated and actual project management issues relating to time, critical path, and milestones are established. Figure 6-4 illustrates the various phases of the EIS development process.

User-System Dialog

In this component of the framework, we can see the most commonalities between the design and development of an EIS and other related tools such as DSS or MDM systems. The dialog system contains an action language for processing the various commands and elements of manipulation. With this language the user is directed in how to use the system. The action language element can be thought of as the incoming communication channel from the executive to the EIS.

In contrast, the dialog component also contains a presentation language that serves as the EIS counterpart to the action language. The presentation language component guides the outflow of information and the form in which this information is

FIGURE 6-4   Development Process

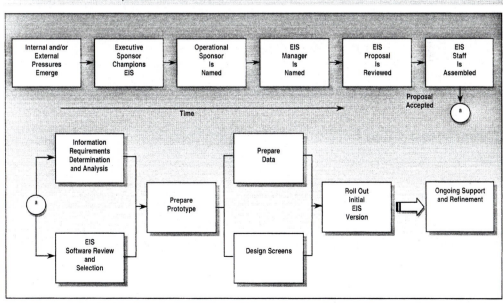

Source: Used with permission from EIS Development Process, from *Building Executive Information Systems & Other Decision Support Applications* by Watson, Houdeshel, and Rainer. Copyright © 1997 by John Wiley & Sons.

presented. Characteristics typical of this component include textual, graphical, and tabular formats, voice annotation, and audio and video capabilities.

The third element in this component is the knowledge base. Covered in greater detail in Chapter 1, the knowledge base is the sum of what the executive knows about using the system and all of the support mechanisms designed to assist in its use. Experience shows that executives simply do not read documentation (unlike you or me, of course). Therefore, the knowledge base must provide the executive with a consistent and context-dependent help system if the EIS is to be used effectively.

The development framework establishes boundaries and guidelines for development of an EIS. In addition to the component elements of the framework, however, Watson, Singh, and Holmes (1995) offer two additional considerations when designing and developing an EIS. First, the EIS must be easy to use. The authors suggested that "because of the nature of the executive user, the system has to go beyond user friendly and be 'user intuitive' or even 'user seductive.'" Second, the EIS must have an acceptably fast response time. Some designers attempt to establish a quantifiable benchmark minimum for response time of 5 seconds or less. Watson, Singh, and Holmes suggest, however, that executive tolerance for response time will vary depending upon the nature of the inquiry; ad hoc queries will elicit greater tolerance for response than simple scanning of prefabricated analyses. The authors cite an unnamed EIS developer who defined acceptable EIS response time when moving from screen to screen as "the time it takes the executive to turn a page of *The Wall Street Journal.*"

SOME EIS LIMITATIONS AND PITFALLS TO AVOID

The development and implementation of an EIS brings significant benefits to an organization, and its potential for improving both competitive advantage and performance is a driving factor in its increasing popularity. Its benefits are not without some caveats, however. Here, we summarize several of the limitations and caveats associated with EIS development.

Cost

Watson, Rainer, and Koh (1991) conducted a survey of organizations using EISs and found the mean development cost to be $365,000. A breakdown of this figure revealed an allocation for software of $128,000, hardware costs of $129,000, personnel costs of $90,000, and the remainder allocated to training. In this same survey, they found the mean annual operating costs for an EIS (including ongoing upgrade and enhancement) to be in excess of $200,000. The majority of this annual operating cost was allocated to personnel and additional training. In other words, the benefits derived from an EIS are costly, and the cost of maintenance of the system after development can easily exceed the original development costs over the life of the system. The decision to adopt an EIS into an organization must be made with the understanding that the ongoing commitment of significant organizational resources is critical if the expected benefits are ever to be realized.

Technological Limitations

The essence of an EIS resides in its ability to bring all of the dispersed data and information necessary to make executive decisions into the executive suite and contain it in an easy-to-use system. The myriad of data sources necessary to accomplish this task and the wide variety of media in which they can reside pose a formidable technical challenge for the EIS designer. To accomplish this seemingly magical feat, developers may need to learn new file structures, data formats, and programming languages as well as enlist the services and support of a variety of data providers and other MIS personnel.

To add to the technical issues facing the EIS designer, the seamless integration of the EIS into the existing computing infrastructure of the organization poses a challenge. As discussed previously, many organizations are still immersed in the transition from older "big iron" environments to the client/server architecture. The presence of this dynamic in the environment must be accounted for in the initial design stages of an EIS. The momentum of this change can often dictate the platform and software selected to design and deploy the EIS. Nonetheless, the EIS must be able to access the data in residence in the legacy system and during data transition to the more modern computing environments.

Organizational Limitations

Aside from the technological issues facing the EIS designer, we must also consider those of an organizational nature. These issues can often be more complex and, thus, more difficult to address than the technical limitations. Millet and Mawhinney (1992) suggested three main categories of potential negative impacts of an EIS on organizations: (1) biased agendas and time orientations, (2) loss of managerial synchronization, and (3) organizational destabilization.

Agendas and Time Biases   Despite the EIS designer's goal of providing the executive with a total information and decision-making package, the system is usually only a part (albeit often a large one) of the totality of information that an executive should ideally consider in making the critical strategic decisions of an organization. The EIS provides information associated with the measurable aspects of the organization and the environment. The less quantifiable aspects of the problem context most often must be obtained from sources other than the EIS. As such, the EIS represents only part of the executive's total agenda. It may become easy to be overly reliant on the EIS, thus focusing the executive's attention on that which can be measured rather than that which is both relevant and necessary. This form of information channeling can cause an executive's agenda to be biased toward a superficial analysis of the environment.

Another potential pitfall associated with EIS use is rooted in the nature of the EIS itself. Because of its ability to produce relevant information with greater frequency and with greater accuracy and depth than an executive is accustomed to, an EIS may lure the executive into concentrating on the more short-run, lower-level decisions within the organization, thus losing focus on bigger-picture decisions. An EIS sometimes promotes a more micromanagement approach to conducting business, disrupting the activities of middle and lower-level managers. Simply knowing that the top executives can monitor their every move via the drill down capabilities of the EIS can force a shifting of time orientation. The lower-level managers will begin to turn their attention to decisions with shorter time horizons in an effort to create improvement in the more closely monitored aspects of their work, thus losing their focus on more long-term performance issues.

Managerial Synchronization   This issue is an extension of the time and agenda issues just discussed. The various managerial processes of an organization not only must be carefully delineated and effectively allocated but also must be coordinated or synchronized toward reaching the goals of the firm. One method of accomplishing synchronization is through a periodic reporting mechanism. Such an approach serves to orchestrate the shared review of key indicators and critical success factors across managerial levels. Even though most EISs can, and do, produce a variety of periodic reports, they can also be used extensively to produce on-demand, ad hoc reports. A heavy reliance on ad hoc reports can sometimes disrupt the stable and well-established reporting cycles designed to synchronize management activities within an organization. The important point here is that while ad hoc reporting is a valuable tool in the executive's EIS arsenal, it must not be used as a replacement for the more stable periodic reporting systems.

Destabilization   By returning to our oft-used cache of airplane metaphors the issue of destabilization can be better understood. The physics associated with flying an airplane are in constant flux across the three dimensions of altitude, forward motion, and direction. A pilot must respond to changes in each of these dimensions with the intention of reaching a goal such as increasing altitude or changing direction while simultaneously performing actions that return the aircraft to stable flight following the attainment of the goal. If the pilot overreacts to a particular short-term flux in one or more of the flight dimensions, the aircraft may destabilize and require additional, more focused actions to take place. The concept of stability is better thought of as an average of conditions over time. The key to stability is not simply to affect an average, but to affect an average based on small variances in change. In the organizational setting, the executive must be positioned to decide rather than to simply react. The fast responses to spur-of-the-moment inquiries made by an executive to an EIS can provide the ability to react swiftly to changes in the organization's operations. It is important, however, that such fast responses do not encourage the executive to react too swiftly by making adjustments to the organization that are too frequent or too strong. Such overreactions by executives can destabilize an otherwise stable organization in much the same manner as an overreactive pilot can destabilize an otherwise smooth-flying aircraft.

FAILURE IS NOT AN ACCEPTABLE ALTERNATIVE

As with any development effort, the possibility of partial or total failure for a particular EIS is always present. An EIS failure occurs when the development effort fails to produce a working system or when the installed system fails to be usable or deliver the desired benefits. Crockett (1992) clearly demonstrated that an EIS development effort that fails to satisfy its targeted users can be a severe setback not only for the organization but for the individuals involved. Competitive edge and opportunity can be lost, many people will be disappointed, careers will undoubtedly be adversely affected, and most important, the organization will likely become reluctant to engage in any future EIS development efforts. As *Apollo 13* Flight Director Gene Kranz put it, "Failure is not an option." Table 6-6 lists many of the factors identified by Crockett that can contribute to the failure of an EIS.

Prevention of EIS failure is not a topic that is readily prescriptive in nature. The need for broad-based executive support for the project is essential, however. Training and regular communication among all the participants are also key elements to success. Finally, being aware of the various factors that can contribute to EIS failure and paying constant attention to minimizing those factors are both important steps toward the successful implementation of an EIS within today's organization.

TABLE 6-6   Factors Contributing to EIS Failures

- Management failures (lack of support, loss of interest, unwillingness to train)
- Political problems (middle management resistance, lack of resource commitment)
- Developer failures (slow development, inadequate needs analysis, doubtful data integrity)
- Technology failures (inadequate speed or capacity, insufficient functionality)
- Costs (development, training, political)
- Time (development, training, maintenance)

6-6: THE FUTURE OF EXECUTIVE DECISION MAKING AND THE EIS

The future of EIS technology and, thus, executive decision making is one where several conditions will merge to transform the technology. Some of these conditions are fairly easy to predict because they exist today, whereas others have yet to emerge. Nonetheless, we will spend some time looking forward to see what the EIS of the future might be.

CONDITIONS OF TRANSFORMATION

Increased Comfort with Computing Technology

One current condition that will continue is the executives' developing comfort level with technology. In the early years of EIS development, a significant roadblock to the acceptance of the technology was executives' lack of experience with hands-on use of computers. An increased focus on training combined with the growing realization that information systems like EISs are valuable to the organization significantly reduces this roadblock. Furthermore, the executive suite is becoming younger. Emerging leaders grew up in the age of technology and developed an early understanding of and comfort level with computer-based systems throughout the organization. As the resistance to computers dissipates, new and more powerful EIS systems will emerge.

Broadening of Executive Responsibilities

The organization will continue to flatten and "rightsize." These conditions will create a leaner, more flexible and responsive structure but will also increase the worker-to-executive ratio. Most of the reduction in workforce will come from staff and middle management levels and the future executive will have direct contact with and responsibility for a much broader span of personnel. We can assume that EIS technology will play a major role in facilitating the management of this flatter organizational structure.

The boundaries of the organization will also continue to expand. Global markets will intensify the competition for market share, natural resources, and labor. With these factors will come continued increases in regulation driven by social and environmental concerns. The scope of responsibility of the executive will clearly include these increasing complexities, and the need for accurate, more diverse, and immediate information will continue to grow.

THE EIS OF TOMORROW

The trend toward the integration of applications and technologies into seamless enterprise-wide systems bodes well for the future of executive information systems. Technological and conceptual advances in telecommunications, information systems, and decision support systems will all contribute to new EIS features and potentially new and more powerful EIS applications. Watson, Houdeshel, and Rainer (1997) suggest that the EIS of the future may become an executive intelligence system.

The Intelligent EIS

The amount of data provided to the executive is literally overwhelming. Even with an EIS, the potential for information overload is constant. Artificial intelligence (AI) can perform some of the data screening for the executive, reducing the amount of time spent searching for relevant data.

The advances in voice input capabilities promote the use of AI. Executives accustomed to delivering verbal instructions would find that voice input reduces both the data entry time and the potential for errors. Properly deployed, voice input and output would clearly add greater flexibility to the EIS and allow for further understanding and comprehension of information. Voice command software is available today, but it is still in a relatively primitive form. The current state of speech recognition system technology, therefore, limits the use of voice input as an interface. Nonetheless, voice annotation technology has already demonstrated its value in increasing comprehension while reducing the need for page after page of reports. As the challenges related to voice recognition technology begin to dissolve, the advent of the intelligent voice-controlled EIS will occur.

Managing the large storage requirements for voice handling presents a major hurdle in voice technology. Physically storing a system that can recognize all the language instruction, accents, and other natural speech phenomena takes huge amounts of magnetic or optical storage space and has proven difficult. In addition, the technology necessary to overcome issues associated with speaker-dependent recognition is still in its infancy. Current systems require the user to "train" the system by participating in a rather protracted preparation exercise. The user is prompted to speak a series of words, phrases, syllables, and numbers repeatedly while the application creates a voice fingerprint for the user. Although this method dramatically increases recognition rates (currently as high as 99.7 percent with the Kurzweil Voice Plus system), it is nonetheless tedious and extremely time consuming, two conditions that are antithetical to the nature of executives. Several speaker-independent recognition technologies are currently under development, however, and when refined, will become an immediate enhancement to current EIS systems.

Another branch of AI is expert systems (ESs). An ES can be used within an EIS to assist the user with appropriate model selection to analyze a problem. Based on rules provided to the ES, the ES can instruct the user on which model would best fit the problem context. An ES is similar to an EIS in that they both contain components that manipulate data. They differ in the way knowledge is maintained, however. An EIS uses predefined models and associated algorithms whereas an ES operation is based primarily on heuristics. We will explore the topic of expert systems further in Chapters 8 and 9.

The Multimedia EIS

A database component is necessary within an EIS for retrieving, analyzing, manipulating, and updating files. A multimedia database management system (MMDBMS) can increase the future EIS user's resources to manipulate text, voice, and images effectively within an integrated database structure. MMDBMSs provide the traditional benefits of a database management system as well as concatenation of voice, transformation of information, rotation of images, scaling of objects, and merging of various data types. The problem with these systems, especially for the executive user, is the complex interface. As the functionality of these systems continues to increase, more applications for their use will be developed. By combining more applications with an easy-to-use system, an opportunity for a competitive advantage develops.

The Informed EIS

We know that most of the decisions made by executives require some element of external data. Strategic decisions require significant access to data about the market, the environment, the economy, regulatory and technological changes, and the competition. Although access to external data via an EIS is not new, the degree to which the EIS will be able to manipulate and assemble those data will be.

Literally thousands of private sector and government-maintained databases currently exist, and the present volume is expected to double by the turn of the century. The information in these databases is available, but the scanning, filtering, and extraction tools that allow for efficient and effective use of those data are still being refined. The challenge for the next generation of EIS designers will be to integrate data access tools into the applications that will allow the EIS to systematically find and organize the necessary information for the executive from the world's data stores and to deliver it to the EIS desktop in a manner that allows it to be readily understood and applied.

The Connected EIS

The Internet and the World Wide Web facilitate the electronic interconnection of companies to their customers and suppliers. The addition of Web-centric groupware technologies such as Lotus Notes moves organizations even closer toward mass interconnectivity. One massive current development is the dawning of electronic commerce (e-commerce). Firms use the Internet to advertise and communicate new product developments to both current and future customers. Emerging virtual markets are making Internet-based commerce and finance a reality.

With the widespread availability of high-bandwidth communications media, a logical extension of this interconnectivity frenzy would include the executive suite. The EIS of tomorrow may allow for controlled access by a variety of stakeholder groups, such as key suppliers, customers, stockholders, and partners, to that part of the EIS that is important to the conduct and maintenance of a particular relationship. This sharing of resources and information will strengthen the relationship between the parties by simultaneously facilitating the coordination of the relationship and the building of a common knowledge base. This concept is simply an electronic extension of today's account manager concept. The EIS of tomorrow will not eliminate the need for human relationship management, but it will serve as a valuable resource for improving the relationship building and maintenance processes.

6-7: CHAPTER SUMMARY

Despite the increasing awareness of the value of information to the successful implementation of organizational strategy, the concept of the executive information system is still in its infancy. As new decision support and information gathering technologies emerge, new and more robust EIS designs will develop. Regardless of its power, however, the purpose of tomorrow's EIS will be the same as today: to provide senior managers with the information they need about their operating environment, internal operations, industry knowledge and events, markets, customers, and suppliers. The future EISs will be bigger and more powerful and will surely differ in the scope of data sources available to them, but their purpose will be unwavering. The EIS will be a common tool found in every executive suite in the Information Age.

Key Concepts

- To address the unique variety of information needs of the CEO, a particular class of decision support technologies has emerged: executive information systems (EISs).

- Definition of an EIS (6-1)

  An EIS is a computer-based system intended to facilitate and support the information and decision-making needs of senior executives by providing easy access to both internal and external information relevant to meeting the stated goals of the organization.

- Design requirements of an EIS (6-1)

  An EIS must be designed and implemented for a particular executive environment.

  An EIS must be designed and implemented based upon a particular executive's information needs.

  Because both of these requirements are extremely fluid, the EIS must be considered an evolutionary tool in an organization, requiring a significant commitment to its ongoing support and development.

- Drill down capability (6-1)

  The drill down capability of an EIS is a process of data decomposition that is selected and controlled by the executive and will be different for every situation. This feature of an EIS allows the executive to seek solutions to problems by employing a "top-down" analysis and a structured investigation.

- Executive activities (6-3)

  By gaining an understanding of the unique nature of work at the top executive level, we can fully appreciate the information needs of top executives. Executive activities can be divided into several basic categories:

  Disturbance management

  This activity requires the immediate attention of executives as well as the deployment of resources to an unexpected occurrence, particularly one that could materially and negatively affect the financial health of the organization.

  Entrepreneurial activities

  These activities are strategic planning tasks usually triggered by real or perceived changes in the external environment. Executives must focus their attention on understanding the dynamic forces in the markets and the global environment and must use the information gathered to predict changes that can be viewed as opportunities to the firm.

Allocation of resources

The authority to deploy resources and the various activities to obtain them are normally performed by top executives. Moreover, top executives must decide to whom and where to allocate the organizational resources because, in general, the demand for resources is greater than their availability.

Negotiation

Executives represent the organization in both internal and external disputes. This role involves responsibility for the resolution of disputes and conflicts and involves a significant amount of negotiation among the parties.

* Given the relevance of the various information attributes to management levels, we can identify the various types of information needed by top executives. (6-3)
* Executive information determination and sources (6-3)

By-product

The primary support comes from traditional processing systems (TPSs) and other management information systems (MISs) that summarize and aggregate the various information by-products of the current operation in the organization.

Null

The null approach involves the constant, but informal, collection of mostly subjective information from trusted sources via "word of mouth." This method relies on the spontaneous exchanges and discoveries that take place during informal tours of an organization.

Key indicator

Top executives monitor only that information that reflects an out-of-nominal condition and gather additional information as a basis for making decisions intended to correct the condition.

Total study

The total study approach gathers information from a sample of top executives in the organization concerning the totality of their information needs.

Critical success factors

The information on the identified critical success factors (CSFs) is constantly gathered and supplied to top executives. This information is used as the basis for making decisions that affect the organization.

* Client/server architecture allows for rapid additions and modifications to be incorporated into business applications and facilitates the widespread access and dissemination of disparate databases located throughout the globe. (6-4)
* EIS components (6-4)

Hardware components

The hardware components of the EIS should be optimized with and conform to the organizational computing resources as well as adapted to the legacy data. Also, the system must be configured with the organization's resources and capabilities so that support is provided to both train executives and facilitate their modifications.

Software components

The individuality of an EIS comes from the software component rather than from the hardware. The software components of an EIS are normally highly specialized and designed to meet the specific needs of specific users.

- An EIS development framework (6-5)

  The development framework provides the terminology, concepts, and guidelines necessary for building an EIS. It can be divided into three major components:

  Structural perspective

  The structural perspective provides a model for understanding the relationships among the various elements and their potential interaction during the various phases of development of the EIS.

  EIS development process

  The development process builds upon the elements and their relationships, contained within the structural model, and adds a time dimension to the framework.

  User-system dialogue

  Action language: The various commands and elements direct users how to use the system. It is the incoming communication channel from the executive to the EIS.

  Presentation language: It serves as the EIS counterpart to the action language. This component guides the outflow of information and the form in which this information is presented. Knowledge base: The knowledge base is the sum of what the executive knows about using the system and all of the support mechanisms designed to assist in its use.

- Two considerations of designing and developing an EIS (6-5)

  The EIS must be easy to use.

  The EIS must have an acceptably fast response time.

- EIS limitations (6-5)

  Cost

  The benefits derived from an EIS are costly and the cost of maintenance of the system after development can easily exceed the original development costs over the life of the system.

  Technological limitations

  The myriad of data sources necessary to accomplish the functionalities of an EIS and the wide variety of media in which they can reside pose formidable technical challenges for the EIS designer.

  Organizational limitations

  Biased agendas and time orientations: This form of information channeling can cause an executive's agenda to be biased toward a superficial analysis of the environment. Also, an EIS can serve to promote a more micromanagement approach to conducting business, which can disrupt the activities of middle and lower-level managers.

  Loss of managerial synchronization: A heavy reliance on ad hoc reports can sometimes disrupt the stable and well-established reporting cycles within an organization that have been designed to synchronize management activities.

  Organizational destabilization: The fast response to spur-of-the-moment inquiries may cause the executive to react too swiftly by making adjustments to the organization that are too frequent or too strong. Such overreactions by executives can destabilize an otherwise stable organization.

- Failure is not an option. (6-5)

  An EIS development effort that fails to satisfy its targeted users can be a severe setback not only for the organization but for the individuals involved.

- Prevention of EIS failure (6-5)

  Broad-based executive support for the project is needed.

Training and regular communication among all the participants is a key element to success.

Be aware of the various factors that can contribute to EIS failure and pay constant attention to minimizing those factors.

- Conditions of transformation in executive decision making (6-6)

Increased comfort with computing technology

Broadening of executive responsibilities

- The EIS of tomorrow (6-6)

The intelligent EIS

Artificial intelligence (AI) can perform some of the data screening for the executive, reducing the time spent searching for relevant data.

The multimedia EIS

A multimedia database management system (MMDBMS) can increase the EIS user resources in order to manipulate text, voice, and images effectively within an integrated database structure.

The informed EIS

The challenge for the next generation of EIS designers will be to integrate data access tools into the applications that will allow the EIS to systematically find and organize the necessary information for the executive from the world's data stores and to deliver it to the EIS desktop in a manner that allows it to be readily understood and applied.

The connected EIS

With the widespread availability of high-bandwidth communications media, a logical extension of this interconnectivity frenzy would include the executive suite. The EIS of tomorrow will serve as a valuable resource for improving relationship building and maintenance.

Questions for Review

1. Define *executive information system.*
2. List the two EIS design requirements.
3. Describe the drill down feature of an EIS.
4. Is the organizational EIS a substitute for other forms of information technology and computer-based systems? Why or why not?
5. List and briefly describe executive activities.
6. List and briefly describe the five basic methods for executive information determination.
7. What is the primary method for establishing the CSFs of an organization?
8. What are the benefits of client/server architecture?
9. Depict the key consideration of the computing hardware environment for developing and deploying an organizational EIS.
10. List and briefly describe the categories of current EIS technologies.
11. Describe the components of an EIS development framework.
12. Identify the three basic components of the user-system dialog.
13. List and briefly describe several EIS limitations.
14. Explain the three main categories of potential negative impacts of an EIS on organizations.
15. How can the failure of an EIS implementation project be prevented?

16. Describe the conditions of transformation in executive decision making.
17. Briefly describe the EIS of tomorrow.

For Further Discussion

1. Analyze an EIS application in the market. Describe its drill down capability and how this function helps executives.
2. Review the categories of executive activities and the information needs for the activities in each category. Relate these factors to a fast-food company. How about a service organization?
3. Find and study a case of disturbance management in an organization. How can an EIS support the executives in this case?
4. Assume you and your team are the top executives of an insurance company. Identify the information you need through key indicator and critical success factors approaches.
5. Review the areas of support that should be provided by an EIS application. Analyze an EIS application product in the market. Describe its functionalities based on these areas of support.
6. Assume you and your team are assigned to develop an EIS for your organization. Design the EIS using the development framework. Identify the factors that may cause the failure of this project. How can you and your team prevent the failure?
7. Use a common development platform such as Excel or Access to develop a proto-typical EIS for your department at work or at school. Use color to highlight exceptions where appropriate and include models for forecasting and prediction. Prepare a report that outlines the steps you took in the development of the system and the problems you encountered during its design.
8. It appears that the EIS is no longer being used exclusively in the executive suite of large organizations. The system is rapidly spreading throughout the organization to all levels of management. Discuss why this phenomenon is occurring and make suggestions about how this diffusion may be facilitated by senior management.
9. Analyze the types of information you use in your daily tasks. Using the various categories of information discussed in this chapter, outline the types you regularly use. Do you see any patterns of information types in your daily activities? Could you benefit from a "personal EIS"?
10. Consider the development of an EIS for the CEO of a major commercial airline. Choose a specific airline and do some basic research on its senior management and its organizational structure.
    - Who would be the target users? List the actual names of the people involved in the EIS use.
    - Who would be the most appropriate project sponsor? Why?
    - What sources and types of information would be made available to the target users via the EIS? What would be in summary form? What levels of detail would be provided? What formats for presentation would you choose?
    - Would the EIS need to be real-time or archival?
    - What limits or controls would you place on various subgroups of the target users?
    - What sources of external data would you include in the EIS?

EIS Product Offerings and Descriptions

This section contains a listing of several DSS application software offerings and their descriptions. This list is by no means comprehensive—DSS products are constantly being introduced, repackaged, and redesigned. It should, however, serve as an effective overview of the various products available and their respective capabilities.

Pilot Decision Support Suite—Pilot Software, Inc.

The Pilot Decision Support Suite is unlike other decision support products. It offers a truly comprehensive solution with predictive data mining, high-performance OLAP, and flexible visualization in an open, plug and play architecture, which is quickly implemented, easily modified, and supports analysis anywhere.

Pilot Designer, the application design environment of the Pilot Decision Support Suite, is the industry's leading solution for rapid data access and visualization. Supporting all Windows graphical user interface standards and a Visual Basic scripting language, Pilot Designer delivers a complete suite of dimensional objects for customizing desktop applications, building libraries, and extending existing analyses. Its tool set can create a variety of visual decision support applications ranging from simple executive information system front ends to complex OLAP applications. With Pilot Designer, decision makers at all levels of an organization have unparalleled access to data, wherever the data elements reside. And they get that information through a wide variety of powerful graphic formats, which combine tabular, geographical and graphical data, text, images, audio, and video. (See *www.pilotsw.com*).

Decision—Comshare, Inc.

Comshare was a pioneer in the EIS business on mainframe computers along with Pilot Software. According to a market study performed by IDC Research, Comshare owns 60 percent of the EIS market by revenue. Comshare's product Commander is known as the prototypical PC-based EIS.

Comshare's latest release, Comshare Decision, is a rich development platform for the creation of custom business intelligence applications that address highly specialized reporting and analysis needs, including sales or market analysis, CRM analysis, performance measurement, and customer/product profitability. A powerful point-and-click developer module simplifies the development of Web-based applications with a wide range of analytic capabilities. Analysis can be performed from an almost limitless variety of perspectives, in any view or combination of views chosen by the user. Comshare Decision enables organizations to get the most out of their investment in OLAP by turning business data into business intelligence for improved decision making.

Comshare Decision is the development platform on which was built Comshare MPC™, Comshare's Corporate Performance Management software. All Comshare Decision modules fully integrate with Comshare MPC modules for planning, budgeting, consolidation, management reporting, and analysis. Comshare customers can extend the value of their current Comshare software by adding powerful, customized analysis. (See *www.comshare.com*).

Tivoli Decision Support—IBM

Tivoli Decision Support taps your IT databanks, transforming these data into critical business information. With Tivoli Decision Support and its companion Decision Support Discovery Guides, executives can make decisions on whether to distribute new software, order memory upgrades for the entire company, or determine the impact on specific business units within the company. Tivoli Decision Support consolidates, transforms, and presents enterprise management data in an easy-to-use view, which reveals hidden patterns and natural relationships among the data. Tivoli Decision Support Discovery Guides organize common topics and provide predetermined questions with graphical and tabular views; disparate data from multiple sources are integrated and presented in a variety of views. Additional questions can be asked easily, with no need to develop complex queries or create new reports. Using today's rapidly emerging online analytical processing (OLAP) technology, Tivoli Decision Support allows exploration—slice and dice and drill through the data—in a variety of ways. Tivoli Decision Support adds context to the decision-making process—not just more data. (See *www.tivoli.com/products/index/decision_support/*).

EIS Pak—Microsoft, Inc.

EIS Pak is a set of tools designed to speed development of EISs by using Microsoft Excel and other mainstream applications. EIS Builder is an add-in development tool aimed at helping developers rapidly create Excel-based enterprise applications without writing macro code. EIS Builder provides graphical query and analysis. It also offers the ability to exchange data with external databases and applications. EIS Pak uses the functionality built into Microsoft Windows applications to simplify advanced analytical charting and text-formatting functions. This product is marketed as capable of meeting the needs of department-level managers. Additional features of EIS Pak include video and sample applications as well as an EIS development guide. (See *www.microsoft.com*).

MicroStrategy 7—MicroStrategy, Inc.

MicroStrategy 7™ is the Scalable Business Intelligence Platform Built for the Internet. Its comprehensive platform architecture provides the security, performance, scalability, and standards critical for the deployment of Web-based query, reporting, and analysis solutions.

The MicroStrategy 7 platform supports the most effective and sophisticated business intelligence and Web-based query and reporting requirements through a number of key benefits. (See *www.microstrategy.com*).

PowerPlay—Cognos

Cognos PowerPlay is the world's best-selling OLAP (online analytical processing) software. It enables users to explore large volumes of summarized data with subsecond response times in a Web, Windows, or Excel environment. With Cognos PowerPlay, users at any business or technical skill level in a company can perform their own multidimensional analysis, create reports, and share them for better decision making.

Cognos PowerPlay draws information from relational databases to model and build PowerCubes. These PowerCubes are data sets with more than 50 million consolidated rows of data and up to 500,000 categories (members). Business rules and calculations (for example, percentage growth and market share change) can be built right into them. Cubes and reports can be deployed to Web clients, or to Windows and Excel clients, all using the same application server. (See *www.cognos.com/products/ powerplay*).

Excel (Spreadsheet)—Microsoft, Inc.

Excel is a high-powered spreadsheet product that attempts to meet business information needs with its information manipulation "bells and whistles." Some features include statistical data analysis, database development, import/export capability to other software, and presentation graphics. IBM Corporation indicated support for a gateway from Excel spreadsheets to the AS/400 minicomputer. This combination will provide a means to exchange data across computer hardware platforms. (See *www. microsoft.com*).

Lotus 1-2-3 (Spreadsheet)—Lotus Development Corporation

EIS programs interface to Lotus 1-2-3 spreadsheets by attaching snapshots of 1-2-3 worksheets to various reports. The EISs compile disparate data and let users work through various levels of detail to find information. The EISs combine spreadsheet data with data from other sources and display them in an easy-to-understand format. An EIS may use 1-2-3 as the front end to examine vast quantities of business data and take advantage of computer users' familiarity with the 1-2-3 format.

Many companies piece together executive information systems out of common products, such as spreadsheets. Lotus 1-2-3 files are compatible with Commander, Pilot Lightship, Forest & Trees, DrillDown, and Information Advisor EIS software products.

Lotus 1-2-3 is not a database manager and therefore does not function well as an EIS data repository. The worksheets grow to a point where they become slow and unwieldy. A better solution is to translate the spreadsheets into products such as SQL Server, dBase, Paradox, or Oracle. Many companies are currently in this position. They are searching for the right products to make the transition but that will not limit their development of a full EIS in the future.

Lotus 1-2-3 for Windows can be used as an EIS front end. Using SmartPak, a new 1-2-3 add-in product, users can modify Lotus menus and customize dialog boxes to create a simple EIS within a spreadsheet. (See *www.lotus.com*).

7

EXPERT SYSTEMS AND ARTIFICIAL INTELLIGENCE

Learning Objectives

- ◆ Define expert system and artificial intelligence
- ◆ Describe the several different reasoning processes used by humans
- ◆ Describe the methods available to create a computer-based reasoning system
- ◆ Explain the concepts and structure of expert systems
- ◆ Understand the predesign activities associated with building an expert system
- ◆ Learn how to evaluate an expert system

EXPERT SYSTEMS ASSIST
IN FRAUD DETECTION

Expert systems can be developed for fraud detection—to put up a red flag for suspicious circumstances. Investigators can then spend time on the highlighted items to stop fraud before it gets out of hand.

A wide variety of industries, including banks, insurance companies, and the U.S. government, use expert systems to detect fraud. Medicare billing fraud, health and property insurance fraudulent claims, credit card fraud, and fraudulent foreign currency exchange are just some of the transactions that can be identified by expert systems.

In the expanding world of digital commerce, the magnitude of transactions makes it difficult for humans to carefully review all the data for fraud, given that a majority are legitimate and need timely service. Indeed, part of the problem is that customers now are accustomed to what computers have done to speed up transactions and expect fast service.

PROPERTY AND CASUALTY INSURANCE CLAIMS

Claims adjusters are under great pressure to process claims quickly, a task that is not getting easier for them as the number of exaggerated losses and bogus claims skyrocketed in the last few years. According to industry estimates, 10 to 15 percent of all claims are fraudulent. The use of the telephone and the computer, instead of personal contact, to gather information accelerates the fraud problem. Now claims adjusters must determine liability, estimate damages, and deal with false or padded claims in a cost-efficient and timely manner.

Extra investigation of a suspicious claim adds expense and delays settlement, but inaction could result in payment of a fraudulent claim and the potential for inviting future bogus claims. It presents a dilemma for even the most seasoned claims adjuster, because most claims contain some suspicious elements. The difficulty comes in determining which claim is most appropriate for denial.

To add insult to injury, identifying a fraudulent or exaggerated claim is only half the problem. Defending the claim denial against lawyers and a jury is the real challenge. Litigation is time consuming, expensive, and exposes the insurer to the potential assessment of punitive damages if the court case is lost.

Enter the expert system (ES) as part of the solution to the property/casualty insurance fraud problem. Claims information can be closely examined by an expert system, which can identify and red flag various kinds of fraud. With the help of an ES, adjusters can adopt the outlook of automatically questioning suspicious claims.

AN EXPERT SYSTEM FOR AUTO BODILY INJURY CLAIMS

Correlation Research, Inc., of Needham, Massachusetts, developed a prototype model of an expert system that contains useful data obtained in conjunction with the Massachusetts Automobile Insurers Bureau. Key variables were collected on claim fraud indicators and what actions were taken by the insurer to counter fraud. The claims adjuster answers 10 to 15 questions on each claim, which allows the system to assign a "suspicion score" to each auto bodily injury claim. The score can be used to screen claims and determine what action to take on each one. Actions might involve paying the claim quickly, getting a second medical opinion, or gathering more information.

This expert system is still evolving but can greatly speed up the decision on how to handle each claim. The database grows as more claims are processed by the expert system—it stores claim characteristics, resulting score, and resulting case settlement. Eventually the expert system will be custom tailored for fraud classifications and cost-effective claim handling. The

(continued)

⟨ **DSS MINICASE** ⟩

(*continued*)

core data needed on each claim may change over time as new ways to make bogus claims are discovered. The cost of gathering information through the expert system must be balanced against its value to the insurance company.

PUBLIC CONCERN

Public sympathy for insurance companies is not as great as it was 20 years ago. People are demanding that insurance regulators control fraud and not pass the cost of paying false claims on to customers via rate hikes. As a result of this public concern, many insurance companies use expert systems with their own database of claim information. What is even more exciting, the National Insurance Crime Board is considering creating an expert system — it could be gigantic given the volume of its National Data Base Services program. This online program would be used by 150 insurance companies, 10 state insurance fraud bureaus, and more than 20 law enforcement agencies.

MEDICAL BILLING FRAUD

Medical billing fraud and abuse can be partially discovered with an expert system. Claims auditing software available in expert systems flags suspicious claims for a real human expert to review manually. These expert systems look for fraud that is a result of the codes used for medical diagnoses and procedures. Misuse of the codes could increase a doctor's Medicare reimbursement. In 1992, health care billing fraud amounted to $84 billion—10 percent of the 1992 U.S. expenditure on health care.

CREDIT CARD FRAUD

Banks are also using expert systems. In 1993 Canada Trust Bank installed Trinzic Corporation's knowledge-based Aion Development System to monitor credit card transaction patterns. It was so successful Canada Trust no longer uses reports from MasterCard International.

Data are reviewed every night and every 2 hours during the business day for deviations from a customer's normal purchase pattern. A score is assigned to the transaction based on how likely it is to be fraudulent. Suspicious scores are routed to the bank's fraud department for a closer investigation. In this way the bank can investigate almost immediately every suspicious transaction. Due to sheer volume, this activity would be impossible using manual labor. Timeliness is the key to preventing further fraud.

FOREIGN CURRENCY EXCHANGE FRAUD

Banks also put expert systems to work watching over currency exchange transactions. New York's Chemical Bank designed an expert system called Inspector. It continuously monitors foreign currency exchanges at Chemical Bank offices around the world. Any questionable transaction is flagged so a human foreign currency expert can review the deal.

Inspector is a great time saver, which offers an important benefit because Chemical Bank handles more than $1 billion a day in foreign currency transactions. One fraudulent transaction could cost the bank millions.

MORE IN THE FUTURE?

Expert systems have found a home in the world of fraud detection. The true potential for expert systems will be realized when they can all be linked so that the full picture can be monitored. With this approach, fraudulent transactions that cross over several insurance companies or banks will be noticed. Expert systems can serve as the watchdog of business transactions. Their vigilance can give human experts time to make personal investigations of suspicious events while the rest of our business deals are quickly and efficiently handled.

7-1: THE CONCEPT OF EXPERTISE

Danish physicist Niels Bohr once defined an expert as one "who has made all the mistakes which can be made in a very narrow field." Although this characterization may be a bit of an exaggeration, it nonetheless frames the realm of an expert. To make all the mistakes possible within a given knowledge domain, one must experience all there is to experience. Thus, given enough information about a particular problem scenario, an expert usually can determine the appropriate solution with a high degree of reliability and with a measurable degree of efficiency over those with less domain experience. This statement may seem rather intuitive and self-explanatory, but the question of just how an expert arrives at an effective solution with such efficiency still remains. The answer to this question is found in the field of logic.

Logical theorem proving is a method of establishing the truth or falsity of particular assertions. It is based on the premise that all information within a particular knowledge domain is related to all other information in that domain in some manner. Therefore, facts or observations about a new scenario within that domain must "fit together." This requirement of fit allows logical processes such as deduction and inference to be used to arrive at a conclusion about the problem under study. Experts use this concept of information fit within a specific knowledge domain to arrive at their decisions.

Of all the situations you can conceive of, whether they involve data interpretation, optimization, planning, diagnosis, or social behavior, most can be expressed in terms of rules. If we think of problem solving as a set of IF-THEN rules, we can begin to see how the experts perform their "magic." They use logic to derive new information from the existing information to arrive at a conclusion. By using the concept of information fit, they can construct an efficient inquiry process to collect the information necessary to create a fit, and thus arrive at a conclusion. As a simple example, consider the following:

KNOWN INFORMATION

- John is Sam's son.
- John is the eldest child.
- Mary is Sam's daughter.
- John and Mary's mother is named Anna.
- Sam has been married to Anna for 50 years.

DERIVED INFORMATION

- IF John is Sam's son, THEN John must be a boy.
- IF Mary is Sam's daughter, THEN Mary must be a girl.
- IF John and Mary have the same mother, THEN John and Mary are brother and sister.
- IF Sam and Anna have been married for 50 years, then John and Mary are their children by either birth or adoption.

The previous example uses the concept of information fit and rules to obtain new information that was not specifically available. Logic suggests that the derived information must be true if the known information is true. From this point, we can collect enough information to make a decision fairly quickly because we know which specific pieces of information are necessary to make the decision. It should be easy to see that by using these concepts (i.e., information fit and seeing a problem context as a set of rules), a computer application could be developed to serve as the "expert" in a problem-solving activity.

EXPERT SYSTEMS AND ARTIFICIAL INTELLIGENCE

The term *expert system* (ES) describes a computer-based application that employs a set of rules based upon human knowledge to solve problems that require human expertise. Expert systems imitate reasoning processes based on the concept of information fit used by human experts in solving specific knowledge domain problems. A non-expert can use an ES to improve his or her abilities to solve complex problems by simulating a dialog with experts in a particular field. Experts can use an ES to simulate a highly knowledgeable assistant. Most commonly, an ES is employed to allow for the propagation of scarce expert resources throughout an organization to increase the consistency and quality of problem-solving activities.

An ES functions as an expert primarily through techniques developed in the field of artificial intelligence (AI). AI research focuses on understanding how humans think, reason, and learn and can be thought of as an intersection between computer science and cognitive psychology. From this understanding, AI seeks to discover and develop practical mechanisms that enable computers to simulate the reasoning processes performed by humans in solving a particular problem. Rich and Knight (1991) define AI as "the study of how to make computers do things which, at the moment, people do better" (p. 3). Although these AI mechanisms are not yet identical to those of humans, they can produce results that are quite similar, and thus useful, to those produced by human decision makers.

In this chapter, we focus on the importance of expert systems and artificial intelligence in the context of decision making and problem solving. We will explore their history, structure, and underlying concepts to better understand their present stage of development and application as well as their potential for future use. Finally, a brief focus on their benefits and limitations lays the necessary groundwork to proceed to Chapter 8, where we take a detailed look at knowledge and the method by which it can be "captured" and harnessed in an ES.

A HISTORY OF ES AND AI

The roots of ESs and AI can be traced back to the mid-1950s and the work of the RAND-Carnegie team. Herbert Simon and Alan Newell of the Carnegie Institute of Technology (now Carnegie-Mellon University) and J. C. Shaw of the RAND Corporation conducted an ambitious series of investigations into the development of computer-based reasoning systems. Their first system, the Logic Theorist, used the concept of reverse reasoning to solve simple problems in propositional calculus using a small set of axioms as a knowledge base. Reverse reasoning begins with the original problem statement and then decomposes, or breaks down, the problem into a series of smaller subproblems that can be solved individually. In the late 1950s, the team embarked on an even more ambitious project that resulted in the development of the General Problem Solver (GPS) system. The GPS, unlike the Logic Theorist, was able to solve problems in a wide variety of problem contexts using general reasoning methods and techniques. The GPS was capable of solving elementary logic problems, chess problems, and even high school algebra word problems. It was the first effective development of a system that used a general approach to problem solving.

By the early 1960s, the basic building blocks for ESs were emerging. Minsky and McCarthy, at the Massachusetts Institute of Technology, invented the programming language LISP, which is a dominant language used in the development of AI-based systems. At this same time, DENDRAL, an ES capable of inferring a structure of molecules by mass spectrography data, was developed at Stanford University. It was a time of rapid advancement of ES technology and a period during which much of the knowledge necessary to build the industrial ESs of the next decade was formulated.

During the 1970s, industry developed expert systems to serve a variety of needs including diagnosis, perception, instruction, learning, theorem proving, game simulation, and pattern and speech recognition. Major organizations including Digital Equipment (with its XCON and XSEL computer configuration ESs), Xerox, IBM, General Electric (with CATS-1, a diesel locomotive troubleshooting ES), General Motors, and Texas Instruments, among many others, embraced and advanced the state of AI and expert systems into their modern-day form. Today, literally thousands of ESs are in operation worldwide as a prosperous market for ES development applications emerges.

7-2: THE INTELLIGENCE OF ARTIFICIAL INTELLIGENCE

As stated previously, AI focuses on understanding how people reason and think and then translates that understanding into computer systems that can perform the same actions. To better understand how AI performs this translation we need to look first at the human side of the equation.

HOW DO PEOPLE REASON?

The scope of this text precludes a thorough discussion of human reasoning processes. An entire field, cognitive psychology, has evolved to focus on the complex processes and conditions that affect human reasoning and response. Nonetheless, we can identify several specific reasoning processes used by humans, which are easily translated into the realm of expert systems and artificially intelligent computers.

Categorization

The most common process associated with human reasoning is that of categorization. When we identify a piece of information as important enough to remember, we categorize it according to one or more characteristics or criteria. Our memories store these categories as a loose set of hierarchies where lower-level pieces of information can "inherit" characteristics from a higher-level category. Figure 7-1 illustrates this concept of categorization.

Depending on the level of detail represented by a particular piece of information, categorization can allow us to reason to a higher level of abstraction. For example, it is logical to reason that if cars are ground-based vehicles and buses are ground-based vehicles, then they must both transport people in a similar fashion. Similarly, categorization

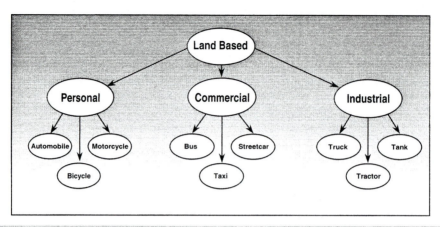

FIGURE 7-1 Example of Concept of Categorization

can allow for reasoning to a lower level of abstraction with greater detail, such as reasoning that if ground-based transportation used to transport people has wheels then cars must have wheels. Categorization allows for rules to be derived from the relationships among the categories.

Specific Rules
Another method humans use to reason is the application of known rules. If a particular rule, or set of rules, is known to exist and be true, then we can use that knowledge to reason our way through a problem context associated with the rules. For example, if we know that a red traffic light means that vehicles facing that light must stop and we know that failure to stop at a red traffic light will result in getting a traffic ticket (or worse), then we can reason that if the light is red we should stop (unless, of course, we want a ticket). Other rules used for reasoning are known as laws. Tax laws allow us to reason whether a particular expense is allowable as a deduction and, if it is, how much of it can be applied. Humans make use of rules by cascading them into a reasoning process that allows them to reach reliable conclusions.

Heuristics
We explored the topic of heuristics in Chapter 2, where we discussed decision processes. Heuristics provide yet another way in which humans reason. Such rules of thumb can be translated or captured for use. Examples such as "If the meal includes red meat, then choose the red wine" or "If the Chicago Bulls are playing at home, they will be favored to win" are heuristics that have been captured and framed as rules. Despite the lack of formality associated with a heuristic we know that searches and decisions using well-formed heuristics can often reduce the time necessary to reach a solution.

Past Experience
Reasoning by past experience incorporates components and activities from both categorization and heuristics. This method can be thought of as a metacategorization whereby humans look at the whole of a situation and attempt to compare it to situations they experienced in the past. If enough characteristics or sequences of events can be matched up, the necessary actions can be reasoned based on what was done in the

past. A common example of reasoning by past experience is found in the use of business cases as study tools in undergraduate and graduate courses. A business case recounts the activities of one or more people or organizations with regard to a particular situation. In addition to detailing the sequences of events and decisions made during the course of the situation, the business case offers the advantage of also being able to record the outcomes of the decisions and use the concept of "20-20 hindsight" to review the appropriateness of those decisions. Humans reason in exactly the same manner. If the current situation appears similar to a situation I experienced in the past, and I know what I did in that situation worked, I can reason that a similar action will be appropriate under the present conditions. Reasoning by this method makes some rather large assumptions—such as history will repeat itself and the present situation really is similar in most respects to the past situation. If these assumptions are valid, however, reasoning by past experience can be an effective decision-making method.

Expectations

One final method of human reasoning uses expectation. Once we experience a particular situation or phenomenon a number of times, we begin to expect it to appear in a certain manner or under a predictable set of conditions. If it occurs as we expect, then we can reason that all is well or that nothing is out of order. If, however, the situation fails to meet our expectations, we can reason that something occurred to change the expected set of conditions.

The people we see and work with every day have unique characteristics and traits that are displayed so regularly that we come to expect their presence. We often encounter a coworker who does not appear to act within the bounds of our expectations and we respond with observations such as "You are not yourself today," or inquiries such as "Is something bothering you today?" Reasoning by expectation is simply a form of pattern recognition. We expect a certain pattern and when it is not present, its absence triggers a series of events and inquiries to determine the reasons for the differences. Note that even though it is similar in nature, reasoning by expectation differs from that of past experience because our expectations are formed via repetitive interaction with a similar set of conditions. Past experience rarely involves multiple experiences of similar scenarios.

Each of these methods employed by humans during the course of reasoning can be framed in terms of rules or patterns that can be recorded in such a way that they can be automated or mechanized. This characteristic of human reasoning processes allows for the development of computers that "reason."

HOW DO COMPUTERS REASON?

The methods employed by AI system designers to create a reasoning system using a computer are based on the same processes and mechanisms used by humans. A designer programs a "reasoning" computer with a set of automated models that simulate each of the main reasoning approaches found in human cognition.

Rule-Based Reasoning

An AI reasoning system uses rules in much the same manner as we do. In fact, the most common form of expert system employs a technique known as rule-based reasoning, in which the computer is given the characteristics of the problem space in the form of input values. It then uses the rules contained within its knowledge base to methodically change the state of the problem space to the desired condition. Each rule is composed of two parts: (1) the operator that performs the state change, and (2) the conditions that determine when an operator may be executed. This rule composition takes the form of an IF-THEN statement as shown here:

IF condition **THEN** operator

If a condition is found to be logically true, then the operator becomes an acceptable action to take and the rule is said to have fired or instantiated. If the condition is logically false, then the operator is ignored and the next rule is accessed. This process continues until either the problem space reaches the desired condition or the rules in the knowledge base are exhausted.

Using a formal set of rules, several types of knowledge can be encoded. For example, inferential knowledge can be represented as rules. This type of knowledge is one whereby a conclusion is reached as a result of one or more premises (facts) being established.

IF premise(s)	**IF** road is under construction
THEN conclusion	**THEN** caution is necessary

A second form of knowledge that can be encoded in a set of rules is procedural knowledge. Here, the conditions take the form of a stated situation and the operator becomes an action to take when the stated situation is logically true.

IF situation	**IF** speed = 55 mph
THEN action	**THEN** issue speeding ticket

The action portion of a procedural knowledge rule can perform any relevant action including calling another rule to test the situation further.

IF situation	**IF** speed = 55 mph
THEN new rule	**THEN** check road conditions
IF situation	**IF** road is under construction
THEN action	**THEN** double speeding violation

A third form of rule-encodable knowledge is declarative knowledge. This form is constructed from antecedents and consequents. If the antecedent (condition portion of the rule) is found to be logically true, then the consequent (operator) must also be true.

IF antecedent	**IF** found guilty of speeding
THEN consequent	**THEN** driver must pay fine

Despite its similarity to human rule-based reasoning, rule formalism in an AI-based system is not without certain disadvantages. Foremost, as the number of rules within the knowledge base grows, the processing efficiency decreases unless some formal structure (such as grouping of rules) is imposed. In addition, it is difficult to encode explicitly static knowledge about objects using an IF-THEN construction. For that type of knowledge an AI-based system must use a different mechanism similar to the human cognitive activity of categorization.

Frames

The concept of frames was first proposed by Marvin Minsky (1975) as a logical extension of a knowledge encoding formalism known as a semantic net. In a semantic network, concepts or entities are represented as nodes and the arcs connecting the nodes represent their relationships. Figure 7-2 illustrates the concept of a semantic net.

The extension of semantic nets to frames created an object-oriented view that allowed knowledge to be partitioned into discrete structures having individual properties. These discrete structures, called slots, can be thought of as similar to fields in a database or categories in your mind. Collectively, the slots within a frame are used to describe the nature of the object stored within the frame:

> A frame is a data structure for representing a stereotyped situation like being in a certain kind of living room or going to a child's birthday party. Attached to each frame are several kinds of information. Some of this information is about how to use the frame. Some is what to do if these expectations are not confirmed. (Minsky, 1975, p. 211)

Frames are simply representations of stereotyped situations or objects that are typical of some category. Each category has certain characteristics that can be inherited by each member of the frame. Figure 7-3 contains an example of a portion of a frame representation for marketable securities.

In addition to slots, which represent the various attributes associated with the object frame, other component elements of frames are important to identify. For example, within each slot is contained one or more facets. These facets describe any data or specific procedures associated with the slot. Several types of facets exist including cardinality (single or multiple values), value type (numeric, text, logical, etc.), and allowable values. In addition, one important element in the frame system is the default value. If no attribute is directly assigned to a particular slot, then the default value is automatically assigned. For example, a frame for life insurance policies is likely to have a slot for "date_of_issuance." If this slot is empty when the frame is saved, then the default value may be the current date. By having default values for slots, the system is assured of always having sufficient information upon which to base a decision.

FIGURE 7-2 Example of a Semantic Network

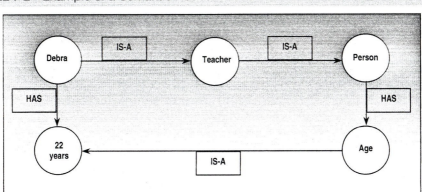

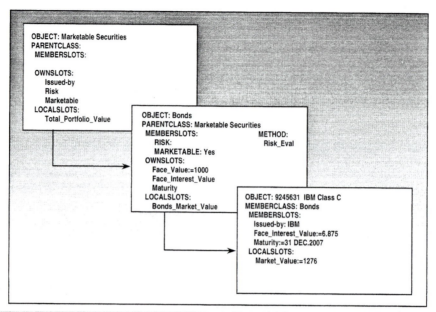

FIGURE 7-3 Example of Frame Hierarchy

Another important type of facet is called the daemon (pronounced "demon"). A daemon is a short procedure that can be triggered whenever a slot is created, modified, or even accessed. Three common daemons in a frame system are the following:

1. **If modified.** This procedure daemon will execute whenever the value of the slot is modified. A common use for this daemon is to record the date, time, and user identification associated with a slot modification.
2. **If deleted.** This daemon executes whenever a value is deleted from a slot. Uses for this procedure may be as with the "If modified" daemon or to prompt the user with a message box of some kind.
3. **If necessary.** This procedure may execute during a problem-solving session to supply some additional value that is needed but not existent in the frame.

The frame concept allows for two types of objects to be represented: classes and instances. As already discussed, objects represented by frames contain slot values that can be inherited down the frame hierarchy. The frame hierarchy is organized by two constructs: subclass links (IS-A) and membership links (INSTANCE-OF). The membership links serve as a classification mechanism and the subclass links serve as a taxonomic mechanism.

This mechanism of inheritance is subdivided into information types based upon the generalizability of the attribute. If an attribute can be inherited by any member of the class, it is stored in a member slot. The attributes associated with the specific object represented by a frame are stored in own slots. Finally, any existing attributes that cannot be inherited and must be only associated with that particular object frame are stored in a local slot.

It should be easy to see that the concept of frames is highly analogous to the human reasoning method of categorization. As with rules, however, frames are subject to limitations. Most notable among them is that frames allow for the representation of descriptive object-oriented information but are not particularly useful for storing information of a more situational nature. For these instances, AI-based systems employ a mechanism that simulates the human process of reasoning by past experience.

Case-Based Reasoning

Case-based reasoning is built on the premise that humans use an analogical or experiential reasoning approach to learn and to solve complex problems. The idea, much like its human counterpart, is to adapt solutions of similar problems to the problem at hand. The process of case-based reasoning involves two primary steps: (1) find those cases in storage that have solved problems similar to the current problem, and (2) adapt the previous solution(s) to fit the current problem context. Figure 7-4 contains a flow diagram of the solution structure in case-based reasoning.

One of the most critical steps in the process is the location and retrieval of one or more relevant cases from the case library. Through a complex set of case indices, cases that are most similar to the current problem can be searched and retrieved efficiently. Each potential case is compared to the present problem using a set of similarity metrics that measures the degree of similarity between the selected case and the current one. Once this process takes place, the contained solutions are analyzed and adapted to the new situation. The process of adaptation consists of a series of modifications to the parameters of the old solutions to fit the new problem context. Finally, the new solution is tested and, if successful, added to the case library. If, however, the test fails, then the adaptation process must be revised or a new set of cases must be retrieved.

Case-based reasoning is most useful in knowledge domains where precedence-based reasoning is appropriate. Domains such as medical diagnosis, audit, legal, and claims settlement commonly use case-based reasoning.

FIGURE 7-4   Nominal Process in Case-Based Reasoning

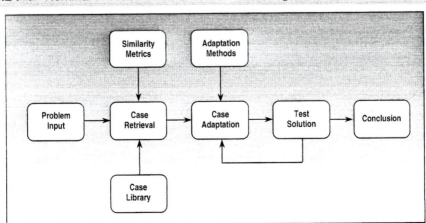

Pattern Recognition

This AI mechanism is most analogous to the human reasoning process of expectations. Pattern recognition includes both visual and audio patterns. As with humans, the degree to which a computer can exhibit intelligent behavior through a pattern recognition system is a function of its ability to perceive its environment and surroundings. If the computer is limited to keystrokes and mouse or trackball movements then its perceptual abilities are also limited to those realms. If, however, additional hardware and software allow the computer to detect sounds and to sense patterns or shapes, then entirely new possibilities for simulating intelligent behavior open up. Advanced pattern recognition systems can detect a specific human voice, a fingerprint, or even identify a person by his or her photographic or video image. Although early pattern matching mechanisms suffered from both speed and resource intensity issues, recent application of new programming algorithms increased pattern recognition reliability and practicality.

Rete Algorithm   One such recent development is known as the Rete algorithm. This algorithm for pattern recognition can handle pattern matching that involves several thousand working memory elements and rules without any severe resource requirements or unacceptable performance losses. This clever algorithm makes use of the fact that the contents of working memory do not change drastically after each rule application but rather exhibit only minor changes from the previous pass. Specifically, the Rete algorithm figures out which rules from the prior cycle did not fire, which rules from the prior cycle will not fire in the next cycle, and which rules from the prior cycle that did not fire will most likely fire in the next. Using this method, the algorithm avoids performing a pattern recognition cycle from scratch each time it must cycle through the rules. By maintaining an internal representation of the state of each rule in working memory, it uses that representation as the basis for repeating the cycle during each subsequent pass until the pattern is matched.

Currently, pattern recognition systems are being marketed to allow for voice-driven commands, voice dictation, computer-generated voice response, photographic analysis and pattern matching, and signature verification systems. This area of AI research has the greatest potential for impact on the design of tomorrow's expert systems.

OTHER FORMS OF ARTIFICIAL INTELLIGENCE

Although the expert system remains at the forefront of widespread application of AI-based systems, several other examples of AI investigation bear mentioning. They are not yet as well developed as the ES, but each has the potential to be a major contributor to the intelligent system of tomorrow. We will take a brief look at each of these developmental AI systems.

Machine Learning

Machine learning involves AI-based mechanisms that allow computers to "learn" from past experiences using examples and analogies. The outcome of machine learning results in a modification of the programmed behavior of the computer or one or more modifications to the stored knowledge the computer program is designed to act upon. Two well-known areas of machine learning research and application are neural networks and genetic algorithms.

Neural Networks   This branch of AI-based systems focuses on creating computer-based mechanisms that simulate the learning processes in the human brain. The human brain consists of thousands of networks of highly interconnected nodes called neurons. Each neuron performs a discrete computation at any given moment, the results of which are transmitted to other neurons along a neural pathway. A single human neuron can send results to as many as 10,000 other neurons in the form of voltages. These signals can either inhibit other neurons from sending signals or excite them into signaling to other neurons on the pathway. This process results in the storage of voltage in certain neurons and not in others. Through a repetitive process of firing and storing voltage, the human neural system learns and adapts to its environment.

In much the same manner, a computer-based neural net uses a series of interconnected mathematical processing elements, also called neurons, that look for patterns in a set of examples and learn from those examples by adjusting the weighted value of the neuron's connection to other neurons. This constant flux in interconnectivity produces specific output patterns much like the human brain. Training the neural net involves the input of numerous related examples followed by feedback on its success or failure in classifying them.

Genetic Algorithms   Originally proposed by John Holland while working at MIT in the 1940s, the term *genetic algorithm* (GA) applies to a set of adaptive procedures used in a computer system and based on Darwin's theory of natural selection and survival of the fittest. Following Darwin's suggestion that species adapt to changes in their environment in an effort to become more dominant, GAs "reproduce" themselves in various combinations in an effort to find a new recombinant that is better adapted than its predecessors. One major advantage to GAs is their ability to examine complex problems without any assumptions of what the correct answer or solution should be. GAs, already being used in conjunction with neural nets and expert systems, solve problems in areas such as scheduling, design, and marketing. We will explore GAs, neural nets, their components, and their application in detail in Chapter 9.

Automatic Programming
This area of AI investigation involves mechanisms that automatically generate a program to carry out some prescribed task. Using this approach, a person who is not a programmer can describe the nature of the task and the specific characteristics and behaviors the program should exhibit to the system without actually knowing how to write the program. The automatic programming software takes this description as input and generates the desired program. Currently, automatic programming is most often used in managerial settings for the generation of programs that produce various reports for decision making.

Artificial Life
Artificial life (AL or Alife) is the term used to describe a relatively new AI-based focus that studies "natural" life by attempting to re-create biological phenomena from scratch within computer-based systems. In contrast to the traditional analytic approach of the life sciences of "taking apart" living organisms to see how they work, AL attempts to "put together" systems that behave like living organisms. The potential for AL lies not only in the development of a better theoretical understanding of biological

phenomena, but also in the practical application of biological principles to other disciplines such as computer hardware and software design, robotics, spacecraft design, medicine, and many other engineering-related endeavors.

AI-based mechanisms such as AL, automatic programming, neural nets, and others stand to become extremely important contributors to the DSSs of tomorrow. When used in combination, such mechanisms could serve as the basis for a wide variety of sophisticated and powerful support systems for decision makers.

7-3: THE CONCEPTS AND STRUCTURE OF EXPERT SYSTEMS

The basic structure of an ES follows the generic structure of a DSS proposed and outlined in Chapter 1. The knowledge base, which is specific to the particular problem domain associated with the ES, is a separate and distinct component to the problem-solving algorithms that can be employed across several domains or tasks. The main difference between a DSS and an ES lies in the ES's containment of real knowledge acquired from experts in the application domain. In this section, we will focus on the component elements that define an expert system. Figure 7-5 illustrates the basic architecture of an ES.

THE USER INTERFACE

The advent of modern ES application generators allows us to see the relative importance of the user interface (UI). An analysis of the code generated to allow for user input, output, and control shows that more than 45 percent of it is directly associated

FIGURE 7-5 Common Expert System Architecture

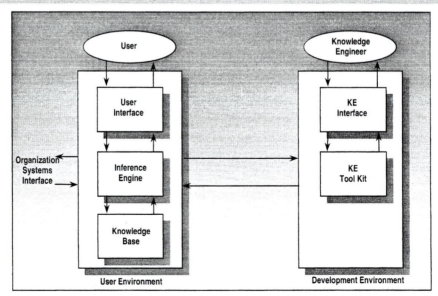

Source: Adapted from Klein and Methlie (1995).

TABLE 7-1   Issues Associated with Better ES Interface Design

- Users should be equal or dominant partners in the design of the UI.
- ES dialogs should be flexible enough to allow users to volunteer information and allow for smooth changes of initiative.
- Explanation facilities must be of high quality and detail.
- A natural language interface may not be appropriate for an expert system.
- ES dialogs should emphasize graphics over text wherever appropriate.

with the user interface of the ES. In addition, most of the up-front analysis and requirements gathering for a new ES design are associated with the human-machine interface functions. In short, the success or failure of an ES can often be attributed to the quality and functionality of its interface.

The focus on design of the UI is primarily on human concerns such as ease of use of the system, simplicity, reliability, error reduction, and the reduction of strain and injury-producing fatigue. The ES designer performs a constant balancing act as he or she maximizes the human concerns while addressing problems associated with storage capacity and hardware constraints. Berry and Broadbent (1987) reached several conclusions regarding the design of a high-quality UI for expert systems. Table 7-1 outlines these conclusions.

The design of the UI should allow for as great a variety of methods for interaction as possible. Such methods include input, control, and inquiry mechanisms that can be selected by the user depending on the particular situation, as well as the individual user preferences. Table 7-2 lists several of the available interaction methods that should be included in an ES interface.

THE KNOWLEDGE BASE

The knowledge base of an ES contains the domain-specific knowledge collected from the sample of domain experts during the design stage. This knowledge consists of all types of knowledge used by the domain expert during the course of solving domain-related problems: object descriptions and relationships, problem-solving behaviors,

TABLE 7-2   Interaction Mechanisms in Expert System Interfaces

- Touch screen
- User-assignable hot keys
- Function keys
- Mouse
- Trackball
- Touchpad
- Light pen
- Voice-activated commands
- Cursor control
- Menuing
- Image mapping

constraints, heuristics, and uncertainties. The success of an ES relies to a great extent on the completeness and accuracy of its knowledge base. An ES subject to incomplete, inconsistent, or inaccurate information in the knowledge base—no matter how efficiently the other components of the ES operate—will simply arrive at an incomplete or erroneous answer at an extremely fast pace.

A distinction must be made between the concepts of data and knowledge when discussing the content of an ES knowledge base. For example, if we are prepared to trust a clerk or an automatic process to collect the desired materials, then the materials in question are data. If, however, we must look to an expert to provide the desired material, then we are talking about knowledge. In other words, a collection of data representing facts is a database. The collection of an expert's set of facts and heuristics is a knowledge base. Unlike a database, a knowledge base contains information at a much higher level of abstraction. As already discussed, the knowledge base is the containment for the rules, frames, semantic nets, scripts, cases, and pattern-matching information necessary for problem-solving within the ES's knowledge domain.

THE INFERENCE ENGINE

If we think of the knowledge base as the brains of the outfit, then the inference engine (IE) becomes the brawn. Here, the processing in an ES occurs, and the knowledge is put to work to produce solutions. The inference engine performs deductions or inferences based on rules or facts. In addition, it is capable of performing inexact or fuzzy reasoning based on probability or pattern matching. The basic process of the IE is called a control cycle. Three steps characterize an inference control cycle: (1) match rules with given facts, (2) select the rule that is to be executed, and (3) execute the rule by adding the deduced fact to the working memory.

The operation of an IE is based on a famous rule of deductive inference known as modus ponens, which says that if A is true and A implies B is true, then B is true. Consider the following:

1. When Mark knows clothing is on sale, he always buys clothes.
2. Mark knows about the clothing sale at the mall.
3. Therefore, Mark buys clothes.

The counterpart rule of deductive reasoning, modus tollens, states that if we are given the implication that A implies B is true, and that B is false, then we can conclude that A is also false:

1. If the sun is shining tomorrow, then we will go swimming.
2. We will not be swimming.
3. Therefore, the sun must not be shining.

An IE uses two basic procedures for applying the two rules of deductive reasoning and for drawing appropriate conclusions: chaining and resolution.

Chaining

Chaining is a simple method used by most IEs to produce a line of reasoning. Using this method the set of rules is organized in a recursive manner so that a fact concluded by one rule is used as the premise for the next. Two types of chaining based upon the direction of the search process are possible in an ES: forward and backward.

Let's investigate how these two procedures work. Consider the following set of rules from a knowledge base:

Step	Rule Base	Workspace
(1)	R1: IF A and B THEN D	A, B
(2)	R2: IF B THEN C	D
(3)	R3: IF C and D THEN E	C, D
(4)		E

In forward chaining, the inference engine begins with the initial content of the workspace and proceeds toward a final conclusion through a series of inference control cycles. During each cycle, the IE searches the knowledge base for a rule whose premises match with the true facts contained in the workspace (step 1). Once found, the antecedent conditions of these rules can be considered as satisfied, the rules can be executed, and the deduced facts will be added to the workspace (step 2). The control cycle of match-choose-execute is then repeated, and additional facts are added to the workspace (step 3). Once the match cycle exhausts the candidate rules in the knowledge base the process ends and the workspace contains the conclusions drawn. This method of reasoning is also referred to as data driven because the process involves a movement from data to goals.

The second method of chaining, backward chaining, causes the IE to work backward from the goal to be proven to the necessary data within the workspace to prove it. Backward chaining can be thought of as a form of hypothesis testing in which the conclusion is proposed and then the data are "collected" to determine support for the hypothesis. Using the same knowledge base as before:

Step	Rule Base	Workspace
(1)	R3: IF C and D THEN E	C, D
(2)	R1: IF A and B THEN D	A, B
(3)	R2: IF B THEN C	

In backward chaining, the IE starts with goal E and then looks to the knowledge base to determine support for the goal. The IE finds that rule R3 concludes with goal E and selects that rule (step 1). Once R3 is selected, the IE can place its premises, C and D, into the workspace (step 2). The next control cycle proceeds to look first for a rule that concludes with C and then one with a conclusion of D. Through rule R1, the IE determines that for D to be true, A and B must also be true. Looking to the workspace, the IE finds A and B stored as true facts (step 3) and concludes support for D as well as C (via rule R2). Backward chaining is also referred to as a goal-directed search because the process starts with a final goal and works backward through the subgoals to the supporting data.

The choice to use backward or forward chaining depends on two primary factors: expert reasoning mode and efficiency. The way in which an expert reasons in a particular domain, the expert reasoning mode, can serve to dictate the appropriate process. If

---

TABLE 7-3 Examples of Backward and Forward Chaining

- ***Situation.*** You wish to fly from Washington, D.C., to San Diego. Unfortunately, all direct flights are booked, so you will have to accept a connecting flight if you are to get to San Diego.
- ***Backward chaining.*** You could check the flights arriving in San Diego and see which cities they are arriving from. Then you could look up the flights arriving in those cities and so forth until you find Washington, D.C.
- ***Forward chaining.*** You could check the flights departing Washington, D.C. and find their destination cities. Then look up the flights leaving those cities and so forth until you find a flight to San Diego.

Source: Adapted from Liebowitz (1990).

---

the expert normally uses problem reduction techniques as a search method, then backward chaining becomes appropriate. If, however, efficiency is an issue because of a large number of goals compared to the amount of input data or known facts, then forward chaining becomes more appropriate. Regardless of the technique employed, however, both methods allow for a logical path to be followed through a knowledge base and toward a satisfactory conclusion. Table 7-3 illustrates the use of both methods in determining the best way to fly from one point to another.

The Blackboard Workspace

The blackboard provides the ES user with an area of working memory to use as a workspace for the various components of the ES. It can be thought of as a sort of electronic scratchpad or notebook where calculations are performed and intermediate hypotheses and decisions are stored during the problem-solving process. Through the blackboard system, the ES can communicate candidate solutions or request additional input. For example, in the diagnosis of a trauma patient in an emergency room, the knowledge base of the ES includes all the rules and reasoning processes related to emergency room trauma treatment. The attending physician using the system enters all of the symptoms and vital signs of the patient into the ES. This initial information is stored in the blackboard. After initial rule selection and hypothesis testing, the ES may suggest that some additional tests be performed. These requests for information are also stored temporarily in the blackboard workspace. When the results of the additional tests are entered, the reasoning process continues until a conclusion is reached. Once the system completes its work, the blackboard area is "erased" and is ready for the next problem-solving session.

7-4: DESIGNING AND BUILDING EXPERT SYSTEMS

EXPERT SYSTEM SHELLS

During the 1980s, perhaps the greatest single challenge to AI research was the development of general-purpose tools for building expert systems quickly and inexpensively. Developers met this challenge by creating systems with reasoning mechanisms independent of the problem domain, which allowed a generic system to be employed with all the problem-specific knowledge contained within the knowledge base. These generic systems were called expert system shells.

One of the earliest successful ES shells was EMYCIN—a general problem processor oriented toward certain types of diagnosis problems. Also developed during this same period were two more generalizable ES shells called OPS5 and ROSIE. Both of these shells used forward chaining as their primary search technique and allowed the developer to create a set of program statements that described the flow of reasoning to be followed during a problem-solving session. Although quite cumbersome by today's standards, these shells made a giant step forward from previously programming an entire ES from scratch using LISP or PROLOG.

Modern ES shells typically contain two primary modules: a rule set builder and an inference engine. The developer uses the former to assist in constructing the initial knowledge base, and the latter serves as the vehicle for reaching conclusions. More recently, with the emergence of an integrated ES environment, a wide variety of knowledge management tools, such as hypertext, graphics, bulletin boards, and messaging, are incorporated along with the fundamental rule-based approach to create expert systems that go beyond the boundaries offered by more traditional systems. With each refinement, AI moves a step closer to the ultimate goal of a truly context-independent problem solver.

BUILDING AN EXPERT SYSTEM

A bit of creative daydreaming should convince you that the scope of managerial application for expert systems is virtually infinite. Despite this potential, however, the targeted nature of an ES requires that the scope and boundaries of its application be clearly identified prior to its design. One method for boundary definition is to identify the type of tasks the ES will be expected to perform. A typology of ES tasks is provided in Table 7-4.

Since the 1970s, several methods associated with the design and implementation of intelligent computer-based systems such as an ES have been proposed. Gerrity (1971) suggested that the key problems in the process were methodological rather than technological. Gerrity's approach to design emphasizes both a descriptive model of the system based on the identifiable system boundaries and a normative model based on the stated system goals and then tries to close the gap between the two models until a satisfactory and functional design is reached.

TABLE 7-4   A Typology of Expert System Tasks

- *Interpretation.* Use sensor data to infer situation descriptions and meaning.
- *Prediction.* Forecast from past and present the likely consequences of given situations.
- *Diagnosis.* Infer faults and malfunctions based on observation and interpretation of data.
- *Planning.* Design actions and plans to achieve stated goals.
- *Design.* Configure object specifications for satisfying particular requirements.
- *Prescription.* Prescribe remedies and solutions for malfunctions.
- *Monitoring.* Compare signals and observations to expected outcomes.
- *Control.* Govern overall system behavior.
- *Instruction.* Diagnose, prescribe, and guide user behavior.

Source: Adapted from Hayes-Roth, Waterman, and Lenat (1983).

In 1978, Keen and Scott Morton extended Gerrity's approach by suggesting that the first step in any intelligent system design must be the establishment of a sociopolitical climate for change and commitment. Once this commitment is achieved, success in the project depends on the identification of the ES problem and the seizing of the ES opportunity.

ES opportunities exist in a variety of locations and sizes throughout the organization. The key is for managers to develop an awareness of such opportunities. Managers not only must look for areas where an ES could serve to propagate scarce organizational expert resources but must also be tuned in to situations in which an ES might serve to enhance the role of an expert by providing necessary assistance. Such situations can free up a human expert to concentrate on other aspects of the job and thus improve productivity. In short, any activity where human experts are overburdened, undersupplied, expensive, or for the most part unavailable are prime candidates for an ES opportunity. Table 7-5 lists several such candidate situations.

PREDESIGN ACTIVITIES

The actual process of design and implementation of an ES is not unlike that of other forms of DSSs, or for that matter, other information systems. As such, we address the common analysis, design, and implementation components associated with all DSS development in Chapters 14 and 15. However, several activities unique to expert system development must be performed prior to formal design.

Finding the Experts

Probably the most important step in successfully designing an ES is the selection of the expert or group of experts that will contribute knowledge to the knowledge base. Logically enough, no expert—no expert system. It is important that the expert be clearly informed of the time commitment associated with the ES development effort. He or she must be willing to participate in the project from start to finish and to expend a significant amount of time and energy in its early stages. It is also important that the expert fully understands the value of the proposed system to the organization in terms of productivity, performance, and quality. At the same time, the system must be positioned to enhance the role of the expert rather than supplant it. An expert who is either unmotivated or threatened by the proposed system, or both, is unlikely to contribute usefully to its successful outcome.

TABLE 7-5   Candidate Situations for ES Opportunities

- Need for diagnosis of a problem situation or variance (audit, troubleshooting, etc.)
- Need to understand the nature of a given situation
- Need to predict the outcome of a current or future event
- Need to control or govern a particular activity or process
- Need to prescribe a solution or course of action
- Need to evaluate and assess a prior event or process

The Development Team

As stated previously, ES development shares a number of elements with other IS development projects, but it also presents some unique issues. Therefore, it is essential that the development team chosen to design and build the system be familiar with the realm of expert systems. The developers should have a functional understanding of the knowledge domain for which the ES is being built. In some cases, one or more members of the development team may also be serving as an expert in the construction of the knowledge base. Quite often, the team is divided early in the process into smaller groups that focus on specific aspects of the system. Some members of the development team will be assigned to the construction of the rule set, others will be focused on the user interface, while still others will play a unique role in the ES design process by serving as knowledge engineers (KEs). The KEs are team members who work directly with the experts to extract and organize the body of knowledge that must be contained in the knowledge base. This knowledge-gathering process is both complex and tedious and requires several unique skills on the developer's part. We will explore the issues associated with the knowledge acquisition and engineering process in the next chapter.

The Application Development Tool

In a conventional IS design project, it is not normally necessary to select an application development tool or language platform in the early stages of development. The focus must first be on the development of a logical model that describes "what" the system will do. The development language is more of a component of the physical solution that focuses on "how" we are going to do it. In the case of ES design, however, it is important that the development tools be determined early on. The iterative nature of prototyping, reviewing, and refining the ES during development makes the selection of the development tool an important predesign decision. The tool must complement the skills of the development team and must provide the appropriate functionality for the problem domain being modeled. Furthermore, the ideal tool can support a number of expert system projects rather than just the current one. In other words, the ideal development tool enhances the productivity of the development team while remaining both flexible and versatile.

Hardware Selection

Again, contrary to most other system development efforts, the selection of the ES hardware platform should be made prior to design. The selected platform must not only support the final ES product and allow for its growth but ideally it should support the selected ES development tool as well. In this way, the prototypes generated during the development process will perform in exactly the same manner in the final product, and no changes in functionality or performance will be incurred due to a change in hardware platform after development.

7-5: EVALUATING THE BENEFITS OF EXPERT SYSTEMS

Given the successful development and implementation of an expert system, a number of benefits can be realized. Their achievement, however, requires significant effort and can only be brought about if the system functionality expectations of the user are met.

Table 7-6 outlines eight basic criteria an ES user may consider in an evaluation of the new expert system's quality and functionality.

Assuming the system meets the criteria set out in Table 7-6 and is accepted by its user community, a number of significant operational benefits to the organization can, and do, emerge.

EXPERT SYSTEM BENEFITS

Increased Timeliness in Decision Making

Sometimes it seems that the availability of a given key piece of information is often inversely related to the immediacy of its need. Even though experts in virtually all knowledge domains are relatively abundant, they are rarely standing next to you, or are even in the same building with you when you need one. Expert systems serve as viable solutions to this problem in knowledge domains where expert advice and input are needed on demand. Unlike human experts, an ES can be on duty 24 hours a day and will never grow weary or become ill. Furthermore, depending upon the scope of knowledge covered by the ES, it can be simultaneously available to many different managers who require additional advice or expertise in related but distinct problem contexts.

Increased Productivity of Organizational Experts

Depending upon the nature of the knowledge domain, a resident expert's time can be in high demand. Because the demands on an organization's expert generally are not made in any prioritized fashion, it is often the case that while the expert is busy consulting with other members of the firm on an issue of moderate operational value, an issue of relative urgency is waiting for his or her attention. The introduction of an ES can offer useful input to those situations of less urgency and, thus, can increase the overall productivity of the resident experts by allowing them to focus on the most challenging organizational problems. Furthermore, this off-loading of day-to-day consultation activities can free up time for the expert to pursue activities of a more creative nature with associated benefits to the organization. Finally, the ability to replicate the ES at multiple organizational sites throughout the world allows for a cost-effective method for all managers to benefit from the input of an expert to their decision-making activities.

Improved Consistency in Decisions

Yet another expected benefit associated with an ES is the increased uniformity of input to decisions and, thus, the increased consistency in decision outcomes. An expert system does not suffer from the same biases and cognitive limitations as its human

---

TABLE 7-6 Criteria for Evaluation of an Expert System

- The system should be responsive and easy to use.
- The design and functionality should conform with current diagnostic standards.
- The system should be able to function with incomplete knowledge.
- The user should always control the consulting process.
- The explanatory facility should be clear and user-friendly.
- The knowledge base should contain generally accepted knowledge.
- The system should be independent of any geographical constraints.
- The system should allow for integration with all other current information systems.

counterpart and, therefore, cannot suffer from lapses of memory or attention to detail. Also, an ES lacks any form of political motivation that could enter into a human expert's analysis of a situation. Although such analysis is most likely still required, it is appropriately left in the hands of the decision maker and is separate from the foundational information used to guide the final decision.

Improved Understanding and Explanation

In much the same manner as a human expert, an ES can provide its user with an explanation for the line of reasoning used during the process of solving a problem. This ability allows the decision maker to critique the expert's thought processes and to decide on the validity (or lack thereof) of the rationale behind the conclusion reached. More often than not, however, the decision maker uses this explanation to further his or her understanding of how an expert arrives at a particular conclusion given a set of initial facts. This increased understanding of the details of a reasoning process can enhance the decision maker's understanding not only of the decision at hand, but of the overall domain knowledge as well.

Improved Management of Uncertainty

Experts must be able to cope with uncertainty in their analysis of a problem. The existence of uncertainty is ubiquitous in all decision-making contexts and an expert must be able to provide a degree of confidence in all advice given in response to a problem. Expert systems are also quite capable of dealing with the uncertainties of conclusions, and this characteristic is yet another way of distinguishing ESs from other traditional IS applications. The method by which an ES handles uncertainty is called fuzzy logic. We will explore this area of intelligent systems in conjunction with our focus on neural nets in Chapter 9.

Formalization of Organizational Knowledge

By incorporating the reasoning processes and rules used by an expert within a particular knowledge domain into an ES, an organization begins the process of codification of its knowledge. The very process of knowledge acquisition allows for a detailed inspection of the organization's approaches to problem solving and thus allows for a better understanding of how the organization's problems are actually solved. Long after the human expert leaves the organization, the knowledge acquired during the development process remains available to future managers as well as the next generation of experts.

PROBLEMS AND LIMITATIONS ASSOCIATED WITH EXPERT SYSTEMS

Despite their widespread acceptance and clear potential for benefiting an organization, expert systems have several limitations that must be acknowledged and dealt with. Table 7-7 lists several factors and problems that must be overcome with regard to ES design, deployment, and use.

In addition to the issues listed in Table 7-7, one should note that an ES is not infallible. Much like its human counterpart, it can and does make mistakes. Because the rule set is simply a model based upon the combined knowledge and reasoning processes of several experts and because each of those experts is subject to error, the ES is also subject to erroneous conclusions. In fact, because we are modeling knowledge rather than exactly mirroring it, the ES suffers from an even greater propensity

TABLE 7-7   Limitations Associated with Expert Systems

- The needed knowledge is not always available.
- Experts use common sense. Programming common sense is not yet a reality.
- Expertise is difficult to extract and encode.
- Experts can recognize a problem outside the knowledge domain much faster than an ES.
- Expert systems cannot eliminate the cognitive limitations of the user.
- An ES is functional only within a narrow knowledge domain.
- Expert vocabulary is often limited and not easily understood by others.
- Human experts adapt to their environments naturally whereas an ES must be explicitly updated.
- An ES has a limited sensory experience compared to human experts.

for error than a human expert. The XCON system, developed by Digital Equipment Corporation to assist sales representatives in assembling bids for complex computer configurations, is considered one of the most successful ES projects in industry. It is often used as an example of a fully developed, mature expert system. Yet, despite its fame and maturity, the XCON system is unable to fulfill about 2 percent of the configurations presented to it. The real question here is whether an organization can become comfortable with giving responsibility for solving complex problems to a computer program known to be fallible. As technology advances, however, these error rates are expected to decline, and the reasoning methods will significantly improve. Another method of identifying an expert system's limitations is to analyze each of the tasks commonly associated with an ES in relation to the specific difficulties encountered with each task. Table 7-8 uses the typology of tasks presented in Table 7-4 and lists several limitations associated with each.

COMMON EXPERT SYSTEM TECHNOLOGIES

Since the emergence of the expert system, its growth has been significant both in terms of numbers of systems and diversity of vertical market application. A section included at the end of this chapter lists and briefly describes many of the more popular and successful commercial ES deployments. Though not comprehensive, this list represents

TABLE 7-8   Limitations Associated with Common ES Task Categories

Task	Problems
Interpretation	Data may be noisy or missing.
	Data may be inaccurate.
Prediction	ES must allow for contingencies and uncertainties.
Diagnosis	Multiple symptoms can confound diagnosis.
Planning	Multiple alternatives with complex scenarios exist.
Design	Conflicting constraints and interaction exist among subdesigns.
Prescription	Multiple problems may exist.
Monitoring	Error conditions and nominal expectations are often context-specific.
Control	Often requires interpretation based on common sense.

the state-of-the–art systems and should provide you with a good start in exploring the diverse applications available through intelligent computer systems.

7-6: CHAPTER SUMMARY

The chapter illustrates the concept of the expert system and its primary method of creation, artificial intelligence. We focused on the significance of both subjects as they relate to the processes of decision making and problem solving.

We looked at the methods available to create a computer-based reasoning system through discussion of human reasoning processes, and we clarified the concepts and structure of expert systems. We also focused on the predesign activities associated with building an expert system. From this focus, we developed a greater understanding of the limitations associated with an ES and, therefore, how to evaluate it. In the next chapter, we will introduce the methods by which expert knowledge is "captured" and stored in an expert system.

Key Concepts

- The definition of expert system (7-1)

  A computer-based application that employs a set of rules based upon human knowledge to solve problems that require human expertise.

- The primary method by which an ES functions as an expert is through techniques developed in the field of artificial intelligence (AI). (7-1)

- AI is focused on understanding how people reason and think and then translating that understanding into computer systems that can perform the same actions. (7-2)

- Several specific reasoning processes used by humans are easily translated into the realm of expert systems and artificially intelligent computers: categorization, specific rules, heuristics, past experience, and expectations. (7-2)

- The methods employed by an AI system designer to create a reasoning system using a computer are based on the following processes and mechanisms: rule-based reasoning, frames, case-base reasoning, and pattern recognition. (7-2)

- The definition of machine learning (7-2)

  Machine learning involves AI-based mechanisms that allow computers to "learn" from past experiences using examples and analogies.

- Two well-known areas of machine learning research and application are neural networks and genetic algorithms. (7-2)

- The main difference between a DSS and an ES is in the ES's containment of real knowledge acquired from experts in the application domain. (7-3)

- The basic architecture of an ES associated with the user environment consists of the user interface, the inference engine, and the knowledge base. (7-3)

- Contrary to most other system development efforts, the selection of an application development tool or language platform and the selection of the ES hardware platform should be made prior to design. (7-4)

- If the expectations of the user in terms of system functionality are met, a number of significant operational benefits to the organization can emerge. (7-5)

- An ES is not infallible. Much like its human counterpart, it can, and does, make mistakes. (7-5)

Questions for Review

1. Define each of the following terms:
   expert system
   artificial intelligence
   facets
   daemon
   machine learning
   neural network
   knowledge base
   expert system shells
   blackboard workspace
   artificial life
2. What is rule-based reasoning?
3. What are frames? Describe how they work.
4. What is pattern recognition?
5. List and explain the different types of human reasoning processes.
6. What is the main difference between a DSS and an ES?
7. Describe the basic architecture of an expert system.
8. What part of an ES's architecture most often contributes to the success or failure of the ES?
9. Explain why it is important in the case of ES design to determine the development tools prior to design.
10. What are the benefits of expert systems?
11. Describe the problems and limitations associated with expert systems.
12. Discuss the criteria for evaluation of an expert system.

For Further Discussion

1. Choose a system using ES technology to support problem solving and describe its benefits and limitations.
2. What kind of organizations do you think most need to use the ES to help make decisions and solve problems? How does it help?
3. You are about to buy a car. Using a rule-based reasoning technique, describe how you make your decision.
4. Identify the differences between two well-known areas of machine learning research and application, neural networks, and genetic algorithms, and give some example systems of each.
5. Analyze the design of the user interface in an ES application. Discuss the reasons why you think it is a good (or bad) design.

Expert System Technologies Hall of Fame

DENDRAL (1965–1983)

The DENDRAL project was one of the earliest expert systems. DENDRAL began as an effort to explore the mechanization of scientific reasoning and the formalization of scientific knowledge by working within a specific domain of science, organic chemistry.

Another concern was to use AI methodology to better understand some fundamental questions in the philosophy of science, including the process by which explanatory hypotheses are discovered or judged adequate. After more than a decade of collaboration among chemists, geneticists, and computer scientists, DENDRAL became not only a successful demonstration of the power of rule-based expert systems but also a significant tool for molecular structure analysis, in use in both academic and industrial research labs. Using a plan-generate-test search paradigm and data from mass spectrometry and other sources, DENDRAL proposes plausible candidate structures for new or unknown chemical compounds. Its performance rivals that of human experts for certain classes of organic compounds, and it resulted in a number of papers that were published in the chemistry literature. Although no longer a topic of academic research, the most recent version of the interactive structure generator, GENOA, has been licensed by Stanford University for commercial use.

META-DENDRAL (1970–1976)

META-DENDRAL is an inductive program that automatically formulates new rules for DENDRAL to use in explaining data about unknown chemical compounds. Using the plan-generate-test paradigm, META-DENDRAL successfully formulates rules of mass spectrometry, both by rediscovering existing rules and by proposing entirely new rules. Although META-DENDRAL is no longer an active program, its contributions to ideas about learning and discovery are being applied to new domains. Among these ideas are the following: induction can be automated as heuristic search; for efficiency, the search can be broken into two steps—approximate and refined; learning must be able to cope with noisy (unfiltered or nonhomogenous) and incomplete data; and learning multiple concepts at the same time is sometimes inescapable.

MYCIN (1972–1980)

MYCIN is an interactive program that diagnoses certain infectious diseases, prescribes antimicrobial therapy, and can explain its reasoning in detail. In a controlled test, its performance equaled that of specialists. In addition, the MYCIN program incorporated several important AI developments. MYCIN extended the notion that the knowledge base should be separate from the inference engine, and its rule-based inference engine was built on a backward-chaining, or goal-directed, control strategy. Because it was designed as a consultant for physicians, MYCIN was given the ability to explain both its line of reasoning and its knowledge. Because of the rapid pace of developments in medicine, the knowledge base was designed for easy augmentation. And because medical diagnosis often involves a degree of uncertainty, MYCIN's rules incorporated certainty factors to indicate the importance (i.e., likelihood and risk) of a conclusion. Although MYCIN was never used routinely by physicians, it substantially influenced other AI research. MYCIN led to work in TEIRESIAS, EMYCIN, PUFF, CENTAUR, VM, GUIDON, and SACON, all described here, and to ONCOCIN and ROGET.

TEIRESIAS (1974–1977)

The knowledge acquisition program TEIRESIAS was built to assist domain experts in refining the MYCIN knowledge base. TEIRESIAS developed the concept of metalevel knowledge, which means that in addition to using knowledge directly, the system can examine it, reason about it, and direct its use. TEIRESIAS makes clear the line of reasoning used in making a diagnosis and aids physician experts in modifying or adding to the knowledge base. Much of this capability was incorporated into the EMYCIN framework. The flexibility and understandability that TEIRESIAS introduced into the knowledge base debugging process provided models for the design of many expert systems.

EMYCIN (1974–1979)

The core inference engine of MYCIN, together with a knowledge engineering interface, was developed under the name EMYCIN, or "Essential MYCIN." It is a domain-independent framework that can be used to build rule-based expert systems for consultation problems such as those encountered in diagnosis or troubleshooting. EMYCIN continues to be a primary example of software that can facilitate building expert systems and has been used in a variety of domains, both medical (e.g., PUFF) and nonmedical (e.g., SACON). The system has been widely distributed in the United States and abroad and is the basis for the Texas Instruments software system called Personal Consultant.

PUFF (1977–1979)

The PUFF system was the first program built using EMYCIN. PUFF's domain is the interpretation of pulmonary function tests for patients with lung disease. The program can diagnose the presence and severity of lung disease and produce reports for the patient's file. Once the rule set for this domain had been developed and debugged, PUFF was transferred to a minicomputer at Pacific Medical Center in San Francisco, where it is used routinely to aid with interpretation of pulmonary function tests. A version of PUFF has been licensed for commercial use.

CENTAUR (1977–1980)

The CENTAUR system was designed to experiment with an expert system that combines both rule- and frame-based approaches to represent and use knowledge about medicine and medical diagnostic strategies. For purposes of comparison, CENTAUR was developed for the same task domain as PUFF, interpretation of pulmonary function tests. CENTAUR performed well, demonstrating the effectiveness of this representation and control methodology.

VM (1977–1981)

The Ventilator Manager (VM) program interprets online quantitative data in the intensive care unit (ICU) and advises physicians on the management of postsurgical patients needing a mechanical ventilator to help them breathe. Although based on the MYCIN architecture, VM was redesigned to allow for the description of events that change over time. Thus, it can monitor the progress of a patient, interpret data in the context of the patient's present and past condition, and suggest adjustments to therapy. VM was tested in the surgical ICU at Pacific Medical Center in San Francisco. Some of the program's concepts have been built directly into more recent respiratory monitoring devices.

GUIDON (1977–1981)

GUIDON is an experimental program intended to make available to students the expertise contained in EMYCIN-based systems. GUIDON incorporates separate knowledge bases for the domain itself and for tutoring, and engages the student in a dialogue that presents domain knowledge in an organized way over a number of sessions. Using the MYCIN knowledge base as the domain to be taught, work in GUIDON explored several issues in intelligent computer-assisted instruction (ICAI), including means for structuring and planning a dialog, generating teaching material, constructing and verifying a model of what the student knows, and explaining expert reasoning. Although GUIDON was successful in many respects, it also revealed that the diagnostic strategies and some of the medical knowledge contained implicitly in the MYCIN rules had to be made explicit in order for students to understand and remember them easily, which led to the development of a new expert system, NEOMYCIN.

SACON (1977–1978)

SACON was implemented as a test of the EMYCIN framework in an engineering context. SACON advised structural engineers on the use of MARC, a large structural analysis program, and served as a prototype of many advisory systems.

MOLGEN (1975–1984)

The MOLGEN project applied AI methods to research in molecular biology. Initial work focused on acquiring and representing the expert knowledge needed to design and simulate experiments in the domain. This work led to the development of UNITS, described next. The second phase of research resulted in two expert systems, representing distinct approaches to the design of genetic experiments. One system used "skeletal plans," which are abstracted outlines of experiment designs that can be applied to specific experimental goals and environments. The other system was based on planning with constraints, in which planning decisions are made in the spaces of overall strategy, domain-independent decisions, and domain-dependent laboratory decisions, and the interaction of separate steps or subproblems of an experiment constitute constraints on the overall problem. These two systems were later synthesized into a third system, called SPEX. Current work, known as MOLGEN-II, is investigating the process of theory formation in molecular biology.

UNITS (1975–1981)

The frame-based UNITS system was developed in the MOLGEN project as a general-purpose knowledge representation, acquisition, and manipulation tool. Designed for use by domain experts with little previous knowledge of computers, it provides an interface that allows the expert to describe both factual and heuristic knowledge. It contains both domain-independent and domain-specific components, including modified English rules for describing the procedural knowledge. Stanford University licensed UNITS for commercial development.

AM (1974–1980)

The AM program explored machine learning by discovery in the domain of elementary mathematics. Using a framework of 243 heuristic rules, AM successfully proposed plausible new mathematical concepts, gathered data about them, noticed regularities, and, completing this cycle, found ways of shortening the statement of those hypotheses by making new definitions. However, AM was not able to generate new heuristics. This failing was inherent in the design of AM; related work on discovering new heuristics was done as part of EURISKO.

EURISKO (1978–1984)

A successor to AM, EURISKO also investigated automatic discovery, with a particular emphasis on heuristics, their representation, and the part played by analogy in their discovery. Several hundred heuristics, mostly related to functions, design, and simulation, guide EURISKO in applying its knowledge in several domains. In each domain, the program performs three levels of tasks: working at the domain level to solve problems; inventing new domain concepts; and synthesizing new heuristics that are specific and powerful enough to aid in handling tasks in the domain. EURISKO applications include elementary mathematics; programming, where it uncovered several LISP bugs; naval fleet design, where it won the Traveller Trillion Credit Squadron tournament; VLSI design, where it created some novel and potentially useful three-dimensional devices; oil-spill cleanup; and a few other domains.

RLL (1978–1980)

RLL (for Representation Language Language) is a prototype tool for building customized representation languages. RLL is self-descriptive—that is, it is itself described in terms of RLL units. It has been used as the underlying language for EURISKO and other systems.

Contract Nets (1976–1979)

The Contract Nets architecture is an early contribution to work on computer architectures for parallel computation. Recently, it received much attention in the literature on multiprocessor architectures for symbolic computation. In the Contract Nets architecture, problem solving is distributed among decentralized and loosely coupled processors. These processors communicate about task distribution and answers to subproblems through an interactive negotiation analogous to contract negotiation in the building trades: The "contract" is given to the processor that can handle the task at the lowest system cost, and failure to complete a task results in its reassignment to another processor.

CRYSALIS (1976–1983)

The CRYSALIS project explored the power of the blackboard model in interpreting X-ray data from crystallized proteins. The overall strategy was to piece together the three-dimensional molecular structure of a protein by successively refining descriptions of the structure. Although the knowledge base was developed for only a small part of the problem, the blackboard model with its hierarchical control structure proved powerful for solving such highly complex problems. Results from CRYSALIS are currently being incorporated in other KSL work and have contributed to improved models of control.

AGE (1976–1982)

The AGE (for Attempt to GEneralize) project sought to develop a software laboratory for building knowledge-based programs. AGE-1, the knowledge engineering tool that resulted, is designed for building programs that use the blackboard problem-solving framework. It can aid in the construction, debugging, and running of a program. A number of academic laboratories as well as industry and the defense community use AGE-1 for various applications.

QUIST (1978–1981)

QUIST combines AI and conventional database technology in a system that optimizes queries to large relational databases. QUIST uses heuristics embodying semantic knowledge about the contents of the database to make inferences about the meanings of the terms in a query. It reformulates the original query into an equivalent one whose answer can be found in the database more efficiently. Then conventional query optimization techniques are used to plan an efficient sequence of retrieval operations.

GLisp (1982–1983)

GLisp is a programming language that allows programs to be written in terms of objects and their properties and behavior. The GLisp compiler converts such programs into efficient LISP code. The compiler has been released to outside users, along with the GEV window-based data inspector, which displays data according to their GLisp description. GLisp is now being distributed from the University of Texas.

XCON (1980 to present)

XCON is probably one of the most famous of all expert systems due to its enormous success. Developed by Digital Equipment Corporation, XCON manages the complex process of configuring the variety of specifications associated with typical customer orders for Digital's products. Before XCON, the configuration of Digital's systems was performed manually by a team of highly skilled computer professionals. Despite their skills, the manual configuration process often resulted in configuration errors or incomplete orders. Following the installation of XCON, however, configuration orders attained an accuracy level of 98 percent compared with 65 percent using the previous manual system. Initial cost savings due to XCON were estimated to be in excess of $15 million with later estimates soaring as high as $40 million per year. XCON still operates today and remains one of the greatest single success stories in the history of expert systems.

8

KNOWLEDGE ENGINEERING AND ACQUISITION

Learning Objectives

◆ Understand the concept of knowledge engineering and how it is distinct from traditional IS development

◆ Compare a decision support system with an expert system

◆ Provide an overview of the methods and tools used in knowledge engineering today and a glimpse of how these will evolve in the future

◆ Understand the basis of knowledge and distinguish it from data and information

◆ Conceptualize the views of knowledge under three different perspectives: representation, production, and states

◆ Comprehend the sources of knowledge and be able to classify different types of knowledge

◆ Identify various methods of knowledge acquisition and management

ROBOTRADER AND CHRISTINE'S BRAIN BACKGROUND

In the early 1990s, the director of research at the British investment house Pareto Partners Ltd. started searching for technical partners to help Pareto automate the stewardship of at least some of the $17 billion in funds it manages. Because financial and military decision makers both face information overload and emotional stress, the partnership of Pareto and the Hughes Electronics Corporation—a missile maker, robot designer, and spy satellite pioneer—became an obvious match.

THE DEVELOPMENT OF ROBOTRADER

In 1993, Christine Downton, an experienced analyst within the trading markets for more than 20 years, flew out to Hughes Research Laboratories in Malibu, California, to "upload" her knowledge of the world's bond markets into a machine. The man at Hughes assigned to squeeze out Downton's experience was Charles Dolan, a systems developer with a doctorate in computer science from UCLA.

Dolan's approach to AI is a mixture of traditional symbolic logic and newer connectionist theories, which proceed from the assumption that intelligent behavior emerges out of an artificial "neural net." Dolan's view is that the two are part and parcel of each other—that within the brain's networks of neurons is this structure that embodies symbols. He tries to create such "knowledge spaces" on the computer, based on the symbolic structures laboriously built into the "wetware" of his willing subjects.

For this task, Dolan developed a system Hughes calls MKAT (Modular Knowledge Acquisition Toolkit)—software tools for extracting and encoding human expertise. MKAT has been used to "knowledge engineer" military skills such as how tank commanders plan an assault on an enemy position. Because knowledge engineering means cross-examining the

expert's thought processes, it often exposes charlatans. Christine Downton, however, is no charlatan. Although Dolan and his Hughes team were highly proficient at knowledge engineering, it still took 8 grueling sessions with Downton spread over 18 months to get a fair sample of those processes, with Dolan switching from tool to tool to try to mimic the complex trains of thought Downton often described.

The result is a set of 2,000 rules called the Global Bond Allocation Strategy. Using electronic market data feeds, the system takes in about 1,800 items of economic information, such as a country's public sector and current account deficits, inflation rates, money supply figures, and so on. After crunching through millions of permutations, it spits out conclusions as a series of recommendations, such as "sell holdings in Denmark and buy bonds in Germany." The recommendations are passed to a flesh-and-blood Pareto trader, who then makes the deals.

Pareto is devoted to a "quantitative" approach to trading whereby all the trading and investment is done using simplified models of what is happening, rather than feelings and theories about why. As such, it seemed natural for Pareto to turn to AI, and AI fit into the firm easily. Robotrader produces recommendations, as any of Pareto's other models do, for which its traders must then find the best market price. It does so at a far more sophisticated level, to be sure, but it fulfills the same basic function.

THE ROBOTRADER

So how has Robotrader performed? As of the end of 1997, Robotrader oversaw US$200 million worth of funds primarily in highly diversified portfolios with relatively low risk levels. The system produces returns of about 3 percent above a bond market benchmark—the kind of hard-working performance that large pension

(continued)

<table>
<tr><td colspan="2">╱ **DSS MINICASE** ╲</td></tr>
</table>

(continued)

funds seek. The returns are not stunning. But then, Robotrader isn't being asked to be stunning; the low risk levels are part of its (reprogrammable) parameters. And they are all the result of the program's own work. Downton resists any temptation to override the system's recommendations, especially when the markets are volatile.

Downton modestly says that no human could process the volume of information that the machine sucks up. She also believes that AI systems will one day lead to radical downsizing in the upper-middle ranks of the finance industry. The functions people perform and for which they charge huge margins will be picked off and automated. The Internet will hasten the process, delivering sophisticated services directly to the consumer. Downton and the rest of the Pareto-Hughes team believe that their artificial intelligence trading system, Robotrader, is one of the first concrete steps toward a shakeout of the financial industry precipitated by new technology.

—Yu-Ting "Caisy" Hung

Simultaneous to the development of the first expert system by Feigenbaum and his colleagues at Stanford came the emergence of a new role in systems analysis, the knowledge engineer (KE):

> The knowledge engineer practices the art of bringing the principles and tools of AI research to bear on difficult application problems requiring experts' knowledge for their solution. The technical issues of acquiring this knowledge, representing it, and using it appropriately to construct and explain lines-of-reasoning, are important problems in the design of knowledge-based systems. . . . The art of constructing intelligent agents is both a part of and an extension of the programming art. It is the art of building complex computer programs that represent and reason with knowledge of the world. (Feigenbaum, 1977, p. 1015)

Although the concept of knowledge engineering can be thought of as a special form of systems analysis, the goals of the two are nonetheless the same. Both knowledge engineers and systems analysts seek to create a thorough specification of an information system that can be successfully implemented. The process of knowledge engineering, however, differs in one key aspect from traditional IS development: The problem context of an ES is unique to the ES and seeks to emulate human expert problem solving. In this sense, each ES is a one-of-a-kind system, and its success is predicated on the skill of the KEs to extract information deeply hidden in the mind of a human expert. From this perspective, we can see that the KE needs to have a high degree of domain knowledge combined with a broad set of system development skills. We can also see why Feigenbaum calls knowledge engineering an art.

Gaines (1995) points out that expert system research is rightfully recognized as a significant contributor to information technology. Despite this contribution, however, it would be disappointing if, in common with many ventures in artificial intelligence research in the past, ES research fails to provide any insights into the nature of human knowledge processes. What is expertise? Why do we value it? How does it arise? What are the underlying social, psychological, and logical processes? What role does it play in the dynamics of the human species? The notion of expertise is central to the professions, career structures, the health care system, the educational system, and so on. It is at the core of how our society functions, and it is the basis on which individuals are valued in that society.

From the narrow point of view of information technology, computer and communications systems support the dynamics of expertise in our society even if they do not yet effectively emulate or replace expertise. A reasonable model of expertise would be valuable in the development of such technology, and various tacit models of expertise are implicit in existing developments. As technology develops and society changes, it would be useful to have an overall model of humanity that contains its processes and products. Such a model would provide some basis for understanding who we are; where we are going; the interplay of our psychology, culture, and technology; and their effect on personal, societal, and technical choices. This long-term objective assumes short-term significance as the goals of knowledge-based systems research advance from emulating the expertise of individuals to emulating that of organizations through enterprise modeling (Petrie, 1992).

In this chapter, we will explore many of the key issues and elements of knowledge engineering and acquisition as they relate to the design and development of an expert system. First, however, we must establish an understanding of the key constructs of knowledge.

8-1: THE CONCEPT OF KNOWLEDGE

Now, at the dawn of the digital era, we are constantly barraged with reports of the importance of knowledge and information and their role in the struggle for global competitive advantage and economic success. Drucker (1993) considers knowledge to be the key resource of tomorrow's organization:

> The knowledge society will inevitably be far more competitive than any society we have yet known—for the simple reason that with knowledge being universally accessible, there will be no excuse for nonperformance. There will be no "poor" countries. There will only be ignorant countries. And the same will be true for companies, industries, and organizations of all kinds. It will be true for individuals too. (p. 80)

Although the terms *data, information,* and *knowledge* are assumed to have common sense meanings, quite often their distinction is not well understood and, thus, they are inappropriately used interchangeably. If we are to engineer knowledge, we must be clear on exactly what it is we are engineering.

WHAT EXACTLY IS KNOWLEDGE?

We can look in any good dictionary and find definitions for the three primary constructs of human thought and reasoning, but to more fully understand how they relate to one another we must understand their evolution.

More than 12 millennia were required for humanity to evolve from oral to written communications. The early stages of this evolution were marked by the emergence of counting. As early as 3100 B.C., we find evidence of an evolutionary process beginning with notched-stick tallies and incised tablets and moving to abstract numerals, ideographic writing, and phonetic coding. Once revealed, writing dominated human communications for the next 4,500 years. By the middle of the fifteenth century, more than 30,000 books existed in Europe. By the year 1500, fewer than 50 years after the invention of the printing press, the number grew to more than 8 million books. At this dawning of the "age of growing abundance of data," we first see the importance of fully understanding the distinctions between the constructs of human thought and reasoning.

The scope of this section precludes a thorough identification and listing of the philosophical perspectives and definitions of data, information, and knowledge. As such, we will establish our definitions within the confines of this text and leave the debate surrounding the various nuances of meaning to those better equipped. For our purposes, we adopt the following definitions:

1. **Data.** Facts, measurements, or observations with or without context. An example of data without context is 60, 62, 66, 72. The same data with context might be the height in inches of Laura, Samantha, John, and Kristine, respectively. The validity and the effectiveness of data are determined primarily by the data's accuracy.
2. **Information.** Data organized in such a manner as to be useful and relevant to a problem solver in making decisions. The key criterion in evaluating information is its usefulness. Information can also be thought of as an event rather than an entity. As such, information "occurs" when a decision maker peruses and understands some structured collection of data.
3. **Knowledge.** The application of a combination of instincts, ideas, rules, procedures, and information to guide the actions and decisions of a problem solver within a particular problem context. In this sense, knowledge is an interpretation made by the mind. Success in explaining the interactions of the problem context is a key element in evaluating the validity of knowledge.

From the preceding definitions, two additional points can be inferred. First, information is personal. One person's information is another person's data. Second, knowledge is not static and, therefore, must change as the environment of the decision maker changes. Knowledge useful in one paradigm or historical era may be completely useless in another. As such, an ES is only useful when its knowledge base contains knowledge from the current paradigm. We could develop an ES to assist doctors during the Civil War in treating the wounded using the knowledge of that era, but its usefulness would be negligible in today's sophisticated medical environments.

KNOWLEDGE PERSPECTIVES

The branch of philosophy known as epistemology deals with the characterization of knowledge as an entity. Although a comprehensive analysis of the nature of knowledge from an epistemological perspective is far beyond our scope, we can nonetheless scratch the surface by reviewing a few basic concepts related to the knowledge construct.

For our purposes it will be helpful to understand the various perspectives regarding what knowledge is. In this regard, three predominant perspectives can be identified: (1) representation, (2) production, and (3) states.

Knowledge as Representation

This perspective of knowledge as an embodiment of a usable representation of some thing was advanced by Newell (1982). He suggested that if a system contains a knowledge representation, such as a model or rule set, of "something . . . , then the system itself can also be said to have knowledge, namely the knowledge embodied in that representation about that thing" (p. 89). It must be noted, however, that this perspective differentiates between the knowledge itself and the representation of that knowledge. The book you are reading is not knowledge but rather a representation of it. If you were unable to read the English language, then the symbols and patterns that serve to communicate such thoughts would be unusable by you and the representation of knowledge embodied in the book would also be useless. The point is that knowledge as representation is only of value if the form of representation can be understood and made useful.

Another important characteristic of this perspective is the distinction made between knowledge representation and the processing required to apply it to a given problem context. Newell suggested that "knowledge cannot so easily be seen, only imagined as the result of interpretive processes operating on symbolic expressions" (1982, p. 89). In other words, a system, such as a DSS or an ES, must possess not only the knowledge representations necessary to solve a particular problem but also the ability to process that knowledge in the form in which it is represented. Implicit here is the notion that each form of knowledge representation in a system will require a complementary knowledge-processing mechanism.

Knowledge as Production

Theorists holding this view see knowledge as a set of inventories in which items are transferred from one inventory to another based on process or external event. The production perspective suggests that learning is a form of knowledge production and that knowledge is "manufactured" as well as acquired. Here, we find the process of decision making to be fueled by knowledge stocks that are either held in reserve until needed or manufactured on demand. This highly metaphoric perspective, while limited in its ability to explain a number of cognitive behaviors, is nonetheless useful in conceptualizing the design of a computer system intended to support a decision-making activity.

Knowledge as States

The third way of viewing knowledge, offered by van Lohuizen (1986), regards knowledge as a set of six hierarchical states. Table 8-1 lists these six states in order of increasing relevance. Each knowledge state can be used to generate a different, more relevant state of knowledge. Problem-solving activities such as gathering, analyzing, evaluating, weighing, synthesizing, and selecting all play a role in the conversion of knowledge from one state of relevance to a higher state. Further, as the state of knowledge increases, the chance for information overload diminishes, extending the quality of the knowledge. The highest state of knowledge, the decision, implies an end to the process of state conversion and a realization of the objective or goal of the conversion process.

TABLE 8-1   The Six States of Knowledge

1. Data	**2.** Information	**3.** Structured information
4. Insight	**5.** Judgment	**6.** Decision

WHERE DOES KNOWLEDGE LIVE?

It will be helpful to this discussion to characterize the sources of knowledge available to the decision maker. Both internal and external sources of knowledge exist and are necessary to the generation of a successful solution product. Further, the acquisition of knowledge from external sources may be either active or passive; that is, knowledge can be acquired either through active communication and messaging between the decision maker and the environment or it may be acquired through simple observation and unobtrusive gathering methods.

Internal sources of knowledge are tapped through knowledge derivation activities. The decision maker must use the existing knowledge of the problem context as a basis for deriving new knowledge through inference, logic, or process of elimination. The decision as to which source or combination of sources to use in solving a particular problem is based on the limits of time, economic resources, and cognitive limitations associated with the problem context. In addition, the decision maker must assess the potential trade-off between the reliability of knowledge acquired internally or externally and the costs and cognitive strain associated with that knowledge. Although it may be easy and inexpensive to acquire a piece of knowledge, its reliability may be such that we may choose to expend greater resources to derive the knowledge needed.

A TAXONOMY OF KNOWLEDGE

Before we can move on to our primary topic of interest, the acquisition and management of knowledge in an ES, we must focus on one remaining issue: the classification of types of knowledge. Because not all knowledge is the same, a classification scheme is useful in both organizing the knowledge for storage and identifying the appropriate type of knowledge to apply in a given situation. To satisfy this need, we adopt the taxonomy of knowledge advanced by Holsapple and Whinston (1988). This classification identifies three primary and three secondary types of knowledge. Table 8-2 lists the types of knowledge within this taxonomy and several examples of each.

The three primary types of knowledge in the taxonomy not only serve as the fundamental inputs and processes associated with problem solving, but are also associated with the ability of a decision maker to recognize the need or opportunity to initiate decision-making activities. Procedural knowledge may be used to analyze descriptive

---

TABLE 8-2   Taxonomy of Knowledge Types

Primary
- *Descriptive.* Data, information, descriptions of past, present, and future situations
- *Procedural.* How to do something
- *Reasoning.* Codes of conduct, regulations, policies, diagnostic rules

Secondary
- *Linguistic.* Vocabulary, grammar, knowledge of gestures
- *Assimilative.* Permissible contents, retention cycles, relevancy filters
- *Presentation.* Modes of communication, graphing, messaging, inverse of linguistic knowledge

---

Source: Adapted from Holsapple & Whinston, 1988.

knowledge, and reasoning knowledge can be employed to either govern the analysis or determine the usefulness and applicability of its outcomes.

The secondary knowledge types can be thought of as peripheral influences on the core process of decision making. Each of the secondary types provides the decision maker with additional channels of inference and knowledge derivation that can "feed" the processes associated with the primary types of knowledge. Basically then, an effective decision maker (or an effective DSS) must be capable of managing each of the six types of knowledge.

8-2: KNOWLEDGE ACQUISITION FOR EXPERT SYSTEMS

The essence of knowledge engineering is the process of knowledge acquisition (KA). Here, knowledge is elicited from experts in a specific domain, gathered, organized, and formalized with the goal of transforming it into a computer-usable representation. The KA process is a complex one that requires a thorough understanding of the various channels and mechanisms for transfer of information from one human being to another. To date, of the numerous methods and approaches to KA offered, no completely generalizable method exists. In this text, we will explore the various steps and processes associated with the more common approaches in an effort to construct a usable prescriptive framework for KA. Figure 8-1 provides a graphical view of the psychological and computational foundations associated with knowledge engineering.

At the top left of the figure is the person regarded as capable of expertly performing some task in some domain. At the top right is the computer regarded as capable of emulating the performance of that task in that domain. The arrow from person to computer indicates that an objective of knowledge acquisition research is to support the required expertise transfer from the person to the computer. The lower portion of the figure illustrates the interplay between the tools employed by the KE and the psychological and computational models developed to represent the knowledge and process contained within the mind of the expert.

MODELING THE TASK

Regardless of the approach, most methods begin with the development of a model of the task or problem domain for which the ES will be designed and built. The primary functions of the task model are to fully define the task under study, assist in the selection of the expert(s), establish the user characteristics and performance criteria for the system, and function as an interpretive framework for protocol analysis of the experts' responses. The task model can be thought of simply as a general competence model of how a typical expert might perform the task or solve the problem of interest. The initial task model represents a decomposition of the task or problem into subtasks and a specification of the flow of control and information between the subtasks. As additional empirical data become available to the KE, the task model will be further developed from its first-order form.

In addition to the task model, a general domain description must be generated. This description, usually synthesized from domain-related reference documents or

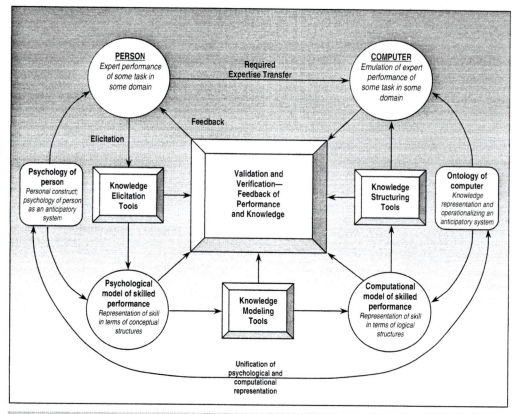

FIGURE 8-1 Conceptual Model of Knowledge Engineering Process

Source: Adapted from Gaines, B. R., and Shaw, M. L. G. *Knowledge Acquisition Tools Based on Personal Construct Psychology,* copyright © 1995, Knowledge Science Institute. Used with permission.

textbooks, consists of both the vocabulary of the domain and the relevant theories and methods associated with the domain. In addition, the general characteristics of the users within this domain must also be included in this description, along with the competence level of the users and their various roles within the task or problem-solving context. Finally, an evaluation of the potential costs and benefits associated with the development of an ES must be performed at this stage.

MODELING THE PERFORMANCE

Performance modeling utilizes models, hypotheses, and cognitive analysis techniques to elicit the real problem-solving knowledge from experts. This process typically occurs through protocol reporting, or verbalization by the expert. The KE elicits knowledge from the expert using verbalization schemes ranging from informal interviewing techniques to highly structured protocol schemes. Following each round of knowledge acquisition, a model of the knowledge is constructed and reviewed by the expert for clarity and accuracy. Any necessary modifications are made by the KE, and the process is repeated. The knowledge acquisition and performance-modeling process proceeds until all case situations identified within the problem space are "solved" from a protocol perspective. In other words, the KE continues until all detailed step-by-step traces of the expert's problem-solving behavior are verbalized and categorized within the problem space. We will explore the process of verbal protocol analysis in further detail shortly.

DIMENSIONS OF KNOWLEDGE ACQUISITION

Kim and Courtney (1988) proposed that knowledge acquisition methods be classified across two dimensions: strategic and tactical. Figure 8-2 illustrates the features of each dimension. As you can see, the strategic dimension focuses on the specific method that drives the KA process, whereas the tactical dimension determines the specific technique used to extract the expert's knowledge.

KE-Driven
Within the strategic dimension, knowledge engineer–driven acquisition is considered the most common approach. In this method, the KE interacts directly with the expert and seeks to model both the task knowledge and the performance knowledge about the domain. Good communication skills along with patience, persistence, empathy, and a reasonable level of intelligence are all important contributors to the success of this process. The primary KA techniques that use this approach include interviewing, protocol analysis, and the repertory grid method.

Expert-Driven
In this approach to KA, the expert encodes his or her own expertise and knowledge and enters it directly into the computer system. In effect, the expert serves two roles: expert and KE. Although the potential for loss of clarity exists (due primarily to the lack of an autonomous KE forcing clarification on key issues), this technique can be useful if the expert can assure the performance of the final model through some independent assessment method. Visual modeling is the primary technique used to construct domain models when using this approach. It allows the expert to visualize real-world problems and to manipulate their elements using a graphical entity representation.

FIGURE 8-2 Knowledge Acquisitions Dimensions

Source: Adapted from Gaines, B. R., and Shaw, M. L. G. *Knowledge Acquisition Tools Based on Personal Construct Psychology,* copyright © 1995 Knowledge Science Institute. Used with permission.

Machine-Driven

This field within AI focuses on machine learning (covered in greater depth in Chapter 9) and works to develop and refine machine-driven approaches to KA. The current technology explores the use of inductive inference engines to extract the knowledge from a set of example cases presented to the computer. The cases, their solutions, and the various attributes that were considered during the problem-solving activity are processed using a computerized algorithm designed to infer rules. Although still in its earliest stages of development, this method promises to be a significant contributor to the next generation of intelligent computer problem solvers.

KNOWLEDGE ACQUISITION TECHNIQUES

Hayes-Roth (1985) proposed that KA occurs in five general stages (see Figure 8-3). Each stage structures KE performance of certain activities and prepares the "deliverables" from that stage to be used as input in the next. For example, the requirements (output) from the identification stage become the input to the activities and processes within the conceptualization stage.

Figure 8-3 clearly illustrates the recursive nature of the general KA process. At the completion of an initial cycle of the process, a series of refinements, redesigns, and reformulations require the KE to revisit various stages of the process until all requirements and elements of knowledge are identified and correctly modeled. This process of recursion can be quite lengthy and tedious and requires constant attention to detail on the part of the KE if it is to be successful. It, however, ensures that the totality of the knowledge domain is captured.

FIGURE 8-3 Five General Stages of Knowledge Acquisition

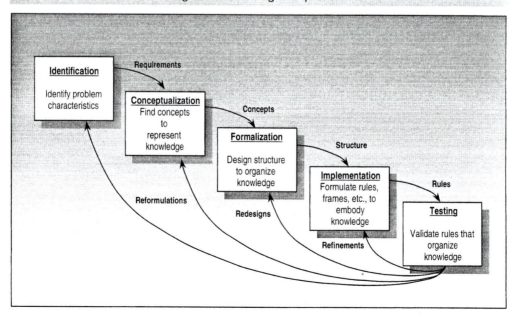

Throughout the KA process, the knowledge engineer must use a variety of elicitation techniques to gather the expert's knowledge. In the next section, we will explore the three most common techniques of the KE-driven approach.

Interviewing Techniques

The interview is probably the most widely used and familiar of all KA techniques. Although simple and relatively easy to perform, interviewing is as much an art as it is a skill, and it requires a significant amount of preparation in order to obtain useful results. From the wide variety of available interviewing techniques, two common classifications emerge: structured and unstructured.

Unstructured Interviews   This type of interviewing technique can best be thought of as normal conversation. The KE engages the expert in conversation with no specific objective or goal in mind and follows a line of inquiry that is driven primarily by the responses provided by the expert to previous questions. The KE may choose to prepare a list of topics to discuss but no formal preparation is performed. The essence of unstructured interviewing is a constant addressing and probing scheme. Topics are addressed either in a breadth-first or a depth-first manner, and then the KE uses probing questions to guide the conversation in whatever direction necessary to fill in the details of a particular dimension. This form of interviewing is best used in the early stages of KA and is essentially an exploratory pass at the knowledge domain in preparation for a more detailed analysis.

Structured Interviews   In contrast to the unstructured interview technique, structured interviews require a significant up-front investment in planning and organizing the topics to be discussed and the sequence and construction of questions to be used. Properly performed, structured interviewing elicits detailed insight into the expert's knowledge base and generates the necessary clarifications, explanations, justifications, and consequences for each case solution to be encoded into computer-usable form. The steps in structuring an interview include selecting and organizing topics, generating specific questions and lines of inquiry, and determining the relationships between the questions and lines of inquiry and the various case solutions under investigation. In this sense, structured interviewing becomes more of an interrogation than a conversation, with questions focused on specific pieces of information or lines of reasoning. Research shows, however, that the semantic construction of the questions (the way in which the questions are formed) asked of the expert can also have a significant effect on the efficiency of the process and the degree of accuracy of the response (Marakas and Elam, 1997).

General Interviewing Techniques   Regardless of the degree of structure chosen for the interview process, several basic tips and techniques can be employed. To begin with, the interviewer needs to start with a few boring but important points—the name and position of the person being interviewed, the date of the interview, the place of the interview, and the main subject of the interview. Also, he or she should try not to ask closed-end questions (ones that can be answered with a yes or no), particularly if the chosen interview approach is unstructured. Unless the objective of the question is simply verification of a previously obtained fact, the open-ended question form is preferable. Open-ended questions generally create a more uninhibited, "stream-of-consciousness" atmosphere that encourages greater detail in the expert's responses.

Whenever possible, questions should be phrased in a stand-alone manner by avoiding the double question: "Is this a step you commonly perform, and is it normal to do it in this way?" Generally speaking, the expert will tend to focus on the answer to the last question first and will not give a thorough answer to the first part of the compound inquiry. In addition, the interviewer should try to avoid framing questions as either leading or hypothetical. In the former case, a question such as "Do you agree that this is the most appropriate way to perform this task?" places the expert in a position of either providing a simple affirmative, thus limiting the level of detail in the response, or having to justify a negative response, thus placing the expert in an unnecessarily defensive position. In the latter case, a question such as "Suppose you didn't possess this level of knowledge—would you still be able to perform this task?" places the expert in a frame of mind that is, most likely, irrelevant to the task under study and, thus, yields little useful knowledge. Finally, as with any KA activity, the interviewer should take the time to plan ahead. Table 8-3 contains the common elements that should be included in a preinterview checklist.

Benefits and Limitations of Interview-Based KA Although interviewing remains the most common method of knowledge elicitation and provides many clear benefits, we must recognize its limitations as well. Interviewing is most effective in the early stages of KA, when the basic structures of domain knowledge are identified, and in the final stages, when the contents of the knowledge base are refined and finalized. The technique is less effective during the phases in which performance knowledge must be acquired. In general, information acquired through interviewing is inherently general, imprecise, incomprehensive, and often inconsistent. Because of the lack of common or definitive structure to the technique, the analysis of the information derived often poses problems. Finally, despite its advantages, interviewing is both time consuming and tedious. Regardless of these caveats, however, interviewing remains an important tool in the KA process.

Verbal Protocol Analysis

Most of the information necessary to model the knowledge of an expert is found in the cognitive processes he or she uses to solve a particular problem or perform a specific task. The true structure of that information is known only to the individual expert and is still beyond the understanding of even our most talented cognitive and behavioral scientists. Our challenge is that, in addition to retrieving that knowledge, we also need to structure it in a manner that is usable by a computer. This representation mismatch is one of the most difficult problems faced by the KE.

One method of KA used successfully to reduce the difficulties associated with representation mismatch is protocol analysis. A protocol is a record or some form of docu-

---

TABLE 8-3 Basic Preinterview Checklist

- Decide what you need to know.
- Ask yourself why this information is needed.
- Determine that an interview is the best method for obtaining this information.
- Determine the appropriate degree of structure for the interview.
- Consider the method by which the answers to your questions will be coded and analyzed.

mentation of the step-by-step information processing and decision-making behavior employed by an expert during a specific task. In most cases, protocols are recorded on audiotape while the expert is actually performing the task or while the expert visualizes its detailed performance. The KE then uses the transcriptions of the recordings to construct a rule set and an accurate performance model of the expert's actions and behavior. Several approaches can be used to collect the protocols including retrospective, introspective, interpretative, and concurrent. However, the concurrent approach, or "thinking aloud," continues to be the most popular and useful; therefore, we will limit our focus to this method.

A concurrent protocol is collected as the expert thinks aloud or verbalizes his or her thoughts while simultaneously performing a task. Figure 8-4 contains a set of eight task instructions given to an expert and the resulting verbal protocols obtained during the performance of each task.

Originally proposed by Ericsson and Simon (1984), this verbal protocol analysis can tap directly into the detailed process information contained in the mind of the expert and can closely reflect the true cognitive processes taking place:

> We claim that cognitive processes are not modified by these verbal reports, and that task-directed cognitive processes determine what information is needed and verbalized. . . . The performance may be slowed down, and the verbalization may be incomplete, but . . . the course and structure of the task-performance will remain largely unchanged. (p. 215)

Limitations of Verbal Protocol Analysis   As with any KA technique, certain benefits and limitations can be associated with this protocol. First, although verbal protocols do provide a dense trace of the expert's cognitive behavior, they do not provide all the necessary details for modeling, and, therefore, additional techniques must be employed. In addition, it is important that the setting for a concurrent protocol session be as close to the natural setting for the task as possible. Also, certain task conditions must be present for the concurrent session to yield useful results. Table 8-4 lists these necessary task conditions.

Finally, for a complete protocol to be obtained it is vitally important that no interruptions occur during the process. The KE should hold any inquiries of the expert until the verbalization is completed.

Repertory Grid Method

Kelly (1955) is credited with providing the KE with yet another powerful technique for knowledge gathering, the repertory grid method (RGM). Kelly conceived of humans as "personal scientists," each with his or her own personal model of the world. The scientist classifies and categorizes knowledge and perceptions and seeks to predict and control events by forming theories and testing hypotheses. Kelly refers to this conceptualization of human thinking as personal construct theory. Each personal scientist's model of the world is made up of individual personal constructs, and the RGM serves as a useful way to elicit and record them. Figure 8-5 illustrates Kelly's conceptualization of a typical repertory grid.

Using the RGM, the expert is presented with objects from the knowledge domain grouped into triplets. The expert is asked to compare the elements of each set to each other and identify one or more distinguishing features that separate any two elements

FIGURE 8-4 Sample Expert Task List and Protocols

1. First of all, write down the name of a subject or author of particular interest to you (a new name if this is the second time you are performing this task Now try to a book on this topic that you would find of interest and briefly write down the name of it.
2. You have heard that Isaac Asimov has written a book on Halley's comet. Check if it is in the library and if you find it, write down the title and location code.
3. Now check if Isaac Asimov has any books in the library from his Foundation series of books. If so write down the number of items in this series that the library keeps.
4. You want to find the UDC code on hazardous substances so that you can browse through the shelves on that and similar topics. Try to find a book on this subject and write down the code.
5. You are looking for a book on pop art, preferably a dictionary. If you find one that matches the description, what is the publisher's name and year of publication?
6. You receive a telephone message to find a book by Sidney Siegell on nonparametric statistics. What is the ISBN number of t his book?
7. For the book 'Fishes of the World,' check and write down how many copies have not been lent out.
8. You have a friend interested in music, decor and dolls. You want to buy her an encyclopedia on one of the topics but with n ot too many pages. Find a suitable book to buy for her.

Key:

?=user query	!=problem	=useful feature
@=assistance given	results of search= 7	achievement=50%

```
T1    Keyword'?
      Shorter versions'many
      ! Some words in German.
      ? How to get to next page.  Gave up 0%
T2    ?How to get back to main menu.
      ! Help not helpful.
      @Assistance given.
      Looked at TIPS
      _Suggested search by author.
      ! Wanted boolean to cut down
      Scanned list.
      Found details 100%
T3    Back to author list.
      _Able to step through details.
      _'v' to narrow search.
      Found book and checked number of copies.
      ! Didn't expect 'u' to get loan details.
      Found number copies of 100%
T4    ! Selected subject no. option but did
      not help to locate a UDC.
      _ Got keyword list.
      ! Selected numbers but delimited with '+'.
      _ Help useful.
      ! Pressed 'Enter' and lost search.
      Restarted search, got list and found subject code 100%
T5    ? Still not sure of option to get back.
      ? Wondered if can enter 2 keywords.
      _ Entered one and found item  100%
T6    Entered incorrectly spelled name.
      Couldn't find book.
      ! Entered 2 worded title but got long list based on one.
      Tried another word but gave up  0%
T7    Entered word in title.
      ? Confused by order alphabetical based strictly on first word.
      ! Pressed enter in error and exited search. Re-entered and
      found number of copies.  100%
T8    ? 's' didn't take to top level.
      ? Entered keyword but confused by context selection.
      ?  Difficult to distinguish book types.
      Entered word from title and got long list.
      ! Wanted to enter two words.
      Found book, partially satisfied  50%
```

TABLE 8-4 Necessary Task Conditions for Successful Concurrent Protocols

- The sample of cases employed must be highly representative of the task under study.
- Each task must have a clearly defined conclusion or point of completion.
- The task must be able to be completed in one protocol session.
- All data must be presented to the expert in a familiar form.
- A test case should be given to the expert prior to the collection of protocols so that he or she may become familiar and comfortable with the verbalization process.

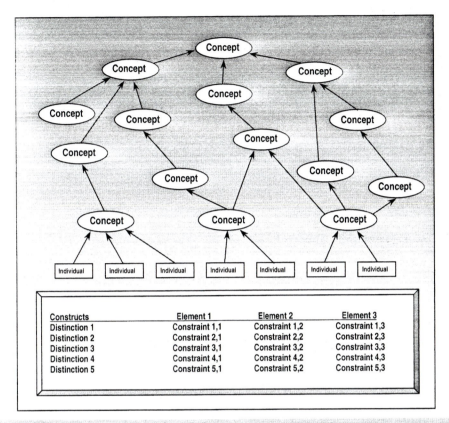

FIGURE 8-5   Typical Structure of a Repertory Grid

from the third. Each successive set is analyzed in this way until all object sets have been distinguished both within and across the entire set of objects. A numeric scale is used to identify the ranking or final grouping of each construct for subsequent analysis. After finalizing the grid, it can be thought of as a representation of the expert's personal model of the domain.

The RGM can also be used to infer similarities in construct beliefs held by multiple experts. Refer to Figure 8-5. Each distinction that may be made about individuals falling under a particular concept from within the grid will form the rows of a matrix; the individuals form the columns, and the constraints that apply to a particular individual relative to a particular distinction constitute the values in the matrix. In simple applications of the repertory grid, these constraints represent the values or beliefs of the individuals on the roles corresponding to the distinctions.

Figure 8-6 shows a basic repertory grid elicited from a geographer about spatial mapping techniques. The mapping techniques used as elements are listed as column names at the bottom. The poles of the constructs elicited are listed on the left and the right as row names. The ratings of the mapping techniques (on a scale of 1 to 9) along the dimensions of the constructs form the body of the grid. For example, "probability mapping" is rated 8 on the dimension "qualitative and quantitative–quantitative," which means that it is construed as primarily "quantitative." Note that the predicates

		1	2	3	4	5	6	7	8	9	10	11	12		
Qualitative and quantitative	1	8	8	6	9	1	9	8	8	9	4	4	4	1	Quantitative
Local	2	9	9	6	3	5	1	9	9	1	4	4	4	2	Global
Autocorrelation not considered	3	1	1	5	4	7	2	3	1	2	9	9	9	3	Autocorrelation considered
Doesn't honor datapoints	4	2	1	3	5	9	9	1	1	9	8	7	7	4	Honors datapoints
Multiple variables considered	5	9	9	9	9	9	9	9	1	9	9	9	9	5	One variable considered
Mathematical curve fitting	6	4	4	8	9	9	1	2	4	9	5	8	8	6	Doesn't fit mathematical curve
Nonparametric	7	9	8	6	1	1	3	6	8	3	8	8	1	7	Parametric
Interval or ratio data	8	9	1	1	5	5	1	1	1	1	1	1	1	8	Nominal data
Requires periodicities	9	6	6	9	9	9	9	1	6	9	9	9	9	9	Doesn't require periodicities
Doesn't fit a trend	10	9	9	1	1	8	1	7	9	1	6	1	1	10	Fits a trend to the data
Heavy computing load	11	7	6	7	8	9	4	4	5	3	1	2	3	11	No computing load
Assumes isotropic surface	12	1	1	4	3	8	9	1	1	9	7	6	6	12	Assumes anisotropic surface
Not as susceptible to clusters	13	8	8	6	9	3	4	7	8	5	1	2	2	13	Susceptible to clusters
Doesn't incorporate geologic model	14	2	2	3	1	9	1	2	2	1	6	6	6	14	Incorporates geologic model
Interpretive	15	9	9	5	9	1	7	9	9	7	3	4	4	15	Representative
Not very important	16	4	5	2	1	9	1	1	6	7	8	9	9	16	Very important
Not very effective	17	4	5	3	1	9	2	4	6	7	9	8	8	17	Very effective
Not widely used	18	3	8	7	5	9	3	3	4	6	2	2	1	18	Widely used
		1	2	3	4	5	6	7	8	9	10	11	12		

1 Probability mapping
2 Trend surface analysis
3 Distance weighted averaging
4 Proximal mapping
5 Hand contouring
6 Bicubic splines
7 Double Fourier series
8 Most predictable surface
9 Triangulation
10 Universal kriging
11 Punctual kriging
12 Nonparametric kriging

FIGURE 8-6 Example of Repertory Grid Analysis for Spatial Mapping Techniques

defined by the pole names may through their linguistic labeling indicate that they themselves are compounds of more primitive predicates. The grid provides the starting point for analysis and refinement, not necessarily in itself a conceptual structure but rather a set of data that must be accounted for by any conceptual structure developed. Techniques such as multidimensional scaling or cluster analysis can then be used to further analyze the grid and identify subtle similarities and differences among the constructs and their elements. The grid of Figure 8-6 is a typical one based on Kelly's original specification. Later developments allow structural relations between elements and between constructs to be specified, and the ratings to be extended to more complex constraints. Most recently, several computer programs were developed to automate the use of the RGM for knowledge-gathering activities.

Benefits and Limitations of the Repertory Grid Method   When a KE faces the task of modeling knowledge for a well-structured problem space, the RGM offers a good choice for elicitation. Domains requiring diagnosis, classification, elicitation of traits, and building of relationships are all appropriate candidates for the RGM. Grid techniques are not well suited, however, for problems of design and planning where unique solutions are derived from components of the problem (Klein and Methlie, 1995). The RGM does not lend itself well to the elicitation of either deep knowledge or performance knowledge.

MULTISOURCE KNOWLEDGE ACQUISITION

Up to this point, we discussed methods by which knowledge is acquired from a single expert. Although it is conceivable that a knowledge base could be effectively populated by a single "master of the domain," it is more likely that multiple sources will be necessary to fully acquire and model the reasoning processes and rules associated with a given problem context. This requirement becomes especially pronounced when the expertise needed for the development of an ES is not particularly well defined or when the development effort is intended to proliferate an expert resource in certain mission-critical environments. In these cases, KA activities must be conducted with multiple sources.

The processes and techniques described so far are applicable in a multiple-expert project, with several important differences. Most notably, a single expert eliminates the chance of unresolved ambiguity or difference of opinion. When multiple experts are used, conflicting views and opinions often arise, which must be resolved. Those conflicts are to be expected given the level of subjective reasoning and heuristics that exist in a typical knowledge domain. In addition, because experts may follow different lines of reasoning in solving a particular problem, this discord can manifest itself in the form of conflicting solutions to the problem. In an effort to minimize such situations, several methods can be used to integrate the knowledge from multiple sources. We will briefly review two of the more common approaches to integration.

Consensus

The techniques and facilities similar to those employed during group decision-making scenarios (see Chapter 5) can be used to achieve consensus among multiple experts in those areas where conflicting views exist. By providing each expert with the judgments and opinions of the others, each can review and revise his or her perspective based on this information. The consensus method may not be able to resolve all sources of conflict, but it is successful in a wide variety of scenarios.

Meta-Analysis

This technique takes a more statistical and quantitative approach than the consensus method and is most useful when expertise involves numerical values such as the assessment of probabilities. Here, the KE weights the individual assessments of the experts to develop a group probability. Also, numerous statistical methods in the domain of multiple-criteria decision making may be useful in resolving multiple-source conflict.

8-3: VALIDATING AND VERIFYING
THE KNOWLEDGE BASE

After capturing the needed knowledge, the KE must evaluate it for usability and accuracy. Two specific issues in this area are the validity of the knowledge and the verification of the knowledge base construction. In many cases, these issues can be addressed at the same time as other knowledge acquisition processes are taking place.

The terms *validation* and *verification* are often used interchangeably and inappropriately. Validation, as part of the evaluation process, focuses on the performance aspects of the knowledge base. In other words, validation looks at whether the system performs with an acceptable level of competence and accuracy. In contrast, verification addresses whether the system conforms to its original specifications. Verification answers the question "Did we build the right system?" Validation provides the answer to the question "Did we build the system right?" Although the process of verification simply involves comparing each of the original system specifications to the final implementation, the process of knowledge validation can involve a variety of tests and control tasks. Table 8-5 lists various validation techniques and measures that may be necessary in the final stages of KA.

It is important to note that a knowledge base can be logically correct without being valid. Validation measures how well the knowledge base conforms to the modeled knowledge domain. In this sense, validation of the knowledge base is a concept external to the system itself—it is an expression of the degree to which the system truly represents reality.

Validity of the knowledge base may be disproved in many ways. Experience, however, indicates three types of faults that primarily occur: (1) factual faults, where an assertion does not correctly represent its associated fact; (2) inferential faults, where a

---

TABLE 8-5   Knowledge Base Validation Measures and Techniques

- *Accuracy.* How well does the system reflect reality? How correct is the knowledge in the knowledge base?
- *Adaptability.* Possibilities for future development or changes.
- *Adequacy.* The portion of the necessary knowledge that is included in the knowledge base.
- *Appeal.* How well the knowledge base matches intuition and stimulates thought and practicability.
- *Breadth.* How well is the domain covered?
- *Depth.* The degree of the detailed knowledge.
- *Face validity.* How credible is the knowledge?
- *Generality.* Capability of a knowledge base to be used with a broad range of similar problems.
- *Precision.* Capability of the system to replicate particular system parameters. Consistency of advice and coverage of variables in the knowledge base.
- *Realism.* Accounting for the relevant variables and relations. Similarity to reality.
- *Reliability.* The frequency of system predictions that are correct.
- *Robustness.* Sensitivity of conclusions to model structure.
- *Sensitivity.* The impact of changes in the knowledge base on the quality of outputs.
- *Technical/operational.* Goodness of the assumptions, context, constraints, and conditions.
- *Turing test.* Ability of a human evaluator to identify whether a given conclusion is made by a real expert or a computer.
- *Usefulness.* How adequate the knowledge is (in terms of parameters and relationships) for solving problems correctly.
- *Validity.* The capability of the knowledge base for producing empirically correct predictions.

Source: Adapted from Marcot (1987).

rule does not correctly represent the domain knowledge; and (3) control faults, where the rules are contextually correct but exert an undesirable control behavior on the conclusion.

8-4: CHAPTER SUMMARY

To fully appreciate the complexities associated with capturing knowledge from experts and encoding it into a computer-based system requires a thorough understanding of the differences between the concepts of data, information, and knowledge. The knowledge engineer must be highly skilled in the process of extracting and organizing expert knowledge if the ES is to be successful.

It should be clear by now that the process of gathering and validating concrete expert knowledge is both a complex and time-consuming activity. To deepen our understanding of expert knowledge, in the next chapter we will shift our attention from general knowledge to a more specific focus on "fuzzy" or approximate knowledge.

Key Concepts

- Both systems analysts and knowledge engineers (KEs) seek to create specifications that will lead to the successful implementation of an information system. The process of knowledge engineering differs in that it seeks to emulate human-expert problem solving unique to a specific expert system.

- A KE needs to have a broad background in systems development, highly developed communication skills, and a high degree of domain knowledge.

- The expertise of individuals in different areas is central to the way society functions.

- Knowledge-based systems are moving from modeling the expertise of one individual to modeling the expertise of entire organizations.

- Distinctions among data, information, and knowledge (8-1)

  Data are facts, measurements, or observations with or without context.

  Information is data organized in such a manner as to render them useful to a problem solver in making decisions.

  Knowledge is the application of instincts, ideas, rules, procedures, and information to guide the actions and decisions of a problem solver within a particular context.

- Three dominant perspectives relating to knowledge are representation, production, and states. (8-1)

  Knowledge as representation

  If a system contains a representation of knowledge, such as a rule set or protocol, then the system itself possesses knowledge.

  Knowledge as production

  Learning is a form of knowledge, and knowledge is manufactured as well as acquired.

  Knowledge as states

  Knowledge can be viewed as a set of six hierarchical states: data, information, structured information, insight, judgment, and decision, in order of increasing relevance.

- Primary versus secondary types of knowledge (8-1)

- Knowledge acquisition (KA) encompasses all methods of gathering and organizing knowledge from experts in a specific domain. The ultimate goal is to translate this expertise into a form implementable by an expert information system. (8-2)

- A KE models the performance of the system by acquiring the practical problem-solving knowledge from experts through models, hypotheses, and cognitive analysis techniques. (8-2)

- Knowledge acquisition is classified by two dimensions: strategic, which explains the driving force behind KA, and tactical, which explains the specific technique used to extract the expert's knowledge. (8-2)

  The strategic dimension includes such methods as KE-driven, expert-driven, and machine-driven.

  The tactical dimension includes three techniques: interviews, protocol analysis, and repertory grid.

- KA generally is a five-step recursive process, as illustrated in Figure 8-3. (8-2)

- When obtaining knowledge from a group of experts, techniques such as consensus and meta-analysis are used to resolve conflicts and to account for differences of opinion. (8-2)

- After acquiring knowledge, a KE must validate and verify its accuracy and usability. (8-3)

Questions for Review

1. Compare knowledge engineering with traditional information systems development.
2. Differentiate among the terms *knowledge, data,* and *information.* Give an example of each.
3. Under the knowledge as representation perspective, what are the two critical requirements a DSS or an ES system must possess before solving a problem?
4. When knowledge is viewed as production, how are the banks of knowledge built upon or improved?
5. What are the six states of knowledge, and how are they transformed into more relevant states in the decision-making process?
6. What are some limiting factors in the information-gathering process?
7. Compare primary and secondary types of knowledge and describe how they are related.
8. What are the primary functions of the task model?
9. Define a *domain description.*
10. What is the primary vehicle for obtaining problem-solving knowledge from experts?
11. When does the knowledge acquisition and performance-modeling process end?
12. Compare and contrast the two dimensions of knowledge acquisition.
13. Compare KE-driven KA with expert-driven KA. Discuss the advantages and disadvantages of each method.
14. What kind of knowledge can be gained from open-ended questions compared with close-ended questions?
15. What is the objective of concurrent protocol analysis, and how does that analysis work?
16. What are the benefits and limitations of the repertory grid method of knowledge gathering?

17. How do the consensus and meta-analysis techniques of KA avoid conflict?
18. Define validity and verification in the context of the knowledge base.
19. What are the three primary challenges to obtaining valid knowledge?

For Further Discussion

1. Interview an expert in a discipline that interests you. Ask that expert to identify a decision he or she makes regularly and attempt to document his or her specific thinking process and assumptions in the decision-making scenario. Do you think a computer could be taught to consider and make this decision?
2. What are the benefits and limitations of structured versus unstructured interviewing techniques? Describe situations in which each would be the preferred technique.
3. Describe an area of personal expertise. How did you acquire your knowledge in this area?
4. Some people feel that expert systems will one day make expert knowledge in some areas a commodity. Explain how you agree or disagree with this claim.
5. Discuss reasons why expert knowledge acquisition and modeling are so difficult and complex.
6. Most experts have mixed feelings about the knowledge acquisition process and goals. Some are proud and honored to be acknowledged and mined as an expert, whereas others claim their decision-making processes are much too complex to model and mimic. As an expert, how would you feel if you were approached by a KE?

9
MACHINES THAT CAN LEARN

Learning Objectives

◆ Understand the types of problems that lend themselves to the application of machine learning systems

◆ Understand the basics of how fuzzy logic processing employs set membership and how linguistic ambiguity can be modeled

◆ Understand the strengths and limitations of fuzzy logic systems

◆ Understand the basic concepts and components of artificial neural networks and their structures

◆ Understand the strengths and limitations of neural computing

◆ Understand the basic components and functioning of genetic algorithms

◆ Be able to determine what type of intelligent system is best suited to different kinds of problems

DSS MINICASE

CHASE MANHATTAN BANK CREDIT SCORING SYSTEM

In 1985, Chase Manhattan Bank began a search for new quantitative techniques to assist senior loan officers in forecasting the creditworthiness of corporate loan candidates. Chase established a 36-member internal consulting organization called Chase Financial Technologies to oversee the development of pattern-analysis network models for evaluating corporate loan risk.

The resulting models, called the Creditview system, perform 3-year forecasts that indicate the likelihood of a company being assigned a Chase risk classification of good, criticized, or charged-off. In addition to the overall forecast, Creditview provides a detailed listing of the items that significantly contributed to the forecast, an ES-generated interpretation of those items, and several comparison reports.

Creditview models run on a Chase Financial Technologies host computer. A user system resides at each user's PC and communicates with the host through telephone lines. In addition, conventional financial statement analysis may be performed using Chase's Financial Reporting System, an independent financial spreadsheet and analysis package. The Financial Reporting System also resides on the user's PC for access to a company's standard financial statements.

The "secret" to the success of Chase's analysis systems lies with an embedded pattern-analysis technology for constructing a hybrid neural network based on sufficient high-quality historical data. Each hybrid net represents a separate "model" produced by the pattern-analysis module. The PLCM (Public Loan Company Model), the first model implemented at Chase, derives from Chase's extensive loan history of large, publicly traded companies and their past financial data. (Chase's client base contains both publicly and privately owned corporations.) The historical data analyzed by the pattern-analysis module to produce forecasting models consist of a large collection of data units. Each data unit contains as much as 6 years of consecutive financial data for a particular company, corresponding industry norms, and the company's status 3 years after the last year of data. (The last of the 6 years is called the "year of the data unit.") The data unit's status is the company's rating—G stands for good, C stands for criticized, and X stands for charged-off. The system uses these data to construct a large set of candidate variables that may or may not indicate a company's future financial condition. These variables become the basis for forming patterns.

A pattern is fundamentally a statement about the value of a particular financial variable or set of variables. A simple pattern may have the following form: C1, V1, C2, where V1 is a financial ratio or variable and C1 and C2 are constants. For example: 1.75, quick ratio, 2.00 could be a simple pattern. Typically, patterns are more complex; several elements of this kind are combined by using *and, or,* and *not.* This example could be one of a small complex pattern:

$$C1 < V1 < C2$$
$$V2 < C3$$
$$C4 < V3 < C5 \text{ and } C6 < V4 < C7$$
$$C8 < V5 < C9$$

where all the Cs are constants and Vs financial variables or ratios. Candidate variables are arranged into thousands of complex patterns and analyzed by the system to produce an optimal set of variables and patterns that form a pattern network called the Forecaster. The criteria for selection of patterns are as follows:

- **Score.** The score (as observed in the historical data) measures the ability of the pattern to differentiate between the

(continued)

⟨ **DSS MINICASE** ⟩

(continued)

categories good, criticized, and charged-off—in other words, the ability of the pattern to classify correctly.

- **Complexity.** Complexity is a measure of how complicated the pattern is (in terms of number of variables), simple patterns within it, and the amount of historical data it satisfies.

- **Spuriousness.** A measure of the likelihood that the pattern's score (how well it predicts) is due solely to chance.

These statistics are used to evaluate the predictive power of the patterns and to ensure that whatever predictive power is uncovered is not by chance. To each pattern and status a probability (called the "precision") exists that a data unit corresponding to the pattern will have that status. The system uses a proprietary network-balancing technique that selects the patterns for the network to maximize precision and minimize bias.

The benefits of this system to Chase are obvious. Chase can now identify the strengths and vulnerabilities in the financial structure of an obligor and forecast the impact of these factors on the firm's financial health 3 years into the future. The savings associated with being able to "predict the future" are a key element in the longevity of Chase Manhattan Bank.

Source: Adapted from NIBS Pte, Ltd. (1996), www.singapore.com/products/nfga.

The advent of the digital computer brought with it a general misconception that the majority of information processing at any given moment in our world is being carried out by an automated device. The ubiquitous nature of the computer allows us to forget about the most complex and powerful information processing device on earth: the human mind. If we look at cybernetics and other disciplines that form the basis of information science, we see that the true nature of information processing is rooted in the actions of living creatures as they struggle to survive and adapt to their environments. Viewed in this light, the information being processed by today's computers accounts for only a small part of the total. Therefore, we can begin to seriously consider the development of information processing devices that mimic the structures and operating principles found in humans and other living creatures.

One of the new multidisciplinary fields of research—neural computing and the development of artificial neural networks (ANNs)—evolved in response to the attractiveness of digital information processors that can simulate the human brain's potential for solving ill-structured business problems. Neural computing involves processing information by means of changing the states of networks formed by interconnecting extremely large numbers of simple processing elements that interact with one another by exchanging signals. This interconnection approach to information processing directly simulates the way the human brain processes information and learns. This chapter will introduce the concept of machine learning by focusing attention on specific methods such as neural computing and genetic algorithms and will discuss numerous applications and domains in which such systems play an integral part.

Up to this point, we successfully developed an understanding of how knowledge can be modeled as rules and relationships contained within the traditional notions of set membership and, thus, stored within the digital realm. As a preface to our focus on machine learning, however, we need to develop a better understanding of the way the human brain actually works. The world of human thought and reasoning is characterized by vagueness, linguistic ambiguity, and fuzzy descriptions.

9-1: FUZZY LOGIC AND LINGUISTIC AMBIGUITY

Fuzzy logic is a relatively recent alternative to the traditional notions of set membership and logic, with their origins in ancient Greek philosophy and applications at the leading edge of AI research (Brule, 1985). Fuzzy logic is a method of reasoning that allows for the partial or "fuzzy" description of a rule. Combining this approach to reasoning with the realm of digital processors results in a class of computer applications that can "learn" from their mistakes and can "understand" the vagaries commonly found in human thought.

LINGUISTIC AMBIGUITY

Our language is replete with vague and imprecise concepts. Sometimes a rule is clear-cut, and sometimes it is difficult (if not impossible) to describe things in terms of well-defined distinctions. Take, for example, the phrase "Dan is very tall," or the phrase "It is extremely hot today." Statements such as these are commonplace in our daily interactions and are representative of a reasoning process of measurable complexity. Yet the translation of these statements into ones of "greater precision" often causes them to lose some of their semantic richness and meaning. For example, the statement, "The current temperature is 97.65 degrees Fahrenheit" does not explicitly state that it is hot, and the statement "The current temperature is 1.1 standard deviations above the mean temperature for this geographic region at this time of the year" is also fraught with many linguistic difficulties. Would it still be hot today if the current temperature were 1.099 standard deviations above the mean? Do I need to know precisely where I am in the world to determine whether it is hot today?

The point is that our language evolves to allow for the conveyance of meaning through semantic approximation rather than precise content. We are quite comfortable with adjectives of categorization that describe intelligent people, midsize automobiles, tall buildings, and powerful computer systems, among many others. This method of categorization enables our expression of general terms and allows us to interpret these generalizations based on the context in which they are made. Although quite useful to humans, these context-based meanings do not lend themselves to the common rule-based or case-based codification schemes necessary for an expert system knowledge base. Fuzzy logic, however, is quite adept at supporting reasoning about these kinds of situations because it focuses on gradation rather than precise distinction.

The kinds of categorizations we often use to describe something do not have precise boundaries. Rather, the categories often encompass a range of values. For example, the term *highly skilled* encompasses a range of values that is context-specific. If the context is a group of elementary school students playing baseball, and one of the young students tends to hit the ball farther than anyone else, she may be referred to as "highly skilled." If, on the other hand, this same student were to be placed in a major league baseball game, the term highly skilled (as it directly relates to her) would no longer be applicable. The "truth" of these categorizations can be thought of as varying much like a light does with a dimmer switch. A switch completely off indicates 0 percent agreement concerning the categorization. A switch completely on means 100 percent agreement; but the switch allows an infinite number of gradations in between.

If we think of the world in terms of the degree to which something is a member of a category or set we can see how fuzzy logic could be used to express many problem contexts. A verbal protocol obtained from the operator of a production line might come in the form of "When the line gets near capacity, I begin to slow the feed." Converting this statement into a set of precise rules could prove problematic, if not impossible. With fuzzy logic, however, rules such as these are completely acceptable and quite easy to accommodate.

THE BASICS OF FUZZY LOGIC

Fuzzy logic is based on an approach to logic that dates back to the days of Plato. Its primary distinction from the early conceptualizations of the world by Aristotle and others is that it defines truth to be a value that is contained within the range of values [0.0, 1.0] with 0.0 representing absolute Falseness and 1.0 representing absolute Truth. It is important to note that fuzzy logic does not mean vague answers but, rather, precise answers that vary mathematically within a given range of values. Fuzzy logic can deal with any degree of precision from the input data and can react just as precisely in returning the results.

Rather than carry around a lot of mathematical baggage, however, let's develop our understanding of fuzzy logic using a commonplace example. Consider the phrase "Dan is very tall." From this phrase we can infer that a subset of all people classified as tall exists, and Dan is contained within that subset. Further, we can infer that Dan is considered an extreme value within the subset of tall people because his membership within the subset is further qualified by the adjective *very*. By formally defining the fuzzy subset TALL_PEOPLE, we can answer the question "to what degree is person x tall?" We must assign a degree of membership in the fuzzy subset TALL_PEOPLE to every member of the set ALL_PEOPLE. The easiest way of defining the set is by creating a membership function based on a person's height. Figure 9-1 illustrates this membership function and shows the shape of a graph of the derived function.

Using the derived membership function for the fuzzy subset TALL_PEOPLE, we can compute values that represent the degree of tallness for any member of the set ALL_PEOPLE. Table 9-1 contains some tallness values for a sample of people drawn from the set. A "precise" mathematical value for degree of tallness is assigned to each person sampled. Using this approach, a rule for determining tallness could be constructed in the form of a "tallness algorithm" that could be contained within a knowledge base for an ES. By developing a network of these algorithms, a complex set of categorizations can be analyzed and a high level of reasoning can be brought to bear on a given problem context. This process is the essence of fuzzy logic reasoning in the development of expert systems and the focus of this chapter: machine learning.

It is important to note, however, that membership functions are rarely as simple as the one used in our example. Often, they involve degrees of membership in multiple subsets based on multiple criteria. For instance, a membership function for the subset TALL_PEOPLE may depend not only on physical height but on chronological age as well ("He's tall for his age"). In fact, it is not uncommon for a particular membership

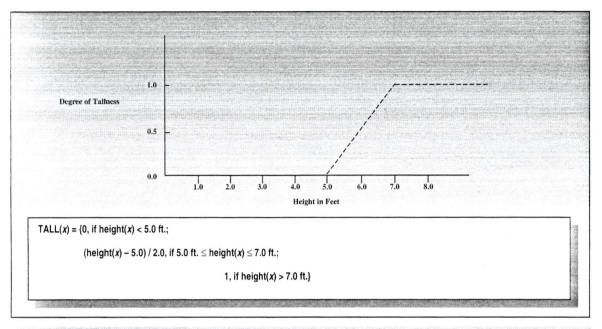

$$TALL(x) = \{0, \text{ if height}(x) < 5.0 \text{ ft.;}$$

$$(\text{height}(x) - 5.0) / 2.0, \text{ if } 5.0 \text{ ft.} \le \text{height}(x) \le 7.0 \text{ ft.;}$$

$$1, \text{ if height}(x) > 7.0 \text{ ft.}\}$$

FIGURE 9-1   Membership Function for Inclusion in Subset TALL_PEOPLE

function to contain elements from a wide variety of criteria and populations. The complexity of such functions is significant and requires a deep level of understanding in sophisticated mathematical concepts to be fully appreciated. This level of understanding is best left to the computer scientists who will build these systems for use by the managerial community. Important here, in the realm of management, is the notion that fuzziness can be codified and that the linguistic ambiguities so commonplace in human interaction can be modeled and systematized in an intelligent computer system.

FUZZINESS VERSUS PROBABILITY

Before we move away from the concept of fuzzy logic, one last point needs clarification. A confusion sometimes arises between the concept of fuzziness and that of probability. Both operate over the same continuous numeric range and at first glance have similarities in the interpretation of their values: 0.0 representing False (or nonmembership)

TABLE 9-1   Sample Values Obtained from Tallness Function

Person	Height	Degree of Tallness
Tom Thumb	2′10″	0.000
Mugsy Bogues	5′3″	0.125
Albert Einstein	5′5″	0.208
Thomas Edison	5′10″	0.417
Michael Jordan	6′6″	0.750
Kareem Abdul-Jabbar	7′2″	1.000

and 1.0 representing True (or membership). However, some fundamental differences between fuzziness and probability are significant.

To fully understand these differences, consider, again, our statement "Dan is very tall." Let's assume that by using our membership algorithm, we assign a degree of tallness value to the statement of 0.80. From this, we can render the statement symbolically as follows:

$$m\text{TALL\_PEOPLE}(\text{Dan}) = 0.80$$

where m is the membership function operating on the fuzzy subset of TALL_PEOPLE.

From a probabilistic approach, we might interpret the degree of tallness value to mean "There is an 80 percent chance that Dan is tall." Conversely, the fuzzy logic approach would yield a statement corresponding to "Dan's degree of membership within the set of tall people is 0.80." The semantic difference between these two statements is critical. The first statement supposes that Dan is or is not tall; it is just that we have only an 80 percent chance of knowing which set he is in. By contrast, the fuzzy statement supposes that Dan is "more or less" tall. In other words, probability deals with the likelihood that something has a particular property, whereas fuzzy logic deals with the degree to which a particular property is present in something. In the former, we are guessing about the presence of a property; in the latter we are assuming the presence of a property and comparing its strength relative to all other members of the set. With probability, we can only determine membership in a set, but with fuzzy logic, we can determine where on the continuum of membership a particular set member resides.

ADVANTAGES AND LIMITATIONS OF FUZZY LOGIC

A truly beneficial aspect of rules is that they allow you to state relationships generally and compactly, as associations (Dhar and Stein, 1997). On the other hand, they do not require you to be as precise as mathematical models, which is good because we know that the complexity of a system increases when variables begin to interact in a non-linear fashion. The acknowledged modern-day "father of fuzzy logic," Lotfi Zadeh, suggested that "as complexity rises, precise statements lose meaning and meaningful statements lose precision." Fuzzy rules offer an attractive trade-off between the need for accuracy, compactness, and scalability as reasoning systems and processes within a particular knowledge domain become more complex. Fuzzy rules generalize the concept of categorization because, by definition, the same object can belong to any set to a certain degree and can belong to multiple sets as necessary. In this sense, fuzzy logic eliminates the problems associated with borderline cases: where the value 1.1 causes a rule to fire but the value 1.099 does not. The net result is that fuzzy logic tends to provide greater accuracy than traditional rule-based systems when continuous variables are involved. In this section, we explore the key benefits derived from the use of fuzzy logic along with identifying several limitations to its use that must be both acknowledged and understood.

Advantages of Fuzzy Systems

Fuzzy logic systems are utilized in a wide variety of applications and can be found in many facets of business and society. Their use in microprocessor-based appliances and products is pervasive, proving their value beyond doubt. Regardless of the application or context, fuzzy logic offers several generalizable advantages and benefits over traditional rule-based logic.

Modeling of Contradiction   Fuzzy logic allows for the modeling and inclusion of contradiction within a knowledge base. Fuzzy rules can be completely contradictory and yet exist in complete harmony. Compared to traditional logic where opposing instructions would result in an inability on the part of the computer to resolve the contradiction, fuzzy logic imparts a certain degree of tolerance to such ambiguities and thus, compromise is allowed. For example, by allowing for membership in multiple sets, a 6-foot-tall person might be simultaneously assigned a degree of membership in the set TALL_PEOPLE of 0.80, a degree of membership of 0.45 in the MEDIUM_PEOPLE set, and a value of 0.01 in the SHORT_PEOPLE set. Using fuzzy logic, the designer exercises complete control over the accuracy of a given conclusion or reasoning process by simply increasing or decreasing the number of rules required and the degrees of sensitivity to membership allowed.

Increased System Autonomy   The rules contained within the knowledge base of a fuzzy system can function completely independently of one another. In a traditional rule-based system, if a single rule is faulty, it can result in outcomes ranging from erroneous conclusions to complete inability of the system to resolve. In a fuzzy system, however, one rule could be faulty and the others will "compensate" for the error. Fuzzy systems actually change the common trade-off relationship between system robustness and system sensitivity. Unlike conventional rule-based systems, properly constructed fuzzy systems actually increase in sensitivity as the robustness of the system is increased. Fuzzy rules will continue to "work" even in circumstances where the whole system is completely changed.

Limitations to Fuzzy Systems

Despite its advantages, fuzzy reasoning presents certain limitations to both the KE and the end user. Its application cannot be construed to be universally better than traditional reasoning methods and, as with all forms of problem-solving strategies, it must be carefully assessed in terms of its appropriateness to a given problem context.

Obstacles to System Verification   Fuzzy reasoning can become an obstacle to the verification of a system's stability or reliability. Under situations of high complexity, it may become impossible to know whether the correct rules are firing. Further, the redefinition of membership associated with fine-tuning a fuzzy system has no set guidelines or prescriptions that are easily followed. As a result, designers may find it difficult to determine whether their actions improve the system or result in a move away from a better solution. One response to this limitation is the use of simulation in the verification of a fuzzy system. Results of multiple simulations can be used to analyze small refinements in set memberships and their relative sensitivities to outcomes derived from the system.

Fuzzy Systems Lack Memory   Basic fuzzy reasoning mechanisms cannot learn from their mistakes and possess no memory. As such, fuzzy logic is not yet capable of optimizing the efficiency of a system. Presently, no precise mathematical method allows for the verification of the correctness of a fuzzy system. Furthermore, the high degree of complexity of a given situation that can be modeled using fuzzy reasoning can result in a literal simultaneous firing of rules. This phenomenon is referred to as *fuzzy set saturation,* which means that the fuzzy set gets so full of inferences that consequent fuzzy sets are overloaded. The end result is that the entire system loses the information provided by the fuzzy rules and the entire fuzzy region begins to "balance itself" around its mean value. The answers to this constant retention of all rules and inferences and the problems of saturation are being addressed by developing systems that can learn from their mistakes and can "learn to forget" information that is no longer applicable to the problem context. Such systems are the focus of our next topic in this chapter: neural networks.

9-2: ARTIFICIAL NEURAL NETWORKS

Artificial neural networks (ANNs) were first proposed in the early 1940s at the University of Chicago as an attempt to simulate the human brain's cognitive learning processes. Their ability to model complex, yet poorly understood, problems for which sufficient data can be collected make ANNs particularly applicable in numerous domains such as business and finance. Their capacity to learn can result in solutions that are superior to those achieved using traditional statistical or mathematical methods.

ANNs[1] are simple computer-based programs whose primary function is to construct models of a problem space based upon trial and error. Conceptually, the process is easily described: A piece of data is presented to a neural net. The ANN "guesses" an output and then compares its prediction with the actual, or correct, value presented as a form of feedback. If the guess is correct, then the network performs no further action. If, however, the prediction is incorrect, then the network analyzes itself in an effort to figure out which internal parameters to adjust to improve the quality of the prediction. Once these adjustments are made, the net is presented with another piece of data and the process is repeated. Over time, the ANN begins to converge on a fairly accurate model of the process.

FUNDAMENTALS OF NEURAL COMPUTING

To better understand how the ANN "learns" from experience, we must begin with an understanding of the biological principles that underlie both human neural processes and artificial neural computing.

The Human Brain

The basic processing element in the human nervous system is the neuron. Our nervous system is made up of a network of these interconnected nerve cells that receive information from various sensors—our eyes, ears, skin, and nose—that are positioned at various places along the network. Figure 9-2 provides a simple representation of a single human neuron and its component parts.

As shown in the figure, the human neuron is composed of a nucleus and connectors called dendrites that are responsible for providing input signals to the neuron and

---

[1]The terms *artificial neural network, neural network, network,* and *net* will be used interchangeably throughout this chapter.

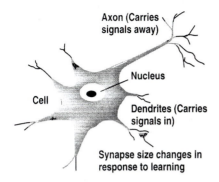

FIGURE 9-2 Typical Human Neuron Cell

axons, which, in turn, carry away the output of the neuron to other parts of the network. The transmission of signals from one neuron to another occurs at the neural synapse via a complex chemical process in which specific substances, called neurotransmitters, are released from one side of the synaptic junction. The effect is to raise or lower the electrical potential inside the body of the neuron. If the electrical potential within a specific neuron reaches a certain threshold, a pulse is sent down the axon and the neuron cell is said to have "fired." These bursts of electricity that occur when a neuron fires transmit information along the network to other neurons. Conceptually speaking, the larger the burst of electricity at the synapse, the more important the information contained within.

Information received at a neuron can have one of two effects: It can either excite the cell or it can inhibit it. If the neuron is excited, it will immediately fire and pass its information along the network to the other neurons. If the neuron is inhibited, however, it will not fire, in effect suppressing the flow of that information along the network. Through this process, each neuron processes the incoming raw input and then determines whether it is important enough to pass along.

The synaptic connections that exist among the neurons can be strengthened or weakened as a result of the passing of time or the gaining of experience. Strengthening of the connection results in learning, whereas the lack of use of a connection over time results in forgetting. This dynamic process results in the establishment of new responses to new stimuli, modifications to existing stimuli, and the complete removal of unused responses.

Putting a Brain in a Box

Following a biological metaphor, the ANN involves an interconnected system of nodes called neurodes that are associated with one or more weighted connections that are equivalent to human neural synapses, inside the memory of a digital computer. The ANN is constructed of multiple layers with the connections running between the layers. Figure 9-3 shows a simple ANN.

As shown in the figure, the ANN is composed of three basic layers. The layer that receives the data is referred to as the input layer and the layer that relays the final results of the net is called the output layer. The internal layer, also referred to as the hidden layer, is where the processing and transformation of the input signal take place and where the type of output signal is determined. The hierarchical network dynamics among the neurodes are determined by a mathematical combination of the weight of

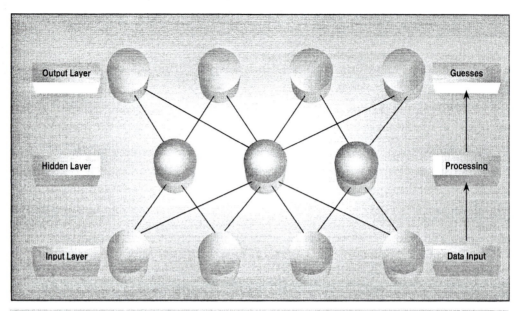

FIGURE 9-3 A Typical Artificial Neural Network Configuration

each input to the neurode and the threshold parameters associated with that neurode. Each pass of the net causes adjustments to these weights in response to the feedback received by the net regarding the accuracy of its last output. Over time, these weight adjustments increase the accuracy in the transformation of the input data. Learning, in a neural network, results from this adjustment of weights.

Inside the Neurode

Figure 9-4 illustrates the component parts of a typical neurode. The basic structure consists of a set of weighted input connections, a bias input, a state function, a nonlinear transfer function, and an output connection. We will explore each of these primary components and their functions in greater detail.

Weighted Inputs   As shown in the figure, each of the inputs to a neurode is a connection from a lower layer of the network. The neurode can, and usually does, have multiple inputs, each with its own associated weight or importance. In the figure, we depict the relative weights of each of the inputs by varying the thickness or style of the line representing that input. The thickness of the line is proportional to its weight or importance. A hollow line indicates a negative weight. The weight of an input determines the importance of its contribution to the output of the neurode. Because all of the weights are added together inside the neurode, the more important inputs will be those with larger weights and the lesser contributors will be those with the smaller weights.

The Bias Input   The bias input is not normally connected to the network and is assumed to have an input value of 1.0 for the state function. Its purpose is to allow for the individual adjustment of the firing threshold of the neurode to facilitate the final adjust-

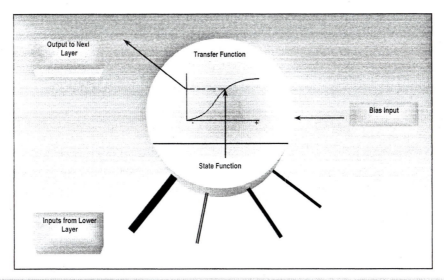

FIGURE 9-4   Typical Neurode Component Structure

ment of the ANN following the learning process. Under normal circumstances the bias input is not used and its value to the state function remains a constant throughout the network. If, however, the need for adjustment of a specific neurode becomes necessary, the bias input for that neurode can be set within a range of 21.0 to 1.0 to allow for the appropriate "bias" in the transfer function.

The State Function   The state function, although conceivably a mathematical algorithm of any form or complexity, is typically a simple summation function. Its purpose is to consolidate the weights of the various inputs to the neurode into a single value that can be passed to the transfer function for processing. The value obtained by the state function determines the degree of impact the combined inputs will have on the transfer function and, thus, on the final output of the neurode. Figure 9-5 illustrates this process.

The Transfer Function   As implied by its name, the primary purpose of the transfer function is to serve as the vehicle by which the summed information is passed on as output. It performs this function, however, in a rather unique manner. Refer to Figure 9-5 and note that the value of the output (and ultimately the threshold at which the neurode will fire) is not linear with respect to the summed inputs. The transfer function acts metaphorically like a dimmer switch for turning the neurode on and off.

Note that in the figure we depict the transfer function in the shape of the typical logistic function. The logistic function is characterized by its "lazy S-shaped" form. Transfer functions can be either continuous (as shown in the figure) or discrete (such as a series of "on" or "off" ranges of values) and can take any appropriate mathematical form. Although the logistic function is the most commonly used, another popular transfer function is the radial basis function, which takes on a more bell-shaped form. The important issue, here, is that the transfer function must contribute a sense of nonlinearity between the summed inputs and the resultant output.

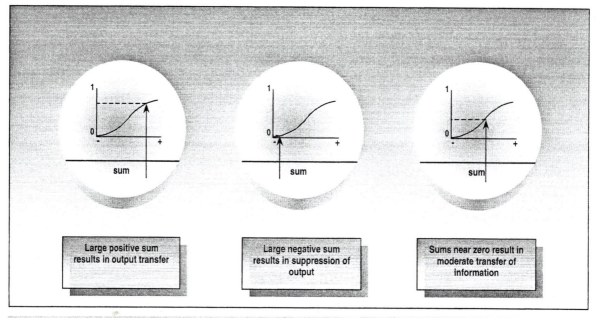

Large positive sum results in output transfer

Large negative sum results in suppression of output

Sums near zero result in moderate transfer of information

FIGURE 9-5 Relationship Between State Function Value and Transfer Function Value

TRAINING THE ARTIFICIAL NEURAL NETWORK

The process of training a neural net to associate certain input patterns with correct output responses involves the use of repetitive examples and feedback, much like the training of a human being. The operation begins by setting all of the connection weights in the net to small random values, which allows the net to begin with no specific "memory" or imprint. Next, the net is presented with a single data example drawn from a training set with known outputs. The net processes this example and then provides a "guess" at the answer based on the example provided.

As you can probably imagine, the first guess provided by the net is usually incorrect because the weights for each of the input connections are not yet set correctly. However, just as humans can learn from their mistakes, so can ANNs. Once the example data are processed, the ANN compares the results of its calculations with the feedback received regarding the desired, correct output and records that comparison in a training record. If the calculation performed by the net compares favorably with the feedback, then no action is necessary. If, however, the guess is deemed incorrect when compared to the feedback, the net begins an iterative process of making small adjustments to the input weights of certain neurodes in an attempt to bring its own output more in line with the feedback. Figure 9-6 depicts this iterative adjustment process.

The actual process by which the net determines an appropriate adjustment to each input weight is a complex mathematical procedure. Essentially, however, it can be thought of as a form of sensitivity analysis in which the size of the error is determined and an adjustment is made to see the effect (and in what direction) of the change on the size of the error. This process continues for each hidden layer in the network until all neurodes have been subjected to the sensitivity analysis and the net is ready for another trial.

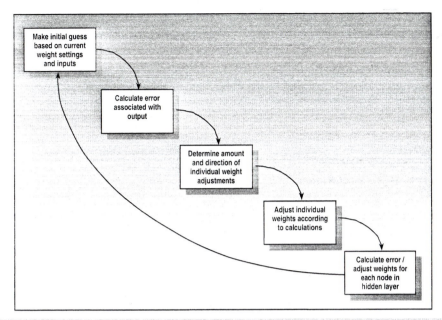

FIGURE 9-6   Typical Training Sequence for Neural Networks

SENDING THE NET TO SCHOOL: ANN LEARNING PARADIGMS

The actual procedure used by a neural network to find the appropriate weight settings is referred to as its learning paradigm. Again, similar to the ways in which humans can acquire knowledge and learn, learning paradigms for ANNs can be loosely classified into those that are largely unsupervised and those that are supervised.

Unsupervised Learning Paradigms

The wide variety of specific unsupervised learning paradigms developed in response to particular problem context needs all possess the same basic characteristics and approaches. Therefore, we will limit our discussion to the general characteristics of all unsupervised learning methods.

The unsupervised nature of an unsupervised learning paradigm simply means that the ANN receives the input data and examples but not any feedback in the form of desired results. To affect its learning process, an unsupervised net begins by developing clusters of the training records it generates based upon similarities it detects in the data examples. The net continues to process data examples, create a training record, and then reclusters the records until a set of definable patterns begins to emerge. With each successive pass, the net finds a pattern more closely matched with the input data than any of the others. Over time, the net refines this pattern recognition until the difference between the input and the output patterns for the training set reach a close approximation of each other.

One way to envision the unsupervised learning process is to imagine a scenario in which you present a group of strangers with a stack of randomly ordered photographs of different situations and ask each of them to classify the photos in some way. Without any specific instructions regarding the method of classification, each stranger will probably choose an approach that is unique, based upon some common characteristic contained within each picture. One stranger might set up a classification based upon the type of scene (indoor, outdoor, day, night, landscape, portrait, etc.). Another may classify the pictures according to the situation depicted (people interacting, pictures of machines, pictures of natural settings, etc.). Yet another may choose to classify the pictures according to their specific photographic characteristics (black-and-white, color, glossy, matte, etc.). Although each grouping would be logical from a given perspective, the relationships among the photos would be different from one grouping to the next. By comparing the relationships within each group, as well as the relationships across groups, we might begin to discover new relationships that were not discernable in any of the previous clusters.

The unsupervised learning paradigm for an ANN works in much the same manner as the situation just described. The net is unsupervised with respect to what it is supposed to discover or conclude. As such, it finds relationships among the input data examples and uses those relationships to create accurate output. Using this approach, a neural net can begin to "specialize" its learning with respect to a specific dimension of the data. A more "organized" form of this approach to the discovery of relationships will be the focus of Chapter 11: Data Mining and Visualization.

Supervised Learning Paradigms

In contrast to the unsupervised approach, the most common supervised learning paradigm is called back propagation. Here, the net receives an input example, generates a guess, and compares that guess to feedback containing the desired results. In this sense, the ANN is being "supervised" by the feedback, which shows the net where it made mistakes and how the answer should look. The name of this technique is based on the fact that the algorithm used to adjust the neurode weights propagates some measure of the calculated error between the guess and the feedback back through the various layers of the network in the direction of the input layer. The most common form of the back propagation algorithm uses a sum-of-squared-errors approach to generate an aggregate measure of the difference error. Following this calculation, a progressive adjusting of the weights along the network is conducted to bring the network "closer" to the correct response. This adjustment process is based on a combination of the calculated error measure and an adjustment increment established by the net trainer. This adjustment increment, or learning rate, is a specification of how much adjustment should occur in each training session. If too large a learning rate is specified, then the net may constantly "overshoot" its optimized weights and never reach the desired level of accuracy. If, conversely, the learning rate is specified in too small an increment, the net may take a long time to reach the desired level of accuracy, if at all.

As with most of the inner workings of an ANN, the mathematics are complex and require a high level of understanding to successfully construct a working ANN. For those with a flair for the calculus, an appendix to this chapter further describes the mathematical foundations of the back propagation algorithm. For others, understanding exactly how it works is not as important as understanding how, and under what conditions, the technology should be applied. Therefore, we turn our attention to some of the advantages and disadvantages that must be acknowledged in the application of neural computing technologies.

BENEFITS AND LIMITATIONS ASSOCIATED WITH NEURAL COMPUTING

One of the most obvious benefits of neural computing is the ability to obtain inferential insights not readily available through the use of other knowledge-based techniques and technologies. In addition to this capability, however, ANNs provide several other advantages over more traditional problem-solving systems. Table 9-2 lists several of those benefits.

A key advantage to ANNs is the elimination of the need for direct input from domain experts. In some cases, soliciting knowledge from a domain expert may be too costly in terms of either economic resources or time involved. In other cases, an expert simply may not exist. Our forays into diverse knowledge domains framed within the physical, biological, and social sciences can often venture beyond the bounds of domain experts. In these cases, ANNs provide a valuable vehicle for the discovery of new relationships and knowledge that is beyond the capabilities of other problem-solving and support technologies.

Another unique advantage of ANNs is their inherent ability to deal with noisy or incomplete data sets. Most often, the availability of clean, high-quality data sets is limited, if not nonexistent, and the problem solver is faced with analyzing data that are poorly distributed and inconsistent. The structural nature of ANNs makes them better suited to deal with such data than more traditional statistical or AI methods. Because each of the neurodes looks at only a small portion of the problem and the neurodes and layers are positioned to look at each of these small elements from different angles, ANNs can often reconstruct missing or corrupt data by inferring what the data "should" look like and then using that inference as an input to its current guess. Such inferences can be modified as necessary along with the weights for each input as the network seeks to reduce the error associated with previous training sessions.

Along these same lines, the ability of an ANN to look at small parts of a large and complex problem also makes it uniquely capable of scaling up as necessary to accommodate problems of increased complexity. Intuitively, more complicated problems can be solved by adding more hidden layers to the network, thus increasing the ability of the network to use the output of neurodes in lower layers and allowing for a greater number of neurodes to interact. In this way, many complicated, highly nonlinear relationships and processes can be modeled effectively.

We must be prepared, however, to acknowledge that these advantages and benefits associated with neural computing do not come without a price. Table 9-3 lists several of

---

TABLE 9-2   Benefits Derived from Neural Computing

- Avoidance of explicit programming and detailed IF-THEN rule base.
- Reduced need for expensive or limited availability experts.
- ANNs are inherently adaptable and do not require update when inputs change.
- Elimination of need for redefined knowledge base.
- ANNs are dynamic and continue to improve with use.
- Ability to process erroneous, inconsistent, or even incomplete data.
- Allows for generalization from specific information context.
- Facilitates the creation of abstractions from diverse data sets.
- Allows for the inclusion of "common sense" into the problem-solving domain.

TABLE 9-3 Limitations to Neural Computing Techniques

- ANNs cannot "explain" their inferences.
- The "black box" nature of ANNs makes accountability and reliability issues difficult.
- The repetitive training process is often extremely time consuming.
- Highly skilled machine learning analysts and designers are still a scarce resource.
- Neural computing technologies generally push the limits of existing hardware.
- ANNs require that a certain amount of faith be imparted to the final output.

the limitations and drawbacks associated with application of neural computing techniques to a problem context.

ANNs are often successfully applied in finding solutions to complex problems involving pattern recognition and nonlinear relationships because of their unique ability to find subtle relationships within data sets. Unfortunately, however, once such subtleties are revealed, the ANN has no mechanism for explaining or justifying them. The fact that an ANN can effectively differentiate items based on inherent, yet latent, characteristics within the data set does not mean that such differentiation is based on the desired set of discriminating characteristics. In fact, it is possible for the ANN to develop an understanding and ability to discriminate between patterns contained within the noise in the data rather than in the data themselves.

One famous example of this potential comes from the military. A neural net was developed to distinguish between pictures containing specific military armaments and those without such elements. In the early training sessions, the net was presented with two sets of photographs: one containing combat tanks and one without any tanks in the pictures. Each of these pictures was converted to machine-readable format and presented to the net for training. Within a relatively short number of passes, the net displayed an excitingly high degree of discrimination between the pictures containing combat tanks and those without. To ensure the success of the training, a new set of photographs was digitized and presented to the net for analysis. The excitement from the training session soon turned to disappointment when the net failed to correctly discriminate the desired elements. An inspection of the training set quickly revealed the problem: The photographs containing tanks were all taken on sunny days, whereas the photos without the tanks were taken on generally overcast days. The net had learned to discriminate between sunny and overcast days rather than to identify images of combat tanks.

The evolution of neural computing and machine learning techniques is rapidly accelerating with new approaches emerging each day that are intended as improvements over the current methods. One such improvement over "conventional" neural computing techniques is the subject of our next discussion.

9-3: GENETIC ALGORITHMS AND GENETICALLY EVOLVED NETWORKS

Recall from our discussion of bounded rationality and optimization in Chapter 2 that humans, although desiring the optimal solution, tend to satisfice and accept a solution of lesser quality than optimum. Even though Simon's explanation suggests that optimization is a laudable, yet unattainable, cognitive goal, we nonetheless continue our quest for the best possible solution to our daily problems. We "know" an optimal, very best solution to our problem exists, if we could only find it.

THE CONCEPT OF OPTIMIZATION

The goal of any problem solver is to arrive at a solution that effectively solves the problem within the constraints (perceived or real) imposed on the problem context. This goal suggests that for a given problem context and set of constraints, there exists an optimal solution based on some predetermined measure of goodness. Although Simon's position on optimizing versus satisficing holds true from a human cognition perspective, in other situations, optimization is not only desirable, but attainable as well. The field of management science successfully developed mathematical techniques intended to derive optimal solutions under a given set of often complex constraints. Such techniques make the best of an imperfect situation by taking the fullest advantage of the limited resources available to the problem. The advent of the computer, combined with these mathematical optimization models, further extends our ability to find the best solution available. Our problem is that as we get more proficient and capable of solving increasingly complex problems, we also develop an appetite for achieving optimal solutions to even more complex problems and constrained contexts. This cycle of complexity stimulates the need for innovative methods of deriving such optimal solutions.

Consider the traveling salesperson problem from Chapter 2. Recall that one of the problems was to determine the number of unique routes without visiting any city along the route more than once. We determined that the need to visit 10 cities yielded a total of 181,440 unique routes.[2] Assuming we have a relatively powerful computer that can evaluate 1 million (10^6) unique routes per second, we could perform an exhaustive search of the problem space in approximately 0.18 seconds—not much time considering the potential return in the form of efficient performance and cost savings. If, however, our zeal for this newfound optimization power suggests that we might want to increase the size of the problem, our limitations for exhaustive search will soon be revealed. By increasing the number of cities to 25, we also increase the number of unique routes to 3.10×10^{23} possibilities. No problem, though. Our computer will figure out the optimal route based on the constraints we have placed on the solution. Unfortunately, however, our computer, operating at a speed of 1 million evaluations per second, will require just a bit longer to process the 25-city problem. At that rate, it will take it somewhere around 10 billion years to perform an exhaustive search and determine the optimal solution.[3] It would appear that conventional approaches to optimization do have their limits.

Recall further from the traveling salesperson problem that we found that a heuristic approach to the solution resulted in a pretty good outcome with a minimum of effort. Such techniques find their way into the realm of machine learning, and one such method, the genetic algorithm, is gaining widespread acceptance and application.

---

[2] Using the formula 0.5(number of cities − 1)!

[3] Assuming 365.25 days per year: 3.10×10^{23} unique routes would require approximately 8.62×10^{13} hours to solve. This approximates to 9,830,411,719 years.

INTRODUCTION TO GENETIC ALGORITHMS

Similar to the conceptual foundations of ANNs, genetic algorithms (GAs) are based in biological theory. In contrast to the neuroscience roots of ANNs, however, GAs find their roots in Darwin's evolutionary theories of natural selection and adaptation.

The theory of natural selection offers some compelling arguments that individuals with certain characteristics are better able to survive and pass on those characteristics to their offspring. A genetic algorithm is an elegantly simple, yet extremely powerful, type of optimization technique based on the ideas of genetics and natural selection. Originally developed by John Holland at MIT during the 1940s, a GA employs a set of adaptive processes that mimic the concept of "survival of the fittest" by regenerating recombinants of the algorithm in response to a calculated difference between the network's guess and the desired solution state. The power of a GA results from the mating of population members and their production of offspring that have a significant chance of retaining the desirable characteristics of their parents, perhaps even combining the best characteristics of both parents. In this manner, the overall fitness of the population can potentially increase from generation to generation as we discover better solutions to our problems. The primary advantage of a GA over conventional unsupervised neural networks is its ability to overcome the combinatorial limitations associated with the development of complex ANNs with intricate combinations of performance criteria.

The Concept of Natural Selection

To better understand the fundamentals of GAs, we must first understand the theoretical foundation upon which they are built. The primary problem faced by all organisms found in nature is that of survival. Those that come up with successful solutions survive and those that fail to solve the problem become extinct. The Darwinian approach to the evolution of species suggests that surviving organisms are able to adapt themselves to the conditions within the environment that best support them and insulate themselves from harmful environmental factors. This adaptation to the environment serves as the basis for the development and use of genetic algorithms.

Basic Components of Genetic Algorithms

In keeping with its root biological metaphor, the GA's smallest unit is called a gene. The gene represents the smallest unit of information in the problem domain and can be thought of as the basic building block for a possible solution. If the problem context were, for example, the creation of a well-balanced investment portfolio, a gene might represent the number of shares of a particular security to purchase. If the problem context focused on the traveling salesperson problem, the gene might represent one of the cities that must be visited on a route. Continuing with the metaphor, a series of genes that represent the components of one possible solution to the problem is referred to as a chromosome. Figure 9-7 illustrates examples of chromosome strings that might be found in a typical GA.

The chromosome is represented in computer memory as a bit string of binary digits that can be "decoded" by the GA to determine how good a particular chromosome's gene pool solution is for the given problem. The decoding process simply informs the GA what the various genes within the chromosome represent. For the traveling salesperson problem, for example, the decoder would know how to convert

```
┌─────────────────────────────────────────────────────────────┐
│ Well-balanced investment portfolio chromosome:                │
│                                                               │
│        {100 300 1000 1000 500 . . . 200 1500}                 │
│                                                               │
│ The decoding function for this chromosome interprets this to mean: │
│                                                               │
│    Buy 100 shares of Stock A, 300 shares of Stock B, . . . etc. │
│                                                               │
│ Traveling salesperson city routing problem:                   │
│                                                               │
│        {Miami Newark Chicago Denver Phoenix . . . Dallas}     │
│                                                               │
│ The decoding function for this chromosome interprets this to mean: │
│                                                               │
│    Start in Miami, go to Newark, go to Chicago, . . ., go to Dallas, return to start │
└─────────────────────────────────────────────────────────────┘
```

FIGURE 9-7 Examples of Genetic Algorithm Chromosome Strings

the genes into cities along the route. This representation of the solution as a bit string is probably the only significant limitation with regard to the application of a GA to a problem context. For the GA to be effective in reaching a solution to the problem, the solution must be able to be represented as a digital bit string. Figure 9-8 outlines the basic processes associated with the operation of a GA.

Initialization   The first step in the creation of a GA is the development of an initial population of chromosomes that are possible solutions to the problem under investigation. This population of initial genetic structures should be constructed in such a way that it represents solutions randomly distributed throughout the solution space.

Evaluation   In the evaluation stage, each chromosome is decoded by the decoder function and evaluated using a fitness function to determine which genetic structures are good and which are not so good. The fitness function is analogous to an objective function commonly found in optimization techniques such as linear programming. The function represents some constraint or requirement to minimize or maximize the use of some resource. In the traveling salesperson example, typical fitness functions might include requirements to minimize time en route, minimize fuel or travel expense, and maximize individual city contact time.

Figure 9-9 illustrates the decoding process using a binary chromosome that represents the cities along a route, their distances from a home base, and the desired contact time in each. In terms of the problem domain, the decoder function and the fitness function are the only two GA components that are specific to the problem context. As such, the GA can be altered with respect to how it ranks solutions simply by changing the nature of the fitness functions. Additionally, the same GA can be used to solve a wide variety of problems simply by changing the decoder function and the fitness functions to those relevant to the new problem domain.

Selection   Once the initial pool of chromosomes is evaluated by the fitness function, the GA experiments with new solutions by iteratively refining the initial solutions so that those with the best fit are more likely to be ranked higher as solutions. In essence, the GA begins to "experiment" with the existing set of chromosomes by combining

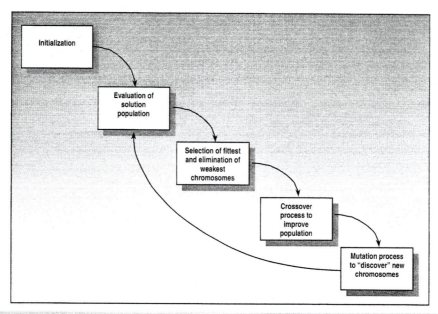

FIGURE 9-8   Basic Process Flow of Genetic Algorithm Problem Solving

FIGURE 9-9   Example of Chromosome Encoding and Decoding

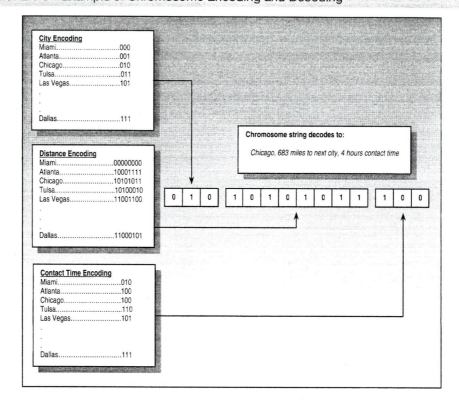

and refining the genes contained within each chromosome. The objective is to produce new chromosomes that form a new generation of possible solutions to evaluate.

In the first step, selection, the GA chooses the fittest species to remain and reproduce within the population of solution chromosomes. Poorer, less fit solutions are eliminated. The most common method for this evolution is called fitness proportional selection. In its simplest form, this method determines the relative fitness of each chromosome to all the other chromosomes in the current generation. If chromosome A is determined to be twice as fit as chromosome B, then chromosome A is given twice the chance of survival as chromosome B. The fittest evolve, and the weaker species "die off." The selection process weeds out the poorer solutions and passes the remaining chromosomes on to the crossover process.

Crossover   Continuing the refinement process, the crossover phase involves the exchange of gene information between two selected chromosomes. Figure 9-10 illustrates this activity in which a portion of one chromosome crosses over into another chromosome, and vice versa.

The crossover operation allows the GA to create new chromosomes that share positive characteristics while simultaneously reducing the prevalence of negative characteristics in an otherwise reasonably fit solution. This process is analogous to the concept of "strengthening the breed" in the field of biogenetics.

One important limitation in the crossover phase, however, is that it can only rearrange gene information that already exists within the population of chromosomes. For example, in our traveling salesperson problem, if we fail to include a city, or a specific characteristic, in the original population, then that value will never become a part of any solution set and, thus, will never be swapped into a better solution chromosome. Just as in nature, however, GAs demonstrate a mechanism for spontaneous evolution of new genetic code.

Mutation   The final step in the refinement process is mutation. The mutation phase randomly changes the value of a gene from its current setting to a completely different one. Figure 9-11 shows the mutation of a chromosome.

FIGURE 9-10   Chromosome Crossover Process

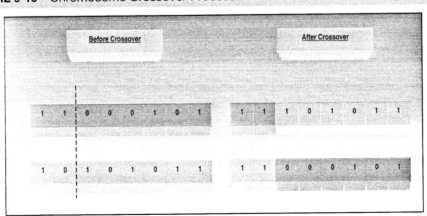

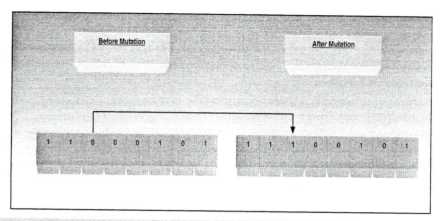

FIGURE 9-11 Chromosome Mutation Process

Most mutations formed by this process are, as is often the case in nature, less fit rather than more so. Occasionally, however, a highly superior and beneficial mutation will occur. Mutation provides the GA with the opportunity to create chromosomes and information genes that can explore previously uncharted areas of the solution space, thus increasing the chances for the discovery of an optimal solution. In conformance with the natural laws, however, mutation is normally set to a low frequency of occurrence and is primarily used to ensure that the probability of searching any point within the solution is never zero.

BENEFITS AND LIMITATIONS ASSOCIATED WITH GENETIC ALGORITHMS

Despite the power of genetic algorithms, some precautions must be taken when setting up or coding a GA problem. Several parameters significantly affect the speed with which an optimal solution is discovered.

One of the most important parameters is population size. The ideal number of initial solution chromosomes is based on a trade-off between time to carry out the processes and degree of diversity in the solution population. Wayner (1991) provided evidence that, for most problems, a population size of 10 appears to be optimal. Fewer than 10 chromosomes causes excessive failures to reach a solution and greater than 10 increases the process time with no measurable advantage.

One of the advantages noted in using GAs to solve complex problems also can be attributed to population size. GAs tend to zero in on a solution much faster than a neural network and generally are highly predictable in their process time. Because the GA is always following the same steps, the total process time is based upon the number of chromosomes in the initial solution population and the number of generations that is chosen to run. A reasonably accurate prediction of time to solution can be derived by multiplying the time necessary to evaluate a single chromosome by the number of chromosomes, and then multiplying that result by the number of generations.

Other parameters that may directly affect the efficiency of the GA include the processes of crossover and mutation. Mutation should be used judiciously to ensure that duplication of solution space members can never occur. Crossover must be set such that an appropriate number of new recombinants can be evaluated without wasting the resources allocated to the GA. If no crossover is conducted, then no new structures will ever become available for evaluation. If all chromosomes in the population are subjected to crossbreeding, then good genes will begin to disappear along with the bad ones. Heuristically speaking, it is recommended that 90 percent of the chromosome population be subjected to crossover with mutation occurring less than 5 percent of the total evaluation time.

The greatest advantage that GAs offer for solving complex problems lies in their ability to "stretch" themselves across a vast solution space in search of the optimal solution. Further, because all initial populations are composed of possible solutions, GAs generally come up with a proposed optimal solution based on the initial population. In other words, with the application of a GA to an optimization problem, you are usually guaranteed to find at least some reasonable solution. In many cases, the proposed solution will be superior to any that were used to seed the initial chromosome population.

Recall from our discussion of Simon and the concept of satisficing that humans are willing to settle for a suboptimal solution as long as it is a good one and meets their criteria for successful outcome. The processes of nature and the evolutionary processes of living organisms tend, also, to conform more to Simon's theories than to those of optimization. It is unimaginable that any population of human species will ever yield a single member that possesses the vision of a Thomas Edison, the charisma and empathy of a Princess Diana, the intellect of a Carl Sagan, and the athletic prowess of a Michael Jordan. We accept the fact that the evolution of our species will be suboptimal, and we must also accept the fact that the solutions we derive will be suboptimal. The important issue is that the evolution of species appears to be constantly improving and is, for the most part, responsible for improvements in quality of life within the species. Likewise, the generation of a suboptimal solution that shows improvement over prior solutions is also beneficial to the advancement of our understanding of complex problems and to our abilities to deal with them. In this regard, GAs play an important part in the decision challenges facing tomorrow's manager.

Another significant benefit associated with the application of genetic algorithms is that they can be used to solve problems that we have no clue how to solve. If we can describe the components of a reasonably good solution and provide a fitness function that is usable by the GA, we can derive one or more solutions that would otherwise be unattainable. This ability to "invent" solutions makes GAs more attractive than conventional expert system applications, where a great deal of explicit knowledge about the domain must exist. In other words, GAs do not need to know how to solve a problem but simply need to recognize a good solution when one presents itself.

One final advantage associated with GAs is that their power does not result from a complex algorithmic perspective, but rather from a relatively simple and widely understood set of concepts. This basis increases the potential for widespread acceptance of a GA approach across an organization composed of individuals without a deep technical background. Almost everyone took at least one class in biology and the concept of survival of the fittest is familiar in almost every knowledge domain. The familiarity with the underlying concepts of genetic algorithms makes their acceptance and credibility relatively easy to establish over other machine learning and AI-based techniques.

9-4: APPLICATIONS OF MACHINES THAT LEARN

MACHINE LEARNING APPLICATION DOMAINS

Table 9-4 contains a brief listing of the types of problem contexts in which machine learning systems such as neural networks and genetic algorithms were successfully applied. Although it is not intended to be comprehensive, the list's diversity illustrates the wide variety of problems and domains in which AI-based systems can be useful.

A number of developmental projects involving ANN technology were reported by the media. For example, Nippon Steel Corporation built a blast furnace operation control support system that makes use of ANNs. The neural network employed in this system comes equipped with functions that enable it to learn the relationship between sensor data and the eight kinds of temperature distribution patterns known from experience to pertain to the overall operation of blast furnaces, and to instantaneously recognize and output that pattern that most closely approximates sensor data input into

---

TABLE 9-4 Typical Applications of Machine Learning Systems

- Predict staffing requirements at different times of the year and for different conditions.
  Brooklyn Union Gas Corp. predicts in advance the number of crew members who will be needed for service calls based on the time of year, predicted temperature, and day of the week.
- Predict which job a job applicant is best suited for.
- Predict which customers will pay their bills.
- Spot odd trading patterns.
  This is how Ivan Boesky, the rogue trader, was caught.
- Predict the properties of chemical mixtures.
- Diagnose diseases.
  A neural net has been developed that outdid an expert system in diagnosing smell disorders.
- Predict the stock market, futures markets, and the like.
- Flag faulty parts on an assembly line.
- Regulate industrial processes using inputs from sensors at different points in the process.
- Classify medical ailments (such as hearing losses), living things, and cells (as cancerous/noncancerous).
- Predict pollution based on the composition of trash coming into an incinerator.
- Predict sales and/or costs.
- Predict a company's corporate bond rating.
- Appraise real estate.
- Predict the outcome of sports events (such as horse racing).
- Predict solar flare activity.
- Predict the length of survival for medical patients with certain ailments.
- Recognize welds that are most likely to fail under stress in nuclear containments.
- Test beer.
  Anheuser-Busch identifies the organic contents of its competitors' beer vapors with 96 percent accuracy.
- Predict which prison inmates could benefit from less expensive alternative programs.

the system. The neural network learns quickly and achieves a better than 90 percent pattern recognition ratio following learning. Because this system performed extremely well during operational testing, Nippon Steel plans to introduce it into other aspects of its operations in addition to blast furnace control, including the diagnosis of malfunctions and other control processes.

A second example is the experimental work started by Daiwa Securities Company and NEC Corporation, which applies neural network technology to the learning and recognition of stock price chart patterns for use in stock price forecasting. NEC previously developed neural network simulation software for use on its EWS 4800 series of workstations, and, by limiting stock price chart pattern learning to a few dozen major stocks, improved the accuracy of this software's forecasting capabilities. Based on these results, the Daiwa Computer Services Company (DCS), an information-processing subsidiary of the Daiwa Securities Group, transferred the NEC system to its supercomputer and taught it to recognize the stock price chart patterns for 1,134 companies listed on the Tokyo Stock Exchange. Since then, DCS put this system to good use in the performance of stock price forecasting.

Yet another recent example is the project at Mitsubishi Electric, which combines neural network technology with optical technology to achieve the world's first basic optical neurocomputer system capable of recognizing the 26 letters of the alphabet. The system comprises a set of light-emitting diodes (LED) that output letter patterns as optical signals, optical fibers, liquid crystal displays (LCD) that display letter patterns, and light-receiving devices that read these letters. This system is capable of 100 percent letter recognition even when slightly misshapen handwritten letters are input.

A fourth example is a development project for a facilities diagnosis system that employs a neural network system at Nippon Oil Company in cooperation with CSK Research Institute. This project is attracting considerable attention because, for the first time, research is examining the application of neural network systems to facilities diagnosis. Initially, the project will be aimed at developing a diagnosis system based on vibration analysis for pump facilities. Nippon Oil operates 1,500 pumps at its Negishi Oil Refinery in Yokohama, Kanagawa Prefecture, alone and must retain large numbers of experienced personnel to maintain these pumps. The company decided to apply neural network technology to pump facilities diagnosis operations in order to reduce the amount of labor required.

Bond rating is another successful ANN application domain. Bond rating refers to the process by which a particular bond is assigned a label that categorizes the ability of the bond's issuer to repay the coupon and par value of that bond. Thus, for example, the Standard and Poor's organization might assign a rating varying from AAA (very high probability of payment) to BBB (possibility of default in times of economic adversity) for investment grade bonds. The problem is that no hard-and-fast rule governs the determination of these ratings. Rating agencies must consider a vast spectrum of factors before assigning a rating to an issuer. Some of these factors, such as sales, assets, liabilities, and the like, might be well defined. Others such as willingness to repay are quite nebulous. Thus, a precise problem definition is not possible.

Still other areas where machine learning systems are regularly applied are credit scoring and target marketing. Credit scoring is used to screen an applicant for credit cards based on known facts about the person applying. These facts usually include such things as salary, number of checking accounts, and previous credit history. Large banks and other lenders lose millions each year from bad debts. Even a small increase in the ability to predict accurately which accounts will go unpaid can result in hundreds of thousands of dollars saved each year for large lenders. To address this problem, major banks and finance companies actively pursue new technologies and systems that can aid in credit prediction.

Machine learning applications also take up a long-standing problem in advertising. For years, advertising agencies and other companies tried to identify and sell to target, or specific, markets. For example, a company selling life insurance might send out an advertisement enclosed in a monthly credit card bill. The company would prefer to send out a small percentage of these advertisements to consumers and keep information on what type of person responds. Once the company obtains data on who responded, it can then build a predictive model to analyze potentially good customers. Thus, a life insurance company may be able to save money by only sending out advertisements to a select 1 million credit card holders who are more likely to buy life insurance, rather than to all credit card holders. Successful target marketing can significantly reduce the marketing expenses each year.

The statistical-based hybrid neural network at Chase Manhattan Bank, discussed in the minicase at the beginning of this chapter, is one of the largest and most successful AI applications in the United States. It addresses a critical success factor in the bank's strategic plan: reducing losses on loans made to public and private corporations. Most of Chase's transactions with corporations involve assessing their creditworthiness. Chase loans $300 million annually and can benefit greatly from tools that improve loan assessment. This assessment allows Chase to mitigate risk and seek out new business opportunities. Financial restructuring deals are promising business opportunities for the bank.

Various international conferences and academic and professional journals and magazines report many recent studies and success stories. An example of a typical multipurpose neural application, NeuroForecaster, is described at the end of this chapter.

THE FUTURE OF MACHINE LEARNING SYSTEMS

A key question that normally arises when reflecting on the advancements in neural computing and other machine learning realms focuses on how close we are to building a truly intelligent machine. For isolated capacities, some ANNs already exceed humans. The development of large-scale networks that mirror complex human endeavors, such as creating a musical work or carrying on a wide-ranging conversation, is not in our foreseeable future.

The greatest obstacle to building such systems is the acquisition of sufficient training data. The speed signal transmission in the human brain is estimated to be approximately 100 meters per second; the speed of a typical copper wire transmission system is at least 1 million times faster. Although it is theoretically possible for a computer to think and learn at a speed 1 million times faster than humans, for it to actually occur the system will need to acquire data at the same speed. This bottleneck is a function of the cognitive limitations imposed on humans to create such training sets and to feed them to the net. In the meantime, we must satisfy ourselves with the development of machines that can learn how to support us in many of our more complex activities such as medical diagnosis, flying an aircraft, sending explorers to other planets, and other endeavors intended to improve our quality of life.

9-5: CHAPTER SUMMARY

We are, rightfully so, fascinated with the processes of the human brain and with the prospects of capturing those processes in a computer-based system. In our quest, however, the lack of clarity and specificity with which the human brain quite comfortably functions on a daily basis looms as a major obstacle to the development of a truly humanlike machine. Nonetheless, the advent of fuzzy systems, genetic algorithms, and neural computing systems takes us another step closer to the goal.

Key Concepts

- Neural computing and the development of artificial neural networks (ANNs) evolved in response to the attractiveness of digital information processors that can simulate the human brain's potential for solving ill-structured business problems.

- Fuzzy logic (9-1)

  Fuzzy logic is a method of reasoning that allows for the partial or "fuzzy" description of a rule. Combining this approach to reasoning with the realm of digital processors results in a class of computers that can "learn" from their mistakes and can "understand" the vagaries commonly found in human thought.

- The essence of fuzzy logic reasoning (9-1)

  Fuzzy logic does not mean vague answers but, rather, precise answers that vary mathematically within a given range of values. By developing a network of mathematical algorithms, a complex set of categorizations can be analyzed and a high level of reasoning can be brought to bear on a given problem context.

- The differences between fuzziness and probability (9-1)

  Probability deals with the likelihood that something has a particular property, whereas fuzzy logic deals with the degree to which a particular property is present in something.

  With probability, we can only determine membership in a set, but with fuzzy logic, we can determine where on the continuum of membership a particular set member resides.

- Advantages of fuzzy systems (9-1)

  Modeling of contradiction

  Fuzzy logic allows for the modeling and inclusion of contradiction within a knowledge base. Using fuzzy logic, the designer exercises complete control over the accuracy of a given conclusion or reasoning process by simply increasing or decreasing the number of rules required and the degrees of sensitivity to membership allowed.

  Increased system autonomy

  The rules contained within the knowledge base of a fuzzy system can function completely independently of one another. Fuzzy rules will continue to "work" even in circumstances where the whole system is completely changed.

- Limitations to fuzzy systems (9-1)

  Obstacles to system verification

  Fuzzy reasoning can become an obstacle to the verification of a system's stability or reliability. Designers may find it difficult to determine whether their actions improve the system or result in a move away from a better solution.

Fuzzy systems' lack of memory

Basic fuzzy reasoning mechanisms cannot learn from their mistakes and possess no memory. As such, fuzzy logic is not yet capable of optimizing the efficiency of a system.

- Fuzzy set saturation (9-1)

The fuzzy set may become so full of inferences that consequent fuzzy sets are overloaded, which results in the entire system losing the information provided by the fuzzy rules in an attempt to "balance itself" around its mean value.

- Artificial neural networks (9-2)

Artificial neural networks are simple computer-based programs whose primary function is to construct models of a problem space based upon trial and error.

- Three basic layers of an ANN (9-2)

Input layer: The layer that receives the data

Output layer: The layer that relays the final results

Internal layer (hidden layer): The layer where the processing and transformation of the input signal take place and where the type of output signal is determined

- The hierarchical network dynamics among the neurodes is determined by a mathematical combination of the weight of each input to the neurode and the threshold parameters associated with that neurode. Learning, in a neural network, results from the adjustment of weights. (9-2)

- Typical neurode component structure (9-2)

The basic structure consists of a set of weighted input connections, a bias input, a state function, a nonlinear transfer function, and an output connection.

Weighted inputs

The neurode can, and usually does, have multiple inputs each with its own associated weight or importance. The weight of an input determines the importance of its contribution to the output of the neurode.

The bias input

The purpose of the bias input is to allow for the individual adjustment of the firing threshold of the neurode to facilitate the final adjustment of the ANN following the learning process.

The state function

The purpose of the state function is to consolidate the weights of the various inputs to the neurode into a single value that can be passed to the transfer function for processing.

The transfer function

The primary purpose of the transfer function is to serve as the vehicle by which the summed information is passed on as output. The transfer function must contribute a sense of nonlinearity between the summed inputs and the resultant output.

- The training for an artificial neural network (9-2)

The process of training a neural net to associate certain input patterns with correct output responses involves the use of repetitive examples and feedback. This iterative adjustment process continues for each hidden layer in the network until all neurodes have been subjected to the sensitivity analysis and the net is ready for another trial.

- ANN learning paradigms (9-2)

The actual procedure used by a neural network to find the appropriate weight settings is referred to as its learning paradigm. The learning paradigms for ANNs can be loosely classified into two categories:

Unsupervised learning paradigms

The unsupervised nature of an unsupervised learning paradigm means that the ANN receives the input data and examples but not any feedback in the form of desired results. Using the clustering approach, a neural net can begin to "specialize" its learning with respect to a specific dimension of the data.

Supervised learning paradigms

The most common supervised learning paradigm is called back propagation. In this approach, the net receives an input example, generates a guess, and compares that guess to feedback containing the desired results. The ANN is being "supervised" by the feedback that shows the net where it made mistakes and how the answer should look.

- Major benefits of neural computing (9-2)

The ability to obtain inferential insights not readily available through the use of other knowledge-based techniques and technologies

The elimination of the need for direct input from domain experts

The inherent ability to deal with noisy or incomplete data sets

The capability of scaling up as necessary to accommodate problems of increased complexity

- Genetic algorithms (9-3)

A genetic algorithm (GA) is an elegantly simple, yet extremely powerful, type of optimization technique based on the ideas of genetics and natural selection. The GA is a set of adaptive processes that mimic the concept of "survival of the fittest" by regenerating recombinants of the algorithm in response to a calculated difference between the network's guess and the desired solution state.

- Basic components of genetic algorithms (9-3)

Gene

The GA's smallest unit is called a gene, which represents the smallest unit of information in the problem domain and can be thought of as the basic building block for a possible solution.

Chromosome

A series of genes that represent the components of one possible solution to the problem is referred to as a chromosome. The chromosome is represented in computer memory as a bit string of binary digits that can be "decoded" by the GA to determine how good a particular chromosome's gene pool solution is for the given problem.

- Basic processes of the operation of a GA (9-3)

Initialization

The first step in the creation of a GA is the development of an initial population of chromosomes as possible solutions to the problem under investigation.

Evaluation

In this stage, each chromosome is decoded by the decoder function and evaluated using a fitness function to determine which genetic structures are good and which are not so good.

Selection

The selection process weeds out the poor solutions and passes the remaining chromosomes on to the crossover process. In this process, the GA chooses the fittest species to remain and reproduce within the population of solution chromosomes. The objective of this process is to produce new chromosomes that form a new generation of possible solutions to evaluate.

Crossover

The crossover phase involves the exchange of gene information between two selected chromosomes. The purpose of this operation is to allow the GA to create new chromosomes that share positive characteristics while simultaneously reducing the prevalence of negative characteristics in an otherwise reasonably fit solution.

Mutation

In order to provide the GA with the opportunity to create chromosomes and information genes that can explore previously uncharted areas of the solution space, thus increasing the chances for the discovery of an optimal solution, the mutation phase randomly changes the value of a gene from its current setting to a completely different one.

• Benefits of genetic algorithms (9-3)

GAs tend to zero in on a solution much faster than a neural network and generally are highly predictable in their process time.

The advantage of GAs in solving complex problems lies in their ability to "stretch" themselves across a vast solution space in search of the optimal solution.

The applications of genetic algorithms can be used to solve problems that we have no clue how to solve.

The power of GAs does not result from a complex algorithmic perspective, but rather from a relatively simple and widely understood set of concepts.

Questions for Review

1. How does fuzzy logic deal with the concept of categorization? How does this method differ from our typical process of categorization?
2. Describe how membership functions often rely on inclusion in multiple sets.
3. Explain the similarities and the differences between fuzziness and probability.
4. List and briefly describe the advantages and limitations of fuzzy systems.
5. What is fuzzy set saturation?
6. Describe the basic structure of an artificial neural network. What is the purpose of each layer?
7. What is the purpose of a transfer function?
8. How does feedback in ANNs work?
9. Briefly describe and compare supervised and unsupervised ANNs.
10. What is the primary advantage of genetic algorithms over ANNs?
11. Describe genes and chromosomes as applied to genetic algorithms.
12. Describe each step in the GA processing: initialization, evaluation, selection, crossover, and mutation.
13. Summarize the benefits of genetic algorithms.

For Further Discussion

1. Discuss the utility of fuzzy logic's ability to model inclusion in multiple sets that intuitively are mutually exclusive or contradictory. In what situations might this prove useful?
2. Use an example to explain the typical neurode component structure described in this chapter.

3. Artificial neural networks deal well with noisy or incomplete data. Describe some situations in which this feature would perform better than other techniques for eliciting patterns from the data.

4. How can mutation enhance a genetic algorithm's ability to arrive at a satisfactory solution? Is mutation necessary?

5. Describe the effect of the number of chromosomes on the performance of a genetic algorithm.

NeuroForecaster and GENETICA

NeuroForecaster is an advanced Windows-based, user-friendly business forecasting tool. It is packed with the latest technologies including neural network, genetic algorithm, fuzzy computing, and nonlinear dynamics. It excels at the following tasks:

1. Time-series forecasting (e.g., stock and currency market forecasts, GDP forecast)
2. Classification (e.g., stock selection, bond rating, credit assignment, property valuation)
3. Indicator analysis
4. Identification of useful input indicators

With NeuroForecaster, you can create neural networks of any size—the only limit is the memory constraint of your computer. It is also an excellent tool for analyzing the effectiveness of neural network architecture (numbers of hidden nodes, hidden layers, transfer functions) for problem solving. It accepts numerical input attributes, patterns, codes, technical indicators, and fundamental indicators, and allows them to be combined to build univariate or multivariate models. Like other numerical tools, it cannot handle descriptive information such as news, rumors, or fiscal policies unless such information is accompanied by numerical information, reflected in other indicators, or can be quantified.

NeuroForecaster is a general-purpose forecasting tool with adaptive learning capability. You can make it into an automatic trading system if you train it with a good trading strategy to generate the buy/sell signals.

GENETICA Net Builder, another neural computing application, is supported by NeuroForecaster 3.0 and above. It searches for the best combination of input data and the most predictable forecaster horizon (i.e., how many steps ahead to forecast), and automatically creates and optimizes forecaster structures and control parameters by evolution and genetic search.

GENETICA is seamlessly integrated with the training process of NeuroForecaster— it determines when to pause the training, purge the poor-performing networks, and evolve new offspring to inherit the knowledge acquired by outperforming parents.

POWERFUL AND UNIQUE FEATURES

- Reads various file formats including MetaStock, CSI, Computrac, FutureSource, ASCII, and VisuaData, displayed in its built-in spreadsheet
- GENETICA Net Builder, which searches for the best input data combination and forecast horizon, and builds the best forecaster networks

- Rescaled range analysis and Hurst exponent to unveil hidden market cycles and check for predictability
- Correlation analysis to compute correlation factors to analyze the significance of input indicators
- Weight and accumulated error index (AEI) histograms to monitor learning process

Back Propagation Algorithm

The primary objective of a back propagation algorithm is the minimization of error between the output of a neural network and the true solution contained within the training data record.[4]

Assuming a logistic transfer function, we can update the weight, ω_{ij}, from a given node, n_i, to the current node, n_j, as follows:

$$\omega_{j(t+1)} = \omega_{j,t} + (\lambda)(\varepsilon\omega_{ij})(n_i)$$

where λ is the learning parameter, the subscript t refers to the number of times the net has been updated, and $\varepsilon\omega_{ij}$ is the sensitivity of node n_j to the change in the weight ω_{ij}.

Recall that the total input to a given neurode is described as

$$s_j = \sum n_i \omega_{ij}$$

where s_j represents the sum of all inputs to the neurode, n_i is the output from the ith neurode in the previous layer, and ω_{ij} is the weight of the input connection between the ith neurode in the previous layer and the current neurode.

The result of this summation is passed to a nonlinear transfer function to yield the total output n_j of neurode j. Typical of the transfer function forms used is the *logistic function*, shown as

$$n_j = \frac{1}{1 + e^{-sj}}$$

With these equations in place, we can determine the overall error for a single pass of the ANN using the following steps:

- Calculate the (RMS) error, E, for the output layer as

$$E = \frac{1}{2} \sum_{\text{output}} (n_j - d_j)^2$$

where d_j is the desired output for output neurode j.

---

[4]This section was adapted from Dhar and Stein (1997).

- Calculate the error term for each output neurode and determine the sensitivity of the error terms to changes in neurode output:

$$\varepsilon o_j = \frac{\partial E}{\partial n_j}$$

$$\varepsilon o_j = (n_j - d_j)$$

- Determine the relationship of change between input and output:

$$\varepsilon s_j = \frac{\partial E}{\partial n_j}$$

$$\varepsilon s_j = \frac{\partial E}{\partial s_j}\frac{dn_j}{ds_j}$$

$$\varepsilon s_j = \varepsilon o_j n_j (1 - n_j)$$

- Next, calculate how much to adjust each weight, w_{ij}, from a given neurode on the layer below the current layer, n_i, to the current neurode, n_j:

$$\varepsilon \omega_j = \frac{\partial E}{\partial \omega_{ij}}$$

$$\varepsilon \omega_{ij} = \frac{\partial E}{\partial s_j}\frac{ds_{ij}}{d\omega_{ij}}$$

$$\varepsilon \omega_{ij} = \varepsilon s_j n_i$$

- Continue this operation on the neurodes in the hidden layers by summing all the contributions of inputs to the errors of the hidden neurodes in the lower layers. The variable εh replaces the variable εo from the previous equations to differentiate the error of the output layers from that of the hidden layers:

$$\varepsilon h_i = \frac{\partial E}{\partial n_i}$$

$$\varepsilon h_i = \sum_j \frac{\partial E}{\partial s_i}\frac{\partial s_j}{\partial n_i}$$

$$\varepsilon h_i = \sum_j \varepsilon s_j \omega_{ij}$$

Using this approach, we can back propagate the error recursively through the entire ANN with all the weights being adjusted to minimize the overall error of the net.

THE DATA WAREHOUSE

Learning Objectives

◆ Explain the goal of the data warehouse and its characteristics

◆ Recognize the differences between an operational data store, a data mart, and a data warehouse

◆ Describe briefly each interconnected element in the data warehouse architecture

◆ Understand the role of metadata in the data warehouse

◆ Describe the components of the metadata

◆ Identify the challenge of implementing a data warehouse

◆ Examine the various data warehouse technologies and the future of data warehousing

CAPITAL ONE

Mass customization transformed the credit card industry from a one-size-fits-all market into a microsegmented market offering thousands of product configurations tailored to the individual. Capital One, one of the top 10 U.S. credit card issuers, was founded on the premise that the credit card business is really an information business and that mass customization is the key to growth and profitability.

Capital One uses information technology to implement a scientific testing approach to targeting profitable business. A strategy is formulated by mining behavioral data from the data warehouse. The target population is segmented and a test cell is established. The test cell is then exposed to the strategy and the results are recorded. An integrated economic evaluation is performed to judge the profit potential of the strategy. The results of the evaluation may lead to a larger-scale rollout, a modification and retesting, or a rejection of the strategy. No matter what the outcome, the data collected from the test become part of the data warehouse for use in evaluating future strategies.

DATA VOLUME

The numbers of data needed to support Capital One's marketing efforts are enormous. The granularity of the segmentation being performed requires all data to be available at the individual account level. Also, the sophistication of the predictive models used requires low levels of transaction detail with a substantial set of measures. With approximately 9 million active accounts, 4,000 products, and 20,000 tests, some with up to 8 years of history, the raw data available are well over a terabyte.

Complex segmentation can potentially require many steps to execute. Each step creates interim files, which need to be stored as input to subsequent steps. With dozens of analysts doing thousands of tests every year, the disk space needed to support analyst work areas accounts for more than 500 gigabytes of storage. Analysts' access to large amounts of table space allow them to create new tables potentially containing millions of rows. Mass updates on these tables are routine because of the complex nature of the segmentations being performed.

DATA STRUCTURE

Rarely do analysts at Capital One ask the same question twice. The lack of a consistent access path to the data makes it almost impossible to utilize standard DSS architectures such as star schemas. Stars require the users to restrict the framing of their questions around predetermined dimensions. With rich sources of data available to the analysts, the number of candidate dimensions would be physically impossible to implement given today's technology.

Most data are stored in slightly denormalized relational formats at a low level of granularity. Few prebuilt aggregations exist for the same reason: Stars are not effective. The analysts pay for the flexibility of the data structures by having to endure longer query turnaround times and more complex query syntax.

DATA WAREHOUSING PRODUCTS

Most data warehouse tools on the market today do not support the mass customization environment. On the data acquisition side of data warehousing, most tools available cannot handle the complex integration of disparate, large-volume data sources. As the tool offerings continue to address the more sophisticated environments, this situation will improve. But for now, companies such as Capital One are forced to build tools in-house.

DATA WAREHOUSING TALENT

Finding the right type of IT professional who can thrive in Capital One's unique culture is a constant challenge. The key characteristics of a successful data warehouse technician include a good balance of business and technical

(*continued*)

DSS MINICASE

(*continued*)

understanding, the ability to be a team player, and a great deal of flexibility. The demand for these types of resources seems endless and makes recruiting data warehousing talent a top priority.

Data warehousing is much more than an IT project for companies embracing the concept of mass customization. Armed with a data warehouse filled with quality information, Capital One used mass customization techniques and scientific testing methods to expand its customer base from one million to nearly nine million in 8 years.

Mass customization is the ultimate use of data warehousing, making it an integral part of the business process. Just like a muscle, a data warehouse increases in strength with active use. With each new test and each new product, valuable information is added to the data warehouse, allowing the analyst to learn from the successes and failures of the past.

During the 1980s, businesses and industries all over the globe participated in a "frenzy" of automation. Almost literally, if it moved, it was computerized. In this regard, the office became the new frontier for analysts and software engineers much as the factory floor had been in the decade prior. This overwhelming concentration on the automation of business processes appeared to offer organizations the opportunity to improve from within and to realize the benefits associated with such improvement through increased profits and reduced costs. Although many mission-critical business processes were improved during this period, the support of decision making throughout the organization remained focused on the operational and functional levels of the firm. Basic stock reports gushed out of the organization's information systems at alarming rates on a daily, weekly, and monthly basis. Often, the data used to construct these recurrent emanations were too old, too detailed, too aggregated, or not integrated. In some cases, the use of such reports led to negative consequences greater than if no information had been used. At the same time this "rain"

(or reign, in some cases) of data was occurring, the window of time to market and to respond to changes in global environments continued to narrow as well. By the end of the 1980s, it became clear to most organizations that the key to survival in the 1990s and beyond would be the ability to analyze, plan, and react to changing business conditions in a much more rapid fashion. It would take more and better information for management at all levels of the firm.

Despite this growing need for more information, every day organizations large and small created billions of bytes of data about all aspects of their business—millions of individual facts about their customers, products, operations, and people—without any formalized initiative beyond the transaction level to organize it. For the most part, these data were literally "locked up" in a thousand computer systems and were, metaphorically speaking, "data in jail."

Only a small fraction of the data that are captured, processed, and stored in the enterprise ever actually make it to executives' and decision makers' attention. The concept of the data warehouse (DW) is part of the response by information technology to meet this identified need. It is a simple concept that, over time, could potentially evolve into a significant contributor to the success and stability of an organization in the global marketplace. The essence of the data warehouse is a recognition that the characteristics and usage patterns of operational systems that automate business processes and those of a DSS are fundamentally different but, nonetheless, symbiotically linked (Kelly, 1994). The data warehouse provides a facility for integrating the data generated in a world of unintegrated information systems. A functional DW organizes and stores all of the available data needed for informational, analytical processing over a historical time perspective. The DW then reintegrates the data generated by a myriad of internal and external information systems to create a sense of unity about the data without surrendering their natural complexities.

10-1: STORES, WAREHOUSES, AND MARTS

The concept of the data warehouse is brand new and, as such, in a state of flux with regard to standardization of terms and definitions. Some definitions focus on data, while others refer to people, software, tools, and business processes. The acknowledged father of data warehousing, W. H. Inmon, provided a clear and useful definition of the DW concept in terms of measurable attributes, which will serve our purposes in this text:

> The data warehouse is a collection of integrated, subject-oriented databases designed to support the DSS (decision support) function, where each unit of data is non-volatile and relevant to some moment in time. (Inmon, 1992a, p. 5)

Inmon's definition of a DW makes two implicit assumptions: (1) the DW is physically separated from all other operational systems; and (2) DWs hold aggregated data and transactional (atomic) data for management separate from those used for online transaction processing.

The requirement of a separate environment for the DW is an essential element in the concept. In most cases, the systems employed in an operational environment are inadequate, in many respects, with regard to decision making and analysis. Primarily, the type, quantity, and quality of the data contained in such environments are not well suited to historical analysis. Warehouse data must be consistent, well integrated, well defined, and most important, time stamped. In addition, the need to merge a wide variety of internal and external environments with an equally wide variety of access methods suggests the need for separate DW systems. Table 10-1 contains a comparison between operational versus data warehouse characteristics.

The blue-collar, distribution-channel metaphor of a "warehouse for data" extends easily to the primary components of a complete data warehouse environment. Although the focus of this chapter is on the warehouse itself, we must briefly examine three additional components of the DW environment: the data store, the data mart, and the metadata.

THE DATA STORE

The operational data store (ODS) is the most common component of the DW environment. Its primary day-to-day function is to store the data for a single, specific set of operational applications. Its function within the DW environment, however, is to feed the data warehouse a stream of desired raw data.

The data organization within an ODS is generally subject oriented, volatile, and current (or near current) and commonly focuses on customers, products, orders, policies, claims, and so forth. Normally, the ODS is fed by one or more legacy systems, and the DBMSs associated with such systems cleanse, transform, and integrate the data into homogenous records of transactions or instances of occurrence. Although the data within an ODS lend themselves favorably to analysis performed by one or more of its legacy systems, the data generally do not integrate easily with data from other non-related systems. Nonetheless, many data stores (both internal and external to the organization) may be drawn upon to feed the organizational data warehouse for the purpose of analysis.

TABLE 10-1   Operational Data Store and Data Warehouse Characteristics

Characteristic	Operational Data Store	Data Warehouse
How is it built?	One application or subject area at a time.	Typically multiple subject areas at a time.
User requirements	Well defined prior to logical design.	Often vague and conflicting.
Area of support	Day-to-day business operations.	Decision support for managerial activities.
Type of access	Relatively small number of records retrieved via a single query.	Large data sets scanned to retrieve results from either single or multiple queries.
Frequency of access	Tuned for frequent access to small amounts of data.	Tuned for infrequent access to large amounts of data.
Volume of data	Similar to typical daily volume of operational transactions.	Much larger than typical daily transaction volume.
Retention period	Retained as necessary to meet daily operating requirements.	Retention period is indeterminate and must support historical reporting, comparison, and analysis.
Currency of data	Up-to-the-minute; real time.	Typically represents a static point in time.
Availability of data	High and immediate availability may be required.	Immediate availability is less critical.
Typical unit of analysis	Small, manageable, transaction-level units.	Large, unpredictable, variable units.
Design focus	High-performance, limited flexibility.	High flexibility, high-performance.

Source: Adapted from Bischoff and Alexander (1997).

THE DATA MART

Although the concept of a central aggregation of disparate, yet relevant, data is appealing, the costs associated with such aggregation across an entire organization may be prohibitive. The need for certain types and sources of aggregated data may exist only within certain business units within the firm and the specific needs of each unit may be tangential to those of the others. As an alternative, many firms adopt a lower-cost, scaled-down version of the DW called the data mart.

The data mart is often viewed as a way to gain entry into the realm of data warehouses and to make all the mistakes on a smaller scale. Further, vendors of data warehousing applications find it easier to deal directly with a small group of isolated users than with the IS department of an entire organization. Although the concept of the "mini-mart" is both appealing and useful, a single caveat regarding its proliferation must be acknowledged: Without careful planning from an enterprise-wide perspective, the data mart can become an isolated island of information that will be inaccessible to others in the firm. Assuming the data marts are constructed within the bigger picture of an enterprise-wide system, they offer a targeted and less costly method of gaining the advantages associated with data warehousing and can be scaled up to a full DW environment over time.

THE METADATA

One additional component of the DW environment is called the metadata. Legacy systems generally do not keep a record of characteristics of the data, such as exactly what pieces of data exist, where they are located, where they came from, and how they can be accessed. The metadata are simply data about data—that is, information that is kept about the warehouse rather than information kept within the warehouse. We will cover metadata in detail in Section 10-3.

THE DATA WAREHOUSE ENVIRONMENT

Figure 10-1 illustrates the flow of data within an organization and the position of the components of the DW environment with regard to other information systems. As shown in the figure, the organization's legacy systems and the relevant data stores of external systems provide the core sources of data for the data warehouse and data mart. During the transfer of data from the various data stores, a process of cleansing and transformation occurs for a greater uniformity of the DW data. Simultaneously, the metadata are collected and associated with the DW data so that potential users can determine the source and general characteristics of the DW data. Finally, the DW or data mart may be employed to create one or more personal data warehouses intended

FIGURE 10-1   Organizational Data Flow and Data Storage Components

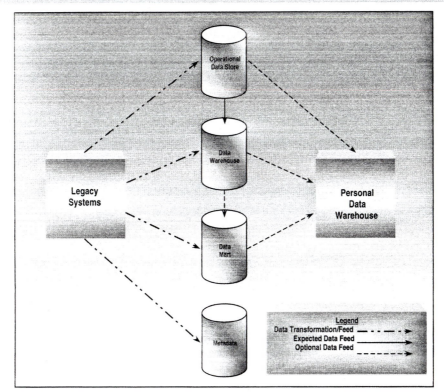

for isolated analysis. In the following sections, we will explore the details of the processes and architectures typically associated with a data warehouse environment.

CHARACTERISTICS OF A DATA WAREHOUSE

So far we established the reasons why data warehousing is an important innovation in decision support, and we formally defined the DW to be

- Subject oriented
- Data integrated
- Time variant
- Nonvolatile

Table 10-2 summarizes these essential characteristics of the DW and provides a brief description of each.

Subject Orientation

The first feature of the DW is its orientation toward the major subjects of the organization, which clearly contrasts with the more functional orientation of the various applications associated with the firm's legacy systems. Figure 10-2 illustrates this contrast in orientations.

As indicated by the figure, the operational world of the organization is typically designed around processes and functions such as inventory or human resources, each of which exhibit specific data needs with most of the data elements local to that process or function. The DW, on the other hand, contains data primarily oriented to decision making and, as such, is organized more around the major subject areas relevant to the firm, such as customers or vendors.

This distinct subject orientation results in several specific differences between typical applications and the data warehouse. For example, design activities in the application world must be equally focused on both process and database design, whereas the DW world is primarily void of process design (at least in its classical form) and tends to focus exclusively on issues of data modeling and database design.

Another specific distinction can be found in the characteristics of the data contained within the DW. Operational data are normally stored in the form of an ongoing relationship between two or more tables based on some established business rule

---

TABLE 10-2 Characteristics of a Data Warehouse

- *Subject orientation.* Data are organized based on how the users refer to them.
- *Integrated.* All inconsistencies regarding naming convention and value representations are removed.
- *Nonvolatile.* Data are stored in read-only format and do not change over time.
- *Time variant.* Data are not current but normally time series.
- *Summarized.* Operational data are mapped into a decision-usable format.
- *Large volume.* Time series data sets are normally quite large.
- *Not normalized.* DW data can be, and often are, redundant.
- *Metadata.* Data about data are stored.
- *Data sources.* Data come from internal and external unintegrated operational systems.

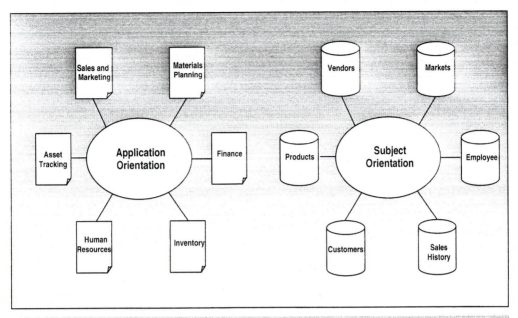

FIGURE 10-2   Application Versus Subject Orientation

such as "Each order must be related to one and only one customer." This business rule creates a relationship between the table containing instances of orders and the table containing instances of customers. One entry in the customer table may be related to many entries in the order table, whereas one entry in the order table will always be related to only one entry in the customer table. In contrast, data in the DW span a range of time and, as such, many business rules (and correspondingly, many data relationships) can be represented in the DW between two or more tables (Inmon, 1992a).

Data Integrated
According to Inmon (1992b), the essence of the DW environment is that the data contained within the boundaries of the warehouse are integrated. This integration manifests itself through consistency in naming convention and measurement attributes, accuracy, and common aggregation. Figure 10-3 illustrates the sharp contrast between the lack of integration found within the operational application environment and that of the DW environment.

Consistent Naming and Measurement Attributes   One of the "freedoms" associated with application design has always been the selection of a naming convention for variables, both as they are represented in the data dictionary and as they appear on the screen. The frequent exercise of this freedom made the inconsistency of applications throughout an organization legendary. For example, the typical data element of gender can (and has) been encoded in operational applications in a myriad of ways. In one application, the variable may be represented as M or F. In another application, the designer may choose to represent it numerically with 1 or 0, or 1 or 2, or possibly 0 or 1. In yet another, the representation may be as an x and a y. As long as these representations are

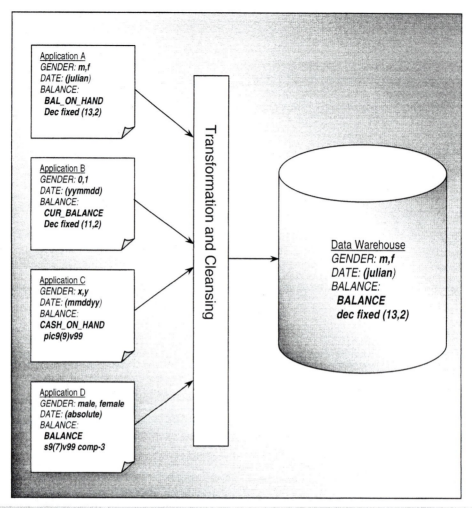

FIGURE 10-3 Integration and Transformation of ODS Data

"understood" by their respective applications and users then no serious problems will occur. However, when the databases associated with these dissimilar applications are loaded into the data warehouse, a decision as to what naming convention will be adopted must be made and a transformation process based on that naming convention must be effected. Therefore, it doesn't particularly matter how gender is represented in the DW as long as it is represented in a consistent and integrated manner. To assure this consistency, each source of data needs an associated conversion process to "scrub" the data into a converted state.

Another result of the need for integrated data is the establishment of a common unit of measure for all synonymous data elements from dissimilar databases. This common measurement must not only serve to integrate the variety of measuring attributes being loaded into the DW but must also create a globally acceptable unit of measure for the final data. In one database, an employee's term of employment may be represented in weeks, whereas in another it may be represented in months or years and decimal years. Just like the conversion of data element names to a common convention, units of measure must also be converted as the data are loaded into the warehouse. This conversion, while serving to standardize the unit of measure, must also create a standard that is universally acceptable to the decision makers and DSS technologies that will use the DW. In some cases, it is an easy decision as to how to represent a particular measurement. Temperature, for instance, will typically be a choice between the Fahrenheit, Celsius, or Kelvin scales. The decision will depend on the intended use of the data. In other cases, however, the decision may be constrained by a wide variety of intended uses for the data element in question. In these cases, it may become necessary to convert the data to some "nonstandard" unit of measure that will allow for the most flexible conversion schema to be employed. In the case of employee tenure, the conversion to a unit of days of employment during data loading of the DW may turn out to be the most flexible choice because this unit will allow easy conversion to any desired output. To extend this concept further, the needs analysis for this data element may suggest that it would be better to not store the length of employee service but, rather, to store the initial date of employment. In this way, a single mathematical process could be employed to convert the data to whatever unit of measure was deemed most desirable.

Whatever the issue, the data must be stored in the DW in an integrated, globally acceptable manner. It is important to the success of a DW that the DSS analyst focus on the use of the data contained in the warehouse rather than on issues of credibility or consistency.

Time Variant

In an operational application system, the expectation is that all data within the database are accurate as of the moment of access. When a customer service representative for your credit card company checks on your current balance, his or her expectation (and yours) is that the value returned will be accurate as of that moment. It would not be particularly useful for the credit representative to tell you that your balance was $459.00 as of 3 weeks ago. In the realm of data warehouses, however, data are simply assumed to be accurate as of some moment in time and not necessarily "right now." Typically, the data are assumed to be accurate at the moment they were loaded into the DW. In this regard, data within a data warehouse are said to be time variant.

The time variance of the warehouse data manifests itself in a variety of ways. Typically, the time horizon for the data in the warehouse is long—from 5 to 10 years. In contrast, the typical operational environment time horizon is much shorter—anywhere from current values to 60 to 90 days. The level of performance associated with high-volume transaction processing necessitates the shorter time horizons in operational applications. In DW environments, however, the desire is generally to analyze data over longer time periods in an effort to reveal trends and temporal relationships.

Another place where DW data display time variance is in the structure of the record key. Every primary key contained within the DW must contain, either implicitly or explicitly, an element of time (day, week, month, year, etc.). In an explicit representation, the time unit may be concatenated (appended) to the primary key (i.e., CUST-ORDER10992, where the second part of the key reflects month and year). In other cases, the time element will be implicitly stated, such as a file that is always loaded at the end of a month or quarter and is named for its associated time period. Regardless of the method employed, every piece of data contained within the warehouse must be associated with a particular point in time if any useful analysis is to be conducted with it.

Yet another aspect of time variance in DW data is that, once recorded, data within the warehouse cannot be updated or changed. In this regard, warehouse data can be thought of as a series of sequential photographs. Using this metaphor, an inaccurate snapshot may be replaced by an accurate one, but once the accuracy of the photos is ascertained, they cannot be altered.

Nonvolatility

In keeping with the restriction of not changing or updating the data contained in a DW, it makes sense that the typical activities of inserts, deletes, and changes performed regularly in an operational application environment are completely nonexistent in a DW environment. Only two data operations are ever performed in the data warehouse: data loading and data access.

This simplicity of data operations creates some extremely powerful differences between operational processing and processing in a DW environment. The design issues in a typical operational application must focus on data integrity and update anomalies. Complex processes must be coded to ensure that the data update processes allow for high integrity of the final product. Such issues are of no concern in a DW environment because data update is never performed. Liberties in the design of the DW databases can be taken to allow for optimal access to the data that could never be allowed in an operational environment. Recall from your study of database design the need to place data in a normalized form to ensure a minimal redundancy. In this regard, the third normal form eliminates any derived data elements, such as those that can be calculated. In an operational application database, a designer would never store the total for a particular order. If this data element is desired it can be easily calculated upon retrieval of the order. In the world of data warehouses, however, designers might actually find it useful to store many such calculations or summarizations not found in the operational data. For example, it might be useful to include weekly or monthly sales figures obtained by aggregating the daily sales figures found in the operational database.

Along with the simplicity of processing in a DW environment comes a relative simplicity in the necessary technology. In the operational realm, the technologies necessary to support issues of transaction and data recovery, roll back, and detection and remedy of deadlock are quite complex. In the realm of data warehouses, all these processes are quite unnecessary.

ISSUES OF DATA REDUNDANCY

The lack of relevancy of issues such as data normalization in the DW environment that are so important to the reduction of data redundancy in the operational realm may suggest the prospect of massive data redundancy within the data warehouse and between the operational and DW environments. Inmon (1992a) pointed out that, counter to that first impression, a minimum of redundancy actually occurs between the data in the operational application databases feeding the DW and the warehouse itself. Several points bear out the truth of this assertion.

First, consider that the data being loaded into the DW are filtered and "cleansed" as they pass from the operational database to the warehouse. Because of this cleansing, numerous data that exist in the operational environment never pass to the data warehouse. Only the data necessary for processing by the DSS or EIS are ever actually loaded into the DW. Also, the DW contains a great deal of summarized data that are never reflected in the operational data store.

Consider also that the time horizons for warehouse and operational data elements are unique. Data in the operational environment are fresh, whereas warehouse data are generally much older. When viewed from a time horizon perspective, the opportunity for overlap or redundancy between the operational and data warehouse environments is minimal.

Finally, recall that the data being loaded into the DW often undergo a radical transformation as they pass from the operational to the DW environment. Because of this transformation and alteration, most of the data that ultimately reside in the data warehouse are not the same data that once resided in the operational environment (at least not from a data integration perspective).

Given these factors, Inmon suggested that data redundancy between the two environments is a rare occurrence with a typical redundancy factor of less than 1 percent.

10-2: THE DATA WAREHOUSE ARCHITECTURE

A data warehouse architecture (DWA) is a method by which the overall structure of data, communication, processing, and presentation for end-user computing within the enterprise can be represented. Figure 10-4 illustrates the various interconnected elements that make up the DWA.

OPERATIONAL AND EXTERNAL DATABASE LAYER

The operational and external database layer represents the source data for the DW. This layer comprises, primarily, operational transaction processing systems and external secondary databases. The goal of the data warehouse is to free the information locked up in the operational databases and to mix it with information from other, often external, sources. An additional objective of the DW is to have a minimal impact on the performance and operation of the systems found in this layer. In other words, the addition of the necessary extraction software to this environment should go unnoticed in terms of performance of the operational applications whose databases are being accessed.

Large organizations frequently acquire additional data from outside databases. The ubiquitous nature of the Web and the Internet makes it easy and economical for firms to access and incorporate such data into their DW. Data related to demographic, econometric, competitive, and purchasing trends typically found in public- or subscriber-access databases via the Internet are treated in the same manner as the ODS data and, following extraction and conditioning for consistency, are loaded into the data warehouse.

INFORMATION ACCESS LAYER

The end user deals directly with the information access layer of the DWA. In particular, it represents the tools that the end user normally uses day to day to extract and analyze the data contained within the DW. This layer consists of the hardware and software involved in displaying and printing reports, spreadsheets, graphs, and charts for analysis

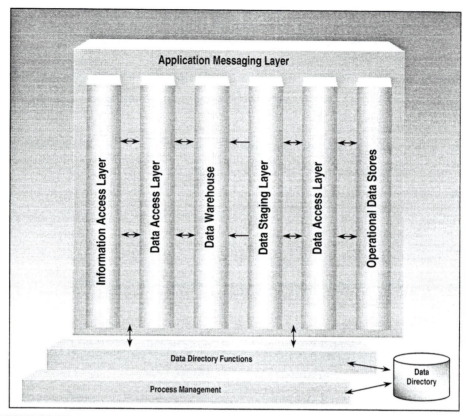

FIGURE 10-4 Components of the Data Warehouse Architecture

and presentation. At the information access layer, the DSSs use the DW data to support the various categories and types of decision making throughout the organization.

DATA ACCESS LAYER

As shown in Figure 10-4, the data access layer serves as a sort of interface or intermediary between the operational and information access layers and the data warehouse itself. This layer spans the various databases contained within the DW and facilitates common access by the DW users. The data access layer not only spans multiple databases and file systems on the same hardware, it also spans the wide variety of manufacturers and network protocols. A successful DW provides end users with universal data access so that, theoretically at least, end users should be able to access any or all of the enterprise's data necessary for them to do their job, regardless of location or information access tool. It is the role of the data access layer to make this access happen.

METADATA LAYER

In order to provide for universal data access, it is absolutely necessary to maintain some form of data directory or repository of metadata information. As discussed briefly in Section 10-1, metadata are data about the data stored within the DW.

Examples of metadata include the directory of where the data are stored, the rules used for summarization and scrubbing, or possibly records of operational data sources.

PROCESS MANAGEMENT LAYER

The process management layer focuses on scheduling the various tasks that must be accomplished to build and maintain the data warehouse and data directory information. This layer can be thought of as the scheduler or the high-level job control for the many processes (procedures) that must occur to keep the DW up to date. Tasks such as periodic download from identified operational data stores, scheduled summarization of operational data, access and download of external data sources, and update of the metadata are typically performed at this layer of the DWA.

APPLICATION MESSAGING LAYER

The application messaging layer transports information around the enterprise computing network. This layer is also referred to as "middleware," but it can typically involve more that just networking protocols and request routing. Application messaging, for example, can be used to isolate applications, operational or informational, from the exact data format on either end, thus facilitating a seamless interface between the uniqueness of a particular data format and the specific format requirements of the analysis tool being used. This layer can also be used to collect transactions or messages and deliver them to a certain location at a certain time. In this sense, the application messaging layer can be thought of as the transport system underlying the DW.

PHYSICAL DATA WAREHOUSE LAYER

The physical data warehouse layer is where the actual data used for decision support throughout the organization are located. In some cases, one can think of the DW simply as a logical or virtual view of data, because, as we will see shortly, in some instances the data warehouse may not actually store the data accessed through it.

DATA STAGING LAYER

The final component of the DWA is the data staging layer. Data staging (sometimes referred to as copy or replication management) includes all of the processes necessary to select, edit, summarize, combine, and load data warehouse and information access data from operational and external databases.

Data staging often involves complex programming, but more and more vendors market data warehousing tools intended to reduce the complexities associated with this process. Data staging may also require data quality analysis programs and other such filters that identify patterns and data structures within existing operational data.

DATA WAREHOUSING TYPOLOGY

As mentioned previously, although the data warehouse may appear to be the source of data for various organizational analysis initiatives and decision-making activities, it may not physically be the location of the data being accessed. Numerous hybrid mechanisms exist to structure a DW, but three basic configurations can be identified: virtual or point-to-point, central, and distributed data warehouses.

Before we review each configuration, we must note that no single approach to configuring a DW schema is best in all situations. Each option fits a specific set of requirements, and a data warehousing strategy may ultimately include all three options.

The Virtual Data Warehouse

A virtual or point-to-point data warehousing strategy allows the end users to access the operational data stores directly using tools enabled at the data access layer. This approach provides a great deal of flexibility as well as the minimum amount of redundant data that must be loaded and maintained; however, it can also put the largest unplanned query load and performance degradation on operational application systems.

Virtual warehousing is often an initial strategy in organizations with a broad but largely undefined need to get at operational data by a relatively large class of end users. In such situations, the likely frequency of requests is low. Virtual data warehouses often provide a relatively low-cost starting point for organizations to assess what types of data end users are really looking for.

The Central Data Warehouse

Central data warehouses are what most people think of when first introduced to the concept of a data warehouse. The central data warehouse is a single physical database that contains all of the data for a specific functional area, department, division, or enterprise. This warehousing approach is often selected when users demonstrate a common need for informational data and large numbers of end users are already connected to a central computer or network. A central data warehouse may contain data for any specific period of time and usually contains data from multiple operational applications.

The central data warehouse is real. The data stored in the DW are physically located in and accessible from one place and must be loaded and maintained on a regular basis. This configuration is the most common of the three basic types and represents the de facto standard for DW implementation due to the wide variety of construction and manipulation tools being offered.

The Distributed Data Warehouse

A distributed data warehouse is just what its name implies: a data warehouse whose components are distributed across a number of different physical databases. As large organizations push decision making down to lower and lower levels of the organization, the data needed for decision making is also pushed down (or out) to the LAN or local computer serving the local decision maker. Many older DW implementations use the distributed approach because initially it was easier to create several small data warehouse databases than to facilitate one all-encompassing one. The advent of modern DW implementation and management applications, however, reduced the need for multiple or distributed DWs.

10-3: DATA HAVE DATA—THE METADATA

JUST WHAT I NEED—MORE DATA!

The real problem with metadata is that the name suggests some high-level technological concept that requires far too much cognitive energy to discuss and understand. With the emergence of the DW as a primary decision support resource, metadata are now considered as much a resource of the organization as the business data they describe.

The standard definition of metadata is "data about data." Although this definition exudes a comforting Zen-like quality to it that makes for a great slogan, it leaves a lot to be desired with regard to providing any useful description. For example, how can we add meaning to data by associating that data with more data? To answer this question we must first understand the primary concept upon which metadata are built.

THE CONCEPT OF ABSTRACTION

To understand metadata, we focus on a relatively simple concept of general semantics called the chain of abstraction. For example, a sofa is a fairly concrete entity. Any particular sofa has a number of descriptive characteristics: It is made of wood, cloth, steel, and leather; it has two arms and a back; it is a particular shape or style; it has several cushions; and so on. We can abstract from that sofa, and others we encounter, to the word *sofa*. In other words, by using the word *sofa*, we can describe a wide variety of specific sofas; in fact, we can describe all sofas ever made. Moving from describing a particular sofa to representing all sofas by using a single word is but one step in the chain of abstraction. We can take further steps. For instance, we could describe the word *sofa* and all the other words we know by the word *word*. The chain of abstraction for anything is essentially unlimited, provided the level of abstraction we use conveys some useful meaning.

Software is simply a link in the chain of abstraction. The word *sofa* that you are reading now, if stored in a computer, would be represented by a string of magnetic flux changes on the oxide surface of a hard disk or as minute pits in the surface of a compact disk. So would a source code statement such as

LET CHECK_BALANCE = CHECK_BALANCE + CREDIT – DEBIT.

The source code statement, in turn, is an abstraction of a banking transaction, which is an abstraction of a bank, which is an abstraction of an industry, which is an abstraction of an economy, which is . . . well, you get the point.

Metadata are simply abstractions from data. They are high-level data that provide us with concise descriptions of lower-level data. The world is full of metadata—consider these examples:

- Author, title, ISBN number, and publisher
- Headlines of stories in a paper
- The business definitions for all data elements in the DW
- Road maps
- Data flow diagrams in a CASE tool's repository

THE KEY TO THE DATA

Metadata are essential ingredients in the transformation of raw data into knowledge. For example, metadata in the form of a field definition tell us that a given stream of bits is a customer's order number, part of a bit-mapped graphic, or the name of a word-processing document we just created. Should the metadata get mixed up or out of alignment, none of the data will make sense. The order number won't match any of our orders; the document we created will not be retrievable; even the graphic will not look quite the way it should, though depending upon how jumbled the metadata get, our eyes may not detect the difference.

It may be helpful to think of metadata as "tongs" with which we can handle raw data (APT, 1996). Without metadata, the data are meaningless. We do not even know where they are or what percentage to take. Take away data definitions, and how could we query a database? All we could hope to recover would be a string of ones and zeroes. In the early days of commercial computing, each application created and handled its own data files. Because the files' metadata were embedded in the application's data definitions, no application could make sense of another application's files. When databases were introduced, one of the greatest advantages they brought was that the metadata were stored in the database catalog, not in the individual programs. The one version of the truth was stored in the database.

THE METADATA IN ACTION

Assume for the moment, that while exploring our organization's data warehouse we find three unique sets of data:

1. 615397 8350621 885214 0051023 6487921
2. A Garrison Group report dated 9/11/96 states that the Asian market for machine tools expanded by 33 percent in 1995
3. Leading sports marketing firms: IMG 45 percent, SportStarz 33 percent, Legends, Inc. 16 percent

How much can we learn from these data? In the first case, the answer is "absolutely nothing." The numbers may be sales figures for a department or region, the population of European cities, or maybe the number of blood cells in a set of samples. The numbers could even represent a sequence of machine code for a computer. These data are typical of tabular data found in a relational database. Meaning can, however, be assigned to the data in two specific ways: from the context or from the metadata. In the former case, these numbers are the result of a query on a given table so we already know their meaning. In the latter, if we associate a metadata description with the data, it will tell us the name of the table and possibly a great deal more.

Example 2 appears to be more straightforward. It is free text and more self-descriptive. One small point, however: The date shown is ambiguous. Does "9/11/95" mean September 11, 1995 (U.S. convention), or November 9, 1995 (British convention)? In this case, the metadata serve to clear up the confusion by indicating that all dates are displayed using "MM/DD/YY."

The third example contains some metadata: We know the data represent leading sports marketing firms. What we don't know is what the percentages represent, what time period is referred to, how the data were collected, or even the source of the information. Without sufficient metadata, the data element in the example is rendered useless.

These examples demonstrate the importance of metadata in the DW environment. Here, data analysts and executives look for useful facts and correlations that they can recognize when they find them—and often, not before. Routine applications are of no use to them: They need to get in among the data, and to do so successfully, they need to understand the data's structure and meaning. Passengers on a train do not need a map, although a timetable may be useful. A driver setting out by road across a foreign country to an unknown village, though, would be unwise to set out without a complete set of large-scale and small-scale maps (APT, 1996). A data warehouse without adequate metadata is like filing cabinets stuffed full of paper with no folders or labels. Try finding anything useful in that!

CONSISTENCY—AVOIDING MANY VERSIONS OF THE TRUTH

Unreliable or missing metadata lead to untenable situations in which one business unit reports that overall corporate profits are up 15 percent, while another business unit says they are down 10 percent. Each functional area uses its own numbers, collected in accordance with its own procedures and interpreted by its own applications. This "algorithmic differential" often results in organizational decision making that lapses into a morass of politics and personalities.

Unlike the individual ODSs established for the benefit of a specific business unit or department, the data warehouse is set up for the benefit of business analysts and executives across all functional areas of the organization. If they need metadata—and they do—then it is the job of the warehouse support staff to make sure they get that information. In this regard, the DW support staff can be thought of as librarians. If you need help finding what you are looking for, they act as guides. If you require no assistance, then you are free to browse at your convenience.

In a DW environment, both the data and the metadata are constantly updated. Organizational decision makers are always on the lookout for new and interesting patterns in the data, which can lead them to investigate and compare information from all corners of the enterprise and beyond. It can also lead to requests for new data sets, which must be replicated from operational application systems or imported from external sources. With each new addition to the DW, the warehouse's metadata map requires extension to accommodate it.

AGREEING ON ONE VERSION OF THE TRUTH

Not only must warehouse administrators keep up with ever-changing data definitions and requests for new and disparate data sets, they must also agree on a single version of the truth. In the corporate world, the saying is that if the revenues for which credit was claimed by all the department managers were totaled, the amount would exceed the organization's actual revenue by several hundred percent. In aggregating all the data elements necessary for a useful data warehouse, the metadata must be organized in such a way that accurate and useful comparisons across time and sources can be made. The greatest challenge developers and maintainers of a DW face is ensuring the integrity and accuracy of the data contained within the data warehouse.

10-4: INTERVIEWING THE DATA—
METADATA EXTRACTION

GENERAL METADATA ISSUES

Inmon (1992b) suggested that, regardless of the specific nature of a given query to the DW, several general pieces of information, derived from the metadata, are important to all decision makers. Table 10-3 lists the generic information essential to using data from a DW.

Data warehouse metadata are not all that different in kind from operational database metadata, although DW metadata are versioned in order to permit historical analysis. The DW metadata must be tagged with some information that lets the user know the general conditions under which the DW data were collected. When collection methods or conditions change, then the metadata version must change as well. In this regard, we can think of metadata versioning as meta-metadata.

COMPONENTS OF THE METADATA

Collecting the right metadata at the right time is a foundational requirement for a successful DW implementation. Although specific metadata considered useful for one DW may not be useful to another, several categories of general metadata can be found in a typical DW environment.

Transformation Mapping

Transformation mapping metadata record how data from operational data stores and external sources are transformed on the way into the warehouse. As the individual data elements from these sources are mapped to the existing DW structures, this mapping should be collected and maintained as metadata. With the advent of modern data warehouse development tools, the mapping process becomes virtually indistinguishable from the process of transformation. Table 10-4 lists several of the types of mappings that must be available as metadata.

Extraction and Relationship History

Whenever historical information is analyzed, meticulous update records must be kept. Often a decision maker begins the process of constructing a time-based report by reviewing the extraction history because any changes to the business rules must be

---

TABLE 10-3   General Metadata Issues Associated with Data Warehouse Use

- What tables, attributes, and keys do the data warehouse contain?
- Where did each set of data come from?
- What transformation logic was applied in loading the data?
- How have the metadata changed over time?
- What aliases exist and how are they related to each other?
- What are the cross-references between technical and business terms?
- How often do the data get reloaded?
- How many data elements are in the DW (to assist in avoiding the submission of unrealistic queries)?

TABLE 10-4   Typical Mapping Metadata

- Identification of original source fields
- Simple attribute-to-attribute mapping
- Attribute conversions
- Physical characteristic conversions
- Encoding/reference table conversions
- Naming changes
- Key changes
- Values of defaults
- Logic to choose from among multiple sources
- Algorithmic changes

ascertained in order to apply the right rules to the right data. If sales regions were real-located in 1994, then the decision maker will know that results prior to that date may not be directly comparable with more recent results.

In addition to the extraction metadata, information regarding the various relationships contained within the DW must be maintained. Data warehouses often implement data relationships differently from operational application databases. Metadata pertaining to related tables, constraints, and cardinality must be maintained, together with text descriptions and ownership records. This information and the history of changes to it can be valuable to decision makers when performing analysis with multiple aggregations of data.

Algorithms for Summarization

A typical data warehouse contains a wide variety of lightly and heavily summarized data, as well as fully detailed records. The summarization algorithms applied to the detail data are important to any decision maker analyzing or interpreting the meaning of the summaries. These metadata can also save time by making it easier to decide which level of summarization is most appropriate for a given analysis context.

Data Ownership

Operational data stores are often "owned" by particular business units or divisions within an organization. In a data warehouse environment, however, all data are stored in a common format and are normally accessible to all, which makes it necessary to identify the originator of each set of data, so that inquiries and corrections can be made to the proper group. It is useful to distinguish between "ownership" of data in the operational environment and "stewardship" in the data warehouse. The administrators of the DW are responsible for the collection, summarization, and dissemination of warehouse data and in this regard are the caretakers or stewards of the data. The administrators of the source ODS, however, are responsible for the accuracy of the transaction-level data and are the actual owners of the data.

Patterns of Warehouse Access

It is often desirable to record patterns of access to the warehouse for the purpose of optimizing and tuning DW performance. Understanding what tables are being accessed, how often, and by whom can alert the DW administrators to ways of improving or simplifying the queries being performed by the end users. Less frequently used data can be migrated to cheaper storage media, and various methods can be employed to accelerate access to the data that are most in demand. Further, the identification and recording of queries can be a valuable resource to the organization because it can facilitate the reuse of queries. Instead of spending the time to figure out how to construct a new query, a decision maker can simply access a repository of past queries and choose the one that most closely resembles the immediate need.

Additional Common Metadata

In addition to the major categories of metadata already discussed, several other less common, yet equally important, categories of metadata can be identified. These miscellaneous metadata components are often context-specific or organization-dependent. When needed for analysis, however, they are as important as the more common categories.

Important members of this class of metadata are the logical business data models. In many instances, users need to understand the logical model that defines the entities, relationships, and rules that exist in a particular business environment where data were obtained. Building a data warehouse without including the source data models is both dangerous and prone to error. When the source data model is available, metadata describing the mapping between the data model and the physical design can be retrieved, thus resolving ambiguities or uncertainties.

Another category of metadata that can make the warehouse much more user-friendly is the recording of aliases. By allowing a table to be queried by "Units produced by each region" rather than "REG_MFG_STATS," aliases makes both the construction and subsequent interpretation of a query more understandable. Aliases are also useful when different business units use their own names to refer to the same underlying data. Careful tracking of aliases for data elements is an important part of the DW metadata.

Development status metadata are yet another important source of information to the DW user. Often, parts of the same data warehouse may be in various stages of development or completion. Status information can be used to convey information to the decision maker regarding, for example, the tables being accessed by a certain query. Such tables might be classified as in-design, in-test, or inactive.

Finally, volumetric metadata can be stored to inform users as to the exact volume of data they are dealing with, to provide them with some idea about how much their queries will cost in terms of time and resources. Volumetrics often include such information as number of rows, table growth rate, usage characteristics, indexing, and byte specifications.

10-5: IMPLEMENTING THE DATA WAREHOUSE

The challenge of providing access to the aggregated data of an organization is not a new one. The 1970s saw the advent of the information center, an ill-fated concept that required a dedicated high-powered computer and severely drained resources in terms of hardware, software, and personnel needed. The 1980s brought an emphasis on data reengineering using the extended relational model. This model, too, suffered from complexities and severe performance degradation issues. The 1990s' answer appears to be the data warehouse. If we are to avoid the problems of the past and realize the successes assumed to be associated with total access to data, IT management and organizational data warehouse champions must not only understand what needs to be done, but also just how to do it. Following a closer look in the next chapter at the data warehouse from a data visualization perspective, in Chapter 12 we will focus in detail on the issues surrounding the implementation of a data warehouse in the modern organization. For our purposes in this chapter, however, we simply need to begin thinking about the unique nature of the data warehouse with regard to implementation.

Denis Kozar (1997), vice president of Enterprise Information Architecture for Chase Manhattan Bank, assembled the "seven deadly sins" of data warehouse implementation. Each of these errors can result in the failure of an otherwise valuable data warehouse initiative. Table 10-5 lists the "seven deadly sins" of data warehousing.

SIN 1: "IF YOU BUILD IT, THEY WILL COME"

Kozar suggested that the first of the seven sins is one of blind faith. It is the failure to recognize the importance of developing a clear set of business objectives for the data warehouse prior to its construction. A successful data warehouse plan considers the needs of the entire enterprise and develops a documented set of requirements to guide the design, construction, and rollout of the project. The data warehouse cannot simply be built in the hope that someone will find a use for it.

SIN 2: OMISSION OF AN ARCHITECTURAL FRAMEWORK

One of the most important factors in a successful data warehouse initiative is the development and maintenance of a comprehensive architectural framework. Such a framework serves as the blueprints for construction and use of the various DW components. Issues such as the expected number of end users, the volume and diversity of data, and the expected data-refresh cycle, among many others, must be considered (and reflected) in the DW architecture.

SIN 3: UNDERESTIMATING THE IMPORTANCE OF DOCUMENTING ASSUMPTIONS

The assumptions and potential data conflicts associated with the DW must be included in the architectural framework for the project. They must be ascertained and codified within the document as early in the project as possible to ensure their reflection in the final product. Several questions must be answered during the requirements phase of the project to reveal important underlying assumptions about the DW. How much data

---

TABLE 10-5   The Seven Deadly Sins of Data Warehouse Implementation

1. "If you build it, they will come."
2. Omission of a data warehouse architectural framework.
3. Underestimating the importance of documenting all assumptions and potential conflicts.
4. Abuse of methodology and tools.
5. Abuse of the data warehouse life cycle.
6. Ignorance concerning the resolution of data conflicts.
7. Failure to document the mistakes made during the first DW project.

should be loaded into the warehouse? What is the expected level of data granularity? How often do we need to refresh the data? On what platform will the DW be developed and implemented? Accurate answers are essential to the success of a data warehouse project.

SIN 4: FAILURE TO USE THE RIGHT TOOL FOR THE JOB

The design and construction of a data warehouse is, in many ways, much different from the construction of an operational application system. A DW project requires a different set of tools than those typically found in an application development effort.

Data warehouse tools can be categorized into four discrete groupings: (1) analysis tools, (2) development tools, (3) implementation tools, and (4) delivery tools. Within each of these categories are specialized tools designed specifically to accommodate the unique design activities associated with data warehouse development.

Analysis Tools

The tools in this category identify data requirements, the primary sources of data for the DW, and the construction of the data model for the warehouse. Modern CASE tools belong to this category. Another analysis tool is the code scanner. These applications scan source code for file or database definitions and data usage identifiers. This information helps to build the initial data model for the warehouse by determining the data requirements contained within the source ODS.

Development Tools

This class of tools is responsible for data cleansing, code generation, data integration, and loading of the data into the final warehouse repository. These tools are also the primary generators of metadata for the warehouse.

Implementation Tools

This category contains the data acquisition tools used to gather, process, clean, replicate, and consolidate the data to be contained within the warehouse. In addition, information storage tools from this category may be used to load summarized data from external data sources.

Delivery Tools

Delivery tools assist in the data conversion, data derivation, and reporting for the final delivery platform. This category includes specific tools for querying and reporting and the generation of and access to data glossaries intended to help end users identify what data are actually contained within the warehouse.

SIN 5: LIFE CYCLE ABUSE

This sin is the failure of the DW developers to realize the differences between the data warehouse life cycle (DWLC) and the traditional system development life cycle (SDLC) methodologies. Although similar, these two approaches differ in one critical aspect: The DWLC never ends. The life cycle of a data warehouse project is an ongoing set of activities that flow from initial investigation of DW requirements through data administration and back again. Typically, as each phase of the DW is completed, a new one is started due to new data requirements, additional user groups, and new sources of data. The DW developers must realize that the project must never end if the warehouse is to remain a viable source of decision-making support.

SIN 6: IGNORANCE CONCERNING THE RESOLUTION OF DATA CONFLICTS

The justification for a new data warehouse initiative is often predicated on the need for greater quality data for decision making within the organization. Although it offers a laudable objective for a DW project, it is simply the tip of the iceberg with regard to actually putting the warehouse into operation. People and organizations tend naturally to be highly protective and territorial when it comes to their data and associated applications. As a result, a great deal of often-tedious analysis must be conducted to determine the best data sources available within the organization. Once these systems are identified, the conflicts associated with disparate naming conventions, file formats and sizes, and value ranges must be resolved. This process may involve working with the data owners to establish an understanding with regard to future planned or unplanned changes to the source data. Failure to allow sufficient time and resources to resolve data conflicts can stall a warehouse initiative and result in an organizational stalemate that can threaten the success of the project.

SIN 7: FAILURE TO LEARN FROM MISTAKES

The ongoing nature of the DWLC suggests that one data warehouse project simply begets another. Because of this tendency, careful documentation of the mistakes made in the first round will directly affect the quality assurance activities of all future projects. By learning from the mistakes of the past, a strong data warehouse with lasting benefits can be built.

10-6: DATA WAREHOUSE TECHNOLOGIES

The real dream of anyone who suffered through the pre-development-tool days of data warehousing is that someday we will be able to place an order with Wile E. Coyote's favorite supplier, Acme. Seconds later, we will receive a big wooden crate with "Acme Data Warehouse" stenciled on the side with everything we need inside, including batteries.

That day may actually come, but current data warehouse products are still quite a ways from the "Acme" ideal. Today organizations buy bits and pieces of complex hardware and software from a number of vendors, like assembling a puzzle. A typical sales pitch by a DW vendor might include "A data warehouse is an architecture, not a product," or "It's a process, not a place," or even something such as "It's 90 percent expertise, 10 percent technology." The translation for all this rhetoric is simple: Good luck making all this stuff work together!

To build a data warehouse that works, developers must be even more resourceful than a cartoon coyote when it comes to architecture, process, expertise, and dozens of other abstractions. But resourcefulness, in itself, may still not be enough to guarantee a successful DW environment. The DW investment requires a thorough evaluation process that probes the promises and pitfalls of integrating data warehouse tools offered by the leading DW vendors.

No one currently offers an end-to-end data warehouse solution, but several companies such as SAS, IBM, Software AG, Information Builders, and Platinum are moving toward that goal, albeit slowly. For instance, here is an example of the type of challenges facing one of the current key data warehouse vendors: IBM.

IBM's premier offering, Visual Warehouse, offers good integration if you run under OS/2 but is much less flexible under other leading operating system platforms such as Windows NT and Novell. In addition, Visual Warehouse is, as yet, unable to manage databases beyond the LAN environment. Larger, more robust databases built around DB/2 Parallel Edition, DB2 MVS, and the new AS/400 parallel database (all IBM offerings) have yet to be accommodated by IBM's leading DW product. Although the company claims it is vigorously working on the problems, it is unwilling to offer any specific time horizons. In other words, even the vendors struggle to make it all work together in harmony.

The good news is that the marketplace is bursting with vendor offerings in the data warehouse arena and, given the plenitude of choices, an organization is likely to find the technology it needs to embark on a DW initiative. The bad news is that the constant state of flux and the high cost of operations make it difficult for the smaller players to stay afloat in this fiercely competitive marketplace, and, as such, the leader board changes daily. Table 10-6 contains a fairly comprehensive listing of the current data warehouse offerings (at the time of this writing, at least).

10-7: THE FUTURE OF DATA WAREHOUSING

It is both highly likely and highly desirable that as the data warehouse becomes a mature part of an organization's decision support infrastructure it will blend into the fabric of the organization and be as anonymous as the data communication network used to move data from place to place. In other words, once the problems currently associated with an inability to access corporate data are completely resolved, an increased effort to find new ways to utilize those data will emerge. This new focus will bring with it several new challenges. This final section identifies several of these challenges facing data warehousing in the future.

REGULATORY CONSTRAINTS

The power associated with the ability to analyze and extract information from large volumes of disparate data continues to spark legislation that seeks to protect individuals from abuse by government or commercial entities that have large volumes of data concerning those individuals. As fears over covert and overt invasions of privacy continue to escalate, the ease with which external data sources can be accessed will decline. This tightening of security will require a concerted effort on the part of all users of data sources to craft a workable set of rules and guidelines that allow for the privacy of individuals while simultaneously facilitating the use of large data sets for meaningful analyses.

TABLE 10-6   Leading Data Warehouse Vendors and Products

DW Vendor	*Product Offering(s)*
Actuate Software	Report Server, Reporting System, Web Agent
Andyne Computing	GQL, PaBLO, Text Tool
Angoss Software	KnowledgeSEEKER
Aonix	Nomad
Applix	TM1 Server, TM1 Client, TM1 Perspective, TM1 Show Business
AppSource	Wired for OLAP
Arbor Software	Essbase, Essbase Web Gateway
Attar Software	XpertRule Profiler
Belmont Research	CrossGraphs
Brio Technology	BrioQuery Enterprise, brio.web.warehouse
Business Objects	BusinessObjects, BusinessMiner
Carleton	Passport
Cognos	Impromptu, PowerPlay, Scenario
CorVu	Integrated Business Intelligence Suite (IBIS)
Computer Associates	CA-LDM, CA-OpenIngres, Visual Express
Concentric Data Systems	Arpeggio
Data Distilleries B.V.	Data Surveyor
Data Junction	Data Junction, Cambio
Data Management Technologies	Time Machine, RQA-Remote Query Accelerator
DataMind	DataMind
Digital Equipment	Alpha Warehouse
Dimensional Insight	Cross Target
Enterprise Solutions	InfoCat
European Management Systems	Eureka
Evolutionary Technologies International	ETI-Extract
Harbor Software	Harbor Light
Hewlett-Packard	Intelligent Warehouse
Holistic Systems	HOLOS
Hyperion	OLAP, Spider-Man
IBM	Data Propagator, DB2 Database Server, Enterprise Copy Manager, Data Hub for OS/2, Data Hub for Unix, Flow-Mark, DataGuide, Application System, Visualizer family, Intelligent Decision Server, Query Management Facility, Intelligent Miner
Informatica	PowerMart
Information Advantage	DecisionSuite, WebOLAP
Information Builders	EDA/Copy Manager, Focus Fusion, Focus Six EIS Edition
Information Discovery	DAta Mining Suite
Informix Software	OnLine Dynamic Server-Unix, OnLine Dynamic Server-Windows NT, New Era ViewPoint OnLine Extended Parallel Server, MetaCube, MetaCube Warehouse Manager

(continued)

TABLE 10-6 Continued

DW Vendor	Product Offering(s)
InfoSAGE	DECISIVE
Innovative Group	Innovative-Warehouse
Integral Solutions Limited	Clementine
Intersolv	DataDirect Explorer, SmartData
Intrepid Systems	DecisionMaster
IQ Software	IQ/SmartServer, IQ/Objects, Intelligent Query, IQ/Vision
Kenan Systems	Acumate ES
Liant Software	Relativity
Lingo Computer Design	Fiscal Executive Dashboard
Logic Works	Universal Directory
Mayflower Software	Sentinel, Information Catalog
Mercantile Software Systems	IRE Marketing Warehouse
MathSoft	Axum
Microsoft	Microsoft SQL Server
NCR	Teradata
NewGeneration Software	NGS Managed Query Environment
Oberon Software	Prospero
Oracle	Oracle8, Discoverer/2000, Oracle Express Server
Pilot Software	Decision Support Suite, Command Center
Pine Cone Systems	Data Content Tracker
Platinum Technology	InfoRefiner, Info Transport, Fast Load, Data Shopper, InfoReports, Object Administrator, Query Analyzer, Report Facility (PRF), InfoBeacon, Forest & Trees
Postalsoft	Postalsoft Library products
Powersoft	InfoMaker
Praxis International	OmniLoader
Precise Software Solutions	Inspect/SQL
Prism Solutions	Prism Warehouse Manager, Prism Change Manager, Prism Directory Manager
Progress Software	EnQuiry
QDB Solutions	QDB/Analyze
Red Brick Systems	Red Brick Warehouse, 5.0, Red Brick Data Mine Option, Red Brick Data Mine Builder, Red Brick Enterprise Control & Coordination
Reduct Systems	DataLogic/R
ReGenisys	extract:R
Sagent	Sagent Data mart
SAS Institute	SAS Data Warehouse, Warehouse Administrator, SAS System, SAS/MDDB
Seagate Software IMG	Crystal Reports, Crystal Info
SelectStar	StarTrieve
ShowCase	STRATEGY

(continued)

TABLE 10-6 Continued

DW Vendor	Product Offering(s)
Siemens-Pyramid	Smart Warehouse
Silicon Graphics	MineSet
Smart Corporation	Smart DB Workbench
Software AG	Intelligon, Passport, SourcePoint, Esperant, ADABAS
Softworks	metaVISION
Spalding Software	DataImport
Speedware	Esperant, EasyReporter, Media
SPSS	SPSS
Sterling Software	Vision:Journey
Sybase	Sybase SQL Server 11, Sybase IQ, Sybase MPP
Syware	DataSync
Tandem	Tandem NonStop
Thinking Machines	Darwin
Torrent Systems	Orchestrate
Trillium Software	Trillium Software System
Visual Numerics	PV-Wave
Vmark Software	uniVerse, DataStage
Wincite Systems	WINCITE
WizSoft	WizWhy

STORAGE OF UNSTRUCTURED DATA

Currently the modern data warehouse is limited to storage of structured data in the form of records, fields, and databases. Unstructured data, such as multimedia, maps, graphs, pictures, sound, and video files, are rapidly increasing in importance throughout organizations. The need to store, retrieve, and combine these new data types will require a new and expanded data warehouse architecture and interface. In the DW environment of tomorrow, a user may be searching for relationships between different types of products. The DW will contain not only structured data for such analysis but may also allow for the scanning and analysis of the contents of images and audio and video files to facilitate the establishment of such relationships. To bring this level of use and functionality to fruition, vendors of DW applications and tools face a number of technological and practical challenges yet to be explored. Issues including how to manage the storage and retrieval of unstructured data and how to search for specific data items must be addressed and resolved if the DW of tomorrow is to accommodate the technology and data being generated today.

THE WORLD WIDE WEB

As with everything it comes into contact with, the World Wide Web will undoubtedly have a significant impact on data warehousing. The ability to access and transfer large numbers of data relatively easily and economically will make the Internet and the Web ideal vehicles to integrate external data into the warehouse environment. Issues of data integrity, accuracy, and quality will have to be addressed and resolved. It is conceivable that third-party enterprises will evolve whose sole purpose is to evaluate and rate the quality and integrity of external data sources. Those quality ratings could be used to determine the degree of value to be placed on the integration of a particular source of external data into the data warehouse. Equally conceivable is the use of the quality rating to determine the price to be paid for access to such data; the higher the quality rating, the higher the price.

10-8: CHAPTER SUMMARY

Due to the overwhelming concentration on the automation of processes by business and industry, organizations, no matter how large or small, create enormous amounts of data every day. The biggest problem with this data explosion is the difficulty in integrating data generated in a world of unintegrated information systems. With data warehousing comes the ability to ask questions of the data that were previously unaskable and to discover new relationships contained within the data that were previously undiscoverable. The concept reintegrates the data generated by the wide variety of internal and external information systems. In the next chapter, we will build upon our understanding of data warehousing by focusing our attention on methods intended to "mine" the hidden resources contained within the data.

Key Concepts

- The data warehouse is "a collection of integrated, subject-oriented databases designed to support the DSS function (decision support), where each unit of data is non-volatile and relevant to some moment in time" (Inmon 1992a, 5). (10-1)
- The operational data store's function is to store the data for a single, specific set of operational applications. (10-1)
- The data mart is often viewed as a way to gain entry to the realm of data warehouses and to make all the mistakes on a smaller scale. (10-1)
- Characteristics of a data warehouse (10-1)

  Subject orientation

  Integrated

  Nonvolatile

  Time variant

  Summarized

  Large volume

  Not normalized

  Metadata

  Data sources
- The data warehouse world is primarily void of process design (at least in its classical form) and tends to focus exclusively on issues of data modeling and database design. (10-1)
- Only two data operations are ever performed in the data warehouse: data loading and data access. (10-1)

- A data warehouse architecture is a method by which the overall structure of data, communication, processing, and presentation that exists for end-user computing can be represented. (10-2)
- Three data warehousing typologies (10-2)

  Virtual data warehouse (point-to-point data warehouse)

  Central data warehouse

  Distributed data warehouse

- Metadata are simply abstractions from data. They are high-level data that provide us with a concise description of lower-level data (data about data). (10-3)
- The "seven deadly sins" of data warehouse implementation.

  Sin 1: "If you build it, they will come"

  Sin 2: Omission of an architectural framework

  Sin 3: Underestimating the importance of documenting assumptions

  Sin 4: Failure to use the right tool for the job

  Sin 5: Life cycle abuse

  Sin 6: Ignorance concerning the resolution of data conflicts

  Sin 7: Failure to learn from mistakes

Questions for Review

1. Define each of the following terms:
   Data store
   Data mart
   Metadata
   Subject orientation
   Data integrated
   Time variant
   Nonvolatile
   Chain of abstraction
   Transformation mapping
2. What unique benefits does a data warehouse provide for management at all levels of the firm?
3. What is a data warehouse? How is it better than traditional information-gathering techniques?
4. Describe the data warehouse environment.
5. What are the characteristics of a data warehouse?
6. List and explain the different layers in the data warehouse architecture.
7. What are metadata? Why are metadata so important to a data warehouse?
8. What are the "seven deadly sins" of building a data warehouse?

For Further Discussion

1. The World Wide Web contains a vast amount of information about data warehousing and is, in fact, a data warehouse itself. Viewing the Web from the perspective of a data warehouse, describe and identify the various warehouse components

and consider how an organization might harness the power of the Web as a useful data warehouse.

2. Proponents of data warehousing state that the concept is highly generalizable and can be used by any industry or knowledge domain. Think of several industries in which data warehousing could be useful in improving the management of information. Can you think of any industries where data warehousing would not be applicable?

3. Find an organization in your area that uses data warehousing. If possible, talk with the warehouse administrator about the trials and tribulations faced during the design and implementation of the warehouse. How did he or she deal with the problems? What problems still exist today?

4. Metadata are everywhere. Find a database of information around your school, work, or home and identify as many pieces of metadata as you can.

DATA MINING AND DATA VISUALIZATION

Learning Objectives

◆ Understand the concept of data mining (DM)

◆ Trace the evolution of decision support activities from verification to discovery

◆ Understand the concept of online analytical processing (OLAP) and its rules

◆ Learn the two approaches used to conduct multidimensional analysis of data—multidimensional OLAP (MOLAP) and relational OLAP (ROLAP)—and explore the different situations suited for MOLAP and ROLAP architectures

◆ Recognize the four major categories of processing algorithms and rule approaches used to mine data: classification, association, sequence, and cluster

◆ Assess current data mining technologies including statistical analysis, neural networks, genetic algorithms, fuzzy logic, and decision trees

◆ Learn the general process of knowledge discovery through examples

◆ Examine market basket analysis procedures

◆ Understand the current limitations and challenges to data mining

◆ Survey the history of data visualization and how it can help with decision-making activities

◆ Consider the typical applications of data visualization techniques

◆ Review several current "siftware" technologies

◆ Conduct several PolyAnalyst and TextAnalyst exercises using actual data sets

THE NATIONAL BASKETBALL ASSOCIATION GETS A "JUMP" ON DATA MINING

Anyone who follows professional basketball knows that the Dallas Mavericks are green, and that's not just one of the colors in their uniforms. Like many NBA franchises, the Mavericks are experiencing the growing pains associated with developing young players and building a winning professional basketball program. They aren't likely to earn an NBA championship anytime soon. Assistant coach Bob Salmi knows this.

But he also knows that by the time Michael Jordan retires again, first from the Chicago Bulls and next time from the Washington Wizards, at least 10 NBA teams will have assembled lineups of comparable talent—including, he hopes, the Mavericks. Given this relatively level playing field, how can a coach create a competitive advantage for his team?

One way is with information—specifically, the information gleaned through Advanced Scout, a data mining application for postgame analysis created by IBM for the NBA to showcase the use of the technology in professional sports.

Salmi uses Advanced Scout to mine for patterns in coaching data, such as winning player combinations. Advanced Scout is synchronized with digital video that is time-stamped by a uniform time clock that tabulates all the statistics—such as rebounding, matchups, and scoring—for all NBA games. Once a seemingly successful pattern is discovered, a coach can cue up the digital video to view additional factors that contributed to those combinations: what plays were run, how they were executed and defended, what other players were involved, and so on.

The data mining approach to postgame analysis is much less time consuming than the old manual method of jotting down stats with pencil and paper and forever rewinding the videotape. That process greatly relied on guesswork and a coach's intuition, and often took all

night. In contrast, Advanced Scout allows for analysis to be performed in the few hours it takes to fly to the location of the next game.

Advanced Scout is based on a data mining technique written in C++ called attribute focusing, which looks for "interesting" patterns and statistical correlations. The key characteristic of the attribute focusing technique is that it is designed for use by lay people, or "domain experts," rather than professional data analysts. The attribute focusing technique's emphasis on the nontechnical user differentiates it from other methods—such as neural networks, decision trees, and regression analysis—typically used in data mining applications like category management, market-basket analysis, and sequence analysis. The complexity of most software tools for these applications makes them better suited to analysts.

Currently, the NBA is mining data on a per-season basis, but now that coaches have two seasons' worth of experience under their belt, they are ready to expand to historical statistical data, going back with Advanced Scout a number of years. Then coaches can use the results not only for postgame analysis but also for contract negotiations with players.

That perspective was clearly illustrated during the 1997 NBA play-off series between the Orlando Magic and the Miami Heat. Like Bob Salmi, Orlando Magic assistant coach Tom Sterner has worked with Advanced Scout since its beginnings. The Heat eventually won the best-of-five series in a hotly contested fifth game. But without Advanced Scout's data mining, it would likely have ended in a three-game Heat blowout.

"We were beaten so badly in games 1 and 2 at Miami—99-64 in game 1 and 104-87 in game 2," Sterner recalls. "After game 2, we ran our analysis and watched the tape to determine what happened. Advanced Scout gave us some interesting pieces of data."

(*continued*)

First, Advanced Scout revealed that the starting backcourt combination of Orlando Magic players Anfernee "Penny" Hardaway and Brian Shaw were 217 in game 2. (Basketball coaches use a plus/minus system based on how many points are scored by or against a team while players are on the court as one indicator of the relative performance of a player or combinations of players.) It also revealed that in the same game the combination of Shaw and point guard Darrell Armstrong—a backup player who usually saw little game time—was 16. Moreover, the combination of Armstrong and Hardaway was 114.

Sterner's conclusion, based on Advanced Scout's analysis: Use Armstrong more in game 3 at Orlando. The results were stunning. "In game 3, with about six or seven minutes left to go in the half, we were down 20 points again," he says. "We brought Darrell into the game, and by the end of the half we were tied, 42-42. By the end of the game, we had won, 88-75. Penny Hardaway had scored 42 points, and Armstrong scored 21. Most importantly, we avoided elimination."

Another example illustrating how a pattern is discovered and interpreted comes from an analysis of the data from a game played between the New York Knicks and the Charlotte Hornets. The data revealed that when *"Glenn Rice played the shooting guard position, he shot 5/6 (83 percent) on jump shots."*

Through data mining, Advanced Scout identified a certain player (Rice), playing a certain position (shooting guard), shooting at a certain rate (83 percent), on a certain type of shot (jump shots). Advanced Scout not only finds this pattern, but points out that it is interesting because it differs considerably from the average shooting percentage of 54 percent for the Charlotte Hornets during that game.

Identifying the exact circumstances of an interesting pattern is something that a coach might not ordinarily detect. Yet it conveys valuable information about a scenario which worked very well for the Hornets but one they used only a few times in the entire game. For the Hornets it suggests a strategy that they should use more often. For the Knicks, it suggests that they might consider a different defensive strategy against Glenn Rice.

By using the NBA universal clock, Advanced Scout can automatically bring up the video clips that show each of the jump shots attempted by Glenn Rice at shooting guard, without requiring the coach to comb through hours of video footage. Those clips show Glenn Rice successfully using his strength and quickness against the player guarding him to free himself up for a jump shot.

"The coach needs to determine how the information relates to his team—his insight is the art," says Sterner. "Why was Phil Jackson of Chicago so successful? Michael Jordan sure helped. But the human element in every team is still important to the success of the team.

"Talent goes a long way to winning. If you have more talent than your opponent, you'll win. When your talent equals theirs, then the competitive edge could be the technology you use to prepare for the game."

Also reinforced is the business case for data mining. A more competitive game is money in the bank for professional sports teams.

"Our fans' faith in the team was restored, and we played two more home games than anybody expected," Sterner says. "That's worth millions of dollars" in terms of the gate, TV advertising, even concession sales. "It's a snowball of positive effects."

Source: askibm@vnet.ibm.com Reproduced by permission from IBM. Copyright 1997 by International Business Machine Corporation.

11-1: A PICTURE IS WORTH A THOUSAND WORDS

The title of this section is, admittedly, an old cliché. We use it when we need to point out that we can derive more information by looking at something than by reading or talking about it. Symbolically it may be true, but if it were literally true, I could deliver this book to you in approximately 350 pictures, if they were the right pictures.

It seems reasonable to assume that a cliché is not intended to be universally applicable but rather applicable under a given set of circumstances. At times, we find it more useful to articulate with words things that are difficult to express with pictures alone. Other times, we might use words for making an inquiry in order to discover something new that is best represented by a picture. In still other situations, a picture is the only method by which certain information can be transmitted effectively (or even at all).

In this chapter, we will explore the new realm of data mining and data visualization. With the realization of the data warehouse comes the ability to ask questions of the data that were previously unable to be asked and to discover new relationships contained within the data that were previously undiscoverable.

WHAT IS DATA MINING?

By its simplest definition, data mining (DM) is the set of activities used to find new, hidden, or unexpected patterns in data. Using information contained within the data warehouse, data mining can often provide answers to questions about an organization that a decision maker had previously not thought to ask:

- Which of our products should be promoted to this customer?
- What is the probability that a certain customer will respond to a planned promotion?
- Which securities will be most profitable to buy or sell during the next trading session?
- What is the likelihood that a certain customer will default or pay back on schedule?
- What is the appropriate medical diagnosis for this patient?

These types of questions can be answered surprisingly easily if the information hidden among the terabytes of data in your databases can be found explicitly and utilized.

An increasingly common synonym for data mining techniques is knowledge data discovery (KDD). This more descriptive term applies to all activities and processes associated with discovering useful knowledge from aggregate data. Using a combination of techniques including statistical analysis, neural and fuzzy logic, multidimensional analysis, data visualization, and intelligent agents, KDD can discover highly useful and informative patterns within the data that can be used to develop predictive models of behavior or consequences in a wide variety of knowledge domains.

For example, from using KDD techniques we know that left-handed women tend to buy right-handed golf gloves. This pattern relates a customer's attributes to product sales. It is also known that AT&T's stock price predictably rises at least 2 percent after every three-day slump in the Dow Jones Industrial Average. One can think of several uses for this single piece of information.

Another example of KDD at work is the relation of product consumption habits to each other: Men who buy diapers also buy beer; people who buy scuba gear take

Australian vacations; people who purchase skim milk also tend to buy whole wheat bread. Finally, the minicase at the beginning of this chapter clearly demonstrates how data mining can be used to assist in play selection in the National Basketball Association. This small sampling indicates only a few of the pattern types that can be found using KDD techniques. The myriad of potential patterns, however, dictates the need for a wide variety of KDD approaches and technologies to assist in finding them.

One of the most recent applications of DM is in the explosive growth area of customer relationship management (CRM). Data mining and CRM software allow users to analyze large databases to solve business decision problems. Data mining is, in some ways, an extension of statistics, with a few artificial intelligence and machine learning twists thrown in. Like statistics, data mining is not a business solution; it is a technology. CRM, on the other hand, involves turning information in a database into a business decision that drives interactions with customers. For example, consider a catalog retailer who needs to decide who should receive information about a new product. The information incorporated into the data mining and CRM process is contained in a historical database of previous interactions with customers and the features associated with the customers, such as age, zip code, and individual responses. The data mining software uses this historical information to build a model of customer behavior that could be used to predict which customers would be likely to respond to the new product. By using this information a marketing manager can select only the customers who are most likely to respond. CRM software can then feed the results of the decision to the appropriate touchpoint systems (call centers, Web servers, e-mail systems, etc.) so that the right customers receive the right offers.

Even more recent is the application of data mining techniques to data collected from visitors to an e-commerce Web site. Companies venturing into e-commerce have a dream. By analyzing the tracks people make through their Web site, they can better optimize its design to maximize sales. Information about customers and their purchasing habits lets companies initiate e-mail campaigns and other activities that result in sales. Good models of customers' preferences, needs, desires, and behaviors help companies simulate the personal relationship that businesses and their clientele had in the good old days.

The foundation of this dream is the log of customer accesses maintained by Web servers. A sequence of page hits might look something like this: Page A => Page B => Page C => Page D => Page C => Page B => Page F => Page G, or more explicitly: Login => Register => Product Description => Purchase.

By analyzing customer paths through the data, vendors hope to personalize the interactions with customers and prospects. Companies will customize the homepage each customer sees, the responses to requests, and the recommendations of items to purchase. If you are a customer of Amazon.com Inc., you may already have noticed such personalization. Vendors can also generate a list of related products.

The business benefits of this customer intelligence are potentially enormous. The number of people who come to a site and purchase will increase, and the average amount per purchase will rise, resulting in a dramatic increase in profitability—that's the dream, at least.

The reality is that achieving this goal is difficult and expensive—but it is possible. First, to be of any use at all, clickstream data require enormous amounts of labor-intensive preprocessing. Even then, extracting meaning is still difficult. Second, many customers are reluctant to have vendors track what they do. Their concern is so great that the government is actively considering privacy regulation to limit Web tracking. Nonetheless, DM is emerging as a major force in deep data analysis. Let's look at why data mining is becoming so important.

VERIFICATION VERSUS DISCOVERY

In the past, decision support activities were primarily based on the concept of verification. In this sense, a relational database could be queried to provide dynamic answers to well-formed questions. The key issue in verification is that it requires a great deal of a priori knowledge on the part of the decision maker in order to verify a suspected relationship through the query. One industry making extensive use of verification querying is the gaming, or casino, industry. The host of the casino can use a database of customer characteristics to develop a unique set of classifications for customers. He or she can then enter a new customer's observable or known characteristics into a query to assist in classifying the customer as a high roller, a souvenir buyer, a ticket purchaser, or any number of other categories related to casino services. Although this approach requires the casino host to manage a large volume of known relationships contained within the database, the ability to categorize a new customer has proven highly profitable.

As casinos embrace more sophisticated computer technologies, the concept of verification continues to evolve into one of discovery. By using siftware, software specifically designed to find new and previously unclassified patterns in data, the casino host can discover new patterns and classifications of customer spending habits that allow for the effective targeting of casino services and events to a specific group of customers.

It is easy to see the vast potential for decision support activities in virtually any domain using KDD. As with any technology, to use KDD effectively we must first understand the foundations upon which it is based. Therefore, our exploration of the new world of data mining must begin at the beginning: the conception of online analytical processing.

DATA MINING'S GROWTH IN POPULARITY

Several reasons can be cited in support of the growing popularity of data mining. Probably the single greatest reason is the ever-increasing volume of data that require processing. The amount of data accumulated each day by businesses and organizations varies according to function and objective. A year 2000 report from the GTE research center suggests that scientific and academic organizations store approximately 1 terabyte of new data each day, even though the academic community is not the leading supplier of new data worldwide.

Another reason for the growing popularity is an increasing awareness of the inadequacy of the human brain to process data, particularly in situations involving multifactorial dependencies or correlations. Our biases formed by previous experience in data analysis often hold us hostage. As such, our objectivity in data analysis scenarios is often suspect.

Finally, a third reason for the growing popularity of DM is the increasing affordability of machine learning. An automated data mining system can operate at a much lower cost than an army of highly trained (and paid) professional statisticians. Although DM does not entirely eliminate human participation in problem solving, it significantly simplifies the tasks and allows humans to better manage the process.

MAKING ACCURATE INDIVIDUAL PREDICTIONS WITH DATA MINING

Although quite valuable in the appropriate contexts, data mining is developing somewhat of an urban legend with regard to its abilities. Scanning data mining articles and texts reveals statements such as, "Data mining will allow us to predict who is likely to buy a particular product," or "We will be able to predict who is likely to cancel their service with us in the next 12 months." This scenario is exciting to consider, but it also tends to defy logic and human nature. Most people do not know what they are likely to do in the coming months or in the next year. It seems unlikely that a software application will be able to determine these actions with near-magical ability.

The real truth to the story is that, in a situation where data mining is used to predict response to a direct marketing campaign, 95 percent of the people picked by the data mining application to be likely respondents will probably not respond. In other words, at the individual level of prediction, data mining prediction will almost always be wrong! This result hardly qualifies it as a crystal ball.

It would seem, then, that data mining is not especially valuable, but the opposite is true. The reason it is so valuable in this scenario, despite appearing to be so inaccurate, lies with an understanding of the correct level of analysis. At the individual prediction level, it is not very good. However, despite the fact that only 5 percent of the people predicted to respond actually did so, this response rate is probably two to five times greater than if no data mining model were used. When dealing with direct marketing campaigns in which the normal expected response rate is 1 percent to 2 percent and the mailing list is 500,000 people, an increase of response rate to 5 percent just gave you an additional 15,000 to 20,000 new customers. If each of those customers represents $10 in profits, you just gained $150,000 to $200,000 at the bottom line. When we look at it from the group perspective, data mining begins to look pretty good.

11-2: ONLINE ANALYTICAL PROCESSING

In 1993, E. F. Codd, the acknowledged founder of relational databases, introduced the term *online analytical processing* (OLAP). Codd suggested that the conventional relational database used for transaction processing had reached its maximum capability with regard to the dimensionality of the views of the data available to the user. He concluded that operational data and operational databases were simply not adequate for answering the types of questions typically posed by managers (a view held by members of the DSS and EIS communities for many years prior to Dr. Codd's revelation). From this conclusion, Codd developed a set of 12 rules for the development and use of multidimensional databases intended to assist decision makers within an organization in freely manipulating their enterprise data models across many simultaneous dimensions. Table 11-1 summarizes Codd's 12 rules for OLAP.

To date, it does not appear that any implementations exist for which all the rules are strictly obeyed. In fact, some argue that it may not even be possible to implement all 12 rules simultaneously (Gray, 1997). More recently, the term *OLAP* has come to represent the broad category of software technology that enables decision makers to conduct a multidimensional analysis of consolidated enterprise data. Along with process, two new terms represent the specific approach used to conduct the analysis: (1) *multidimensional online analytical processing* (MOLAP), and (2) *relational online analytical processing* (ROLAP).

TABLE 11-1   Codd's 12 Rules for OLAP

1. Multidimensional view
2. Transparent to the user
3. Accessible
4. Consistent reporting
5. Client-server architecture
6. Generic dimensionality
7. Dynamic sparse matrix handling
8. Multiuser support
9. Cross-dimensional operations
10. Intuitive data manipulation
11. Flexible reporting
12. Unlimited levels of dimension and aggregation

MULTIDIMENSIONAL OLAP—MOLAP

Analyzing data across multiple dimensions is much easier to visualize than to describe. Figure 11-1 shows how sales data might be analyzed across the dimensions of time, product, and market region.

As the figure shows, the data can be viewed as though they were stored in a three-dimensional array, or cube, with each side of the cube representing a single dimension. The intersecting cells of the three dimensions contain the actual data of interest and each of the dimensions can contain one or more members. For example, the market region dimension might have north, south, east, west, and central as its members and the product dimension would contain members representing each of the products being sold. The members of the time dimension could be months, quarters, years, or specific fiscal periods that represent particular sales cycles.

FIGURE 11-1   Multidimensional Analysis of Data

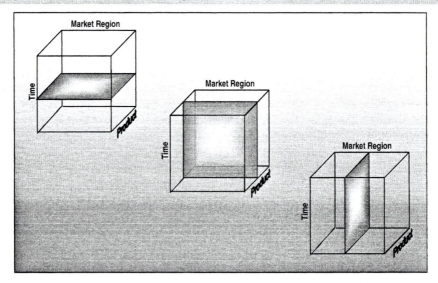

Although three dimensions of analysis may be useful in a limited setting, most multidimensional analysis is conducted using many more than three dimensions. In fact, MOLAP organizes and analyzes data as an *n*-dimensional cube.[1] The MOLAP cube can be thought of as a common spreadsheet with two extensions: (1) support for multiple dimensions, and (2) support for multiple concurrent users.

In a hypercube, the data are stored as a multidimensional array where each cell in the array represents the intersection of all of the dimensions. Using this approach, any number of dimensions may be analyzed simultaneously and any number of multidimensional views of the data can be created. In such a design, however, many cells in the hypercube may not have a value. For example, if the hypercube is analyzing a sales system across product, region, time, sales volume, and ratio of actual versus budgeted sales, it is conceivable that not all products will have been sold in all stores or regions during any given time period. In general, as the number of dimensions of the hypercube increases, so does the number of potentially empty cells. This phenomenon, called *sparcity,* can significantly increase the storage requirements of a MOLAP hypercube by requiring that storage space be allocated to all cells rather than only to those containing a value. New products are emerging, however, that incorporate special physical storage techniques such as data compression and complex indexing mechanisms that can reduce the negative impact of sparcity and thus ensure the fast access to hypercube cells.

One of the current limits to MOLAP is its scalability. Although it is good at handling summary data it is not particularly well suited to handling large numbers of detailed data. Currently, MOLAP architectures are limited to data warehouses under approximately 50 gigabytes. To accommodate data sets larger than the current limitations and to address issues of scalability, the database world is, once again, embracing the relational model as an alternative approach to MOLAP.

RELATIONAL OLAP—ROLAP

In ROLAP, a large relational database server replaces the multidimensional database server. This "super" relational database contains both detailed and summarized data, thus allowing for "drill down" techniques to be applied to the data sets. In those cases in which a specific needed summarization is not contained within the database, the ROLAP client tool can build it dynamically. The ROLAP approach is a trade-off between flexibility or scalability and performance. On the plus side, ROLAP implementations offer robust administration tools and open structured query language (SQL) interfaces that allow vendors to build tools that are both portable and scalable. The negative side is that ROLAP requires a significantly large number of relational tables to handle the massive volume of data and dimensional relations. The extreme processor overhead needed for table joins and index processing results in significantly degraded performance over MOLAP implementations.[2]

---

[1] The term *cube* is used to describe the *n*-dimensional space occupied by the data. Once the number of dimensions increases beyond three, however, it is no longer a cube in the geometric sense. A data cube with more than three dimensions is, therefore, referred to as a hypercube.

[2] A table join is a basic database operation that links rows, or records, of two or more tables by one or more columns in each table. Index processing involves the creation, maintenance, and use of a lookup table that relates the value of a field in an indexed file to its record in that file. This allows for a lookup to be performed on a field value other than the primary key. Both of these operations require significant amounts of processing power, especially for large databases.

One method being employed to reduce the processing overhead associated with ROLAP is the denormalization of the tables into a star schema. Figure 11-2 illustrates this approach to data organization.

At the center of a star schema is a central fact table. This table contains numerical measurements that exist at the intersection of all dimensions. If any combination of dimensions does not yield a value, then no zero value is stored. The facts in the central fact table represent quantities of data that can be aggregated without losing their meaning and that need to be described by more than two dimensions (Inmon, Welch, and Glassey, 1997). The central fact table streamlines the processing associated with access to the facts contained within the fact table.

FIGURE 11-2 Typical Star Schema Data Organization

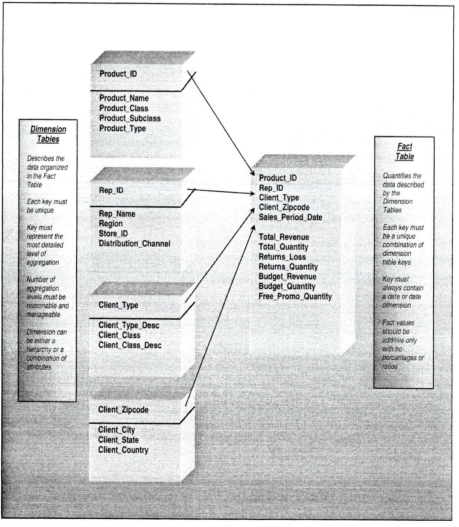

Source: Managing the Data Warehouse, by Inmon, Welch, and Glassey, copyright © 1997 by John Wiley & Sons. Reprinted with permission of John Wiley & Sons, Inc.

The dimension tables surround the central fact table. These tables describe or categorize the data contained in the fact table. A concatenated (compound) key in the central fact table is made up of the keys from all of the dimension tables and results in a row in the fact table for every unique combination of the domains of all the keys of all of the dimension tables. Using this approach allows the performance of multidimensional analysis on data sets larger than the current 50-gigabyte limit imposed on MOLAP implementations. ROLAP architectures are especially appropriate when dynamic access to combinations of summarized and detailed data is more important than the performance gains offered by the MOLAP approach using only summarized or preconsolidated data.

11-3: TECHNIQUES USED TO MINE THE DATA

With the popularity of data mining growing at a lightning-fast pace, the cadre of new and innovative techniques to mine the warehouse data is exploding as well. Many of the new techniques are refinements of previous methods, although some can truly be classified as major innovations. Because of a lack of standardization across vendors, however, innovations in data mining are often limited to a particular vendor platform and, thus, cannot be used across the board to advance the state of the art. Rather than concentrate on vendor-specific techniques and mining methods, we will focus on developing an understanding of the basic categories of mining techniques currently in use. Regardless of the specific technique, data mining methods may be classified by the function they perform or by their class of application. Using this approach, four major categories of processing algorithms and rule approaches emerge: (1) classification, (2) association, (3) sequence, and (4) cluster.

CLASSIFICATION

The classification approach includes mining processes intended to discover rules that define whether an item or event belongs to a particular subset or class of data. This category of techniques is probably the most broadly applicable to different types of business problems. The technique involves two subprocesses: (1) building a model, and (2) predicting classifications.

For example, suppose we want to look for previously undetermined buying patterns in a customer base. A classification model can be constructed that maps the various customer attributes (e.g., age, gender, income, etc.) with various product purchases (e.g., luxury automobiles, concert tickets, clothing, etc.). Given an appropriate set of predicting attributes, the model can be used against a list of customers to determine those most likely to make a particular purchase in the next month. The data records isolated by the data mining classification model could then be used to feed a selection query against a customer database in order to generate a targeted promotional contact or mailing list.

Other typical questions of classification include "Which households will likely respond to a forthcoming direct mail campaign?" "Which stocks in this portfolio will go up after the next major stock market correction?" "Which insurance claims currently under process are most likely fraudulent?" By building and refining a predictive model of the business problem, data mining classification methods can often provide useful and highly accurate answers to questions.

Generally speaking, classification methods develop a model composed of common IF-THEN rules. Because the idea is to gain insight into probable members of a class, the standard approach to determining whether a specific rule is satisfied is relaxed to allow for three possible conditions and, thus, three possible subclasses:

1. ***Exact rule.*** Permits no exceptions—that is, each IF object is an exact element of the THEN class. This approach creates the highest probability class of members: 100 percent probability.
2. ***Strong rule.*** Some exceptions allowed but an acceptable range of exceptions is prescribed. This approach creates a subclass of strong probability members: 90 to 100 percent probability.
3. ***Probabilistic rule.*** Relates the conditional probability $P(\text{THEN}|\text{IF})$ to the probability $P(\text{THEN})$. This approach creates a measured probability subclass of members: x percent probability.

ASSOCIATION

Techniques that employ association or linkage analysis search all details or transactions from operational systems for patterns with a high probability of repetition. This approach results in the development of an associative algorithm that correlates one set of events or items with another set of events or items. Patterns derived from the algorithm are generally expressed as, for example, "Eighty-three percent of all records that contain items A, B, and C also contain items D and E." The specific percentage supplied by the associative algorithm is referred to as the confidence factor of the rule. Associations can involve any number of items on either side of the rule.

A common example of the use of association methods is *market basket analysis.* Using a linkage approach, a retailer can mine the data generated by a point-of-sale system, such as the price scanner at the grocery store. By analyzing the products contained in a purchaser's basket and then using an associative algorithm to compare hundreds of thousands of baskets, specific product affinities can be derived. Example outcomes of an association method might be "Twenty-nine percent of the time that the brand X blender is sold, the customer also buys a set of kitchen tumblers," or "Sixty-eight percent of the time that a customer buys beverages, he or she also buys pretzels." This type of information can be used to determine the location and content of promotional or end-of-aisle displays (such as a 10-foot-high display of pretzels at the end of the aisle where the beverages are sold). Even though common associations such as yogurt and skim milk or wine and cheese are relatively intuitive, data mining using a linkage approach can find less obvious, yet nonetheless useful, associations such as men who buy diapers also buy beer (really, it is true). We will explore market basket analysis in greater detail in the next section.

SEQUENCE

Sequencing or time series analysis methods relate events in time, such as the prediction of interest rate fluctuations or stock performance, based on a series of preceding events. Through this analysis, various hidden trends, often highly predictive of future events, can be discovered.

Common applications of sequence analysis methods can be found in the direct mail industry. Sequences are often analyzed as they relate to a specific customer or group of customers. Using this information, a catalog containing specific product types can be target mailed to a customer associated with a known sequence of purchases. For example, a known buying sequence might be that parents tend to buy promotional toys associated with a particular movie within two weeks after renting the movie. This sequence would suggest that a flyer campaign for promotional toys should be linked to customer lists created as a result of movie rentals. Another sequential pattern might be the determination of a set of purchases that frequently precedes the purchase of a microwave oven. By monitoring buying patterns of customers, particularly using credit card transactions, highly targeted mailing lists can be generated to focus promotions and marketing campaigns on those customers most likely to be persuaded to buy.

One additional technique within this class focuses on the determination of similar sequences. In a typical sequential analysis, the output is a pattern representing a sequence of events over time. In a similar sequential analysis, however, the goal is to find groups of timed sequences. One of the most common examples of this approach is a large retailer using a similar sequence approach to find unrelated departments with similar sales streams. This information can be used to determine more profitable promotions, customer flow, or store layouts. Similar sequence techniques can successfully balance investment portfolios by identifying stocks or securities with similar price movements.

CLUSTER

In some cases, it is difficult or impossible to define the parameters of a class of data to be analyzed. When parameters are elusive, clustering methods can be used to create partitions so that all members of each set are similar according to some metric or set of metrics. A cluster is simply a set of objects grouped together by virtue of their similarity or proximity to each other. For instance, a clustering approach might be used to mine credit card purchase data to discover that meals charged on a business-issued gold card are typically purchased on weekdays and have a mean value of greater than $250, whereas meals purchased using a personal platinum card occur predominately on weekends, have a mean value of $175, and include a bottle of wine more than 65 percent of the time.

Clustering processes can be based on a particular event, such as the cancellation of a credit card by a customer. By analyzing the characteristics of members of this class, clustering might derive certain rules that could assist the credit card issuer in reducing the number of card cancellations in the future.

DATA MINING TECHNOLOGIES

By now you should begin to realize the potential power of data mining with regard to providing new answers to old questions and to the development of new knowledge and understanding through discovery. Unlimited types of questions can be asked and answered. Numerous techniques are available to assist in mining the data, along with numerous technologies for building the mining models. Most of these technologies are covered in greater detail in other chapters, but for purposes of continuity, they are mentioned briefly again here.

Statistical Analysis

Statistical analysis, despite requiring specialized capabilities to truly grasp all its importance, is the most mature of all data mining technologies and is the easiest to understand. If 69 percent of people who purchase product X using a credit card also purchase product Y, and product Y never sells independently, then it is relatively easy to build a model predicting product Y sales with an accuracy of 69 percent. Of greater interest, of course, is to be able to predict the sales of product X.

At this point, the traditional statistical analysis methods and data mining methods begin to diverge. Traditional statistical modeling techniques such as regression analysis are fine for building linear models that describe predictable data points; however, complex data patterns are often not linear in nature. Further, traditional statistical methods can frequently be negatively affected or problematic if the data are not well described by a linear model or if the data set contains a large number of outliers.[3] Data mining requires the use of statistical techniques—which are beyond the scope of the discussion in this text—that are capable of accommodating the conditions of nonlinearity, multiple outliers, and nonnumerical data typically found in a data warehouse environment.

Neural Networks, Genetic Algorithms, and Fuzzy Logic

As discussed in Chapter 9, neural networks attempt to mirror the way the human brain works in recognizing patterns by developing mathematical structures with the ability to learn. By studying combinations of variables and how different combinations affect data sets, it is possible to develop nonlinear predictive models that "learn." Machine learning techniques, such as genetic algorithms and fuzzy logic, can derive meaning from complicated and imprecise data and can extract patterns from and detect trends within the data that are far too complex to be noticed by either humans or more conventional automated analysis techniques. Because of this ability, neural computing and machine learning technologies demonstrate broad applicability to the world of data mining and, thus, to a wide variety of complex business problems.

Decision Trees

Recall from our discussion of problem-structuring tools in Chapter 4 that decision trees offer a conceptually simple mathematical method of following the effect of each event, or decision, on successive events. For example, in a simple decision tree involving the performance of an activity indoors or outdoors, if "indoors" is selected from the initial choice set, then the next decision will more likely be "upstairs/downstairs" rather than "sun/shade." By continually breaking data sets into separate, smaller groups, a predictive model can be built. Decision trees used in data mining applications assist in the classification of items or events contained within the warehouse.

In the appendix to this chapter, a complete outline of an actual decision tree analysis for Saudi Arabian Airlines is discussed. This analysis, using PolyAnalyst's Decision Trees exploration algorithm, determined what attributes influence the percentage of passengers flying in the first-class section. The analysis helped predict the optimal percentage of first-class seats for each flight, thus allowing Saudi Arabian Airlines to maximize revenue and increase customer satisfaction levels.

---

[3]An *outlier* is a data point that is unusually distant from the mean of the data set. In some cases, an outlier may represent simply an extremely low probability point. In other cases, it may be an indicator of a more complex relationship than is currently being modeled or assumed.

THE KNOWLEDGE DISCOVERY SEARCH PROCESS

Although no exact rules must be followed for mining a data warehouse and each inquiry must be considered individually, some guidelines can be established. Table 11-2 contains the sequence of events in a generic data mining "expedition."

One way to better understand the data mining process is to actually see it in operation. Although we cannot do that completely within the pages of a book, we can look at examples of some queries that might be constructed during a typical data mining session.

For example, a typical model-building SQL statement might take the following form:

CREATE MODEL promo_list

income character input, age integer input . . . respond character output

Note the similarity of the CREATE MODEL statement to the standard SQL CREATE TABLE statement. Data mining software designers intentionally establish this format because the newly created model is actually the same as a table or a view available for subsequent SQL processing. The CREATE MODEL statement creates a model that will relate various inputs, such as level of income (high, mid, or low) and age, to a desired output, such as a direct mail response rate (respond 5 yes or no). Bear in mind that this example is purposely simplistic and that the number or type of inputs that could be considered is not subject to any practical limit. A real application would typically include from several dozen to 100 or more such attributes.

To provide the model with a data set to process, it is simply a matter of inserting the data into the model using a standard SQL statement such as:

INSERT INTO mail_list SELECT income, age, respond

FROM client_list,

WHERE mail = "Q2_Southeast"

This process automatically creates additional views of the model table that can be used for understanding the relationships and predicting future outcomes (mail_list_UNDERSTAND and mail_list_PREDICT tables). Once the model is built, it represents the best information available to the decision maker about the profile of

---

TABLE 11-2   General Process of Knowledge Discovery

- *Select a topic for study:* Develop an understanding of the business problem.
- *Identify a target data set(s):* Determine what data are relevant for study.
- *Clean and preprocess the data:* Identify missing data fields, data noise, etc.
- *Build a data model:* Use the mining software to construct a mathematical model "explaining" the varying impacts of the inputs on the outputs.
- *Mine the data:* Search for patterns of interest (not all patterns identified by the model will be "interesting").
- *Interpret and refine:* Review the results of the initial mining and use the results to refine the model, as necessary, to gain additional insight into identified patterns of interest.
- *Predict:* Use the refined model to predict the output for a set of inputs where the output is not yet known.
- *Share the model:* Once validated, make the model available to other warehouse users.

people who respond to the organization's direct mail campaigns. To view the information generated by the model, an SQL statement is constructed to select from the table:

> **SELECT * FROM mail_list_UNDERSTAND**
> **WHERE input_column_name = "income" and**
> **input_column_value = "high" and**
> **output_column_name = "respond"**
> **and output_column_value = "yes"**
> **ORDER BY importance, conjunctionid**

In order to generate a mailing list for a new regional promotion in Miami, an SQL statement could be constructed to access the PREDICT table for only the records from which a positive response is predicted:

> **SELECT name FROM client_list, mail_list_PREDICT**
> **WHERE city = "Miami" AND respond = "yes"**

Notice that the model and its associated views, once created, are treated simply as tables in the database. They can be viewed and joined as appropriate to deliver the most benefit from the data mining process. Also, the model tables are available to anyone with access to the warehouse and the ability to generate SQL, not just the person who created them. Other users may choose to use this model as a template with their own modifications. Although the actual process is much more involved than this example, the same basic steps are followed and the same types of SQL statements are constructed.

NEW APPLICATIONS FOR DATA MINING

As data mining matures, new and increasingly innovative applications for it emerge. Although a wide variety of DM scenarios can be described, two new categories of applications can be identified: (1) text mining, and (2) Web mining.

Applications that support text mining quickly summarize, navigate, and cluster documents contained in a database. This allows the analyst to perform semantic information retrieval with text exploration focusing on a certain subject. Previous text mining attempts used keywords and frequency counts for text extraction. Modern applications provide solutions based on semantic network analysis, which uses Artificial Neural Networks (see Chapter 9) to extract semantic information from the text. This information can be used to create summarizations, concept-based searches, or semantic text-based navigation. Table 11-3 lists common functionalities found in modern text mining applications.

An extension of text mining is Web mining. Web mining is an exciting new field that integrates data and text mining within a Web site. It enhances the Web site with intelligent behavior, such as suggesting related links or recommending new products to the consumer. Web mining is especially exciting because it enables us to perform tasks that were previously difficult to implement, including personalized e-CRM, automated site navigation, and real-time e-business intelligence. Several advantages can be realized through Web mining:

- Unobtrusively learn the interests of your visitors, based on their interaction with the Web site. User profiles are modified in real time as more information is learned.

TABLE 11-3 Examples of Common Functions Found in a Text Mining Application

Functionality	Description
Distilling the meaning of a text	Formation and export of an accurate semantic network of the text or textbase. A semantic network is a set of the most important concepts from the text and the relations between these concepts weighted by their relative importance. This network concisely represents the meaning of a text and serves as a basis for all further analysis.
Accurate summarization of texts	The quality of the summary is provided by a balanced combination of linguistic and neural network investigation methods. The size of the summary is controlled through the semantic weight threshold.
Subject-focused text exploration	User-specified dictionaries of excluded and included words allow the investigation to focus on a chosen subject.
Efficient navigation through a text base	The knowledge base can be navigated with hyperlinks from concepts in the semantic network to sentences in the documents that contain the considered combination of concepts. Individual sentences are in turn hyperlinked to those places in original texts where they have been encountered.
Explication of the text theme structure	A tree-like topic structure representing the semantics of the investigated texts is automatically developed. The more important subjects are placed closer to the root of the tree.
Clustering of texts	Breaking links representing weak relations in the original semantic network enables clustering of the text base.
Semantic information retrieval	Natural language queries are analyzed for semantically important words and all relevant sentences from the text-based documents are retrieved. In addition, a subtree of concepts related to the query is formed, which facilitates a simple search refinement.

- Automatically match the best available resource to the interests of the visitor. This capability allows you to target banner ads, suggest related links, or provide dynamic, personalized content.
- Perform real-time response prediction. "Is this visitor going to make a purchase?"
- Perform real-time prospect valuation. "How much is this visitor going to spend?"
- Predict when a visitor is about to leave your site, and provide incentives to stay.
- Identify and act on cross-sell and up-sell opportunities.
- Reveal clickstream patterns in your site. "What paths do most users follow?" and "What paths do my most valuable users follow?"
- Increase overall user satisfaction of your site.
- Record all customer interactions through the Web site in the most efficient manner.
- Transform and store these data in a format suitable for further analysis.
- Use data for learning customer interests, preferences, and possible courses of action.

- Analyze efficiency of the Web site resources and architecture.
- Generate reports for executive managers.
- Recognize repetitive customers and access their profiles.
- Utilize all harvested knowledge to personalize communications with each customer.

Web mining applications typically run as a service in conjunction with a server operating system such as Windows 2000 or NT. They can be configured to monitor and gather data from a wide variety of locations and can analyze the data across one or multiple Web sites.

11-4: MARKET BASKET ANALYSIS: THE KING OF DM ALGORITHMS

As you will see from your exploration of the PolyAnalyst software provided to you with this text, 20-plus data mining and visualization algorithms are available, each of which is appropriate in certain analysis scenarios. Although the PolyAnalyst and TextAnalyst tutorials will familiarize you with the available algorithms, it is beyond the scope of this text to provide a detailed look at them all. For that reason, we focus on the most widely used and, in many ways, most successful data mining and visualization algorithm: *market basket analysis.*

Market basket analysis is one of the most common and useful types of data analysis for marketing.[4] It determines what products customers purchase together; it takes its name from the idea of customers throwing all their purchases into a shopping cart (a "market basket") during grocery shopping. Knowing what products people purchase as a group can be helpful to a retailer or to any other company. A store could use this information to place products frequently sold together into the same area, while catalog or e-commerce merchants could use it to determine the layout of their Web site, e-catalog, and online order form. Direct marketers often use market basket analysis results to determine what new products to offer to their current customers.

In some cases, the fact that items sell together is obvious—go through the drive-up at any fast-food restaurant and you will probably hear, "Would you like fries with that?" However, sometimes the realization that certain items sell well together is far from obvious. Recall the well-known example from the previous section about the supermarket performing a market basket analysis and discovering that diapers and beer sell well together on Thursdays. Though the result does make sense—couples stocking up on supplies for themselves and for their children before the weekend starts—it is not the sort of relationship one would normally think of when considering where to place products on the shelf or throughout the retail area. Computer data mining tools and market basket analysis eliminate the need for a person to focus on what products consumers would logically buy together. Instead, the customers' sales data speak for themselves. It is a prime example of the current trend toward data-driven marketing.

---

[4]The information in this section has been adapted from Ananyan, S. (2001), "Market Basket Analysis White Paper," All permissions granted.

Once a firm knows that customers who buy one product are likely to buy another, it can market the products together or make the purchasers of one product the target prospects for another. If customers who purchase diapers are already likely to purchase beer, then a beer display just outside the diaper aisle will increase that likelihood. Likewise, if customers who buy a sweater from a certain mail-order catalog show a propensity toward buying a jacket from the same catalog, then sales of jackets can be increased by telephone representatives who describe and offer the jacket to customers who call in to order the sweater. By targeting customers who are already known to be likely buyers, the effectiveness of marketing—whether in the form of in-store displays, catalog layout design, direct offers to customers, or some other practical approach—is significantly increased. Thus, market basket analysis can improve the effectiveness of marketing and sales tactics using customer data already available to, and often already collected by, the company.

THE BENEFITS OF MARKET BASKET ANALYSIS

To a retailer, knowing which products are highly likely to sell together is the marketing equivalent to card counting in blackjack. It provides a distinct advantage in the highly competitive and often opportunistic world of consumer behavior. The most obvious effect is the increase in sales that a retail store can achieve by reorganizing its products so that things that sell together are also found together. This strategy facilitates impulse buying and helps ensure that customers who would buy a product don't forget to buy it simply because they did not see it. In addition, customers will begin to feel comfortable in their assumption that whatever they need, they will find at a particular outlet, thus improving customer satisfaction. Every time they are reminded to buy an item because of intelligent placement of that item in the retail area, this customer assumption will become reinforced. World Wide Web or catalog merchants get the same benefit from conveniently organizing their catalog or e-commerce Web site so that items that sell together are found together. It is commonplace to see suggested products that are associated with the product being purchased displayed on the same screen. This savvy marketing probably can be attributed to market basket analysis.

Outside of the store environment, market basket analysis provides somewhat different benefits, though equally useful ones. For a direct marketer, it is far preferable to market to existing customers, who are known to buy products and have a history with the company. The company's database already holds a significant amount of information about these people. After running a market basket analysis, a direct marketer can contact its prior customers with information about new products shown to sell well with the products they already bought; chances are, they will be interested. In addition, even when making sales to new customers, telephone representatives can offer buyers of a product discounts on any other products they know sell with it, in order to increase the size of the sale.

Finally, market basket analysis even contributes outside the realm of marketing. It can be useful for operations purposes to know which products sell together in order to stock inventory. Running out of one item can affect sales of associated items; perhaps the reorder point of a product should be based on the inventory levels of several products, rather than just one. In addition, market basket analysis can be used wherever several different conditions lead to a particular result. For example, by studying the occurrence of side effects in patients with multiple prescriptions, a hospital could find previously unknown drug interactions about which to warn patients.

Market basket analysis offers several advantages over other types of data mining. First of all, it is undirected. It is not necessary to choose a product that you want to focus on in order to run a basket analysis. Instead, all products are considered, and the data mining software reveals which products are most important to the analysis. In addition, the results of market basket analysis are clear, understandable association rules that lend themselves to immediate action, and the individual calculations involved are simple.

ASSOCIATION RULES FOR MARKET BASKET ANALYSIS

Association rules are a common undirected data mining technique and complement market basket analysis. All association rules are unidirectional and take the following form:

Left-hand side rule IMPLIES Right-hand side rule

Notice that association rules are unidirectional; they only go in one direction. In a restaurant market basket analysis, we might find that CAVIAR IMPLIES VODKA but the reverse VODKA IMPLIES CAVIAR may not hold. In addition, both the left-hand side and the right-hand side of the rule may contain multiple items or combinations of items such as the following:

Yellow Peppers IMPLIES Red Peppers, Bananas, and Bakery

It should be obvious to you by now, that any given market basket is chock full of potential rules, since any one item in the basket may imply all of the other items in that basket. As discussed earlier, however, data mining is not valuable at the individual prediction level of analysis. To draw rules from a single basket would certainly not prove useful to marketing to the wider community. Only when these rules are formed from an analysis of thousands of market baskets can we begin to use them in a predictive sense.

To make effective use of a predictive rule derived from market basket analysis, three distinct measures of that rule must be considered: (1) support (sometimes referred to as prevalence), (2) confidence (also referred to as predictability), and (3) lift.

Support

The *support measure* refers to the percentage of baskets in the analysis where the rule is true, that is, where both the left-hand side and the right-hand side of the association are found.

Confidence

The percentage of baskets from the analysis having the left-hand side item that also contain the right-hand side item is found via the *confidence measure*. This measure is different from support in that confidence is the probability that the right-hand side item is present given that we know the left-hand side item is in the basket.

Lift

The third measure of associative rule power, *lift*, is probably the closest to being useful on its own. It compares the likelihood of finding the right-hand side item in any random basket. Lift measures how well the associative rule performs by comparing its performance to the "null" rule (that the left-hand-side item is present without the right-hand-side item). In this sense, lift can also be thought of as *improvement*, because it measures the improvement of the prediction over time. A typical example of an associative rule with its measures would look something like this:

Green Peppers IMPLIES Bananas

Lift = 1.37

Support = 3.77

Confidence = 85.96

An interpretation of this rule suggests that the vast majority of people in this market basket analysis bought bananas, including those who bought green peppers. Although not terribly interesting by itself, what happens when we combine it with two other associative rules generated by the market basket analysis algorithm?

Red Peppers IMPLIES Bananas

Lift = 1.43

Support = 8.58

Confidence = 89.47

Yellow Peppers IMPLIES Bananas

Lift = 1.17

Support = 22.12

Confidence = 73.09

In combination, we begin to see a pattern emerge: Because bananas are universally popular, green peppers sell in about the same quantities as either red or yellow peppers; they just aren't as predictive. One reason may be that red and yellow peppers are produce items typically imported to the region under study, whereas green peppers are indigenous to the region. This factor would make red and yellow peppers generally more expensive and could imply a certain snob appeal to red and yellow peppers over the more common green ones. Given this set of rules, the store may want to try repositioning the red and yellow peppers away from the more common green peppers and closer to the other "exotic" imports such as fresh morels or other imported vegetables. Another experiment would be to triple the price of a few green peppers and display them with their higher-priced cousins. It is possible that the combination of all three colors would sell together at a higher price than if they were marketed individually.

Method

In order to perform market basket analysis, it is necessary to first have a list of transactions and what was purchased in each one. Consider the following simple example of convenience store customers, each of whom bought only a few items.

Transaction 1: Frozen pizza, cola, milk
Transaction 2: Milk, potato chips
Transaction 3: Cola, frozen pizza
Transaction 4: Milk, pretzels
Transaction 5: Cola, pretzels

Each customer purchased a different basket of items, and at first glance, no obvious relationship exists between any of the items purchased and any other item. The first step of a basket analysis, however, is to cross-tabulate the data into a table, allowing you to see how often products occurred together. These five convenience store purchases result in the following table:

	Frozen Pizza	Milk	Cola	Potato Chips	Pretzels
Frozen Pizza	2	1	2	0	0
Milk	1	3	1	1	1
Cola	2	1	3	0	1
Potato Chips	0	1	0	1	0
Pretzels	0	1	1	0	2

The central diagonal of the chart shows how often each item was purchased with itself. Though it is significant for figuring some reliability statistics, it does not show how items sell together, and can be ignored for now. Look at the first row—of the people who bought frozen pizza, one bought milk, two bought cola, and none bought potato chips or pretzels. This finding hints at the fact that frozen pizza and cola may sell well together, and should be placed side-by-side in the convenience store. Nowhere else in the table do we find an item that sold together with another item as frequently, which suggests an actual cross-selling opportunity. Compare it to the second row—of people who bought milk, one bought frozen pizza, one bought cola, one bought potato chips, and one bought pretzels. It seems milk sells well with everything in the store, which limits good cross-selling opportunities. This finding makes sense for a convenience store, because people often come to a convenience store specifically to buy milk, and will buy it regardless of what else they might want.

Results

A real example would usually contain much more than five products and thousands more than five transactions. As a result, the distinction between products that sell well together and products that do not would be much sharper. Also, a market basket analysis of large amounts of data would be performed using data mining software, rather than being entered into a table by hand as in our example. You will conduct some of this large data set analysis in your exercises with PolyAnalyst.

As shown, the results of a market basket analysis are particularly useful because they take the form of immediately actionable association rules. These rules allow a store to know right away that promotions involving frozen pizza and cola will pay off. Whether it places the cola display right next to the frozen pizza, advertises the two products together, or attaches cola discount coupons to the frozen pizza boxes, the convenience store will probably be able to increase sales of both items through directed marketing. And unlike most promotions, this promotion is almost sure to pay off—the convenience store has the data to back it up before even beginning the campaign.

This example demonstrates the best kind of market basket analysis result—*actionable*. Unfortunately, two other kinds of association rules are sometimes generated by market basket analysis: the *trivial* and the *inexplicable*. A trivial rule is one that would be patently obvious to anyone with some familiarity with the industry at hand. For instance, the discovery that hot dog buns sell well with hot dogs would not surprise the owner of a grocery store, and would in fact not be at all useful for promotion purposes—people will buy hot dog buns with their hot dogs regardless of any marketing campaign encouraging them to do so. Another example of a trivial rule would be the discovery that people who purchase an extended warranty for a television generally purchase a television—the warranty would be pointless without the television. The data mining software can only point out which items sell well together; it is up to the user to rely on his or her own business knowledge to determine which rules are valuable to the business.

Finally, market basket analysis occasionally produces inexplicable rules. These rules are not obvious, but also do not lend themselves to immediate marketing use. An example of this type of rule is one hardware store chain's discovery that toilet rings sell well only when a new hardware store is opened. No obvious reason can be found for this tendency—why do people only need toilet rings when a new store opens? In addition, even though the company could offer a sale on toilet rings during new store openings, it cannot tell whether this promotion will be successful, because it is still rather mysterious why they sell better at new openings at all. An inexplicable rule is not necessarily useless, but its business value is not obvious and it does not lend itself to immediate use for cross-selling.

Limitations to Market Basket Analysis

Though a useful and productive type of data mining, market basket analysis does have a few limitations. The first involves the kind of data needed to do an effective basket analysis. A large number of real transactions is required to obtain meaningful data, but the data's accuracy is compromised if all of the products do not occur with similar frequency. Thus, in our convenience store example, if milk is sold in almost every transaction, but glue only sells once or twice per month, putting both of them into the same basket analysis will probably generate results that look impressive without being statistically significant, and acting on these results is not likely to benefit profitability. With only one or two glue customers, the data mining software can confidently state what sells well with glue, but the correlation may only be true for the one or two customers analyzed. However, this limitation can be overcome by classifying items into a taxonomy as described in the next section.

Second, market basket analysis can sometimes present results that are actually due to the success of previous marketing campaigns. If the convenience store consistently put cola discount coupons on the frozen pizza, the fact that cola and frozen pizza sold well together probably does not surprise them. In this sense, it does not provide any new information; it just shows that previously existing marketing campaigns are already working. In fact, the previous campaign may even be overshadowing a real relationship. Perhaps people would normally prefer to buy beer with pizza, but buy the cola because of the discount. In this case, the convenience store is missing out on a potentially better promotion.

PERFORMING MARKET BASKET ANALYSIS WITH VIRTUAL ITEMS

Suppose a marketer wants to consider more than just which items sell together in developing their promotions. It may be important to know which items sell better to families with children, or to repeat customers, or to new customers. In such cases, the sales data can be augmented with the addition of virtual items. A virtual item is not a real item being sold, but is treated as one by the data mining software. So if a new customer calls a catalog and orders a sweater and a jacket, this transaction can be entered into the database as:

Item 1: Sweater

Item 2: Jacket

Item 3: (new customer)

Thus, when the data mining software is used to determine which items sell well together, it may discover that some items sell particularly well with the (new customer) virtual item. This connection could tell the catalog company which items are so interesting as to lure new customers, as opposed to only selling to long-time catalog buyers. By using virtual items, data about the customers themselves, or which store the items sold at, or which sales representative sold the item can be considered in the analysis without changing the method by which it is performed. By adding the store number or sales representative number as a virtual item, patterns can be found that exist only in certain places or are brought out by certain salespeople. As far as the data mining software is concerned, (new customer) or any virtual item is a real item like any other.

Virtual items are also useful for testing the effects of promotions. By adding virtual items to represent promotions or discounts, it is possible to see how these affect crossselling. They can also be used to compare urban and suburban sales, seasonal or time-of-day differences, or gift-wrapped purchases versus those that people bought for themselves.

Measures of Association

Referring back to our table of transactions, we can calculate our measures of association for each rule:

	Frozen Pizza	Milk	Cola	Potato Chips	Pretzels
Frozen Pizza	2	1	2	0	0
Milk	1	3	1	1	1
Cola	2	1	3	0	1
Potato Chips	0	1	0	1	0
Pretzels	0	1	1	0	2

The support measure for the rule "Cola IMPLIES Frozen Pizza" is 40 percent. Of five total records, two of them include both Cola and Frozen Pizza. Note that support considers only the combination, and not the direction, as the support for the rule "Frozen Pizza IMPLIES Cola" is also 40 percent. Support can also be used to measure a single item. For example, the support for the item "Milk" is 60 percent, because it occurs in three of the five records. Measuring the support of a single item is where the central diagonal of the table can be useful.

Recall that the confidence of an association rule is the percentage of baskets from the analysis with the left-hand-side item that also contain the right-hand-side item. This percentage can be calculated by dividing the support for the combination by the support for the condition. For example, the rule "Milk IMPLIES Potato Chips" has a confidence of 33 percent. The support for the combination (Potato Chips + Milk) is

20 percent, occurring in one of the five transactions. However, the support for the condition (Milk) is 60 percent, occurring in three of the five transactions. This gives a confidence of 20 percent / 60 percent = 33 percent.

Note also that confidence is unidirectional—the confidence of the rule "Potato Chips IMPLIES Milk" is 20 percent / 20 percent = 100 percent. However, this rule is based on only one transaction! Thus, like a high support, a high confidence alone does not indicate that a rule is necessarily a good one. This example also shows what happens when certain items with extremely low sales are thrown into a basket analysis with high sales. One customer's purchase of two items together can create an extremely high-confidence rule that may not mean much. This problem is overcome by using taxonomies, as described later in this section.

As discussed previously, both support and confidence must be used to determine whether a rule is valid. However, sometimes both of these measures may be high, and yet still produce a rule that is not useful. Take these results for example:

Convenience store customers who buy orange juice also buy milk with a 75 percent confidence.

The combination of milk and orange juice has a support of 30 percent.

At first glance, this statement sounds like an excellent rule, and in most cases, it would be. It shows high confidence and high support. However, what if convenience store customers in general buy milk 90 percent of the time? In that case, orange juice customers are actually less likely to buy milk than customers in general. In such cases, we also need to consider our measure of lift.

The lift measure, the likelihood of finding the right-hand-side item in any random basket, is calculated as follows:

$$\frac{\textbf{Support (Condition + Result)}}{\textbf{Support (Condition)} \times \textbf{Support (Result)}}$$

It can also be defined as the confidence of the combination of items divided by the support of the result. So in our milk example, based on the assumption that 40 percent of the customers buy orange juice, the improvement would be:

$$\frac{\textbf{30\%}}{\textbf{40\%} \times \textbf{90\%}} = \textbf{0.83}$$

The result is a lift measure of less than 1. Any rule with a lift of less than 1 does not indicate a real cross-selling opportunity, no matter how high its support and confidence, because it actually offers less ability to predict a purchase than does random chance.

As a side note, it is possible to negate a rule that has a lift of less than 1 and thereby produce a rule with a lift greater than 1. For example, we could change this rule into "Orange juice DOES NOT IMPLY Milk" with a 25 percent confidence. The purchase of orange juice without milk, therefore, has a support of 10 percent. This new rule offers a lift measure of 1.21. Unfortunately, as is probably obvious from that rule, negated rules are not particularly useful for marketing. Knowing that customers who buy one product will not buy another one is usually not helpful for marketing products to customers or placing the products in a store or catalog.

Taxonomies

The most common obstacle to performing a good market basket analysis is the presence of low-support items. The fact that 100 percent of purchasers of mushroom pizza also buy broccoli seems like a good rule, unless only one person purchased a mushroom pizza. However, data mining software will produce such results, because they have a high confidence and improvement, probably much higher than those of any item that sold a larger number of times.

This problem can be dealt with in two ways. One way is to create a support threshold. Any combination with support below a certain percentage will be dropped from the analysis. If the support threshold was set at 5 percent, it follows that because the support of a combination is always less than the support of any single item, all items with a support of less than 5 percent can also be dropped from the analysis. Thus, in this case, mushroom pizza would not even be considered in the analysis, and would thus not produce its 100 percent-confidence, high-improvement rule.

Unfortunately, the support threshold method's major disadvantage is that it eliminates some potentially valuable data from consideration. This drawback brings us to the best way to deal with low-support items: the creation of a taxonomy. A taxonomy is an orderly hierarchy of items and item categories, dividing things such that each item put into the basket analysis occurs with a similar level of support. This process aggregates low-support items into groups and analyzes the group as a single item, while breaking down high-support items into smaller units for analysis.

For example, look at the following list of items and their support levels:

Grape Popsicles	1%
Cherry Popsicles	3%
Orange Popsicles	3%
Lime Popsicles	2%
Frozen pizzas	70%

Obviously, these results will not do for basket analysis. If someone buys a grape Popsicle and any other item, it will show an extremely high confidence and improvement rule linking grape Popsicles with whatever else the person bought. To come up with a confidence or improvement this high, frozen pizza buyers would have to buy another item almost every time.

The solution is to aggregate some items and break down others. The items that should be used in the analysis would look more like:

Popsicles (all)	9%
Frozen pizzas (pepperoni)	12%
Frozen pizzas (cheese)	15%
Frozen pizzas (Supreme)	11%
Frozen pizzas (sausage)	10%
Frozen pizzas (combination)	15%
Frozen pizzas (vegetarian)	7%

By combining all the Popsicles into a single item, while breaking the frozen pizzas down into smaller items, comparable support levels were found for all of the items. The support levels do not have to be the same, but if one item shows support more than an order of magnitude above another item, the smaller support items will probably dominate the association rules produced.

Taxonomies can be created aggregating items all the way up to "Frozen Food" or splitting them down all the way to the UPC bar code or SKU price level. By finding comparable support levels for all items, you ensure the production of association rules whose confidence and lift can be meaningfully used for comparison.

Multidimensional Market Basket Analysis

Thus far, we looked only at association rules involving two items. However, sometimes better rules emerge when more than two items are considered:

Plant and Clay Pot IMPLIES Soil.

Glue and Scissors IMPLIES Paper.

Though these rules are trivial, they also illustrate that while sometimes a single item will not give much insight into a customer's future product purchases, a pair of items might. The same goes for higher numbers of items.

Performing a basket analysis that considers higher numbers of items in groups is done iteratively. First, pairs are found, then sets of three, then four, and so on. The number of calculations required to perform the analysis varies exponentially with the number of products to be considered simultaneously. The number of calculations for n items is proportional to the number of items to be considered at a time raised to the nth power. As a result, a pruning method has been developed to minimize calculation time by eliminating items as the number of items to be considered simultaneously increases. To perform a multidimensional market basket analysis, a minimum support threshold, say 2 percent, must be set. The data mining software first eliminates all items that have less support than this minimum threshold and then conducts an analysis comparing only pairs of items and generates a set of association rules.

At this point, the second round of pruning occurs. Any two items that, as a pair, have a support less than the minimum threshold are eliminated from consideration as conditions of an association rule. Then, these pairs of items are checked against all the items in the analysis (as results) and another set of association rules is generated.

This process continues, next eliminating all sets of three items that as a group fall below the minimum support threshold. In some environments, such as a convenience store, it is quite possible that customers buy so few items at a time that no rules involving more than two or three items will ever have the minimum support necessary to be considered significant. In contrast, in an environment like a large grocery store, where customers buy more than 100 items at a time, rules of 10–12 items may be significant.

Performing basket analyses considering more than two items at a time results in the development of multidimensional tables that can be difficult to visualize. However, the use of data mining software allows meaningful rules to be found in these data despite the difficulties in representing them.

USING THE RESULTS
Store Layout Changes

The results of market basket analysis can indicate how stores can change their layout to improve profitability. If the market basket analysis shows that lightbulbs and gardening tools sell well together in a hardware store, the obvious response is to put the lightbulbs next to the gardening aisle. However, a better response might be to put a shelf of the store brand of lightbulbs, a high-profit item for the store, next to the gardening aisle, leaving the rest of the lightbulbs where they are. By making it most convenient for the customer to buy high-profit items, the store owner can maximize profit. The market basket analysis shows that this tactic will probably work, because customers will already be looking to buy the item.

This same tactic is equally valid for "stores" that take some form other than the supermarket floor—anywhere that a customer browses for items is appropriate for reorganization based on market basket analysis. A catalog or Web page can also be reorganized to direct the attention of customers who are likely to buy a certain product toward high-profit items.

Product Bundling

For companies without a physical storefront, like mail-order companies, Internet businesses, and catalog merchants, market basket analysis can be more useful for developing promotions than for reorganizing product placement. By offering promotions in which buyers of one item get discounts on another they are likely to buy, sales of both items may be increased. In addition, market basket analysis can be useful for direct marketers in reducing their number of mailings or calls. By calling only customers who previously showed a desire for a product, the cost of marketing can be reduced while increasing the response rate.

11-5: CURRENT LIMITATIONS AND CHALLENGES TO DATA MINING

It is important to remember that despite the potential power and value of data mining to the business world, it is still a new and underdeveloped field. Most current developers of commercial data mining products are relatively small and generally license or sell their products to larger, more established software vendors for incorporation into existing software products. Several of the challenges that significantly limit the advancement of data mining products are identified in this section.

IDENTIFICATION OF MISSING INFORMATION

Until such time as data mining becomes commonplace and legacy application databases are replaced by newer "warehouse friendly" databases, warehouse designers will continue to grapple with the conversion of data from an ODS into a homogenous form for the warehouse. This transformation, albeit quite thorough and technologically sophisticated, cannot yet detect whether the original data set contains the necessary elements for effective mining. For example, the data contained in an ODS are normally not inclusive of domain knowledge. In other words, not all knowledge about a particular application domain is present in the data. We know from past discussion that the data within an ODS are normally limited to those needed by the operational application associated with that database. Even though application-relevant queries can be successfully made on the data, more generalizable queries may not be possible. Data mining applications need to include mechanisms for "inventorying" the data sets so that attribute sufficiency can be determined prior to loading the data into the warehouse. For instance, if it is known that decision makers may wish to diagnose potential cases of malaria from a patient database, it is also known that all patient data sets loaded into the warehouse must include the patient's red blood cell count. Without these data, no diagnosis can be effectively made.

DATA NOISE AND MISSING VALUES

Virtually all operational databases are contaminated to some degree by errors. Data attributes that rely on subjective measurements or judgments can give rise to errors so significant that some examples may even be misclassified. Errors in either the values of the attributes or the classification of data are referred to as data noise. Mining applications must address the problem of data noise in order to minimize its debilitating effect on the overall accuracy of rules generated from the data. Currently, data mining systems are limited to the treatment of noise via statistical techniques that rely on known distributions of data noise. Future systems must incorporate more sophisticated mechanisms for treating missing or noisy data that include inference of missing values, Bayesian techniques for averaging over the missing values, and other methods of data inference.

LARGE DATABASES AND HIGH DIMENSIONALITY

Operational databases are inherently large and dynamic; their contents are ever changing as data are added, modified, or removed. Rules derived from a data set at one moment in time may become less accurate as the data change. This need for timeliness of the data creates a parallel need for increased dimensionality of the data for purposes of discovery. In other words, to ensure that discovered patterns are not "local" to a given time period, data patterns must be constantly updated by an expanding set of time-sensitive data values. This need in turn creates a problem space of significant breadth and depth that requires increasingly greater computing power to search. The spiraling nature of this problem must be addressed by future discovery applications that can portion the problem space into smaller, more manageable chunks without losing any of the intrinsic attributes of the data contained therein.

11-6: DATA VISUALIZATION: "SEEING" THE DATA

Data visualization is the process by which numerical data are converted into meaningful images. The raw data may come from any number of different sources, including satellite photos, undersea sonic measurements, surveys, or computer simulations, to name just a few. Typically, these sources create data that are difficult to interpret because of the overwhelming quantity and complexity of information and the embedded patterns. The human brain is capable of processing a significant amount of visual information, instantly recognizing millions of different physical objects. Data visualization techniques are intended to assist in analyzing complex data sets by mapping physical properties to the data, thus taking advantage of human visual systems. Reflectance and other lighting effects, color, direction and size of shadows, relative sizes of and distances between objects, speed, curvature, and transparency are just a small sample of the characteristics that help us visualize data.

For example, Table 11-4 contains an example of some real-life weather balloon data. As you can see, our ability to extract any useful information from looking at the numbers is virtually nonexistent.

Using a data visualization technique that allows for the creation of a three-dimensional model of the sensor data reveals the shape in Figure 11-3. The various shadings contained within the figure indicate relative degrees of thunderstorm activity with the darkest portions of the figure indicating the most violent storm activity.[5] The ability to create multidimensional structures and models from raw data is one of the most important innovations in decision support technologies. In this section we continue our

TABLE 11-4 Sample Weather Sensor Data

Offset	X	Y	Z	Vector
0.000000	−17.833000	6.661000	0.011000	−0.118000
0.000000	−17.773001	6.683000	0.015000	−0.122000
0.000000	−17.673000	6.718000	0.009000	−0.143000
0.000000	−17.563999	6.757000	0.008000	−0.163000
0.000000	−17.461000	6.802000	0.011000	−0.165000
0.000000	−17.375000	6.865000	0.012000	−0.149000
0.000000	−17.297001	6.940000	0.009000	−0.127000
0.000000	−17.239000	7.016000	0.010000	−0.114000
0.000000	−17.200001	7.091000	0.018000	−0.116000
0.000000	−17.170000	7.167000	0.030000	−0.133000
0.000000	−17.169001	7.256000	0.050000	−0.148000
0.000000	−17.187000	7.345000	0.064000	−0.152000
0.000000	−17.226000	7.429000	0.074000	−0.153000
0.000000	−17.290001	7.509000	0.088000	−0.152000
0.000000	−17.375999	7.583000	0.106000	−0.146000
0.000000	−17.488001	7.645000	0.112000	−0.145000
0.000000	−17.620001	7.692000	0.118000	−0.156000
0.000000	−17.768000	7.724000	0.126000	−0.158000
0.000000	−17.931000	7.737000	0.133000	−0.143000
0.000000	−18.106001	7.736000	0.128000	−0.134000
0.000000	−18.284000	7.719000	0.121000	−0.132000
0.000000	−18.450001	7.688000	0.121000	−0.129000

---

[5]Normally data visualization images are rendered in color so that colors, rather than shades of gray, can be used as data value indicators. Because we are limited to a gray scale medium for this text, we will determine data values using relative shades of gray.

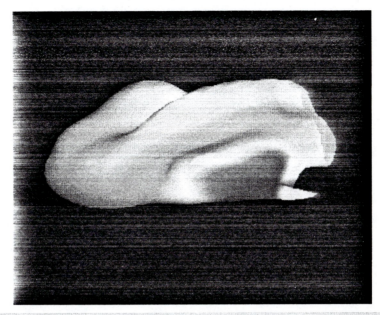

FIGURE 11-3   Data Visualization of Weather Sensor Data Depicting Storm Cell Activity

discussion (begun in Section 11-2) of multidimensional analysis and examine the visualization of data across *n* dimensions.

A BIT OF HISTORY

The early concepts of data visualization originated in the statistical and scientific disciplines. Most of the early work involved a series of two-dimensional analyses of multidimensional or multivariate data sets. Such analyses involved the use of static images and graphs that could then be sequenced to affect a quasi-layering of the data across dimensions.

Much of the advancement in data visualization can be credited to the National Center for Supercomputing Applications (NCSA) at the University of Illinois at Champaign-Urbana. One of the first practical applications of multidimensional data analysis was the Los Angeles smog project conducted by NCSA. By creating a computer animation of smog data superimposed over a three-dimensional map of the Los Angeles basin, NCSA was able to pinpoint locations of major contributors to pollution and to accurately predict smog levels and movement over a wide area of the basin.

Some of the newest developments in data visualization have come from the work conducted at Xerox PARC in the area of virtual reality. Three-dimensional visualization programs allow the user to "fly through" large data sets, view the data from infinite angles, and examine and rearrange object representations of the data interactively. Military and industrial simulations are two examples of the practical application of these innovative data analysis methods. Computers can be used to display realistic visuals of tank combat in urban areas or large tankers docking in busy harbors, thus allowing for learning through experience and avoiding the messy cleanup associated with mistakes made during the early phases of training.

HUMAN VISUAL PERCEPTION AND DATA VISUALIZATION

If you were to go outside right now, your sense of vision would immediately detect a variety of objects—automobiles, buildings, people, trees, dogs—all organized in a neatly coherent and meaningful framework. Your brain would be processing all of these objects by assembling edges, movements, and distances into multidimensional wholes for which you would seamlessly retrieve identities and labels. This apparently effortless processing is both continuous and subconscious.

Data visualization is so powerful not only because the human visual cortex dominates our perception, but because the process of converting objects into information occurs so quickly. Using data visualization, massive amounts of information can be presented, thus accelerating the identification of hidden patterns contained within the data. Stop for a moment and contrast how easily you processed the image presented in Figure 11-3 with how difficult it was to process the rows and columns in Table 11-4, and you will immediately realize the value of data visualization as an analytical tool.

Applying the old adage of a picture being worth a thousand words, we may better come to appreciate the value of data visualization by simply looking at several examples of complex data sets from a variety of knowledge domains represented in visual form.

The graphic in Figure 11-4 represents a model of a dynamic data set related to the connectivity, relative throughput, and usage of a private global computer network. The lightest shaded lines connecting the nodes indicate the lowest values of throughput and the darkest shades indicate the highest values. The relative vertical size of each of the ground-based and satellite-based nodes represents the current number of active processes or users accessing that node. Although this figure is a static representation of network activity, these data could be easily converted into a dynamic animation of the network, which would allow analysts to see patterns of usage over time and indications of peak or overload conditions at a given node.

Figure 11-5 is a static screenshot of an interactive visualization of the multiple variables affecting the monitoring of a natural gas pipeline. The underlying map and pipeline network diagram shows each of the compressor stations, with the total flow through each station represented by the height of each station. Although not easily detectable in gray scale, the large station in the foreground indicates an alert condition (shown in bright red in a color rendering), in this case highlighting a station with a particularly high flow volume. Drill down permits the operator to explore the situation—pointing to a station elicits a pop-up text report of all the underlying data, or pop-up charts and graphs, or detailed graphics, such as the state of each turbine within the station, shown as small, light-colored bars on top of the station.

The visualization in Figure 11-6 shows the benefit that three-dimensional representation can have on the most mundane printed reports. Instead of seeing just a yield curve and the overnight impact on the portfolio, the manager is enticed by an interactive yield curve of "what-if" interactions, without having to wait for reports detailing various scenarios.

If you ever received one of those telephone survey calls around dinnertime or during the most exciting part of a televised sporting event or movie, then you know how annoying they can be. Your opinions are, nonetheless, important and the process of polling is often quite expensive. Frequently, the subject of the poll, while interesting to the pollster, is not something you are particularly interested in, and the pollster must randomly call

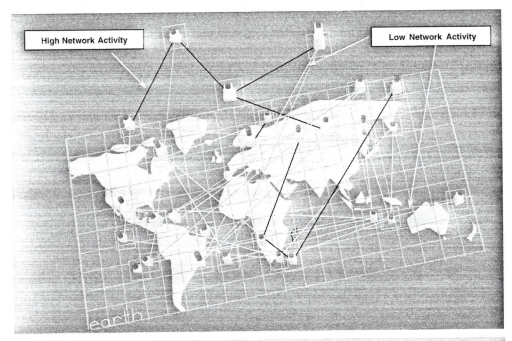

FIGURE 11-4   Data Visualization of Global Private Computer Network Activity

FIGURE 11-5   Natural Gas Pipeline Analysis

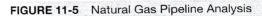

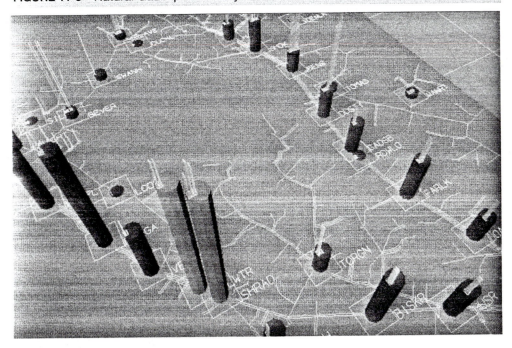

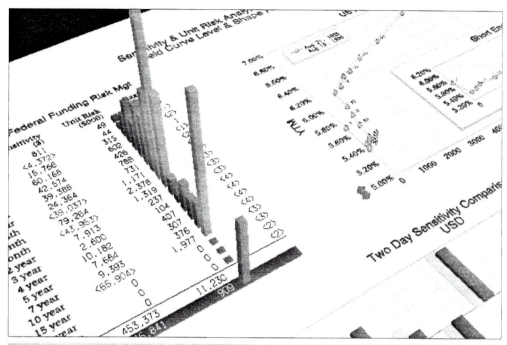

FIGURE 11-6 Risk Analysis Report

thousands of homes until enough interested parties express their opinions. Using data visualization, however, a polling application could be developed that would allow people to participate on only those issues that they feel strongly about. Consider the following scenario: A new poll question is advertised on TV or radio with a 1-800 phone number. Interested voters call the 1-800 number and press 1, 2, or 3 based on whether their vote is yes, no, or other. A database correlates the votes and can even verify through caller identification that no originating phone number votes twice. The data visualization application converts the collected opinion data into a three-dimensional map of the calling area and depicts the frequency of answers as differently shaded vertical bars (such as illustrated in Figure 11-7). The user clicks on the area that he or she is interested in to see the results in that area and can successively click until he or she gets down to poll results by districts.

GEOGRAPHICAL INFORMATION SYSTEMS

A geographic information system (GIS) is a special-purpose digital database in which a common spatial coordinate system is the primary means of reference. Comprehensive GISs require a means of (1) data input from maps, aerial photos, satellites, surveys, and other sources; (2) data storage, retrieval, and query; (3) data transformation, analysis, and modeling, including spatial statistics; and (4) data reporting, such as maps, reports, and plans.

The many definitions offered for GISs emphasize their various aspects. Some miss the true power of the GIS—that is, its ability to integrate information and to

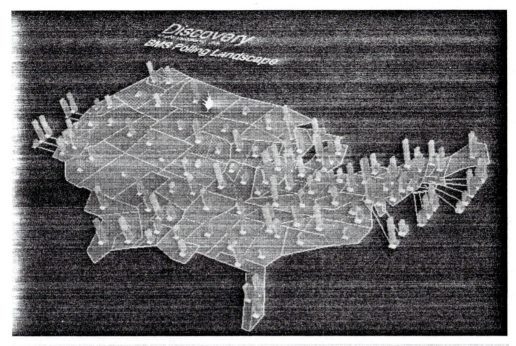

FIGURE 11-7   Interactive Telephone Polling Discovery

help in making decisions—but all include the essential features of spatial references and data analysis.

For the purposes of this text, we define a GIS as follows: a system of hardware, software, and procedures designed to support the capture, management, manipulation, analysis, modeling, and display of spatially referenced data for solving complex planning and management problems.

In other words, a GIS is both a database system with specific capabilities for spatially referenced data and a set of operations for working with those data.

Spatial Data

Spatial data are elements that can be stored in map form. These elements correspond to a uniquely defined location on the Earth's surface. Spatial data contain three basic components: points, lines, and polygons.

- *Points.* Points are single locations in two- or three-dimensional space. Example: The dot representing a city on a map of the United States.
- *Lines.* Lines can be isolated, within a tree structure, or elements of a network structure. Example: River or road systems.
- *Polygons.* Polygons can be isolated, adjacent, or nested. Example: State boundaries or contour lines on a map.

Attribute Data

Along with spatial data, a GIS must be able to handle attribute data as well. Simply put, attribute data are the description of the spatial data seen on a map. For example, a map of Pittsburgh, Pennsylvania, will have corresponding "attribute" data that describe it, such as elevation numbers, land use designations, and boundary information. This information is usually kept in tabular form and managed as a normal database. If something on the map changes (for example, city zoning areas), the attribute data can be modified, and the map will reflect the changes.

The GIS is often referred to as the "spreadsheet of the 1990s." In the same way the computer spreadsheet changed the way people organized and used information in the 1980s, so is the GIS today, only in a more powerful way. The GIS facilitates wise use of limited resources by clarifying characteristics and patterns over space.

Examples of decision-making scenarios in which a GIS may be appropriate include the following:

- Does it make sense to put a megamall here?
- Should legislative district boundaries go here or there?
- Do we expand the existing airport here or build a new one there?
- Will the current school facilities be sufficient for the number of students in 10 years?
- Which pockets of endangered environment should we protect?
- What is the impact of waste facilities on local health patterns?
- Where might restocking of native species be environmentally wise?
- Are we adequately prepared to service the local and surrounding population in the event of various possible disasters?

APPLICATIONS OF DATA VISUALIZATION TECHNIQUES

We live in an age of fierce competition and ever-increasing needs for more and faster information. The power of data visualization is one response to meeting these needs and it appears that its value is generalizable across a wide variety of application domains. Currently, industries ranging from banking, where data visualization is used in credit scoring and risk analysis, to government, where data visualization is used in fraud analysis and drug enforcement, are making effective use of available data visualization techniques and applications.

Table 11-5 contains a brief listing of typical data visualization business applications.

11-7: SIFTWARE TECHNOLOGIES

Although the market is in a constant state of flux with the entry and exit of data visualization product vendors on a daily basis, a number of vendors are establishing a stronghold in the marketplace as they develop a significant brand loyalty among their customers. This next section briefly outlines the characteristics of several of the more prominent players in the field.

RED BRICK

Red Brick offers a number of cases in support of the use of its data mining technology, two of which are H.E.B. and Hewlett-Packard.

H.E.B., of San Antonio, Texas (sales of approximately $4.5 billion, 225 stores, 50,000 employees), was able to bring about a category management application from design to

TABLE 11-5   Typical Applications of Data Visualization Techniques

Retail Banking
- Customer/product cross-selling analysis
- Electronic banking management
- Credit risk
- Product pricing strategy

Government
- Budget analysis
- Resource management
- Economic analysis
- Fraud detection and drug trafficking analysis

Insurance
- Asset/liability management
- Actuarial modeling
- Workflow management and analysis

Health Care and Medicine
- Claims analysis
- Patient behavior analysis
- Therapy analysis

Telecommunications
- Call-center management
- Network operations management
- Service policy analysis
- Market analysis
- Loading pattern analysis

Transportation
- Yield analysis
- Asset utilization
- Fleet management

Capital Markets
- Risk assessment
- Derivatives trading
- Institutional sales systems
- Retail marketing

Asset Management
- Portfolio performance analysis
- Asset allocation
- Portfolio optimization

rollout in under 9 months because it kept the requirements simple and utilized database support from Red Brick and server support from Hewlett-Packard Company.

Previously, the marketing information department would take ad hoc requests for information from users, write a program to extract the information, and return the information to the user a week or so later—not timely enough for most business decisions and in some cases not what the user really wanted in the first place.

The organization implemented a change to category management in 1990. The category manager is characterized as the "CEO" of the category with profit and loss responsibilities, final decision over which products to buy and which to delete, and where the products are to be located on the shelves. The category manager also decides which stores get which products. Although H.E.B. stores are only within the state of Texas, it is a diverse market: Some stores near Mexico have 98 percent Hispanic customers, while suburban Dallas stores may have only 2 percent Hispanic customers. The change to category management centralized all merchandising and marketing decisions, removing these decisions from the stores.

As category managers built up their negotiating skills, technical skills, and partnering skills over 3 years, the need for more timely decision support information grew. An enterprise-wide survey of users to determine requirements took until September 1993. The final system was delivered in March 1994, with the application up and running without problems since then. The company maintains 2 years of data by week, by item (257,000 universal product codes, or UPCs), and by store, which amounts to approximately 400 million detail records. Summary files are maintained by time and total company only, which can be an advantage.

To meet the goal, all queries would be answered in 4 seconds, but some trend reports dealing with large groups of items over long time periods take 30 to 40 seconds. The users are not always technically oriented, so the design is intentionally simple. The system is ad hoc to the extent that the user can specify time, place, and product.

H.E.B. feels that category managers now make better fact-based decisions to determine which products to put in which stores, how much product to send to a store, and the proper product mix. Historically, the company promoted buyers from the stores based on their considerable product knowledge. Now, category managers come from other operational areas such as finance and human resources. The system supports people with diverse backgrounds because it gives those with limited product knowledge the equivalent of years of experience.

Another example of Red Brick technology in the marketplace can be found at Hewlett-Packard (HP), a premier global provider of hardware systems. HP is known for manufacturing high-quality products, but to maintain its reputation it depends on delivering service and support through and after product delivery.

The Worldwide Customer Support Organization (WCSO) within Hewlett-Packard is responsible for providing support services to its hardware and software customers. For several years, the WCSO used a data warehouse of financial, account, product, and service contract information to support decision making. WCSO Information Management is responsible for developing and supporting this data warehouse.

Until 1994, WCSO Information Management supported business information queries with a data warehouse architecture based on two HP3000/Allbase systems and an IBM DB2 system. It was a first attempt at collecting, integrating, and storing data related to customer support for decision-making purposes. As WCSO users increasingly relied on the data warehouse, they began to demand better performance, additional data coverage, and more timely data availability.

The warehouse architecture failed to keep pace with the increased requirements from WCSO users. Users wanted to get information quickly. Both load and query performance were directly affected as more data were added. WCSO decided to investigate other warehouse alternatives that would significantly improve load/query performance, be more cost effective, and support large amounts of data without sacrificing performance.

HP chose to use Red Brick software on an HP9000, and the project began with the consolidation of the existing three databases into a single data warehouse named Discovery. This downsizing provided significant cost savings and increased resource efficiencies in managing and supporting the warehouse environment. Today, Discovery supports approximately 250 marketing, finance, and administration users in the Americas, Europe, and Asia-Pacific regions. They pull query results into their desktop report writers, load information into worksheets, or use the data to feed executive information systems. User satisfaction rose dramatically due to Discovery's vastly improved performance and remodeled business views.

ORACLE

For large-scale data mining, Oracle on the SP2 offers its users robust functionality and excellent performance. Data spread across multiple SP2 processor nodes are treated as a single image affording exceptionally fast access to large databases. Oracle Parallel Query allows multiple users to submit complex queries at the same time. Individual complex queries can be broken down and processed across several processing nodes simultaneously. Execution time can be reduced from overnight to hours or minutes, enabling organizations to make better business decisions faster.

Oracle offers products that help customers create, administer, and use their data warehouse. Oracle's large suite of connectivity products provides transparent access to many popular mainframe databases and allows customers to move data from legacy mainframe applications into the data warehouse on the SP2.

Some of the examples of its technology at work include the following:

- John Alden Insurance, based in Miami, Florida, uses Oracle Parallel Query on the SP2 to mine health care information, which permits orders-of-magnitude improvements in response time for typical business queries.
- ShopKo Stores, a $2-billion, Wisconsin-based mass merchandise chain that operates 128 stores throughout the Midwest and Northeast, chose the SP2 to meet its current and projected needs for both data mining and mission-critical merchandising applications.
- Pacific Bell and Qwest, both telecommunications providers, use the Oracle Warehouse, introduced in 1995, to improve their ability to track customers and identify new service needs. Pacific Bell's data warehouse provides a common set of summarized and compressed information upon which to base decision support systems. The first system analyzes product profitability, and similar decision support systems are in development for marketing, capital investment, procurement, and two additional financial systems.

- Qwest implemented a warehousing system to analyze intra–area code calling data from its three operating companies. Running Oracle7 Release 7.2 on a nine-CPU symmetric multiprocessing system from Pyramid, Qwest's initial centralized architecture supported use by 20 executives and marketing specialists. The next phase delivered warehouse access to more than 400 service representatives, which will ultimately be expanded up to 4,500 service representatives.

INFORMIX—DATA WAREHOUSING

As a major player in the field of data mining, Informix claims a number of success stories. For example, Associated Grocers, one of the leading cooperative grocery wholesalers in the northwest United States, with revenues of $1.2 billion, is replacing its traditional mainframe environment with a three-tiered client/server architecture based on Informix database technology. The new system's advanced applications cut order-fulfillment times in half, reduced inventory carrying costs, and enabled the company to offer its 350 independent grocers greater selection at a lower cost.

In 1991, Associated Grocers embarked on a phased transition from its mainframe-based information system to open systems. The company initially used IBM RS/6000 hardware, and subsequently included Hewlett-Packard and NCR. In evaluating relational database management systems, Associated Grocers developed a checklist of requirements including education/training, scalability, technical support, solid customer references, and future product direction.

After selecting Informix as its company-wide database standard, Associated Grocers then assembled the rest of its system architecture using a three-tier model. On tier 1, the "client" presentation layer, graphical user interfaces use Microsoft Windows and Visual Basic. Tier 2, based on Hewlett-Packard hardware, runs Micro Focus COBOL applications on top of the OEC Developer Package from Open Environment Corporation, which helps Associated Grocers develop DCE-compliant applications. The third layer, the data layer, is the INFORMIX-OnLine database.

Associated Grocers' pilot Informix-based application provides real-time inventory information for its deli warehouse. In the past, merchandise was received manually, and pertinent product information was later keyed into Associated Grocers' financial system. In contrast, the new system recognizes merchandise right at the receiving dock. Handheld radio frequency devices allow merchandise to be immediately scanned into the Informix database. Product is assigned to a warehouse location and its expiration date is noted. When orders are filled, products with the earliest expiration dates are shipped first.

As an extension to the deli warehouse system, the new postbilling system provides separate physical and financial inventories. Previously, merchandise could not be released for sale until the financial systems had been updated, which typically occurred overnight. The new Informix-based system allows for immediate sale and distribution of recently received merchandise.

A third Informix-based application enables Associated Grocers to sell unique items economically—that is, slow-moving merchandise that is ordered monthly versus daily. Rather than incurring the high cost to warehouse these items, Associated Grocers created a direct link to outside specialty warehouses to supply the needed items on demand. Independent stores simply order the merchandise from Associated

Grocers. The order goes into Associated Grocers' billing system, which transmits it to the specialty warehouse, which immediately ships the merchandise to Associated Grocers. The specialty items are loaded onto Associated Grocers' delivery trucks and delivered along with the rest of an independent store's order.

SYBASE

As testimony to the interest and activity in data warehousing, recent surveys (conducted by Meta Group, Inc.) show that more than 70 percent of *Fortune* 1000 companies have data warehousing projects budgeted or underway at an average cost of $3 million and a typical development time of 6 to 18 months.

Conventional warehousing applications today extract basic business data from operational systems, edit or transform them in some fashion to ensure their accuracy and clarity, and move them by means of transformation products, custom programming, or "sneaker net" to the newly deployed analytical database system. This extract-edit-load-query system might be acceptable if business life were simple and relatively static. New data and data structures are added, changes are made to existing data, and even whole new databases are added on a regular basis.

Sybase Warehouse WORKS was designed around four key functions in data warehousing:

1. Assembling data from multiple sources
2. Transforming data for a consistent and understandable view of the business
3. Distributing data to where they are needed by business users
4. Providing high-speed access to the data for those business users

The Sybase Warehouse WORKS Alliance Program provides a complete, open, and integrated solution for organizations building and deploying data warehouse solutions. The program addresses the entire range of technology requirements for data warehouse development, including data transformation, data distribution, and interactive data access. The alliance partners are committed to adopting the Warehouse WORKS architecture and APIs, as well as to working closely with Sybase in marketing and sales programs.

SILICON GRAPHICS

New solutions for data mining are extending the advances in data analysis realized through breakthroughs in data warehousing. Sophisticated tools for three-dimensional visualization, coupled with data mining software developed by Silicon Graphics, make it possible to bring out patterns and trends in the data that may not have been realized using traditional SQL techniques. These "nuggets" of information can then be brought to the attention of the end user, yielding bottom-line results.

Using fly-through techniques, the user can navigate through models on consumer purchasing and channel velocity to follow trends and observe patterns. In response to what the user sees, he or she can interact directly with the data, using visual computing to factor critical "what-if" scenarios into the models. By making it possible to go through many such iterations without overburdening IS staff with the need for analytical assistance, the user can eliminate days—even months—from the review process.

IBM

IBM provides a number of decision support tools to give users a powerful, easy-to-use interface to the data warehouse. IBM Information Warehouse Solutions, in keeping with their commitment to provide open systems implementations, offers the choice of decision support tools that best meet the needs of the end users.

IBM announced a Customer Partnership Program to work with selected customers to gain experience and validate the applicability of the data mining technology. This program offers customers the advantage of IBM's powerful new data mining technology to analyze their data looking for key patterns and associations. For example, Visa and IBM announced an agreement in 1995 that changed the way in which Visa and its member banks exchange information worldwide. The structure facilitates the timely delivery of information and critical decision support tools directly to member financial institutions' desktops worldwide.

IBM Visualizer provides a powerful and comprehensive set of ready-to-use building blocks and development tools that can support a wide range of end-user requirements for query, report writing, data analysis, chart/graph making, business planning, and multimedia databases. As a workstation-based product, Visualizer is object-oriented, which makes it easy to plug in additional functions such as those mentioned. Visualizer can also access databases such as Oracle and Sybase as well as the DB2 family.

A number of other decision support products are available from IBM based on the platform, operating environment, and database of the user. For example, the IBM Application System (AS) provides a client/server architecture and the widest range of decision support functions available for the MVS and VM environments. AS is the decision support server of choice in these environments because of its capability to access many different data sources. IBM Query Management Facility (QMF) provides query, reporting, and graphics functions in the MVS, VM, and CICS environments. The Data Interpretation System (DIS) is an object-oriented set of tools that enables end users to access, analyze, and present information with little technical assistance. It is a LAN-based client/server architecture with access to IBM and non-IBM relational databases as well as host applications in the MVS and VM environment. These and other products available from IBM provide the functions and capabilities needed for a variety of implementation alternatives.

11-8: CHAPTER SUMMARY

"Seeing" the data is becoming a major component in decision support and the formation of organizational strategies. The coming "Age of Information" will bring with it increased demands for organizing and using the multitude of information and knowledge resident within a typical organization, and the discovery of hidden structures and patterns within that information will be a key activity. Through this technology we will fundamentally transform our understanding of the concept of information from its present form of "something we need to know" into its future form of "something we could otherwise never have known."

Key Concepts

- Data mining (DM) is the set of activities used to find new, hidden, or unexpected patterns in data. A synonym for data mining techniques is knowledge data discovery (KDD). (11-1)

- The online analytical processing (OLAP) category of software technology enables decision makers to conduct multidimensional analysis of consolidated enterprise data. Two approaches can be used to conduct the analysis. (11-2)

Multidimensional OLAP (MOLAP)

MOLAP organizes and analyzes data as a hypercube, an *n*-dimensional cube, which allows a number of dimensions to be analyzed simultaneously and any number of multidimensional views of data to be created. Although MOLAP is good at handling summarized data, it is not particularly adept at handling large amounts of detailed data.

Relational OLAP (ROLAP)

In ROLAP, the multidimensional database server is replaced with a large relational database server. ROLAP architectures are especially well suited to those situations in which dynamic access to combinations of summarized and detailed data is more important than the performance gains offered by the MOLAP approach using only summarized or pre-consolidated data.

- Categories of processing algorithms and rule approaches (11-3)

Classification

By building and refining a predictive model of the business problem, data mining classification methods can often provide useful and highly accurate answers.

Association

By searching all details or transactions from operational systems, an associated algorithm that includes the rules that will correlate one set of events or items with another can be developed.

Sequence

Sequencing and time-series analysis are used to relate events in time and, therefore, discover hidden trends for predicting future events.

Cluster

By creating clusters of data according to some metric or set of metrics and analyzing the characteristics of members in the class, clustering might derive certain rules.

- Data mining technologies (11-3)

Statistical analysis

Data mining requires the use of statistical techniques capable of accommodating the conditions of nonlinearity, multiple outliers, and nonnumerical data typically found in a data warehouse environment.

Neural networks, genetic algorithms, and fuzzy logic

By utilizing these machine learning techniques to derive meaning from complicated and imprecise data, patterns and trends within the data can be detected and extracted.

Decision trees

By continually breaking data sets into two separate smaller groups, a predictive model can be built. This technique is often used in data mining applications to assist in the classification of items or events contained within the warehouse.

- General process of knowledge discovery (11-3)
    1. Select a topic for study.
    2. Identify a target data set.
    3. Clean and preprocess the data.
    4. Build a data model.
    5. Interpret and refine.
    6. Predict.
    7. Share the model.
- Current limitations and challenges to data mining (11-5)

  Identification of missing information

  Even with thorough and sophisticated technologies, we cannot yet detect whether the original data set contains the necessary elements for effective mining. Therefore, data mining applications need to include mechanisms for "inventorying" the data set so that a determination of sufficiency in attributes can be made prior to loading the data into the warehouse.

  Data noise and missing values

  Currently, data mining systems are limited to the treatment of noise via statistical techniques that rely on known distributions of data noise. Future systems must incorporate more sophisticated mechanisms for treating missing or noisy data.

  Large databases and high dimensionality

  Dimensionality ensures that discovered patterns are not "local" due to the constant update of the data by an expanding set of time-sensitive data values.
- Data visualization (11-6)

  Data visualization is the process by which numerical data are converted into meaningful images. The ability to create multidimensional structures and models from raw data can assist in analyzing complex data sets by mapping physical properties to the data, thus taking advantage of human visual systems. The identification of hidden patterns contained within the data can be accelerated.

Questions for Review

1. Define data mining.
2. Describe the evolution of decision support activities from verification to discovery.
3. What is online analytical processing (OLAP)?
4. Explain the concept of multidimensional online analytical processing (MOLAP).
5. Describe how relational online analytical processing (ROLAP) works.
6. Compare the two approaches of conducting OLAP analysis. What are the differences between them?
7. Explain the technique of classification for mining data.
8. How does the association technique apply to data mining?
9. List and briefly describe several data mining technologies.
10. List and briefly describe the knowledge discovery search process.
11. Describe the three measures of association used in market basket analysis.
12. What are the current limitations and challenges to data mining?
13. What is data visualization?
14. What is text mining? How does it differ from typical data mining?
15. What are some of the functions of Web mining?

For Further Discussion

1. After gaining an understanding of the evolution of decision support activities from verification to discovery, find an example of this evolution and what makes it possible.
2. Analyze a data mining product utilizing the concept of OLAP in the market. Describe which approach(es) and technique(s) it applies and how it works.
3. Analyze a data mining product in the market. Identify the benefits of this product and discuss its limitations.
4. How can data visualization help in decision making?
5. Compare the siftware technologies discussed in Section 11-7. What are their common characteristics? What are the differences among them?

PolyAnalyst Exercises

1. POLYANALYST: SUMMARY STATISTICS AND LINK ANALYSIS

Comparing characteristics of cars manufactured at different locations
Consider the *Autompg.csv* data set provided in the PolyAnalyst Examples folder.

CASE DESCRIPTION:

The data consists of 398 records characterizing various car types. For each car type the following attributes are provided: the miles-per-gallon value (mpg) measured for each car model in a test performed in 1982, the number of the engine cylinders (cyl), the cylinder displacement in cubic inches (displ), the engine power (power), the car weight in pounds (weight), a number of seconds required to accelerate to the speed of 100 miles per hour (accel), the car's production year (year), the country of production (origin: United States, Europe, or Japan), and the name of the model (model).

Tasks:

a) Load the file Autompg.csv in PolyAnalyst and select the number of cylinders (cyl) to be a categorical attribute.
b) Use Rule Assistant to create a new attribute representing the car age at the time of the experiment out of the year of production of the car and create a new data set "Explored" where Age attribute is included instead of the production year. Plot a histogram illustrating the distribution of the age of cars included in the experiment; use Chart Wizard to reformat the histogram to appear in the depicted form; save the picture in BMP format; and insert this picture in your report. What conclusions can you make about the age of cars considered in the experiment?
c) What is the statistical mean and standard deviation of the car engine power, mpg, and acceleration time, accel?
d) Split the Explored data set in three data sets containing only cars manufactured at each particular location and determine the distribution of the number of cylinders in cars manufactured at different locations compared to the overall distributions. What conclusions can you make? Support these conclusions with the relevant graphs.
   Hint: Use PolyAnalyst Summary Statistics engine.

e) Depict the relation between the location of the car production and the number of cylinders in this car with the help of Link Chart of PolyAnalyst. What are the most prominent positive and negative correlations that you see? What conclusions can you make? Is it easier to arrive at the conclusions utilizing Link Chart or Summary Statistics engine? What are the benefits and drawbacks of each method?

f) Compare cars manufactured at different locations on all their characteristics at once. What conclusions can you make? Support your conclusions by including the graphs saved from PolyAnalyst in your report.

Hint: Use PolyAnalyst Snake Chart.

2. POLYANALYST: LINEAR REGRESSION

Discovering simple relations in medical data
Consider the *2med.csv* data set provided in the PolyAnalyst Examples folder.

CASE DESCRIPTION:

The data for this problem are taken from an archive of a large heart surgery hospital. Each record corresponds to one patient. The record fields, or attributes, are as follows: *file number ID (FILE), sex, age, diagnosis, weight, body surface area (bsa)*, and *height*. The purpose of this exercise is to find whether the weight of a patient can be reliably predicted based on other attributes.

Tasks:

a) Start PolyAnalyst and load *2med.csv* data set. Exclude attributes *FILE* and *bsa*. Launch the Linear Regression exploration engine with the weight attribute as a target. Interpret the results and record the accuracy of the prediction.

b) Note that it might be somewhat more reasonable to expect that *weight* is linearly proportional to body volume rather than the height of a patient. Create a new attribute "cube_of_height" representing the third power of weight and include this attribute instead of *height* in the same analysis. Interpret the results and compare the accuracy of the obtained model to the previous step.

c) Plot a chart displaying the dependence of the weight against the height of patients. Add the obtained linear regression rules to the same chart. Use the sliders on the right-hand side of the chart to test the dependence of the models on other attributes.

d) What other PolyAnalyst exploration engines can be used for developing a model predicting the value of *height* (continuous variable) based on other independent attributes?

3. POLYANALYST: DECISION TREE

Determining profile of nonbuyer of Land Rover Discovery
Consider the *Lrover.csv* data set provided in the PolyAnalyst Examples folder.

Note: The data in this example are real, but both the data and the company name are disguised for privacy reasons.

CASE DESCRIPTION:

To better understand the lifestyles of potential purchasers of the Discovery SUV produced by Land Rover, the marketing research manager commissioned a study of consumers' attitudes, interests, and opinions. A questionnaire was designed with 30 statements covering a variety of dimensions, including consumers' attitudes toward risk, foreign versus domestic products, product styling, spending habits, self-image, and family. The questionnaire included a final question of attitude towards purchasing the Land Rover Discovery.

The respondents used a nine-point Likert scale, where a value of "1" meant that they definitely disagreed with a statement, and "9" meant that they definitely agreed. A total of 400 respondents were obtained from the mailing lists of *Car and Driver, Business Week,* and *Inc.* magazines, who were then interviewed at their homes by an independent surveying company.

Tasks:

a) Read through the corresponding PolyAnalyst Tutorial to learn what questions were asked, and how the marketing research manager was able to build a profile of a typical buyer of a Land Rover Discovery.
b) Consider nonbuyers as respondents who expressed little interest in the possibility of purchasing a Land Rover Discovery (mark their Attitude as 1 or 2). With the help of the Decision Tree algorithm, determine a profile of a typical nonbuyer and interpret your results.
c) Compare the profiles of typical buyers and nonbuyers. What recommendations to the management of Land Rover you can make regarding the marketing positioning of Discovery?

4. POLYANALYST: MARKET BASKET ANALYSIS

Discovering purchase patterns in transactional data
Consider the *Grocery.csv* data set provided in the PolyAnalyst Examples folder.

CASE DESCRIPTION:

Transactions are the lifeblood of any corporation. It is common knowledge that companies record transactional data in order to fulfill orders, manage the supply chain, facilitate accounting, process product returns, and support their daily operation in many other ways. Daily records of customers, products, dates, and amounts provide an unbiased corporate history.

The technology that helps solve the task of discovering purchase patterns in transactional data is called market basket analysis (MBA). This technology finds which products sell together well and what drives these sales. The key sale drivers are identified in the form of association rules, which can capture relations of the types: one-to-one (the purchase of *cereal* often implies that *milk* will be purchased in the same transaction) or many-to-one (the purchase of a *computer* and *printer* will most probably imply that the customer is going to purchase the corresponding *connecting cable*). Association rules are usually unidirectional: for example, a rule that *steak* will be purchased when *barbeque sauce* is purchased does not necessarily imply that the opposite rule holds true.

The data in the file *Grocery.csv* are provided in transactional format. In this format, each transaction (or basket) is marked by an ID in one data column, and the other data column contains all products purchased in this transaction. Therefore, each shopping basket may contain several products. In the considered file, the attribute *Customer* contains a unique identifier for each shopping basket and the attribute *Product* lists all products associated with every basket.

Tasks:

a) Launch PolyAnalyst and load the file *Grocery.csv* in the system. What are 15 most commonly purchased and 15 least commonly purchased products from the grocery store?

b) Use the PolyAnalyst Transactional Basket analysis algorithm to learn which products are most commonly purchased together and what the corresponding association rules are. List those groups of products discovered by the system, which we could intuitively predict to be often purchased together.
Hint: Use the following settings for the TB exploration engine:
Min. Support: 1 percent
Min. Confidence: 30 percent
Min. Improvement: 2 percent

c) Provide the definitions of Support, Confidence, and Improvement as the measures of the quality of the results obtained by Basket Analysis. Interpret the key product associations discovered in the Transactional Basket analysis performed in the previous step and interpret the discovered rules according to these definitions. Provide a written interpretation of the relationship found between *Hot Dogs, Hot Dog Buns,* and *Sweet Relish* in terms of Support, Confidence, and Improvement.

d) Based on the achieved results, what types of recommendations would you make to the manager of the grocery store in order to utilize the discovered cross-sell opportunities to increase sales?

5. POLYANALYST: TEXT ANALYSIS

Determining occupational trauma hazards through text analysis
Consider the *UnitedMutual.csv* data set provided in the PolyAnalyst Examples
folder.

Note: The data in this example are real, but both the data and the company name are disguised for privacy reasons.

CASE DESCRIPTION:

The Research Center of United Mutual, a health insurance company with more than 1,000 offices throughout the world, was tasked with determining the causes of accidents and injuries, and identifying appropriate methods for preventing these accidents. The goal of the project was to drive down the incidence of occupational injuries and reduce the disabilities arising from those that do occur. The main source of accidents and claims data available is the Call Center data, which contains natural language textual notes entered in the database by Call Center operators upon interviewing claimants.

The important fields and their definitions are listed here:

Cause

Reported cause of injury descriptive (natural language text data reported by the insured and entered in the database by a Call Center operator).

Diagnosis

Doctor report of patient's injury (also unstructured text data).

Localization

Trauma localization (category selected from a predetermined drop-down list).

Tasks:

a) Count all records describing cases involving trucks (in all common meanings of this word in the sense of a vehicle for hauling something). What senses of the word *truck* have you selected to work with?

   Hint: Use PolyAnalyst Text Analysis exploration engine and allow the system to include word generalizations.

b) How many cases out of those selected in the first step do not contain the word *truck* itself but contain related words (such as, for example, *tractor* or *van*)? How many cases were treated erroneously as related to trucks?

c) Compare the distribution of trauma localization for cases involving trucks with all cases. What are the main differences between the most represented trauma localizations in two cases?

d) List trauma localizations that occur unusually frequently in the cases involving trucks (even if the absolute number of these cases is not high). List trauma localizations that occur unusually rarely in cases involving trucks. Which PolyAnalyst instrument did you use in order to most readily arrive at your results?

6. TEXTANALYST: SUMMARIZATION

Document summarization and semantic search for information

Consider the *Web_Intelligence.txt* file provided in the Data_TA folder on the Megaputer software CD.

CASE DESCRIPTION:

Industry analysts who process large numbers of documents are often overloaded with work and seek automated tools to reduce that burden. When an analyst is monitoring a particular subject or when, say, a venture capitalist wants to assess the value of a proposal and must search the Internet, both end up with a huge collection of documents. Some of those documents contain key answers they are searching for, but the majority of the collected documents are usually irrelevant to their research. Analysts must skim through all the collection to decide which documents are worth further investigation. The technology for automated document summarization can dramatically increase the effectiveness of this work and save analysts vast amounts of time.

"Web Intelligence" is an eight-page white paper discussing the benefits and techniques of Web data mining. The objective of this exercise is to carry out semantic analysis, automated summarization, and a natural language search for information with the help of the text mining tool TextAnalyst, offered by Megaputer Intelligence. TextAnalyst operates via unique neural network technology combined with some linguistic analysis, which allows the system to analyze large volumes of unstructured text quickly and efficiently.

Tasks:

a) Launch TextAnalyst and load the file *Web_Intelligence.txt* in the system. Browse through the automatically created Semantic Network (a list of most important terms and relations between these terms in the text) and locate with the help of TextAnalyst all the sentences in the text that deal simultaneously with the terms *website* and *prospects*. Include the found sentences in your report on the problem. What is the meaning of the numbers to the left of each term included in the Semantic Network? What does it mean when two numbers appear to the left of a term?

b) Run the automated summarization of TextAnalyst. Does the summary generated by the system provide you with a sufficient initial understanding of the subject of the text? Compare the size and quality of the summaries generated by TextAnalyst with a minimum semantic importance threshold set to 90 and 99. Include both summaries in your report, listing the semantic weight of each sentence in the summaries.

c) Run a natural language query against the considered text. A good sample query would be: "How does data mining help in learning visitor interests?" Include the response generated by the system in your report. How many fragments found by the system are relevant with respect to your query?

d) More difficult: What is the basic idea of the search mechanism implemented in TextAnalyst? Why do you think the terms that had not been present in your query were still presented in the list of terms in the Query control window? Can you trace their relation to your initial query?

7. TEXTANALYST: KEY CONCEPT EXTRACTION

Extracting knowledge from customer surveys
Consider the *ITT_survey.txt* file provided in the Data_TA folder on the Megaputer software CD.

Note: The data in this example are real, but both the data and the company name are disguised for privacy reasons.

CASE DESCRIPTION:

One of the basic tasks of a text mining system is to identify automatically key concepts and links between them in documents. The created semantic network of concepts and relations serves as the foundation for many further analysis techniques, as well as being displayed graphically to provide a convenient navigation mechanism for the considered texts. The background knowledge about the considered application domain can be utilized through customized user dictionaries.

ITT set an online survey soliciting customer comments about the quality of their service as a provider of Internet access. The goal of ITT management was to monitor the overall satisfaction of its customers with the Internet access service and to identify the main issues perceived by its customers as problems. Knowledge of these issues could help the company address the identified problems and thus improve the satisfaction of its customers.

Tasks:

a) Launch TextAnalyst and load the file *ITT_survey.txt* in the system. The obtained results do not take into account the presence of synonyms in the text, but these preliminary results are already quite useful, because they reveal the main topics customers are concerned about. These topics include e-mail, ads, navigation bar, page, service, search engine, and so on. List in your report other topics that are most important to customers. Which of these concepts might be of primary concern to ITT managers? Why?

b) Pull out customer comments dedicated to *ads*. How many sentences were retrieved? Include the results in your report. Do customers perceive ads as a benefit or a drawback of the provided service? What is the ratio of positive to negative comments related to ads?

c) As useful as they are, these results can be significantly improved by making the following observation: Some terms can be used interchangeably within the considered domain. For example, the terms *mail* and *e-mail* refer to the same subject, e-mail, in the present context. This conclusion is made based on a visual evaluation of the results furnished by TextAnalyst. Launch the Dictionary Editor module of TextAnalyst and add the following terms and their synonyms, as used by the survey respondents, to the dictionary:

   advertise (synonyms: ad, advertising, and advertisement, and even add)

   toolbar (synonyms: bar and menu)

   rid (synonym: remove)

   Hint: When adding words with their synonyms to the dictionary, mark the main added words as *exception words*, as defined in the TextAnalyst User Manual.

   Add "don't" to the dictionary as *not analyzed word*. Save the resulting dictionary under a different name and then link TextAnalyst to this new dictionary, so that the new synonym list is utilized in the further analysis. Close and reopen TextAnalyst in order for all the performed changes to take effect.

d) Load again the same file *ITT_survey.txt*. Observe that with the new dictionary, TextAnalyst obtains more accurate and informative results. Summarize the most significant differences between the newly obtained results and the results generated in the first step of the analysis. What issues did you find to represent the main problems for customers when they use the ITT Internet access service? Obtain and copy to your report all text fragments corresponding to the three main problems as perceived by customers.

   Hint: Because the concept page is too unspecific and can be related to many different situations, you need to ignore this concept in your analysis.

e) *More difficult:* Export the resulting semantic network to CSV format. Open these CSV results in Microsoft Excel, sort the results in order to obtain the list of the most important concepts in descending order, and then plot an Excel graph illustrating the frequency of occurrence of the top 30 concepts representing customer comments and suggestions.

8. RECOMMENDATION MODULE

Making intelligent product recommendations to assist call center operators
Install Online Recommendation system from Megaputer Intelligence on your
machine and launch Online Recommendation Demo through the regular
Windows Start menu.

Note: The data in this example are real, but both the data and the company name are
disguised for privacy reasons.

CASE DESCRIPTION:

Scores of transactions are recorded and stored by thousands of companies daily. The
advent of e-commerce that requires recording millions of transactions daily accelerated
the growth of volumes of stored data. The analysis of transactional data can help improve
the quality of business decisions and increase the value of every customer interaction.

The purpose of a recommendation system is to provide the most probable additional purchases in response to any transaction performed by the customer. Customers
might enjoy seeing an accurate and unobtrusive recommendation for possible other
products of interest to them. These recommendations can help them better navigate
through the store and reduce their shopping time.

MITA Group performs analytical research for various high-tech industries ranging
from broadband and cellular communications to biotech sector. The company analysts
create industry-specific reports as a service to the players in the respective market. The
average price of the reports ranges from $7,000 to $10,000, and the volume of business-
to-business sale transactions with these reports is rather low. The point of sale is a call
center, where operators handle requests for particular reports from customers. The utilization of the Recommendation module from Megaputer Intelligence helped call center operators identify the best cross-sell opportunities on the fly in each particular case.
This recommendation of the most relevant additional reports of interest to the individual customers simultaneously generated additional revenue to the company and
increased customer satisfaction.

Tasks:

a) Launch the Online Recommendation (OR) demo and view the *Transactions* table
in the opening Microsoft Access database demo. It is the main source of data for the
application. The two most important fields are *Company_Name,* which represents
the customer that purchased products, and *Product_Name,* which represents the
purchased report. In our application, the data are so sparse (few products are purchased by a single customer) that we can view all purchases performed by a single
customer as a single transaction in order to identify the best cross-sell opportunities. What are the four main industries that MITA Group covers? Which industries
have the largest number of reports dedicated to them? How many individual purchase records are included in the Demo data?
Note: Often, a vendor would want to recommend not only products with a high
probability of being purchased, but to recommend those products that have the
highest margin. This issue is addressed in the OR module by incorporating the
Margins table, where the business user can specify different margins for products
and influence the recommendations made in each case.

b) Click the *Create* button on the *Online Recommendations* form in Access demo. OR Module will process historical transactional data contained in the database and distill and store in a recommendation table all frequent purchase patterns for each product. With the creation of the recommendation table, you can select a product from a drop-down list of all products in the lower part of the form. For example, select *4F Cellular* (the real report name: *3D Cellular*) and click *Add*, which implies that the customer purchased this report. What other products of interest the system recommends might the customer be interested in? What recommendations have sufficiently high probability (the number in the square brackets) to be recommended to customers? How many products from the biotech sector are included in the recommendations returned by the system? Why?

c) Set the *Number of Recommendations* to 4 to include only the most important recommendations, and select one of the products recommended by the system, for example, *Core Ultra-fast nets: Market options for Ultra-fast Switching, Routing, and Crossconnect in DASA nets* as the next purchase by the same customer. How did the list of recommendations returned by OR Module change?

d) Now assume that you assist the next customer. Click *New Customer* on the form to "forget" the last transactions. Select the report *Diagnostic Imaging Equipment and Systems Global Market* as purchased by the new customer. What are additional reports recommended by the system? How many reports dedicated to broadband communications do you see recommended? Why? Which products can indeed be recommended, taking into account our certainty in the outcome? Does it help the business if we try to recommend more?

e) *More difficult:* Determine manually from the Access *Transactions* table why OR Module recommended the products you see in the list. Provide simple mathematical reasoning for your conclusion.
   Note: It is relatively easy to trace the reason for the system decision in this case because the data are so sparse and so few transactions are considered. In more realistic situations involving millions of products and transactions, as well as more than one product in the basket, this analysis might become a formidable task.

f) What other businesses, in addition to Call Centers, could successfully utilize an expert system with the results obtained by Online Recommendation module? What would be a typical corresponding system implementation?

APPENDIX TO CHAPTER 11

SAUDI ARABIAN AIRLINES—
DATA ANALYSIS PROJECT

Objective and Exploration

The objective of the performed analysis was to determine what attributes influenced the percentage of passengers flying in the first-class section. These influential attributes could thus be manipulated to influence the number of first-class passengers present on each flight to increase revenue. The analysis also helps predict the optimal percentage of the first-class seats for each flight, thus allowing Saudi Arabian Airlines to maximize the revenue and increase customer satisfaction.

The data provided for the analysis contained various characteristics of flights originating from or arriving to major cities in Saudi Arabia: Riyadh (RUH), Jeddah (JED), Medina (MED), and Mecca (DMM).

To simplify the analysis, we began by creating a data set that consisted of flights departing from a single location, designated by **JED_DEP,** which listed all flights departing from Jeddah. Breaking the departure field down to one location allowed us to concentrate on the flight analysis of just this location: The analyses for other locations can be performed similarly. Next, we created a variable that indicated the season when the fight took place called **D_Season.** This variable indicates whether any relationship is evident between the number of first-class passengers and a certain season. Third, we created two ratios to allow comparison of the prices of first-class tickets to economy-class tickets (**FtoY**) and business-class tickets to economy-class tickets (**JtoY**) on each individual flight. Fourth, we created an attribute named **FC_percent** that indicates the percentage of first-class passengers on a given flight.

Customer-provided attributes used in the analysis include the following:

* **REVPAX** is a given attribute that indicates the total number of passengers on the flight.
* **L_MAILKILO** is the total weight of the Mail on the flight in kilos. Here, more analysis is required to determine how this variable is applicable to the model.
* **FREIGHT** is the total amount of freight weight in kilos on the flight.
* **L_COMAT** is the total amount of commercial mail weight in kilos on the flight.
* **FC_PREV** is the total number of first-class passengers on the flight.
* **BC_PREV** is the total number of business-class passengers on the flight.
* **EC_PREV** is the total number of economy-class passengers on the flight.

Derived/Added attributes used in the analysis include the following:

* **F** gives the price of the first-class ticket for the flight.
* **J** gives the price of the business-class ticket for the given flight.
* **Y** gives the price of the economy-class ticket for the given flight. (**Note: F, J,** and **Y** are actionable attributes that management could manipulate to change consumers' response to purchasing first-class tickets.)
* **JED_origin** indicates the departure is from JED, which is used to break the data set down to a single airport.
* **Weekday** indicates whether the flight took place on a weekday. (We assumed the number of passengers who fly on weekends would differ from the number of passengers who fly on weekdays.)
* **Flight_class** indicates whether a flight is primary or secondary.
* **FC_percent** indicates the percentage of the first-class passengers on each flight.
* **FC_perc_class** indicates whether the number of first-class passengers is high, low, or zero.
* **FtoJ** indicates the ratio of the first-class ticket price to the business-class ticket price.
* **FtoY** indicates the ratio of the first-class ticket price to the economy-class ticket price.
* **D_Season** indicates one of the four seasons in which the flight took place. (We felt this attribute would help in determining when the airline industry increases were due to passengers who do not travel on a regular basis—for example, people who only travel during summer vacations.)
* **Flight_class** is a derived variable that indicates the value, as "Yes" if the **FLIGHTNO** variable is less than 1,000 and "NO" if the **FLIGHTNO** is greater than or equal to 1,000. (This attribute was created in order to separate primary flights serving popular routes, which were given three-digit flight numbers, and supplementary flights serving less-popular routes and having four-digit flight numbers. Flight_class attribute was created after observing the difference in the number of passengers carried by flights with three- and four-digit flight numbers.)

We divided the percentage of first-class passengers carried by individual flights into three categories: 0, to indicate the category contained no first-class passengers; low, to indicate less than 6 percent of the passengers are first class; and high, to indicate 6 percent or more are first-class passengers. We used the percentage value of the number of the first-class passengers rather than the absolute number of first-class passengers on each flight, because the latter would give a solution based mainly on the plane's size. The percentage of the first-class passengers on each plane was split by 6 percent to give us three almost evenly populated categories, with 6 percent as the mean number of first-class passengers on all the flights. The resulting new attribute, named **FC_perc_class,** provided the target variable in our exploration. Creating this categorical attribute allowed the use of the Decision Trees exploration engine in order to predict whether a considered flight will have a large or small percentage of first-class passengers.

With the data initially explored and all derived attributes applied to the data set **JED_DEP,** we then created a testing dataset called **JED_DEP_Check10P** by randomly sampling 10 percent of records from the **JED_DEP** data set. These data were not used when training the model but were used to test the created model for significance. A complement to this data set produced a data set that contained 90 percent of records of flights originating from JED. This data set was called **Training;** it contains 16,350 records of the **JED_DEP** data set.

First, to identify a small set of variables that influence the percentage of first-class seats on an airplane most significantly, we run the Find Dependencies (FD) exploration engine with the **FC_perc** attribute selected as a target and only some independent variables included. The first round of the FD exploration suggested that two attributes, **L_COMAT** and **Flight_class**, are the most important predictors for **FC_perc**, which indicates that the amount of commercial mail and whether the flight is a primary flight can determine what percentage of first-class passengers it will carry. The second round of FD, with **L_COMAT** and **Flight_class** that were identified in the previous round excluded from the exploration, suggested that three other most important attributes are prices **F, J,** and **Y,** which is not surprising. Although this result is interesting, we would like to find out *how* various attributes influence the percentage of first-class passengers.

To create a model to predict the target variable **FC_perc_class,** we used PolyAnalyst's Decision Trees exploration engine. This engine clearly indicates the most influential attributes (using a graphical decision tree) in determining the target variable: **FC_perc_class.** The Decision Trees exploration model named **DT_FC_perc_class** was the first algorithm run, and it returned a decision tree using the attribute **DEST** as the initial split comprised of approximately 44 different nodes with a high classification probability of 59.35 percent. (Individual classes were predicted with errors of 27 percent, 60 percent, and 36 percent, respectively.) By testing this model on the **JED_DEP_Check10P** data set, we can see that the created model delivers only slightly worse results on the data that were not used in training. This conclusion increases our confidence in the significance of the model. This model can be used to determine the number of first-class seats that should be reserved to a given destination. For example, flights destined for AMS, BWN, BRU, MAA, CMB, CPH, DAC, DUS, ISB, LAX, MCT, and THR should reserve a low number of first-class seats because a low number of the flights to these locations contain passengers in the first-class section. At the same time, flights to AUH, AMM, CAI, DXB, and KRT have a large percentage of first-class seats on them. To further investigate other actionable attributes that influence the target, we create a second Decision Trees model.

Next, we ran Decision Trees again, but this time excluded the **DEST** variable. The Decision Trees exploration model named **DT_No_Destination,** returned the following classification statistics:

Classification probability: 64.44 percent
Classification efficiency: 46.42 percent
Classification error for class "0": 29.29 percent
Classification error for class "1": 53.80 percent
Classification error for class "2": 23.88 percent

These statistics show that the second Decision Trees model provides a higher classification probability than the first Decision Trees model. Thus, if the second model proves to be significant through testing it on unseen data, it would be the better model in predicting the objective. The classification error for class "1" (low percentage of first-class passengers) is relatively high, but it is not of great concern because we are more interested in whether the percentage of first-class passengers is high or none.

The Decision Trees exploration engine made the initial split on variable **F**, which is the first-class price for a ticket. **F**, as the initial splitting attribute, indicates that it is the most important variable in determining the objective. The following decision tree was produced by the algorithm; for easier visibility the tree is split into two different pictures by the initial split on variable **F**.

In the figure, the nodes' color indicates the predicted classes: Blue is class "High"; red is class "0"; and green is the class "Low." The shade of each node relates to the share of records that correspond to it, where bright nodes have a higher number of corresponding records and light nodes contain fewer records. The Decision Trees algorithm found the attributes **Flight_class**, **REVPAX**, **FtoJ**, **FtoY**, **D_Season**, and **L_MAILKILO** to be important attributes in predicting the target attribute. One can follow individual branches of this tree to see how these attributes predict either a large or small portion of passengers flying first class, or none at all.

Business Discussion

Note: This business analysis covers just one branch of the Decision Trees model.

In determining the attributes that predict the percentage of the first-class passengers, the decision tree indicates that price of the first-class ticket is the most influential as the initial split. (Note: Nodes closer to the root have a stronger influence on the model.) If the first-class ticket price is less than $2,380, then 52 percent of these flights will contain passengers of the High first-class section. If the first-class ticket price is more than or equal $2,380 then only 14 percent of these flights will contain passengers of the High first-class section.

For the higher first-class ticket prices, the next most influential parameter is whether the flight is a primary flight or secondary flight. Here, we assumed that three-digit flight numbers refer to primary flights, while four-digit flight numbers indicate secondary flights. For the secondary flights, the majority of the passengers purchase either business or economy tickets. For the primary flights, a much higher percentage of the passengers are first class. This statistic would indicate the need to reserve a much larger section for first-class passengers on primary flights and small sections for secondary flights. However, we could be wrong in our assumption here since secondary flights may not offer first-class seats.

For the higher first-class ticket prices and primary flights, the next most influencing parameter in determining our objective is the total number of passengers a given fight carries. It is assumed that lower-revenue-producing flights use smaller planes. These planes can either accommodate first-class passengers or they cannot, because the flights either contain a high number of first-class passengers *or* they contain a high number of business and economy passengers. For higher-revenue–producing flights the probability is higher that the flights will contain a large number of first-class passengers. We assumed the higher-revenue–producing planes to be larger planes and in turn have the ability to accommodate first-class arrangements.

For the higher first-class ticket prices, primary flights, and higher-passenger-booked planes, the next most influencing attribute in reaching our object is the ratio of first-class ticket price to business-class ticket price. This ratio indicates that when the value is greater than or equal to 1.28, there is a higher chance that more passengers will be flying in the first-class section. Here, this result seems to be paradoxical, but the Decision Trees exploration engine found it to be soundly based on the data. This finding may indicate that higher-ratio flights offer better first-class service, which consumers may desire. Thus, providing a higher, more-expensive first-class service, could increase the number of first-class passengers on board a flight, and thus increase the ratio.

```
Root
  F<2.38e+003
    Flight_class=yes
      REVPAX<16.5
        REVPAX<10.5
        REVPAX>=10.5
      REVPAX>=16.5
        FtoJ<1.28
          FtoY<1.46
            F<1.45e+003
            F>=1.45e+003
          FtoY>=1.46
            REVPAX<129
              REVPAX<30.5
              REVPAX>=30.5
            REVPAX>129
        FtoJ>=1.28
          FtoJ<1.28
            REVPAX<96.5
            REVPAX>=96.5
          FtoJ>=1.28
            L_MAILKILO<138
              REVPAX<70.5
              REVPAX ②=70.5
                F<1.39e+003
                F>=1.39e+003
                  L_MAILKILO<56.5
                    REVPAX<240
                    REVPAX>=240
                  L_MAILKILO>=56.5
            L_MAILKILO>=138
              F<1.39e+003
              F>=1.39e+003
                F<1.69e+003
                F>=1.69e+003
    Flight_class=No
      REVPAX<250
      REVPAX>=250
        REVPAX<395
        REVPAX>=395
  F>=2.38e+003
    FtoY<1.5
```

```
        REVPAX>=395
  F>=2.38e+003
    FtoY<1.5
      REVPAX<61.5
        REVPAX<16.5
        REVPAX>=16.5
          FtoY<1.41
          FtoY>=1.41
            FtoY<1.5
            FtoY>=1.5
      REVPAX>=61.5
        REVPAX<386
          FtoY<1.41
            F<3.14e+003
            F>=3.14e+003
          FtoY>=1.41
            Flight_class=No
            Flight_class=Yes
              D_Season=2
                REVPAX<110
                REVPAX>=110
              D_Season=4
                FtoY<1.5
                FtoY>=1.5
              D_Season=1
              D_Season=3
        REVPAX>=386
    FtoY>=1.5
      Flight_class=Yes
        REVPAX<49.5
          REVPAX<16.5
          REVPAX>=16.5
            FtoJ<1.3
            FtoJ>=1.3
        REVPAX>=49.5
          FtoY<1.5
            FtoY<1.5
            FtoY>=1.5
              REVPAX<103
              REVPAX>=103
          FtoY>=1.5
      Flight_class=No
```

For the higher first-class ticket prices, primary flights, higher-passenger–booked planes, and lower first-class to business-class price ratio, the next most influencing parameter is the ratio of first-class ticket price to economy-class ticket price. A high ratio means a higher number of first-class passengers on these flights. We assumed this parameter to be due to better first-class service, which usually attracts customers.

For the higher first-class ticket prices, primary flights, higher-revenue–producing planes, lower first-class to business-class price ratio, and a high first-class to economy-ticket price ratio, the next most influencing variable is the very high-passenger-booked planes. These nodes indicate that planes with a large number of passengers are more likely to have more people in the economy sections rather than planes that hold fewer than 129 passengers. The assumption here is that planes that can handle many passengers allow for more room by not having as many first-class seats that tend to take up more space, thus not allowing for as many first-class tickets. To increase the number of first-class passengers you could increase the space allowed for the first-class area in the plane.

Model Testing

After analyzing the results of Decision Trees, the algorithm was tested on data that were not used for training in order to manually test the model for significance. PolyAnalyst contains a unique feature that allows the models to be tested for their ability to successfully predict outcomes of future situations. The testing results returned statistical values indicating that the Decision Trees algorithm proved to be successful on the unseen data. The following classification statistics can be compared to the classification statistics of the Decision Trees algorithm in showing the significance of the model.

Classification probability: 64.54 percent
Classification efficiency: 45.38 percent
Classification error for class "0": 33.22 percent
Classification error for class "1": 52.05 percent
Classification error for class "2": 22.29 percent

Conclusions

The performed analysis suggests the following conclusions:

1. The attribute ratios **FtoJ** and **FtoY** can be manipulated by changing the ticket prices to influence the number of first-class passengers aboard each individual flight. Increasing the benefits of the first-class section results in higher percentage occupancy of the first-class seats.
2. The primary flights could use planes that accommodate more first-class passenger seats, and secondary flights could decrease the area of the first-class section to allow for more economy and business seats. Using the first Decision Trees model, you could increase or decrease the number of reserved first-class tickets to increase profit based on the destination of the flight from JED.
3. Flights destined for AMS, BWN, BRU, MAA, CMB, CPH, DAC, DUS, ISB, LAX, MCT, and THR should reserve a low number of first-class seats because a low number of the flights to these locations carry passengers in the first-class section.
4. At the same time, flights to AUH, AMM, CAI, DXB, and KRT have a large percentage of first-class seats on them. The company should proactively manipulate the attribute ratios **FtoJ** and **FtoY** in order to increase the occupancy rates of the first-class seats on flights to these destinations.

Source: Provided by Richie Kasprzycki, Analyst at Megaputer Intelligence. R.Kasprzycki@megaputer.com. All permissions granted.

DESIGNING AND BUILDING THE DATA WAREHOUSE

Learning Objectives

◆ Understand the enterprise model approach to building a data warehouse

◆ Explore the issues related to defining the project scope

◆ Examine the concepts associated with economic justification of the project

◆ Review the various analysis tools used to gather system requirements

◆ Explain the design of a project plan for construction of a data warehouse

◆ Understand the process of economic feasibility analysis and the importance of intangibles

◆ Review the various data warehouse architectures and development methodologies

◆ Determine the project success factors associated with data warehouse implementation

⟨ **DSS MINICASE** ⟩

SALES BLOSSOM AT EFLOWERS.COM
WITH WEB MINING

eFlowers.com came to be when Bill McClure, chairman and CEO of Flowers Direct LP and Universal American Flowers LP, decided to sell flowers over the Internet. The company obtained nationwide publicity in April 2000 by acquiring its domain name in exchange for agreeing, in addition to a cash payment, to send a dozen long-stem roses to the previous owner's wife every month for the rest of her life.

When McClure founded eFlowers.com, he had already built two substantial businesses selling flowers wholesale to supermarkets and directly to consumers over the telephone. Together with eFlowers.com, these businesses occupy a 35,000-square-foot fully refrigerated facility and employ more than 100 full-time employees.

eFlowers.com leverages its experience and a strong business infrastructure to surpass other Web florists by offering the freshest product and the most creative designs. Today, it takes the company no more than 3 days to deliver cut product direct from its farms in South America—two days faster than the industry standard. According to eFlowers, flowers are more than just a decorative accessory. Flowers have the power to deliver the sender's thoughts and feelings, just as those emotions were meant to be expressed.

THE BUSINESS CHALLENGE

eFlowers.com experienced problems with a low-end traffic analysis solution for their Web site. Potential traffic builders, advertisers, and investors used the number of unique visitors as their primary metric, yet the low-end tool was only able to measure the number of visitor sessions. The problem grew large when eFlowers' partners began expressing their concerns over the accuracy of the numbers and the overall validity of the application used to collect the metrics.

Inability to track referrals from various search engines hampered the company's efforts to improve its search engine positioning. Because most search engines charge per click-through, it also meant that eFlowers.com had no way to validate the actual numbers they were paying for. Finally, the traffic analysis tool provided no assistance in addressing another critical issue: extremely short sales periods during holidays. The company's marketing team needed immediate feedback on the performance of sales promotions in order to make adjustments that could have a major financial impact.

THE SOLUTION

Virtually all of the partners who expressed concern over the tool were users of WebTrends, a popular Web mining application. Their recommendations weighed heavily in eFlowers.com's decision to adopt WebTrends as their Web mining solution because the credibility of the numbers is so important. eFlowers.com found the WebTrends solution to be a blessing because it required virtually no support infrastructure, which eliminated the need to purchase and set up hardware, install software, and maintain everything. All they had to do was paste a bit of JavaScript code on each of the pages they wanted to analyze. The cost was reasonable, the process simple, and on the few occasions they ran into snags, they received excellent technical support from WebTrends.

THE RESULTS

Implementing a robust Web mining solution immediately improved their credibility with traffic builders and potential advertisers. They can provide information in a format that everyone is used to seeing, and the WebTrends name meant instant credibility.

(continued)

The fact that Web mining is able to provide unique user statistics is especially important, and the service saved eFlowers.com time by eliminating disagreements. For example, if a search engine tells them that they received 252 referrals but the Web mining system says it was only 158—that statistic ends the argument. Just as important is the additional information the service provides. Having continual, accurate information on referrals from each search engine helps eFlowers.com increase traffic by allowing them to focus marketing efforts on sites where they have a low number of referrals. The Web mining solution goes beyond reporting the source of the traffic by providing a count of keywords used to reach the eFlowers.com site. Then, if they see they are getting very little traffic from a search engine for a keyword that is generating a lot of traffic from other sites, the marketing staff can change the metatags or headlines to try and improve the results.

The ability of the Web mining application to track transactions helped the company significantly increase revenues during key flower holidays. The specials they run during holiday periods generate a significant part of eFlowers.com revenues. The problem they encountered in the past was that it often took a day or two before they were able to generate meaningful figures from their back-end systems on which promotions were taking off and which ones were falling flat. By the time eFlowers.com received the information, a lot of sales were already lost. Now, the marketing and sales staff can query the Web mining application and get a real-time determination of exactly how their products are moving. Based on that information, they can make decisions such as moving a popular promotion to the homepage, dropping a promotion that isn't working, ordering new inventory of a popular item, or reducing the price of something that isn't selling. By closely tracking what is happening in the early hours of the holiday, eFlowers.com can make decisions that affect sales over these hot selling periods. For Thanksgiving 2000, the Web mining solution helped eFlowers.com determine which centerpieces were the best sellers. The products were moved to the homepage, and they beat their projected sales targets for the period.

12-1: THE ENTERPRISE MODEL APPROACH TO DATA WAREHOUSE DESIGN

In Chapter 10, we explored the concept of a data warehouse (DW) and looked briefly at some of the challenges associated with implementing one within a modern organization. In this chapter, we extend our focus to specific issues regarding the construction and implementation of an organizational data warehouse.

Regardless of the level of sophistication of an organization's strategic deployment of technologies, the data warehouse poses a significant challenge to the technology infrastructure. If the data warehouse project is to be successful and generate information for the widest possible audience, the first step in planning a DW must be to define the information requirements of the enterprise in a holistic sense. This definition normally requires a description of the business at the enterprise level in terms of its various information characteristics. These activities constitute the creation of an *enterprise model* (EM).

ENTERPRISE MODEL DEFINED

The enterprise model of a firm consists of a number of separate models that, when properly integrated, provide a coherent picture of the enterprise. The various submodels may describe the enterprise in terms of strategy, organization, data, processes, or culture. The goal is to ascertain the level of alignment between the business and its cadre of systems.

Although all of the components of a fully specified EM will be of interest to the DW designers, two specific elements of the model are particularly important: (1) the corporate process model, and (2) the corporate data model.

The corporate process model represents a highly structured description of the elementary processes within the enterprise that identify the interrelationships among the different processes. The corporate data model describes the entities generated by, or required by, the elementary processes carried out by the enterprise. We will explore the content and construction of each of these models in greater detail later in this section. For the moment, it is only important for us to realize the benefits of developing an enterprise model prior to launching a data warehouse venture of any size.

The long-term benefit of the construction of an enterprise model is found primarily through the increased integration of the business processes throughout the firm. Simply constructing the model does not, however, create this benefit. The increased integration is a direct result of the redesign of the processes themselves and of the information systems that support them. Most organizations cannot, however, afford the luxury of having a fully integrated set of business processes. They need, or simply want, an integrated view of their data immediately. The construction of an enterprise model can deliver a short-term benefit to the organization by serving to integrate the data, if not their associated processes. The organization can use its enterprise model to determine which data to offload to the data warehouse from its currently disintegrated data model. The DW can then serve to integrate the offloaded data according to the desired enterprise data model before moving on to the longer-term (and more costly) goal of total integration of the business processes.

TOP-DOWN DATA WAREHOUSE DESIGN

The decision to construct an accurate enterprise model prior to commencement of a data warehouse is heavily dependent on which approach to DW construction the organization chooses to adopt. A top-down approach to DW design is firmly based on the enterprise model itself. It implies a strategic rather than an operational perspective of the data.

Many organizations are reluctant to accept the daunting task of constructing an enterprise model before beginning the more urgent data warehouse initiative. The perception is that too much organizational change will be generated by organizational, competitive, and economic uncertainties for the model to ever be truly accurate at any given point in time. Another common reason for resistance is that the construction of a holistic model of the enterprise will likely identify deficiencies throughout the organization that could be potentially damaging to individuals and groups and disrupt an otherwise stable power structure. Finally, IS personnel, continually under the gun to deliver high-quality systems, may not feel that the resources necessary to construct the enterprise model can be effectively diverted to an activity that does not result in the delivery of a new system. Regardless of the reason for resistance, building an enterprise model means putting the *important* before the *urgent*. It is precisely because of the constant fluctuation and change in the business environment and the relatively poor productivity in the IS function that the enterprise model needs to be built first. The model serves as a jointly created charter of an agreed course for the future and the proper alignment of the organization's information systems with its business goals and objectives.

BOTTOM-UP DATA WAREHOUSE DESIGN

In contrast, a bottom-up approach to DW design focuses more on making use of data available in the current operational systems. The decision of which approach to take can ultimately affect the nature and functionality of the final DW. Wherever possible, the top-down approach brings more benefit to the project, albeit with much more effort.

To be clear, however, an organization can build a successful DW without first going through the process of constructing an accurate and strategic enterprise model. If this direction is chosen by the organization, two significant factors must be given careful consideration. First, no enterprise model, regardless of how well it is constructed, will solve the immediate problem of integrating data on existing operational systems. In other words, the construction of an enterprise model is not a substitute or alternative to building a data warehouse. Second, if the chosen route is to bypass the enterprise model, the data warehouse will most likely end up a solution to some of the organization's information needs but certainly not all of them. If this "80 percent right" approach is acceptable to the organization, then the enterprise model step can be skipped altogether.

THE CONCEPT OF ENTERPRISE INTEGRATION

Enterprise modeling and its associated software and hardware standards are at the heart of the concept of integration. We will revisit this concept later in Chapter 15 with a focus on the DSS. For now, we are interested in its application to the data warehouse. To be effective, integration must occur on three distinct levels: (1) horizontal, (2) vertical, and (3) enterprise.

Horizontal Integration
Horizontal integration can be thought of as the most basic form of integration because it seeks to ensure that each application under development or in operation is fully integrated within its own boundaries and to eliminate any inconsistencies in the final software product. This level of integration is often achieved without any reference to an enterprise model and is limited to providing quality within each isolated software application.

Vertical Integration
Often much less prevalent in organizations is *vertical integration*. It is the means by which the application designer ensures that the software application is in harmony with its stated business requirements. To make a comparison across applications, some form of high-level enterprise model (at least from a strategic perspective) must exist. Vertical integration is a move toward enterprise integration because the determination is based on the mission, goals, objectives, and critical success factors of the business.

Enterprise Integration

At this level of integration, consistent definitions of all data and processes across the enterprise will occur. To arrive at this level, the organization engages in a literal refinement of all naming conventions used to identify, describe, and define objects within the enterprise. Once this task is completed, the data and processes throughout the organization and all interactions between them will be standardized. This level can only be achieved via the construction of an enterprise model that has been validated by all business users of the information systems within the organization and where strict compliance to all standards set by the model are observed by all software developers within the firm.

Although it is beyond the scope of this text to discuss the detailed steps in constructing an enterprise model, Table 12-1 contains a brief listing of the various activities and techniques of enterprise modeling.

12-2: THE DATA WAREHOUSE PROJECT PLAN

As we have seen so far, no easy prescription or recipe precedes the formal initiation of a data warehouse project. Each organization is unique and, thus, few of these activities can be repeated across organizations. Regardless of the situation, however, the first item on the agenda must be an assessment of the organization with regard to its readiness to undergo DW development and implementation.

DATA WAREHOUSE PROJECT DEFINITION AND READINESS ASSESSMENT

An organization's readiness for a data warehouse can be assessed using five key factors. It is not necessary for the organization to achieve high scores in each of the factors to proceed, but rather for the key players to have a clear understanding of the project and an awareness of any potential vulnerabilities. If you find that you are unable to confidently give your organization a passing grade on the combined factors, however, it may be time to pull the plug on the project and revisit the issue later. Weaknesses in any given readiness factor will not correct themselves via time alone. When identified, a weakness in readiness should be addressed before proceeding with the DW development effort. Each of the five factors of readiness is discussed briefly.

Strong Management Sponsorship

Strong management sponsorship for the DW project may be the single most critical factor to its success. Strong project sponsors generally possess a clear vision of the data warehouse's impact on the organization. They also hold a strong conviction with regard to their vision, enough to allow themselves to be held accountable for it.

One strong sponsor is good; multiple sponsors from different areas of the business are even better. Effective sponsors are realistic and will be able to accept and address the short-term problems normally associated with a typical DW endeavor.

Compelling Business Motivation

By itself, a data warehouse will do nothing. Its value lies in its role as an enabler of specific business processes and strategic initiatives. In this sense, your organization can be considered ready on this dimension when a clear and easily articulated motivation for

TABLE 12-1   Activities Associated with Construction of an Enterprise Model

Activity	Description
Entity identification	Entities are the main building blocks of the DW and will be identified by nouns that occur within the organization. Typical examples include: **CUSTOMER, ORDER, EMPLOYEE, INVOICE, PRODUCT.**
Entity relationship diagramming	Every identified entity within the organization must be described along with a depiction of the relationships, ordinalities, cardinalities, and optionalities associated with each relationship. The identified relationships will ultimately aggregate into the business rules under which the organization operates. A typical example of such a relationship would be: **Each CUSTOMER may place one or more ORDERS.**
Elementary process identification	The identification and description of all high-level processes within the organization. Each logical unit of work identified should occur as a result of a response to some event. Those found to not conform to this requirement should be assessed with the intent of eliminating or redesigning them. A typical example of the description for each high-level process should include **NAME, PROCESS DESCRIPTION, TRIGGER EVENT, LOCATION, FREQUENCY OF OCCURRENCE.**
Entity life cycle analysis	This activity associates the data model and the process model for each business area as well as validates the completeness and consistency of both. A typical example of the outcome of this activity would be: **Each ORDER may be related to a number of elementary processes that can change the state of the entity from PLACED to CONFIRMED to CANCELLED to REORDERED.**
Event analysis	This activity describes the events clustered around interdependent processes such that the analyst can subdivide the enterprise into lower-level functions.
Association diagramming	This technique captures for analysis the association that exists between two objects resident in the enterprise model. Analysis results are usually presented in matrix form.
Critical success factor analysis	This activity identifies the high-level conditions critical for the enterprise to function effectively in the marketplace. A typical example of a CSF would be: **The organization will possess a thorough understanding of its customers' behaviors.**
SWOT Analysis	SWOT analysis identifies the strengths, weaknesses, threats, and opportunities associated with a specific course of action.
Information needs analysis	This activity guides the key information needs of the decision makers at the strategic and operational levels. A typical example of this activity might provide the following knowledge: **The key information need of a certain operational decision maker is to know how many units of the product were sold within a given week.**
Current systems evaluation	This analysis provides the basis for determining the distance between the current information systems architecture and the constructed conceptual model of the enterprise. This analysis demonstrates the ability (or lack thereof) of the existing information systems architecture to meet the demands of the business, which provides a key input to the justification of a DW project.

having the DW is present. A warehouse that can demonstrate an alignment with the stated strategic mission of the organization can be considered to display compelling motivation for its existence.

Level and Quality of IS/Business Partnership

In an ideal world, one would never hear the phrase "IS and the business." IS is simply a facet of the business, just like marketing or finance. The degree to which you can determine the conscious elimination of the phrase is one way to measure the strength of the IS portion of a business and its potential to make a positive contribution to the DW initiative. The firm cannot build a successful DW without significant effort from IS and the IS group cannot build a successful DW without the rest of the business functions as its partners. The good news is that a data warehouse may the perfect project to bring all of the functions of the business together to form a more cohesive culture.

Analytic Culture of the Organization

My good friend, Alan Dennis, is often fond of turning a common phrase with regard to decision making: "You can lead a group to information, but you can't make them think."[1] It offers an appropriate way of thinking about the current analytic culture of the organization with regard to DW readiness. If the organization does not place a high value on information and analysis, then its readiness for a DW becomes questionable. The most successful data warehouses can be found in organizations that reward fact-based decision making. If the culture in your organization is better described as heuristic rather than holistic, you may want to reconsider your readiness for DW.

Data Warehouse Feasibility

This factor is concerned specifically with the feasibility of converting the existing organizational data into a common form for storage in the data warehouse. If the current data model indicates that the typical organizational data are questionable with regard to accuracy, redundancy, colocation, or even physical existence, then a data warehouse should not be in your immediate future. Further, if common business rules and definitions in the form of data relationships do not currently exist, the timeline for launching the DW initiative will be severely extended.

Kimball and his colleagues (1998) developed a data warehouse litmus test, which makes it relatively easy to see how an organization stands up to the challenge. Table 12-2 contains each of the readiness factors along with a description of what both high and low readiness look like. Look over the chart and see how your organization, or one that you know is contemplating a DW project, scores. Use a weighting of 60 percent for the sponsorship category, 15 percent each for the business motivation and feasibility categories, and 5 percent each for the two remaining categories of readiness.

ADDRESSING DATA WAREHOUSE READINESS SHORTFALL

As already discussed, stellar grades on all categories will not automatically ensure a successful DW initiative, and less than stellar grades on one or two categories do not mean the project should not go forward. If the litmus test for readiness identifies a

---

[1]Dr. Alan R. Dennis is the John T. Chambers Chair of Internet Systems in the Kelley School of Business at Indiana University.

TABLE 12-2   Litmus Test for Data Warehouse Readiness Determination

DW Readiness Factor	Low-Level Readiness	High-Level Readiness
Strong management sponsor	Not widely respected. Hard to gain access to. "Let me get back to you." "Good luck with the project." "Can we get this done in a month?" "What's a data warehouse?"	Widely respected and high clout. Easily accessible. Decisive with regard to problem resolution. Active, vocal, and visible sponsor of the project. Demonstrates realistic expectations with regard to project completion. Demonstrated understanding of DW concepts.
Compelling business	"So what's the point of this again?" "Can we afford to do this?" Nebulous, blurry vision of the project. Multiple views of the solution. Project viewed as tactical rather than strategic. Project viewed as a cost savings mechanism. Inability to satisfactorily quantify payback.	Project viewed as necessary for survival. "We can't afford to not do this." Clear articulation of the project vision. Clear and consistent view of the solution. Project viewed as strategic rather than tactical. Project viewed as a revenue generation opportunity. Clearly articulated and demonstrated payback.
Level and quality of IS/business partnership	Business engages outside consultants with IS knowledge. Business creates internal DW team without IS participation. "We can trust our current systems to be accurate." "It will take years to get IS involved."	Business and IS work as a team from the beginning. IS is actively engaged in all business activities. Business has strong confidence in current systems. IS is quick to respond to ad hoc project requests.
Analytic culture of the organization	Decisions are still made from the "gut." User community generally does not ask for more data. Current reports are not aggressively employed. Finance believes they own the bottom-line performance figures.	Fact-based decision making is prevalent. Business users are constantly asking for data. Current reports are widely used for other related analysis projects. Information is openly shared throughout the organization.
Data warehouse feasibility	DW project would require a large-scale purchase of all new technology. All experienced personnel are committed to other "highly strategic" projects. Data reliability is in question throughout the organization.	Organizational information systems architecture is robust and stable. Experienced human resources are available for the project. Data quality is perceived to be high throughout the organization.

Source: Adapted from Kimball, Reeves, Ross, & Thornthwaite. *The Data Warehouse Lifecycle Toolkit.* John Wiley & Sons Publishing, 1998.

weakness in one or two areas, then several techniques can be used to address the short-fall and get the organization ready for the big project.

In this section, we identify several techniques commonly used to address readiness shortfall in one or more areas. Although the techniques are presented as isolated activi-ties, they are more commonly used in conjunction with one another to address any readiness shortfall.

High-Level Business Requirements Analysis

The basic tools and techniques associated with business requirements analysis are described in any good systems analysis and design text.[2] Therefore, we will defer any discussion of the details of interviewing, survey preparation, JAD, and direct observa-tion. If a readiness shortfall is discovered during the litmus test, it may be time to con-duct a thorough business requirements analysis to determine exactly what the business needs and where the disconnect is between their actual needs and their perceived needs. Generally speaking, a high-level business analysis effort should answer several key questions essential to the success of the data warehouse initiative:

- What are the key strategic business initiatives as perceived by management?
- What are the key performance indicators or success metrics to be used for each of the key business initiatives?
- What are the core business processes that management regularly monitors and wishes to affect positively through one or more key business initiatives?
- What is the potential impact on each of the existing performance metrics with improved access to higher-quality business process information?

The answers to these questions will identify the area(s) of the business that need atten-tion to correct the overall DW readiness shortfall.

Business Requirements Prioritization

This technique is adapted from the formal step of project prioritization advocated by James Martin in his Rapid Application Development (RAD) methodology. Following the identification of key strategic initiatives, you will probably find that the organiza-tion believes several initiatives are important rather than settling on one. Until some method of prioritization can be agreed upon, any attempts to build organizational con-sensus for a data warehouse project will be difficult, if not impossible to achieve.

Although various techniques can be used to determine an unbiased ranking of projects on the basis of priority, the important issue is for the characteristics that drive a prioritization project to be carefully selected and agreed upon. Often a less complex approach will be more widely accepted than a highly complex mathematical method, such as analytical hierarchy process (AHP), and will be more easily understood by the various constituencies involved.[3]

One approach to the prioritization project is to rank the set of initiatives across two dimensions: (1) perceived impact on the core business, and (2) feasibility of near-

---

[2]The reader is referred to Marakas, G. M. 2001. *Modern Systems Analysis and Design: An Active Approach.* Upper Saddle River, NJ: Prentice Hall.
[3]AHP is a mathematical ranking technique that can create an unbiased set of metrics to determine the exact order of priority for a set of characteristics or events. Although quite effective, it can also be quite complex and often yields results similar to that of other less complex approaches.

term completion. With the first dimension, each person assigns a rating on a scale from 1 to 10 with regard to the potential dollar payback to the organization, its strategic significance, availability of alternative solutions, political strength, and so on. Each characteristic should be calculated in terms of dollars with an appropriate level of justification for each estimate provided.

This ranking of the projects and initiatives, based on potential impact on the business, can then also be prioritized in terms of feasibility of near-term completion. Feasibility can be determined in terms of data availability, ease of development, availability of necessary resources, and human factor requirements related to overall experience with similar projects. Using a simple 2 x 2 matrix approach, the various projects under consideration can be plotted into one of four quadrants. Figure 12-1 illustrates a typical plot of eight identified projects.

As you can see from the figure, Project 6 appears to represent the only project of the group that demonstrates both high business impact and high near-term feasibility. Based on this analysis, Project 6 would get an immediate nod. What would the next project likely be?

Proof of Concept

This technique stems from the widely used software development approach of prototyping. In this case, however, proof of concept allows for a relatively low-cost approach to demonstrating the perceived benefits and feasibility of a given project. It can take

FIGURE 12-1   Example Project Prioritization Matrix

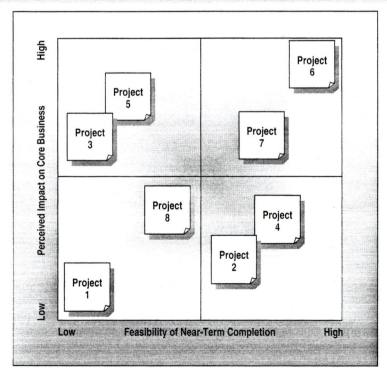

the form of a small pilot study or isolated rollout of a technology to demonstrate its ability to succeed in a relatively low-risk environment. Once the small-scale proof of concept is established, the necessary buy in for its large-scale counterpart is much easier to obtain.

DEFINING THE DATA WAREHOUSE PROJECT SCOPE

After the overall organizational readiness is determined to be within acceptable boundaries, the data warehouse project can begin. The first item on the agenda is the formal definition of the project scope. It establishes an agreed boundary for the project and defines not only what the project is, but equally important, what the project is not.

Interestingly, one of the first challenges associated with project scope definition is the determination of exactly what it is we are scoping. Are we defining a project scope for the near-term requirements determination and DW design activities? Are we scoping a project that will result in the delivery of the first generation of the warehouse? Are we providing a project scope for a 3-year phased rollout? It is somewhat axiomatic that the farther one tries to see into the future, the more blurry their vision becomes. It is, therefore, important to determine the scope of the scope in terms of how far into the future one can see with 20-20 vision.

One of the unwritten rules concerning initial project scope definition is that the project manager wants to make as few promises as possible while simultaneously painting a broad enough picture to effectively identify the benefits and costs associated with the effort. To this end, several guidelines can be used for developing the preliminary scope for a DW project. Table 12-3 lists and briefly describes these guidelines.

The primary deliverable from this activity is the formally documented statement of project scope. Although it is clearly destined to change over time, this document provides the roadmap for each of the future development stages and reminds everyone what the objective of the project is. The more one gets involved in the details of an endeavor, the greater the likelihood that they will begin to forget the objective of their activities. The statement of project scope makes for a useful reminder in such times of temporary memory loss.

One last point to address before leaving project scope definition is the discussion of *scope creep*. This phenomenon is often found with projects that are complex and highly organizational in nature. Scope creep occurs when the initial scope of the project continues, sometimes imperceptibly, to expand as affected parties begin to think of features they would like to see incorporated into the project. Over time, scope creep can result in inflated budgets, missed deadlines, and projects that never seem to end. It is important to recognize the distinct difference between project scope refinement and scope creep. The former is a natural result of the gathering of more detailed information and requirements. The project still fits in the same-sized box, it just fits more snugly. The latter always results in the project needing a continually larger box in which to reside.

DEFINING THE BUSINESS JUSTIFICATION FOR A DATA WAREHOUSE PROJECT

Once project scope is successfully established and agreed to by all related parties, the process of making the business case for the project can begin. This exercise formally articulates the various arguments that justify the allocation of resources necessary to

TABLE 12-3 Guidelines for Developing Initial DW Project Scope

Project Scope Guideline	Description
Joint effort between IS and other business functions.	While the specific business requirement upon which the project scope is being developed may not be driven by IS, all relevant business functions, including IS, must materially participate in the development of the project scope for the DW.
Initial scope is meaningful and manageable.	*Meaningful* refers to the value to or impact on the organization derived from successfully addressing a well-defined business requirement.
	Manageable translates into *doable*. The value of starting small and growing cannot be overstated at this stage. By starting with smaller, quicker-to-market projects, the organizational knowledge as it relates to DW issues can be greatly enhanced without the fear of large-scale failures.
Initial focus is on a single business requirement from a single-source process.	Scope should be defined in terms of a single business process that requires a bounded set of data sources. Projects attempting to extract and integrate information from multiple business processes suffer from an exponential growth in the data staging effort necessary. Satisfy one constituency at a time.
Number of initial users is limited.	In general, an initial rollout limited to the needs of 20 to 25 users is considered manageable. Once the core user base can be established and stabilized, a plan to roll out to a larger community of users can be executed.
Success criteria are developed in conjunction with project scope.	The scope should be driven by the expectations of the business community with regard to the DW. To this end, success criteria should be established simultaneously with the definition of project scope to ensure the expectations are properly managed.

design, construct, and deliver the DW. As with the definition of project scope, all related parties, including IS, must be involved in the construction of the business case for the DW.

The business case is really no mystery or magical exercise, although some people fear it as such. The justification for the project simply identifies and quantifies the appropriate anticipated benefits and costs, both tangible and intangible, to a level of accuracy that is both reasonable and from which common financial performance measures can be derived. Two distinct areas of concentration can be identified: (1) investment (cost), and (2) benefits (value). Each of these areas can be explored independently of the other and, when appropriately combined, can provide a clear justification (or lack thereof) for the proposed DW initiative. Remember, if the project cannot be adequately justified before it begins, no such justification will be forthcoming after money and time are already invested in it. At that point, it simply becomes sunk cost and wasted resources. Better to face that issue before the money is gone rather than after.

ISSUES IN MAKING THE BUSINESS CASE

One way to view the justification stage of the project is to think of the proposed data warehouse as a business case for a major capital investment by the organization. If we adopt this approach, we can identify three perspectives from which the argument to pursue the investment may be made: (1) facts, (2) faith, or (3) fear.[4] Figure 12-2 provides several examples for each of these perspectives.

In the late 1980s, economic researchers discovered the *productivity paradox.* Despite an immense investment in information technologies—more than $1 trillion since the beginning of the PC revolution in about 1980—productivity growth in the United States has been either stagnant or weak. Growing productivity, more than anything else, contributes to expanding opportunity and a better material life. The effects of computerization, such as the speeding up of production and consumption and the ubiquity of computers, are clear, but wages and productivity stalled during the years of heavy investment in information technologies.

MIT researchers Erik Brynjolfsson and Lorin Hitt (1998) completed a comprehensive study of productivity in 380 large firms that together generate yearly sales in excess of $1.8 billion. They found that computing technologies were far from unproductive: They were significantly more productive than any other type of investment these companies made. The gross return on investment averaged about 60 percent annually for computers, including supercomputers, mainframes, minis, and micros. And IS staffers were more than twice as productive as other workers.

Although many reasons explain why the productivity paradox appears to exist or, more recently, why it is a myth, one fact remains indisputable: If an investment cannot be justified in fact before it is made, then it will never be justifiable in fact after it is made. One theory behind the inability of researchers and economists to find a justifiable basis for investment in information systems is because many of them were never justifiable in the first place.

This point brings us back to facts, faith, and fear. Many IT investments in the past were made based on faith: "Look, we need to do this if we are to grow as an organization and remain technically competitive with the marketplace. You really have to trust me on this one." Others were made based on fear: "If we don't implement this new system, our competitors will eat us alive!" The important point here is that the feasibility assessment of an information system, at this point in the development process, must be made purely on fact and must be devoid of faith-based statements or threats of extinction. If the facts support the implementation of the proposed solution, then it is justifiable on all dimensions and should be implemented. If not, then the present is precisely the time to realize the potential for failure and deal with it prior to the unwarranted investment of millions of dollars of organizational resources.

ECONOMIC FEASIBILITY ANALYSIS

This issue of business justification is not unique to data warehouse proposals. Regardless of the nature of the project, we must assess the *economic feasibility* of the proposed system. This dimension identifies the financial and net economic impacts to the organization of the proposed system. Is it worth doing? Do the benefits outweigh the costs?

---

[4]I am in debt to my good friend and colleague, Dr. Bradley C. Wheeler, for allowing me to use his excellent conceptualization of making the business case.

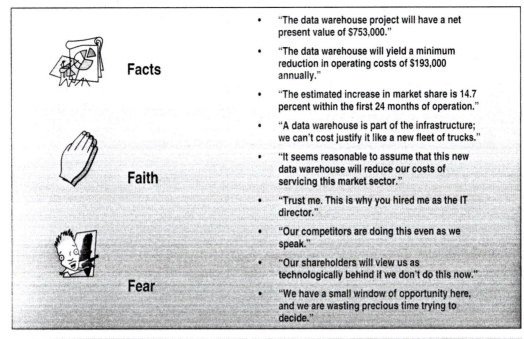

Facts
- "The data warehouse project will have a net present value of $753,000."
- "The data warehouse will yield a minimum reduction in operating costs of $193,000 annually."
- "The estimated increase in market share is 14.7 percent within the first 24 months of operation."

Faith
- "A data warehouse is part of the infrastructure; we can't cost justify it like a new fleet of trucks."
- "It seems reasonable to assume that this new data warehouse will reduce our costs of servicing this market sector."
- "Trust me. This is why you hired me as the IT director."

Fear
- "Our competitors are doing this even as we speak."
- "Our shareholders will view us as technologically behind if we don't do this now."
- "We have a small window of opportunity here, and we are wasting precious time trying to decide."

FIGURE 12-2   Three Bases of Project Justification

This activity can be thought of as a cost-benefit analysis, but it is actually much more complex. A great number of the expected benefits from a new data warehouse system may appear to be intangible (i.e., improved customer service, improved customer satisfaction, increased employee morale). We will soon see that this complexity can be managed and, using common financial analysis techniques, the true economic value of a system can be determined.

Although economic feasibility assessment may be arguably the most important of all dimensions of justification, it must be performed last if it is to be comprehensive in its analysis. The true economic impact of a system must account for all components, including required changes to the technology and the organization, additional specialized human resources or training, and compliance with, or management of, any material legal or political constraints. Further, the final decision to invest in the proposed system will be made primarily on the outcome of the economic analysis rather than any specific information requirements or favorable feasibility dimension. Thus, to ensure that all other dimensions of feasibility can be reconciled in favor of the system, we perform the economic assessment last. If it passes this analysis, then it is ready for the next step.

Identifying the Costs and Benefits

It is often said that the good parts of an investment are a lot easier to identify than the bad parts. This generalization is equally true in the identification of the benefits and costs associated with a proposed data warehouse initiative. We will begin by identifying and quantifying the benefits, both tangible and intangible, of the new DW.

By definition, a *benefit* is something that, either directly or indirectly, increases profit or decreases cost. Benefits are the desirable side of the equation and the goal is to design a DW that has more benefit than cost. The task then is to identify all the benefits and, as accurately as possible, quantify them in terms of dollars and cents. Benefits can be classified as either tangible or intangible.

A *tangible benefit* is one that can be identified with certainty and easily expressed in dollars. Table 12-4 identifies some common tangible benefits associated with a typical information system.

Intangible benefits, although believed to be directly associated with the operation of the new information system, cannot be identified with certainty or easily expressed in dollars. The intangible benefits, even though they are difficult to quantify, contribute to the overall economic analysis of the system and can improve the benefit side of the economic feasibility assessment. Table 12-5 summarizes several common intangible benefits associated with a new information system.

Just as with the benefit side of the analysis, the cost side contains both tangibles and intangibles. Tangible costs can be identified with certainty and easily expressed in dollars. The intangible costs are not easily identified with certainty and cannot be readily expressed in terms of dollars. One additional classification of costs distinguishes

TABLE 12-4 Typical Tangible Benefits Associated with a New Data Warehouse

Benefit Category	Common Examples
Cost reduction	Reduction in labor or head count
	Reduction or elimination of overtime
	Consolidation of jobs or employee roles
	Reduction in supply usage
	Less paperwork
	Smaller inventory needs or carrying costs
	Efficiencies in distribution
	Less need for travel
	Efficient use of utilities
	Lower costs of hardware and/or software
	Less maintenance
	Increase in product/process quality
	Improved production throughput or costs
	Reduction in overall cost of funds
	Improved subcontractor or external vendor control
	Reduction in or improved effectiveness of training
Revenue increase	Introduction of new products
	Decreased time to market
	Improved product quality
	Increased efficiency in sales processes
	Product enhancements
	Improved advertising support and target marketing
	Effective bidding tools
	Development of, or access to, new markets

TABLE 12-5   Typical Intangible Benefits Associated with a New Data Warehouse

- Improved employee morale
- Improved corporate or public image
- Increase in perceived quality of products or services
- Perceived decrease in time to market by customers
- Improved decision making
- More timely information
- Increased organizational flexibility
- Improved resource allocation and control
- Increased strategic or competitive advantage
- Improved public and community relations
- Improvements in addressing environmental concerns
- Reduced employee turnover
- Increased quality of work for employees
- Proactive attention to ethical issues
- Proactive addressing of legal issues
- Increased workplace and/or community safety

between those associated with data warehouse development and those dealing with data warehouse operation. Development costs are typically incurred once during the development project, while operating costs generally follow the implementation of the system and are considered to be ongoing. Table 12-6 contains examples of both tangible and intangible costs typically associated with a new data warehouse.

Tangibles and Intangibles

The most difficult problem in performing a thorough economic feasibility assessment lies with the intangibles. They are, admittedly, difficult to identify and even more difficult to quantify. For this reason, the tendency is to ignore them in the preparation of the assessment. Yielding to this tendency, however, can be a most serious mistake in a business justification exercise.

Think of it this way: The intangible benefits are like icing on a cake. They are not the primary reason for pursuing the new DW, and their presence or absence in the analysis will probably not make or break the decision to pursue the project. If you are wrong about the intangible benefits, so what?

Unfortunately, however, the same cannot be said for the intangible costs. The fact that they can be identified at all suggests that they have the potential to negatively impact the economic assessment. They represent one or more potential "black holes" where money can go in but can never be recovered. Failing to quantify the intangible costs as accurately as possible can be disastrous. If you are wrong about the intangible costs, then what? To ensure an accurate analysis, all costs and benefits, both tangible and intangible, must be identified and quantified as accurately as possible. The question then becomes, "How do we make that which is intangible tangible?" The answer in its simplest form is, we guess.

The validity of an economic assessment that is based on completely unquantified components becomes somewhat difficult to accept. If we are to obtain an accurate assessment of the economic feasibility of the new system, we must take the position

TABLE 12-6 Typical Costs Associated with a New Information System

Cost Category	Common Examples
Tangible development	Development personnel
	Analysis and design consulting fees
	Predevelopment training
	Materials and supplies
	Vendor installation and consulting
	Hiring costs for new operating personnel
	Hardware and software acquisition or development
	Physical plant acquisition and/or conversion
	Documentation preparation and distribution
	Data conversion costs
Tangible operating	Maintenance and upgrades (hardware and software)
	Annual or renewable software licenses
	Repairs (hardware and software)
	Operational personnel
	End user training
	Connectivity and communication charges
	Materials and supplies
	Equipment lease payments
	Depreciation of system assets
Intangible	Potential disruption to existing productivity and environment
	Loss of customer goodwill
	Reduction in employee morale
	Diversion of attention to daily responsibilities

that there is no such thing as an intangible cost or benefit. They are all costs and benefits, some of which can be accurately quantified and some that require a reasonable estimation process. To that end, the intangibles must be calculated using a logical set of underlying assumptions that lead to an estimate. The estimate, although probably not 100 percent accurate, is nonetheless much closer to reality than simply ignoring the cost or benefit altogether. In reality, all of the numbers in an economic justification are estimates—some are just more accurate than others. Let's look at an example.

Suppose the issue is to determine the potential cost of a temporary reduction in employee morale associated with the first 6 months of implementation for the new data warehouse. This intangible cost, identified through past experience, suggests that a certain number of employees will be distressed by the intrusion of the new technology into their environment and their productivity will be temporarily reduced as a result of this distress. A series of surveys and focused interviews reveals that approximately 10 percent of our workforce will experience this loss of productivity based on their concerns expressed during the information gathering process. Further, we know from reviewing other similar DW projects and by consulting industry professionals that the probability of this reduction in morale occurring is about 60 percent. Our problem is that we do not know the dollar value of a 60 percent chance of a 10 percent reduction in employee morale. What we need is a logical surrogate measure for employee morale. In other words, we need something we can quantify to logically represent something we cannot.

Suppose we make the assumption that the overall morale of our workforce is directly related to the profits of our company. In other words, if our employees are unhappy, then we will not sell our products or services and will, therefore, not make any money. We could argue that morale is directly related to company revenues but, for purposes of illustration, profit becomes a more conservative approach to the problem. Given this assumption, we still do not know what a 10 percent reduction in employee morale is worth but we now know what a 100 percent reduction in morale would cost: 100 percent of our annual profits! Consider the following:

100 percent reduction in employee morale = Nominal annual profits

Nominal annual profits = \$2,000,000

100 percent reduction in employee morale = \$2,000,000

10 percent reduction in employee morale = (0.1)(\$2,000,000) = \$200,000

60 percent probability of a 10 percent reduction in employee morale = (0.6)(\$200,000) = \$120,000

By performing this analysis, on either intangible costs or benefits, using assumptions that can be agreed upon as logical, we quantify the intangible. Although this approach still may not yield an accurate assessment of the cost or benefit, it nonetheless provides a working boundary for the problem. Other assumptions can be considered and tested until one is found that all agree will provide enough reliability to be useful. An estimate is just that: an estimate. The important issue is that a reasonably derived estimate is infinitely more useful in assessing the economic feasibility of a project than no estimate at all.

ECONOMIC FEASIBILITY MEASURES

Numerous financial methods and approaches to the assessment of economic feasibility—often referred to as a test of *cost-effectiveness*—can be employed. For our purposes, we will examine the use of three common approaches: (1) net present value (NPV), (2) internal rate of return (IRR), and (3) breakeven analysis.[5]

All of the assessment approaches mentioned share a common concept called the *time value of money*. In essence, this concept suggests that a dollar today is worth more than a dollar in the future. The reasoning behind this concept is that if you have a dollar today, you can invest that dollar in some interest-bearing manner and have more than a dollar in the future. In assessing the economic feasibility of a project, we must consider the time value of money because we must incur cash outflows today, in the form of dollars spent to design, develop, acquire, and implement the proposed system, so that we can enjoy cash inflows in the future through the benefits expected from the new system. To ensure we are comparing "apples to apples," we convert all future

---

[5]A detailed coverage of each of these methods is beyond the scope of this text. The explanations provided here are intended to demonstrate the basic use of the assessment approach in a manner that will allow for its application. For more detailed explanations for these methods, the reader is referred to any good financial analysis textbook.

dollars in the present value of today's dollars. In this way, we can accurately assess the value of the system over its useful life in today's dollars.

Net Present Value

Probably the most common technique for assessing the economic feasibility of an investment is the *net present value* approach. This method calculates the present value of a series of cash outflows and expected future cash inflows. The logic behind this technique is that if the net of all current and future outflows and all current and future benefits using a reasonable cost of capital or rate of return (called the discount rate) is positive, then the investment is a good one. If it is negative, then the investment will not yield the necessary returns, and it should be abandoned in favor of one that will. This technique can be used to compare two or more competing investment alternatives, as well. The one with the largest NPV will be the one that should be chosen based on the value of its return to the organization. Figure 12-3 contains a spreadsheet model used to conduct a net present value analysis of a project.

Note that each of the expected cash outflows and inflows for the project is calculated and then *discounted* back to today's dollars by applying a factor based on an acceptable rate of return for the organization. This factor can be thought of as the opportunity cost associated with investing those dollars in other projects including stock, bonds, or other less risky investments. In many cases, the NPV analysis is conducted using a discount rate deemed to be risk-free to determine the relative level of risk in the project. Probably the most common risk-free rate is based on the return on a U.S. Treasury bill and the assumption that the United States will not go bankrupt or out of business.

It is also important to note that the actual value calculated in an NPV analysis is not an important number. What is important is whether the final calculation is positive or negative. If it is positive, then the investment will yield a return greater than the required return. If it is negative, then the project, at least in its present form, is not economically feasible. The present value of a dollar for any period in the future can be easily calculated using the following formula:

$$PV_n = 1 / (1 + i)^n$$

where

$$PV_n = \text{present value of \$1 } n \text{ years from now}$$
$$i = \text{the accepted discount rate or rate of return}$$

Thus, the present value of a dollar 3 years from now assuming a discount rate of 10 percent is:

$$NPV = PV_1 + PV_2 + PV_3 + \ldots + PV_n$$
$$PV_3 = 1 / (1 + 0.10)^3 = 0.751$$

This calculation suggests that $1 received 3 years from now is the same as receiving 75.1 cents today if a 10 percent rate of return is required. As shown in the calculations and in Figure 12-3, the *NPV* of an investment is simply the sum of the present value calculations for each period.

Although simple enough to calculate, most financial textbooks contain detailed tables of discount factors for a dollar at various interest rates and for various periods. Table 12-7 contains a partial listing of discount factors using common interest rates and

FIGURE 12-3 Spreadsheet Model of Net Present Value Analysis

	Year 0	Year 1	Year 2	Year 3	Year 4	Year 5	Totals
Net economic benefit		$ 920,168.30	$ 926,977.32	$ 934,286.92	$ 941,703.65	$ 949,228.60	
Discount rate (8.25%)	1.0000	0.9238	0.8534	0.7883	0.7283	0.6728	
PV of benefits		$ 850,040.00	$ 791,067.06	$ 736,540.37	$ 685,808.14	$ 638,603.49	
NPV of all BENEFITS		$ 850,040.000	$ 1,641,107.06	$ 2,377,647.42	$ 3,063,455.56	$ 3,702,059.05	$3,702,059.05
One-Time COSTS	(831,579.65)						
PV of Equipment Depreciation		$ (56,086.46)	$ (51,811.97)	$ (47,863.25)	$ (44,215.47)	$ (40,845.70)	
Recurring costs		$ (325,576.80)	$ (341,855.64)	$ (358,948.42)	$ (376,895.84)	$ 395,740.64	
Discount rate (8.25%)	1.0000	0.9238	0.8534	0.7883	0.7283	0.6728	
PV of recurring costs		$ (300,763.79)	$ (291,733.93)	$ (282,975.17)	$ (274,479.38)	$ (266,238.66)	
NPV of all COSTS	$(831,579.65)	$(1,511,089.71)	$(1,854,635.61)	$(2,185,474.03)	$(2,504,168.89)	$(2,811,253.25)	$(2,811,253.25)
Overall NPV							$ 890,805.80
Overall ROI							32%
IRR							38%
Breakeven Analysis							
Yearly NPV cash flow	$(831,579.65)	$ 549,276.21	$ 499,333.13	$ 453,565.19	$ 411,328.75	$ 372,364.83	
Overall NPV cash flow	$(831,579.65)	$ (661,049.71)	$ (213,528.55)	$ 192,173.39	$ 559,286.67	$ 890,805.80	
Project breakeven occurs at 2.576 years							

TABLE 12-7	Partial Table of Values for the Present Value of a Dollar			
Period	*8%*	*10%*	*12%*	*14%*
1	0.926	0.909	0.893	0.877
2	0.857	0.826	0.797	0.769
3	0.794	0.751	0.712	0.675
4	0.735	0.683	0.636	0.592
5	0.681	0.621	00567	0.519
6	0.630	0.564	0.507	0.456
7	0.583	0.513	0.452	0.400
8	0.540	0.467	0.404	0.351

discount periods. A more complete listing can be obtained from any good financial analysis reference book.

Internal Rate of Return

Another equally popular method of assessing the economic feasibility of a project, closely related to the NPV approach, is to calculate its *internal rate of return* (IRR). The IRR is mathematically more complicated that calculating an NPV, but it is actually the rate of return of the project when the NPV is zero. The result of an IRR calculation is the true net return on the investment expressed as an interest rate. The internal rate of return of an investment is mathematically defined as the largest number d that satisfies the equation:

$$x = \sum_{t=1}^{T} \frac{R_t}{(1 + d)^t}$$

where

T = the expected life of the project in years

X = the total cost of the project

R_t = the expected net return in year t

Given the obvious complexity of the preceding calculation, it is much better to use a computer when determining an IRR.[6] Most spreadsheet programs include a simple function for calculating IRR. As shown in Figure 12-3, the calculated IRR of our project is 38 percent.

Breakeven Analysis

The objective of a *breakeven analysis* is to determine at what point over the expected life of the project (if ever) the benefits derived from the project equal the costs associated with implementing it. The first step in determining the breakeven point is to calculate the NPV of the yearly cash flows for the project. Next, a running total of the overall NPV cash flow during each period of the project must be determined. The year in which

---

[6]A related calculation sometimes employed in investment analysis is return on investment (ROI). Although useful as an analysis tool, its applicability in assessing the economic feasibility of a proposed project is limited because it takes into account only the net results at the endpoints of the investment (i.e., the beginning and the end of the project). Because it accounts for the net cash flows during each period, IRR is preferred over ROI.

the overall NPV cash flow for the project is positive is called the *payback period.* To determine the actual breakeven point for the project, the following formula can be used:

$$\frac{\text{Payback Period NPV Cash Flow} - \text{Overall NPV Cash Flow}}{\text{Payback Period NPV Cash Flow}}$$

Referring to Figure 12-3, we can see that the project will reach a breakeven point in approximately the seventh month of year 2.

Another equally effective method to determine the breakeven point of a project is to simply plot the expected costs against the expected benefits on a graph. The point at which the two lines intersect is the breakeven point. Figure 12-4 illustrates the graphical approach to the assessment.

DEVELOPING THE DATA WAREHOUSE PROJECT PLAN

The next step in the process is the development of a formal *project plan,* which involves looking at staffing needs, time estimates, constraints, and other project management activities. Put on your project manager hat, and let's get started.

Project Staffing Issues

Any data warehouse project, regardless of size or scope, requires a number of different roles and skills to be successful. Rarely will these roles align themselves in a one-to-one fashion with individuals. Instead, it will more likely be the case that certain individuals will serve in several roles throughout the DW project. When determining initial staffing requirements for the project, you should actively seek synergies across roles and match those synergies to individuals who possess the necessary skill set to successfully perform the duties required.

Table 12-8 lists the various roles associated with a typical DW project along with a brief description of each. Table 12-9 illustrates a typical staffing plan for the user requirements definition phase of a typical DW project.

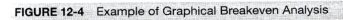

FIGURE 12-4   Example of Graphical Breakeven Analysis

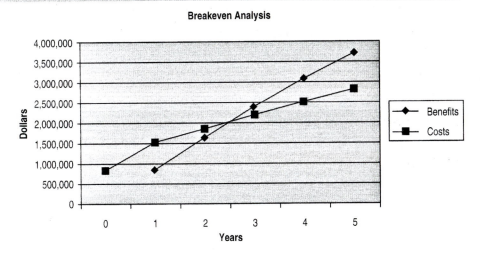

TABLE 12-8 Typical Staffing Roles Associated with a Data Warehouse Project

Staffing Role	*Role Description*
Project Sponsor	Typically the business owner(s) of the project and those who bear the direct financial responsibility for the project.
Project Manager	Responsible for the day-to-day coordination of project activities and tasks. Will supervise all roles but will work closely with the Business Community Liaison.
Business Community Liaison	This role will work daily with the Project Manager as well as serve as the central communication channel regarding the project to the rest of the business community.
Business Systems Analyst	Responsible for leading the business requirements definition stage of the project. Additionally, this role is responsible for the creation of the initial dimensional model for the project.
Data Modeler	Responsible for the detailed data analysis and development of the dimensional model for the DW.
DW Database Administrator	The DBA translates the dimensional model into a set of physical table structures. In addition, the DBA is responsible for determining initial aggregation, partitioning, and indexing strategies for the DW. Upon completion of the DW, the DBA will also be responsible for the day-to-day operational support of the database, ensuring data integrity, database availability, and DW performance.
Data Staging Designer	Responsible for the end-to-end design of the production process to extract, transform, and load the data in preparation for the DW.
End User Application Developers	Responsible for the creation and maintenance of end user applications associated with the DW. In addition, this role is generally responsible for loading the metadata for the data access tool.
DW Educator	Responsible for educating the business end users on the content and structure of the DW, as well as the various end user applications and the data access tool.
Technical/Security Analyst	Responsible for the design of the technical infrastructure and security strategy for the DW.
Technical Support Specialist	These specialists focus on issues related to mainframe systems software, client/server systems, and networking. In addition, this role serves as the primary support for the DW upon its completion.
Data Staging Programmer	Responsible for the programming of applications needed to automate data staging extraction, transformation, and load processes.
Data Steward	Also referred to as the data administrator, this role is responsible for gaining organizational consensus on common definitions for conformed DW dimensions and facts. In addition, this role is responsible for the ongoing maintenance of the DW data dictionary.
DW Quality Assurance Analyst	Responsible for ensuring that the data loaded into the DW are accurate.

TABLE 12-9   Typical Staffing Plan for DW User Requirements Phase

Requirement Definition Task	EU	BS	ISS	BD	PL	PM	SA	DM	DBA	DSD	DE	AD	TA	TS	DSP	DS	QA
Prepare interview team						1	2	2									
Select respondents	3	3	3	1	1												
Schedule interviews					2	1											
Conduct user kickoff	2	2	2	2	2	1	2	2									
Conduct interviews	2	2		2	2	5	1	5				5					
IS data discovery						5	1	1	2	2		5			2		
Analyze interviews					2	2	1										
Document findings	3			3	2	2	1	2									
Publish requirements	4	4	4	4	2	2	1	2	4	4	4	4	4	4	4	4	4
Revise project scope	3	3	3	2	1	2	2	2	2	2	5	2	5	5	2	5	5
User acceptance Review	5	4	4	2	1	2	2	2	2	2	5	2	5	5	2	5	5

Legend	Description
EU	Business End Users
BS	Business Sponsor
ISS	IS Sponsor
BD	Business Driver
PL	Business Project Lead
PM	Project Manager
SA	Systems Analyst
DM	Data Modeler
DBA	Database Administrator
DSD	Data Staging Designer
DE	DW Educator
AD	Application Developer
TA	Technical/Security Analyst
TS	Technical Support Specialist
DSP	Data Staging Programmer
DS	Data Steward
QA	Quality Analyst
1	Primary responsibility for the task
2	Involved in the task
3	Provides input to the task
4	Informed of task results
5	Optional involvement in the task

The Formal DW Project Plan

If we identify two key characteristics of a well-designed DW project plan, they would be high integration and high detail. The former is necessary to ensure that the various subplans developed by each of the DW staffing roles can be integrated into a cohesive and logical project plan for the data warehouse. The latter characteristic suggests that a high level of detail for each proposed task in the plan be described with sufficient detail so as to ensure no misunderstanding or confusion. In addition, high detail implies that the project plan will be maintained in an up-to-date manner to include the latest iteration of all dependencies and task assignments. Although no specific template is available for developing a DW project plan, several guidelines as to its content can be offered:

Required resources: All human, financial, and material resources should be clearly defined and tied to a specific task in the project plan.

Current estimated schedule: A current estimate of the number of days for each stage in the project as well as the total estimated project duration.

Task commencement date: The date the project, and each of its associated tasks, is scheduled to begin.

Current estimated completion date: The date the project, and each of its associated tasks, is scheduled to be completed.

Project status: The current status, often represented as a percentage of total effort, of the project and each of its associated tasks.

Task dependencies: Clear and detailed identification of tasks that must be completed prior to the commencement of this task.

Late flags: A mathematical calculation based on the difference between the expected completion date for both the project and its associated tasks and the current date. Normally expressed in terms of a positive or negative number of days. Positive numbers indicate project tasks ahead of schedule.

The single most important thing to remember regarding the project plan is that, as a living document, it will require multiple, sometimes daily, updates. It is the roadmap for the project and must always accurately reflect the current status of the project if it is to be of any value.

12-3: SPECIFYING THE ANALYSIS AND DESIGN TOOLS

Once the project plan is completed and approved and the business user requirements gathering has begun, we can begin to focus on the logical modeling processes necessary to create an implementation-independent model of the proposed data warehouse. Our intention here is to transform the legacy data resources throughout the organization into the final DW data structures. These models will also provide the basis for designing the data extraction and transformation strategies for the project, an estimation of the overall size and administrative needs of the central DBMS, and the prototyping of end user applications.

DIMENSIONAL MODELING APPROACH TO DW LOGICAL DESIGN

Through your studies in the field of information systems analysis and design, you probably recognize entity-relationship diagrams (ERD). These diagrams graphically depict the logical entities, relationships, and data structures in a relational data environment. Although the ERD approach could serve as a modeling tool for the DW, its several disadvantages make it less desirable in this domain. Instead, the logical design technique known as dimensional modeling (DM) is more often chosen when building a data warehouse. DM differs from the ERD approach in several important ways and, currently, is considered to be the only viable technique for effective design of a DW. To be sure we can make a clear distinction between the two techniques, however, it might be useful to provide a brief review of the ERD approach to data modeling. For those of you who are comfortable with your understanding of the approach, just skip down to the next section. For those of you who aren't, I promise it won't take too long.

Entity-Relationship Modeling

Entity-relationship modeling (ERM) is a disciplined approach to structuring data such that the microscopic relationships among the data elements are revealed. The goal is to remove all redundancy in the data and to create a set of stable relationships that can be easily translated into a physical set of tables or databases. This technique now provides the mainstay of transactional systems designs because it stores transactions in simple and deterministic ways. Even complex lookups are controlled by a single record key data element, and the use of indexed lookup is easily accomplished using a relational approach.

The real problem lies with the efficiency and effectiveness with which the ERM approach reaches its stated goals. In a typical organizational data structure, we find situations where a transaction as simple as taking an order can create dozens of tables linked together by a cacophony of spider web-like joins that are confusing at best. At the enterprise level, the ERM will contain literally hundreds of logical entities, and enterprise resource planning (ERP) installations can number in the thousands. This situation can bring even the most stalwart data query designers to their knees. As such, the ERM approach creates situations that are counterintuitive and counterproductive to the concept of a data warehouse:

- Business end users cannot be expected to remember or even fully understand the complexities of en enterprise-level ERM. Such a model is not easily navigated and offers no simple graphical interface to make the job easier.
- Generally speaking, end user application software cannot readily query an ERM. A common example is the cost-based optimizer applications that attempt to query but are notorious for suggesting the wrong choices.
- The ERM approach tends to defeat the purpose of a DW, namely high performance and intuitive retrieval of relevant data.

To combat these problems and to facilitate other issues associated with DW design, the concept of dimensional modeling was developed.

Dimensional Modeling

Similar to ERM, dimensional modeling (DM) is a logical design technique to provide access to the data contained in the DW in a highly efficient, effective, and intuitive manner. The DM approach differs significantly from the more conventional ERM technique.

Every DM is composed of three basic elements. The first element is a central table containing multipart keys called the *fact table*. Surrounding the fact table are two or more smaller tables referred to as the *dimensional tables*. Each dimensional table contains a single-part primary key that directly corresponds to exactly one of the component elements of a multipart key in the fact table. Joining the dimensional tables to the fact table is a set of relationships referred to as a *star join*. Figure 12-5 illustrates a dimensional model for a typical retail sales process.

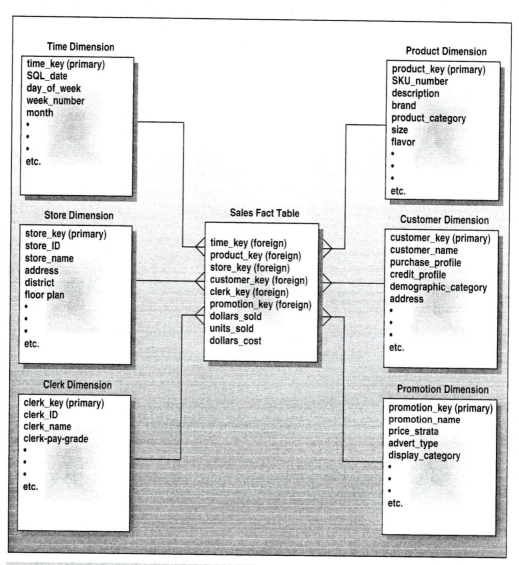

FIGURE 12-5 Dimensional Model for a Typical Retail Sales Process

Source: Adapted from Kimball, Reeves, Ross, and Thornthwaite. *The Data Warehouse Lifecycle Toolkit.* John Wiley & Sons Publishing, 1998.

Note the many-to-one relationships between the fact table and each of the dimensional tables as illustrated in the figure. Because the fact table contains a multipart key made up of two or more foreign keys, the relationship between it and any single dimensional table will always be many-to-one. Also, as shown in the figure, in addition to the multipart foreign keys, a typical fact table also contains one or more numerical facts that occur for the combination of keys that define each record.

ERM versus DM

Certainly, the model illustrated in Figure 12-5 contains several characteristics reminiscent of an ERD, but it is clearly not an ERD. Ironically enough, the real difference between ER models and dimensional models lies in their relationship to one another.

The key to understanding this relationship is to realize that a single ERD can be broken down into multiple fact table diagrams (dimensional models). If we envision the ERD as a model that represents every possible business process and rule throughout the enterprise, we can quickly understand why it is so complex and unwieldy for data query purposes. The ERD represents on one diagram multiple processes and business rules that never actually coexist in a single data set at any consistent point in time. In contrast, the dimensional model represents a holistic characterization of a single business process. As such, in a DW environment where the data are organized into a set of star joins via dimensional modeling, a single fact table can be queried independently from all others with a simple query.

We can identify several additional advantages to the dimensional model that are lacking in the ERM approach. First, the dimensional model can be more readily thought of as a standardized and predictable framework. Therefore, a user interface can be constructed to allow the end user to browse the various dimensional tables associated with a relevant fact table for the purposes of establishing the constraints in the query and thus facilitating the design of query tools and report generators. This predictability in the framework also offers measurable advantages with regard to processing.

Another advantage to the star join schema is its graceful extension and scalability in accommodating unexpected new data elements and/or new design decisions. It allows new data rows to be easily added to existing tables without reloading the tables. Further, none of the query or reporting tools needs to be reprogrammed to accommodate the new data. Finally, and probably most exciting, all old applications can continue to run without any changes and without yielding different results.

One final point regarding the differences between ERM and DM approaches is that, despite its shortcomings, there is a place for the ERD in the data warehouse. The ERD should be used in all legacy OLTP applications based upon relational technology. This approach ensures the highest levels of transaction performance and data integrity. In addition, the ERD may be quite useful in designing the data staging activities associated with data cleaning and loading. Don't just focus on the DM and forget the ERD. If used appropriately, each will serve to make the DW design stronger and more efficient.

DESIGNING A DW FACT TABLE

Even though the details associated with the design of a large-scale DW logical model are beyond the scope of this text, we can look at a typical fact table design process in order to better understand the steps associated with its design. In general terms, the logical design of a dimensional schema can be described in four basic steps: (1) choosing the data mart, (2) determining fact table granularity, (3) determining the dimensions, and (4) determining the facts. We will briefly discuss each of these steps in their logical sequence in the following sections.

1. **Choosing the Data Mart.** Recall from Chapter 10, the data mart is often viewed as a way to gain entry into the data warehouses and to make all the mistakes on a smaller scale. Further, vendors of data warehousing applications find it easier to deal directly with a small group of isolated users than with the IS department of an entire organization. When developing a fact table, the concept of a data mart can be broadened slightly to include any operational legacy source of data. Typically, these sources include elements such as purchase orders, sales, payments, and shipments. In some cases, legacy data may reside in multiple data marts, bringing an additional level of complexity to the problem. Once the source of data is identified as viable and accessible, however, the first step toward a fact table will be complete.

2. **Fact Table Granularity.** Data granularity refers to the smallest defined level of data to be used in the fact table. In other words, the degree of granularity determines exactly what constitutes a fact record in the table. This step, sometimes referred to as "declaring the grain," attempts to create the finest possible degree of granularity for the fact table. The finer the grain, the more robust the design will be. Examples of fine granularity records for a fact table might include a sales transaction, an ATM transaction, a daily sales product total, or even a single line item on an order. Generally speaking, sufficient granularity can be found at the transaction, snapshot, or line-item levels depending upon the nature of the data source.

3. **Fact Table Dimensions.** The first two steps in the process lead to a straightforward selection of the dimensions. In some cases, the chosen level of granularity dictates the dimensions for the table. In other cases, certain decisions or trade-offs may be required. Regardless of the situation, however, the fact table must ultimately represent a set of simultaneous measurements at the specified level of granularity. For this reason, the dimensions can be thought of as those data elements that take on a single value in the context of the measurements set forth by the definition of the fact table. Further, the granularity of any single element in a dimensional table cannot be lower than the granularity of the records in the fact table. In other words, if the fact table granularity is specified at the month level, then the dimensions cannot be specified in days or weeks.

4. **Determining the Facts.** At the final step in the process, the facts to be contained in the fact table are selected. In most cases, if the level of granularity is set at the transaction level, then the only useful fact would be the amount of the transaction. If the snapshot level is used, however, many more open-ended facts can be stored because any summary activity fact would be considered relevant at this level. Snapshot tables offer the most flexible extension of the facts contained in the fact table. Line-item fact tables can also contain several facts; a typical line item can be broken down into its subelements—quantities, gross totals, adjustments, net amounts, taxes, and others.

The details associated with the development of fact tables for the DW are extensive. Further, a typical data warehouse can be expected to contain hundreds, if not hundreds of thousands, of fact tables. As you can see, the development of the data warehouse is an often tedious and lengthy process. During this stage, the designers and sponsors need to remind themselves of the long-term value to be achieved by a DW. Otherwise, it can become easy to wonder why you are performing these tedious and meticulous activities.

12-4: WAREHOUSE ARCHITECTURE SPECIFICATION AND DEVELOPMENT

The next phase in the DW project is the specification and design of the technical architecture associated with the DW. Data warehouse architecture describes the elements and services of the warehouse, and details how the components will fit together and how the system will grow over time. Whether ad hoc or planned, an architecture always evolves, but experience shows that planned architectures stand a better chance of succeeding. Regardless of the exact business requirements for the DW, a planned data warehouse architecture must identify certain elements if it is to be useful in the design and construction of the DW. We will briefly outline each of these required architectural elements in the following sections.

COMMON SOURCES

The DW architecture must identify the best system to obtain each required dimension key and metric used in the anticipated DW environment. It involves determining the best source system in the business to obtain "Customer ID" information, for example. Once the source system is identified, the first incremental data mart team builds an extract and transformation process to populate its incremental data mart. This extraction process needs to be stored in a central repository where other teams can utilize it when they need the same information.

Many times, the different elements of the organization served by individual data marts cannot agree on a common source system. In this case, you must integrate these two sources into a common source for the various data marts in the organization.

COMMON DIMENSIONS

Every business looks at its activities in a variety of ways common to most user groups in the organization. Popular categorical examples include *customer, product, time, geography,* and *employee.* A primary goal of the DW architecture is to identify common business dimensions that are shared across multiple targeted user groups for multiple incremental data marts in the organization.

COMMON BUSINESS RULES

Business rules provide the algorithms and logic used to calculate metrics and derive classification and structure. Various business units commonly use a variety of ways to calculate standard business metrics such as "sales" or "net profit." It is the job of the DW design team during the formation of the enterprise architecture to identify as many common business rules as possible. It is also a necessity to identify all the different ways the business calculates the same metrics, classifications, and structure. If the designers fail to, or are unable to, gain consensus on these business rules, the DW will need individual columns identifying each method of calculation.

COMMON SEMANTICS

Semantic terms are what the business uses to label itself, its elements, its structure, its metrics, and its activities. As elsewhere in life, semantic differences between different elements of the organization lead to many challenges. When two different groups use the same term for two different entities, or use two different terms for the same entity, confusion and frustration can result. Enterprise-wide consensus for semantic terms may be challenging to obtain, but certainly necessary.

COMMON METRICS

Organizations use a variety of methods, referred to as metrics, to measure the operations of the business. Common metrics include *units, dollars, hours,* and other measures of *output, throughput,* or *productivity.* Metrics are fundamentally what the business is about and how it measures itself.

The creation of the DW architecture is an absolute prerequisite for success and its absence will guarantee long-term failure of the design team's efforts. It is most tempting when faced with the need for only a single incremental data mart solution to avoid or defer this step. An initial single solution, however, soon leads to a proliferation of "single solutions" that pop up across the landscape of the organization. Without a common enterprise-wide DW architecture to lay the groundwork for common sources, dimensions, metrics, semantics, and business rules, the business end users ultimately face multiple versions of the truth, mass confusion, and frustration about semantic differences and a lack of data mart integration.

Figure 12-6 illustrates a generic technical architecture configuration for a typical DW. The individual components can be found in your DW, but the exact nature of the components will differ depending on your business requirements and the overall complexity of your extraction and transformation processes.

FIGURE 12-6 Generic Technical Architecture for a Typical Data Warehouse

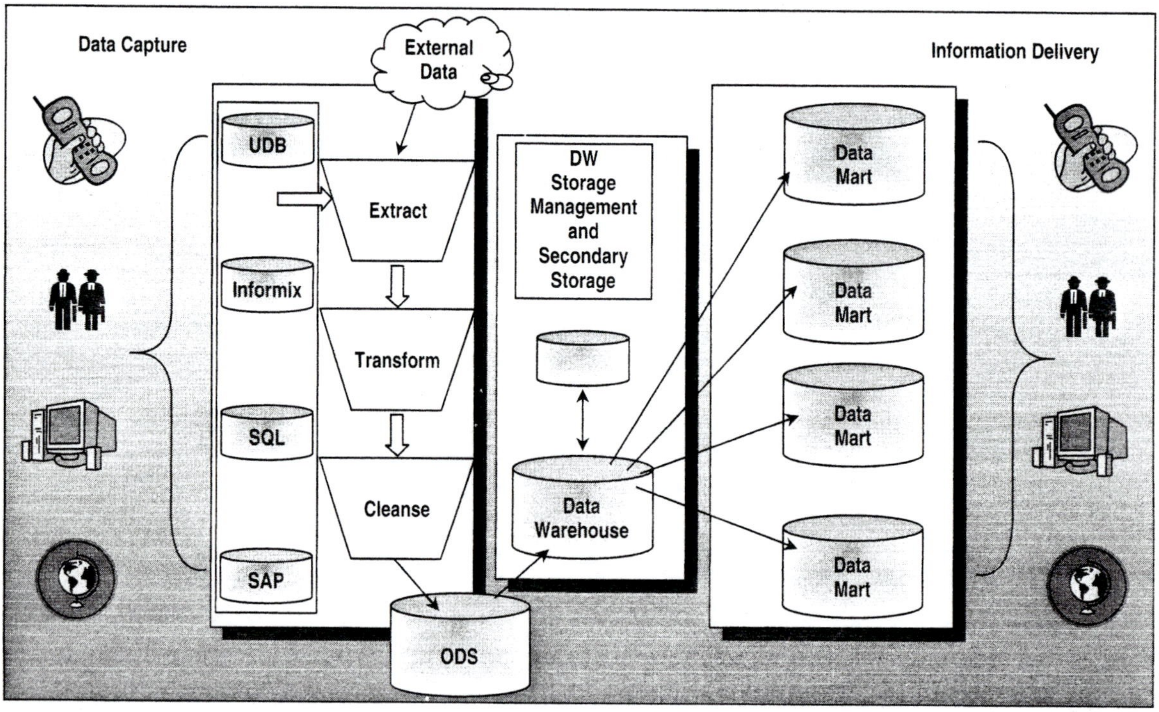

DW ARCHITECTURE KEY COMPONENT AREAS

A complete data warehouse architecture includes all data and technical elements. We can categorically break down the DW architecture into three broad areas. The first, data architecture, centers on business processes. The next area, infrastructure, includes hardware, networking and operating systems, and desktop machines. Finally, the technical area encompasses the decision-making technologies needed by the users, as well as their supporting structures. Each of these categorical areas is detailed in the following sections.

Data Architecture

As stated previously, the data architecture portion of the overall DW architecture is driven by business processes. For example, in a manufacturing environment the data model might include orders, shipping, and billing. Each area draws on a different set of dimensions. But where dimensions intersect in the data model the definitions must be the same—the customer that buys is the same that builds. So data items should have a common structure and content, and involve a single process to create and maintain.

As the designers work through the architecture and present data to the business end users, tool choices will be made, but many choices disappear as the requirements are set. For example, product capabilities are beginning to merge, like MOLAP and ROLAP. As we discussed in Chapter 11, MOLAP is most efficient when the query or queries stay within the cube. It is fast and allows for flexible querying, within the confines of the cube. Its weaknesses are size (overall and within a dimension), design constraints (limited by the cube structure), and the need for a proprietary database. Nonetheless, as product capabilities continue to evolve in functionality, tool choice becomes an even greater contributor to overall DW success.

Infrastructure Architecture

Given the need for all the required hardware platform and boxes, often the data warehouse grows to become its own IS shop. Indeed, lots of "boxes and wires" accompany data warehousing, mostly used for databases and application servers.

The issues with hardware and DBMS choices are size, scalability, and flexibility. In about 80 percent of data warehousing projects, businesses can get enough power to handle their needs.

In terms of the network, check the data sources, the warehouse staging area, and everything in between to ensure enough bandwidth to move data around. On the desktop, run the tools and actually get some data through them to determine if enough power is available for retrieval. Sometimes the problem is simply with the machine, and the desktops must be powerful enough to run current-generation access tools. Also, remember the need to implement a software distribution mechanism.

Technical Architecture

The technical architecture is driven by the metadata catalog. Most DW experts follow the idea that "everything should be metadata-driven." The services should draw the needed parameters from tables, rather than hard-coding them. An important component of technical architecture is the data staging process, which covers five major areas:

1. *Extraction:* Data come from multiple sources and are of multiple types. Data compression and encryption handling must be considered at this area, if applicable.

2. *Transformation:* Data transformation includes surrogate key management, integration, denormalization, cleansing, conversion, aggregation, and auditing.
3. *Loading:* Loading is often done to multiple targets, with load optimization and support for the entire load cycle.
4. *Security:* Administrator access and data encryption policies.
5. *Job control:* This element includes job definition, job scheduling (time and event), monitoring, logging, exception handling, error handling, and notification.

The staging box needs to be able to extract data from multiple sources, so designers of the architecture must be specific when choosing key products. It must handle data compression and encryption, transformation, loading (possibly to multiple targets), and security (which is often considered a major challenge at the front end). In addition, the staging activities need to be automated. Many vendors' offerings do different things, so it is becoming common for organizations to use multiple products.

A system for monitoring data warehouse use is valuable for capturing queries and tracking usage, and performance tuning can also be helpful. Performance optimization includes cost estimation through a "governor" tool, and should include ad hoc query scheduling. Middleware can provide query management services. Tools for all of these and other related tasks are available for the front end, for server-based query management, and for data from multiple sources. Tools are also available for reporting, connectivity, and infrastructure management. Finally, the data access piece should include reporting services (such as publish and subscribe), a report library, a scheduler, and a distribution manager.

A Word About Metadata

Recall from Chapter 10, our discussion of metadata. The standard definition of metadata is "data about data." Consider the creation and management of data via the DW in terms of the following sequence:

1. Warehouse model
2. Source definitions
3. Table definitions
4. Source-to-target maps
5. Map and transformation information
6. Physical information (table spaces, etc.)
7. Extracted data
8. Transformed data
9. Load statistics
10. Business descriptions
11. Query requests
12. The data itself
13. Query statistics

To demonstrate the importance of metadata in the architecture, of the steps listed, only three involve any "real" data—7, 8, and 12. All of the other steps involve metadata. Using this lens, it becomes easy to see that the whole data warehouse process relies on the clear definition and accessibility of the metadata. For architecture definition, the major technical elements of a metadata catalog should include:

Business rules: Definitions, derivations, related items, validation, and hierarchy information (versions, dates, etc.)

Movement/transformation information: Source/destination information, as well as DDL (data types, names, etc.)

Operations information: Data load job schedules, dependencies, notification, and reliability information (such as host redirects and load balancing)

Tool-specific information: Graphic display information and special function support

Security rules: Authentication and authorization

DEVELOPING A DW TECHNICAL ARCHITECTURE

When developing the DW technical architecture model, the architecture requirements document is typically drafted first. Next to each business requirement are listed the architecture implications. These implications are then grouped according to architecture areas (remote access, staging, data access tools, etc.).

We must acknowledge and recognize that developing a data warehouse architecture is difficult and, thus, a "just do it" approach is probably not a good solution. Numerous prescriptions for architecture development can be found, but a simple approach consisting of a four-layer process is often sufficient: (1) business requirements, (2) technical architecture, (3) standards definition, and (4) application product development.

As discussed earlier in this chapter, business requirements essentially drive the architecture, which would suggest the value, and necessity, of talking to business managers, analysts, and power users. From these interviews, major business issues, as well as indicators of business strategy, direction, frustrations, business processes, timing, availability, and performance expectations, can be derived. Document everything well and often!

From an IT perspective, talk to existing data warehouse/DSS support staff, OLTP application groups, and DBAs, as well as networking, OS, and desktop support staff. Also speak with architecture and planning professionals. Here you want to get their opinions on data warehousing considerations from the IT viewpoint. Learn whether existing architecture documents, IT principles, standards statements, organizational power centers, and so on are available.

Few standards exist for data warehousing, but standards may be available for a lot of the components. Regardless of what standards they support, major data warehousing tools are metadata-driven. However, they seldom share metadata with each other and vary in terms of openness. The key here is to research and shop for tools carefully and use the architecture as your guide.

How detailed does a data warehouse architecture need to be? The question to ask is this: Is this enough information to allow a competent team to build a warehouse that meets the needs of the business? As for how long it will take, the architecture effort will grow exponentially as more people are added for its development (i.e., it becomes "techno-politically complex"), and the more complex the resulting system needs to be (i.e., "functionally complex").

Like almost everything in data warehousing, an iterative process is best. So begin with the high-leverage, high-value aspects of the process. Then, use your success to make a case for additional phases. Table 12-10 summarizes the benefits associated with a sound data warehouse architecture.

TABLE 12-10 Benefits Typically Realized Through a Sound Data Warehouse Architecture

Benefit	Description
Provides an organizing framework	The architecture draws the lines on the map in terms of what the individual components are, how they fit together, who owns what parts, and priorities.
Improved flexibility and maintenance	It permits quick addition of new data sources, offers interface standards, and allows plug and play. The model and metadata allow impact analysis and single-point changes.
Faster development and reuse	Warehouse developers are better able to understand the data warehouse process, database contents, and business rules more quickly.
Management and communications tool	Defines and communicates direction and scope to set expectations, identify roles and responsibilities, and communicate requirements to vendors.
Coordinate parallel efforts	Multiple, relatively independent efforts have a chance to converge successfully. Also, data marts without architecture become the stovepipes of tomorrow.

12-5: DATA WAREHOUSE PROJECT SUCCESS FACTORS

By now, you probably understand that developing a sound architecture for the DW is considered the key to a successful data warehouse initiative. You should also see that, like any other complex information system, the architecture of a DW must be a living document, which means that, throughout its life, it will, and should be expected to, change. As time moves forward and the data warehouse becomes institutionalized in the organization, the velocity of change in the architecture document will slow, but it will probably never become static. As new requirements emerge, new architecture becomes necessary.

At this point, we have covered the basics. If your intention is to become conversant in DW issues, then you can congratulate yourself on a job well done. If you aspire to become an expert then thousands of pages of information await you. In either case, the data warehouse is rapidly becoming a standard fixture in the modern information-driven organization and understanding its concepts and uses will become de facto literacy.

To that end, it seems like a good time to set forth a set of guidelines for DW project success. Such guidelines are intended to be prescriptive in nature but should be viewed as probably necessary but definitely not sufficient for a successful DW venture. Essentially, these guidelines, combined with strong business justification and a great deal of tenacity, will probably result in project success and a data warehouse that grows daily in its value to the organization. Table 12-11 lists these success guidelines and briefly describes each.

TABLE 12-11   Guidelines for a Successful Data Warehouse Project

Have a strong project sponsor	Two sponsors are always better than one. Regardless, the business sponsor must be committed to the project and prepared to defend it with resources.
Generage user buy in	Business user buy in is as important as corporate sponsorship. The end users must see the value of the project as it directly relates to their needs.
Identify business needs	The project must be constructed to meet the business needs of the supporters. You must clearly identify these needs and motivations before the project begins.
Start with a narrow scope	Do one or two things well and expand as your successes become realized.
Understand the organizational culture	The organization has certain cultural norms and power relationships. The success of the DW will be dependent on how well it conforms to the existing cultural fabric.
Create clear requirements documents	Who will use the system? How will they use it? What are the criteria for measuring success? Remember, you cannot manage what you are not measuring and you cannot measure what you have not defined.
Determine availability of necessary resources	Make an accurate assessment of the current and necessary resources with regard to their availability.
Define all data requirements	Create a clear enterprise-wide data architecture and define all necessary fact tables and dimensions.
Define all communications requirements	Where are the databases? How will they be accessed? What external databases must be accessed? Are the existing communication links sufficient, or will more bandwidth be required?
Use a best-of-breed approach to application selection	Realize that the best package for your DW may consist of several commercial applications. Each manufacturer will have a specialization. Use that specialization to create a package that best fits the business needs of the DW users.
Prototype	Prototype often during the requirements determination stages and use the business user feedback to create a closer iteration to their expectations. Realize that in some ways, a DW is always a prototype for the next iteration.
Train and support	Be ready to train the users and to support their requests for more features, tools, and analysis.

12-6: CHAPTER SUMMARY

Because of its unique use and potential value to the organization, a data warehouse can, in most cases, be thought of as any other complex information systems development effort. DW projects proceed through requirements determination, architecture specification, logical and physical modeling, implementation, and maintenance. The real key is to ensure strong justification for the project. This admonition should be applied to all information systems development efforts, but the enterprise nature of the DW makes it even more of a necessity. The more tangible the benefits, the more likely the necessary buy in from the business constituents will be realized.

In the next chapter, we will return our focus to the world of decision support systems by exploring the DSS from a systems perspective. The understanding you gained in this chapter by taking a holistic, enterprise-wide perspective of a project should come in quite handy.

Key Concepts

- The enterprise model of a firm consists of a number of separate models that, when properly integrated, provide a coherent picture of the enterprise.

- The various submodels may describe the enterprise in terms of strategy, organization, data, processes, or culture. This exercise determines the level of alignment between the business and its cadre of systems.

- A top-down approach to DW design is firmly based on the enterprise model itself. Such an approach implies a strategic rather than an operational perspective of the data.

- A bottom-up approach to DW design focuses more on making use of whatever existing data are available in the current operational systems.

- To be effective, integration must occur on three distinct axes: (1) horizontal, (2) vertical, and (3) enterprise.

- An organization's readiness for a data warehouse can be assessed using five key factors.

  Strong management sponsorship

  Compelling business motivation

  Level and quality of IS/business partnership

  Analytic culture of the organization

  Data warehouse feasibility

- The first item on the agenda is the formal definition of the project scope.

- It establishes an agreed boundary for the project and defines not only what the project is, but equally important, what the project is not.

- Once project scope is successfully established and agreed to by all relevant parties, the process of making the business case for the project can begin.

- This exercise formally articulates the various justifications for the allocation of resources necessary to design, construct, and deliver the DW.

- Any data warehouse project, regardless of size or scope, requires a number of different roles and skills to be successful.

  Rarely will these roles align themselves in a one-to-one fashion with individuals. Instead, it will more likely be the case that certain individuals will serve in several roles throughout the DW project.

  When determining initial staffing requirements for the project, you should actively seek synergies across roles and match those synergies to individuals who possess the necessary skill set to successfully perform the duties required.

- Similar to ERM, dimensional modeling (DM) is a logical design technique for providing access to the data contained in the DW in a highly efficient, effective, and intuitive manner. In other aspects, the DM approach differs significantly from the more conventional ERM technique.

Every DM is composed of three basic elements. The first element is a central table containing multipart keys called the fact table. Surrounding the fact table are two or more smaller tables referred to as the dimensional tables. Each dimensional table has a single-part primary key that directly corresponds to exactly one of the component elements of a multipart key in the fact table. Joining the dimensional tables to the fact table is a set of relationships referred to as a star join.

- Regardless of the exact business requirements for the DW, a planned data warehouse architecture must identify certain elements if it is to be useful in the design and construction of the DW.

Common sources

Common dimensions

Common business rules

Common semantics

Common metrics

- A complete data warehouse architecture includes all data and technical elements.

Data architecture

Infrastructure

Technical

- For architecture definition, the major technical elements of a metadata catalog should include:

Business rules: Definitions, derivations, related items, validation, and hierarchy information (versions, dates, etc.)

Movement/transformation information: Source/destination information, as well as DDL (data types, names, etc.)

Operations information: Data load job schedules, dependencies, notification, and reliability information (such as host redirects and load balancing)

Tool-specific information: Graphic display information and special function support

Security rules: Authentication and authorization

Questions for Review

1. Describe the concept of an enterprise model and its importance to a successful data warehouse project.
2. What are the two most important components of a fully specified enterprise model?
3. Describe the two basic approaches to designing an enterprise model. What are their relative advantages and disadvantages?
4. Compare and contrast horizontal, vertical, and enterprise integration.
5. What are the five organizational readiness factors for a data warehouse?
6. What methods are available to address data warehouse readiness shortfall?
7. Describe the process of defining the project scope for a data warehouse. What are some of the important elements in this process?
8. What is scope creep?
9. What are the primary elements of an economic feasibility analysis?
10. Why are intangibles so important in constructing the business justification for a data warehouse?
11. Describe the component elements in a fact table.

12. What are the four steps in developing a dimensional schema?
13. What are the key component areas of a data warehouse architecture?
14. Identify and discuss the five areas associated with the data staging process.
15. What major technical elements should be found in a metadata catalog?

For Further Discussion

1. Using the techniques discussed in this chapter, conduct a thorough feasibility analysis of the purchase of a new computer system for your personal use. Assume a 3-year analysis period and use a reasonable rate of return on your investment. Can you justify it from a feasibility analysis perspective? Does it indicate a positive NPV?

2. Contact a local organization's IT department and see whether you can arrange a time to discuss the various processes and activities they are involved in that relate to the development of a data warehouse. What do these processes have in common? Are any of the processes outsourced? If so, what is the rationale for outsourcing these particular activities and not others? Could an organization conceivably outsource all DW activities and just manage the relationships?

3. Identify three intangible costs and three intangible benefits associated with a software development project. Create a logical approach to converting them to expected values. Be sure to clearly state the logic behind your surrogate measures.

13

THE SYSTEMS
PERSPECTIVE OF A DSS

Learning Objectives

◆ Develop a clear understanding of the concept of a system

◆ Understand the need for a systems perspective in DSS deployment

◆ Examine the concept and value of functional decomposition

◆ Define the DSS information systems architecture

◆ Recognize the factors contributing to information quality

◆ Focus on the role of the Internet in DSS development and use

ANATOMY OF A DATA WAREHOUSE FAILURE

It is often said that "the road to hell is paved with golf courses." For Jake Bonaventure, the CEO of Ability Systems, Inc., his trip netherward began with a day on the links in the autumn of 1999 with a software vendor. At the time, Jake was particularly vulnerable to a "business-transforming" pitch. He knew he needed to make technology changes—and fast. His teleservices company, founded with $200 in the late 1970s and now a $100 million success, stood at a crossroads. Intent on choosing the straightest path through a double-digit growth period, Jake was searching for technological help. So when the vendor tempted him with visions of integrated data flow and information on demand, Jake just couldn't resist.

Historically, Ability Systems' outbound (telemarketing) and inbound (catalog sales) business units operated as totally separate companies. The company went public in 1994, and rapid growth put major pressure on its antiquated and proprietary systems. The software vendor made a convincing case that a data warehouse was the solution to Ability Systems' and Jake's problems.

With 2000 already shaping up to be a banner year for Ability Systems, however, the timing for a data warehouse project could hardly be worse. The company planned to expand from six call centers to 116, implementing new, open switching systems in the new centers to enable automatic dialing and call routing. In addition, information systems (IS) were updating all of Ability's internal management systems by deploying new human resources and general ledger software.

Jake expected the can-do culture that he'd nurtured from the early days of Ability to carry it through this period of exponential growth and technological change. He believed that making all the systems changes—including building the data warehouse—in a short time frame was just a matter of getting the right

people for the job. That approach always worked in the past.

Based on the few technology tidbits obtained from the software vendor on the fairway, Jake was convinced he could have a 500-gigabyte production data warehouse up and running in 4 months despite the fact the existing IS staff was already stretched to the limit. Before the project team was on board, he set the project deadlines and a budget of $250,000.

Because no one in-house had data warehousing experience or time to devote to the project, five outside people were hired. The outsiders included a manager of MIS, Jackie Pemberton, brought on in part to manage the data warehousing project, and a director of MIS, both with proven data warehousing track records and a combined total of nearly 30 years of experience in the field. Pemberton was also put in charge of the general-business systems software rollout already underway.

Unrealistic time and resource allocations alone might not have grounded Ability's data warehouse had the business ranks been clamoring for the information it could provide. But because they lacked any previous exposure to an analytical environment before, the users did not know what they were missing. Indeed, the business unit managers were quite content with the canned reports they could get from their current DOS-based database. The few who needed more analysis entered the report numbers into a spreadsheet and did rudimentary manipulations.

The lack of demand for a new reporting system foreshadowed a virtually insurmountable problem: Down the road, the users would not be willing to commit the time and effort required to make the warehouse a success. The users never really understood what a data warehouse could do.

The new director of MIS assembled the initial project team, consisting of Pemberton, two

(continued)

senior managers from Sales and Telemarketing, and a database administrator as well as two outside consultants with expertise in data warehouse deployment. Almost immediately, Pemberton, the director of MIS, and the consultants pushed back on the scope of the project, the preset deadlines, and budget, but Jake stuck to his guns. Ultimately, he grudgingly accepted the idea of a pilot in 5 months rather than insisting on the full-blown production warehouse. Jake never really seemed to understand the magnitude of the undertaking. Despite the early uncertainties, optimism prevailed at the project launch. "Our Director of MIS had so much positive energy. I really thought together we could make this happen," says Pemberton.

The two outside consultants saw the process of gathering user requirements for the warehouse as critical. Along with Pemberton, they embarked on 3 painstaking months of interviewing the key users as 2000 began. Instead of merely asking users what data they needed from a data warehouse, they invited them to talk in general terms about their jobs, homing in on how their job performance was evaluated and how they managed people.

As they collected user requirements, Pemberton and the consultants set about creating a business model that would capture the business professionals' requirements in their own terms. Independent of technology, this model would define the business dimensions (for example, looking at the business in terms of products, locations, or time periods), attributes, relationships, facts, and logical navigation paths, all of which would translate to the design of the warehouse.

The bad news was that the model revealed a highly complex set of business requirements and an inconsistent group of data "facts" that would populate the warehouse. Unlike a retail data warehouse in which the quantity of a particular SKU sold at a particular time becomes an unalterable "fact," performance of customer

service representatives—what Ability was trying to measure—proved much more subjective and obscure. Business managers used their own customized spreadsheets into which they re-entered the data they wanted to examine from the original database reports. Because the managers looked at things differently (for example, some defined "revenues" as actual revenues; others considered them estimated revenues), defining the fact groups became an ordeal that required sorting through literally hundreds of calculations based on subjective assumptions. This process alone took nearly a month, which meant the team could not start building the relational format and user interface.

Then came the biggest blow to date. With the pilot deadline at hand, Ability's IS veterans, who always believed their jobs were threatened by the data warehousing project, finally admitted to the project team that populating the warehouse was not possible. The only data available was basic customer and transaction information captured by Ability's proprietary telecommunications switching systems as a by-product of call routing.

Panicked at the thought of breaking that news to the executive sponsors, the team jury-rigged a way to populate the pilot by parsing the DOS-based database reports and manipulating the report data into a relational database format. But the handwriting was on the wall—without replacing the proprietary switching systems, there would be no data warehouse.

By this point, Pemberton and her team were in overdrive, working 15+ hours a day, 6 days a week. Twice-weekly trips to Ability's other major corporate office in the next state also took their toll. Pemberton described it as "an emotional nightmare."

The pilot contained a small summary-level set of data that the team manipulated and manually loaded into the database. After the pilot was complete in August, the team faced an

(continued)

<DSS MINICASE>

(continued)

unpleasant revelation. Even if there had been pristine source data, the users weren't having any of it. The users were quick to point out that the system was simply giving them what they already had in a format that did not match their original hard copy.

Undaunted, Pemberton assembled a team of 57 IS staff and business users and in a few weeks created a detailed plan for reengineering the outbound business processes and updating their systems. With her heart in her mouth and passion still unspent, she presented her plan to the executives in October 2000, telling them it would take 2 years to reengineer before they could even begin the data warehouse. She said she believed nothing less than the survival of the company was at stake. Her words fell on deaf ears. "They said, 'Thanks for your work, but no thanks,'" says Pemberton. No one spoke in favor of her proposal at the meeting.

Jake Bonaventure canceled the data warehousing project in October 2000. From Jake's point of view, the entire project had been a fiasco. The anemic pilot was delivered 4 months later than the initial (highly unrealistic) deadline for the fully functional warehouse. Although Jake had budgeted a paltry $250,000 for the project, the team had spent nearly $750,000 on hardware, software, and services.

Besides wasting money and time, the project cost Ability Systems 50 percent of its IS staff, about half of whom quit. Currently, the company is reengineering its outbound business processes with an eye toward another data warehousing attempt. But in the meantime, Ability's stock price took a beating, losing more than two-thirds of its value between October 2000 and September 2001. It was clear that Ability simply bit off way more than they could chew.

So much for believing everything you hear on the golf course.

Warning Signs That the Ability Systems, Inc., DW Was Destined to Fail

No prelaunch objectives or metrics

Many major systems projects underway simultaneously

Budgets and deadlines set by CEO before project team was on board

No insider presence on data warehouse project team

An overburdened project manager

Source data availability unconfirmed at the outset

No user demand for sophisticated data analysis

No routine meetings of executive sponsors and project manager

No initial involvement of business managers

13-1: WHAT IS A SYSTEM?

We really cannot consider our exploration of decision support systems complete without focusing on one of the most important elements of a DSS, that of the concept of *system*. Exploring the volumes written simply in an attempt to fully define the concept is beyond our scope in this text. For our purposes, we need only to acquire and understand a definition that we can use to better understand that which we are charged with the responsibility of building.

One general way to define a system is to think of it as a part of the universe with a limited extension in space and time. Using this definition, it is logical that more, or stronger, correlations will exist between one part of a given system and another, than between the same part of the given system and parts outside of the given system. Although accurate in its description, using this definition also tends to give one a headache.

Maybe Aristotle's statement of composition will make it clearer:

The whole is more than the sum of its parts, the part is more than a fraction of the whole.

Even though it predates the concept of systems analysis in general and decision support systems specifically by a few millennia, Aristotle's perspective gives us an initial picture of what a system is. When the component elements of a system work together in some usable fashion, we gain something beyond the mere sum of the component elements.

A system is an interrelated set of elements, with an identifiable boundary, that work together to achieve some common objective or goal.

According to the most widely used definition, a system is a set of interacting elements that form an integrated whole. A city, a cell, and a body, then, are systems. And so are an automobile, a computer, and a washing machine! For that matter, a problem can be thought of as a system, too.

Implicit in this definition are specific components with specific relationships (interacting elements), a purpose or goal for the system (integrated), and some type of identifiable boundary (whole). So, a system is a set of interrelated elements, with an identifiable boundary, that function together to achieve a common goal. Using this definition and drawing from the previously mentioned definitions, we can look at the characteristics of the three criteria for a system: interrelated elements, boundaries, and a common goal.

The concept of interrelatedness suggests that the elements of a system are interdependent. In other words, if one element of a system fails or is malfunctioning, then it will affect some or all of the other elements in the system. These elements, often referred to as *subsystems*, work together to achieve the goals or objectives of the system. Going back to Aristotle's conception, we can also conclude that an effective system produces results that could otherwise not be achieved by each element acting individually, also known as synergy—the total output of the system is greater in value than the sum of its individual elements.

The concept of a boundary suggests that a system is definable within the context of all other systems and that its limits can be established. Further, the existence of a boundary implies that the elements of the system must be contained within it and that any element not contained within the defined boundary of the system must, therefore, not be a part of the system. Elements not contained within the boundary of a system are said to be a part of the environment of the system rather than a part of the system itself. Finally, if we assume that certain systems are within our span of control, particularly information systems, then we can also assume that the elements contained within the system boundary are within our control. Those that are a part of the environment are not controllable.

Last, but not least, the common goal or purpose of a system is, quite simply, its reason for being. If a system outlives its usefulness or can no longer provide the necessary functionality, then the purpose is no longer important and the system is no longer necessary.

SYSTEM CLASSIFICATIONS

Depending on what level of detail or characteristic you choose to focus, you may confront as many ways to classify systems as there are systems. For our purposes, however, we will adopt a common and useful classification scheme consisting of two categories: open systems and closed systems. Figure 13-1 contains a basic model for the two system types.

Closed-Stable-Mechanistic

A generally self-contained design characterizes a *closed system,* often referred to as a stable or mechanistic system. This class of systems seldom interacts with the environment in order to receive input or to generate output. As a consequence, closed systems tend to be both highly structured and routine in operation and environmental changes tend not to materially affect them.

An excellent example of a closed system is a terrarium. Figure 13-2 shows a picture of a typical terrarium. This enclosed glass container contains a stable, self-sustaining world for the plants and animals that live inside. By carefully selecting the proper materials and inhabitants for a terrarium, all of the necessities for the miniature world can be provided by other inhabitants of it. Food, water, moisture, oxygen, and carbon dioxide are produced by some components and used by others, thus sustaining the system.

FIGURE 13-1   Comparison of Characteristics for Open and Closed Systems

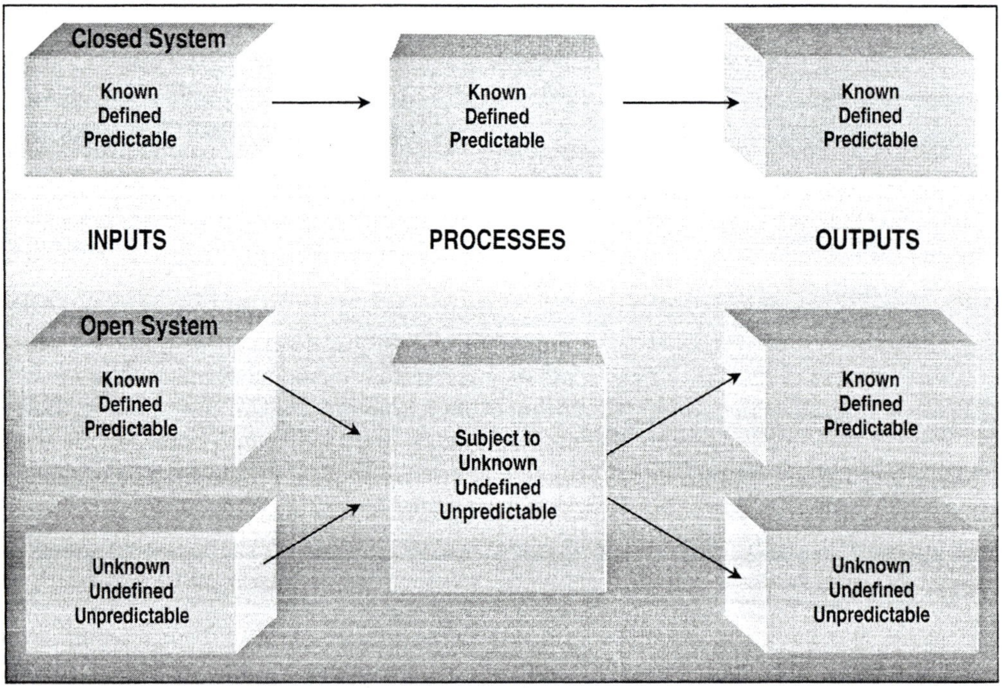

FIGURE 13-2   A Typical Terrarium—A Closed System

One important characteristic of a closed system is that, while it is self-sustaining, it is not perpetual. All known systems must eventually interact with the environment in some manner or they begin to deteriorate and decay. For long-term sustainability, a closed system must eventually be replenished with new materials and sources of energy. In other words, a closed system does not have to interact with its environment to exist, but it does have to eventually interact with its environment to survive.

Open-Adaptive-Organic

In contrast to the closed system, the *open system,* often called an *adaptive* or *organic system,* tends to be less structured and routine in operation than the closed system. In this category, entities that exist both internal and external to the system are important. Further, the interactions of the various components with each other and with the environment, while probabilistic, constantly change in ways more unpredictable than those in a closed system.

A distinguishing characteristic of an open system is its adaptability to changes in both internal and external conditions. The truly perfect open system operates in a self-organizing manner in the sense that it can change its organization and structure in direct response to changes in its environment. Although not perfect, two examples of open systems of the greatest interest to systems analysts are the business organization and the information system.

The Subsystem: Functional Decomposition

Recall from our definition of a system that one of its characteristics is that it contains interrelated elements. For this reason, we take a system apart and study each of its individual components. At this point, however, things can get a little confusing because each of the elements of a system, called *subsystems,* can also be thought of as systems, and each of the interrelated elements of the subsystems of the original system can be thought of as systems and ... well, you get the picture. This confusion is easily resolved by setting a specific goal before beginning the process.

The process of breaking a system down into its component elements is called *functional decomposition,* and it represents a critically important aspect of designing a DSS. By using a structured process of decomposition, a designer can break a system down into smaller and less complex subsystems for easier analyses. Functional decomposition allows us to study a single part of a system and to consider its refinement or modification independently from the larger system. By continuing to decompose subsystems into smaller subsystems we can also learn something about the original system that may not have been apparent prior to the decomposition effort. Figure 13-3 illustrates the concept of functional decomposition by using a city block as the original system under study.

As you can see from the figure, the original system (the city block) is functionally decomposed into its fundamental elements, its buildings. Each of these subsystems can be further decomposed into subsystems. This process can continue, theoretically at least, ad infinitum. So the question becomes, "How do we know at what layer of decomposition to stop the process?" The answer depends on what you are trying to find out.

For example, let's assume that the reason we are analyzing the city block is because we want to buy it as an investment. In this case, we would certainly want to look at each building individually, thus decomposing the block into the next layer of component elements. We may want to look at each of the floors and rooms within each building to determine occupancy and possible uses for the space. This decomposition would take us into the next layer of subsystems. If we are really serious we may even look closely at the finish materials such as doors and windows to assure ourselves that the building is built to our standards. This level would represent yet another decomposition layer. Would we need to have the doors, windows, and bricks analyzed to determine the raw materials used in their construction? Probably not. In other words, although we could

FIGURE 13-3 Example of Functional Decomposition

Continually redefining the system under study into subsystems until reaching a point where no further value is gained from additional subsystem identification.

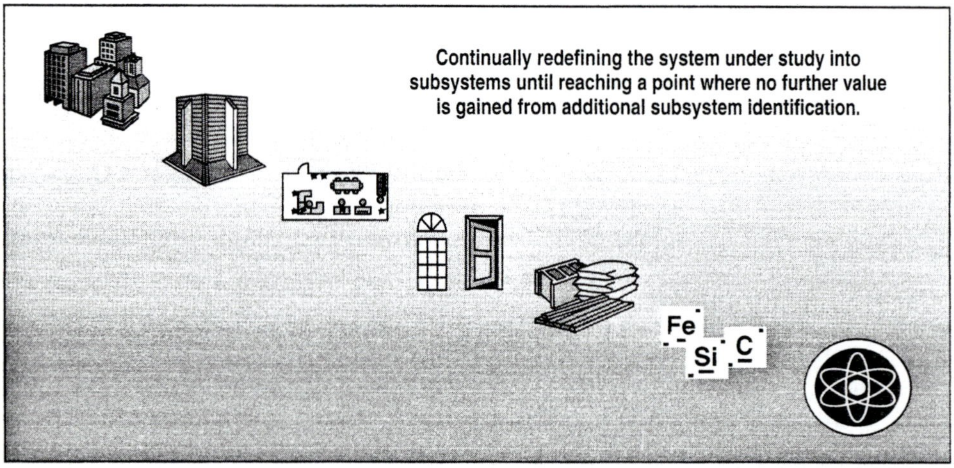

continue to functionally decompose the subsystems into smaller subsystems, we would not gain any useful information at each subsequent layer beyond what we had before. In this case, continuing to decompose the system would not provide any additional benefit. We therefore choose to stop at the layer of detail that provides the most beneficial and useful information to us.

Now consider another example. Suppose we were hired to analyze a particular city block because an unusually high level of maintenance is associated with the buildings located there. In this case we would certainly decompose the system into the layers discussed in the previous example, and we may discover the problem. More than likely, however, we would need to continue decomposing the system beyond an inspection of the doors, windows, and bricks into the layer that reveals the raw materials and even possibly to the layer that reveals their chemical composition. A more microscopic perspective might be required to determine the cause of the maintenance problems: substandard building materials. Through functional decomposition we arrived at the root of the problem and can then turn our attention toward proposing an effective solution to the problem.

In the context of DSS design, functional decomposition allows us to think of the DSS as a series of subsystems, or modules, each of which can operate independently or in conjunction with other modules to produce a prescribed outcome. The same concept can be applied during the early stages of requirements determination in which we uncover the scope of the decisions requiring support by the system. In this context, functional decomposition allows us to break the decision into its component elements and to study each of them independent of the others in an effort to bring as much support to the decision process as possible. Decisions are subsystems made up of smaller, more focused decisions. The simplicity is apparent when you look at it from this perspective.

13-2: DSS IN THE CONTEXT OF INFORMATION SYSTEMS

Until now, we discussed the decision support system in terms of its variations. An exploration of GSS, EIS, expert system, ISA, and the other forms helped in more fully understanding the concept, and reality, of a decision support system. In the spirit of functional decomposition, however, we must also explore where the DSS resides in the realm of all information systems. In this section, we look at the DSS from the perspective of information systems so that we can fully appreciate its role in the whole scheme of things.

Simply put, a DSS is a specific type of information system. At first glance this assessment may seem a bit anticlimactic, but once we know that a particular information system is a DSS, we can immediately draw many conclusions about it that differentiate it from all other types of information systems.

MULTIPLE ASSOCIATED AND DISTRIBUTED DATA STORES

One particular characteristic of a DSS is that it is usually associated with multiple data stores, often taking many forms and residing in a distributed (nonlocalized) fashion. In some cases, one or more of these data stores may be controlled or maintained by the DSS itself, while in other cases the associated data store may be maintained by the organization within which the DSS resides. In yet other scenarios, one or more of the associated data stores may be completely external to the organization and, therefore, to the DSS.

UNIDIRECTIONALITY OF DATA FLOW

With the exception of the data stores controlled and maintained by the DSS itself, most of the data and their associated data stores used by a DSS are populated by an application other than the DSS. All external databases fall into this category. Further, most internal databases and data warehouses also fit this profile. Most of the data stores associated with a typical DSS are actually populated by a transaction processing system or a data aggregation application. For this reason, the DSS contributes little data to its storage schema—it generally takes data rather than gives data.

NARROW BOUNDARY OF END-USER COMMUNICATION

All software applications communicate with their associated end users, but a DSS necessarily dictates a much more narrow boundary of potential end users, sometimes simply a single end user. Depending on the nature of the system, the end user may be positioned as an external entity residing outside the system boundary; he or she may simply provide input to and receive output from the DSS. In other situations, the end user may be modeled as a part of a larger decision-making process in which the DSS is simply one of the subprocesses involved. In this case, the end user would reside within the system boundary.

HIGH-LEVEL USER CONTROL

Compared to other types of information systems, a DSS can be controlled directly by its end user(s). In the typical usage scenario, the decision maker provides the DSS with specific information regarding the problem domain and the DSS uses that information to determine what model to invoke and what data to extract from its associated data stores. Compare this scenario to a transaction-processing system that dictates what data the user will enter, where it will be entered, in what form it must be entered, and whether it is ready to be committed to the database.

Figures 13-4 and 13-5 illustrate a general schema for a DSS.

In Figure 13-4, we see two examples of context diagrams for a typical DSS. The diagram on the left depicts the DSS as a bounded system in which both the external data sources and the end user decision maker reside outside of the system boundary. This type of system would typically be found in an environment where the DSS provides support to the decision process in several different forms and may or may not be used in all decision scenarios for which it was designed.

The right portion of Figure 13-4 shows a context diagram for a DSS in which the decision maker is positioned inside the system boundary and the external data stores remain as sources residing outside of the system boundary. This type of DSS design suggests a system in which the DSS is an integral part of the decision-making process and in which the decision maker is guided by or heavily reliant on the output of the DSS for all relevant decisions within that domain. Although both design choices are

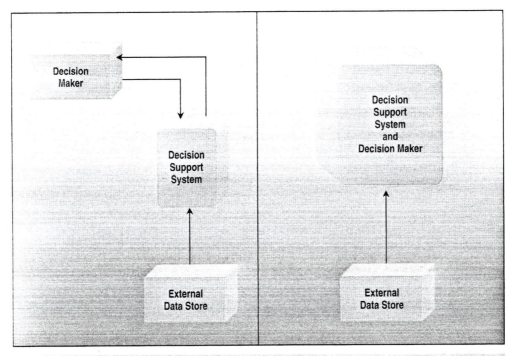

FIGURE 13-4   Context Diagrams of Two DSS Design Approaches

viable, the decision as to which one to adopt will be dictated by the nature of the decision environment and the relative dependency on the DSS.

Figure 13-5 illustrates a much broader view of the generalized DSS. This perspective is not linked to any particular DSS application or decision-making environment and is equally representative of a DSS that assists in medical diagnosis or a DSS used in the loan approval process for a bank.

Given our ability to conceptualize a DSS in a generic sense, the design of a specific DSS application depends simply upon the answers to several questions regarding its purpose:

- What is (are) the specific objective(s) of the DSS application? (The answer must be defined in terms of the specific decision being made and the specific outputs required of the DSS.)
- What are the external sources and recipients for the DSS under design, and under what conditions will the DSS communicate with each?
- What is the exact nature of the data flows between the DSS application and each of the previously identified external entities?
- What data will reside within the boundary of the DSS application? How will the required data stores be populated? Under what conditions will externally acquired data be stored within the DSS system boundary?
- What are the detailed temporal processes contained within the DSS application? What are the data needs for each of these processes?

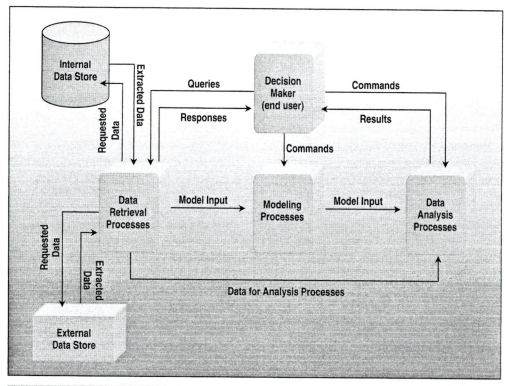

FIGURE 13-5 Processes and Data Flows Within the Generalized DSS

The answers to these questions may not be readily apparent in the early stages of design of the DSS, but they must all be answered in detail prior to active development of the system. Once all the questions are sufficiently answered, a clear system perspective of the DSS will emerge and a successful development process can begin.

13-3: INFORMATION QUALITY ISSUES IN DSS DESIGN

The general system adage of "garbage in equals garbage out" is equally applicable to the design considerations for a DSS application. Within the realm of decision making, information can be thought of as anything that reduces uncertainty in the environment. As discussed in Chapter 2, the more relevant information we possess, the less uncertainty about the outcome we must endure. Using this approach, we can think of information in terms of granularity or bits. Finer granularity in the bits of information leads to greater clarity. Consider the following examples:

- Picking the winner of the Super Bowl using information from all NFL teams is more likely to be correct than by using information only from teams assigned to the NFC Central Division.

- Being told that your new computer will be delivered on Wednesday, August 7, 2002, between the hours of 11:00 A.M. and 1:00 P.M. conveys a much finer granularity of information than being told that your new computer will be delivered "sometime in August."
- Communicating that "Stephanie Essington received an A+ in her Seminar on Learning Disabilities" creates less uncertainty than saying " Stephanie did well in her seminar."

Even though more information is highly correlated with reduced uncertainty, it is not as simple as gathering all available information before making a decision. Given our limited ability to process large amounts of information (see Chapter 2), we can easily become overwhelmed by information not limited to our exact needs at the moment of the decision. This generalization is further complicated by the degree of structure associated with the decision at hand. Relatively structured problems require much less information than those of a more ill-structured nature. Extremely unstructured problems may remain uncertain even after large volumes of information are realized. Consider the following:

- You want to see a new movie that just came out. The information required to make your decision is limited to when the show begins and where the movie is shown. This decision is relatively structured and, therefore, only a small amount of information is required to reduce uncertainty to an acceptable level.
- You are the chief product manager for a software development company. You need to decide whether to approve the development of a new software product for use by a particular vertical market sector. Your decision to approve the new product depends on expected development costs, production costs, expected sales demand, expected pricing structure and revenues, and budgetary constraints regarding funds to develop and test the new product. This type of decision is ill-structured and, thus, requires much larger amounts of fine granularity information to reduce uncertainty to acceptable levels.
- You are the CEO for a large retailer. You must decide on a long-range strategic plan to position your company as the leading retailer in your sector. You are actually answering the question, "What will our business need to look like in 5 years to become the market leader?" This highly unstructured decision requires a large amount of fine granularity information and still retains a significant amount of uncertainty with regard to its outcome.

In each of the preceding examples, the amount of information required was closely related to the relative structuredness of the decision at hand. To add greater complexity to each situation, the examples all assumed that the required information was available and that all information received was accurate. Under the equation laid out at the beginning of this section, poor quality information will likely lead to high uncertainty and poor decision making.

It seems almost intuitive to say that higher-quality information leads to higher-quality decisions, but one must also consider the fact that higher-quality information generally costs more to produce. Given this constraint, the quality of the information necessary to make a decision becomes a cost benefit analysis between the cost of the information and the sensitivity of the decision to information quality. We must find ways to analyze this sensitivity to determine whether the higher-quality information is worth its cost to obtain.

INFORMATION QUALITY SERVICE LEVELS

If you plan to provide a service to another person or organization, somewhere along the line you will encounter the need to negotiate a service level agreement (SLA). An SLA defines the scope and level of service expected by the community receiving the service. A typical SLA describes each aspect of a service provision, details the level of acceptable service, and states the reporting obligations of all parties for that aspect of the service provision. Further, an SLA should contain a definition of service expectations consisting of an acceptably high standard and a realistic budget allocation. Depending on the service, the recipient may not be well served by low performance expectations that could be achieved with ease but would not provide a sufficiently efficient and cost-effective outcome. Likewise, the recipient may not benefit from service levels set so high they cannot be reached reasonably. Because service provisions are often dynamic, an SLA should not be static, but rather able to respond to changes in the needs of the recipient and the capabilities of the service provider.

Information can be considered a form of service to an end user. The data, and the information derived from it, are not normally in the possession of an end user but must be supplied either on demand or on a regularly scheduled basis. Regardless of the scenario, the factors that determine the quality of information can be defined such that a wide variety of information quality and service levels can be realized. In simple terms, the degree to which information can effectively contribute to a decision process, hence its value to that process, depends entirely on its quality.

Given this option, we may simply choose to accept nothing but the highest quality of information from the most reputable sources. If cost were not an issue, then this perspective would be an appropriate one. Unfortunately, just like any other product or service, quality is closely related to cost. It is why a Ferrari is more expensive than a Hyundai, or at least partly why.

When we refer to the quality of information, we are actually assessing how closely that information matches its intended purpose. If we need to find out how fast we are traveling on a bicycle, then a speedometer divided in increments of 5 miles per hour (and probably accurate to only 2 to 3 miles per hour) provides more than sufficient information quality. Using that same level of information quality to state the financial condition of a large, publicly traded organization would be sadly inadequate. Conversely, having a bicycle speedometer calibrated down to the hundredth of a mile per hour would provide rich data but not much more information. To assess the quality of the information needed, we much first ascertain the sensitivity of the decision to the quality of the information available.

In the world of DSS development, information quality is a central issue. Each decision that must be made requires certain pieces of information, each with their own unique quality levels. Some decisions can use lower quality and, thus, relatively inexpensive information. Others will require information at the highest quality levels with no expense spared. The challenge to the DSS designer, then, is to ascertain the information quality level needed and then to assess the quality of the various sources from which the information could be obtained. No easy task, to be sure.

FACTORS IN DETERMINING INFORMATION QUALITY

One piece of good news to this challenge is that an agreed-upon set of factors can be used to determine both the level of information required and the quality of the information available. Figure 13-6 illustrates the 11 factors associated with information quality. Each of these factors will be discussed briefly in this section.

Relevance

Information can be considered relevant if it can be directly applied to the task at hand or the decision under study. Its overall degree of relevance is a function of how closely the information being supplied matches the needs of the decision maker.

Information relevance can be thought of as a binary variable—it is, or it is not. Although most decision makers are generally inundated with volumes of information, the best ones can screen out unnecessary elements. Even good decision makers, however, face a significant cost in time and effort to conduct such a screening. Knowing what information is relevant to a given situation depends mostly on one's level of detailed understanding of the business and the environment in which it operates.

So how do we determine the relevance of all of the possible information available to us? In many cases, we guess. This guess, however, is fairly well informed by the results of the preliminary requirements determination activities. We will, however, be faced with many available information sources for which relevance is possible but not certain. In these cases, we find it better to err on the side of gathering and storing too much information rather than not enough. This general rule is, of course, tempered by

FIGURE 13-6   Factors Determining Information Quality

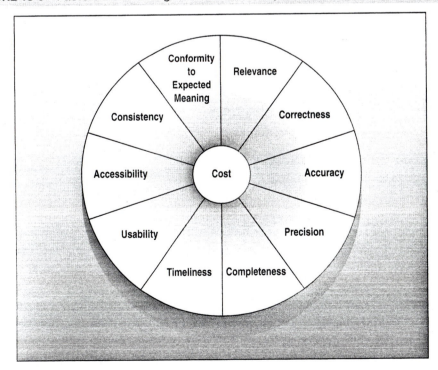

the cost of gathering and storing the information. Remember too that information needs may change over time and, therefore, the relevance of a particular piece of information may vary. As you can see, relevance determination is a constant balancing act.

Correctness

The concept of correctness is often used synonymously with *precision* and *accuracy*. As you will see, the three terms, although related, are unique in their definition and concept. Information correctness is the degree to which the information is representative of reality. If we were to look at the "real world" we would discover a consistency between what we find and what the information suggests we will find. Using this perspective, not all correctness situations are absolute.

In some cases, correctness is absolute and without error tolerance. A postal code or a telephone number is either correct or it is not. If it is not correct, it is useless for our purpose. In other situations, however, information can be deemed correct, in that it refers favorably to the real world, but not be an exact representation of the actual value in the real world. This information is referred to as an *approximation* and can be as useful as the real thing. It is here where we begin to see the difference between correctness, precision, and accuracy.

Consider the mathematical construct pi (π). If we state that $\pi = 3.1416$, we are correct. As long as we realize that pi, being an infinite number in reality, has been approximated for our use, then we will encounter no difficulty. Whether our "correct" statement is sufficiently accurate is a decision left to the decision maker using it.

We can also apply the concept of correctness to alphanumeric information as well. If I spell a person's name phonetically, for example, Mykull Jordun, I can be considered correct because my representation is sufficiently close to its real-world counterpart. What could also be said is that, while correct, it is both imprecise and inaccurate.

Accuracy

Unlike correctness, which is the degree of similarity to a real-world entity, accuracy is the measure of closeness. This factor of information quality applies most readily to those pieces of information that allow for some error tolerance. Such items include numerical quantities, text strings, and even pictures. Accuracy can also be applied to statistically derived information. For example, the statement "the confidence interval of the actual value is stated at the 90 percent level" suggests that, while not absolute, we are accurate to within a 10 percent margin of error.

Applying this factor to information quality allows us to determine whether the information accuracy is "close enough" to its true value to be considered useful. Once again, the impact of accuracy on information quality is a function of the situation in which the information will be used. Being off by 5 percent in determining the outside temperature will not significantly affect our decision as to what clothing to wear, but being off 5 percent in descent speed of a spacecraft will result in a landing that is either "too high" or "too low." Neither of these outcomes would produce satisfactory results.

Precision

Precision refers to the maximum accuracy with which a piece of information can be represented. Another way of thinking about precision is to equate it to granularity of measurement. The greater the precision is, the finer the granularity of measurement. Too little precision can bring predictably bad results, while excess precision may only increase the cost of the information without providing any increase in value. In addition, excess precision can actually make the information harder to use.

Oftentimes, precision is used to imply accuracy. We could state that the approval rating for a particular elected government official is 71.36719 percent. Using this approach, many people may be tempted to believe that this figure represents an exact measure of the approval rating when in fact, the actual level of precision for the measure is 68 ± 4 percent. The former figure, while appearing to be more precise, is actually less informative than the latter figure, which also conveys the true margin of error. Reports with six digits behind the decimal point may look impressive, but in reality their usefulness may be quite limited.

In DSS design, the information quality factor of precision is quite important. In many cases, the designer may actually find that it would be more informative to the end user to provide less, rather than more, precision. Consider these examples:

- We are easily capable of stating a corporation's earnings per share (EPS) to tenths or even hundredths of a cent. Typically, however, they are stated to the nearest cent because it is considered enough precision to effectively compare earnings across firms and to make accurate profitability projections.
- A graph can often convey necessary information far more quickly than the table of data from which it is derived. The numbers in the table may be higher in precision than the scale on the graph, but for the purposes of analysis, the graph is much easier to use with no loss of quality.
- The balance sheet for a *Fortune* 500 company displays the value of the assets and liabilities rounded to the nearest thousand, ten thousand, or even million. For the purposes intended, lowering the precision level makes the balance sheet more useful and easier to understand.

One final note with regard to precision: The DSS designer must think of the precision of a piece of information or data in terms of internal and external precision. We may choose to store the data with a level of precision out to six decimal places for the purposes of calculation, but we may display the results of the calculations at a much lower level of precision for clarity.

Timeliness
Three interrelated elements affect the timeliness of a piece of information:

1. When is the information needed?
2. When is the information available?
3. When was the underlying data for that information collected?

For information to be considered timely, it must first be available in time for its intended use. If a weather forecast for the next 48 hours takes 49 hours to produce, its usefulness will be limited to confirming what the weather was an hour ago. DSS designers must be constantly aware of the deterioration of information value over time.

In addition to availability, timely information reflects the relationship between when it is made available and when the underlying data to produce it were collected. Using our same weather forecast example, a 48-hour forecast prepared with data collected last week is of questionable usefulness, at best. Similarly, a bank balance system that authorizes withdrawals based on balance calculations from 2 days ago will also be problematic.

Usability

Information is considered usable by how quickly and easily its intended user can figure out what to do with it. If minimal effort is necessary to understand it, then its usability is considered high. Information that requires large amounts of time or cognitive effort to decipher would be considered limited in usability.

The quality factor of usability is directly related to presentation method. As already discussed, often a graph will be more understandable than would the table from which the information is derived. Presentation format can also be extended to choice of font, point size, bolding, spacing, shading, and so forth. In DSS design, all facets of presentation format that may affect usability must be given careful consideration. Consider the following:

Given the global nature of the business environment, DSS designers must also consider differences in language when determining usability. At its most basic form, information presented in a language not known or understood by the end user will possess little usability. In other situations, differences in language can make the decision much more complex. Until 1994, the word *llamo* meaning "I call" would appear alphabetically after the word *lugar* meaning "to place," because, up until that time, *Ll* was considered a separate and distinct letter appearing alphabetically between the letters *L* and *M* in the Spanish alphabet. After the decision was made to change it to better conform to the standards of the English alphabet, many such examples could be found that affected the usability of a given DSS output.

Consistency

Information consistency refers to the degree to which similar pieces of information are stored and presented in a similar and predictable fashion. This factor of information quality also affects the handling of multiple pieces of information applied or created in a particular time period. Consider the following examples:

- A plant manager wishes to compare the output of his manufacturing facility for a particular product to that of his closest competitor. He retrieves the data for product output for the last year from his company's information system. He then requests the same information from a public external database that houses production data for all companies in that industry. He finds that his plant's production output is more than 400 percent greater than his nearest competitor. He is overjoyed and immediately begins planning a trip to his boss's office to discuss a big raise.

- A bank manager wishes to determine the productivity of the loan officers throughout the branches. She decides to instruct a software application to retrieve last year's loan origination volume and divide it by the number of loan originators employed throughout the bank. Upon obtaining the results and comparing them to an industry or geographic sector average, she finds that the average loan volume per loan officer is 40 percent lower than the industry average. She concludes that the ability of the bank's loan officers to generate loans is substandard and at an unacceptable level.

In both of these examples, the conclusions drawn by the decision makers were wrong. The error in both cases can be traced to an issue of consistency.

In the first example, the plant manager failed to pay attention to the unit of measure for production figures stored in the public database. In his database, production figures for that product are stored in annual increments. In the public database, however, the production figures are stored as average quarterly production for the previous year. By failing to realize that he was comparing information stored and presented in an inconsistent manner, he overestimated his company's position in relation to the competition. By performing the analysis using consistent information, he would realize that he was simply maintaining parity with the competition.

In the second example, the issue of consistency was not with units of measurement but was, instead, a problem with inconsistency in reporting periods. She was comparing last year's loan volume with the current year's head count of loan officers. Because the company recently expanded the number of loan officers, she reached the conclusion that something was wrong. By dividing last year's loan volume by last year's head count of loan officers, she would have realized that the bank was actually far above the industry average in loan originations.

Conformity to Expected Meaning

For information to be information it must conform to the expected meaning of the end user. If the DSS performs for only one intended user, then the information it provides must conform to that end user's expectations with regard to meaning and relevancy. If the DSS is intended to support more than one end user, then the expectations of all end users must be taken into consideration. In some cases, the expectations of multiple end users may vary enough that the DSS must be designed to present the same information in a different manner to each of the potential end users.

One example can be demonstrated with the phrase "last year." To one end user, it may mean the most recently ended calendar year. To another, it may mean the previous fiscal year. Although each end user may be considered correct in his or her own way, the DSS must either "know" their individual definitions or must be clear in defining the term before the information is generated.

Information Cost

The cost of a particular piece of information is a measure of all the resources expended to obtain it, translated into some commonly accepted financial terms. The ideal that all information should be free is far from reality. Cost sits squarely in the middle of the other information quality factors because it is usually calculated as a trade-off in the degree of presence or absence of the remaining factors. Increased timeliness may actually decrease accuracy. Increased correctness may affect timeliness. All of these trade-offs will, in their own way, alter the total cost of the information. Even though the cost of many sources of information drops each year, the cost of other sources of more refined and immediately available information continues to climb. The DSS designer must be constantly aware of the true cost of each piece of information required or generated by the DSS to accurately determine its economic feasibility to the organization.

13-4: DEFINING THE DSS INFORMATION SYSTEM ARCHITECTURE

Despite the unique nature of most DSS applications, several considerations that parallel the development of any other large-scale software application must be made. One of the most important considerations is the degree to which the proposed DSS conforms to and integrates with the existing enterprise information systems architecture. The *architecture* of an information system refers to the manner in which the various pieces of the system are laid out with respect to location, connectivity, hierarchy, and internal and external interactions.

When we speak of an information systems architecture, we are not referring to the exact make and model of computer, disk drive, or monitor in the system. Rather, we are focused on three specific higher-level issues: (1) interoperability, (2) compatibility, and (3) scalability.

INTEROPERABILITY

DSS *interoperability* controls the degree to which information can be delivered to the exact locus of a decision or point of use in an effective and efficient manner. It ensures that the DSS under design can access and deliver its information to the appropriate end users at whatever location or time period they may need it. If the DSS itself were the only consideration, the issue of interoperability would be a moot one. We would only need to ensure that the end user and the DSS could get together when necessary. Unfortunately, however, the modern DSS must integrate into a much larger enterprise information environment of various information systems and platforms. In addition, most DSS applications must also access data stores that are either under the control of another application or reside entirely outside the organizational boundary. For this reason, the interoperability of the DSS in relation to other systems in the architecture becomes a highly relevant issue, which we explore in much greater detail in Chapter 15.

COMPATIBILITY

The issue of *compatibility* focuses on the degree to which the DSS under design will work in harmony with other existing platforms and data stores within the organization. It is rare that the data contained in an organizational data store, particularly those accessed and created by a DSS, are of limited use to anyone in the organization other than those who created them. In fact, most organizations are moving toward a minimally redundant data model with a declining number of unique data repositories. In return for this monumental effort, the organization enjoys the benefits of large-scale data sharing and leveraging. If we accept that each piece of information generated comes with an associated cost, then we can reduce the cost of information gathering and dissemination within the organization by increasing the overall compatibility of data stores with all applications throughout the organization. This architectural issue requires a holistic perspective on the design of all applications and data stores throughout the organization.

SCALABILITY

The *scalability* of a particular application or platform is the degree to which it can be expanded or scaled up to accommodate an increase in processing requirements due to bottlenecks throughout the system. Considering the scalability of all platforms and designs reduces the likelihood an organization will later need to scrap an entire system because of its inability to accommodate larger or faster processing requirements. It represents probably the single most difficult issue to address when developing an enterprise-wide information system architecture.

ELEMENTS OF A TYPICAL DSS ARCHITECTURE

The DSS architecture for an organization is frequently defined as a subset of the organization's entire information systems architecture. Despite this subsystem approach, the DSS architecture must reflect a number of elements similar to, if not identical to, the overall architecture for the organization. Figure 13-7 illustrates an example of an organization's DSS architecture as a subset of the larger organization's information systems.

As the figure indicates, a DSS architecture must consider the spectrum of applications that may be necessary in a given environment. Such applications must address the organization's needs in the area of strategic, tactical, and operational decisions, the relative degree of structuredness of the decision being made, and the various levels and divisions of the organization that may be affected by these decisions.

FIGURE 13-7   Example of DSS Architecture at Indiana University

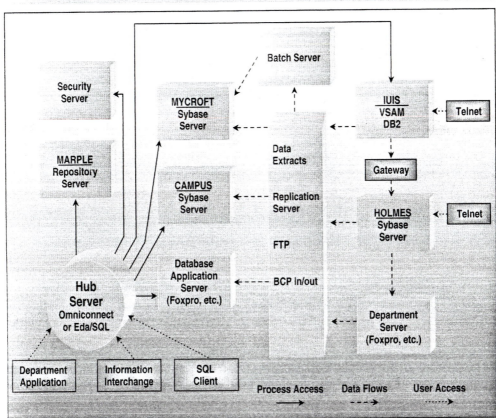

Regardless of the environment, a robust and well-defined DSS architecture should contain details about the following elements:

- *Databases:* A comprehensive listing of all databases, external and internal, along with a statement of who is responsible for the accuracy, currency, and security of each database
- *Models:* A comprehensive listing of all underlying models, their sources of data, and the party responsible for maintaining them
- *End users:* A comprehensive listing of all end users, their locations, job titles, levels of education, and any other factors that may affect DSS access or use
- *End user tools:* A listing of all software tools an end user may use to access the databases and/or the models
- *Administration tools:* A listing of all software tools used by system administrators to manage the databases and the underlying models
- *Platforms:* A detailed description of the hardware and operating system platforms employed by the DSS; a statement of any organizational policies with regard to product or vendor standardization
- *Communications:* A detailed description of the networking and communication capabilities through which the DSS is interconnected

Once these items are thoroughly articulated and verified, a generic DSS architecture will begin to emerge. Figure 13-8 illustrates one such conceptualization.

Once a decision is made to move from a conceptual DSS architecture to a specific one, issues associated with type of platform, centralization and decentralization of the data, and client server or file server configuration will arise. Although details of these deployment issues are beyond the scope of the discussion in this textbook, the reader can consult any available introductory text on information systems for more information. Here, however, we can provide some insight into these issues by supplying a list of questions that need to be asked when making these determinations. Individually, the answers to these questions provide only a small element of the decision. In concert, however, the answers help the DSS designer in making these important decisions. Table 13-1 contains a list of questions to ask in determining DSS platform requirements.

13-5: THE ROLE OF THE INTERNET IN DSS DEVELOPMENT AND USE

The Internet is the world's database and is rapidly becoming the world's leading source of information. Given the pervasive nature of the Internet and the World Wide Web, the information available through these vehicles will become essential to the successful deployment and use of the modern DSS. Further, the ease with which applications can be written and deployed using HTML, JavaScript, and other Web standards will allow for a more rapid deployment of a DSS application to a much wider community of end users regardless of their physical location. In the DSS of the future, the Internet will become the de facto platform and data access mechanism.

It is important to note that despite the increased reliance on the World Wide Web in the design and deployment of a DSS, the same basic issues associated with design,

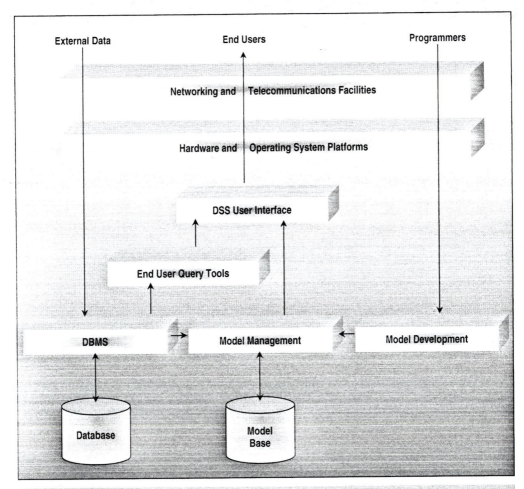

External Data
End Users
Programmers

Networking and Telecommunications Facilities

Hardware and Operating System Platforms

DSS User Interface

End User Query Tools

DBMS → Model Management ← Model Development

Database

Model Base

FIGURE 13-8 Example of a Generic DSS Architecture

TABLE 13-1 Questions to Ask in Determining DSS Platform Requirements

Do any current corporate policies constrain or dictate platform choices?

What is the size and distribution of the proposed end user community?

Will all users employ the same basic set of applications, models, and tools?

Could the DSS reside on any of the existing hardware platforms without compromising future capacities?

Will the end users access the system via their existing desktop or laptop computers or will a separate access terminal be required?

To what extent must the existing organizational system be able to share data with the DSS platform?

Do the necessary development tools exist within the organization to effectively deploy the DSS or must new development tools be acquired?

What database capabilities will be required by the DSS? Is read-only sufficient or must the DSS also be allowed to write back to the organizational databases?

What is the expected processing power required for the DSS application under full load?

Will the end users be responsible or capable of performing basic system administration tasks or will the system require a dedicated administrator?

interface, information quality, and overall suitability for purpose must still be determined. In addition, because of the public access nature of the Internet, data security becomes an even greater concern in the design of the DSS. The Ford Motor Company certainly does not want General Motors to be able to access their DSS or the data used to determine possible new designs and features for forthcoming products. Because both entities are connected to the same network, additional security measures will need to be incorporated into the DSS design to ensure that only authorized end users are allowed access. Internet security is still in its infancy and as new ways of locking up the data are developed, new ways of picking those locks will also begin to emerge. A DSS designer must expand his or her understanding of the role of the Internet in DSS design to insure a successful and secure use of it.

ADVANTAGES OF THE INTERNET AS A DSS SERVER

Several obvious advantages to using the Internet as a DSS server can be easily identified. First, the ubiquitous nature of Internet connectivity means that a typical DSS end user need not be local to the DSS to use it. Using common browser technology, a DSS user can access the system as if they were at their desks from virtually anywhere in the world.

Another advantage to using the Internet as a DSS server lies with the hardware-independent nature of most Internet browsers and applications. Because the World Wide Web can be easily accessed via any type of available hardware, end users having Windows, MAC-OS, LINIX, UNIX, or even a home television Web service can easily share and access the DSS application. Therefore, total cost of ownership for a particular DSS application will be lower and, thus, generate a higher measurable rate of return to the organization.

Finally, the World Wide Web and modern browser interfaces enjoy widespread literacy across potential end users. Almost anyone with any computer experience is familiar, if not proficient, in using a Web browser interface. As such, using the Internet as the DSS server will reduce the learning curve associated with the application. Given the unique nature of a DSS, however, training will still be required to familiarize the end user with the specific capabilities and limitations of the DSS application itself.

DISADVANTAGES OF THE INTERNET AS A DSS SERVER

No opportunity is without its downside, and the Internet is no exception. When considering the Internet as a DSS server, the DSS designer must take into consideration several potential disadvantages.

First, in all but the most modern of technology-based environments, Internet access is still relatively slow. Standard dial-up modems and telephone line access to the Internet is still a long way from providing high-speed access to the Internet. A Web-based DSS may, therefore, require a larger investment in additional telecommunications resources beyond the more conventional local area network DSS platform.

Being facile at Web design does not mean one will be equally facile in DSS design. These two skills must be considered separate and distinct. If the Internet is to be used as a DSS server, both sets of skills will be necessary to effectively develop and deploy the DSS application. This need for multiple skill sets further complicates the already complex nature of DSS design.

In some cases, Web access is paid for using a "per-minute" approach. Even in situations where unlimited Web access is available, it is often deployed throughout a network from a single access point. Applications such as a DSS, which may require large amounts of processing power and bandwidth, may unacceptably degrade network and access point performance and force rather expensive upgrades.

The current standard for Web-based applications is JAVA. Although showing great promise, JAVA is not yet capable of providing fast, reliable performance in complex application environments, primarily because it is interpreted, rather than compiled into machine code. This method tends to slow down processing and can result in complex mathematical processes that require large amounts of RAM and processor power to execute.

In summary, the Internet and the World Wide Web hold great potential for DSS design and deployment. Although much work needs to be done to overcome the inherent disadvantages, we must not ignore its possibilities in future DSS design endeavors.

13-6: CHAPTER SUMMARY

This chapter focused on the DSS from a system perspective and identified several design issues that must be considered with regard to the modern DSS. In later chapters, we will explore specific DSS design and implementation issues and will develop a thorough understanding of the complexities associated with design and deployment of a DSS application in today's computing environments.

Key Concepts

- A system is an interrelated set of components, with a common, identifiable boundary, working together to reach some common objective or goal.

- Open versus closed systems

   A generally self-contained design characterizes a *closed system,* often referred to as a stable or mechanistic system. This class of systems seldom interacts with the environment in order to receive input or to generate output.

   A distinguishing characteristic of an open system is its adaptability to changes in both internal and external conditions. The truly perfect open system operates in a self-organizing manner in the sense that it can change its organization and structure in direct response to changes in its environment.

- The process of breaking a system down into its component elements is called *functional decomposition.*

- A DSS is a specific type of information system.

   Multiple associated and distributed data stores

   Unidirectionality of data flow

   Narrow boundary of end-user communication

   High-level user control

- Given our ability to conceptualize a DSS in a generic sense, the design of a specific DSS application depends simply upon the answers to several questions regarding its purpose:

   What is (are) the specific objective(s) of the DSS application? (The answer must be defined in terms of the specific decision being made and the specific outputs required of the DSS.)

What are the external sources and recipients for the DSS under design, and under what conditions will the DSS communicate with each?

What is the exact nature of the data flows between the DSS application and each of the previously identified external entities?

What data will reside within the boundary of the DSS application? How will the required data stores be populated? Under what conditions will externally acquired data be stored within the DSS system boundary?

What are the detailed temporal processes contained within the DSS application? What are the data needs for each of these processes?

- Factors in determining information quality

  Relevance

  Correctness

  Accuracy

  Precision

  Timeliness

  Usability

  Consistency

  Conformity to expected meaning

  Information cost

- When we speak of an information systems architecture, we are not referring to the exact make and model of computer, disk drive, or monitor in the system. Rather, we are focused on three specific higher-level issues: (1) interoperability, (2) compatibility, and (3) scalability.

- Regardless of the environment, a robust and well-defined DSS architecture should contain details about the following elements:

  Databases: A comprehensive listing of all databases, external and internal, along with a statement of who is responsible for the accuracy, currency, and security of each database

  Models: A comprehensive listing of all underlying models, their sources of data, and the party responsible for maintaining them

  End users: A comprehensive listing of all end users, their locations, job titles, levels of education, and any other factors that may affect DSS access or use

  End user tools: A listing of all software tools an end user may use to access the databases and/or the models

  Administration tools: A listing of all software tools used by system administrators to manage the databases and the underlying models

  Platforms: A detailed description of the hardware and operating system platforms employed by the DSS; a statement of any organizational policies with regard to product or vendor standardization

  Communications: A detailed description of the networking and communication capabilities through which the DSS is interconnected

Questions for Review

1. What is a system?
2. Discuss the concept of functional decomposition of a system.
3. What is the difference between an open system and a closed system?

4. What conclusions can be drawn with regard to a DSS versus other types of information systems?
5. Define the concept of an information system architecture.
6. What are the three high-level issues associated with an information system architecture?
7. What are the benefits to developing an enterprise-wide information architecture?
8. Compare and contrast a typical DSS architecture with an enterprise-wide architecture.
9. What are the factors that must be considered in designing a DSS architecture?
10. Define information quality and discuss its importance to DSS design.
11. What are the factors associated with information quality?
12. Discuss the relative advantages and disadvantages to using the Internet as a DSS server.

For Further Discussion

1. Consider the DSS architecture for a typical retail environment. What databases will be necessary? For what types of decisions would we expect to use the DSS? What underlying models will be required?
2. Using a World Wide Web search engine, locate several examples of software packages that claim to include some form of decision support capabilities. Make a comparative listing of their hardware and software requirements to determine those most likely to be operational across multiple platforms and architectures.
3. Using Figures 13-7 and 13-8, draw comparisons between the generic DSS architecture and the specific one shown from Indiana University. Can you find the similarities between the two illustrations?
4. Assume your job includes responsibility for developing a set of standards for evaluating decision support systems. What factors would you include in your assessment?

14

DESIGNING AND BUILDING DECISION SUPPORT SYSTEMS

Learning Objectives

♦ Examine the two basic DSS development strategies

♦ Comprehend the various approaches to DSS analysis and design

♦ Understand the DSS development process (DDP)

♦ Learn the differences between the traditional system development life cycle (SDLC) approach and the DDP

♦ Study the process of prototyping

♦ Assess the two basic kinds of prototypes: throwaway prototypes and iterative prototypes

♦ Review the benefits and limitations of prototyping

♦ Consider the skill set needed by DSS developers

♦ Learn the concept of end-user computing

♦ Recognize the advantages and risks of end-user DSS development

♦ Evaluate the criteria for selection of DSS development tools

RAPID PROTOTYPING THE ALLKAUF INFORMATION SYSTEM

During the summer of 1994, the management of the German retail chain Allkauf decided to implement a company-wide executive information system. Erhard Jusche, managing director of the Allkauf Group, explains: "In the past we have worked very successfully—using our experience and intuition. Now we want to use modern technology to create an easily accessible information base for present and future generations of management." Understanding the needs of its customers is a top priority at Allkauf. It includes knowing exactly what product is sold in which store and when. The company's new EIS would need to deliver that kind of information within 5 seconds!

Allkauf owns and operates a chain of 75 superstores, each with more than 65,000 square feet of shopping area stocked with more than 80,000 different products. Because of the company's size, the task of collecting and integrating the enormous amount of information needed for the EIS was monumental. One of the key requirements for the new system was rapid response time. The size, complexity, and requirements of this system made it clear from the beginning that only the latest technology would do: client/server architecture, multiuser facilities, Windows, multidimensional modeling facilities, and full EIS functionality. When Allkauf went looking for a vendor that could meet all of its system needs at once, it soon found out that such a vendor was a scarce commodity. Only two vendors were able to meet the stringent demands of the new system, and Allkauf finally selected Comshare.

The Allkauf information system (AIS) is designed to cover three functional areas: standard reporting, exception reporting, and ad hoc analysis. Among the three primary functions, ad hoc analysis is considered the most important because Allkauf wants all of its users to be able to analyze any data according to their individual needs.

The AIS was built using a step-by-step "evolutionary prototyping" approach. Two

Allkauf analysts developed the first application in only 1 month. This first system component monitors sales results using dynamic reporting by directly accessing the data held on the company's OLAP server. Data can be represented in tables or in graphics, sorted and color coded, and users can drill down by line item. One of the primary requirements of the system was met, too: Response times for queries are typically under 5 seconds.

The second module, the short-term income statement, was up and running by the middle of March 1995. The third module contained all of the statistical information on all items on sale in all superstores and was initially intended for use by the 30 members of the central buying department. The most significant feature of this application is a single dimension with nearly 200,000 item members. Only Comshare's new Essbase version 4.0 was able to meet this requirement. This version was released in March 1996. In the meantime, Allkauf developed three less challenging applications using the existing Essbase version.

The use of an evolutionary approach to development produced prototypes that users were able to respond to quickly, and, therefore, developers were able to modify to meet the needs of the users. Allkauf analysts believed that a more structured approach, such as a typical life cycle method, would not have added materially to the quality of the system and, more important, would have delayed the availability of the three primary modules. It is important to note, however, that Allkauf did not sacrifice its highly structured development approach that it employs for all its major transactional information system development projects.

Using the AIS, Allkauf can support its business much more effectively and save valuable time in business analysis. Allkauf management is convinced that it has chosen exactly the right time to gain a competitive advantage using its EIS.

We are now at the point in our journey into the world of decision making and decision support where, for a brief instant, we must turn our attention to the technology itself. One of the most challenging problems associated with the DSS is its design and implementation. This chapter focuses on the complexities and design issues regarding the construction of a modern DSS, and Chapter 15 will look at the various issues surrounding the implementation of a DSS and its integration into the organization.

From past discussion, you are aware of a wide variety of decision support systems, each with its own set of tools, assumptions, and underlying models. Although the "generic" DSS can be described in terms of a generalized set of components (see Chapter 1), the final product will necessarily possess characteristics and functionality unique from all other systems (no matter how similar). Because no one best DSS can be developed, it stands to reason that no single best way to design and build one exists. Some DSS projects can be completed in a matter of days whereas other systems take years to develop and implement. Still others are never truly finished but, rather, exist in a dynamic state of refinement and modification.

Studies of DSS development methodologies (Arinza, 1991; Saxena, 1992) identified more than 30 different approaches to the design and construction of DSS technologies. We will not look at all defined methodologies currently in use; however, we will present a variety of strategies that embody the spirit and complexity of the domain of DSS design. Most important, the premise of this chapter and the next is that despite the outward similarities between a DSS and an organizational application system, the design and implementation processes for each are decidedly different. To demonstrate, we begin with an overview of the basic strategies associated with DSS development.

14-1: STRATEGIES FOR DSS ANALYSIS AND DESIGN

BASIC DSS DEVELOPMENT STRATEGIES

From the many different approaches to DSS development, two common strategies can be identified: (1) programming a customized DSS, and (2) employing a DSS generator. Because each approach is unique, the choice of which one to adopt often depends on the organizational setting or problem context. In fact, it is quite possible for a complex DSS undertaking to use both approaches in combination during the various design stages of the project. We will briefly explore the two strategies here, and will look in greater detail at the various tools used in each later in the chapter.

Programming a Customized DSS
This strategy employs either a general-purpose programming language (GPL) such as PASCAL or COBOL or a fourth-generation language (4GL) such as Delphi or Visual C11. Although early DSS designs were built using the GPL approach, most modern systems use a combination of 4GL and modeling applets to boost programmer productivity and decrease development time and effort. Despite the advent of specialized applications intended to support the DSS development process, a large organizational DSS intended to interface with a variety of existing operational systems is usually

based on a commercial programming product to allow for the development of "one-of-a-kind" interfaces and conduits between the DSS and the other organizational applications.

Employing a DSS Generator

A DSS generator is an application system that eliminates the need for programming thousands of individual instructions or code in the design and construction of a DSS. One of the most common forms of DSS generator is an electronic spreadsheet, such as Excel, Lotus 1-2-3, or Quattro Pro. Literally thousands of individual and organizational DSS applications use a DSS generator as the basic development foundation. Several commercial add-ins such as @RISK, a sophisticated probability assessment tool, are available to assist in the development of various types of DSS analysis mechanisms using an electronic spreadsheet as the primary DSS generator. More sophisticated generators such as MicroStrategy's DSS Architect (see Figure 14-1) allow the designer increased flexibility over the conventional spreadsheet. Although considerably more efficient than using the programming language approach, the DSS generator strategy is nonetheless limited in its flexibility and level of complexity compared to 4GLs or other available strategies.

One recent improvement in this area is the advent of domain-specific DSS generators. Such systems assist in the generation of a highly structured DSS intended for a specific functional area. Examples of domain-specific DSS generators include SAS for complex statistical applications and Commander FDC for financial analysis.

FIGURE 14-1   MicroStrategy's DSS Architect

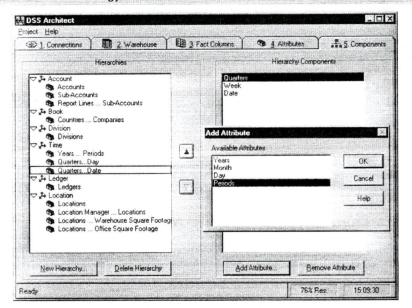

THE DSS ANALYSIS AND DESIGN PROCESS

A number of analysis and design approaches can be applied to the process of DSS development. Here we explore each of the common processes in some detail and compare their contributions and limitations within a DSS development setting.

System Development Life Cycle

A common perspective with regard to system design and development is found in the system development life cycle (SDLC) approach. The SDLC portrays the process as a series of recursive phases, each with its own set of required inputs, activities, and outputs. Figure 14-2 illustrates the various phases and the recursive nature of the SDLC.

In the problem definition phase, analysts assess the nature of the organization's problem and document the problem context and the organizational environment. Then, a feasibility analysis is performed to determine whether the problem context outlined in the previous stage can be effectively addressed by one or more applications integrated into an information system. Activities during this stage include conversion of the existing physical system into a series of logical models to look at the embedded processes in an implementation-independent manner. Initial assessments of available technologies, human and economic resources, and political and regulatory constraints are conducted during this phase.

During systems analysis, the analysts focus on the determination, collection, and documentation of specific requirements for the new system. Based on these requirements, the design phase begins with a detailed model of the various system component processes and data elements as well as of their interactions and interrelationships. Modifications to the resultant logical model reflect the identified requirements of the new system and improve on or eliminate any weaknesses in the old system. During the

FIGURE 14-2 Classical System Development Life Cycle

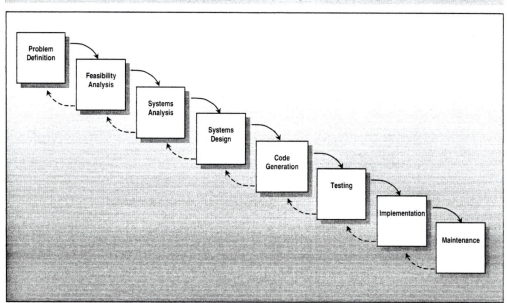

programming phase, the logical model for the new system is converted into a physical system via the development and acquisition of software and hardware necessary to meet the needs of the system's users. Following the testing phase, where the final system is put through a series of trial runs to ascertain its performance relative to the stated requirements, the implementation of the system takes place and the final installation activities are performed. Once the system is operational, the maintenance phase begins. Here various refinements and incremental enhancements are applied to the operational system to effect performance and functionality improvements to the production system.

Advantages and Disadvantages of the SDLC Approach

The primary advantage in using the SDLC in DSS development is that it brings a necessary structure and discipline to the DSS development process. When the SDLC was first introduced in the late 1970s, it was considered a traditional approach within the various engineering disciplines, but still somewhat revolutionary within the realm of computer programming.

Following its introduction, the SDLC was the method of choice for the development of transaction processing systems. In recent years, however, its use extended into the development of a widespread set of software applications, including DSS. It is particularly common today in situations where a formal, and often contractual, relationship exists between the developers of a DSS and the end users of the system and when the SDLC's requirement of providing written deliverables following each stage of the process is desirable.

The major complaint associated with the use of the SDLC in DSS development is it rigidity. The requirements in DSS systems often change quite rapidly. In these situations, the SDLC's structure may force too much structure on end-user requirements too early in the development process. It is, in fact, considered one of the SDLC's major strengths in that it prevents change in the requirements rather than encourages it. Given the more fluid nature of a typical DSS application, however, the SDLC may not be the most appropriate development strategy to adopt.

ROMC Analysis

An alternative to the SDLC approach is ROMC analysis (Sprague and Carlson, 1982). This approach focuses the analysis effort on developing understandings of representations (R), operations (O), memory aids (M), and controls (C).

Using this approach to DSS design, the analyst characterizes the various representations available for use as methods of communication between the DSS user and the DSS application. Examples of representations include graphical displays, charts, tables, lists, stock reports, input forms, and menus, among many others.

In operations analysis, the analyst identifies those activities necessary for the DSS to perform or facilitate the generation and delivery of the various representations contained within the system. Such activities include the interpretation, production, and packaging of relevant knowledge contained within the DSS.

Memory aid components provide support to the user of the various identified representations and operations. Examples of memory aids include databases, work spaces or blackboard systems, and embedded triggers that alert DSS users of the need to perform specific operations relevant to the task at hand.

Finally, control mechanisms help the DSS extract or synthesize a particular decision-making process from the available representations, operations, and memory aids. Examples of controls include mechanisms to assist the user in submitting specific requests or queries to the DSS, functions that assist the user in tailoring the DSS to his or her unique problem-solving style or tendencies, and modules that assist the user in learning to use specific elements within the DSS via examples rather than trial-and-error discovery.

Functional Category Analysis

Yet another methodology for the design of a DSS is functional category analysis (Blanning, 1979). This method identifies the specific functions necessary for the development of a particular DSS from a broad list of available functions including selection, aggregation, estimation, simulation, equalization, and optimization. Table 14-1 lists and briefly describes the various functional categories.

Functional category analysis organizes the key functions of the proposed DSS into a useful arrangement, thus allowing the DSS designer to perform a more focused and detailed analysis.

DSS DEVELOPMENT PROCESS

Despite the many similarities between the design and construction of an organizational DSS and that of transactional application systems, the unique nature of the semi-structured or unstructured problems typical of the objective for developing a DSS dictates that an equally unique approach to design be employed. Often the specific information needs of managers in a given problem context are not clear in the early stages of DSS design and thus are not easily identified. To facilitate the collection of DSS requirements and functions, a process that emphasizes prototyping is employed. In this section, we identify a general process of system development that is tailored to the special needs and challenges of the DSS designer. Because each DSS design project will be unique, however, not all activities identified may be performed. A simple DSS project may allow for a reduced approach involving only the essential activities of DSS

TABLE 14-1   Functional Category Analysis

Functional Category	Activities Performed
Selection	Locating knowledge within the knowledge base for presentation or use as input to the new knowledge derivation process
Aggregation	Creation or derivation of summary statistics such as averages, subtotals, frequencies, and groupings
Estimation	Creation or derivation of model parameter estimates
Simulation	Creation or derivation of knowledge regarding expected outcomes or consequences of specific actions within the organizational environment
Equalization	Creation or derivation of knowledge regarding the conditions necessary to maintain equilibrium or consistency within the problem context
Optimization	Derivation of knowledge regarding what set of parameters serve to maximize or minimize a given performance measure within a set of defined constraints

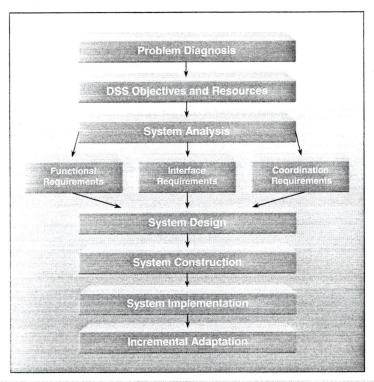

FIGURE 14-3 Generalized DSS Development Process

design, whereas a more complex project may involve all of the outlined activities and phases of the process. For our purposes, however, we will discuss the DSS development process (DDP) in terms of a generalized set of activities and phases of development that are typically associated with DSS design. Figure 14-3 illustrates the phases contained within the process.

The first step in DSS development is the formal identification and recognition of a problem context requiring decision support. Recall from Chapter 2 that problems manifest themselves as a collection of symptoms. The totality of symptoms identifies the underlying problem and, thus, the opportunity for decision support.

Opportunities for decision support can present themselves in many ways. In addition to support for identified problems within the organization, a DSS can assist in the discovery of new knowledge that can advance the competitive position of the firm or improve its ability to reach a specific market segment. Using the data mining and visualization techniques discussed in Chapters 11 and 12, a manager may be able to identify buying patterns in isolated segments of the market that can be parlayed into increased market share for the firm. In another situation, the use of a DSS may facilitate the discovery of organizational problems that would otherwise go undetected, such as embezzlement or theft. These examples show that the manager must be constantly alert for opportunities to use decision support in the course of daily activities throughout the organization.

Identification of DSS Objectives and Resources

Once the opportunity for decision support is identified, the specific objectives and key decisions to be supported by the DSS must be described. In addition, a determination of available resources including hardware, software, current technology, and available knowledge must be made. During this phase, the designer must carefully identify the general objectives of the DSS. These objectives should clarify the function of the proposed DSS with regard to the various types of knowledge to be managed, the capacity of knowledge to be made available to the decision maker, and the general performance characteristics of the system. In addition, the types of support to be made available to the user by the DSS must be specified. Here the designer must determine exactly what role the DSS will be expected to play within the identified problem context. Table 14-2 lists several general types of support a DSS can provide.

Along with the identification of the objectives for the proposed DSS must come the methods by which the success of those objectives will be evaluated. Specific and objective standards of performance must be established. For example, consider the following set of objectives:

- Improve the quality of decisions made within the organization.
- Improve the quality of a particular raw material by more than 12 percent.
- Reduce the nominal decision time for a particular analysis activity by 10 percent.
- Increase the market share for product X.

Despite the apparent value of each of the stated objectives to the firm, only two of them represent objectives that can be accurately assessed. The first and last goals are stated in a way that prevents an objective assessment of them. The first example, the improvement of decision quality within the organization, is a lofty and laudable goal, but it cannot be determined without first identifying the criteria for a quality decision. Even so, one might argue that if any improvement in decision quality, however minuscule, is realized via the DSS, the objective will have been reached. In this case, the investment of $1 million for the development of a DSS that results in an improved decision quality netting the organization 10 cents would be sufficient evidence of goal attainment. Try and sell that concept to your boss.

The same problem exists with the last of the four stated objectives. Any increase in market share for product X would be sufficient to satisfy the goal. The second and third objectives, however, allow for the objective assessment of not only the value of the goal but whether it has been achieved. Although some objectives are necessarily difficult to quantify or are seemingly intangible, the ultimate success of a DSS

TABLE 14-2 Types of Support Provided by a DSS

- Identify the need for decisions
- Identify specific problems that require attention
- Solve or assist in solving problems
- Help compensate for cognitive limitations of human decision makers
- Provide assistance in the form of advice, analysis, or evaluation
- Enhance user creativity, imagination, or insight
- Facilitate interactions in multiparticipant decision-maker settings

development project rests on the establishment of explicit goals and the methods used to assess them.

System Analysis

The activities of this phase of the DSS development process result in a detailed set of requirements for the DSS. According to Holsapple, Park, and Whinston (1993), three primary categories of system requirements for the DSS can be established: (1) functional requirements, (2) interface requirements, and (3) coordination requirements.

Functional Requirements   This set of specifications for the DSS focuses on its capacity for the storage, recall, and production of knowledge useful to the problem context. An example of this type of requirement might be the capability of a particular DSS to store a variety of product sales projections, recall specific components or characteristics of one or more projections, and estimate the effect on sales volume of one or more changes to the underlying assumptions or variables contained therein.

Interface Requirements   The heart and soul of a DSS is arguably related to the quality and usefulness of its interface. The interface requirements focus on the communication capabilities of the DSS. During this phase, the designer must determine the various channels and methods of communication that will be made available to the DSS user and the conditions under which they will be made available. Menuing, report structures, command interface, and output formats are all identified during this phase of the development process. In addition, the developer must identify the various types of requests that might be made of the DSS by the decision maker and the appropriate types of responses the DSS must be able to make as a result.

Coordination Requirements   In addition to establishing the specific functions and communication mechanisms associated with the proposed DSS, the designer must determine the coordination requirements, including the timing of events associated with the decision-making process, the facilitation of access to relevant information, and the integration of various modeling tools contained within the DSS. An example of a coordination requirement might be the necessity for one event to have occurred before another action can be initiated (for instance, sales projections for prior fiscal periods would need to be updated to actual figures before initiating a future projection process).

System Design

The determination of specific physical components, structure, and development platforms is made during the system design stage of the DSS development process. One of the primary activities in this phase is the selection of a set of development tools to be used in the construction of the DSS. Once the development tools are determined, a design can be created that takes advantage of the specific strengths and features of those tools while simultaneously avoiding known weaknesses associated with the platform. We will take a closer look at the various development tools and platforms available for DSS design later in this chapter.

System Construction

During the system construction phase, the designer uses an iterative prototyping approach in which small, yet constant, refinements are made to the system based on feedback received from testing and user involvement. This process of refinement is continuous during this phase and often results in significant changes to the initial design specifications. Each iteration of the prototype provokes the DSS user into verbalizing needs and desires not yet reflected in the design. In addition, the prototype can be used to incrementally determine the various requirements associated with interconnecting the DSS with other existing organizational application systems. We will focus on the activities associated with prototyping later in this section. For now, know that the design phase often represents the majority of the effort and time associated with the development of an organizational DSS.

System Implementation

The goal of the system implementation phase is to test, evaluate, and deploy a fully functional and documented DSS. This phase includes an all-important final determination and evaluation of the degree to which the DSS meets the users' needs. As in the design phase, modifications may be necessary to fully realize the potential of the DSS and to fully implement the identified objectives of the decision makers. Also performed during this phase is the training of the DSS user group with regard to specific capabilities, functions, and structure of the system. Users are also trained in methods associated with maintenance and refinement of the system over time. At the conclusion of this set of development activities, a fully deployed and functional decision support system tailored to the specific needs and characteristics of the problem context is available to the organization. The final step in the process, incremental adaptation, can then be initiated.

Incremental Adaptation

This final stage in the DSS development process is a continual revisiting of the activities of the earlier stages in an effort to enhance the capabilities of the DSS based on knowledge gained as a result of its use. Over the operating life of an organizational DSS, new needs manifest themselves and many innovative functions are developed in response to those needs. In addition, as technology changes in the environment, the desire to incorporate those changes and improvements into the DSS may result in the development process starting again on a major revision to the existing design. As you can see, the development of a DSS is truly an evolutionary process that can, and should, result in a highly effective support mechanism for organizational decision making.

SDLC VERSUS DSS DEVELOPMENT PROCESS

Several general approaches to the design and development of a DSS range from highly staged and structured to highly iterative and unstructured strategies. To further understand the need for a unique development process in the design of a DSS, we must look at the two extremes of the development strategy continuum, the SDLC and the DDP, in greater detail.

The SDLC evolved out of analysts' and developers' experience with computer-based information systems. The sequential and structured nature of the process is one of its primary strengths in that it provides a vehicle for programmed problem solving while simultaneously minimizing the inherent biases and cognitive limitations associated with human problem-solving activities. The life cycle approach to system development is characterized as a top-down design philosophy, which implies that the exact needs and specifications of the system are determined first and then followed by the design and construction of a system that meets those exact needs. Practicing analysts are quick to point out, however, that the SDLC is an idealized abstraction of the actual process and that often a more iterative bottom-up design approach may become necessary to facilitate the development of a particular system or component. Nonetheless, its strength clearly lies in its simplicity and ability to impose necessary structure on the design process. The SDLC continues to be the single most useful approach to the development of computer-based information systems. It is, however, this strength that renders it inadequate for the effective design and construction of an organizational DSS.

The underlying cause for this inadequacy is related to the stated objective of a DSS: support for semistructured problem contexts. The use of the SDLC presumes that the structure of the problem to be solved or the nature of the problem context in which the DSS will operate is fully known and identifiable prior to the initiation of the design phase. In most system projects where the SDLC is appropriately employed, the problem context, managerial preferences, decision-making processes, and environmental conditions are, for the most part, identifiable and largely static. Although the initial activities in the SDLC approach are associated with the gathering of knowledge by the analysts, the process assumes that such knowledge is readily available and categorized according to a set of system requirements. This assumption is simply untenable within the realm of DSS design and construction. The lack of understanding on the part of the DSS designer is only one variable in the development equation. More often than not, the problem context, the managerial preferences, the decision-making processes, and the environmental conditions are also unknown to the user and tend to vary greatly throughout the development process. This "mental migration" of system requirements commonly (and necessarily) associated with the development of a DSS is counter to the assumptions of convergence commonly associated with the life cycle approach.

> Over time the initially unstructured or semi-structured planning issue that originally motivated the DSS project migrates in the minds of both the user and the DSS designer. This occurs when the traditional life-cycle design methodology begins to enforce premature closure on the original problem definition so that the specifications can be "frozen." The resulting DSS system design, therefore, also tends to migrate over the developmental time interval. (Moore and Chang, 1983, p. 184)

It follows that the design of a DSS requires a process uniquely constructed to allow for the largely evolutionary design approach necessary in DSS development. This approach emphasizes prototyping activities.

PROTOTYPING

The prototyping approach provides a common and increasingly popular method of system development. Although opinions differ regarding the appropriate use of prototyping as part of a life cycle approach, the use of iterative, or evolutionary, prototyping in the design and construction of a DSS appears to be an expedient and efficient method of "hitting the moving target" of DSS user requirements. Although no commonly prescribed methodology for prototyping exists, several researchers (Courbon, Grajew, and

Tolovi, 1980; Henderson and Ingraham, 1982) offered a useful description of the task sequence associated with developing an iterative prototype.

The early stages of the prototyping approach contain several similarities to the classic SDLC methodology. The primary differences begin to occur following the initial gathering of requirements and the development of the first round of prototypes. Once the first prototype is in place, a repetitive and incremental process begins in which increasingly smaller, but constant, changes are made to the prototype until a stable system accurately reflects the needs and desires of the DSS users. This process requires a significantly higher level of interaction between the analyst and user, and the nature of the cooperation between the two is generally more intense than in an SDLC-based design effort. This cooperative effort is characterized by a repetitive shift in responsibility throughout the project. While a particular iteration of the prototype is being constructed, the analyst shoulders the responsibility and the users are not directly involved. When the iteration is complete and ready for preview, however, the DSS users assume responsibility for determining what is good, what is bad, and what needs to be added or removed from the functionality of the system. Contrary to the user's more passive or reactive involvement in the SDLC approach, the DSS user is an integral and active part of the usability and evaluation activities during DSS development. In addition, both parties cooperate in the identification and location of additional data needed for input to the DSS during this iterative activity. Once completed, the prototyping approach supplies a highly specific application usable in a narrow problem context and often by only a few decision makers or problem solvers.

THROWAWAY VERSUS ITERATIVE PROTOTYPES

Two basic kinds of prototypes can evolve from the development process. The throwaway prototype is for demonstration purposes only and is then discarded. The advantage to developing a throwaway prototype lies with the increased speed—compared to a life cycle approach—with which a quasi-functional application can be put before the user and with the relative cost savings associated with development. By reducing the time necessary to develop a working version of the project, the value of the application can be demonstrated to senior management and financial supporters much earlier in the project. This expediency can often draw the long-term support necessary for the successful implementation of the DSS application. Moreover, the cost of development, in the early stages at least, is significantly lower than with an SDLC design effort because the initial success of the application can be more readily determined early in the prototyping process. If, for whatever reason, the developer is unable to design and implement the DSS with the currently available technologies and development tools, the plan can be more easily reconsidered and revised earlier in the design process.

The alternative to the throwaway system is the development of an iterative prototype (also referred to as an evolutionary prototype). Rather than being discarded following demonstration, the iterative prototype is redeveloped and continually refined until it completely satisfies the requirements and needs of the DSS users, and then any necessary integration with other existing organizational systems is performed. In other words, the prototype "evolves" into the final production system. Unlike the throwaway system, the iterative prototype is a much more complex and formidable design effort. In both types, however, the basic process of development remains the same. The requirements of the system, often inexplicable or even initially unknown to both the user and the analyst, are eventually discovered, documented, and embedded in a fully operational DSS.

BENEFITS AND LIMITATIONS OF PROTOTYPING

As stated previously, the prototyping approach to the design and construction of a DSS appears to be superior to the more conventional life cycle process. Several clear bene-fits can be identified with the adoption of this design approach. The significant reduc-tion in development time and generally lower cost compared to an SDLC approach makes prototyping an attractive alternative in today's fast-paced managerial environ-ment. In addition, the immediate nature of user response and feedback regarding sys-tem functionality can often result in a greater degree of support from senior manage-ment because they can more easily see the project's advantages to the firm. Finally, the iterative nature of the prototyping process, at least theoretically, promotes an increased user understanding of the system and its range of capabilities.

Many of the strengths and benefits associated with the prototyping approach can also contribute to its limitations. Although the SDLC approach is admittedly slower and more cautious than a pure prototyping process, that increased caution often con-

14-2: THE DSS DEVELOPER

Developers of decision support systems are often as diverse as the systems they create. The skills and backgrounds of DSS developers range from the experienced profes-sional analyst to the novice first-time developer. Within the population of experienced professionals is an equally broad spectrum of experience ranging from analysts who specialize in the development of DSS applications to those who, although experienced in the development of organizational systems, lack experience in the design of a DSS application. In contrast to the professional DSS developer who is formally trained in either computer science or business information systems, the novice developer is typi-cally a managerial decision maker within the organization who perceives the need for computer-based support in a one-time or recurrent problem context. He or she is rarely trained in the formalities and complexities of systems analysis and design and may be experiencing the development process for the first time. Novice developers do possess one significant advantage over the formally trained and more experienced ana-lysts, however: They possess a more intimate knowledge of what they want the DSS to accomplish and, with the right set of tools, can take advantage of the synergy associated with the developer and the user being the same person.

NECESSARY SKILL SET

Regardless of the DSS developer's experience or organizational role, several key skills are essential to the success of the endeavor. As you will see, the professional developer has an advantage in certain skill areas, but the novice may have an edge over the pro-fessional in other areas. For example, as already mentioned, the novice may know exactly what functions are expected of the system, whereas the professional must work to extract that understanding from the DSS users. Conversely, the professional is more likely to respond to the complexities of tool selection and system design more readily than a novice developer with no formal training in these subjects. In the following subsections, we briefly outline and discuss the skill set needed by the developer for a successful DSS design effort.

Understanding the Problem Domain

The development of any organizational application, especially one intended for decision support, requires a thorough understanding of the problem domain. In some cases, the necessary level of understanding may approach that of domain expertise, while in other situations, a more general knowledge of the problem domain is sufficient. The problem-centric nature of a DSS, however, demands that both the developer and the user be more than conversant in the specific characteristics of the problem context. The DSS developer must possess not only the knowledge to develop the computer-based application but also knowledge of the details surrounding the problem under study. A DSS developer with expertise in the medical profession may be valuable in the development of a system to support initial trauma center decisions regarding patient care but probably will not be effective in the development of a product allocation DSS for a consumer manufacturing firm.

Understanding Specific User Requirements

Just as the designer must understand the problem context, he or she must also understand the needs of the DSS users. This understanding encompasses both the functions of the proposed system as well as the specific interface requirements for communication with the system. Getting the DSS users involved early in the analysis and design of the system is necessary for the designer to develop this skill.

Understanding the Available Development Technologies

The analyst and DSS users use their combined skills and knowledge to select a DSS development tool or platform. A number of technologies can provide the basis for DSS development. For example, a spreadsheet may be an appropriate platform for building a DSS intended to provide what-if analysis, whereas a rule management platform may be more suitable when designing a DSS to determine the most appropriate corrective action in a complex manufacturing process. Still other situations may call for development of a system around a case-based reasoning engine. The greater the familiarity a developer has with the intricacies of the technology, the greater the chances of successful tool selection and, thus, successful DSS development.

Access to Appropriate Knowledge

Even the most experienced and skilled DSS developer must still be able to identify, locate, and represent the relevant knowledge appropriate for decisions made in the specific problem context for which the DSS is being developed. In many instances, the responsibility for the identification of relevant knowledge is shared equally by the analyst and the DSS users, but the burden of accurate representation of that knowledge falls almost exclusively on the developer. The DSS user can only confirm that the knowledge is appropriately represented by thoroughly testing each iteration of the DSS. This necessary skill is closely aligned with the need for a thorough understanding of the problem domain. A developer who is not familiar with a specific problem domain may not be aware of the existence of knowledge in the form of specific procedures or modeling techniques relevant to the DSS. In such cases, the developer may either waste time and resources by "reinventing the wheel" or may design a less effective system.

END-USER DSS DEVELOPMENT

The novice DSS developer comes from a group engaged in end-user computing. End users are those individuals who fall outside the confines of the formally defined IS department. End-user computing includes activities such as electronic mail in business, word processing to develop documents, and designing and implementing a computer-based information system, such as a DSS. End-user DSS developers build computer-based systems either to solve organizational problems or to assist in the pursuit of decision-making activities.

End-user developers play a variety of organizational roles and exhibit a variety of computer skill levels. End users are found at all levels of the organization, from the shop floor to the executive suite, and in all functional areas, from accounting to marketing to materials planning. In addition, their experience and skill level associated with developing and using a DSS are equally as diverse, ranging from a first-time user to the department computer guru. Comparable to this diversity is the range of applications developed by end users and the degree of formality associated with the chosen development methodology.

Because the typical end-user developer lacks formal training in system development methods, most end-user-developed applications tend to evolve from a relatively informal, often ad hoc process. Although this informality poses no serious problem in a small and isolated DSS development project, it can result in serious negative consequences when applied to a large and complex DSS development effort. Without the rigor and discipline of a formal design methodology, complex DSS development projects can fall prey to defects related to a lack of direction, divergence of system objectives, and imprecision of system requirements and specification.

ADVANTAGES OF THE END-USER-DEVELOPED DSS

The most obvious advantage gained from end-user DSS development is a major reduction in delivery time of the application. Assuming the end user possesses the skills necessary to complete the project successfully, the delay often experienced in getting the information systems department actively involved in a development effort can be avoided. The DSS project can be initiated literally overnight and, depending on the complexity of the design, can be completed within the span of a few hours to a few weeks. As you know, the value of a DSS lies solely with its effectiveness in supporting a successful decision process. The faster the DSS can be put into operation, the faster the organization can realize the benefits it provides.

Another major benefit of end-user development is the elimination of the time-consuming process of gathering and formalizing the end-user specifications for the system. Users are often unable to verbalize their needs with the same degree of clarity with which they can envision them. In end-user development, the analyst and the user are the same person, which facilitates the rapid transfer of envisioned needs and requirements into a working prototype. End users may not be adept at explaining what is needed but they will undoubtedly know it when they see it.

A third benefit of end-user DSS development is in the reduction of implementation problems following the design phase of the project. Often the same issues of communication between the analyst and the users in understanding the complexities of the system are found during the implementation training process. Not only does the analyst have a difficult and time-consuming task of identifying and formalizing the users' needs during the requirements gathering phase of the project, but he or she must transfer the operational aspects of the new system back to the end users during the implementation phase. In the case of end-user development, the user is immediately and intimately familiar with the operation of the DSS and can proceed from development to operation and use with a minimum of effort and time.

The final advantage of end-user DSS development is a consequence of the previous three advantages: lower cost of development. The reduction in time and organizational resources associated with end-user development often translates into huge cost savings for the organization. This savings, combined with the increased speed with which the benefits of the operational DSS can be realized, makes the concept of end-user DSS development an attractive alternative to the more conventional analyst-user life cycle approach.

RISKS IN END-USER DSS DEVELOPMENT

Along with the advantages of end-user DSS development come certain inherent risks that must be carefully managed. The most obvious concern is the quality necessary in the final product to make it a reliable and useful decision aid. End users often ignore or bypass conventional control mechanisms and testing procedures intrinsic to formal, structured development methodologies. This lack of rigor during the development process can often lead to serious deficiencies and sometimes catastrophic consequences. Something as simple as a formula in a spreadsheet that fails to accurately account for all subtotals in a grand total can result in the loss of millions of dollars if it is not detected during a testing phase and the users rely on the results provided by the DSS in their decision making. In other cases, deficiencies in the functionality of the DSS can go undetected during the development process and can manifest themselves during a crucial decision-making activity.

Another common risk associated with end-user development is the lack of quality documentation. Professional developers lament the tedium of documentation but realize the importance of the process and the necessity for accuracy and thoroughness. End users may acknowledge the importance of accurate and thorough documentation but they rarely demonstrate their concerns by actually doing it. The focus of the end user is on completion of the application. Documentation is, more often than not, an afterthought (if a thought at all). As long as the same individual who developed the system uses the system, the lack of comprehensive documentation is not a major problem. In some cases, however, an end-user DSS can evolve into an integral part of a functional area's decision processes. Should the developer leave the organization, the knowledge associated with the internal workings of that system generally leaves with the developer. Years later, when a modification to the otherwise reliable DSS becomes necessary, no one in the organization can decipher the source code sufficiently to make the necessary changes. At this point, the organization is faced with either not making the desired improvements or changes or starting the development effort from scratch and designing a new DSS that incorporates the necessary functions (and, one would hope, is well documented).

A third area of concern is the potential lack of necessary security measures built into the system due to the end user's lack of familiarity with proper application security controls. In most cases, a lack of security is not a threat to the integrity of the organizational data because the typical end-user-developed DSS is a stand-alone application used only by a select few members of the organization. In some cases, however, the end-user-developed application may need to access data from one or more organizational data stores. Then, the end-user application becomes a direct conduit not only to the organization's proprietary data but, in some cases, to other operational application systems as well. By failing to include the same level of security and control to the end-user-developed application typically part of more formally designed and developed systems, the end user potentially leaves an unlocked door to proprietary and otherwise secure organizational data and information.

These risks (and many others not discussed here) can be effectively managed so that the expected benefits associated with end-user development can be realized. A novice developer, despite his or her lack of formal training, can still acquire an understanding of the important elements of good design and can develop an attitude of professionalism that will increase the prospects of a successfully developed and implemented DSS.

The management of risk in end-user development is the subject of extensive academic and applied research. Several frameworks focus attention on the proper application of security and control (Walls and Turban, 1992), on overall risk reduction techniques (Alavi and Weiss, 1986), and on specific error-location and reduction techniques in spreadsheets (Galletta et al., 1996). Figure 14-4 contains a model of factors that influence risk in end-user-developed applications that can be useful in developing guidelines for end-user development activities within an organization.

More recently, organizations address the risks associated with end-user development through internally developed education programs. The concept of the information center (IC) arose out of the need for end-user support in the design and development of computer-based applications. Often associated with the MIS department of an organization, the IC assists the end user with issues of project selection, scope, and selection of appropriate development tools. In addition, the IC offers a resource for technical assistance for the end user while still encouraging the creativity and autonomy generally associated with end-user development projects. The existence of an information center within an organization is a sign of a strong commitment to end-user computing and application development.

14-3: TOOLS FOR DSS DEVELOPMENT

As DSS implementation within the modern organization becomes more common, it ushers in new and more powerful DSS development tools. Tools for specific decision support techniques, such as spreadsheet management or text management, are now commonly found on most business-computing desktops. Multiple technique development tools that incorporate two or more design capabilities such as spreadsheet, text, and graphical presentation techniques are also becoming increasingly available. Finally, highly sophisticated DSS development tools, referred to as DSS generators,

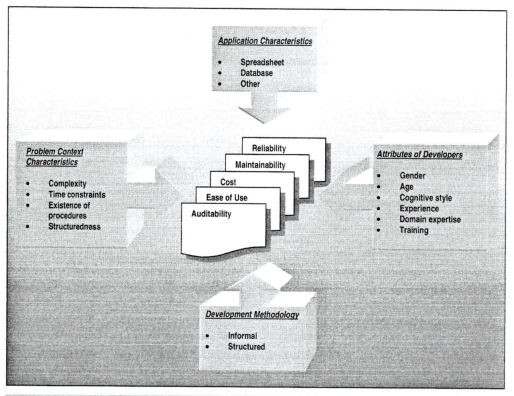

FIGURE 14-4 Factors Influencing Risks and Outcome Characteristics of End-User-Developed Applications

Source: Adapted from Janvrin and Morrison (1996), p. 348.

also facilitate the development of equally sophisticated and complex DSS applications. In this section, we examine the various tools and methods of classifying them.

DEVELOPMENT TOOL CLASSIFICATION

A wide variety of schemes and frameworks attempt to classify DSS design and development tools. Some methods classify the tools according to the development techniques offered by the tool. Others look at the specific role played by the tool during the course of DSS development. Still others focus on the type of interfaces generated by the tool. A thorough understanding of the various DSS development tools can provide both the experienced professional and the end-user developer with a better chance of choosing the most appropriate development platform for the task at hand.

A common and easily generalizable classification scheme for DSS development tools was proposed by Sprague and Carlson (1982). Figure 14-5 illustrates this hierarchical classification scheme.

The development tools are classified according to three levels of technology: (1) DSS primary development tools, (2) DSS generators, and (3) specific DSS applications.

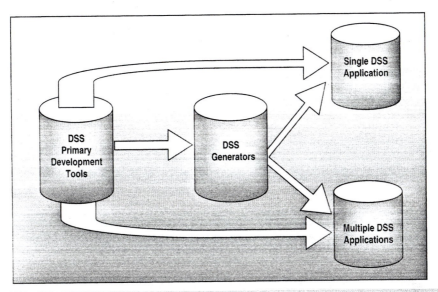

FIGURE 14-5 DSS Development Tools Classification

DSS Primary Development Tools

As implied by their name, the primary development tools are the lowest level of DSS development technology. In this category, we find the programming languages, code and text editors, graphics development applications, and database query mechanisms employed during the development of either a DSS generator or a specific DSS application. A detailed discussion of these elements is beyond the scope of this text, but a great deal of literature addresses the programming of DSS applications if one needs additional information (e.g., Lotfi and Pegels, 1996; Sprague and Carlson, 1982).

DSS Generators

According to Sprague and Carlson's classification, a DSS generator is a "package of hardware/software which provides a set of capabilities to build specific DSS[s] quickly and easily" (1982, p. 10). A wide variety of commercially available DSS generators can be found ranging from Microsoft's Excel, a spreadsheet package found on most business-computing desktops, to highly sophisticated and often expensive applications such as MicroStrategy's DSS Agent. Regardless of the level of sophistication, however, all DSS generators possess integrated and diverse functionality, including decision modeling, report design and generation, presentation graphics, and basic database management capabilities.

The main advantage of DSS generators over primary DSS development tools is convenience. Issues such as integration among the tools, access to multiple tools, import and export of data, and nonstandardized command structures across tools are all eliminated with the use of a DSS generator. The tight integration among the various functions of the DSS generator allows the developer to concentrate on the design process rather than on getting two tools to work together or to transfer data.

One important item to note about DSS generators is that their name is not completely accurate. In most cases, a DSS generator does not actually "generate" anything. Rather, it is simply an integrated set of tools and functions that assists in the design and implementation of a DSS. In reality, the true "DSS generator" is the developer.

Specific DSS Applications

The third level of DSS technology is the specific DSS application. In certain knowledge domains, decision makers face problems that, although semistructured, are widely experienced and generalizable across a large set of scenarios. In these cases, a commercially developed DSS application can be acquired rather than internally developed. One example of this type of problem context is the use of DSSs in the medical profession. Even though each specific situation encountered by a medical professional is unique, the vast knowledge base of medicine is for the most part generalizable across the human race. For this reason, adoption of a commercially available DSS that can assist in diagnosis or treatment of medical conditions or illnesses is a more expedient, economical, and reliable way to acquire the necessary decision support than internal DSS development using a generator.

Referring again to Figure 14-5, we can see that the relationships between the three elements of the classification are not strictly hierarchical in nature. DSS tools can be used to construct a DSS generator, which can be used to develop a single DSS or possibly many different DSS applications. Those same tools can be used to directly develop a specific DSS application. Likewise, a commercial DSS generator can be acquired by an organization to develop a wide variety of specific DSS applications. The choice of sequence depends on the specific needs of the decision maker and on the nature of the problem context.

DEVELOPMENT TOOL SELECTION CRITERIA

The evaluation of whether to use a selected set of primary DSS development tools or to acquire an existing DSS generator is a complex decision in its own right and often involves a significant amount of research and analysis. A number of criteria must be considered when making the decision to build from scratch or buy a commercial development generator. Table 14-3 contains a brief listing of the various criteria that are important in the selection of a DSS generator.

Within each of these categories, numerous questions must be answered before deciding to acquire the DSS generator. Does the data management system allow for creation of individual or personal databases? Does the user interface generator provide

TABLE 14-3 Selection Criteria for DSS Generators

- Data management functions
- Model management functions
- User interface capabilities
- Compatibility and degree of connectivity
- Available hardware platforms
- Cost
- Quality and availability of vendor support

support for a wide variety of input and output devices? What are the ongoing maintenance and upgrade costs associated with a particular vendor's application? What technical support is available for this application? Remember that the realm of decision
support is complex, varied, and often unpredictable in terms of specific needs. The DSS
generator must allow for the broadest possible spectrum of development support to
achieve the necessary economies of ownership and to ensure long-term usefulness.

14-4: DSS USER INTERFACE ISSUES

It is often stated that "a software application is only as effective as its interface." In the
case of a DSS, this adage is possibly even more fitting than in other application environments. Because the purpose of a DSS is to work in harmony with one or more decision makers, the DSS interface necessarily possesses certain unique characteristics and
requirements over applications, such as transaction processing, or simple data entry
systems. The majority of the unique characteristics of the DSS interface stem from the
equally unique characteristics of the typical DSS end user:

- DSS end users play a role in the organization that is filled based on some skill set
  other than basic computing skills. As such, the typical DSS end user may not possess a high degree of computer literacy or facility.
- DSS end users are generally afforded more latitude in exercising individual judgment than other knowledge workers.
- The types of decisions DSS end users make generally have a greater impact on
  the performance of an organization than other knowledge workers.
- DSS end users generally spend more time performing tasks that do not require a
  computer and, therefore, only use the DSS for a small portion of their typical day.
- The unique nature of the decisions in which the DSS will play a part necessitates
  the accommodation of end-user personal preferences.

Because of these, and other, unique characteristics of the DSS end user, certain
interface issues become extremely important if the DSS is to be a success. Several factors associated with the design of the DSS can be directly related to the quality of the
user interface:

Learning curve: How long does it take the DSS end user to effectively learn his or her
  task? Effective interface design can contribute significantly to lowering the learning curve of a new DSS user and, therefore, contributing to the end product with
  much greater efficiency.

Operational recall: How difficult is it for the DSS user to refresh themselves in the operation
  of the DSS after not using it for a period of time? Recall that the DSS, unlike a transaction processing system, is used for only part of the decision process and may, therefore, sit idle for extended periods. The quality and simplicity of the interface can assist
  the user in recalling procedures more quickly than a complex interface might allow.

Task-related time: How long does the typical decision task take? Although a certain
  percentage of task-related time can be attributed to the execution and response
  time of the DSS, proper interface design can significantly reduce wasted time in
  the decision-making process.

System versatility: To what extent does the system provide facilitation in a variety of end-user tasks? A DSS is generally designed and implemented to provide assistance to a specific range of tasks, but over time, new tasks related to its use often arise. Generally speaking, adding further functionality to a DSS is less of a problem when it involves an interface designed in a flexible manner to allow for scalability and expansion.

Error-trapping and support: What is the range of errors that can be made by the DSS end user, and what are their relative severities? Certain errors must be considered as severe when they will most likely lead to an erroneous decision. These types of errors generally cannot be managed to any great extent by the DSS because their source is probably a bad model or an ill-advised conclusion. Other errors, however, are less severe but must still be identified and corrected if the DSS is to be used effectively. Proper interface design can serve to minimize the time lost due to these less severe error types. One example is to not have the user reenter a large list of numbers or attributes simply because he or she made an error on the second to the last entry. In addition, the interface can provide useful feedback to the user in the event an error is detected such that a clear understanding of the nature of the error and the appropriate corrective response can be achieved.

Degree of system adaptability: To what extent is the DSS designed to adjust to an individual user's use of the system? Some users will find it natural to enter dates as month-day-year while others may find it more appropriate to enter dates as day-month-year. The interface can offer the end user a choice for such scenarios. Another example of system adaptability may be the provision for an end user to elect to use a graphical instruction method, a keyboard shortcut, or a command line method to issue instructions.

Management of cognitive overload: To what extent does the DSS reduce the need for the user to remember things while using the system? We know that human cognitive processes are limited (recall the theory of seven, plus or minus two). The DSS interface can make extensive use of informative labels for open screens and hot tips for iconic commands to reduce the degree of cognitive overload on the part of the user.

Degree of personal engagement: To what extent is the DSS enjoyable to use? The interface can play a significant role in providing an engaging experience for the user during use, which is not to suggest that cartoons or jokes should be included in the interface but rather the inclusion of timely messages intended to keep the user informed. Examples of these types of messages could be keeping a constant stream of communication going with the user so that he or she knows what the system is doing at any given time, and providing warnings with regard to processes or commands that may take a significant time to execute. Providing progress reports for processes that are necessarily time-consuming, and various other methods, can significantly minimize end-user frustration with the DSS.

Degree of guidance and structure: To what extent does the interface provide tacit or explicit guidance to the end user? In some cases, guidance can come in a structured manner that literally walks the user through a complex set of procedures. In other cases, guidance can come in the form of providing default values for certain parameters.

Although certainly not exhaustive in nature, the preceding considerations are necessary when developing the final user interface to the DSS. Some of these considera-

TABLE 14-4   Prescribed Sequence for the Development of the DSS Interface

1. Determine the exact set of possible end users.
2. Determine the exact nature of use of the DSS for each identified end user.
3. Determine the sequence of steps or events each end user will employ to accomplish their task(s).
4. Create a process diagram or decision tree for each task identified in step 3 and review it with the end user for accuracy and completeness.
5. Ascertain which of the steps in each process will require direct interaction between the user and the DSS.
6. Determine the exact nature of the information requirements for each of the interactions identified in step 5.
7. Select an appropriate set of dialog approaches (menus, command prompts, windows, etc.).
8. Create a process diagram of the flow of all possible dialog, and review it with the end user for accuracy and completeness.
9. Design the interface screens to accommodate all requirements as determined in the previous steps.
10. Test it, analyze it, change it, test it, analyze it, change it. . . .
11. Update all decision diagrams as conditions change.
12. Create a bulletproof (idiotproof?) dialog for the DSS because the user will do something totally unexpected at some point.

tions can also be thought of as necessary in the design of any software application, but the unique nature of the DSS makes these issues even more critical to success.

In developing a DSS user interface, a prescribed sequence of events can be followed to ensure that all issues are given proper consideration. Table 14-4 contains such a prescribed development sequence.

14-5: CHAPTER SUMMARY

The design and development of a DSS is a significant undertaking that can result in huge benefits to the organization if done right. The selection of the development tools, methodology, and the gathering of requirements are all precursors to a successful DSS development effort. Designing and constructing the DSS are only half the battle, however. Once the system is complete, it must be fully implemented and integrated into the organization if any of its benefits are to be realized. We will focus on the issues of DSS implementation in the next chapter.

Key Concepts

- Basic DSS development strategies

  Program a customized DSS

  This strategy employs either a general-purpose programming language (GPL) or a fourth-generation language (4GL).

Employ a DSS generator

This strategy employs application systems that eliminate the need for programming thousands of individual instructions or code in the design and construction of a DSS.

- DSS analysis and design process

System development life cycle (SDLC)

The SDLC portrays the analysis and design processes as a series of iterative and recursive phases, each with its own set of required inputs, activities, and deliverables. These processes are problem definition, feasibility analysis, systems analysis, systems design, code generation, testing, implementation, and maintenance.

ROMC analysis

This approach focuses on the analysis effort developing understanding of representations (R), operations (O), memory aids (M), and controls (C):

Representations: The analysis focuses on characterizing the various representations available for use as methods of communication between the DSS user and the DSS application.

Operations analysis: The analysis is focused on identifying those activities necessary for the DSS to perform or facilitate the generation and delivery of the various representations contained within the system.

Memory aids: Memory aids are the components intended to provide support to the use of the various identified representations and operations.

Controls: Controls are mechanisms that help the DSS extract or synthesize a particular decision-making process from the available representations, operations, and memory aids.

Functional category analysis

Functional category analysis focuses on the identification of specific functions necessary for the development of a particular DSS from a broad list of available functions including selection, aggregation, estimation, simulation, equalization, and optimization.

- DSS development process (DDP)

The development of a DSS employs a unique approach because of its nature of dealing with semistructured or unstructured problems.

Problem diagnosis

The first step in DSS development is the formal identification and recognition of a problem context requiring decision support.

DSS objectives and resources

During the problem definition phase, the specific objectives of the DSS and key decisions to be supported by the DSS must be carefully identified. Further, specific standards of performance must be established and detailed in a manner that allows for an objective assessment of their attainment.

System analysis

Within this phase, a detailed set of requirements—including functional, interface, and coordination requirements—for the DSS is generated.

System design

During the system design stage of the DSS development process, the determination of specific physical components, structure, and development platforms is made.

System construction

During the system construction phase, the designer uses an iterative prototyping approach that allows for small, yet constant, refinements to be made to the system based on the feedback received from testing and user involvement.

System implementation

The goal of the system implementation phase is to test, evaluate, and deploy a fully functional and documented DSS.

Incremental adaptation

The final stage in the DSS development process is a never-ending revisiting of the activities contained within the earlier stages in an effort to enhance the capabilities of the DSS based on experiences and knowledge gained as a result of its use.

- The prototyping process requires a significantly higher level of interaction between the analyst and user, and the nature of the cooperation between the two is generally much more intense than in an SDLC-based design effort.

- Contrary to the user's more passive or reactive involvement in the SDLC approach, the DSS user is an integral and active part of the usability and evaluation activities during DSS development.

- Two basic kinds of prototypes

Throwaway prototypes

The throwaway prototype is intended for demonstration purposes only and is discarded after its usefulness as a demonstration tool is depleted. The advantages of using throwaway prototypes include the increased speed over a life cycle approach, the expediency of gaining long-term support, and the lower cost in the early stage.

Iterative prototypes (evolutionary prototypes)

The iterative prototype is redeveloped and continually refined until it completely satisfies the requirements and needs of the DSS users, and then any necessary integration with other existing organizational systems is performed.

- Benefits of prototyping

The significant reduction in development time and generally lower cost over an SDLC approach make prototyping an attractive method in today's fast-paced managerial environment.

The more immediate nature of user response and feedback regarding system functionality can often result in a greater degree of support from senior management.

The iterative nature of the prototyping process promotes an increased user understanding of the system and its range of capabilities.

- Limitations of prototyping

A slower and more cautious pace permits greater attention to detail in the development of comprehensive documentation and a more thorough understanding of the system's benefits and corresponding costs, which may be lost in a pure prototype process.

A prototype development process increases the likelihood that system maintenance will be more difficult than in a comparable SDLC-based system.

- Necessary skill set for the DSS developer

Understand the problem domain

Understand the specific user requirements

Understand the available development technologies

Have access to appropriate knowledge

- End-user computing

End-user computing refers to the involvement of end users in the development of a computer-based system. End-user DSS developers are those individuals who build computer-based systems either to solve organizational problems or to assist in the pursuit of decision-making activities. The identifiable characteristics of the population of end-user developers are the wide variance in organizational role and individual computer skill level.

- Advantages of an end-user-developed DSS

A reduction in delivery time of the application

The elimination of the time-consuming process of gathering and formalizing the end users' specifications for the system

The reduction of implementation problems following the design phase of the project

Lower cost of development due to the reduction in time and organizational resources associated with the development of the system

- Risks of end-user DSS development

The final product will lack the necessary quality to make it a reliable and useful decision aid.

The final product will lack quality documentation.

The lack of necessary security measures built into the system may potentially result due to the end user's lack of familiarity with proper application security controls.

- DSS development tool classification

The DSS primary development tools

The primary development tools are the lowest level of DSS development technology, such as programming languages, code and text editors, and graphics development applications.

The DSS generators

A DSS generator is a "package of hardware/software which provides a set of capabilities to build specific DSS[s] quickly and easily." The main advantage of DSS generators over primary DSS development tools is convenience.

The specific DSS applications

In certain knowledge domains, because the problems faced by decision makers are widely experienced and generalizable across many scenarios, a commercially developed DSS application may be preferable to one that is internally developed.

Questions for Review

1. What are the two basic strategies for DSS analysis and design?
2. Explain domain-specific DSS generators.
3. List and briefly describe the processes of the system development life cycle (SDLC) approach.
4. Describe the functional category analysis approach. What is its most significant benefit?
5. During the system analysis phase of the DSS development process, what kinds of requirements should be identified?
6. Describe the major task(s) of the system design and construction phases of the DSS development process.

7. What are the strengths and weaknesses of the traditional SDLC approach?
8. What is prototyping?
9. List and briefly describe the two kinds of prototypes. Compare their advantages and limitations.
10. Compare the SDLC and the DDP in terms of user roles and the level of user involvement.
11. List and briefly describe the benefits and limitations of prototyping.
12. What skills are necessary to be a DSS developer?
13. Explain the concept of end-user computing.
14. Identify the advantages and risks of end-user DSS development.
15. Classify the DSS development tools.
16. How do you evaluate the selection of DSS development tools?

For Further Discussion

1. Use the ROMC analysis approach to analyze a DSS development project.
2. Why do we need a unique development approach to the DSS other than the traditional SDLC?
3. Discuss the importance of quantifying DSS objectives.
4. Compare DDP with SDLC. Discuss the major differences between these two system development approaches
5. Discuss the diversity of the DSS developers within organizations and the effects of this diversity.
6. Observe a decision-making process in an organization you are familiar with. Assume that you are developing a DSS for this process. List your considerations for selecting the development tool(s).

15

IMPLEMENTING AND INTEGRATING DECISION SUPPORT SYSTEMS

Learning Objectives

◆ Understand that the essence of implementation is the introduction of change

◆ Learn several theoretical models of change

◆ Based upon the sources of project initiation, identify the six patterns of implementation

◆ Examine the frameworks for system evaluation: overall software quality, attitudinal measures of success, technical measures of success, organizational measures of success

◆ Learn how to measure user satisfaction toward a DSS

◆ Review the four categories of measurement in a generalized framework to measure the success of a DSS: system performance, task performance, business opportunities, and evolutionary aspects

◆ Comprehend the risk factors in DSS implementation projects

◆ Demonstrate how to formulate possible implementation strategies for dealing with identified risk factors

◆ Consider the importance of integration

◆ Investigate the concepts behind global DSS integration

◆ Recognize the factors that can result in resistance to changes associated with a new system

<hr>

⟨ **DSS MINICASE** ⟩

3COM ASSIST CUSTOMER SERVICE
WEB SITE

3Com Corporation has a problem its competitors envy. Since the company's founding in 1979, sales skyrocketed to nearly $2.3 billion in 1996. As one of the data networking industry's largest and fastest growing companies, 3Com serves more than 32 million users in 32 countries worldwide.

One critical corporate challenge is how to provide an ever-expanding customer base with the world-class anytime, anywhere global support that is the company's hallmark. After the number of its customer support personnel more than doubled over the last few years, 3Com concluded that ongoing staff expansion is not a viable long-term customer service strategy.

"We can't continue hiring at the present rate, or our support organization will outgrow the company," Bob Noakes, manager, Internet commerce marketing, says. "To preserve our quality of product support, we need to give customers alternative and equally satisfactory ways to resolve problems without calling us."

SPEEDING PROBLEM RESOLUTION

To create more options for product support, 3Com decided to enhance its customer service offering on the World Wide Web. The Web's tremendous round-the-clock accessibility worldwide makes it an unparalleled vehicle to enhance customer service. 3Com is a key player on the Internet, able to connect millions of people worldwide with its Internet access solutions. Still, 3Com believes it can do much to enhance its Web offering. The company's initial Web technical support provided no information, and customers relied on search mechanisms to find solutions on their own.

To bring intelligence to its Web site, 3Com adopted Inference Corporation's CBR technology. By merging existing support information with CBR, 3Com created an interactive troubleshooting tool with hot links that gives customers step-by-step guidance to problem solving. Anyone with a Web browser can access the service regardless of the user's operating platform.

MINIMUM DEVELOPMENT AND MAXIMUM BENEFIT

3Com ASSIST was built using Inference's CasePointÆ WebServer, Windows NT version; CBR Express; CasePoint; CBR Tester; and CBR Search Engine for Windows.[1] Inference's CBR software uses an approach similar to a doctor's medical diagnosis. The computer system is given details of a series of cases illustrating common problems, together with the accepted path to resolve them. The software leads a caller with a query through a series of questions and answers to identify a solution.

PUTTING KNOWLEDGE TO WORK

3Com is known for the superior quality and reliability of its network adapters, the interface devices that connect computers to networks. The EtherLink III adapter is 3Com's highest volume product, accounting for roughly 40 percent of the company's business.

The company has sold more than 32 million EtherLink IIIs, and although only a low percentage ultimately requires support, that number is nonetheless large and growing. Because the product generates the highest volume of customer support calls, Noakes expects that its inclusion on 3Com ASSIST will make a substantial contribution to the company's call avoidance strategy.

<hr>

[1]Inference, CasePoint, CasePoint Search Engine, CasePoint WebServer, CBR Express, CBR Express Tester, and CBR Generator are trademarks of Inference Corporation.

(continued)

```
                      ╱─────────────────────╲
                      │     DSS MINICASE      │
                      ╲─────────────────────╱
```

(continued)

The 3Com Impact External Digital Modem is a new but not highly complex product that experienced a high percentage of calls per shipment initially. "The modem's ISDN technology is unfamiliar to many users, and we're also dealing with less sophisticated customers," Noakes says. "3Com ASSIST is an ideal way to reduce calls per shipment."

QUICK RESOLUTION

"By putting a tool to resolve problems directly in our customers' hands, we expect to promote call avoidance," Noakes says. "Equally important, we hope to turn the information we receive from customer inquiries into self-help."

3Com hopes that half the people using products supported by 3Com ASSIST will be able to resolve their problems on the Web. Customers can avoid waiting and actively solve their own problems.

After starting with two product lines, 3Com plans to expand 3Com ASSIST to include more products. "One goal is to be better at capturing information when customers call," Noakes says. As 3Com ASSIST goes forward, the company will work on integrating CBR with other methods to capture information. "Since CBR is OLE compliant, we expect to integrate the system with Clarify, multimedia, other databases, online documentation and marketing information."

Check out how 3Com Corporation integrated Inference's CBR technology into 3Com ASSIST by visiting www.infodeli.3com.com/wcp/profile1.htm.

15-1: DSS IMPLEMENTATION

FOR ALL THE MARBLES . . .

By now, the need for a unique approach to the design and construction of a DSS should be evident. Equally important is the complex process of implementing the DSS and integrating it into the organization. It is probably the most important step in the entire DSS design process because without successful implementation, the greatest DSS ever created will go unused or perhaps even unnoticed. The implementation process is, metaphorically speaking, "for all the marbles."

The nineteenth-century author Washington Irving once observed:

> There is a certain relief in change, even though it may be from bad to worse; as I have found in traveling in a stagecoach, that it is often a comfort to shift one's position and be bruised in a new place.

Implementation is, in fact, the introduction of change. Although it is often referred to as if it were an "event"—as in "When we implement the system . . ." or "Following implementation . . ."—it is more accurately thought of as a set of activities focused on the successful introduction of the DSS into the organizational environment. As such, the position of the implementation phase in a classic SDLC model is somewhat misleading. By the end of this chapter, you will see that implementation is truly a dynamic activity that actually occurs throughout the entire development process and simply completes itself during the implementation phase of the project. Contrary to the other steps in the DSS development process where each phase marks an initiation of a set of activities, the implementation phase marks a completion of activities. Further, following Irving's observations about riding in stagecoaches, successful DSS implementation may require a series of incremental shifts within the organization that, at the time, may be painful to some while a relief to others.

INTRODUCING CHANGE INTO THE ORGANIZATION

A rich and extensive body of literature discusses the subject of change—its characteristics, the steps to take to achieve it, and the ways to measure its success. Pervasive in this literature is the recognition that the process by which the change is introduced is, in many cases, more important to its acceptance and success than the nature of the change itself. Although numerous models of change have been advanced, two elegantly concise ways of describing the process can be found in the Lewin-Schein theory of change and the Kolb-Frohman change model. We will briefly explore the components of each of these approaches in an effort to understand the concept of change.

The Lewin-Schein Theory of Change

According to the Lewin-Schein theory of change (Schein, 1956), the process of change occurs in three basic steps:

1. **Unfreezing.** The creation of an awareness of the need for change and a climate receptive to change.
2. **Moving.** The changing of the magnitude and/or direction of the forces defining the initial need for change through the development of new methods and the learning of new attitudes and behaviors.
3. **Refreezing.** Reinforcement of the desirable changes that occurred and the establishment of a maintainable and stable new equilibrium.

As you can see, the Lewin-Schein theory is simultaneously both structured and fluid. It is structured in the sense that the description of the three steps implies a specific order of events necessary for successful implementation. Yet it is fluid in the sense that the activities within each of the steps relate dynamically to the nature of the change, the magnitude of the change, and the environment within which the change is taking place. Zand and Sorensen (1975) directly applied this theory of change in a study that focused on a large sample of projects associated with the implementation of a variety of management science methods within organizations. The researchers found that success in handling the issues encountered at each step in the process was strongly correlated with the overall success of a given project. Table 15-1 lists the key issues identified by Zand and Sorensen at each stage of the change model.

Kolb-Frohman Model

A slightly more elaborate offering by Kolb and Frohman (1970) contrasts with the Lewin-Schein model. This model of change contains seven steps and is considered to be more normative than that of Lewin-Schein. The essence of the Kolb-Frohman model is the assumption that successful implementation depends on a specific pattern of actions between the users and analysts. An empirical study by Ginzberg (1975; 1976)

TABLE 15-1 Favorable and Unfavorable Forces During Stages of Lewin-Schein Change Model

Stage of Change	Favorable Forces	Unfavorable Forces
Unfreezing	• Top managers felt the problem was important to the company. • Top management became involved. • Unit management recognized a need for change. • Top management initiated the project. • Both top management and unit management were open and candid during discussion. • Unit managers were willing to revise some of their initial assumptions.	• Unit managers were unable to state their problems clearly. • Top management felt the overall problem was too big. • Unit management felt threatened by the project. • Some unit management resented the project. • Unit management lacked confidence in the analysts. • Unit managers felt they were capable of handling the project alone.
Moving	• Unit management and analysts gathered data jointly. • All relevant data were accessible and available. • New alternatives were devised. • Unit management reviewed and evaluated all alternatives. • Top management was advised of options. • Top management participated in the development of a solution. • All proposals for solutions were improved sequentially.	• Analysts were often not effective in educating unit management. • Unit management did not participate in the development of new solutions. • Unit management often did not fully understand the proposed solution of the analysts. • Analysts felt the project was concluded too quickly.
Refreezing	• Unit management tried the solution. • Frequency of utilization demonstrated the superiority of the new solution. • Analysts initiated positive feedback after early adoption and use. • Final solution was widely accepted after initial success. • Unit management expressed satisfaction with the new solution.	• Analysts did not try to support new managerial behavior after the solution was used. • Analysts did not try to reestablish stability after the solution was used. • Results were often difficult to quantify or measure.

Source: Reprinted from "Theory of Change & Effective Use of Management Science," by Zand, Dale E., and Sorenson, Richard E., published in *Administrative Science Quarterly,* Vol. 20, no. 4, by permission of *Administrative Science Quarterly.*

applied this model of change in the development of a series of hypotheses suggesting a strong relationship between the degree to which issues were successfully resolved at each of the seven stages and the overall success of the implementation process. His results indicated that projects that conformed closely to the normative Kolb-Frohman process showed a significantly greater degree of success than those projects that measurably deviated from the model. Table 15-2 lists the seven phases of the model and provides a brief explanation of the activities within each phase.

The purpose of reviewing these two accepted theories of change is to develop an understanding of the change process as it occurs during a typical DSS implementation. The models are not intended to be prescriptive but, rather, are intended as a descriptive framework within which the implementation process can be conducted.

PATTERNS OF IMPLEMENTATION

Alter (1980) suggested that the initial impetus behind the development of a DSS can be categorized in the following terms: (1) user stimulus, (2) managerial stimulus, or (3) entrepreneurial stimulus.

As the first two category names imply, the stimulus for a DSS project can result from the perceived needs of the users or the perceived needs of management. The third

TABLE 15-2	The Kolb-Frohman Normative Model of Change in System Development
Scouting	User and designer assess each other's needs and abilities to see if there is a match. An appropriate organizational starting point for the project is selected.
Entry	User and designer develop an initial statement of the goals and objectives. Commitment to the project is developed. User and designer develop a trusting relationship and a "contract" for conducting the project.
Diagnosis	User and designer gather data to refine and sharpen the definition of the problem and goals for the solution. User and designer assess available resources (including commitment) to determine whether continued effort is feasible.
Planning	User and designer define specific operational objectives and examine alternative ways to meet these objectives. Impacts of the proposed solutions on all parts of the organization are examined. User and designer develop an action plan that takes account of the solutions' impacts on the organization.
Action	User and designer put the "best" alternative into practice. Training necessary for effective use of the system is undertaken in all affected parts of the organization.
Evaluation	User and designer assess how well the goals and objectives (specified during the diagnosis and planning stages) were met. User and designer decide whether to work further on the system (evolve) or to cease active work (terminate).
Termination	User and designer ensure that "owernship" of and effective control over the new system rest in the hands of those who must use and maintain it. User and designer ensure that the necessary new patterns of behavior have become a stable part of the user's routine.

source assumes one or more persons from inside or outside the organization make an effort to sell the organization on the idea of developing a DSS. Building upon these three sources of initiation, Alter identified six generic DSS implementation patterns that differ in terms of degree of user initiation, degree of mandated use, and degree of user participation in the design and development. Each scenario is descriptively named to suggest its underlying characteristics. Figure 15-1 illustrates Alter's six generic implementation patterns.

Join Hands and Circle Round

This scenario is the ideal and most commonly employed, according to the normative literature and reported empirical findings on implementation. Assuming all other factors remain the same, higher levels of user initiation and user involvement in a DSS development project are associated with higher probabilities of success. In this scenario, it is assumed that no obvious solution can be determined in advance and that the user is ready to become involved in a cooperative problem-definition and problem-solving endeavor.

Service with a Smile

Here the user is simply looking to buy a product rather than a service. The form and content of the product are relatively clear-cut and predetermined. The main goal in this scenario is the completion of the DSS to specifications within the time and budget constraints set forth. Similar to Join Hands pattern, the degree of user initiation is quite high. In contrast to the previous scenario, however, the degree of user participation in development is relatively low.

FIGURE 15-1   Six Generic DSS Implementation Patterns

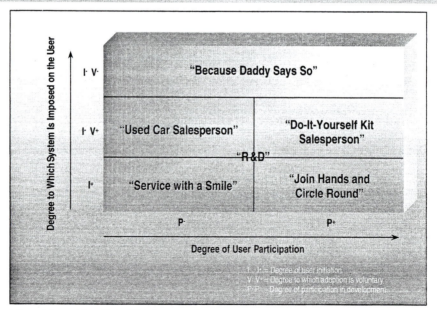

Source: Adapted from Alter, S. L. 1980. *Decision Support Systems: Current Practices and Continuing Challenges.* Reading, MA: Addison-Wesley.

Do-It-Yourself Kit Salesperson

As shown in Figure 15-1, the degree of user initiation in this implementation scenario is small but the degree to which adoption is voluntary is relatively high. This scenario is an effort to convert a low-initiation, low-participation situation into a more favorable one. In this case, the user must be convinced that the DSS is necessary to the success of the firm and must be encouraged to participate in its development.

Used Car Salesperson

This common scenario is characterized by a consultant or salesperson attempting to sell the need for a DSS to the user. It is not unusual for this situation to yield significant benefits to the organization because many successful innovations often originate outside the settings in which they are applied. This same scenario, however, has a comparatively high risk of implementation difficulties stemming from the external initiation of the project.

Because Daddy Says So

The fifth implementation situation is also considered a common one in which the senior management of the firm mandates the development and use of a DSS. Despite its commonplace occurrence, this scenario is considered to be the least effective method of introducing decision support technologies into an organization. Without sufficient user initiation and support, the DSS will never become satisfactorily institutionalized so that its value can be fully realized.

R&D

The sixth and final scenario identified by Alter lies squarely in the middle of all the others and suggests that the results of an internally initiated research and development effort can emerge into the regular implementation stream through any of the other five scenarios.

The identification of the six types of DSS implementation situations provides insight into the types of activities that can be considered positive steps toward a successful implementation project. In the next section, we will build upon this insight and focus on the development of a framework for DSS implementation strategies that can be applied to specific situations and development needs.

15-2: SYSTEM EVALUATION

KNOWING SUCCESS WHEN YOU SEE IT

Implicit in the process of implementation is the goal of success. If the implementation is a success then the effort is deemed worthy and sufficient. If, on the other hand, the implementation is viewed as a failure, then it is quite possible that nothing of the project can be salvaged and the question of what went wrong becomes the focus of all participants. Although the goal of success may be implicit, the measure of success remains less than clear. Just exactly what constitutes the successful design and implementation of a DSS? How do the designer and the users know success when they see it? In this section we will look at methods proposed to measure implementation success and several indicators of success that resulted from various implementation research efforts.

FRAMEWORKS FOR SYSTEM EVALUATION

Success is a somewhat elusive construct. One person's measure of success may be another's minimum acceptable level of expectation. Although no generalizable set of standards measures success of a DSS implementation, unless a set of localized standards is developed it will be difficult, if not impossible, to determine the degree of success of the project. The literature contains a number of approaches to measuring success, each with its own unique criteria.

Overall Software Quality

Boehm et al. (1978) proposed a framework for measuring success that focuses on the characteristics, or quality, of the software. Table 15-3 lists and briefly describes the elements identified in this framework.

Dickson and Powers (1973) suggested a more macro set of criteria in the form of specific quantitative measures:

- Ratio of actual project execution time to estimated project time
- Managerial attitudes toward the system
- Ratio of actual cost to develop the project to the budgeted costs

---

TABLE 15-3   Characteristics of Software Quality

Portability	Degree of platform or device independence: Software can be executed on a variety of hardware configurations.
Reliability	Degree of completeness: All of the software components are present and each is fully developed.
	Degree of accuracy: Software outputs are sufficiently precise to satisfy their intended use.
	Degree of consistency: Software contains uniform notation, terminology, and symbology within itself, and its content is traceable back to the requirements.
Efficiency	Degree of device efficiency: Software fulfills its purpose without wasting resources.
	Degree of accessibility: Design of software facilitates the selective use of its components.
Human-Engineering	Degree of communicativeness: Software facilitates the specification of inputs and provides outputs whose form and content are easy to assimilate and which are useful.
Testability	Degree of structuredness: Software possesses a definite pattern of organization of its independent parts.
Understandability	Degree of self-descriptiveness: Software contains enough information for the reader to determine its objectives, assumptions, constraints, inputs, outputs, components, and status.
	Degree of conciseness: No excessive information is presented.
	Degree of legibility: Software function and those of its component statements are easily discerned by reading the documentation or code.
Modifiability	Degree of augmentability: Software easily accommodates expansions in data storage requirements or component computational functions.

Source: Reprinted from *Characteristics of Software Quality,* © 1978, by permission of Barry Boehm.

- The degree to which managers' needs are satisfied
- Impact of the project on the computer operations of the firm

A close consideration of the criteria proposed by Dickson and Powers reveals that success, from their perspective, relates more to efficiency than effectiveness (recall Chapter 2). But even though efficiency may be an important element in measuring success, it must be subordinated to effectiveness if the goals of the project are to be realized.

Attitudinal Measures of Success

Another approach to the assessment of DSS design and implementation success is by measuring the attitudes of the users of the system with regard to various aspects of its use. One common approach is to focus on the degree to which the system is actually used by the intended user group. Measures such as the number of inquiries made during a given period or the number of accesses of the system during a specific set of activities provide potential indicators of success. Although initially attractive, primarily due to the ease with which they can be obtained, such measures fail to account for whether system use is mandated by the organization or whether alternative decision support mechanisms are available to the users. If use is mandated, then measuring the number of times the system is accessed does not necessarily indicate the success of the system. Furthermore, if no alternative decision support mechanisms exist for a particular problem context, then access of the system may be a measure of its being "better than nothing" rather than true user preference. The problems associated with directly measuring system use while still attempting to measure the users' attitudes toward a given system can be avoided by using the concept of user satisfaction.

The logic behind user satisfaction as a measure of success is that the users will view a DSS as favorable if they perceive it to be effective in supporting the decision-making process. The more effective the system appears to be, the more satisfied the users will be with the system. Ives, Olson, and Baroudi (1983) developed a 40-item measure of user satisfaction that synthesizes the work of several researchers in this area. Although it is a popular measure and appears to be reliable across various projects, its use in the context of a DSS development effort can be problematic. DSS users tend to base their responses to the questionnaire on their most recent experience with the DSS rather than on their overall experience with the system. Contrary to a typical organizational application where one experience is similar and easily generalizable to all others, the interaction with a DSS is not nearly as predictable. For this reason, measures of user satisfaction may vary greatly over time with regard to a particular DSS.

An alternative to measuring user satisfaction was proposed by Davis (1989). He used Likert scales[2] to measure attributes of two constructs associated with success: (1) perceived usefulness, and (2) perceived ease of use. The former construct focuses on the user's perception of whether the system brings utility or value to the activity within which it is used. The latter focuses on the user's perception of how easy the tool is to use. The distinction between these two constructs can be illustrated with a simple example. Suppose you are faced with the task of removing a large tree from the middle of an otherwise barren field. One tool you might consider is a bulldozer, and another is a chain saw.

---

[2]A Likert-type item consists of a single statement followed by a usually five-point choice with each choice phrased to indicate that the choices are equally distant from each other; for example, strongly agree, agree, no opinion, disagree, strongly disagree.

The bulldozer may actually elicit a higher degree of perceived usefulness over the saw because it could easily push the tree over in one motion and move it out of the way with little effort. The chain saw, however, for a variety of reasons, may elicit a higher perceived ease of use over the bulldozer. Factors ranging from familiarity with tool use, accessibility, environmental constraints, and other such issues can result in one tool being perceived easier to use in spite of it being perceived as less useful. The key measure of DSS success using Davis's approach is for the system to elicit both a high degree of perceived usefulness and a high degree of perceived ease of use. Table 15-4 lists several elements contained within each of the two constructs as they relate to DSS development and implementation.

Technical Measures of Success
A third approach to measuring DSS success is to determine whether the system does what it is supposed to do. In this regard, the technical functionality of the system determines system success. One advantage to focusing on the technical aspects of the system is that, for the most part, they are easily measured and readily accessible. For example, assuming the existence of a documented set of user requirements for the DSS, the degree to which the system accomplishes its original objectives, such as providing useful advice, may be an acceptable measure of DSS success. Another measure of success in this realm might be the number of DSS features consistent with the stated information needs of the users. Still another measure might be the adequacy of advice or explanations provided to the user during a specific problem-solving activity or, quite possibly, the number of cases submitted to the DSS for which no advice was offered. When an expert system is a component of a DSS, technical success may be measured by comparing the advice offered by a live expert to that of the DSS when both are presented with an identical problem. Depending on the nature of the problem context, technical measures of success may be adequate to determine the overall success of the DSS implementation project.

Organizational Measures of Success
A final category of success measures focuses on the degree to which the system meets or exceeds certain organizational needs or expectations. For example, the direct payoff to an organization from its use of a particular DSS, either through cost reductions, increased revenues, or both, may be a useful measure of DSS implementation success. Ratios of direct benefits to direct costs are also commonly used to determine issues of organizational success.

Meador, Guyote, and Keen (1984) proposed a set of conditions for which organizational appropriateness and, thus, DSS success can be ascertained. Table 15-5 lists these criteria for DSS success.

TABLE 15-4 Characteristics of Davis's Success Measures

Perceived Usefulness	*Perceived Ease-of-Use*
• Increases user productivity • Enhances choice effectiveness • Improves choice performance • Increases ease with which choices can be made	• Increases user understanding of interaction with system • Increases overall flexibility of system • Facilitates steeper learning curves • Increases likelihood of skilled application of system

TABLE 15-5   Criteria for a Successful DSS

- Improves the way decision makers think about problems.
- Fits well with the organization's planning methods.
- Fits well with the political approach to decision making within the organization.
- Results in alternatives and choices that are implemented.
- Is considered both cost-effective and valuable relative to its development costs.
- Is expected to be used for a measurable period of time.

MEASURING DSS SUCCESS

One thing is clear regarding the question of what constitutes success and what criteria should be used to determine its degree: All of the ways in which success can be addressed are important to some aspect of the DSS implementation. That being the case, we can incorporate the various approaches to measuring success into a generalizable framework for DSS evaluation. Klein and Methlie (1995) suggested a framework for evaluating a DSS that contains four categories of measurement. Table 15-6 contains the four categories and the various measures of success within each.

System Performance
The first of Klein and Methlie's categories focuses on the quality of the computer system. Issues such as system response time, availability, usage time, reliability, and quality of system support, among others, are identified and measured. These measures can be obtained using a variety of methods including direct observation, event logging,

TABLE 15-6   A Framework for DSS Success Evaluation

System Performance
- Efficiency and response time
- Data entry
- Output format
- Hardware
- Usage
- Human-machine interface

Task Performance
- Decision-making time, alternatives, analysis, quality, and participants
- User perceptions of trust, satisfaction, usefulness, and understanding

Business Opportunities
- Costs of development, operation, and maintenance
- Benefits associated with increased income and reduced costs
- Value to the organization through better service, competitive advantage, and training

Evolutionary Aspects
- Degree of flexibility, ability to change
- Overall functionality of the development tool

Source: Adapted from Klein and Methlie (1995).

and attitude or perceptual construct surveys. As discussed previously, the overall quality of the performance of the DSS is often highly correlated to user acceptance of the system.

Task Performance

This category of assessment takes a micro focus on performance and addresses issues related to the functionality of the DSS within the specific problem context for which it was developed. Ideally, a DSS is intended to provide the support that will result in an improved decision outcome. Unfortunately, however, the degree of uncertainty associated with a typical semistructured or unstructured decision context makes a focus on the quality of the outcome somewhat untenable in terms of performance evaluation. Once the decision is made, the outcome is often out of the control of the decision maker. Therefore, we can agree that a high-quality decision does not necessarily result in a high-quality outcome. Furthermore, a high-quality outcome can occur by chance, even in the face of a poor-quality decision. The point is that we assume a relationship between the quality of the decision made and the quality, or desirability, of the outcome realized. As such, we measure task performance by focusing on that which we can control (decision quality) instead of that which we cannot (outcome quality). Decision quality can be assessed in terms of time spent in the decision process, number of alternatives evaluated, and span of information searched. Additionally, qualitative measures dealing with trust or confidence, satisfaction, and understanding can also be included in this measure.

Business Opportunities

Klein and Methlie's third category measures the DSS's effect on certain organizational factors. The development and implementation of a DSS normally requires a significant commitment of organizational resources represented by both dollars and time. The effects of that commitment can be used to determine the level of success achieved in this area. This category is primarily quantitative in nature and includes measures that focus on increases in revenue, cost reductions, increases in training effectiveness, increases in competitive advantages, and changes in productivity, among many others.

Evolutionary Aspects

How well the DSS adapts to changes within the problem context and environment is the focus of this fourth category of performance measurement. Providing support to ill-structured decisions and problem-solving tasks is subject to the changes that can occur in the users' decision-making behavior, the problem characteristics, and circumstances under which the decision must be made. The ability of a DSS to adapt to these dynamics is often a function of the original development tool selected and the ability of the user to make necessary changes to data or models. Despite the highly qualitative nature of this measurement category, perceptions of flexibility and adaptability influence the overall performance quality of a DSS.

RISKS IN DSS IMPLEMENTATION PROJECTS

Recall from Chapter 4 that risk is a concept rooted in probability assessment. Often one cannot know the exact probability of one or more negative events occurring during the course of a project, nor can one ever be sure that all possible negative outcomes have been identified and assessed. So the bad news is that we cannot completely determine the scope of the possible risks and their exact probabilities of occurrence. However, the good news is that any identification of potential risk and any quality assessment of probability directly contribute to increased quality of the DSS implementation effort and, thus, the success of the project. To perform a risk assessment in any environment, one needs simply to know what risks are possible and to attempt to determine conditions that suggest an increased likelihood of failure.

Alter (1980) identified eight basic clusters of risk factors that can be used to assist in determining the degree of uncertainty during the DSS implementation process. Table 15-7 lists each of these clusters of risk factors, its effect on the project, and the typical way in which it presents itself.

DSS IMPLEMENTATION STRATEGY

A thorough risk analysis conducted using the factors outlined in Table 15-7 precedes the formulation of possible strategies for dealing with either the identified risk factors themselves or their expected consequences.

As with any organizational application development project, the choice of implementation strategy is based on a series of considerations. In the case of selecting an appropriate DSS implementation strategy, the choice depends on determinations of resource requirements and availability, likelihood of successful completion of the project, and the specific situational constraints associated with a specific strategy. Alter (1980) identified four general categories of DSS implementation strategies, each with its own set of unique characteristics and situational constraints. Table 15-8 summarizes the four strategies and lists several situations in which each would be considered appropriate.

It is important to note that the various strategies contained within the framework are not meant to be universally useful. For example, even though the strategy of avoiding change may minimize difficulties in implementing a new DSS, it may not be a viable strategy if the primary objective of the new DSS is to foster or promote change. In other words, the selection of an implementation strategy is a function of the stated objectives of the system and of the environment in which it will be implemented.

In the next section, we turn our attention away from the big picture of DSS implementation to the more focused but equally important activities of system integration. Without an effective integration of the DSS into the existing application infrastructure of the organization, the odds are small that the DSS will become an institutionalized component of the organization's daily decision processes.

ISSUE-BASED MANAGEMENT APPROACH TO DSS DEVELOPMENT AND IMPLEMENTATION

A new perspective on DSS design and implementation is emerging. Although it still embraces the understanding that DSS development and its associated life cycle are somewhat different from more traditional application development challenges, the concept of *issue-based management* can be successfully applied to the DSS development and implementation realm.

Simply defined, issue-based management takes a process-centric perspective with regard to the design of an information system and its associated applications. Using

TABLE 15-7   DSS Implementation Risk Factors

Risk Factor	Problem	Typical Situation	Result
Nonexistent or unwilling users	Lack of commitment to use the system	System not initiated by potential users and developed without their participation	Disuse; uneven use; lack of impact
Multiple users or implementers	Communication problems; inability to incorporate interests of many people	System involving voluntary use by many individuals or coordination among many people	Uneven use
Disappearing users, implementers, or maintainers	No one available to use or modify the system	Worst case: System is the vehicle of a person who leaves, or system initiator leaves before system is installed	Reduced use or disappearance of the system
Inability to specify purpose or usage pattern	Overoptimism on part of system designer and advocates	Assumption that non-computer personnel will figure out how to use the system	Disuse
Inability to predict and cushion impact	Lack of motivation to work or change work pattern without receiving benefits	No benefits from the system to people in the "feeder role"; forced changes in organizational procedures	"Why bother" syndrome; fear and/or annoyance
Loss or lack of support	Requirements for funding; obstruction by uncooperative people	Lack of budget to run system; lack of management action to use system effectively	System death or disuse
Lack of experience with similar systems	Unfamiliarity leading to mistakes	Developing an innovative system aimed at substantive change rather than automation per se	Technical problems; bad fit of solution and problem; misuse or disuse of system
Technical problems and cost-effectiveness	Cost of maintaining or improving system	Advocacy situation: No adequate way to estimate value of system either before or after potential improvements	Failure of system to meet needs; either limps on or is discarded

Source: Adapted from Alter, S. L. (1980). *Decision Support Systems: Current Practices and Continuing Challenges.* Reading, MA: Addison-Wesley.

this approach, the designers focus on the issues and objectives associated with each step in the development and implementation process rather than using the more traditional approach of focusing on the individual decision maker and the individual semi-structured problems normally encountered and requiring decision support. The proposed advantage to this method is that it allows the design and implementation of the DSS to become much broader in scope and more easily modified to support a wider variety of organizational decisions and, thus, a wider variety of potential decision

TABLE 15-8   DSS Implementation Strategies

Implementation Strategy	*Typical Situation or Purpose*	*Pitfalls Encountered*
1. Divide the project into manageable pieces	To minimize the risk of producing a massive system that doesn't work.	
Use prototypes	Success of the effort hinges on relatively untested concepts. Test these concepts before committing to a full-fledged version.	Reactions to the prototype system (in an experimental setting) may differ from reactions to the final system in day-to-day use.
Use an evolutionary approach	Implementer attempts to shorten feedback loops between self and clients and between intentions and products.	Requires users to live with continuing change, which some may find annoying.
Develop a series of tools	To meet ad hoc analysis needs by providing databases and small models that can be created, modified, and discarded.	Limited applicability. Expense of maintaining infrequently used data.
2. Keep the solutions simple	To encourage use and to avoid scaring away users.	Although generally beneficial, can lead to misrepresentation, misunderstanding, and misuse.
Be simple	Not an issue for inherently simple systems. For other systems or situations, it may be possible to choose between simple and complicated approaches.	Some business problems are not inherently simple. Insisting on simple solutions may result in skirting the real issue.
Hide complexity	The system is presented as a "black box" that answers questions using procedures not presented to the user.	Use of "black boxes" by non-experts can lead to misuse of the results because of misunderstanding of the underlying models and assumptions.
Avoid change	Given a choice of automating existing practice or developing new methods, choose the former.	New system may have little real impact. Not applicable to efforts purporting to foster change.
3. Develop a satisfactory support base	One or more components of the user-management support base is missing.	Danger that one support-gaining strategy will be applied without adequate attention to others.
Obtain user participation	The system effort was not initiated by users. The usage pattern is not obvious in advance.	With multiple users, difficulty of getting everyone involved and incorporating everyone's interests. With sophisticated models, reduced feasibility of user participation in model formulation and interpretation.
Obtain user commitment	The system has been developed without user involvement. The system is to be imposed on users by management.	It is difficult to obtain commitment without some kind of quid pro quo or demonstration that the system will help the user.

(continued)

TABLE 15-8 Continued

Implementation Strategy	Typical Situation or Purpose	Pitfalls Encountered
Obtain management support	To obtain funding for the continuation of the project. To obtain management action in forcing people to comply with the system or to use it.	Management enthusiasm may not be shared by users, resulting in perfunctory use or disuse.
Sell the system	Some potential users were not involved in system development and do not use it. System is not used to full potential by the organization.	Often unsuccessful unless real advantages can be convincingly demonstrated.
4. Meet user needs and institutionalize system	A system is to have many users in an ongoing application.	Because strategies under this heading are somewhat incompatible, emphasis on one may exclude another.
Provide training	The system is not designed in close cooperation with all potential users.	Frequent difficulty in estimating the type and intensity of training that is needed. Initial training programs often require substantial reformation and elaboration.
Provide ongoing assistance	The system is used by an intermediary rather than a decision maker. The system is used with the help of an intermediary who handles the mechanical details.	If the system is used by an intermediary, the decision maker may not understand the analysis in sufficient detail.
Insist on mandatory use	The system is a medium for integration and coordination in planning. The system purports to facilitate the work of individuals.	Difference between genuine use and half-hearted submission of numbers for a plan. Difficulty in forcing people to think in a particular mold.
Permit voluntary use	Avoid building resistance to a hard sell by allowing voluntary use.	Generally ineffective unless the system meets a genuine felt need or appeals to an individual user intellectually or otherwise.
Rely on diffusion and exposure	It is hoped that the enthusiasts will demonstrate the benefits of a system to their colleagues.	Ineffective; perhaps as much an excuse for lack of positive action as it is a real strategy.
Tailor systems to users' capabilities	Users differ in their ability and/or propensity to use analytic techniques.	Not clear how to do so. In practice, systems seem to be built to users' requirements, not their capabilities.

Source: Adapted from Alter, S. L. 1980. *Decision Support Systems: Current Practices and Continuing Challenges.* Reading, MA: Addison-Wesley.

makers. Although still in its infancy, several large-scale successfully completed international development projects used an issue-based management approach; its potential value to the DSS development community is gaining momentum.

A thorough description and analysis of the issue-based development approach is clearly beyond the scope of this text. For a brief overview, however, a comparative analysis of the conventional approach to DSS development and the issue-based method is provided in Table 15-9.

TABLE 15-9   Conventional Versus Issue-Based Approaches to DSS Development and Delivery

Area of Interest	Conventional Approach	Issue-Based Approach
Focus	• The decision maker • Single decisions • Making decisions • Generation of alternatives	• Decision-making issues • Interaction of decision issues • Focusing attention on decision issues • Setting of agendas
Favored domains	• Operational decisions • One-shot decisions • Functional applications • Department applications	• Strategic decisions • Recurring decisions • Cross-functional applications • Organization applications
Design and delivery	• The individual decision maker • Interaction between decisions not incorporated • Prototyping design • Design approach becomes the system	• Group decision making and consensus • Integration and consensus drive the process • Prototyping design and delivery • Delivery approach becomes the system
EIS readiness	• No tracking component • Emphasizes convergent structuring of data • Major transformation required to provide EIS functionality	• Incorporates tracking component • Balances divergent exploration and convergent structuring of the data • Easy transition to EIS functionality
Relevant emerging technologies	• Expert systems • Artificial intelligence	• Idea processing and associative aids • Multimedia connectivity platforms • Object-oriented programming

15-3: THE IMPORTANCE OF INTEGRATION

In some cases, a DSS may be developed and implemented in a manner such that it requires no special access or interface to other organizational applications and simply operates as a stand-alone decision support tool. With the increasing popularity of expert systems, executive information systems, and data mining applications, however, the isolated DSS is becoming virtually extinct. The costs associated with the development of an organizational DSS dictate that the widest possible community of decision makers be able to access the technology. Furthermore, the growing need for multiple and disparate sources of information requires the modern DSS to be "connected" in some manner to a large population of existing applications and data stores. The following discussion centers on this connectivity or integration of the DSS into the existing organizational computing infrastructure.

Integrating the DSS into the organization simply means that the new application is merged into the existing computing infrastructure in a way that gives the appearance of a seamless architecture to the user. This appearance of one agency rather than separate hardware, software, communications, and data access contributes significantly to the perception by the users of ease of use and usefulness that are so important to the success of a DSS implementation.

Another important benefit associated with integration comes from the various synergies created from simultaneous access to multiple decision support and development tools that facilitate the movement of models and data between the various applications. Once the decision maker is provided with a wide variety of integrated tools and support mechanisms, he or she can focus attention on using each of the tools to reach a specific objective within the problem context. Instead of diverting effort away from the problem at hand in order to achieve some application-related objective, such as the transfer of data from one DSS to the next or the modification of a model in one application using a tool contained in another, the decision maker can concentrate on solving the primary problem.

TYPES OF INTEGRATION

Two general categories of DSS integration can be identified: (1) functional integration, and (2) physical integration.

In functional integration, the various decision support functions of the DSS are integrated and linked to those of the existing infrastructure. This linkage provides common menu access, inter- and intra-application transfer of data and tools, and a common application interface at the same desktop client or workstation. In this way, single or multiple users can access all available organizational decision support mechanisms and resources on demand.

Physical integration involves the architectural bundling of the hardware, software, and data communication characteristics associated with the new DSS into the existing set of physical systems. In many cases, physical integration begins before the DSS is even designed because the need for integration with the existing infrastructure will, in some cases, determine which DSS development tools to employ and which software platforms to adopt for development.

The activities of both physical and functional integration are often quite technical and tend to be unique to each organizational environment. For this reason, any detailed discussion is beyond the scope of this text and is best left to the computer scientists who devote themselves to understanding the inner world of the machinery. It is sufficient for our purposes simply to realize the importance of integrating the DSS into the existing computing applications and to acknowledge the complexities associated with accomplishing this necessary objective.

A MODEL FOR GLOBAL DSS INTEGRATION

Numerous proposed models focus on the integration of DSS, ES, and EIS systems into existing computing architectures. Each of the models takes its own approach; for example, some are problem driven, some application driven, and some function driven. Furthermore, each proposed model of integration contains its own set of terms and titles ranging from management support system (MSS) to expert support system (ESS) to intelligent decision support system (IDSS). Regardless of the approach, however, the common bond among all of these proposed models of integration is the goal of global connectivity and access to all organizational communication channels and decision support mechanisms. Figure 15-2 depicts a generalized global integration concept for decision support within an organization.

RESISTANCE AND OTHER COMPLETELY NORMAL REACTIONS

One of the most common problems that arises during the implementation and integration of virtually any computer-based information system, including a DSS, comes in the form of the resistance by certain individuals or groups to the changes associated with the new system. The most important thing to realize about user resistance to new systems and resistance to change in general is that it is a normal and, in some cases, healthy human response.

Change tends to disrupt a person's frame of reference, particularly if it appears to suggest a future where lessons learned from past experiences will not hold true, or will be potentially unreliable. Technological change can be the most pervasive and the most formidable faced by the typical organizational member. Resistance to change is often most noticeable when such change is viewed as a crisis or a response to an emergency. In the case of an impending new DSS, which may not be completely understood or may appear to require significant effort to master, users may react in several ways. They may simply deny the change. They may actually distort information about the new system so that they convince themselves and others that the new system will not really affect the status quo. In other cases, however, they may engage in efforts, either overt or covert, to derail the new system, thus eliminating the source of the undesirable change (Marakas and Hornik, 1996). The importance of effective integration in order to reduce resistance to change cannot be overstated. No matter how important the new system is to the attainment of organizational objectives, resistance to change can result from a number of factors:

- *Self-interest.* If users achieved status, privilege, or self-esteem through effective use of an old system, they will often see the new system as a threat. If the plan threatens paid overtime by reducing effort needed in a particular problem context, users may fear the impact on their bank balance.
- *Fear of the unknown.* Users may be uncertain of their ability to learn new skills, their aptitude with new systems, or their ability to take on new roles.
- *Conscientious objection or differing perceptions.* Users may sincerely believe that the new system either is inappropriate or will be ineffective. They may view the

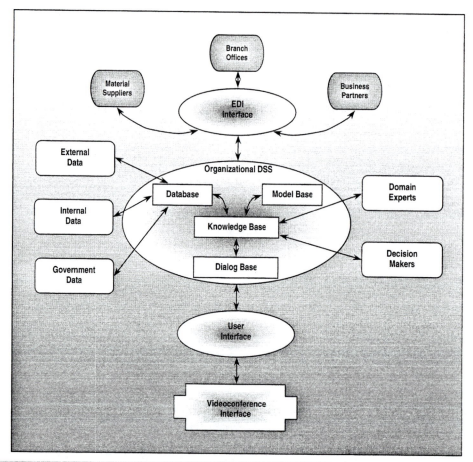

FIGURE 15-2   Generalized Globally Integrated DSS

Source: Adapted from Min and Eom (1994).

situation from a different viewpoint, or they may have aspirations for themselves or the organization that are fundamentally opposed to those of the designers of the new system.

- *Suspicion.* Users may not trust the new system or the advocates of the development project.
- *Conservatism.* Organizations or factions of people within them may simply be opposed to change. This attitude can result from a feeling that everything is okay, from being out of touch with customers, from lack of exposure to better ways of doing things, or from slowness of decision making.

Table 15-10 lists several potential resisters to a new DSS application within the organization.

The important point here is that if we can understand the roots of possible resistance to change, we can plan for it and overcome it before it becomes a significant obstacle.

TABLE 15-10   Potential Resisters to DSS Implementation

- *Managers.* Some may fear loss of job through automation or loss of importance.
- *Users.* Some may resist any form of computerization and others may experience difficulties adapting to user-DDS interfaces.
- *IS personnel.* Some may fear loss of power if technologies reside outside their sphere of control or influence.
- *Experts.* Some may fear a loss of importance or complete job loss.
- *Nonexperts.* Some may fear inability to be recognized in an environmental dependent upon decision support technologies.
- *Unions.* Resistance to change is often an effective vehicle to increase membership.

15-4: CHAPTER SUMMARY

With this chapter, we complete the cycle started in Chapter 1. The implementation of the organizational DSS is as important, if not more so, as the design of the application itself. Organizations must be aware of the importance of committing sufficient resources to the implementation and integration processes to ensure a successful and useful DSS project. In the remaining chapters, we look at supplementary issues related to decision support within the modern organization: the role of creativity in decision making and the future of DSS technologies.

Key Concepts

- DSS implementation (15-1)

  Implementation is the introduction of change through a set of activities focused on the successful introduction of the DSS into the organizational environment.
- Models of change (15-1)

  Lewin-Schein theory of change

  According to this theory, the process of change occurs in three basic steps: unfreezing, moving, and refreezing. Success in handling the issues encountered at each step in the process strongly correlates with the overall success of a given project.

  Kolb-Frohman change model

  This model contains seven steps. The essence of this commonly used model is the assumption that the probability of successful implementation depends on a specific pattern of actions between users and analysts. Researchers indicate that projects that conform closely to the normative Kolb-Frohman process show a significantly greater degree of success than those projects that measurably deviate from the model.
- DSS development project initiation sources (15-1)

  The initial impetus for the development of a DSS can be categorized in terms of three potential sources:

  User stimulus

  Managerial stimulus

  Entrepreneurial stimulus
- DSS implementation patterns

  The six generic DSS implementation patterns differ in terms of degree of user initiation, degree of mandated use, and the degree of user participation in the design and development. (15-1)

Join Hands and Circle Round

This scenario is considered the ideal situation. It is assumed that no obvious solution can be determined in advance and that the user is ready to become involved in a cooperative problem-definition and problem-solving endeavor.

Service with a Smile

In this situation, the form and content of the solution are relatively clear-cut and predetermined. The degree of user initiation is quite high; however, the degree of user participation in development is relatively low.

Do-It-Yourself Kit Salesperson

This scenario is an effort to convert a low-initiation, low-participation situation into a more favorable one. In this case, the user must be convinced that the DSS is necessary to the success of the firm and must be encouraged to participate in its development.

Used Car Salesperson

This scenario is characterized by a consultant or salesperson who attempts to sell the need for a DSS to the user. It has a comparatively high risk of implementation difficulties stemming from the external initiation of the project.

Because Daddy Says So

This situation is a common one in which the senior management of the firm mandates the development and use of a DSS. It is considered the least effective method of introducing decision support technologies into an organization.

R&D

This scenario suggests that the results of an internally initiated research and development effort can emerge into the regular implementation stream through any of the other five scenarios.

- The identification of the six types of DSS implementation situations provides insight into the types of activities that can be considered positive steps toward a successful implementation project. (15-1)

- Frameworks for system evaluation (15-2)

Overall software quality

The measuring of success focuses on the quality of the software.

Attitudinal measures of success

The measuring of success focuses on the attitudes of the users of the system with regard to various aspects of its use.

Technical measures of success

The measuring of success focuses on determining whether the system does what it is supposed to do. In this regard, the technical functionality of the system determines system success. The advantages of this method are that the technical functions are easily measured and accessible.

Organizational measures of success

The measuring of success focuses on the degree to which the system meets or exceeds certain organizational needs or expectations.

- Measurement of user satisfaction (15-2)

The logic behind user satisfaction as a measure of success is that the user will view a DSS as favorable if it is perceived to be effective in supporting the decision-making process. The more effective the system appears to be, the more satisfied the user will be with the system.

- A generalized framework for DSS success evaluation (15-2)

  System performance

  In this category, the quality of the computer system becomes the focus. The overall quality of the performance of the DSS is often highly correlated to user acceptance of the system.

  Task performance

  This category of assessment takes a micro focus on performance and addresses issues related to the functionality of the DSS within the specific problem context for which it was developed.

  Business opportunities

  This category measures the factors that contribute to the organizational aspects of the DSS.

  Evolutionary aspects

  The degree to which the DSS adapts to changes within the problem context and environment is the focus of this category of performance measurement.

- Eight basic clusters of risk factors in DSS implementation projects (15-2)

  Nonexistent or unwilling users

  Multiple users or implementers

  Disappearing users, implementers, or maintainers

  Inability to specify purpose or usage pattern

  Inability to predict and cushion impact

  Loss or lack of support

  Lack of experience with similar systems

  Technical problems and cost-effectiveness

- Four general categories of DSS implementation strategies (15-2)

  Divide the project into manageable pieces

  Keep the solution simple

  Develop a satisfactory support base

  Meet user need and institutionalize system

- The selection of an implementation strategy is a function of the stated objectives of the system and of the characteristics of the environment in which it will be implemented. (15-2)

- The importance of integration (15-3)

  The costs associated with the development of an organizational DSS dictate that the widest possible community of decision makers be able to access the technology.

  The growing need for multiple and disparate sources of information requires that the modern DSS be "connected" in some manner to a large population of existing applications and data stores.

  The integrating of the DSS into the organization contributes significantly to the perception by the users of ease of use and usefulness, factors that are important to the success of a DSS implementation.

  The potential for simultaneous access to multiple decision support and development tools can facilitate the movement of models and data between the various applications.

- Types of integration (15-3)

  Functional integration

  In functional integration, the various decision support functions of the DSS are integrated and linked to those of the existing infrastructure.

Physical integration

Physical integration involves the architectural bundling of the hardware, software, and data communication characteristics associated with the new DSS into the existing set of physical systems.

• Global DSS integration (15-3)

Global DSS integration creates a global connectivity and access to all organizational communication channels and decision support mechanisms.

• Several factors can result in resistance to changes associated with the new system. (15-3)

Self-interest

Fear of the unknown

Conscientious objection or differing perceptions

Suspicion

Conservatism

Questions for Review

1. Describe the relationship between system implementation and change.
2. Describe the Lewin-Schein theory of change and its characteristics.
3. What are the seven steps of the process of change in the Kolb-Frohman model?
4. What are the possible sources of initial impetus for the development of a DSS?
5. Briefly describe the basic concept Alter used for classifying implementation patterns. What is the value of this classification?
6. List and briefly describe the six generic DSS implementation patterns.
7. List and briefly describe the frameworks for system evaluation.
8. What are the various methods of measuring user satisfaction?
9. What are the differences between the evaluation of system performance and the evaluation of task performance?
10. Describe the generalized framework for DSS success evaluation introduced in this chapter.
11. Identify the risk factors in DSS implementation projects.
12. What are the differences between the conventional approach to DSS development and the issue-based approach?
13. List and briefly describe the types of integration.
14. Is resistance to change natural? Why or why not?

For Further Discussion

1. Observe the implementation of a DSS in an organization with which you are familiar. Identify its pattern of implementation.
2. Use the generalized framework for DSS success evaluation to evaluate the success of a DSS implementation project in an organization with which you are familiar.
3. Discuss the considerations for formulating and selecting implementation strategies. Discuss the importance of integration.
4. Study a successful case of system integration. Describe the type(s) of integration used. Discuss the effects of resistance to changes associated with the new system.

16

CREATIVE DECISION MAKING AND PROBLEM SOLVING

◆ Explore three perspectives on the theory of creativity: psychoanalytical, behavioral, and process

◆ Review five basic categories of ways of thinking: logical, lateral, critical, opposite, and groupthink

◆ Understand why it is important for decision makers to impart intuition and creativity to the decision process

◆ Recognize the categories of creative problem-solving techniques and their basic concepts

<DSS MINICASE>

FISHING FOR NEW IDEAS

Marsh Fisher was first captivated by creativity in 1964 when he attended a writing class at UCLA. Much to his amazement, he discovered that he lacked the ability to ad lib and generate ideas as quickly as his fellow students. As he drove home, however, he thought of a funny idea and wondered why he could not think of those same ideas in class. As Fisher pursued the elusive ability to make creative connections, he realized that his own production of creative ideas was limited primarily by his memory abilities and the variety of associations generated by his life experiences.

In general, the human mind is much better at recognizing information than recalling it, which explains why multiple-choice tests can be so much easier than essay exams. Fisher believed that his limitations to recall and to make a variety of associations were roadblocks that might be overcome with the help of computer software. Therefore, when he retired as cofounder of Century 21 Real Estate Corporation in 1977, he devoted himself full-time to developing a software package that would help people generate ideas by expanding their limited memory capabilities, helping them make associations, and asking probing questions.

Through his years of studying the creative process, Fisher concluded, "Creativity is about as magical as the skill required to add two plus two. Both can be taught and learned. And the more one practices any discipline, the more proficient one becomes."

The software package that resulted from his research is IdeaFisher: a 25-megabyte associative database (compressed to 7 megabytes) designed to stimulate thinking about virtually any subject and capable of being tailored by the user to include industry- or product-specific terms and links. IdeaFisher contains two databases that are linked in a unique manner to perform these tasks. The first database, the QBank, contains nearly 6,000 questions organized to clarify problems, modify ideas, and evaluate solutions. The second, the IdeaBank, contains more than 70,000 idea words and nearly 800,000 associated links. It is somewhat analogous to a huge free-association thesaurus.

The psychological foundation of Idea-Fisher rests on the principles of association, memory retrieval, and the use of analogy and metaphor. Thinkers interact with and use the idea words to stimulate ideas and associations in their own memory banks. New connections and associations are stimulated and a tremendous number of ideas can be generated in an extremely short period of time.

IdeaFisher speeds up the creative process by mimicking the way the human mind organizes and remembers experiences through the formation of associations to link words and concepts together. These idea associations invoke different mental images about the subject being considered, thus stimulating new viewpoints and ideas. Further, these associations can be used to generate ideas for new products or services, new markets or uses for existing products or services, advertising or promotional campaigns, special events or programs, training programs, presentations, stories or scripts, and corporate or product names.

A typical example of the use of IdeaFisher comes from Jim Shenk, manager of contracts and program management with CEC Instruments in San Dimas, California, who used the software to facilitate a strategic planning process. "We needed to do some strategic thinking for the division so we used IdeaFisher to help guide us through the process. The first thing it does is ask the questions that are so obvious that you usually don't ask them . . . and, all too often, don't really know the answer to . . . such as 'What business are we in?' and 'Why do our customers buy from us?'" As noted earlier, IdeaFisher offers nearly 6,000 questions to help stimulate thinking.

"We asked ourselves a lot of questions and the answers began to lead us toward an oppor-

(*continued*)

tunity. We have been heavily dependent on the aerospace industry, and this opportunity helped us create a market outside that industry, in the commercial aviation market.

"I've also used the software to help set up a mission statement and for understanding what our business is all about. It was extremely helpful for thinking through those questions. I also use the Strategic Planning Module, which has a lot of interesting questions specifically organized for planning, as well as the Presentation Planning Module." (A business and grant proposal module is also available.)

It is important to remember that Idea-Fisher does not create anything for you. It is not like a spreadsheet or a database program that will produce something. IdeaFisher just helps stimulate your own thinking and keeps you focused on questions that most of us tend to think are too obvious to even be considered. In actual fact, we can't answer many of those questions because we really have not thought about them . . . and when we do think about them enough to answer them, we find they lead us in directions that we might not have discovered before.

"IdeaFisher is a great way to find 100 new ideas . . . even if you reject 99 of them, so what? If you get one that's usable or opens up a new

opportunity, it makes the process worthwhile," says Shenk.

Clayton Lee, Houston-based inventor of the Orbiter, an impact-free trampoline treadmill, used IdeaFisher to reduce the unit cost of an add-on to the Orbiter . . . from $2,000 a unit to approximately $100 per unit. The vast reduction in cost opened up new markets. Said Lee, "IdeaFisher puts more thinking back into the marketplace. It helps develop our minds, which is something we've forgotten how to do. Thinking is no longer an elective skill."

Ron Sargent, a fluid engineer who designed the first cruise control for GM, the Porta Potti, and the Dancing Waters at Disney World's EPCOT Center, states, "We look at IdeaFisher almost as an open-ended platform, an AutoCAD for creativity."

IdeaFisher is a powerful thinking tool that can be used in a wide variety of ways. In addition to the previous examples, IdeaFisher has been used to write sermons, design tapestries, develop university courses, create product names, and invent a tree shaker modification for the orchard industry. It even played a part in Vice President Al Gore's reinventing government project where it was used by the Department of Commerce in a series of focus group meetings to help transform complaints into suggestions.

Despite the advances in artificial intelligence and computer-based decision support mechanisms, we still face making certain underlying assumptions about the human decision-making process that are just that: assumptions. For example, in the context of decision models, we often face the assumption that all alternative courses of action are known to the decision maker or are easily ascertained. In most unstructured problem contexts, however, this assumption is simply untenable. We know we must generate new ideas if an acceptable alternative is to be realized. Often this new idea generation is something that just happens during the normal course of problem solving. In other words, we know some things are happening, but we just do not fully understand their role in either the process or outcomes. One of these is the role of creativity in decision making. In this chapter, we will explore the concept of creativity and identify what is currently known about its role in managerial decision making. Through this investigation we can begin to see why the study of creativity is important in the field of DSSs.

16-1: WHAT IS CREATIVITY?

The reasonable man adapts himself to the world. The unreasonable man persists in trying to adapt the world to himself. Therefore, all progress depends upon the unreasonable man.

—GEORGE BERNARD SHAW

So, what do we really know about creativity? Can it be characterized as an act, an intentional process, an ideology, or a bit of all of these? Throughout history, the human spirit celebrated and affirmed creativity, yet it is clearly more than a cultural phenomenon. Where do our creative ideas and our ideas about creativity come from? Why are some of us viewed as more creative than others?

One way to think about creativity is as an ability to see the same things as everyone else but to think of something different. Creativity as a concept summons almost as many definitions of itself as the number of new ideas it generates. From philosopher to layperson, each person seems to have his or her own definition of what creativity is. Often the definition takes the form of "I don't really know what it is, but I know it when I see it." No matter the origin or focus of the definition, however, all seem to agree that creativity involves the ability to generate novel and useful ideas and solutions to problems and challenges.

Creativity involves the translation of our unique gifts, talents, and vision into some form of external reality that is both new and useful. Often creativity can involve the combining of existing objects intended for one purpose into a new object that serves a completely different purpose. When NASA realized the need to develop a low-friction coating for spacecraft heat shields to keep astronauts from burning up when reentering Earth's atmosphere, someone else saw the same coating as a way to solve the problem of eggs sticking to the frying pan: Teflon. When astronaut James Lovell and the crew of *Apollo 13* faced running out of oxygen while trying to get themselves and their crippled spacecraft back to Earth from the moon, creativity helped them and their team figure out how to use unrelated components from the lunar lander to fashion a carbon dioxide filter for the command module so they could recycle their oxygen. When the wine press and the die punch were developed in the seventeenth century, their respective inventors saw devices useful for making wine and for manufacturing castings for metal parts. Gutenberg, on the other hand, saw the same objects as the parts necessary to build a printing press capable of mass-producing manuscripts. Lucky for us that he did, too. Imagine reading this textbook on handwritten scrolls!

Increasingly, the problems we face have little or no precedent. As a result, we find ourselves in a constant struggle to find effective solutions that are familiar and easily understood. Compounding this struggle is the fact that we can easily become blinded by our own thinking and are often unable to break out of our customary heuristic approaches to problem solving (Marakas and Elam, 1997; Tversky and Kahneman, 1974).

Creativity is an important element in the generation of new ways to do old things and ways to do things yet undone. These new alternatives are essential to achieving the competitive edge so necessary to success and survival in the world's markets. Because a DSS is intended to support the decision-making process and an essential element in that process is the creative generation of new ideas, it makes perfect sense that the two concepts should be entwined.

16-2: CREATIVITY DEFINED

To venture toward an accepted definition of creativity, we can begin by looking at the socially constructed definition of a creative person. A creative person does things never done before. In this sense, important instances of creativity often include discoveries of new knowledge, invention of new technology, the composition of beautiful works of art and music, or the analyzing of a situation in a new way.

To further refine our definition of creativity, we must distinguish among three related, but unique, characteristics: (1) intelligence, (2) academic achievement, and (3) creativity.

Intelligence is the ability to learn and think. Academic achievement results in the degrees one receives after sitting through years of lectures, examinations, theses, and dissertations. If we compare these constructs to each other and to creativity, we can observe several conditions:

- Most individuals who are associated with the creation of things of significance are deemed intelligent.
- Many individuals with high academic achievement do not have a creative bone in their body or thought in their head. Even though they can solve complex problems, someone else must first formulate the problem for them (i.e., provide an equation).
- Individuals who are both intelligent and deemed highly creative often do not display a history of high academic achievement.

Thus, intelligence and academic achievement are not evidence of creativity.

Often, those not accustomed to being classified as creative place pejorative labels on those who are in an effort to characterize the nonconventional personality traits often found in creative individuals. We regularly encounter labels such as *eccentric, geek,* and *nerd* in conversations about a creative individual. Such labels characterize creative individuals as social anomalies and offer the "ordinary" person an excuse for not being able to compete with these anomalies. In addition, such labeling serves to marginalize creative individuals by alleging that they are either defective in some way or possess a distinct personality disorder.

Despite this social ignorance about creative individuals, we can generate a wide variety of formal definitions for the construct. If we consult a dictionary, we may find something like:

> *Creative:* characterized by originality and expressiveness, imaginative, generative, groundbreaking, innovative, original, handmade.

Although generous in their use of adjectives, dictionaries fall short of providing us with a useful definition of creativity. A review conducted by Seiffge (1974) noted that more than 100 definitions for creativity are available within the literature. Amabile

(1983) offered a definition that, although still somewhat nebulous, is used by a wide variety of researchers (Marakas and Elam, 1997):

> A product or response will be judged to be creative to the extent that it is a novel and appropriate, useful, correct or valuable response to the task at hand. Thus, a product or response is creative to the extent that appropriate observers independently agree it is creative.

Continuing along this path, Ripple (1977) offered several contentions regarding creativity that move us closer to operationalization:

> Creativity is a conceptually identifiable phenomenon; it can be measured and/or assessed; it has distinctive characteristics and development patterns; and its development and expression can be facilitated through educational training intervention programs. Thus, creativity can be learned.

Ackoff and Vergara (1981) echo these characteristics with their definition of the construct:

> Thus, creativity lies in the ability to redirect a line of thought taken in solving a problem. Because redirection is cognitive, it emerges from a specific problematic situation and it can be changed by instruction. Therefore, it can be learned.

This focus on defining creativity could easily command an entire manuscript, but here we must eventually settle on a definition to build upon when investigating barriers to, and enhancement of, creativity. For this purpose, I believe the definition offered by Ackoff and Vergara works well:

> We define creativity in problem solving and planning as *the ability of a subject in a choice situation to modify self-imposed constraints so as to enable him to select courses of action or produce outcomes that he would not otherwise select or produce, and are more efficient for or valuable to him than any he would otherwise have chosen.*

With this definition, we can proceed to explore the various enhancements and barriers to our creative potential. It should be noted, however, that most of the work conducted in this area, to date, is predominately descriptive in nature. Even those who posit that creativity can be increased by instruction and practice provide little or no such instruction and often do not specify the relevant types of practice. It does not mean that prescriptions for enhancing creativity are not available, but their development is not derived from either operational definitions of creativity nor any theories that explain it.

16-3: THE OCCURRENCE OF CREATIVITY

Often, individuals renowned for their creative output may be highly diligent, often bordering on the obsessive (Standler, 1998). Creative individuals seem to *need* to express their creativity, a situation that led society to shamefully exploit many of the great innovators throughout history. Being creative is extraordinarily difficult work, but essential to progress. Thus, it seems counterintuitive that society often takes great delight in denying resources to the creative people who need them the most. Given this obstacle, the characteristics of the creative individual are often associated with traits such as persistence, tenacity, arrogance, and stubbornness.

When creativity emerges, it often occurs in the form of an intuitive flash of insight in which the more or less complete idea is revealed. Equations, hypothesis testing, and analysis often come much later in this process. One of the principal prescriptions associated with being creative comes in looking for alternative ways to view phenomena or alternative ways to ask a question. The extremes of questions range from those whose answers are trivial to those requiring extraordinary effort. Although it is relatively easy to ask a question that is couched in one of the extremes, it is surprisingly difficult to find questions that lie near the mean and also result in an answer worth knowing.

Several oft-cited examples of such intuitive flashes can be found in the literature on creativity. One such example is that of George de Mestral's observation of how common cockleburs seem to have a natural penchant for attaching themselves to one's clothing. His transformation of this nuisance resulted in a rather useful product: Velcro.

Another common example is Arthur Fry's development of the Post-It removable note at 3M Corporation in 1974, based on a polymer adhesive that formed microscopic spheres instead of the more conventional uniform coating, developed by another 3M scientist, Dr. Spencer Silver. The characteristic that made Dr. Silver's adhesive virtually useless because it took literally years to set intrigued Arthur Fry, who was looking for a better bookmark for his church hymnal. Ignoring the conventional wisdom that every adhesive must be strong, Fry decided to try Silver's "poor" adhesive and subsequently developed a highly successful office product.

When one asks a question, an implicit constraint on the domain of the answer is in place. One generally is limited to answering the question within the context of the question. Because of this constraint, creativity rarely emerges from an answer but rather as a direct result of the question. During the late 1800s, a medical student, berated by his professor for carelessly allowing his culture dish to become contaminated with mold, realized that this contamination killed his bacteria and ruined the lesson being taught. During this period, many patients died from bacterial infections and medical students spent a great deal of their training learning about the various bacteria harmful to humans. In retrospect, neither the professor nor the student asked the proper question. Because the focus of the experiment was to grow the correct bacterium, no one bothered to inquire as to why the bacteria died. The creative question would have been "Can the property of molds to kill bacteria in vitro be used to cure bacterial infections in vivo?" In 1928, Alexander Fleming isolated penicillin from the common mold *Penicillium* for which he received the Nobel Prize in 1945. Fleming's discovery came from asking the proper question that professors of bacteriology could have asked, but did not, 50 years prior. From these examples, we learn that one can neither predict nor schedule creativity. It just seems to occur when the conditions are right.

It would appear many components influence creativity in individuals. Individuals seldom fluctuate wildly in their day-to-day or hour-to-hour creativity, but some individuals are generally more creative than others most of the time. To begin, without the abilities necessary to perform a creative act, it becomes highly unlikely that such an act will emerge. Conversely, however, just because a person possesses the ability to do something, does not guarantee they will ever do it. Individuals need motivation. In the context of creativity, a creative person is generally motivated to take advantage of opportunities in the environment that allow for the generation of a new idea or a new perspective. This self-motivated fluency in generating creative ideas is the most prominent characteristic of a creative individual.

Nicholas deWolf, the cofounder of Teradyne Corporation, often encouraged his engineers to increase their motivation toward creativity. One of his favorite quotes was:

> To select a component, size a product, architect a system, or plan a new company, first test the extremes of the domain and then muster the courage to resist what is popular and the wisdom to choose what is best.

Similarly, Albert Einstein, often regarded as a highly creative individual, developed the theory of relativity by thinking about what happens to matter when traveling at extreme speeds such as the speed of light. Other fellow physicists took heed of Einstein's motivation to be creative by questioning what would happen at the limits of very small sizes and energies, which resulted in the recognition of the laws of quantum mechanics.

THEORIES OF CREATIVITY

An ongoing debate among psychologists rages over the origins of creative thought. This debate continues to spark a wide variety of theories to explain why some people seem to be more creative than others.

The psychoanalytic perspective maintains that creativity is a preconscious mental activity. In other words, creative thinking occurs in our subconscious thoughts and, as such, is not directly accessible to our conscious thoughts. In contrast, the behavioral perspective argues that creativity is nothing more than a natural response to stimuli within our individual environments and that certain combinations of stimuli can lead to more creative behavior than other combinations. A third perspective, the process orientation view, sees creativity as a property of a thought process that can be acquired and improved through instruction and practice. Recent studies indicated that individual creativity is not as strong a function of individualized traits such as inventiveness or independence as previously thought and can, therefore, be learned and improved. This finding suggests that the potential for creative thinking exists to a greater or lesser degree in everyone (Marakas and Elam, 1997). Another result of this view is an influx of commercial products into the realm of the DSS intended to foster and enhance creativity in decision makers and organizational problem solvers at all levels of the firm.

It is generally agreed that to "teach" creativity, one must break down rigid thinking that blocks the generation of new ideas. In this regard, the enhancement of creativity is a process of change. By eliciting and facilitating different ways of thinking, creativity can be enhanced and new ideas can be generated.

DIFFERENT WAYS TO THINK

When we think about a particular problem context, the way in which we conduct our thinking can significantly affect on the generation of alternatives or the selection of an appropriate alternative from a choice set. Using a common classification scheme, five basic categories of ways of thinking can be identified: (1) logical, (2) lateral, (3) critical, (4) opposite, and (5) groupthink.

Logical Thinking

One way to think about a problem is for the decision maker to build on his or her experimental and analytical abilities. Logical thinking is perhaps the most common, most widely used, and most often recommended approach to solving a problem. This method of thinking is rooted in the model-building and quantitative methods of management science and is an integral part of the design and development of a computer-based DSS.

Lateral Thinking

Lateral thinking was originally identified by Edward de Bono (1970), a British physician and psychologist, as a method of providing an escape from conventional "vertical" lines of thought. The method is based upon the premise that the human mind naturally processes and stores information in accordance with a specific pattern of thought and action. Because of this logical categorization process, the mind becomes hindered in any attempt to change these recognized patterns of thought. Lateral thinking disrupts these patterns through the introduction of discontinuity. Table 16-1 compares the characteristics of conventional vertical thinking with those of a lateral thinking process.

Three major activities are available to promote lateral thinking processes: (1) awareness, (2) alternatives, and (3) provocation.

1. **Awareness.** The activities in this category are intended to redefine and clarify current ideas. Before any new ideas can be generated or any old ideas rejected, the range of current ideas must be fully identified and understood. Activities such as

TABLE 16-1   Characteristics of Vertical and Lateral Thinking

Vertical Thinking Process	*Lateral Thinking Process*
Concerned with stability and the identification of absolutes for judging various relationships.	Concerned with both change and movement and with trying to find new ways to look at things.
Seeks to find the "right" answer by using YES/NO justification at each step of the process.	Avoids looking for the absolute "right" or "wrong" answer and focuses attention on what is different.
Analyzes ideas with regard to their probability of success.	Analyzes ideas with regard to how they might be useful in generating new ideas.
Strives for continuity of process by logically proceeding from one step to the next.	Constantly strives for the introduction of discontinuity by encouraging illogical jumps from one step to another.
Rejects any information not considered to be immediately relevant and selectively chooses what to consider in the generation of new ideas.	Chance intrusions are welcomed and nothing is considered irrelevant.
Focuses primarily on the obvious and tends to progress using established patterns of thought.	Focuses on progress via avoidance of the obvious.
Guarantees that at least a minimally acceptable solution will be found.	Increases the odds that a new or innovative solution will be found but avoids making any guarantees.

the direct identification of the dominant ideas in the problem context, a review of common boundaries of the problem space, and identification of typical assumptions made about the problem are necessary to promote the awareness required to think laterally. The important thing to note here is that awareness activities are intended only to identify current ideas and not to evaluate them. The process of evaluation comes later.

2. **Alternatives.** In this second category of activities, a conscious effort is made to produce as many different ways as possible of looking at the problem context. The object is to provide the decision maker with a wide variety of approaches without regard to which one might be the best. To facilitate this process, an alternative can be generated using any number of assumptions without further justification of those assumptions. This flexible form of problem analysis frees the decision maker from the boundaries of traditional justification of assumptions and focuses attention on the "what if we could do it this way" part of alternative generation. Using techniques such as rotation of attention (looking at the problem from a different perspective), establishment of a quota of alternatives (forcing the generation of a given number of choices), and problem fractionation (breaking the problem into random subdivisions without regard to logical boundaries), the decision maker can begin the process of generating new ways of doing old things.

3. **Provocation.** The activities in provocation assist directly in the development of new ideas through introducing discontinuity into the thought process by forcing a change in the way the problem is viewed. Change from both within the problem context and external to the problem context can be provoked. Change from within can be introduced by using a reversal or backward approach to looking at the problem. For example, suppose we are faced with a situation in which parking meters are being used to discourage local commuter parking in a particular area. Reversal of the problem context would require analysis from the perspective of encouraging parking. From this perspective, we might suggest providing any out-of-town shopper with a ticket to park free one day each week while shopping. This solution could result in an increase in out-of-town shoppers parking near the retail areas and, thus, the discouragement of parking by daily commuters. In lateral thinking, it is not so much the correctness of the reversal that is important, but rather the simple fact that the perspective is reversed.

Another method of change from within is to employ exaggeration. In contrast to a reversal, the direction of change is one of increasing the characteristics and boundaries of the problem rather than simply reversing them. For example, suppose our problem is one of quality control of several products manufactured by our production facilities. Exaggeration could be used to view the problem as if every product we made were faulty. In looking at the problem from that perspective, we might discover new and innovative ways of completely redesigning the production facility to improve the quality of all of our products.

Change from outside the problem context can also be used to provoke lateral thinking. The most common method of introducing change from outside the problem context is to use analogies. Translating the problem into a completely different context, developing and refining solutions for it, and then translating those solutions back into the original problem context, can lead to the discovery of new and creative alternatives. Suppose, for example, our problem is to find a way to conserve the water used during a waste disposal process. The current process simply allows the soluble waste products to collect in a container of water; then they are periodically flushed away into a sewer or other carry-off with the water. The water facilitates the movement of the waste through the carry-off and into a more permanent collection point. The problem arises because the water mixed with the waste product requires that the permanent collection facility be large enough not only to accommodate the volume of waste generated but also to accommodate the volume of water used to move it. We need an analogy to view this problem in a new way.

One analogy to our problem might be to compare it to how logging operations use rivers to transport their cut trees to convenient loading points. The loggers simply push the cut trees into the river and then let the current of the river move the logs down to a collection point where the logs can be loaded onto trucks for transportation to a sawmill. When the logs are collected, the vehicle by which they were transported (the water in the river) is left to be used again by other natural processes such as rain and irrigation. The reason this process works is because the logs are not soluble in water and therefore are never really mixed with the water. This lack of solubility allows for the items being transported and the vehicle of transport to be easily separated upon reaching the desired destination. What if we did this same thing with our solid waste? By using a liquid to transport the waste that does not allow the waste material to dissolve, say oil, we can transport the waste to its collection point, recover the oil, and recycle the whole process, thus eliminating the need to store both the waste product and the oil. Voilà, introduction of change from without.

Critical Thinking

This method of thinking takes the position that certain elements within a problem context are most critical to any solution outcome. By focusing on the critical elements only, a solution with an immediate and measurable impact on the problem can be crafted. One common approach to problem solving based on the critical thinking method is called the Pareto Law (also commonly referred to as the 80-20 rule). Figure 16-1 illustrates a hypothetical Pareto distribution of parts of a product in relation to their individual cost.

As shown in the figure, 80 percent of the cost of the product is represented by only 20 percent of the parts used to manufacture it. If we wish to control the production costs for this product, we could control 80 percent of the costs by focusing our attention on only that 20 percent of the total parts. We could, therefore, design a system that continuously monitors those particular parts while managing the remaining 80 percent of the parts using some form of exception reporting or control. Critical thinking allows for the partitioning of any problem into important and unimportant elements.

Opposite Thinking

Opposite thinking is a method of problem solving whereby the decision maker simply takes the perspective of someone other than herself or himself. It is a form of "standing in another's shoes." Using this method, a decision maker can often gain insight into why a particular problem exists in the first place. Consider the following problem:

Lynne is probably the most valuable member of the software development staff at Trident Software. Whenever a big job comes along that looks as

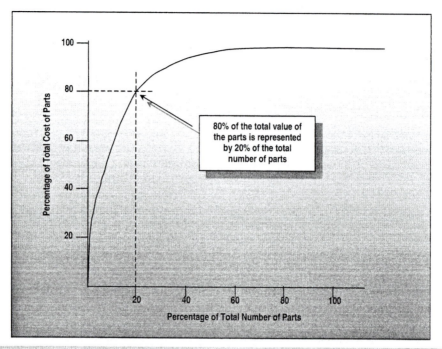

FIGURE 16-1   A Pareto Distribution of Parts Necessary to Build a Product

though it can't be solved, Lynne seems to come to the rescue with the perfect cost-effective solution for the client. When the company finally gained the attention of a major client it had been courting for several months, much of the credit could be attributed to the successes Lynne engineered with two of the client's biggest competitors. The client wants to schedule planning meetings during the last two days of next week and cannot offer much flexibility in scheduling due to some previous government commitments. Lynne insists that she cannot be available on those days. When pressed for a reason, she reveals that next week is the first anniversary of her father's death and she needs to be with her mother in Indiana. Lynne acknowledges the importance of the meetings but remains firm in her position that she must be with her mother on those specific days. If Trident wants the business, they must be able to meet next week and they must be able to deliver Lynne for the meetings. Got any ideas?

One way of looking at this problem is from Lynne's perspective rather than from Trident's. Lynne believes her mother will be comforted by her presence and feels obligated to spend time with her mother during this period. Logically speaking, Lynne is not so concerned about being in Indiana as she is in being with her mother. Standing in her shoes, the answer begins to become clear. Why not bring Lynne's mother to her instead of Lynne going to her mother? When asked, Lynne sees the win-win situation and agrees. Opposite thinking can often produce new perspectives and, thus, new solutions.

Groupthink

Because groupthink was covered in a detailed manner in Chapter 5, we will mention it only briefly in this context. Despite its negative connotations, it does represent an alternative way of thinking and can be used effectively to achieve group involvement in activities such as idea generation and brainstorming (discussed later in this chapter).

INTUITION

Although not the same as creativity, intuition is often identified as an important element in creative decision making and problem solving. Managers who can harness their intuitions can often respond more quickly to a given situation and apply both experience and judgment. Consider the following example:

> In Marseilles, France, . . . a suspect on board a fishing vessel was thought to be smuggling heroin. Unfortunately, when the naval patrol boarded the vessel, they could not find any drugs. As the naval patrol prepared to depart, one officer noticed that the boat's concrete ballast was located in the front of the ship rather than at its normal position in the center. When the ballast was examined, the patrol discovered that it was hollowed out and contained the largest cache of heroin ever found. The intuition of the naval officer helped solve the problem. (Rowe and Boulgarides, 1994, p. 172)

In the realm of DSS design, mechanisms must be developed to allow the decision maker to impart intuition to the decision process as a supplement to other problem-solving resources, including creativity.

BARRIERS TO CREATIVITY

Much has been written regarding methods by which creativity can be enhanced or promoted. In contrast, relatively little research delves into specific scenarios and conditions that inhibit the creative process or the emergence of creative thought and action. In most cases, the thinking is that by doing certain things, creativity will emerge and, implicitly, by not doing them, creativity will not emerge. Unfortunately, any given condition may be necessary but not sufficient to ensure creative output. Despite all of the mechanisms favoring creativity, certain barriers, both artificial and intrinsic, may still inhibit our creative actions and thoughts. Before we explore the prescriptions for enhancing creativity, we need to understand the barriers that must be overcome if these prescriptions are to have any chance of success.

SELF-CONSTRAINING BELIEFS

One of the most commonly identified barriers to creativity is referred to as self-constraining beliefs. Under this condition, problem solvers often make assumptions regarding potential outcomes or "rules of engagement" that are fabricated or untrue. Each decision maker facing a problem situation, either consciously or unconsciously, formulates some concept or model of it (Ackoff and Vergara, 1981). Because of certain erroneous assumptions about the environment or problem space, this model is flawed. Thus, instead of acknowledging the true difficulty of a problem-solving scenario via a sound and accurate model of it, the participant makes the problem more difficult by assuming certain constraining conditions that do not exist.

A classic example of this common barrier to creativity is found in the familiar nine-dot puzzle problem presented in Chapter 2. In this problem, the decision maker is presented with the task of drawing exactly four straight lines to cover all nine dots without lifting the writing instrument being used to draw the lines. Although never stated explicitly, most people incorrectly assume that no lines may be drawn outside the perimeter of the square formed by the dots. Since all possible courses of action tested by the problem solver will share this erroneous constraint, no possible solution will present itself. However, if this self-constraining belief is relaxed, the solution becomes easy to envision and execute.

In some cases, problem solvers may even be aware of one or more of their self-constraining beliefs. In these cases, the problem solver tends to rationalize the constraints as being imposed by either someone else or the environment itself. Ackoff and Vergara (1981) offered the example of an academic department chair who was unwilling to face the consequences of firing a tenured professor. Because of this unwillingness, the department chair erroneously assumed that he or she is not allowed to dismiss tenured faculty and will even use this self-imposed constraint to justify his or her actions to others.

This issue of self-constraining beliefs can start a cascade effect that eliminates the possibility of a creative outcome. The ease with which an individual can remove these self-imposed barriers often depends on how strongly he or she believes in them or perceives them to be out of their locus of control. The more firmly an individual believes in the uncontrollability of a constraint, the more likely he or she is to reconcile the inconsistencies by formulating additional constraining assumptions.

Fears, Beliefs, and Stresses

In addition to self-constraining beliefs, several other barriers to creativity can be found within an individual's control. Issues related to fear of criticism, a general lack of confidence, or some other negative affect such as stress, can all effectively deter creative thoughts or behaviors. In many situations, our greatest barrier to creativity is our belief that we are just not creative. These personal disaffirmations create a self-fulfilling prophecy that prevents us from ever seeking a creative outcome. The opposite is also true as we shall see when we explore methods of enhancing our creative actions and outcomes.

We often struggle with an internal fear related to criticism. Although no one likes criticism from others, the possibility that our ideas will be shunned or categorized as pedestrian or commonplace can erect an impenetrable barrier to the generation of novel and innovative thoughts. Bear in mind that what we may fear as mundane may actually appear quite creative to those around us.

Criticism can also be self-imposed. By dwelling on our fears of criticism from others, we often begin to exercise self-doubt and negative thinking about ourselves. Put these two forces together and you stand a good chance of never generating a creative thought or behavior as long as you live!

Our belief structure can also negatively affect our ability to be creative. One who possesses a strong belief in some context is necessarily limited in their response options related to that context. This sense of conviction can act as a filter of the information we receive from external sources. Anything that tends to contradict our belief structure will be "filtered out" so that we can remain comfortable in our own personal reality and unaware of our opportunities to think and act creatively.

A strong ego identity with a particular belief structure can further magnify this filtration response. In this case, we find ourselves compelled to aggressively defend our belief, often in a manner destructive to our creativity, ourselves, and those around us. One must not be void of belief structures to be creative, but rather one needs to be especially aware of how their beliefs could potentially limit creativity.

Routines and Rigidity

To be sure, not all barriers to creativity are self-imposed. The environment in which we live can often either enhance or prevent our creativity from emerging. Extremely hectic environments tend to deter one from taking opportunities to reflect and ponder. This lack of introspection can be a major barrier to creative thought. A "noisy" environment can be further exacerbated by spending the majority of our time in environments that are sterile and, therefore, unable to feed the senses.

Environments in which quick production of thought is the norm can also inhibit creativity. Such environments are often characterized by rigid rules and processes that preclude flexibility in thought or action. This rigidity prevents us from conducting the information gathering, the interactions, and the incubation of thought necessary for creative output. Much of the literature on barriers to creativity suggests an inverse correlation between the emergence of creativity and rigidity in schedule and process. This generalization is not to say that creativity will automatically emerge in a free form, unstructured environment, but rather that highly structured and rigidly enforced environments can stifle creativity to the point of nonexistence.

16-4: CREATIVE PROBLEM-SOLVING TECHNIQUES

A review of the literature on the subject of creative problem solving will quickly suggest as many different techniques to apply to a problem-solving context as there are problems that need solving. VanGundy's "Techniques of Structured Problem Solving" (1988) contains more than 100 detailed techniques for fostering creativity in a wide variety of problem contexts. This news is both good and bad for the DSS designer. It is good news when a need to enhance or foster creative thinking under a given set of circumstances arises and a specified method for accomplishing it can be found. It is bad news in that, because the nature of DSS design and use is to support semistructured problem contexts, deciding which creative problem-solving techniques to incorporate into the design becomes a major decision in and of itself. But there is more good news: The vast majority of creative problem-solving techniques applicable in an electronic decision support mechanism can be categorized into an easily manageable taxonomy consisting of four basic categories: (1) serendipity, (2) free association, (3) structured relationships, and (4) group techniques.

SERENDIPITY

The originator of the concept of serendipity is Mother Nature. Evolution is often a function of several serendipitous events converging on a moment. In our quest to enhance our demonstrated levels of creativity, we must acknowledge the role of serendipity in that process.

Although it appears that we are, as yet, unable to control the emergence of serendipitous events in our lives, we do have methods by which we can enhance its probability of occurrence. One method is to actively pursue a study of currently unexplained phenomena. In conducting this investigation, use your portfolio of unsolved problems as a guide while browsing libraries, attending conferences and trade shows, and interacting in seemingly nonrelated events. On more than one occasion, while copying a journal article, I encountered the title page of an unrelated article that either spawned an idea for a new research project or filled a void in an ongoing one. This is serendipity at work.

Numerous anecdotes support the role of serendipity in creative outcomes. William Shockley, the father of the modern transistor, describes the process by which it was invented as "creative failure methodology." A multidisciplinary team at Bell Labs was formed to invent the MOS transistor and ended up instead with the junction transistor and the entirely new science of semiconductor physics. Alexander Graham Bell was inspired to develop the telephone after reading an account, in German, that described an invention Bell believed had the function of a telephone. After demonstrating his first working prototype he learned that because of his language barrier, he had completely misunderstood the original German report, which described an invention with a function much different from a telephone.

According to his own story (and in sharp contrast to the apple-falling-on-his-head legend), Sir Isaac Newton conceived the concept of gravity when he observed an apple falling from a tree while, at the same time, noticing the moon in the night sky. These simultaneous, and admittedly serendipitous, images inspired him to speculate whether the same laws governing the falling apple also kept the moon from falling from the sky. This speculation led him to develop the laws of mechanics and universal gravitation that now serve as the primary foundations of science and engineering.

FREE ASSOCIATION TECHNIQUES

The techniques in this category are all focused on two simple goals: divergent thinking and the generation of ideas. Of the several principles that guide the techniques of free association, probably the most important is to defer judgment. Divergent idea generation relies on the complete suspension of analysis and judgment. If each time an idea is generated it must be fully analyzed and judged, then the number of possible alternatives to consider will be significantly reduced, diminishing the odds of generating a new and innovative solution to the problem.

Additional principles guiding the techniques in this category include the assumptions that quantity begets quality, the crazier the better, and to combine is to improve. The first maxim simply assumes that with deferred judgment, more ideas will emerge, and with more ideas, the laws of probability suggest that more quality ideas will be part of the set. The second principle suggests that divergent thinking requires a certain propensity for risk taking. Conservative and cautious thinking approaches generally do not yield breakthrough ideas. The third principle calls for not only a generation of completely divergent ideas but the combination of divergent concepts and ideas into new and improved ones, as well. In 1912, a magazine advertisement for the new Oldsmobile quotes Mr. Olds himself as saying, "I do not believe that a car materially better will ever be built." What a visionary Mr. Olds must have sounded like at the time. Fortunately for us, however, a few people since 1912 managed to combine ideas and improve somewhat on Mr. Olds's 1912 prognostication.

Brainstorming

Probably the most common free association technique used in the DSS realm is that of brainstorming. This method can be extremely effective at both the individual and group levels in generating a long list of ideas quickly and efficiently. Building upon the principles outlined, brainstorming techniques focus on quantity and variety and require the deferment of all judgment, criticism, and analysis until the list of ideas is completed. Although the process typically leads to an initially overwhelming number of alternatives, the process of culling the list down to a more manageable size is normally accomplished with limited effort. Brainstorming can be conducted either individually or collectively and can be unstructured or structurally facilitated. In a multi-participant setting, brainstorming can often stimulate the phenomenon of idea hitchhiking, where one idea leads to another and then another with each subsequent iteration becoming more refined and often more implementable. Most important, brainstorming can be easily incorporated into a DSS as either a part of a guided process or a stand-alone module that can be adopted as desired by the users. In a DSS setting, additional features such as list combining, ranking, and culling can also be built into the system to facilitate the brainstorming activity.

A number of commercial products intended to facilitate the idea generation and brainstorming functions are emerging. One of the most successful products in this arena is IdeaFisher (see the case at the beginning of this chapter), which contains an associative lexicon of the English language and can easily and quickly create thousands of cross-references and word associations intended to facilitate idea generation. Figure 16-2 contains examples of typical screen layouts in IdeaFisher.

Another highly successful electronic brainstorming product is contained within the Ventana Corporation's GroupSystems product. Although marketed as a GDSS product (see Chapter 5), the brainstorming facilities included in the product are considered some of the most sophisticated free association tools available. Figure 16-3 contains examples of screens from GroupSystems.

STRUCTURED RELATIONSHIPS

In this category of creative problem-solving techniques, the focus is on the generation of new ideas via a process whereby two or more objects, products, ideas, or concepts are forced together or combined to produce new objects or ideas. Although it is generally the case that elements related to each other will tend to produce practical ideas more than unrelated elements, such ideas also tend to be more mundane and less unique than those produced from unrelated elements.

Osborn's Idea Checklist

A classic technique that falls into this category uses checklists that cover many potential perspectives and sources of creative solutions to problem contexts. The best known example of this approach is Osborn's (1963) 73 Idea-Spurring Questions. The questions require the user to transform the decision context into a variety of new perspectives and

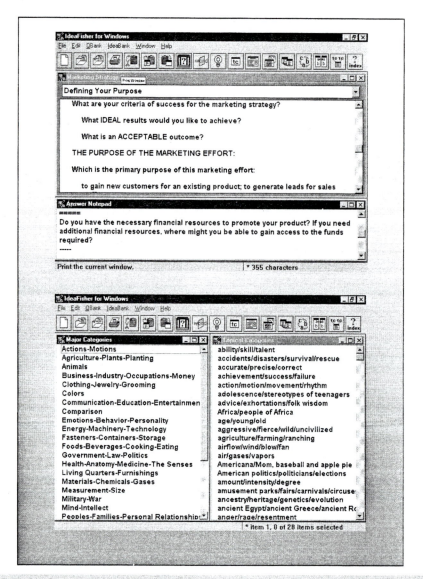

FIGURE 16-2 Screenshots from IdeaFisher

shapes, thus forcing a new formulation and combination of the elements contained within. Table 16-2 contains a complete list of Osborn's transformation questions.

Morphological Forced Connections

Koberg and Bagnall (1976) suggested another forced connection technique that emphasizes the morphological (i.e., the science of changes in living things) attributes of design problems. The technique requires the user to write down attributes of a problem, list as many alternative options under each attribute as possible, and then consider all possible combinations and permutations of the alternatives. The analysis is most

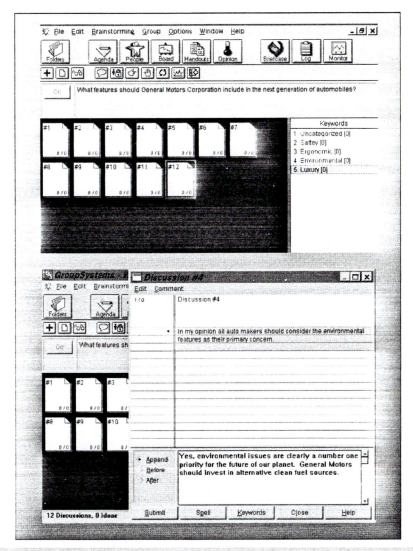

FIGURE 16-3 Screenshots from GroupSystems

appropriately performed in a matrix format and can be easily delivered via a DSS. Table 16-3 contains an example of a morphological analysis for a drug smuggling problem context.

NASA uses morphological forced connection modules extensively in many of its DSSs used to support the establishment of scientific objectives for space exploration activities. Action phrases such as "Measure the tidal deformations in . . ." are combined with targets such as "the interior of Jupiter" to create a possible scientific objective.

The real value of a forced connection technique lies not in its ability to find all possible combinations but rather in its ability to create a framework within which all possible combinations exist and can be selectively screened to determine the most appropriate candidates.

TABLE 16-2 Osborn's 73 Idea-Spurring Questions

- **Put to other uses.** New ways to use as is? Other uses if modified?
- **Adapt.** What else like this? What other ideas does this suggest? Does the past offer a parallel? What could I copy? Whom could I emulate?
- **Modify.** New twist? Change meaning, color, motion, sound, odor, form, shape? Other changes?
- **Magnify.** What to add? More time? Greater frequency? Stronger? Higher? Longer? Thicker? Extra Value? Plus ingredient? Duplicate? Multiply? Exaggerate?
- **Minify.** What to subtract? Smaller, Condensed? Miniature? Lower? Shorter? Lighter? Omit? Streamline? Split up? Understate?
- **Substitute.** Who else instead? What else instead? Other ingredient? Other material? Other process? Other power? Other place? Other approach? Other tone of voice?
- **Rearrange.** Interchange components? Other pattern? Other layout? Other sequence? Transpose cause and effect? Change pace? Change schedule?
- **Reverse.** Transpose positive and negative? How about opposites? Turn it backward? Turn it upside down? Reverse roles? Change shoes? Turn tables? Turn other cheek?
- **Combine.** How about a blend, an alloy, an assortment, an ensemble? Combine units? Combine purposes? Combine appeals? Combine ideas?

Source: Osborn, A. O., (1963). *Applied Imagination.* Reprinted with permission from the publisher, The Creative Education Foundation Press, 1050 Union Road, Buffalo, NY 14224.

Analytic Hierarchy Process

It is often difficult to conceptualize all the different elements that make up a decision. As a result, the error of failing to include one or more elements, or including elements that are not important in the decision, commonly occurs. In addition, the cognitive energy necessary to prioritize decision elements may make it difficult to keep

---

TABLE 16-3 Example of a Morphological Analysis Grid for Drug Smuggling

Problem Components	Component Alternatives	
Type	A. Cocaine	B. Heroin
	C. Amphetamines	D. Marijuana
Source	E. Thailand	F. Local sources
	G. Turkey	H. United States
Importation method	I. Air	J. Sea
	K. Courier	L. Produced locally
Distribution method	M. Large-scale, highly organized	N. Hobby
	O. Small-scale, poorly organized	
Sponsors	P. Organized crime	Q. Triad
	R. Political terrorists	S. Individual

Possible morphological connections include:

- Cocaine (A) from the United States (H) produced locally (L) and distributed on a large-scale, highly organized (M) basis by organized crime (P).
- Heroin (B) from Turkey (G) imported by air (I) and distributed on a small-scale, poorly organized (O) basis by an individual (S).

track of all previous priority rankings and may lead to inconsistent priority judgments. In an attempt to counter these problems, a methodology was developed by Thomas Saaty at the University of Pennsylvania in the early 1980s called the analytic hierarchy process (AHP).

AHP is a mathematically based theory and comprehensive methodology for use in decision making. It employs two key aspects:

1. Data from the various variables that make up the decision
2. Judgments about these variables from decision makers

AHP supports the decision-making process by allowing decision makers to organize and evaluate the relative importance of selected objectives and the relative importance of alternative solutions to a decision. AHP provides a way to measure the consistency of judgments and to reevaluate inconsistent judgments. Finally, this methodology offers a theoretical grounding for consistent decision making.

To determine the best overall action to take, AHP requires the following steps:

1. The structuring of a decision into a hierarchical model
2. Pairwise comparisons of all objectives and alternative solutions

First, as stated previously, every AHP decision begins with a model in the form of a hierarchy. The general form of the model is composed of four elements:

1. **Goal.** The desired outcome of the decision
2. **Criteria.** Sometimes called the objectives; the elements that comprise the goal
3. **Subcriteria.** The elements that make up the criteria under which they fall (the node directly above)
4. **Alternatives.** The solutions or choices available

Decomposing a decision into this format allows decision makers to focus on each and every part of a complex problem.

Once the model is built, the next step is to evaluate the elements by making pairwise comparisons. A pairwise comparison is the process of comparing the relative importance, preference, or likelihood of any element with respect to the element in the level above. Comparisons are usually top-down, both across nodes and within nodes. Consider the following examples:

1. Is criterion 1 more preferable/important/likely than criterion 2, with respect to the goal?
2. Is subcriterion 1 more preferable/important/likely than subcriterion 2, with respect to criterion 1, with respect to the goal?

Because we are seldom consistent when making comparative judgments, AHP assumes inconsistency in judgments. AHP attempts to measure this inconsistency via a mathematical formula called an inconsistency ratio, where a value of 1.0 is considered complete inconsistency (i.e., inconsistent 100% of the time), less than 0.10 is considered acceptable consistency (i.e., inconsistent only 10% of the time), and a value greater than 0.10 suggests a need to reexamine the judgments made with an eye toward improving consistency (i.e., inconsistent greater than 10% of the time).

After all preferences are recorded, and are of sufficient consistency, data corresponding to the subcriteria are introduced into the model. This process of prioritizing the alternatives is referred to as synthesis.

By taking these two elements—(1) consistent preferences and (2) data on subcriteria—AHP generates the global weights of the nodes by combining the local priorities throughout the entire model. Via synthesis, it arrives at the overall priorities of the alternatives, thus providing decision makers information on which alternative is the best choice.

An example of an AHP decision hierarchy is demonstrated with the following situation: The objective is to decide whether to admit an applicant to an MBA program. To begin, the decision must be broken down into its constituent elements. The applicant's academic, professional, and personal credentials are the main components upon which the admission decision will be based. These components represent the decision criteria. Under each of these criteria are the subcriteria: the elements that make up their respective criteria. For example, the essence of an applicant's academic credentials are the overall undergraduate GPA, major GPA, GMAT score, quality of the undergraduate institution, and so on. Finally, the alternatives consist of the possible choices: in this case, the range of possible applicants. Each alternative, or applicant, will provide the data for each subcriterion, in order to conduct synthesis. By performing the complete set of pairwise comparisons and ranking the alternatives based upon this method, AHP can assist the decision maker in reaching a ranking that reflects the relative contribution of each of the subcriteria to the final decision and applicant selection.

GROUP TECHNIQUES

As the name implies, this category comprises creative techniques focused on enhancing and fostering creativity within a multiparticipant problem-solving context. A key element present in these techniques is the improvement of group interaction. The assumption is that participants in a problem-solving exercise naturally create synergies that generate creative ideas if they are stimulated by some form of regular and flexible interaction. Once the interaction is initiated, the process tends to build upon itself and generates creative ideas.

Nominal Group Technique

Delbecq, Van de Ven, and Gustafson (1975) developed a widely used and highly successful group interaction mechanism known as the nominal group technique (NGT). This technique builds on the concept of brainstorming in a multiparticipant setting and may use a variety of media, including paper-based, verbal, and electronic, to facilitate the activity.

The name describes how the process works. It is a process for a group of people who become a group in name only (hence the name, nominal group) when they are using the technique. The purpose of NGT is to eliminate social and psychological dynamics of group behavior that tend to inhibit individual creativity and participation in multiparticipant decision-making (MDM) contexts. While the group uses the technique, they avoid the normal problems of a few individuals doing all the talking, the rest listening, and very few people taking the time to actually think about the issue at hand. Individuals can be more creative, and everyone is given a structured opportunity to participate. It minimizes the common problems often encountered in small group meetings organized for the purpose of generating ideas, planning programs, and problem solving. Table 16-4 lists each step of NGT.

TABLE 16-4   Nominal Group Technique

Silent Generation of Ideas in Writing
- Provides time to think
- Provides a creative setting
- Provides focus and uninterrupted thought
- Encourages each member to search for ideas
- Avoids competition and status differences
- Avoids conformity pressures
- Avoids evaluation and closure
- Avoids polarizing on ideas

Recorded Round-Robin Listing of Ideas on Chart
- Structures equal sharing and participation
- Encourages problem identification
- Encourages each member to build on other members' ideas
- Depersonalizes ideas
- Tolerates conflicting ideas
- Reinforces concentration: hear and see ideas
- Provides written permanence

Discussion and Clarification of Each Idea on Chart
- Each idea is as important as another
- Equal time to each idea
- Clarifies ideas

Preliminary Vote on Priorities
- Provides focus on important issues
- Structures equality in choices
- Allows a "trial run"
- Avoids a premature decision
- Avoids dominance by strong members

Discussion of Preliminary Vote
- Clarifies misunderstandings
- Encourages minority opinions
- Promotes "criticizing" ideas on wall—not people
- Provides preparation for decision

Final Vote on Priorities
- Structures an independent judgment from each member
- Provides closure
- Promotes sense of accomplishment
- Motivates involvement in future phases of planning and problem solving
- Provides a written record of the ideas generated

Delphi

Recall that in Chapter 5 we briefly mentioned the MDM technique called Delphi. This technique was developed at the RAND Corporation (a well-known think tank of the 1950s and 1960s) to elicit expert opinion on how many Soviet atomic bombs it would take to do a specified amount of damage to various locations throughout the United States. A number of research groups used the technique as well as many business groups and private corporations within a DSS setting including Bell Canada, Honeywell, AT&T, Owens-Corning, General Dynamics, TRW, Skandia Insurance Company, Weyerhaeuser, and Imperial Chemical, among many others.

A key element in the Delphi technique that separates it from NGT is that the participants are all anonymous and, in most cases, are widely geographically dispersed. The Delphi questionnaires are generally presented to the members of a group in the form of carefully prepared written questions, although oral questions are sometimes used. The questions normally require subjective estimates, assessments, or projections by the group members.

The first round of questionnaire responses is analyzed, usually statistically (e.g., average, variance, median, quartile, range). The result of this analysis plus the respondents' initial estimates are then provided as feedback to the original participants, who reevaluate their estimates and revise them if appropriate, knowing the group's response. Several iterations of this process are conducted until convergence (in the form of decreasing variance) of response is achieved.

Studies show that a Delphi-developed consensus is more effective and more accurate than a consensus developed through verbal interaction. The reasons relate to the domination of the opinions of certain personality or authority types in face-to-face group dynamics; those opinions that dominate are not necessarily the most correct. The quiet, reflective mood of the Delphi results in better projections than the noise of a meeting. Also, the Delphi is generally a more efficient use of the time of a group of experts and can be easily incorporated into a DSS.

The operating assumption of the Delphi technique is that those respondents whose original projections involved less confidence will be more inclined to revise their response, knowing the group's response, than those whose estimates involved more confidence or knowledge.

16-5: CREATIVITY AND THE ROLE OF TECHNOLOGY

Until recently, little empirical evidence supported the role of technology in either the enhancement or inhibition of creativity. Elam and Mead (1990) first provided a direct empirical link between the use of technology in the context of a problem-solving scenario and the enhancement of creative output with regard to the solution. Marakas and Elam (1997) further investigated these findings and demonstrated that even though the technology offers an effective and novel delivery vehicle, the underlying process imposed on the decision maker is the primary causal agent in the enhancement of creative solutions and outcomes. Further, when the appropriate process is combined with an effective technology mechanism, the results are greater than those realized in either a process-only or technology-only environment.

The real question then becomes, "Where should we go from here?" Our knowledge of computers as machines of programmed logic, of rules, and of human-designed boundaries or limits suggests that we must better understand the underlying processes through which this nebulous concept of creativity acts and emerges. Wherever technology can be deployed to remove the cognitive burden and drudgery of solving complex problems, it is reasonable to assume that more, and more appropriate, responses may result. Having said this, we must also remember that the strategy and process are what actually produce the solution, not the tool. If the presence of a whiteboard in a classroom encourages, supports, or facilitates a successful learning strategy, the credit for learning must, nonetheless, be credited to the strategy, not the whiteboard. This same perspective must be extended to the role of technology in the creative process. We may find it novel and amusing to incorporate technology into our problem-solving and idea-generating activities, but we must also recognize our yet immature understanding of what creativity is and what we must do to realize its potential in each individual. One end of this continuum of understanding is exemplified in the following quote:

> ... media are mere vehicles that deliver instruction but do not influence student achievement any more than the truck that delivers our groceries causes changes in our nutrition. Basically, the choice of the vehicle might influence the cost or the extent of distributing instruction, but only the content of the vehicle can influence achievement. (Clark, 1983, p. 445)

The other end of this continuum can be easily defined by building upon Clark's metaphor. The delivery truck may not be the direct causal agent for better nutrition but the advent of modern, better-refrigerated trucks vastly facilitates the range of foods we may easily access. In a similar fashion, when combined with a detailed understanding of the creative process, technology may offer each of us new and promising tools and techniques through which unique and more creative outcomes can be realized.

16-6: CHAPTER SUMMARY

As components of the decision-making process, creativity, intuition, and innovativeness are yet to be fully understood or employed. It is important, however, that we realize their value in contributing to effective solutions and that we design our support mechanisms to embrace and enhance their contribution.

Key Concepts

- Creativity

  Creativity is an ability to see the same things as everyone else but to think of something different. It involves the ability to generate novel and useful ideas and solutions to problems and challenges.

- Theories of creativity

  Psychoanalytical perspective

  Creativity is a preconscious mental activity. Creative thinking occurs in our subconscious thoughts and is not directly accessible to our conscious thoughts.

Behavioral perspective

Creativity is a natural response to stimuli within our individual environments. Certain combinations of stimuli can lead to more creative behavior than other combinations.

Process perspective

Creativity is a property of a thought process that can be acquired and improved through instruction and practice.

- Ways of thinking

Logical thinking

This method of thinking is rooted in the model-building and quantitative methods of management decision science and is an integral part of the design and development of a computer-based DSS.

Lateral thinking

This method of thinking is based on the premise that the human mind naturally processes and stores information in accordance with a specific pattern of thought and action. Lateral thinking disrupts these patterns through the introduction of discontinuity. Three major activities are available to promote lateral thinking processes: awareness, alternatives, and provocation.

Critical thinking

By focusing on certain critical elements within a problem context, a solution with an immediate and measurable impact on the problem can be crafted.

Opposite thinking

Opposite thinking is a method of problem solving whereby the decision maker simply takes the perspective of another person. It is a form of "standing in another's shoes."

Groupthink

Groupthink as an alternative way of thinking can be used effectively to achieve group involvement in activities such as idea generation and brainstorming.

- In the realm of DSS design, mechanisms must be developed to allow the decision maker to impart intuition to the decision process as a supplement to other problem-solving resources, including creativity. (16-1)
- Creative problem-solving techniques

Free association techniques

The techniques in this category are all focused on a single goal: divergent thinking and the generation of ideas. Several principles guide the techniques of free association:

1. Defer judgment
2. Quantity begets quality
3. The crazier the better
4. To combine is to improve

The most common free association technique used in the DSS realm is brainstorming.

Structured relationships

These techniques focus on the generation of new ideas via a process in which two or more objects, products, ideas, or concepts are forced together or combined to produce new objects or ideas. Two common techniques in this category are Osborn's idea checklist and the morphological forced connection technique from Koberg and Bagnall.

Group techniques

These techniques focus on enhancing and fostering creativity within a multiparticipant problem-solving context. The assumption is that participants in a problem-solving exercise will naturally create synergies that generate creative ideas if they are stimulated by some form of regular and flexible interaction. Common techniques in this category include the nominal group technique and the Delphi technique.

Questions for Review

1. What is creativity? Try to explain it from different perspectives.
2. Explain the basic concept of logical thinking.
3. Describe the basis of lateral thinking.
4. List and briefly describe the three major activities in promoting lateral thinking processes.
5. What approaches can provoke changes in lateral thinking?
6. List the major principles of free association techniques.
7. Briefly describe the major concept of a structured relationship technique in problem solving.
8. Describe the primary assumptions of nominal group technique in problem solving. What are the benefits of using this technique?
9. Describe the role of serendipity in creative thinking. Can you provide examples of your own?
10. Describe some of the common barriers to creative thinking.

For Further Discussion

1. Discuss the importance of creativity and intuition in decision making.
2. Study and describe a case in which the critical thinking approach (e.g., the Pareto Law) can be applied in the problem-solving process.
3. Briefly describe a problem occurring in an organization with which you are familiar. Use the technique of brainstorming to find the solutions.
4. Use a structured relationship technique to solve the problem identified in the previous question.
5. Information about intelligent agents (IAs) is plentiful on the World Wide Web. Find some Web sites that discuss the use of IAs. Hint: Try Firefly, IBM, or BargainFinder.

INTELLIGENT SOFTWARE AGENTS, BOTS, DELEGATION, AND AGENCY

Learning Objectives

◆ Examine the world of delegation and agency in cyberspace and networks

◆ Learn the basic concept of intelligent software agents (ISAs)

◆ Recognize the characteristics of intelligent software agents

◆ Understand the types of problems intelligent agents can solve

◆ Explore the future applications of intelligent software agents

MYERS INDUSTRIES SEARCHES INTELLIGENTLY

Consider the following: You manufacture custom-designed parts to the exact specifications of each customer using extremely costly raw materials and highly sophisticated machinery. A customer with whom you have never done business before, places a large and lucrative order for several custom parts for a new automotive product. Because you have never done business with this company before and the cost of getting stuck with expensive custom parts that are no good to any of your other customers is high, you act quickly with the necessary due diligence to assess this new customer and to protect yourself against potential losses. When time is of the essence and information is needed, where else do you turn but to the Internet? Do a keyword search on any supplier or customer and you are likely to unearth a wealth of information. The problem is finding the time or tools to sift through the mountains of information to get vital data.

Seeking to address this problem, Computer Associates added intelligent agent technology to its BizWorks e-business management software to give corporate strategists and managers the ability to pose questions to internal and Web-based systems and get back only information that is pertinent.

BizWorks eBusiness Intelligence Agents enable enterprise managers to define both the parameters and frequency of Web searches. The returned data are evaluated based on business rules set by the user, and actions can be triggered within internal systems, such as enterprise resource planning or procurement. Unlike standard keyword search tools, the BizWorks' intelligent search agents use natural language processing to decipher the context in which a question is asked. More important, once the parameters are supplied to the agent, they go off and collect the data you need automatically while you go off and attend to other business tasks.

One of the first users of the new intelligence tools is Myers Industries, an international manufacturer of custom plastic and rubber products. The company makes both consumer and industrial products such as automotive repair parts, flowerpots, and storage containers.

About 18 months ago, the Akron, Ohio, firm, which operates 25 plants in six countries, began using BizWorks intelligent agent technology to integrate and analyze data from a variety of internal sources. These sources included three enterprise resource planning systems used in different operating units, process automation software running on mainframes, and even data gathered from machines on the shop floor.

The agents use a set of business rules programmed into the system to look for trouble areas in the company's processes. The software also enables upper management to log into a secure portal and create reports, checking on the efficiency of the company's overall processes, for example, as well as more fine-grained reports about error rates on batches of products produced for specific accounts.

Myers senior management soon realized the value of intelligent agent technology for rapidly gathering targeted data. They then deployed the agent technology to check up on the creditworthiness of potential customers of custom parts. The agents give Myers the ability to incorporate data from outside the enterprise into its process planning, which provides the company a strategic advantage.

For instance, a prospective customer may want to place a large order with particular specifications. To fill these orders, Myers usually incurs heavy up-front costs to retool equipment and make other special preparations. This initial expense exposes the company to a serious financial risk if the customer defaults on the contract, especially when it is unlikely that the custom products could be sold elsewhere.

(continued)

<DSS MINICASE>

(continued)

To protect itself, Myers programmed an intelligent agent that searches about 500 Web sites and newsgroups for information about financial reporting, legal filings, news reports and other items that might provide clues about a potential customer's financial health.

The price tag for this technology is remarkably inexpensive given its potential to protect against big losses. The $40,000 investment in the agent technology can be credited for no production run stoppages, to date, as a result of the information collected by the agent. Just one instance in which a high-risk customer of expensive custom parts can be identified before the production run begins will be all that is needed to pay for the technology many times over.

17-1: A WORLD OF DELEGATION AND AGENCY

To delegate is to entrust a representative to act on your behalf. Delegation involves the discretionary authority to autonomously act on behalf of another. Such actions include making decisions, committing resources, and performing sometimes menial tasks.

Although you may not realize it, you are involved in delegacy in almost every activity you pursue. Anytime you run an errand for someone, do the grocery shopping, or even take out the garbage, you are acting as an agent in some capacity. In many cases, your tasks as an agent may involve delegation of some portion of your responsibility to another agent. If you agree to perform a certain task for another, you take on the role of an *autonomous agent.* In this situation, the "responsibility" for completing a task is delegated to you, and within certain guidelines you are empowered to act on behalf of the person who delegated the responsibility to you. In many cases, you may be able to complete the delegated task without any help. In other cases, you may need the help of additional people. When you do, you become an agent who must rely on one or more additional agents. Although autonomous agents possess a high degree of self-determination, they may be required to achieve a goal that is made easier, satisfied more completely, or only possible with the aid of other, similarly autonomous agents. The key to success in these situations is the strength of the trust relationship between you and your agents. For delegation to be successful a relationship between the agent delegating the goal or task and the agent to whom it is delegated is required. Furthermore, after successful delegation, responsibility for the task concerned is not passed on but is instead shared. For example, the manager of a business unit, in delegating a task, although still responsible for its completion is no longer solely responsible for its execution. The manager must, however, ensure that the employee to whom the task is delegated acts appropriately (i.e., by completing the task, asking for help, or further delegating the task).

Delegation is all around us primarily because it provides us with many benefits. First, the ability to successfully delegate reduces an individual's workload. We are often charged with a scope of responsibility far greater than the available time in which to act. Also, in some cases our responsibilities include many subtasks that can be quite tedious and not necessarily the highest and best use of our time and skills. It is here that we must turn to the concept of delegation to ensure that our responsibilities are met via a parallel rather than a sequential process.

Yet another area where delegation becomes a useful managerial tool is the strategic deployment of information systems. The various information systems deployed in an organization are all intended, in one form or another, to transfer work from the human assets in the organization to the computers and networks. By delegating through the computer, tedious and time-consuming activities such as information finding, retrieval, and filtering can be accomplished in a much more expedient and efficient manner. Another situation in which delegation through an information system can be useful is the personalization of human-computer interaction. Using sophisticated filters and agents, we can get some of our work requiring the use of a computer done without actually having to sit down and manipulate the computer through all of the necessary steps and actions. In some cases, these agents and software-based filters can help us perform our computer-related tasks while we are physically disconnected from the computing resource. Much like the concept of delegation to another person, these software agents can share our responsibilities via our guidance rather than through our direct control.

Computer-based information systems are as ubiquitous as automobiles and toasters, but exploiting their capabilities still seems to many to require the training of a rocket scientist. VCR displays blinking a constant 12:00 around the world testify to this conundrum. As interactive television, palmtop diaries, and "smart" credit cards proliferate, the gap between millions of untrained users and an equal number of sophisticated microprocessors will become even more sharply apparent. With people spending a growing proportion of their lives in front of computer screens—informing and entertaining one another, exchanging correspondence, working, making decisions, shopping, and falling in love—some accommodation must be found between limited human attention spans and increasingly complex collections of software and data.

Even the most sophisticated computer currently responds only to what interface designers call *direct manipulation*. Nothing happens unless a human being gives commands from a keyboard, mouse, or touch screen. The computer is merely a passive entity waiting to execute specific, highly detailed instructions. In their basic form, they provide little help for complex tasks or for carrying out actions (such as searches for information) that may take an indefinite amount of time or effort.

If untrained consumers are to employ information systems and networks effectively, direct manipulation will give way to some form of delegation. Researchers and software companies set high hopes on the concept of *intelligent software agents* (ISA), which "know" users' interests, requirements, and objectives and can act autonomously on their behalf. Instead of exercising complete control (and taking responsibility for every move the computer makes), people will be engaged in a cooperative process in which both human and computer agents initiate communication, monitor events, and perform tasks to meet a user's immediate or long-term goals.

The concept of *delegacy* for software agents centers on persistence. "Fire-and-forget" software agents stay resident, or persistent, as background processes after being launched. By making decisions and acting on their environment independently, software agents reduce human workload by generally only interacting with their end clients when it is time to deliver results. An example of this type of delegation is the

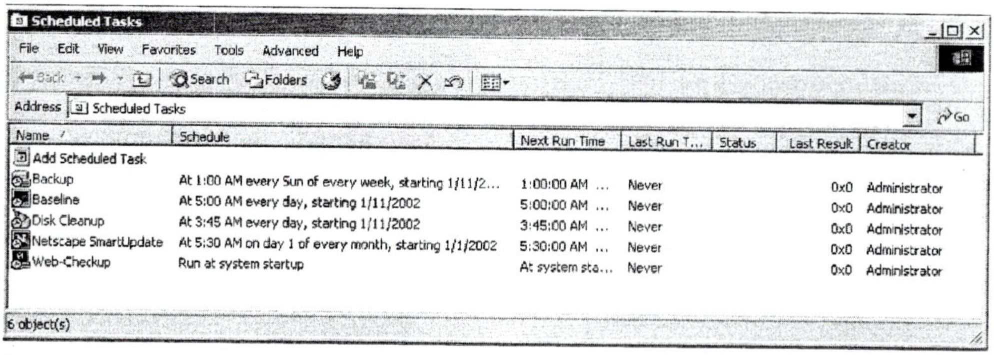

FIGURE 17-1   Example of a Simple "Fire and Forget" Task Delegation Scheduler

Task Scheduler found in most versions of Microsoft Windows (see Figure 17-1). Additionally, this type of automation can lead to super human performance in terms of volume and speed.

Delegacy for ISAs is far more absolute. ISAs are capable of generating and implementing novel rules of behavior that human beings may lack the opportunity or desire to review. Because ISAs can engage in extensive logical planning and inferencing, the relationship of trust between the client and the agent is, or must be, far greater, especially when the consumption of client resources is committed for reasons unexplained or multiple complex operations are actuated before human observers can react.

In the world of ISAs, the average person will have many alter egos—in effect, digital proxies operating simultaneously in different places. Some of these proxies will simply make the digital world less overwhelming by hiding technical details of tasks, guiding users through complex online spaces, or even teaching them about certain subjects. Others will actively search for information their owners may be interested in or monitor specified topics for critical changes. Yet other agents may have the authority to perform transactions (such as purchasing certain online goods or services) or to represent people in their absence (such as a simple out-of-office reply to e-mail). As the proliferation of paper and electronic pocket diaries already attest to, software agents will play a particularly helpful role as personal secretaries—extended memories that remind their bearers what their account numbers are, where they put things, whom they talked to, what tasks they already accomplished, and what tasks remain to be finished.

This change in functionality will most likely go hand in hand with a change in the physical ways people interact with computers. Rather than manipulating a keyboard and mouse, people will speak to agents or gesture at things that need doing. In response, agents will appear as "living" entities on the screen, conveying their current state and behavior with animated facial expressions or body language rather than windows with text, graphs, and figures. Figure 17-2 shows several examples of simple software-based agents developed through Microsoft's Agent technology that can be programmed to perform a wide variety of tasks.

Agents can come in almost any form imaginable. Also, many agent-based programs are widely available on the Internet. Figure 17-3 shows the homepage for one of the largest collections of agents and agent-based programs on the Web—The Agentry (available at www.agentry.net).

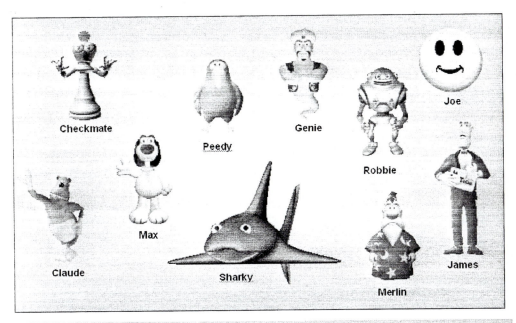

Checkmate

Peedy

Genie

Joe

Robbie

Max

Claude

Sharky

Merlin

James

FIGURE 17-2 Examples of Characters Used to Represent Intelligent Software Agents

Source: www.agentry.net

Whether person-to-person or person-to-ISA, a principal who delegates authority to an agent must make her or his intentions clear. The agent should then follow the principal's instructions faithfully. As with delegation from person-to-person, misunderstandings may occur at the interface between a human principal and an ISA—when a principal does not clearly define intentions, when an agent does not fully comprehend the instructions, or when the two parties interpret identical instructions differently.

AGENCY DIVERSIFICATION AND PERSONALIZATION

Although not yet widely apparent, long-term developments in the area of information exchange, as well as in the area of the Internet and intranets, are moving toward increasing *diversification* of the entire information market, which in turn enables increasing *personalization* of information exchange.

This increasing diversification, and most certainly the increasing personalization of information, presents a logical next step. In many areas (of our lives, in an organization's business, etc.), it is common practice to farm out certain activities or responsibilities to others. In many of our daily but also many not-so-daily tasks, we distribute the need to possess certain knowledge and experience to specialists and organizations that have made this task their primary activity or core competency. For instance, we could go out and visit as many bookshops as possible and take as many subscriptions to magazines and journals as possible, but we chose to do things differently. We visit a library instead, or we buy topical magazines, to relieve us of the task of gathering, selecting, and editing the news and information that best suit our information needs. An important reason for consolidating these tasks is because this activity or task does not belong to your core (or main) activities. In plain English, it means that doing it yourself, or learning how to do it yourself, would just cost too much time and money.

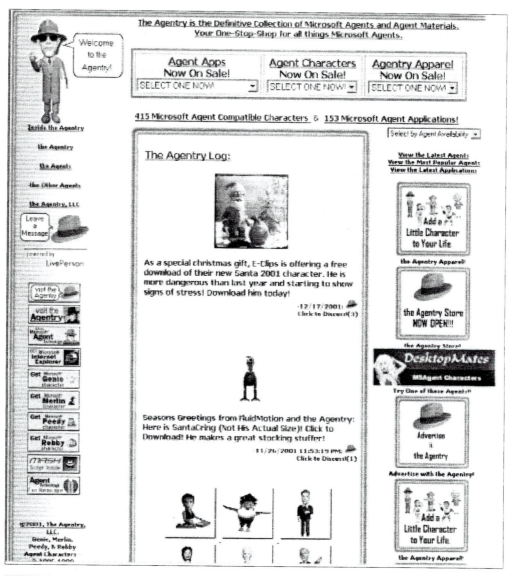

FIGURE 17-3   Homepage for The Agentry—ISA Support Group

When looking at the current state of affairs on the Internet, the need to outsource one or more Internet-related tasks and activities grows larger each day. If the Internet is to become the basis for the future information and service marketplace, then things will have to change, because using it now is time-consuming, laborious, and quite often not very satisfying. Many users feel lost and are unable to cope with the seemingly endless amounts of information available to them. The first signs of such changes are already apparent in the form of techniques and ISA products and various kinds of personal, often Web-enabled, *awareness services*. Although these options are far from being the perfect solution, the general public is accepting and using them with great eagerness. Of course, a portion of the population will choose to satisfy their information needs all by themselves because they are dissatisfied with the selections offered by third parties or just because they like doing it. However, the expectation is that many people will happily rely on the capabilities of others to perform the activities for them. Further, we can expect to see as many possibilities and alternatives available to fit a person's needs as there are individuals. Some will want extensive services and premium content and will be quite willing to pay the price for such services. Others will use free or nearly free services such as the public library or ad-subsidized information sites because they are not willing (or able) to pay a high price for obtaining the information they need.

The emergence of a large number of people needing large amounts of diverse information brings with it two primary implications:

1. Not one or a few, but *many* ways and forms will be available in which information can be offered and obtained, enabling individuals or organizations to choose the way(s) that suits them best.
2. This whole process of offering and obtaining information and services through the electronic marketplace will be enhanced and catalyzed in various ways, and will better fit the personal needs and preferences of each individual (user, supplier, etc.). This added value and catalyzing "force" is called *agency*.

TYPES OF AGENCY

To make it possible to use the Internet and the current and future electronic marketplace on a higher conceptual level and in a task-oriented way, we need some sort of cement on which to build it and some kind of oil to make the process run smoothly. The concept of agency will serve as both the glue and the lubrication. We can think of agency as *the techniques, concepts, and applications to personalize, customize, elaborate, delegate, and catalyze the processes in the online marketplace.* The key characteristic of agency is that it does not influence the information, content, or services that it presents or enables. Agency makes the processes in the information chain work better and more smoothly, and it makes them more user-friendly but it does not alter or influence the actual data or information it is charged with gathering.

The current and future online marketplace will require the need for three types of agency:

1. **Supplier-driven agency,** which is closely related to Information Push. Current and future examples of this kind of agency are push technologies, ISAs, and Web-enabled television.
2. **User-driven agency,** which is closely related to Information Pull. Current and future examples of this kind of agency are mobile intelligent software agents (MISAs, described later in this chapter) and personal newspapers.
3. An agency that makes the two previous agencies converge and is related to both Information Push as well as Information Pull will focus on **intermediary services.** Current and future examples of this kind of agency are (human or computer) information brokers and intermediaries.

Agency will enable people to focus primarily on *what* it is they want to do (e.g., which information they need, which task they would like to get done), and much less

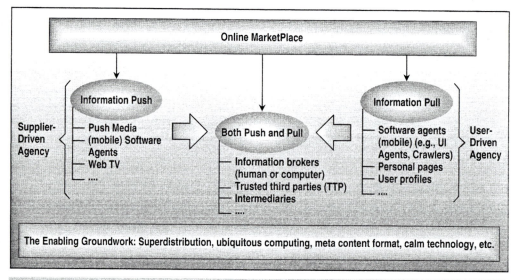

FIGURE 17-4 Predicted Structure of the Future Online Marketplace

on *how* they should best do it (e.g., where to look for information or where to offer it) and which applications, services, and techniques can best accomplish the task. This focus shift is not only necessary because it saves us time and because it makes life a lot easier, but also because many of the newcomers on the future online marketplace will be nontechnical by nature and disinclined to acquire a high degree of technical literacy. If this marketplace is to be open and ready for everyone, it must not have high technological barriers to entry. Agency will shift the focus from people complying with the constraints imposed by the tools to a situation in which the tools conform to the constraints imposed by the people.

Figure 17-4 contains a structural overview of the information market as it could emerge in the near future. Next to each of the agencies, related concepts, techniques, and applications are given. Bear in mind that these examples are by no means an exhaustive list.

17-2: WHAT IS AN INTELLIGENT SOFTWARE AGENT?

Although creativity remains one of the last bastions of human cognitive endeavors, the ISA as an emerging technology is rapidly finding its way into all computer-related realms, including that of the DSS, by facilitating users in the delegation of work to a computer. ISA technology is truly a glimpse into the future of DSSs and tomorrow's problem solving, because intelligent software agents are capable of performing many of the necessary decision support tasks formerly designated as uniquely human activities. They can perform such tasks as finding and filtering information, customizing views of information, and automating work. In this next section we will summarize the characteristics that differentiate agents from other software, examine several proposed classification schemes for intelligent agents, and identify several current intelligent agent technologies that can be used to add agents to new or existing DSS applications.

INTELLIGENT SOFTWARE AGENT THEORETICAL CONCEPTS

The concept of an agent is an important one for both managers and computer scientists. To assist in organizing all the characteristics of ISAs, we can conceptualize software agents as members of three primary divisions: (1) agent theory, (2) agent architecture, and (3) agent languages.

Agent Theory

Agent theory answers the question of what an agent is, as well as the mathematical formalisms for representing and reasoning about the properties of agents. How do the various components of an agent's cognitive makeup conspire to produce rational behavior? What is the relationship between these components? What formalisms are appropriate for expressing aspects of agent theory? Do we need logic-based formalisms? If not, is another type of mathematical framework appropriate?

Agent Architecture

This division of conceptualization can be thought of as software engineering models of ISAs. Researchers in the area of *agent architecture* address the problem of designing software and hardware systems that will satisfy the properties specified by the agent theorists. What structure should an artificial intelligent agent have? Is reactive behavior enough or do we need deliberation as well? How can we integrate reactive and deliberative components cleanly? What is the relationship between an agent theory and its associated architecture?

Agent Languages

This last conceptual division, *agent languages,* focuses on the development and deployment of software languages for programming and experimenting with ISAs that embody the principles proposed by agent theorists. What are the right primitives for programming an intelligent agent? How are these primitives related to the theory of an agent or its architecture? Can we realistically hope to execute agent specifications in complex, perhaps multimodal languages? Should we aim for simple agents with limited internal complexity or for agents with complex reasoning abilities?

CHARACTERISTICS OF THE ISA

We discussed throughout this text how the pace and complexity of decision making and problem solving in tomorrow's organization are truly increasing. However, ease of use fails to keep up with the tremendous amount of advanced functionality now available. The result is that DSS applications are becoming more and more daunting for beginning, and even veteran, users. The information and processing that should be available are simply not accessible.

In our lives, when we find ourselves in a position where time and activities overtake us, we seek help in the form of assistants—people who take care of things we could do ourselves but prefer not to. In the DSS world, intelligent software agents play the role of such assistants. ISAs function by allowing users to delegate their work to the agent software. ISAs are useful in automating repetitive tasks, assisting the user in remembering critical dates or events, or intelligently summarizing complex data. More important, just like their human counterparts, intelligent agents can learn from the user and even make recommendations to you regarding a particular course of action.

As with any cutting-edge technology, the formal definition of the concept tends to be both varied and custom-tailored to the definer's specific vision of the technology. The world of intelligent agents spawned numerous early definitions and conceptualizations, each with its own unique perspective on just what an ISA is, or should be. Table 17-1 summarizes the current range of definitions for intelligent agents, their sources, and basic assumptions.

The notion of an agent can be traced back to the Latin expression *agens,* meaning "the cause of an effect, an active substance, a person or a thing that acts, or a representative." A review of the various definitions shown in Table 17-1 reveals two subtle commonalities: (1) An agent is one who acts, or who can act; and (2) an agent is one who acts in place of another person with permission from that person. Building on these two common characteristics of intelligent agents, Franklin and Graesser (1996) offered a formal definition of intelligent software agents that embodies the essence of the prior definitions and to which we will subscribe in this text:

> An autonomous intelligent software agent is a system situated within and a part of an environment that senses that environment and acts on it, over time, in pursuit of its own agenda and so as to effect what it senses in the future.

This definition is broad enough to avoid the restrictive, targeted nature of other definitions, but it offers a useful boundary within which to explore intelligent software agents and their use. Within the context of the DSS, we believe that the concept of the ISA should be focused enough to define a specific mechanism for analyzing systems, such as semistructured problem spaces, but at the same time be expansive enough, as necessary, to allow for creative and innovative uses for the technology. In this sense, not every program is an agent. Intelligent software agents are, by definition, computer programs, but a computer program must possess several unique characteristics to be classified as an ISA.

Table 17-2 provides a listing of the various identifying characteristics of intelligent software agents that differentiate them from other computer-based programs.

Autonomy

An agent must display a measure of *autonomy* from its user. In other words, once initiated it exercises control over its own actions. This characteristic is good because when you delegate something to your agent, you expect it to work independently on your request no matter what happens around it. To this end, a software agent must be able to display a certain level of spontaneous execution and preemptive or independent action for the benefit of its user. In this respect, ISAs differ from other computer programs, which tend to respond only to direct manipulation and otherwise function without any awareness of the conditions in which they are operating.

Reactivity

An agent must be relatively *reactive;* that is, an ISA must sense changes in its environment and respond in a timely fashion. This characteristic of agents is also at the core of delegation and automation. Just as you tell your assistant, "When x happens, do y," an agent is always waiting for x to happen! Finally, in order to carry out the wishes of the user, all agents must be continuously operational, even when the user is gone.

TABLE 17-1   Summary of Current Definitions of Intelligent Software Agents

Agent Name	*Agent Definition*
MuBot Agent	Represents two orthogonal concepts: the agent's ability for autonomous execution and the agent's ability to perform domain-oriented reasoning.
AIMA Agent	Anything that can be viewed as perceiving its environment through sensors and acting upon that environment through effectors.
Maes AGent	Autonomous agents are computational systems that inhabit some complex dynamic environment and act autonomously in this environment, and by doing so realize a set of goals or tasks for which they are designed.
KidSim Agent	A persistent software entity dedicated to a specific purpose. "Persistent" distinguishes agents from subroutines; agents have their own ideas about how to accomplish tasks, their own agendas. "Special purpose" distinguishes them from entire multifunction applications; agents are typically much smaller.
Hayes-Roth Agent	Intelligent agents continuously perform three functions: perception of dynamic conditions in the environment; action to affect conditions in the environment; and reasoning to interpret perceptions, solve problems, draw inferences, and determine actions.
IBM Agent	Intelligent agents are software entities that carry out some set of operations on behalf of a user or another program with some degree of independence or autonomy, and, in doing so, employ some knowledge or represenation of the user's goals or desires.
Wooldridge-Jennings Agent	A hardware or (more usually) software-based computer system that enjoys the following properties: • *Autonomy.* Agents operate without the direct intervention of humans or others and have some kind of control over their actions and internal state. • *Social ability.* Agents interact with other agents (and possibly humans) via some kind of agent communication language. • *Reactivity.* Agents perceive their environment (which may be the physical world, a user via a graphical user interface, a collection of other agents, the Internet, or perhaps all of these combined) and respond in a timely fashion to changes that occur in it. • *Proactiveness.* Agents do not simply act in response to their environment; they are able to exhibit goal-directed behavior by taking the initiative.
SodaBot Agent	Software agents are programs that engate in dialogs and negotiate and coordinate transfer of information.
Foner Agent	Agents collaborate, are autonomous, trustworthy, and degrade gracefully in the face of communications mismatch.
Brustoloni Agent	Autonomous agents are systems capable of autonomous, purposeful action in the real world.
FAQ Agent	Agents possess attributes of autonomy, goal orientation, collaboration, flexibility, self-startedness, temporal continuity, character, communicativeness, adaptiveness, and mobility.

TABLE 17-2	Common Characteristics of Intelligent Software Agents	
Autonomy	Cooperation	Graceful degradation
Personalizability	Risk and trust	Anthropomorphism
Discourse	Domain	Mobility

Personalizability

The whole point of an ISA is to enable a user to perform a task, such as information gathering or data analysis, better than he or she could do alone. Because each decision maker is unique and each problem context is different from the last, an ISA must be educable in the task at hand and in how to perform it. This characteristic of *personalizability* is displayed by a learning agent that can acquire the information necessary to function, in part, by initially monitoring the actions of its user.

Discourse and Cooperation

To ensure that an ISA shares the agenda of its user and can carry out the task in the manner desired, some form of discourse or two-way feedback is required. This discourse allows both entities to make their intentions and abilities known to the other and, through this feedback, agree on something resembling a contract about what is to be done, by whom, and when.

In addition to feedback or discourse with the user, ISAs may need to invoke one or more additional ISAs to help them accomplish a task. In this sense, an ISA must possess the ability, when necessary, to interact and communicate with other related ISAs. These ISAs are considered "social" and can communicate with other agents through proprietary means or some common language standard.

Risk, Trust, and Domain

As discussed in the introduction to this chapter, the concept of an intelligent software agent implies the notion of delegation. If we do not *trust* the entity to carry out the task delegated to it, then we are faced with performing the task ourselves. Even with the required level of trust in the agent, delegating responsibility for a task to an external agent exposes us to the *risk* that the agent will do something wrong. The use of intelligent software agents requires a balance between the risks associated with relinquishing control of an operation and our level of trust in the technology. The user, therefore, needs a reasonably accurate mental model of not only what the agent will do (hence, the level of trust we ascribe to it) but also the problem *context and domain* of interest (hence, the degree of risk associated with an error on the part of the ISA).

Knowledge of the domain within which the ISA will reside and operate is an important element in the successful deployment of ISAs. If the domain is a localized decision simulation, then the degree of trust associated with employing the agent can be relatively low, which also means the associated degree of risk is likely to be quite low. If, on the other hand, the agent is being deployed in a domain where its responsibility includes monitoring the position of the control rods in a nuclear reactor and notifying its user when a certain set of conditions exists, then the degree of trust needed in the ISA is, by necessity, quite high and the level of risk associated with its use is also substantial. In these cases, the use of ISAs must be accompanied by additional control mechanisms intended not only to back up the ISA but to monitor its performance as well.

Graceful Degradation and Cooperation

The characteristic of *graceful degradation* is a key element that differentiates an ISA from a simple computer program. This concept relates closely to the concepts of risk, trust, and domain. In the event that the agent experiences difficulty communicating with its user (even in situations where one or the other party may not realize it) or encounters a domain mismatch (one or both entities are simply out of their element and, again, may not realize it), the agent should be able to complete a portion of the task assigned instead of simply failing to operate. In situations where the use of ISAs is appropriate, completion of a portion of the task is generally a better outcome than failing to run at all.

Anthropomorphism

Anthropomorphism is the ascription of humanlike characteristics to an otherwise nonhuman entity (Marakas, Johnson, and Palmer, 2000). Although commonly employed, this characteristic of ISAs is the subject of great debate. Anthropomorphism is evident in a wide variety of situations, such as the assumption that a watercraft is female in gender ("She's a fine craft") or that computers are interactive social entities ("My system has a virus, and it infected the whole lab"). Some agents, such as Merlin or Peedy[1], strive to be believable, in that they are represented as an entity visible or audible to the user, and may even have aspects of emotion or personality. Intelligent software agents are often designed to display humanlike tendencies and actions in situations where possible interaction with users other than the agent owner might be desirable. One such example of the use of anthropomorphism in the design of ISAs is the concept of an avatar.

An *avatar* is defined as an embodiment or concrete manifestation of a principle, attitude, view of life, or the like. In a virtual reality environment (VRE), your avatar is your signature, your trademark, and the symbol of your physical presence. Users with ISAs that work within a VRE may have hundreds of avatars: some are idiosyncratic, some are pictographic, some iconoclastic, but, typically, most of the enduring avatars have been those associated with recognizable symbols of popular culture—cans of Spam, Winnie the Pooh, or Tarzan. As avatars grow more common and complex, and more ambitious in terms of their ability to do things—to simulate conversational exchange, to exhibit dynamically generated behaviors—we will rely more and more upon visualization skills to establish online identity. The design challenges here are considerable: strategic, visual, conceptual, choreographic. Figure 17-5 shows a screen shot of a typical virtual world application in which each participant is represented by his or her chosen avatar. In such environments, participants can freely interact, converse, and even collaborate on creating a highly personalized space within the environment. Notice that some of the options available to communicate with others include prespecified movements such as doing the Macarena, waving, and executing karate moves, among others.

Mobility

Some agents are *mobile* and, when necessary, can move from machine to machine or across different system architectures, networks, and platforms. Agents that move can get closer to data they may need to process and, moreover, they can do so without

---

[1]Merlin and Peedy are two common examples of simple ISAs that can be downloaded from several locations on the World Wide Web. Both are examples of the Microsoft Agent software currently available at www.microsoft.com.

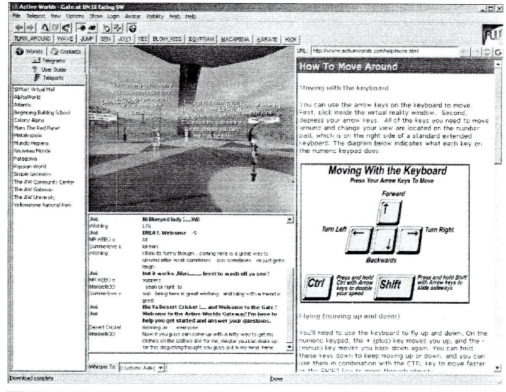

FIGURE 17-5 On-Screen View of the ActiveWorld Virtual Community

Source: www.agentry.net

network delays. A *transportable agent* is a program that can migrate from machine to machine in a heterogeneous network. The program chooses when and where to migrate. It can suspend its execution at an arbitrary point, transport to another machine, and resume execution on the new machine. The agent can perform arbitrarily complex processing at each machine in order to ensure that the message reaches the intended recipient. Figure 17-6 illustrates an example of a mobile agent carrying a mail message.

Transportable agents offer several advantages over the traditional client/server model:

1. **Efficiency.** Transportable agents consume fewer network resources because they move the computation to the data rather than the data to the computation.
2. **Fault tolerance.** Transportable agents do not require a continuous connection between machines.
3. **Convenient paradigm.** Transportable agents hide the communication channels but not the location of the computation.
4. **Customization.** Transportable agents allow clients and servers to extend each other's functionality by programming each other.

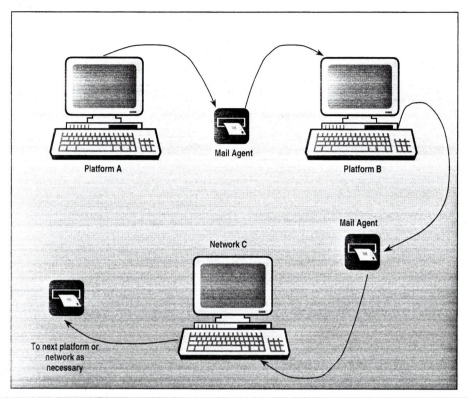

FIGURE 17-6 Illustration of a Transportable Mail Agent

17-3: CLASSIFICATION OF INTELLIGENT SOFTWARE AGENTS

Intelligent software agents can be classified according to several subsets of properties and characteristics. Although all agents must possess the characteristics of reactivity, autonomy, goal orientation, and temporal continuity, other characteristics allow for their classification in either a hierarchical or categorical manner.

HIERARCHICAL CLASSIFICATION OF INTELLIGENT AGENTS

Franklin and Graesser (1996) proposed a "biological" metaphoric classification scheme for ISAs that takes the form of a tree with "living creatures" at the root and individual species at its leaves. Figure 17-7 contains this hierarchical classification scheme.

CATEGORICAL CLASSIFICATION OF INTELLIGENT AGENTS

Another method of classification of ISAs is organizational versus personal agents (also referred to as public, or shared, versus private agents) in which the differentiation is based on whether the agent is executing a business process or task on behalf of an

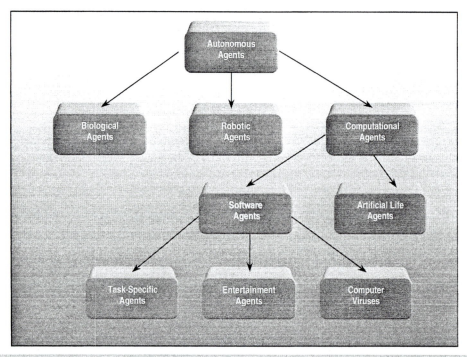

FIGURE 17-7 Franklin and Graesser Hierarchical Classification of Intelligent Agents

organizational application or on behalf of a specific user. Personal agents are more widespread in today's DSS environments but the deployment of organizational ISAs is escalating. The pervasive nature of collaborative technologies such as Lotus Notes makes the use of organizational agents for tasks such as e-mail sorting and filtering or document work-flow management increasingly desirable.

Brustoloni (1991) offered a method of classifying ISAs based on a three-way categorization into regulation agents, planning agents, and adaptive agents. Table 17-3 provides a brief description of each category of agent within this classification method.

Yet another classification method for agents was proposed by Lee, Cheung, and Kao (1997). This method classifies ISAs according to their level of intelligence and power. Table 17-4 contains the Lee, Cheung, and Kao taxonomy of software agents.

TABLE 17-3 Brustoloni Taxonomy of Software Agents

Classification	*Definition*
Regulation Agent	Reacts to each sensory input as it comes in and always knows what to do. This agent neither plans nor learns.
Planning Agent	Performs planning functions using case-based or randomizing algorithms. This agent cannot learn.
Adaptive Agent	These agents can learn while simultaneously performing planning.

TABLE 17-4 Lee, Cheung, and Kao Taxonomy of Software Agents by Level
of Intelligence

Intelligence Level	*Definition*
Level 0	Agents retrieve documents for a user under straight orders. The user must specify the exact location of the desired documents. Example: typical Web browser.
Level 1	Agents-conduct a user-initiated search activity. Agent can match user-supplied keywords with indexed information. Example: Internet search agents (i.e., Yahoo, Alta Vista, etc.).
Level 2	Agents maintain profiles on behalf of their users. Agents can monitor various information sources and notify user whenever relevant information is located or new information is discovered. Example: Web-Watcher.
Level 3	Agents learn and deduce from user-specified profiles to assist in the formalization of a query or target search. Example: DiffAgent.

THE TYPES OF PROBLEMS INTELLIGENT SOFTWARE AGENTS CAN SOLVE

To increase our understanding of ISA technology, we examine some of the various practical problems that intelligent software agents can solve. The list of problems discussed in this section is not meant to be exhaustive, but rather illustrative of general types of problem contexts in which deployment of ISAs may be useful. Consider the following:

> Corinne is up to her neck in information. Her position as a researcher for a small but rapidly growing retail industry consulting firm is both exciting and challenging. She is regularly asked to gather information on a wide variety of subjects relevant to the firm's clients and to "keep her eyes open" for new developments in areas that relate to projects the firm is currently working on. Although Corinne really enjoys the "thrill of the hunt" for information related to a new project, she often finds herself swamped with data that seem to take forever to wade through to find what she refers to as "the keepers." An even bigger problem is the constant struggle to meet the mandate of "keeping her eyes open" for important events. She just knows a better way exists somewhere. Maybe she needs to hire some help.

Corinne could benefit enormously from the employment of several ISAs to assist her in her daily work. The task of wading through information to find the "keepers" is tenable when only a few pieces of data are involved, but as the number of data grows, and as the rate of arrival of new data increases, the task rapidly becomes daunting and untenable. Intelligent software agents could be used to customize information to Corinne's preferences, thus saving her time in handling it and sorting through it.

What about her problem of keeping up with current events? These events could be real-world events like competitive announcements or emergencies, or they could be computer events like the release of a new version of a design document. Regardless of the nature of the event, intelligent software agents continuously monitor various information sources for keywords that indicate an event of interest to one of Corinne's clients or relevant to one or more of the firm's projects. When an event of interest occurs, the ISA could notify Corinne, download appropriate documents to a specified location, schedule a meeting with a specified group of people, or all of these activities.

ISAs are currently employed in a wide variety of organizational situations. Imagine a customer help desk where an ISA can take the basic parameters of a customer's problem and use them to retrieve relevant technical documents from a database for use by the support personnel. The business value of delegating intelligent software agents to handle these and many other types of problems comes from getting the right information at the right time, without having to do it all yourself or rewrite the base applications.

CLASSIFICATION OF ISA TASKS AND APPLICATIONS

The potential application of ISAs is limited only by the needs or desires of the community of users. The range of applications that make use of ISAs includes personalized information management, electronic commerce, and management of complex commercial and industrial processes. This seemingly infinite range of applications for ISA technology can be generally divided into five categories. The following section provides a brief discussion and examples of each of the basic categories of ISA applications.

Watcher Agents

A *watcher agent* searches for the emergence of specific information. It can be instructed to report information of a specific nature from a wide variety of disparate databases and information sources or only from a select few. The watcher agent does not seek information in the form of retrieval but rather monitors its assigned information sources until a relevant piece of information emerges. In general, this category of ISAs is used to facilitate a timely awareness of events relevant to its user. An example of a watcher agent would be an ISA that alerts its user whenever a news story is published that contains information relevant to its assignment.

Learning Agents

In contrast to the watcher agent, the *learner agent* is tailored to its user's individual preferences by "learning" from the user's past or current behavior. In this category, ISAs that facilitate or assist the user in performing some periodic task may be found. For example, suppose a user deploys a learning agent to separate important or relevant e-mail messages from those considered junk mail or noncritical to the user's responsibilities. Without the learner agent, the user would be limited in this activity to setting up a set of filters or rules that would act anytime a message with a particular set of characteristics is received. Using the learner agent, the basic rules for filtration could be provided to the ISA but it would also monitor the filing and deletion of those messages that were not separated by the filtration rule set. By monitoring the subject, sender, content, and actions of the user with regard to these messages over time, the learning agent will be able to predict the actions of the user and will "learn" how to assist the user in sorting the e-mail messages received. If a particular sender's mail is generally filed in a certain place and subsequently replied to, the learning agent can alert the user that a message has been received and that a reply document is ready to be sent. Once the user writes the reply, the ISA can automatically file the message in the appropriate spot. In other situations in which a message from a particular sender or type of sender is regularly deleted without being read, the learner agent could suggest that the user unsubscribe from the message service or even perform the unsubscribe process for the user.

Shopping Agent

This category of ISA is becoming one of the most popular applications of agent technology in existence. The *shopping agent* can be designed to facilitate and assist with a wide variety of online shopping activities. One common application of the shopping agent is to search the Internet for vendors offering a particular product and then retrieve those vendor offerings with the best prices and delivery terms. Other applications of agents in this category could be the deployment of an agent that constantly searches for products of a unique or rare nature, such as rare artwork or other collectable items. Once discovered, the shopping agent can retrieve a summary of the product offering, compare it to a known list of such items owned by its user, alert the user to its existence, and even inform the user with regard to current market values that might apply to the rare item in question. Imagine providing your shopping agent with your Christmas list, including the names and addresses of the people you are shopping for, and empowering it to find the items at the best price and availability, order them gift wrapped, purchase them with your credit card, and have them shipped directly to each recipient. No more last-minute shopping for that special person.

Information Retrieval Agents

This common category of ISA application is designed to help its user search for desired information in an intelligent fashion and retrieve and organize the information in a useful and timely manner. The most common application of this category of ISA is the familiar *search engine* used by Web surfers to locate Web sites relevant to a particular topic of interest. Information retrieval agents can be found in a wide variety of complexities. Some, such as those available through sites such as Yahoo! or Alltheweb.com, retrieve information via a keyword and metatag search algorithm and return their findings ranked by the probability of relevance. Other more sophisticated ISAs in this category can search not only the keywords and metatags contained within the HTML code at the site, but can also search the text, audio, and even video elements stored at a particular site to create an even richer set of potentially relevant Web sites. Figure 17-8a contains the first page of a typical information retrieval search result obtained from Yahoo! Figure 17-8b contains results from the same search using rival information retrieval agent, Alltheweb.com.

Helper Agents

The final categorical type of ISA is referred to as the *helper agent*. The agents that fall in this generalized class perform tasks on behalf of their user in an autonomous fashion and without human interaction. One common example of this type of agent is agents that assist Web site owners in registering their site with available search engines throughout the Internet. The agent is deployed such that anytime it finds a search engine that does not have its user's site registered, it will automatically and autonomously complete the registration process. In addition to simple registration activities, these types of agents can allow their users to specify the numbers of pages deep into the search engines they wish to check, the keywords they want checked against their site, and the URLs they want checked. Further, they can monitor the ranking of the user's site against all other relevant sites and, if so programmed, can execute periodic searches through the various search engines to raise the ranking of its associated Web site in terms of number of search hits. This activity will result in the agent's assigned site being listed closer to the front of a search inquiry rather than two

Search Results

Your search: George M Marakas

Web Page Matches

1. AIS - George Marakas
   AIS Home. Welcome to the home page of **George M. Marakas**
   Associate Professor. Office: BU560F Phone ...
   http://www.indiana.edu/~aisdept/people/marakas.html
   More Results From: www.indiana.edu

2. Amazon.com: buying info: Decision Support Systems in the 21st ...
   ... Was this review helpful to you? Customers who bought titles by **George M.**
   Marakas also bought titles by these authors: ... Explore similar authors ...
   http://www.amazon.com/exec/obidos/ASIN/013744186X/
   More Results From: www.amazon.com

3. eLibrary Author Select
   George M. Marakas Indiana University 10th and Fee Lane 560F Bloomington, IN 47405
   USA, PHONE: (812) 855-2381 FAX: EMAIL: gmarakas@indiana.edu URL: Information ...
   http://ids.csom.umn.edu/isworld/facdir/eLibrary.cfm?LName=Marakas&FName=George

4. Catalog
   ... Systems Analysis and Design: An Active Approach, 1/e **George M. Marakas**, Kelley
   School of Business, Indiana University 2001 / 0-13-022515-0 / Prentice Hall. ...
   http://vig.prenhall.com/catalog/academic/course1,4095,134,00.html
   More Results From: vig.prenhall.com

5. Pearson Technology Group - Systems Analysis and Design. An ...
   ... Systems Analysis and Design: An Active Approach 1/e **George M. Marakas** Published November
   2000 by Prentice Hall Copyright 2001, 483 pp., Cloth ISBN: 0-13-022515 ...
   http://www.pearsonptg.com/book_detail/0,3771,0130225160,00.htm
   More Results From: www.pearsonptg.com

6. Companion Website to Support Decision Support Systems in the ...
   ... Decision Support Systems in the 21st Century by **George**
   M. Marakas. Select a chapter: 1 ...
   http://cw.prenhall.com/marakas

7. Barnes & Noble.com - Decision Support Systems in the Twenty- ...
   ... No items in cart. Bibliography Books by **George M. Marakas** About the Book
   Publisher Information. From the Book Table of Contents, Related Titles. ...
   http://shop.barnesandnoble.com/textbooks/booksearch/isbninquiry.asp?isbn=013744186X
   More Results From: shop.barnesandnoble.com

8. Kelley School MBA Program | Curriculum
   ... R. Dennis Dr. Joseph Fisher Dr. Les Heitger Dr. Patrick E. Hopkins Laureen Maines
   George M. Marakas Dr. Anne P. Massey Dr. Robert W. Parry Dr. James H. Pratt Dr ...
   http://www.bus.indiana.edu/mba/faculty/roster.cfm
   More Results From: www.bus.indiana.edu

FIGURE 17-8a Retrieval Results for Yahoo! Query on "George M. Marakas"

or three pages in. For those sites competing for business on the World Wide Web, it can create a big competitive advantage.

INFORMATION OVERLOAD AND FILTERING

By now, you are probably a veteran user of the Internet and the World Wide Web. It is clear to you that the one resource most readily available to the "connected world" is information. Some of it is useful, some of it is useless, but all of it is available, with more

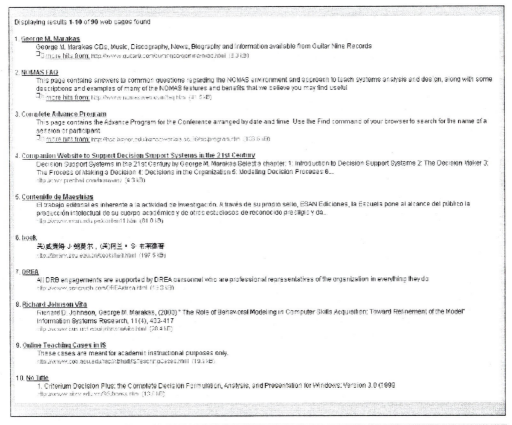

FIGURE 17-8b   Retrieval Results for the AllTheWeb Query on "George M. Marakas"

of it each day. This explosive growth in available information results in the condition commonly referred to as *information overload*. We know from Chapter 2 that the typical decision maker is limited in his or her cognitive ability to process large volumes of information. Because of this limitation, having too much data or information can be as debilitating as having too little or none. Intelligent software agents are being deployed in an effort to rescue us from this world of information overload. The categories of ISAs discussed in the previous section all focus on information gathering, which is useful when we are faced with the task of finding relevant facts and information about a pending decision or task. More often than not, however, we are faced with the opposite problem: Of the enormous amount of information available to us, only a small portion of it is relevant to our task at hand. It is here where *information filtering* becomes a key capability of an ISA.

Despite the obvious advantages of the modern e-mail system, we all reach the point at which our ability to overcome the slow speed characteristics of "snail mail" places us in an information overload condition. Some organizations receive so much e-mail that they actually employ clerical workers to sift through the incoming e-mail, answer basic queries, and then forward the remainder on to more specialized workers. By deploying an ISA-based application to assist in this filtration process, companies are again realizing both effectiveness and efficiency in their e-mail systems. The filtration agent can read each incoming e-mail and refer to a software-based *knowledge chart* to determine who should receive the query. Systems such as these can quickly save organizations large amounts of time and money.

A popular ISA deployed for e-mail filtration is called Maxim. One of the early prototypes out of the MIT Media Lab, Maxim is described as a "personal digital assistant" that exploits agent technology in order to manage and filter e-mail. The program can learn to prioritize, delete, forward, sort, and archive e-mail messages on behalf of a user by electronically "looking over the shoulder" of a user as he or she works with the e-mail and by making internal predictions about what a user will do with the e-mail. Once Maxim achieves a particular level of accuracy in its predictions, it offers suggestions to the user about how best to handle the e-mail. Maxim can even deploy a small character face that changes expression depending upon the actions being taken by its user.

About the same time that Maxim was being developed, the MIT Media Lab also designed an ISA-based Internet news-filtering program known as *Newt*. After a human user provides Newt with a series of examples of news articles that would and would not be of interest, the application uses this information-specific feedback to develop an internal model of the user's preferences. Newt ultimately employs this model to filter and thereby select those items of news that would be of interest, without any need for the human user to browse the items. Newt is also capable of retrieving articles on the basis of explicit rules provided by the user. Once the user reviews the retrieved articles, feedback given to Newt allows the agent to be trained further on which articles to retrieve and which to ignore.

WHAT SORTS OF THINGS CAN ISAs DO?

Consider the following examples that use an intelligent agent and illustrate some of the important ways in which intelligent agents help solve real problems and make today's computer systems easier to use.

CUSTOMER HELP DESK

A customer help desk consultant's job is to answer calls from customers and find the answer to their problems. When customers call with problems, in some cases the employee manually looks up answers from hardcopy manuals; in other cases a searchable CD-ROM collection can be used. Some companies even offer searches over the Internet. Instead of hiring help desk consultants, or having the customers search the Internet for an answer, with ISA-based technology, the customer describes the problem and the ISA automatically searches the appropriate databases (either CD-ROM or the Internet). Once the search is complete, the ISA presents a consolidated answer with the most likely first.

WEB BROWSER INTELLIGENT SOFTWARE AGENT

A Web browser ISA is an agent that tracks what Web sites were visited and then customizes the view of the Web by automatically keeping a bookmark list, ordered by how often and how recently a user visited the site. It allows the search for any words stored in the user's bookmark track and takes the user back to the site thus avoiding a search involving multiple site hits. The ISA can also help find where the user has been by showing all the different tracks taken in the past starting at the current page. It could also let the user know via notification when sites of interest are updated.

PERSONAL SHOPPING ASSISTANT

IBM's Personal Shopping Assistant uses ISA technology to help the Internet shopper or the Internet shop owner find the desired item quickly without browsing page after page of the wrong merchandise. With the Personal Shopping Assistant, stores and merchandise are customized as the ISA learns the shopper's preferences as he/she enters any online mall or stores or looks at specific merchandise. It can also arrange the merchandise so that the items most preferred are the first ones displayed. Finally, Personal Shopping Assistant automates the shopping experience by reminding the user to shop when a birthday, an anniversary, or even a sale for a particular item occurs.

17-4: INTELLIGENT SOFTWARE AGENTS IN E-BUSINESS

A few years ago, ISAs were regularly hyped as being the next big thing in e-commerce. In their early days, e-commerce agents largely flopped because users new to the Internet buying experience were hesitant to turn over shopping, negotiating, and buying tasks to invisible software applications. More recently however, as buyers become more comfortable with making their purchases via the Internet, agent technology aimed specifically at furthering electronic commerce is reemerging. For example, tools now exist that help consumers determine what to buy (product brokering) by guiding them through a large product feature space. It allows consumers to specify constraints on a product's features. A *constraint satisfaction search engine* then returns an ordered list of only those products that satisfy all the consumer's chosen preferences. Other ISA-based applications can be programmed and deployed to recommend products via a "word of mouth" recommendation mechanism called *automated collaborative filtering* (ACF). Essentially, these agent applications use the opinions of like-minded people to offer consumer recommendations. A common application for this type of system is currently being used to recommend commodity products such as music and books. Figure 17-9 shows the results of a word-of-mouth recommendation engine used by Amazon.com, a leading Internet retailer.

Still other ISA-based shopping applications compare various merchant alternatives. This type of application is referred to as a *merchant brokering* agent. When a user provides the name of a particular product, for example the CD titled *The Deric Rush Band—Wood and Steel,* the merchant brokering agent searches a number of merchant Web sites and determines and compares various price differentials. Once it creates an optimal set of merchant options, the agent presents the results to the user and the user can authorize the purchase of the product. In some cases, the user can preauthorize the agent to buy the product if a specified set of constraints is satisfied.

Customer Reviews

Avg. Customer Review: ★★★★★

Write an online review and share your thoughts with other customers.

1 of 7 people found the following review helpful:

★★ **Pen or writing implement?**, May 18, 2001
Reviewer: **A reader** from Miami, Fl United States
Why does he use all these unnecessary, fancy, confusing, mind bending words? The author loses and confuses the reader.

Was this review helpful to you? (YES) (NO)

12 of 15 people found the following review helpful:

★★★★★ **It's a mistake to buy any other book**, December 12, 1999
Reviewer: debby_h (see more about me) from United States
It's rare to read a text book cover to cover, but you'll find it easy to do with Marakas' DSS text. He writes as if he is lecturing in class - the examples are clear (and lively, which is rare in academia!), the language flows and the presentation of the material makes it easy even for beginners in the field (like me) to understand. Don't miss out on this text!

Was this review helpful to you? (YES) (NO)

7 of 10 people found the following review helpful:

★★★★★ **This book is the killer click.**, November 19, 1999
Reviewer: **Ubirata Lima** from Buenos Aires, Argentina
Excellent book. Very practical approach to an extremely complex and soft subject.

Was this review helpful to you? (YES) (NO)

FIGURE 17-9 Example of Word-of-Mouth Recommendation Engine

One recent innovation in agent technology relevant to electronic commerce is Tete-a-Tete (T@T). The feature that distinguishes this agent technology from its predecessors is the ability to negotiate in a cooperative rather than a competitive style. T@T can also negotiate across multiple terms of a transaction including warranties, delivery times, service contracts, return policies, loan options, gift services, and other merchant value-added services. The agent technology proved to be so successful that it is now marketed commercially by Frictionless Commerce, Inc.

FUTURE APPLICATIONS OF INTELLIGENT SOFTWARE AGENTS IN ELECTRONIC COMMERCE

The problem with technology is that it is often impossible to identify its effects on a society. Consider the now-ubiquitous computer. In the mid-1940s, when digital computers were first built, leading pioneers presumed that the entire country might need only a dozen or so. In the mid-1970s, few expected that within a decade the PC would become the most essential occupational tool in the world. Even fewer people realized that the PC was not a stand-alone technology, but the hub of a complex technological system that contained elements as diverse as online publishing, e-mail, computer games, and electronic gambling.

In this same vein, it is unclear whether ISA technology will appear in electronic commerce as part of an evolutionary or revolutionary process. Much will depend on the future infrastructure and architecture of the Internet, including the chosen agent standards, whether a homogeneous or heterogeneous architecture is adopted, and, most important, whether ISA interoperability standards will be required. The extent to which agent technology will require an interoperability standard exemplifies one of the many difficult choices that developers of agent technology face. Currently, a great deal of debate surrounds the issue of what the appropriate agent paradigm is in electronic commerce. One of the most heated arguments focuses on whether the negotiation protocol of an e-commerce ISA should be competitive or cooperative in nature. Because merchants tend to strive for highly cooperative, long-term relationships with their customers in order to maximize loyalty, customer satisfaction, and reputation, it is generally believed that more cooperative multiagent decision analysis tools instead of competitive negotiation protocols, such as online auctions, will become the standard. If this approach becomes the norm, which presently appears to be the case, an interoperability standard will indeed be necessary. It is yet another in a long line of cyber laws issues to be addressed in the coming years.

If it turns out that open standards are further developed and adopted, one might expect that electronic commerce will shift away from its current mode of interaction—a mode that is in many ways constrained by the fact that transactions take place within a closed system. In the future, a move toward more open, "public" systems seems likely. This type of system will, of course, require much greater agent mobility. In the open marketplaces of the future, the specific negotiation protocols for given transactions will likely not be predetermined. These negotiation protocols would be left to the predilections of those who design, create, and employ the intelligent software agents involved in those particular transactions.

The future shift toward more open systems will significantly affect the legal treatment of automated electronic commerce, as well. The current closed systems offer the commercial advantage of clarifying all of the legal rules in advance. Recall, for example, that from the earliest days of electronic data interchange (EDI) through today's deployment of extensible markup language (XML) Web sites, human users are required to adopt certain predetermined "rules of engagement," many of which were built directly into the system. In the open systems of the future—where intelligent software agents will be free to roam the Internet in search of transaction partners without any preexisting commitment to the same rules of engagement as those preferred by agents encountered along the way—the threat of commercial uncertainty looms large. In today's rather unsophisticated marketplace, agents are purposely constrained to extremely simplistic negotiations in order to foster trust and confidence in the human users. Consider, then, the kind of legal clarification that might be required in the following future world:

Debby relies on a mobile ISA to orchestrate her Friday evenings. Launched months ago, her ISA waits in a quiet corner of the electronic marketplace for most of the week; however each Friday at exactly 12 noon it takes the following steps:

1. Debby's agent keeps a record of the films it selected on past occasions to prevent selecting one of those films again.
2. The ISA travels to one of the many video retailing Web sites on the Internet. It uses the agent programming language's GO instruction and a ticket that designates the video Web site by its authority and class.

3. Her ISA meets with the video agent that resides in and provides the service of the video Web site. It uses the MEET instruction and a petition that designates the video agent by its authority and class.

4. Debby's ISA asks the video agent for the catalog listing for each romantic comedy in its inventory. Her ISA selects a film at random from among the recent comedies, avoiding the films it selected before. Her ISA then orders the selected film from the video Web site agent, charges it to Debby's credit card, and instructs the video Web site agent to transmit the film to her home at 7 P.M. that evening. The video Web site agent compares the authority of Debby's agent to the name on the credit card and determines the transaction to be valid.

5. Debby's ISA goes next to the Domino's pizza Web site by using the GO instruction and a ticket that designates the pizza Web site by its authority and class.

6. Her ISA meets with the pizza Web site agent that resides in and provides the service of the pizza Web site. It uses the MEET instruction and a petition that designates the pizza agent by its authority and class.

7. Debby's ISA orders one medium-sized pineapple and eggplant pizza for home delivery at 6:45 P.M. The agent charges the pizza, as it did the video, to Debby's credit card. The pizza Web site agent, like the video agent before it, compares the authority of Debby's agent to the name on the credit card and determines the transaction to be valid.

8. Debby's ISA returns to its designated resting place in the electronic marketplace. It uses the GO instruction and a ticket that designates that place by its place name and network address, which it noted previously. All that remains is for the ISA to notify Debby and her companion Bernie of their evening appointment.

9. The agent creates two new agents of Debby's authority and gives each the catalog listing of the selected film and Debby's and Bernie's names. Its work complete, the original ISA awaits another Friday.

10. One of the two new agents goes to Debby's mailbox site and the other goes to Bernie's. They use the GO instruction and tickets that designate the mailbox places by their class and authorities.

11. The agents meet with the mailbox agents that reside in and provide the services of the mailbox sites. They use the MEET instruction and petitions designating the mailbox agents by their class and authorities.

12. The agents deliver to the mailbox agents electronic messages that include the film's catalog listing and that remind Debby and Bernie of their date. The two agents terminate and the mailbox agents convey the reminders to Debby and Bernie.

It does not require much imagination to conceive of adaptations in the use of this ISA technology that would generate transactions much more sophisticated than the straightforward consumer purchases envisioned in the preceding description. Imagine, for example, a similar agent technology applied by an industrial manufacturer that, instead of ordering pizza and a video, supports a team of software agents, each of which is dispatched to perform a particular task that will be carried out in conjunction with the tasks performed by other agents on the team. For example, after an agent designed to monitor the manufacturer's supply of certain subcomponents discovers that the supply is low, it launches into action several merchant brokering agents that are then dispatched to search the Internet for the lowest prices for various subcomponents needed to manufacture the ultimate product. Once the appropriate merchants' sites are discovered and evaluated, other agents step in to negotiate the terms and conditions upon which those separate subcomponents might be purchased (including product warranties, freight rates, delivery dates, exemption clauses, etc.). Other agents assist with the information and communications pertaining to placing the orders and arranging for the shipping and receiving of the subcomponents, while a different agent would initiate electronic payment schemes. Still other agents would deal with the marketing and sales of the ultimate product, once manufactured. Notice that the advent of electronic cash mechanisms—especially in cases where the goods bought and sold are information products not requiring a physical medium in order to execute the transaction—no longer requires human users to ratify or "physically consummate" agent-made agreements. Thus, one ends up in a future world in which agreements are negotiated and entered into without any need for human traders to review or even be aware of particular transactions.

A world such as this could undoubtedly create various advantages for human entrepreneurs. Such a world would spare human users from having to find, negotiate, and deal with buyers and sellers. A truly intelligent technology applied in this manner would depersonalize the process of negotiation, avoid misunderstandings resulting from language barriers, and perhaps even free people to perform other important tasks or pursue more meaningful relationships. These systems would also allow more accurate business records to be kept because software agents could build databases that, among other things, keep track of all interactions (whether or not the particular negotiation resulted in the formation of a contract). The proper integration of the information on such databases could not only reduce transaction costs but could lead to pricing that is closer to optimal.

Agent Deceit

Of course, such a world would also create various disadvantages too. As programmers of ISA technology become more adept, it will become possible for them to design deceitful and perhaps even malicious agent protocols. Then the need for ISA-based solutions to these ISA-created problems might become necessary. For example, regulator ISAs roaming the marketplace could potentially ensure that no illegal activity occurs. It is difficult at present to know or even imagine whether ISA technology could ever rise to the occasion. Even if such technology became possible, it is not clear that regulator ISAs could effectively operate in the future open systems of an indeterminate number of potential marketplaces. Nor is it clear that we would want them to.

Agent Malfunction

Deceit aside, it is also quite possible for agent technology to malfunction or in some other way carry out decision processes that do not comply with the intentions or purposes of the human user who employed the particular agent or, for that matter, the human designer of the software agent. As we all know, software is, by nature, unreliable.

The failure of a complex program is not always due to human negligence in the creation or operation of the program, although examples of such negligence are abundant. Although it is at least theoretically possible to check to see whether a program output is correct in a given instance, it is still unproven that programs can be verified as a general matter; that is, that they are correct over an arbitrary set of inputs. In fact, it appears highly unlikely that even programs that successfully process selected inputs can be shown to be correct generally.

Software reliability cannot be conclusively established because digital systems in general implement discontinuous input-to-input mappings that are intractable by simple mathematical modeling. This point is particularly important: Continuity assumptions cannot be used in validating software, and failures are caused by the occurrence of specific, unpredicted combinations of events, rather than from excessive levels of some identifiable stress factor.

The long-term operation of complex systems entails a fundamental uncertainty, especially in the context of complex ISA environments, including new or unpredictable environments. That, of course, is precisely the situation in which ISAs are forecast to operate.

In addition to unreliability on the part of a software agent, the intentions of a human user may not always be carried out even when the agent technology is performing reliably. Because mobile agent technology aims to allow agents to be cross-software compatible, human users often will not know when or even where their agents are executing. When one software agent operates in conjunction with others in a cooperative agent system across platforms and operating systems, as described in the preceding example, it will become next to impossible to distinguish between them and determine which agent did not properly perform its task. The biggest danger of any network-wide system that allows ISAs is that some of the agents will deliberately or accidentally run amok. Agents can be compared with viruses; both are little programs that seize control of a foreign machine. Another commonality between some software agents and viruses is that they will sometimes mutate in order to perform their tasks. As a result, both are subject to *polymorphism,* a phenomenon that makes it difficult to isolate a particular program because its identity is not always consistent over time. Thus, if a particular ISA carries out its function through a series of continuous mutations of specific bits of its program, or *codelets* as they are often called, it will not be long before that agent will become unrecognizable to the human user who originally created and deployed it.

The future of ISA technology in the world of e-commerce is full of question marks. Although it is by no means clear precisely what intelligent software agents will look like or how they will operate in the years to come, it is virtually certain that ISAs will play a major role in the next wave of e-commerce. ISAs will be deployed to assist human interaction through the various stages of a transaction from product and merchant brokering through to negotiation, sale, distribution, and payment. It is not unreasonable to predict that, in time, ISA-based technology will become sufficiently sophisticated to perform many if not all of these sorts of tasks without human oversight or intervention. Such possibilities would perhaps require programmers to develop polymorphic systems capable of generating creative intelligence. Some of the decisions entailed by these systems would by nature be pathological, that is, at least some of the outcomes generated by future agents would be unintended. Still, a look at the future reveals the technological and commercial promise of autonomous ISAs is both immediate and apparent.

17-5: DESIGNING AND DEPLOYING INTELLIGENT SOFTWARE AGENTS

Given the infancy of the intelligent software agent in our increasingly wired world, it should come as no surprise that prescriptions for design and implementation of ISAs are not yet readily available. Several researchers, however, provide descriptions of approaches and guidelines for design and development that address many of the issues in this area (see Figure 17-10). This section provides a brief overview of several of the commonly applied approaches to ISA design and implementation.

THE GAIA METHODOLOGY

Gaia is a general methodology that supports both the microlevel (agent structure) and macrolevel (agent society and organization structure) of agent development. It is by no means, however, a "silver bullet'" approach because it requires that interagent relationships (organization) and agent abilities are static at run time. The motivation behind Gaia is that existing methodologies fail to represent the autonomous and problem-solving nature of agents; they also fail to model agents' ways of performing

FIGURE 17-10   Proposed Approaches for the Design and Implementation of ISAs

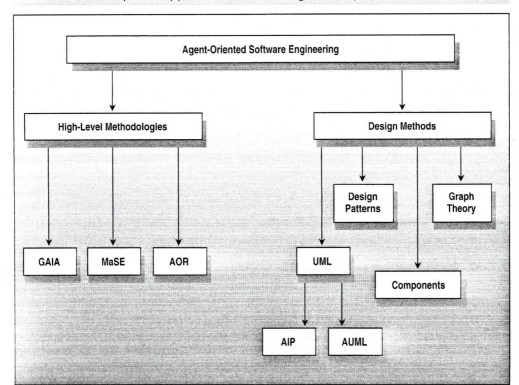

interactions and creating organizations. Using Gaia, software designers can systematically develop an implementation-ready design based on system requirements.

The first step in the Gaia analysis process is to find the *roles* for the various agents to be deployed in the system. Once that step is achieved, the second step is to model any expected or desired interactions between the roles identified. Roles consist of four attributes: responsibilities, permissions, activities, and protocols.

- *Responsibilities* are of two types: (1) liveness properties in which the role must add something good to the system, and (2) safety properties in which the role is to prevent and disallow that something bad happens to the system.
- *Permissions* represent what the role is allowed to do, in particular, which information it is allowed to access.
- *Activities* are tasks that a role performs without interacting with other roles.
- *Protocols* are the specific patterns of interaction (e.g., a seller role can support different auction protocols, such as "English auction").

Gaia's formal operators and templates represent roles and their associated attributes. It also employs schemas for the representation of interactions.

In the Gaia design process, the first step is to map roles into agent types, and then to create the right number of agent instances of each type. The second step is to determine the services model needed to fulfill a role in one or several agents; and the final step is to create the acquaintance model for the representation of communication between the agents.

Due to the restrictions of Gaia, it is of less value in the open and unpredictable domain of Internet applications. On the other hand it offers a good approach for developing closed-domain agent systems.

THE MULTIAGENT SYSTEMS ENGINEERING METHODOLOGY

Another suggested approach to ISA design and implementation is the Multiagent Systems Engineering methodology (MaSE). MaSE is similar to Gaia with respect to generality and the application domain supported, but MaSE goes further in supporting automatic code creation through the MaSE tool. The motivation behind MaSE is the current lack of proven methodology and industrial-strength tool kits for creating agent-based systems. MaSE leads the designer from the initial system specification to the implemented agent system. Domain restrictions of MaSE are similar to those of Gaia, but in addition it requires that agent interactions are one-to-one and not multicast.

The MaSE methodology is divided into seven sections (phases) in a logical pipeline. Figure 17-11 graphically illustrates the MaSE approach.

Capturing goals, the first phase, transforms the initial system specification into a structured hierarchy of system goals by first identifying goals based on the initial system specification's requirements and then ordering the goals according to importance in a structured and topically ordered hierarchy.

Applying use cases, the second phase, creates use cases and sequence diagrams based on the initial system specification. The use case is an object-oriented design tool that presents the logical interaction paths between various roles and the system itself. Sequence diagrams are used to determine the minimum number of messages that must be passed between roles in the system.

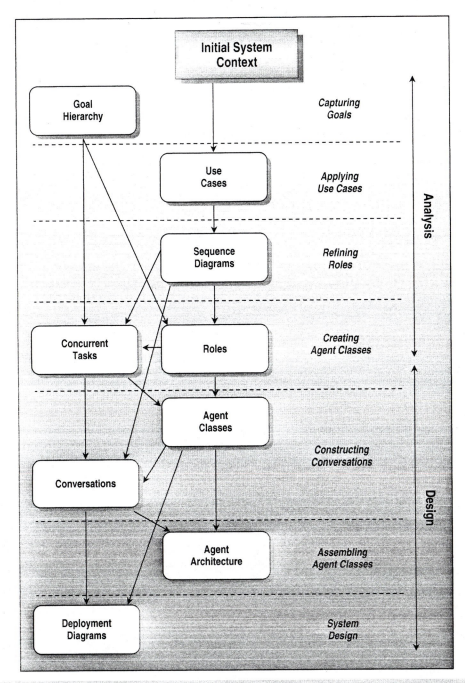

FIGURE 17-11   Illustration of MaSE Phased Agent Development Methodology

The third phase, *refining roles,* creates roles that are responsible for the goals defined in phase 1. In general each goal is represented by one role, but a set of related goals may map to one role. Together with the roles, a set of tasks is created to define how to reach goals related to the role. Tasks are defined using another common object-oriented design tool, state diagrams.[2]

The fourth phase, *creating agent classes,* maps roles to agent classes in an agent class diagram. This diagram resembles object class diagrams, but the semantic of relationships is high-level conversation as opposed to the object class diagrams' inheritance of structure.

The fifth phase, *constructing conversations,* defines a coordination protocol in the form of state diagrams that define the conversation state for interacting agents.

In the sixth phase, *assembling agent classes,* the internal functionality of agent classes is created. Selected functionality is based on five different types of agent architectures: belief-desire-intention (BDI), reactive, planning, knowledge-based and user-defined architecture.

The final phase, *system design,* creates actual agent instances based on the agent classes. The final result is presented in a deployment diagram. Visions of the future for MaSE include completely automatic code generation based on the deployment diagram.

THE AGENT-OBJECT RELATIONSHIP METHOD

The agent-object relationship (AOR) modeling approach is inspired by two widely applied models of databases: the entity-relationship (ER) metamodel and the relational database (RDB) model.

The purpose of the ER metamodel is to transform relations between different types of data (entities) into an implementation-ready (database) information system design. This transformation is well supported for static entities or objects, but falls short in modeling active entities or agents in an information system. The purpose of the AOR model is to extend the ER model by providing the ability to model relations between agents in addition to static entities.

In AOR, entities can be of six types: agents, events, actions, commitments, claims, and objects. *Commitments* and *claims* are dualistic in that commitments of one *agent* are seen as claims against other agents. Organizations are modeled as a group of sub-agents. Each of the subagents has the right to perform certain *actions,* but they are also committed to duties such as monitoring claims and *events* relevant for the agent organization. The interpretation of duties and permissions seems to correspond with services and permissions found in the Gaia methodology.

In addition to these methodologies, several ISA design and development approaches have been inspired by the methodologies and standards of the object-oriented software engineering field.

---

[2]Although beyond the scope of this text, the reader can find a more detailed explanation of the use case, state diagram, and other object-oriented design tools in any modern systems analysis text. The reader is referred to Marakas, G. M. 2001. *Systems Analysis and Design: An Active Approach.* Upper Saddle River, NJ: Prentice Hall.

UML

The universal modeling language (UML) is a graphical representation language originally developed to standardize the design of object classes. It now includes extended support for designing sequences, components, and in fact all parts of an object-oriented information system design.

Using UML as the foundation, several researchers suggested an architecture-centric design method for multiagent systems. The method is based on standard extensions of UML using the object constraints language (OCL), and it supports the transformation of agent-oriented modeling problems into object-oriented modeling problems. In the transformation process, relations between agents are transformed to design patterns, which are then used as relations between object classes. This process contrasts with the more commonly applied relation types between object classes such as inheritance. The result of this method is that designers and developers are able to use existing UML-based tools in addition to their existing knowledge and experience from developing object-oriented systems.

Building upon this foundation, other researchers suggest a three-layer representation of agent-interaction protocols (AIPs). AIPs are defined as patterns representing both the message communication between agents and the corresponding constraints on the content of such messages. In contrast to the UML-based architecture approach, AIP requires changes to the UML visual language as well as the expressed semantics. The representation requires changes of the following UML representations: packages, templates, sequence diagrams, collaboration diagrams, activity diagrams, and state charts.

In the first layer, the communication protocol (i.e., type of interaction) is represented in a reusable manner applying UML packages and templates. The second layer represents interactions (i.e., which type of agents can communicate with whom) between agents using sequence, collaboration, and activity diagrams as well as state charts. In the third layer, the internal agent processing (i.e., why and how the agent acts) is represented using activity diagrams and state charts.

Expanding this approach, further extensions to UML called agent UML (AUML) represent all aspects of agents using AUML. Its creators submitted AUML to the UML standardization committee as a proposal for inclusion in the forthcoming UML 2.0. According to the suggestion, UML must include richer role specification that requires modification of the UML sequence diagram format. To be able to represent agents instead of operations as interface points, the UML package definition requires modification. Agents' mobility allows them to move between different agent systems autonomously. In order to represent this capability in UML, the deployment diagram definition must change.

Several researchers propose the application of four agent-oriented UML diagrams at the highest abstraction level of agent-oriented software engineering, namely the agent level. It is similar to the AIP approach in the sense that it requires no changes to the UML standard itself. The first is the *ontology diagram* used to model the world as relations between entities using the UML static class diagram format. The second is the *architecture diagram* for modeling the configuration of a multiagent system by applying the UML deployment format. Diagram three is the *protocol diagram*, which is intended to represent the language of interaction and is based on the UML collaboration diagram format. This protocol diagram corresponds to AIP's first layer model of the communication protocol. The fourth is the *role diagram* based on the UML class diagram; it is used to represent the functionalities of each agent role.

THE DESIGN PATTERN APPROACHES

Design patterns are reoccurring patterns of programming code or components in the software architecture. The suggested classification scheme for design patterns in a mobile agent context provides one approach to ISA development and usage. This approach also suggests various patterns belonging to each of the classes. The purpose is to increase reuse and quality of code and, at the same time, reduce the effort of development of mobile agent systems. The design pattern classification scheme has three classes: traveling, task, and interaction. Patterns in the *traveling class* specify features for agents that move between various environments, such as the forwarding pattern that specifies how newly arrived agents can be forwarded to another host. Patterns of the *task class* specify how agents can perform tasks, or how multiple tasks can be performed on multiple hosts, for instance. Patterns of the *interaction class* specify how agents can communicate and cooperate. An example of an interaction class pattern is the facilitator, which defines an agent that provides services for identifying and finding agents with specific capabilities.

THE COMPONENTS APPROACH

Components are logical groups of related objects that can provide certain functionalities. This function might sound quite similar to agents, but components are not autonomous. By grouping related objects, components allow more coarse-grained reuse than the combination of single classes from scratch. It offers an effective and popular development approach in the software industry.

One suggestion presents a three-tier architecture that enables composition of agents by applying reusable components. The first tier is *interactions* that are built up by agent roles and utterances. The second tier is *local information and expertise* that enables the storage of information such as execution states, plans, and constraints of the agent. *Information-content,* the third tier, is passive and often domain-specific, because it is often used to wrap legacy systems (e.g., a mainframe database application).

AGENT ACCESSIBILITY GUIDELINES

A variety of perspectives guide the potential design and deploy ISAs. Although all show some merit, none have yet received sufficient consensus and acceptance to be considered *de facto* standards. In the meantime, we can refer to a simple set of agent accessibility guidelines proposed by Jacobs et al. (2001). These guidelines can assist ISA developers in ensuring that their agent designs are usable by the widest variety of end users (particularly those with various disabilities or physical challenges). A closer inspection of these guidelines reveals them to be applicable to general systems design as well as to more targeted ISA design and implementation. Table 17-5 provides a listing of these guidelines followed by a brief description of each.

(1) Support Input and Output Device Independence
Because people use a variety of devices for input and output, ISA developers need to ensure redundancy in the user interface. Operation of the user interface may require a

TABLE 17-5   Intelligent Software Agent Accessibility Guidelines

Agent Accessibility Guideline	*Description*
(1) Support input and output device independence.	Ensure that the user can interact with the user agent (and the *content* it renders) through different input and output devices.
(2) Ensure user access to all content.	Ensure that users have access to all content, notably *conditional content* that may have been provided to meet the requirements of the Web Content Accessibility Guidelines 1.0.
(3) Allow configuration not to render some content that may reduce accessibility.	Ensure that the user may turn off rendering of content (audio, video, scripts, etc.) that may reduce accessibility by obscuring other content or disorienting the user.
(4) Ensure user control of rendering.	Ensure that the user can select preferred styles (colors, size of rendered text, synthesized speech characteristics, etc.) from choices offered by the user agent. Allow the user to override *author-specified styles* and *user agent default styles.*
(5) Ensure user control of user interface behavior.	Ensure that the user can control the behavior of viewports and other user interface controls, including those that may be manipulated by the author (e.g., through scripts).
(6) Implement interoperable application programming interfaces.	Implement interoperable interfaces to communicate with other software (e.g., assistive technologies, the operating environment, plug-ins, etc.).
(7) Observe operating environment conventions.	Observe operating environment conventions for the *user agent interface,* documentation, installation, etc.
(8) Implement specifications that benefit accessibility.	Support the accessibility features of all implemented specifications. Implement W3C Recommendations when available and appropriate for a task.
(9) Provide navigation mechanisms.	Provide access to content through a variety of navigation mechanisms: sequential navigation, direct navigation, searches, structured navigation, etc.
(10) Orient the user.	Provide information that will help the user understand browsing context.
(11) Allow configuration and customization.	Allow users to configure the user agent so that frequently performed tasks are made convenient, and allow users to save their preferences.
(12) Provide accessible ISA documentation and help.	Ensure that the user can learn about software features that benefit accessibility from the documentation. Ensure that the documentation is accessible.

variety of input devices (keyboard, pointing device, voice input, etc.) and output modalities (e.g., graphical, speech, or braille rendering).

Though it may seem contradictory, enabling full ISA operation through the keyboard is an important part of promoting device independence in today's ISAs. In addition to the fact that some form of keyboard is supported by most platforms, several reasons make this approach practical. For some users (e.g., users with blindness or physical disabilities), operating an ISA with a pointing device may be difficult or impossible if it requires tracking the pointing device position in a two-dimensional visual space. Keyboard operation does not generally require as much movement "through space." Furthermore, some assistive technologies that support a diversity of input and output mechanisms use keyboard APIs for communication with some ISAs. People who cannot or do not use a pointing device may interact with the user interface with the keyboard, through voice input, a head wand, touch screen, or other device.

As a way to promote output device independence, this guideline requires support for text messages in the user interface because text may be rendered visually, as synthesized speech, and as braille.

(2) Ensure User Access to All Content

This guideline requires the ISA to provide access to all content through a series of complementary mechanisms designed so that if one fails, another will provide some access. Not all content is rendered at all times. Automatic decision by the ISA about when and where to render conditional content is preferred, but manual choice by the user may be necessary for access. Structure is preferred (both the author's specified preferences and the user's structured access), but unstructured access may be necessary for access to all content. Rendering according to format specification is preferred, but a source view of text content may be necessary for access (e.g., because of user-side error conditions, authoring errors, inadequate specification, or incorrect ISA implementation). For example, the user may have to look at URLs for information, HTML comments, XML element names, or script data. The ISA should respect authoring synchronization cues for content that changes over time, but also needs to allow the user to control the time intervals when user input is possible.

Configuration and control of rendering are important for access. Ensuring access to conditional content benefits all users because some users may not have access to some content due to a technological limitation (e.g., their mobile browser cannot display graphics) or simply a configuration preference (e.g., they have a slow Internet connection and prefer not to download movies or images).

(3) Allow Configuration Not to Render Some Content That May Reduce Accessibility

Some content or behavior specified by the author may make the ISA unusable or may obscure information. For instance, flashing content may trigger seizures in people with photosensitive epilepsy, or may make a Web page too distracting to be usable by someone with a cognitive disability. Blinking text can affect screen reader users, because screen readers (in conjunction with speech synthesizers or braille displays) may re-render the text every time it blinks. Distracting background images, colors, or sounds may make it impossible for users to see or hear other content. Dynamically changing Web content may cause problems for some assistive technologies. Scripts that cause unanticipated changes (viewports that open, automatically redirected or refreshed pages, etc.) may disorient some users with cognitive disabilities. This guideline requires the ISA to allow configuration so that, when loading Web resources, the ISA does not render content in a manner that may pose accessibility problems.

(4) Ensure User Control of Rendering

Providing access to content (see guideline 2) includes enabling users to configure and control its rendering. Users with low vision may require that text be rendered at a size larger than the size specified by the author or by the ISA's default rendering. Users with color blindness may need to impose or prevent certain color combinations.

For dynamic presentations such as synchronized multimedia presentations created, users with cognitive, hearing, visual, and physical disabilities may not be able to interact with a presentation within the time frame assumed by the ISA author. To make the presentation accessible to these users, ISAs rendering multimedia content (audio, video, and other animations) need to allow the user to control the playback rate of this content, and also to stop, start, pause, and navigate it quickly. ISAs rendering audio need to allow the user to control the audio volume globally and to allow the user to control independently distinguishable audio tracks.

ISAs with speech synthesis capabilities need to allow users to control various synthesized speech rendering parameters. For instance, users who are blind and hard of hearing may not be able to make use of high or low frequencies; these users have to be able to configure their speech synthesizers to use suitable frequencies.

(5) Ensure User Control of User Interface Behavior

Control of viewport behavior of the ISA is important to accessibility. For people with visual disabilities or certain types of learning disabilities, it is important that the point of regard—what the user is presumed to be viewing—remain as stable as possible. Unexpected changes may cause users to lose track of how many viewports are open, which viewport has the current focus, and so on. This guideline includes requirements for control of opening and closing viewports, the relative position of graphical viewports, changes to focus, and inadvertent form submissions and micropayments.

(6) Implement Interoperable Application Programming Interfaces

This guideline addresses interoperability between a conforming ISA and other software, especially assistive technologies. The checkpoints of this guideline require implementation of application programming interfaces (APIs) for communication. Three types of requirements are important within this guideline:

- What information must be communicated through an API
- Which APIs or types of APIs must be used to communicate this information
- Any additional characteristics of these APIs

It is generally believed that, in order to promote interoperability between a conforming ISA and more than one assistive technology, it is more important to implement conventional APIs than custom APIs, even though custom APIs may enable superior access. When conventional APIs do not allow users to satisfy the requirements of these checkpoints, however, developers may implement alternative APIs in order to conform to this document.

(7) Observe Operating Environment Conventions

Part of ISA accessibility involves conforming to the following conventions of the user's operating environment.

- Complying with operating environment conventions for ISA user interface design, documentation, and installation.
- Incorporating operating environment-level user preferences into the ISA. For instance, some operating systems include settings that allow users to request high-contrast colors (for users with low vision) or graphical rendering of audio cues (for users with hearing disabilities).

Following operating environment conventions increases predictability for users and for developers of assistive technologies. Platform guidelines explain what users will expect from the look and feel of the user interface, keyboard conventions, documentation, and other elements. Platform guidelines also include information about accessibility features that the ISA should adopt rather than reimplement.

(8) Implement Specifications That Benefit Accessibility

Developers should implement open specifications. Conformance to open specifications benefits interoperability and accessibility by making it easier to design assistive technologies (also discussed in guideline 6).

(9) Provide Navigation Mechanisms

Users should be able to navigate to important pieces of content within a configurable view, identify the type of object they navigated to, interact with that object easily (if it is an enabled element), and review the surrounding context (to orient themselves). Providing a variety of navigation and search mechanisms helps users with disabilities (and all users) access content more efficiently. Navigation and searching are particularly important to users who access content serially (e.g., as synthesized speech or braille).

Sequential navigation (e.g., line scrolling, page scrolling, sequential navigation through enabled elements, etc.) means advancing (or rewinding) through rendered content in well-defined steps (line by line, screen by screen, link by link, etc.). Sequential navigation can provide context, but can be time-consuming. Sequential navigation is important to users who cannot scan a page visually for context and also benefits users unfamiliar with a page. Sequential access may be based on element type (e.g., links only), content structure (e.g., navigation from heading to heading), or other criteria.

Direct navigation (e.g., to a particular link or paragraph) is faster than sequential navigation, but generally requires familiarity with the content. Direct navigation is important to users with some physical disabilities (who may have little or no manual dexterity and/or an increased tendency to push unwanted buttons or keys) and to users with visual disabilities. It also benefits "power users." Direct navigation may be possible with the pointing device or the keyboard (e.g., keyboard shortcuts).

Structured navigation mechanisms offer both context and speed. ISAs should allow users to navigate to content known to be structurally important: blocks of content, headers and sections, tables, forms and form elements, enabled elements, navigation mechanisms, containers, and so on. For information about programmatic access to document structure, see guideline 6.

ISAs should also allow users to configure navigation mechanisms (e.g., to allow navigation of links only, or links and headings, or tables and forms, etc.).

(10) Orient the User

All users require clues to help them understand their "location" when browsing: where they are, how they got there, where they can go, what is nearby. Some mechanisms that provide such clues through the user interface (visually, as audio, or as braille) include the following:

- Information about the current state of the user's interaction with content: where the viewport is in content (shown, for example, through proportional scroll bars), which viewport has the current focus, where the user has selected content, a history mechanism, the title of the current document or frame. These clues need to be available to the user in a device-independent manner.
- Information about specific elements, such as the dimensions of a table, the length of an audio clip, the structure of a form, and whether following a link will involve a fee.
- Information about relationships among elements, such as between table cells and related table headers.
- Information about the structure of content. For instance, a navigable outline view can accelerate access to content while preserving context.

Orientation mechanisms such as these are especially important to users who view content serially (e.g., when rendered as synthesized speech or braille). For instance, these users cannot "scan" a graphically displayed table with their eyes for information about a table cell's headers, neighboring cells, and other features. ISAs need to provide other means for users to understand table cell relationships, frame relationships (what relationship does the graphical layout convey?), form context (have I filled out the form completely?), link information (have I already visited this link?), and other content information.

This guideline also includes requirements to allow the user to control some ISA behavior (form submission and activation of fee links) that, if carried out automatically, might go unnoticed by some users (e.g., users with visual disabilities) or might disorient others (e.g., some users with a cognitive disability).

(11) Allow Configuration and Customization

Web users can access a wide range of capabilities and need to be able to configure the ISA according to styles, graphical user interface configuration, keyboard configuration, and other preferences. Most of the checkpoints in this guideline pertain to the input configuration: how ISA behavior is controlled through keyboard input, pointing device input, and voice input.

(12) Provide Accessible ISA Documentation and Help

Documentation of the user interface is important, as is documentation of the ISA's underlying functionalities. Although intuitive user interface design is valuable to many users, some users may still not be able to understand or be able to operate the native user interface without thorough documentation (e.g., a user with a visual disability may not find a graphical user interface intuitive without supporting documentation).

This guideline contains three types of requirements:

1. Accessibility of the documentation.
2. Minimal requirements of what must be documented. Documentation should include much more to explain how to install, get help for, use, or configure the ISA.
3. Organization of the documentation.

USING AGENT DEVELOPMENT PLATFORMS

Given the complexity associated with the construction and deployment of ISAs, it is understandable why the software development market spends a significant amount of time in the development of platforms and environments that make the design of an ISA as simple as possible. Even though numerous commercial offerings exist, they all share many of the same basic functions and features. This section outlines the functions set normally found in a professional ISA design platform.

COMMON FUNCTION SET FOR ISA DESIGN PLATFORMS

Today's ISA design platforms are generally marketed as integrated software development tools that allow software developers with no background in intelligent systems or intelligent agent technologies to quickly and easily build intelligent agent-based applications. The ISA platform reduces development time and development costs while simplifying the development of high-performance, robust agent-based systems.

Most ISA build platforms provide graphical tools for supporting all phases of the agent construction process. Programming software agents (sometimes called agent-oriented programming) specify intuitive concepts such as the beliefs, commitments, behavioral rules, and actions of the ISA. In addition, an ISA design platform makes it much easier to create, debug, and test multiagent systems. The software developer need only model the communications dialogs between agents using the protocol tools and the design application will automatically construct the required behavioral rules required for implementing these conversations. This capability significantly reduces the amount of time required for building multiagent systems.

Typical ISA design platforms include the following features:

* Tools for defining the agents that comprise an agency.
* Tools for defining interagent conversations or protocols.
* Tools for associating agent protocol roles with individual agents.
* A viewer that allows the developer to control individual agents and examine the message traffic between agents.
* Tools for automatically generating behavioral rules required for interagent communications.

In addition, a good ISA development platform makes it easy to add a graphical user interface to an agent or an agent-enabled application. Developers can import existing classes, thus allowing agents to utilize legacy code. Special purpose modules for building agents that handle e-mail, read and post to network news groups, and analyze documents and FTP files are also available.

Figure 17-12 contains a screenshots from AgentBuilder, one of the most popular ISA development platforms.

17-6: THE FUTURE OF INTELLIGENT SOFTWARE AGENTS

It is quite possible that intelligent software agents will be one of the most important advancements in the DSS environment in the next decade. In the early part of the twenty-first century, virtually every significant computer-based application will have

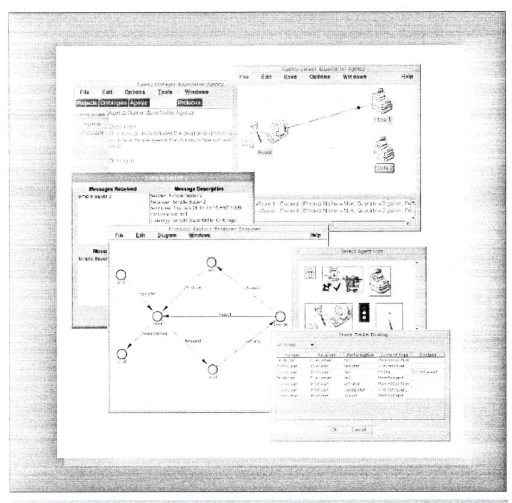

FIGURE 17-12 Examples from AgentBuilder Screens

some form of agent enablement (Janca, 1996). Several reasons can be cited for this conclusion:

1. Desktop applications are becoming extremely "feature rich." For this reason, users can master only a small part of their capabilities. ISAs can mask the complexity of new applications and help the user accomplish what he or she wants.
2. Sources and volumes of information are burgeoning. ISAs can help do the data mining and can assist in locating the most productive data mines.
3. The current bandwidth limitation in decision support exists between the tip of the user's nose and the surface of the computer screen. Greater computing bandwidth means more data can get to the user more quickly, but the user is still subject to a limited cognitive processing capacity and a limited number of hours in the day available to work. ISAs can work around-the-clock and can help manage the data flow by filtering and sending only that information the user considers essential.

4. Many client desktops and servers are now powerful enough to support the deployment of multiple ISAs to help users and processes easily.

5. The rapid increase in the use of the Internet and World Wide Web creates a much more complex computing environment. This new environment is commonly referred to as "network computing," which implies that we are moving from a world of simple connections (i.e., a terminal-to-host, or a client-to-server) to a more complex world of multiple servers and services interconnected like a highway network. In this new environment, everything is available, but changes occur by the second and the decision maker must figure out how to discover them. ISAs can create a cohesive whole out of this seemingly random mess.

6. Both academic and commercial research are now beyond the point of mere theory in their understanding of ISAs, and experimental systems are freely available and in use on the Internet.

7. Large custom applications, such as Lotus Notes, are significantly agent-enabled, further broadening the experience base.

As of this writing, more than 50 commercial vendors offer agent-enabled software and services. Their products are spread across virtually every application area, including Internet applications. The present challenge is to make it easy to add intelligent software agents to any application, new or existing. ISAs are not a concept of the future; they are in use today helping make applications easier to use, and their usage is increasing rapidly.

17-7: CHAPTER SUMMARY

The widespread dissemination of intelligent software agents presents enormous social, economic, and political considerations. ISAs will, in effect, bring about a social revolution the magnitude of which will rival the advent of the personal computer. Almost anyone will have access to the kind of support staff that today is the mark of the privileged. As a result, they will be able to digest large amounts of information while simultaneously engaging in a wide variety of unrelated activities. The ultimate ramifications of this change are impossible to predict but, to be sure, the change will be significant.

The shape of the changes that agents bring, will, necessarily, depend on how they are deployed. Many questions remain to be answered, and many more remain to be asked. For example, should users be held responsible for the actions of their agents in the same manner they are held accountable for the actions of their children or employees? How can we ensure that an agent will maintain our privacy by protecting all of the personal information it accumulates about its user?

Should agents be free to automate the bad habits of their users or should the system be designed to try and teach them better ones? And, if so, who defines "better"? As our cyber ecosystem grows in its sophistication and complexity, will it be possible to ensure enough processing power and bandwidth for the infinite agent-based tasks and activities human beings want to accomplish? Our knowledge in this area, thus far, can only hint at the possibilities.

Key Concepts

- Intelligent software agent (ISA) is capable of generating and implementing novel rules of behavior that human beings may lack the opportunity or desire to review.
- According to Franklin and Graesser (1996), "An autonomous agent is a system situated within and a part of an environment that senses that environment and acts on it, over time, in pursuit of its own agenda and so as to effect what it senses in the future."
- The concept of intelligent agents is an emerging technology that facilitates users in the delegation of work to a computer. Intelligent agents are capable of performing many of the necessary decision support functions formerly relegated to human beings.
- Two common characteristics of intelligent agents

  An agent is one who acts, or who can act.

  An agent is one who acts in place of another person with permission from that person.
- Characteristics of intelligent software agents

  Autonomy

  Personalizability

  Discourse

  Cooperation

  Risk and trust

  Domain

  Graceful degradation

  Anthropomorphism

  Mobility
- Transportable agents offer several advantages over the traditional client/server model:

  Efficiency

  Fault tolerance

  Convenient paradigm

  Customization
- Classification of intelligent agents

  Hierarchical classification

  Hierarchical classification is a "biological" metaphoric classification scheme for ISAs that takes the form of a tree with "living creatures" at the root and individual species at its leaves.

  Organizational versus personal agents

  This classification is based on whether the agent is carrying out a business process or task on behalf of an organizational application or on behalf of a specific user.

  Brustoloni taxonomy of software agents

  This classification is based on a three-way categorization of ISAs into regulation agents, planning agents, and adaptive agents.

  Lee, Cheung, and Kao taxonomy of software agents

  This method classifies ISAs according to their level of intelligence and power.

Questions for Review

1. What is an intelligent agent?
2. Identify and discuss two characteristics of intelligent agents.
3. What is a learning agent?
4. How does the concept of delegacy apply to the design and construction of ISAs?
5. Explain why graceful degradation of an ISA is important.
6. What are the advantages of transportable agents over the traditional client/server model?
7. List and briefly describe the methods of classifying ISAs.
8. Compare and constrast the three types of agency.
9. Define the following: *agent theory, agent architecture,* and *agent language.*
10. What is a learner agent? A shopping agent?
11. What can go wrong with an ISA?

For Further Discussion

1. Analyze an intelligent software agent in the market. Characterize its functionality. Discuss the types of problems it can solve.
2. Discuss why it is important for the user of intelligent software technology to maintain a balance between the risks of ISA use and the trust of the user in the ISA.
3. Information about ISAs is plentiful on the Web. Find some Web sites that discuss the use of ISAs. Hint: Try Firefly, IBM, or BargainFinder.
4. You already studied artificial intelligence, fuzzy logic, and neural networks. How do these topics relate to the design and implementation of an ISA?
5. Pick a task you can fully describe that requires the help of others acting on your behalf. Describe the same task using ISAs. What would be the various roles and characteristics played by your ISAs?
6. Go to www.clickmusic.co.uk/Clickmusic_Web_Guide/Shopping/Shopbot/ and see whether you can find the best price for your favorite CD. The prices will be returned in British pounds but you will still be able to determine the lowest available price.

DECISION SUPPORT IN THE TWENTY-FIRST CENTURY

Computers in the future may weigh no more than 1.5 tons.
—*POPULAR MECHANICS,* FORECASTING THE RELENTLESS MARCH OF SCIENCE AND INNO-
VATION, 1949

I have traveled the length and breadth of this country and talked with the best people,
and I can assure you that data processing is a fad that won't last out the year.
—EDITOR OF BUSINESS BOOKS FOR PRENTICE HALL, 1957

We are at the end of our journey (at least for now), which simply means that you now possess a sufficient understanding of the application of current decision support technologies to use them effectively during the course of your managerial activities. The journey continues, however, because even as you read this text, new and innovative DSS technologies are emerging that will require acceptance and assimilation by managers into their world. This issue is one of the first problems we must address.

A common and natural hesitation to squarely confront the central, long-term challenge facing an organization—the formidable nature of emerging technologies—seems to take hold of most managers. Recent history makes it evident that discounting the future can be costly. Over the long term, new technologies will arise and take hold. These innovations inevitably lead to novel products and processes, sometimes supplanting entire industries or creating whole new businesses. Coping with the continual flow of new technologies is a monumental task that all decision makers face. If the organization is to benefit from the increased power that new decision support technologies offer, managers must seize the opportunities these technologies present, while simultaneously guarding against the pitfalls they bring with them.

The objective of this final chapter is to provide a glimpse into the future of decision making and DSS-related technologies. To be sure, it is a formidable task. One look at the abundance of futuristic technologies we see in the latest offerings from Hollywood provides some understanding of the size of this undertaking. Some of these prototypes of tomorrow gradually materialize, but the majority remains the pursuit of forerunning researchers and inventors. The fundamental problem, as described by John Rennie, editor-in-chief of *Scientific American,* then is that "most technology predictions ... are simplistic and hence, unrealistic." He goes on to point out that externalities such as market forces, government policies, socioeconomic conditions, whims of fashion or fad, and even the vagaries of the human nature all contribute to whether a technological innovation can blossom and be absorbed into the lives of the ordinary you and me. This important and insightful point should not be lost on decision makers.

This chapter is not an attempt to perform the impossible: to predict that which is unpredictable. The objective is to focus on emerging trends and innovations in decision support technology and to explore the possible changes in the way we think and solve problems that may result from these innovations. The purpose of this chapter is to provoke each of you into exploring the possibilities that you will assuredly experience.

18-1: WHERE WE ARE AND WHERE WE HAVE BEEN

I think there is a world market for maybe five computers.
—THOMAS WATSON, CHAIRMAN OF IBM, 1943

640K ought to be enough for anybody.
—BILL GATES, COMMENTING ON THE TYPICAL AMOUNT OF PERSONAL
COMPUTER MEMORY, 1981

No successful look into the future can be accomplished without some grounding in the current state of affairs. We, therefore, begin our prognostications with a look at the wide variety of domains in which DSS technology has been effectively integrated and applied within the modern organization.

DSSs have been successfully applied to a wide variety of problems. Application domains where DSSs play an important role include urban traffic management, health care and medical diagnosis, environmental planning, farming, forestry, and agriculture, among many others. The following sections outline further only a few of the countless important areas of DSS application.

ENVIRONMENTAL DECISION MAKING AND IMPACT ASSESSMENT

Environmental decision support systems (EDSSs) can be used to assess the impact of natural resource development. Several commercial systems available are being used for environmental monitoring and impact assessment. One major area of application is in the field of water resource management. DSSs to support water reservoir decision analysis developed by several organizations (both government and commercial) include tools to support water delivery maintenance and planning and have been in use since the late 1980s. Other DSSs were developed to assist decision makers in the planning of complex irrigation systems.

AGRICULTURE

Irrigation systems are primarily deployed in an effort to improve food production in a region suffering from a lack of natural water supply for crops. However, irrigation management supported by DSS technology is only one application related to agriculture. DSSs focusing on the overall improvement of agricultural production processes include those developed to assist in the identification of disease and treatment decisions related to both crops and agricultural animals. The use of such systems contributes to the world's food resources and plays a major part in the agricultural development of third world countries.

FORESTRY

Several DSSs were developed to assist forestry- and natural resource–related decision making. For example, a DSS called TEAMS provides a tactical planning system to aid forest managers in developing site-specific treatment schedules. Reforestation problems and financial issues related to forest management are also being assisted by domain-specific DSSs. Most recently, a DSS was developed that embeds a linear programming model to evaluate New Zealand forests privatized by the government.

MANUFACTURING

Deciding on appropriate levels of investment in industrial and manufacturing enterprises can be a difficult undertaking. DSSs function as ubiquitous elements in the realm of industrial investment decisions. Further, DSSs serve in environments that adopt industry-wide analysis and planning techniques such as MRP (materials requirements planning) and MRP II (manufacturing resource planning). The area of numerically controlled machine tools is only one in which computer-based decision support and artificial intelligence systems are being used successfully in manufacturing.

MEDICINE

Recall from Chapter 7 that DSS and expert system technologies such as MYCIN and DENDRAL served in the medical profession for many years. More recently, DSSs to support hospital services planning, such as patient loads and staffing forecasts, were developed in response to the escalating cost of these services. A wide variety of medical decision making is currently supported by DSS technologies. For example, a DSS to assist in the development of proper nutritional balance for diets is being marketed commercially. Other uses of DSSs by the medical profession include tropical disease diagnosis, simulation of epidemics, and creation of pharmaceutical interaction scenarios.

ORGANIZATIONAL SUPPORT

Numerous examples of DSS applications in support of common organizational decision-making activities can be found. Specific instances of these applications include DSSs that assess the risk in international investments, DSSs that guide decisions involving the management of assets and liabilities, and DSSs that participate in the development of organizational investment strategies and capital budgeting decisions. It is commonly accepted that the use of a DSS can improve the organizational decision maker's capabilities by improving his or her ability to visualize pertinent financial data.

This list of current DSS application areas is by no means exhaustive. The list does, however, illustrate both the scope of and interest in practical applications of DSS technologies. The next section will begin our discussion of the future of DSSs and the succeeding sections will address the future of IT-related technologies: expert systems and executive information systems.[1]

---

[1]Many of the predictions set forth in these sections have been built upon the work of Kersten and Meister (1993) and Dobrzenieki (1994).

18-2: THE FUTURE OF DECISION SUPPORT SYSTEMS

But what . . . is it good for?
—ENGINEER AT THE ADVANCED COMPUTING SYSTEMS DIVISION OF IBM ON THE MICROCHIP, 1968

This "telephone" has too many shortcomings to be seriously considered as a means of communication. The device is inherently of no value to us.
—WESTERN UNION INTERNAL MEMO, 1876

One ultimate mission of tomorrow's DSSs will be to apply information technologies to enhance the productivity of information workers in the new "Information Age" in dealing with problems that vary in complexity and structure. Alvin Toffler (1970) warned of an impending flood of information so severe that people would become paralyzed and unable to choose between options. The problem of information overload is a reality; it is estimated that the amount of data collected by a typical modern organization doubles every year. Given that a typical knowledge worker can only effectively analyze about 5 percent of those data, the need for support in the area of decision making appears to be crucial. In this regard, a number of challenges face the DSS designers and users of tomorrow.

DSS INTEGRATION

As discussed in Chapter 15, one of the major challenges facing DSS use is an issue of integration. A common dialog interface throughout the organization is necessary to allow users to easily and effectively access all available information resources. The window of connectivity between the DSS and the various operational data stores should be transparent and enable the integration of various architectures and platforms on which separate resources might reside. In this regard, a standardized graphical user interface (GUI) provides compatibility and easy accessibility to all applications and data. This type of standardization is the primary reason for the worldwide adoption of Microsoft Windows and its related products. A major problem in DSS development, however, is the lack of appropriate GUIs to help integrate the various architectures and platforms. From the perspective of the typical decision maker, the GUI can be a determining factor as to whether the DSS will succeed or fail when it comes to implementing the system in the work environment.

Therefore, the concepts of information representation must be addressed by DSS designers and users. What forms of information representation will be required to face the problems and decisions of tomorrow? Will we continue to rely on traditional reporting formats such as charts, maps, or diagrams? Will we need new types of graphics such as dynamic graphical models and reports that allow for multidimensional representations?

The integration of components of expert systems and other AI approaches with organizational DSSs presents a major focus. The knowledge base becomes a form of database or model base, the inference engine can be viewed as a knowledge base management system, and the language system of the ES is now effectively a part of the DSS dialog system. One of the challenges for the future will be to introduce even tighter integration between the DSS and the organizational applications, thus extending the "IQ" of the DSS and the decision maker even further.

DSS CONNECTIVITY

Connectivity represents an extremely important aspect of the next generation DSS, especially with regard to communications. Although our present ability to connect desktop clients through LANs (local area networks), WANs (wide area networks), and gateways is an important first step, the next challenge is clearly the standardization of communication protocols, communication channels, bandwidths, and data transfer rates to facilitate the increasing demands for interchange of large data sets, graphical databases, digital images, and video.

The ability to connect to other networks is important to the organization because it provides a diverse and global channel for resources. The major drawback here is the potential security problems attributable to open network links through unsecured gateways. One way to minimize these potential security issues is the standardization of communication protocols that minimize these disparities.

DSSs IN DOCUMENT PROCESSING

Improvements in the access and management of organizational document resources in addition to organizational and external data are essential to the future strength and effectiveness of the DSS. New search and structuring technologies, such as concept retrieval, hypertext, and multimedia, are under development by both research and commercial efforts with an eye toward creating effective enabling technologies. Probably the single greatest manifestation of this effort is the recent emergence and growth of groupware products such as Lotus Notes. The world is rapidly getting connected, which bodes well for the next round of decision support tools.

The proper representation of knowledge enables systems to better mimic experts. This ability will translate into competitive gains, especially if the expert systems are used in critical areas that offer high profit margins. Access to documents from widespread and diverse sources with the use of quick search algorithms will also serve to enhance organizational competitiveness. Ensuring that communications are upgraded so that the DSSs can interface with the Internet and the World Wide Web will enable organizations to remain abreast of evolving technologies and innovations in decision making and thereby maintain their competitive edge in the emerging electronic marketplace.

VIRTUAL REALITY IN A DSS ENVIRONMENT

Virtual reality (VR) technology enables individuals to actively immerse themselves in a simulated environment. This offspring of computer graphics relies on the development of more sophisticated hardware and software programs to make the environments more "real." VR presentation environments range from theater-style viewing on large screens to computer monitor displays to helmets equipped with stereoscopic screens and headphones. The experience is multisensory: Sight, sound, and touch are the most common. The technology facilitates the viewer's understanding of interrelationships among contextual elements and provides a means by which the viewer can learn to respond effectively and efficiently to the available data.

Scope of Impact

VR is predicted to dramatically affect such diverse areas as manufacturing, education and training, medical interventions, military preparedness, and entertainment. For example, engineers engaged in computer-aided design (CAD) will be able to interact with their designs for the early detection of design flaws that are not obvious with current technologies until prototype construction. Impact on the educational system could be significant. People tend to learn more easily through experiential exercise rather than through memorizing rules. VR offers such a tool. Many types of training could be carried out efficiently and effectively through VR. The potential for high economic returns based on VR research and development is encouraging entrepreneurial activity, and giants such as Boeing and AT&T are investing millions.

Areas of Concern

VR environments may be so enticing as to become addictive to viewers. A more insidious side effect could be that certain users would be incapable of distinguishing between reality and virtual reality, leading to actions that could be dangerous to themselves or others. Likewise, VR could be used to manipulate users as well. U.S. congressional hearings, chaired by Al Gore in 1991, concluded that the United States is not investing sufficiently in VR. It has been called the "manifest destiny for computers," but the issues of control and manipulation may lead to a code of ethics for cyberspace.

18-3: THE FUTURE OF EXPERT AND ARTIFICIAL INTELLIGENCE SYSTEMS

> Everything that can be invented has been invented.
> —CHARLES H. DUELL, COMMISSIONER, U.S. OFFICE OF PATENTS, 1899

> Professor Goddard does not know the relation between action and reaction and the need to have something better than a vacuum against which to react. He is clearly no expert and seems to lack the basic knowledge ladled out daily in all high schools.
> —*NEW YORK TIMES* EDITORIAL ABOUT ROBERT GODDARD'S REVOLUTIONARY ROCKET WORK, 1921

Two primary issues must be addressed regarding the future of expert systems: (1) future AI requirements for intelligent databases, and (2) knowledge management.

ARTIFICIAL INTELLIGENCE REQUIREMENTS FOR INTELLIGENT DATABASE SYSTEMS

The advancement of expert systems in the realm of decision making will require a significant focus on the development of database systems that can contain and manage agents of artificial intelligence. The concept of intelligent database systems (IDSs) can be best illustrated by drawing an analogy to a typical health care system. In this domain, the health care providers such as doctors, nurses, and medical technicians can be considered analogous to software intelligent agents, each with individual and shared knowledge and reasoning abilities and assigned to provide the best possible care for patients. The level of care they can deliver, however, often depends on the complex relationships concerning authority, roles, and responsibilities encountered by these agents as they interact and cooperate with one another. In other words, the knowledge possessed by these agents can only be effectively applied within the rules and regulations defined by the health care environment itself.

Applying this same logic to the domain of expert systems and intelligent software agents, the ability for two or more agents to cooperate intelligently to achieve a common goal evokes the problem of interoperability. The advent of an IDS will provide systems support for interoperability (management and access to shared and private objects). The development of such systems might include the integration of AI knowledge representation and reasoning with database models and processing to produce a super-object model. The problems or tasks within the domain will then be solved or executed by agents cooperating to determine the best solution using the available resources.

Although the concept of intelligent software agents attached to expert systems is attractive, distributing such work across multiple domains requires the system to possess a variety of knowledge and associated reasoning capabilities much more powerful than today's systems. This knowledge and reasoning capability will be characterized by the nature and amount of knowledge and reasoning required, the degree of distribution and sharing among the system's agents, and the precision and completeness of, as well as the means for, acquisition, augmentation, and learning of domain-related knowledge. The representation, modeling, controlling, and managing of large volumes and differing data types of persistent, shared, distributed knowledge and associated reasoning clearly pose major challenges for intelligent database systems.

One promising response to that challenge that is currently under development is the high-performance storage system (HPSS). An HPSS is software that provides hierarchical storage management and services for extremely large storage environments. The technology may be of particular use in those situations such as management of large rule sets having present or future scalability requirements, which are demanding in terms of total storage capacity, file sizes, data rates, number of objects stored, and number of users. A central technical goal of HPSS is to move large files between storage devices and parallel or clustered computers at speeds many times faster than today's commercial storage system software products allow, and to do it in a way that is more reliable and manageable than is possible with current systems. HPSS is the result of a collaborative effort by leading U.S. government supercomputer laboratories and industry to address real, urgent, high-end storage requirements.

KNOWLEDGE MANAGEMENT

In anticipation of the increased size and usefulness of tomorrow's expert systems, questions surrounding issues of maintenance and management begin to surface. These issues center on improvement with regard to methods of gathering and acquiring expert knowledge and ensuring that the knowledge base contains the most current information available. Current research is focusing on several potential approaches to extend and capture knowledge for an ES. The first method involves software engineering practices that are used for large conventional programs for the maintenance of the knowledge base. The second builds support for rules into an efficient system for managing large relational databases. The problem of scaling, however, occurs when faced with the need to compute a million rules over several million pieces of data. To overcome the problem of scaling in this context, systems must be designed is such a way that the rule support mechanisms are tightly coupled within the DBMS, thus allowing the rules to be used efficiently for large applications, integrity control, referential integrity, transition constraints, and protection.

A third potential approach is to use the declarative form of rule specification to provide ES implementers with some form of abstract standard that will detail and define the type of answers from the knowledge base. The problem here is to find knowledge representation that is declaratively well founded and procedurally effective. Finally, a promising approach focuses on the depth and breadth of knowledge. The advent of a deep knowledge base for an expert system facilitates the possibility of solving complex search problems. A system possessing broad (general) knowledge combined with a variety of specific concepts and situations could easily provide support for multiple problem context generalization and analogy. Together with suitable procedures for deployment and use, such an ES should be able to address different subject areas, understand English-like statements, and possibly learn to enhance its own problem-solving capabilities.

Advancements in Knowledge Acquisition and Representation

In conjunction with the intelligence component of an expert system, mention must also be made of the future of knowledge acquisition and representation. We know from Chapters 7 and 8 that the modeling of expert behavior is a complex and often difficult task. Not all knowledge can be captured by production rules; knowledge can exist through causal information or mathematical relationships as well. The ultimate design goal for expert system knowledge acquisition in the next century will be to design systems that allow experts to encode their own knowledge directly into the computer, thus removing the role of the knowledge engineer from the knowledge acquisition phase. This goal may be difficult to achieve in the near future, however, because the functioning of the knowledge engineer is currently understood as more of an art than a science. The current state regarding the transfer of knowledge involves asking the expert to introspect about the decision-making process, and such translations still involve codifying experiences based on sensations, thoughts, memories, and feelings. We are not yet capable of building a system that can handle the complexities of those concepts, but we most likely will be soon.

In the near future, however, improving the processes by which expert knowledge is coded into machine language by knowledge engineers will become a focus, because the current procedures only try to mimic expertise at a basic level. In this regard, a number of questions must be answered. Will direct interaction between the expert and the ES be more productive than acting through the knowledge engineer? Can we capture and represent knowledge that can be applied to a variety of problem domains? Can multiple sources of knowledge be captured and incorporated in a single ES so that they are able to interact with other expert systems tools with respect to the problem domain? Finally, can we automate the knowledge acquisition process using technologies such as machine learning?

18-4: THE FUTURE OF EXECUTIVE INFORMATION SYSTEMS

There is no reason anyone would want a computer in their home.
—KEN OLSON, PRESIDENT, CHAIRMAN, AND FOUNDER OF DIGITAL EQUIPMENT
CORPORATION, 1977

Drill for oil? You mean drill into the ground to try and find oil?
—DRILLERS WHOM EDWIN L. DRAKE TRIED TO ENLIST IN HIS PROJECT TO
DRILL FOR OIL, 1859

The advancement of executive information systems, to date, depended on the continued successful migration away from mainframe computer systems. This trend helped to eliminate the need for executives and senior managers to learn different computer operating systems and substantially reduced the costs of EIS implementation. This "downsizing" of computers in terms of operational footprint does not mean that greater demands for processing power will not be made with regard to tomorrow's EIS. Future executive information systems will be based on super personal computers that dynamically organize and integrate a wide variety of existing and future software application packages into a useful EIS. An additional impetus will be not only to provide a system that supports senior executives but to satisfy the information needs of middle management as well. In this sense, the EIS of tomorrow may be more appropriately called an organizational information system (OIS).

Several functions just now appearing will become commonplace in the future OIS. One recent addition is the inclusion of a module to perform visual information access and analysis (VIAA). VIAA modules provide access to both organizational and external information through visual screens that combine text, numerical data, graphical data, and images. The visual screens offer users quick and easy access to data, improving their decision-making capabilities.

An OIS that employs VIAA modules can be thought of as the second generation of executive information systems, one that takes advantage of the profound increases in information processing speed and capability found in the latest personal computers or workstations. The typical EIS and the OIS differ in several respects, however.

- Originally the EIS was designed for senior executives. OIS systems will be designed for use by all levels of company personnel.
- Even modern EISs typically operate in closed, proprietary systems in which the output to the user depends on the weakest component of an integrated set of organizational systems. For example, the overall system may possess excellent graphics capabilities and be based upon a powerful fourth-generation language but be linked to one or more legacy database systems. As manufacturers begin to provide solutions to the conversion of data from older legacy applications and databases, users will be able to "snap together" products from different software vendors to form a complete OIS solution. This approach will allow the "best-of-breed" components to be integrated into a customized product based on individual end-user and organizational needs.

- Many older-generation EISs still limit user access to preprocessed data only. OIS applications will enable users to access real-time data instantly regardless of its location. Improvements in data conversion based on current standards such as dynamic data exchange (DDE) will allow OIS applications to reflect automatically the most current information when the underlying data or images change. This capability will provide users at all levels of the organization with fast access to the most up-to-date data available.

Many EIS software vendors are already incorporating VIAA functions into their next generation of products. The latest EIS software developments are responding to the changing needs of their users and making the systems accessible to many different layers of management within a company. The abilities to access data already stored and to incorporate the best features of other software applications are beginning to be recognized by the software developers as the means to increase their customer base. As new products are developed and the customer base is broadened to several management layers within a company, the gap between the EIS and other computer-assisted analysis tools, such as the DSS, will narrow.

This trend toward the integration of all organizational applications and technologies makes the future especially promising for executive information systems. Extensive technological and conceptual advances in information systems as well as in the telecommunications area suggest that the realization of a truly functional OIS is not far in the future.

18-5: THE FUTURE OF INTELLIGENT SOFTWARE AGENTS AND DELEGATION

Sure, the truth is out there, but on the Internet, it's hard to find. With millions of Web pages, getting what you want is now more difficult than ever. For users baffled by information overload, the Web has become more than a little anonymous. The solution to this problem may lie with intelligent software agents (ISA), which have the potential to transform the nature of Web surfing and make it a more personal, productive, and lucrative enterprise for users and vendors.

As ISAs come of age, you can expect highly personalized content for entertainment, news, products, and other links to appear automatically on your favorite Web sites. This personalizing will happen, literally, behind the scenes.

Sophisticated ISAs can learn on their own by following your example. They can watch how you browse during a session and discover what you might be interested in, tailoring their behavior accordingly.

Searching for plane tickets, a stock bargain, or a good book? As commercial ISAs continue to appear, they will be able to hunt down just what you want. If properly authorized, they can even place orders and charge your credit card for you.

ISA development is also driven by a number of aggressive start-up companies and backed up by leading-edge academic research in computer science. The world of agents is clearly heating up.

Now that we have search engines producing hundreds of hits for almost any conceivable query, the problem lies in knowing what really interests users. For this purpose, the ISAs of the present and near future will make the greatest impact. *Personalized content*—delivering just what you want—is the goal of many of the ISA technologies under consideration, and many strategies exist for trying to provide it.

Agents are somewhat indebted to certain technologies from the 1980s that never caught on. Such technologies—namely, artificial intelligence (AI) and expert systems—as we have seen, failed to live up to high expectations.

The next generation of applied research, the intelligent agent, presents a greater likelihood of success, because it involves new models of computer "intelligence." New technologies such as *collaborative filtering* (developed by Firefly and Net Perceptions) offer a productive model that fits within an extraordinary range of consumer tastes. Your interest in media (such as books and CDs) or content (such as news stories) can be ascertained with collaborative filtering.

Where the older AI technology tried to make computers think like people (which had only limited success), collaborative filtering applies human thought, in the form of a database of user preferences, to new items with extraordinary powers of prediction. This consumer-centered approach is a hit with many Web masters and delivers obvious applications for catalog and content-based sites.

Traditional AI approaches will still be available, too. Several ISA products use research in areas you possibly never encountered, such as neural networks, fuzzy logic, natural-language processing, and collaborative filtering. For example, to accomplish pattern recognition and visual processing, ISAs might use neural networks, which in turn use parallel processing (one of the staples of cognitive science and AI).

Meanwhile, fuzzy logic supplies computers with sufficient data to codify fine distinctions that people make all the time (such as the concept of "warm" rather than "hot" or "cold"). Natural-language processing allows computers to operate using English-like statements instead of arcane programmer-oriented language. Autonomy's client-side program uses natural-language queries to learn the information you want.

DEALS IN CYBERSPACE

In the near future, ISAs for buyers and sellers could meet on the Web and actually make deals in cyberspace. These agents could search the Internet for a desired product and price, even ordering the product automatically by using your credit card number. Many vendors are drooling over the prospect of having autonomous ISAs hunt down bargains.

For this approach to be used over the public Internet (it is currently being used on intranets), standards definitions for such commerce (principally, security) need to be implemented. For ISAs to work properly, servers of all kinds would need to be able to run mobile agents safely and securely.

Without broad support for standards, an agent cannot possibly move around from server to server. Nevertheless, this vision holds a lot of potential. A host of useful business applications awaits, but time will tell whether this technology can become widely accepted.

THE CHALLENGES YET TO BE ADDRESSED

To realize all of the hype and promise of ISAs, society will have to grapple with certain issues through various legislations, and those issues will be problematic. They include the following:

- **Privacy:** How do you ensure your agents maintain your much needed privacy when acting on your behalf?
- **Responsibility:** When you relinquish some of your responsibility to software agent(s) (as you would do implicitly), be aware of the authority that is being transferred to it/them. How would you like to come back home after a long, hard day at work to find out you are the proud owner of a used car negotiated and purchased courtesy of one of your (Kasbah) software agents? How do you ensure the agent does not run amok and run up a huge credit card bill on your behalf?
- **Legal issues:** Imagine your agent (which you probably bought off-the-shelf and customized) offers some bad advice to other peer agents resulting in liabilities to other people. Who is responsible? The company who wrote the agent? You who customized it? Both? One can envision a new raft of legislation that will need to be developed in the future to cover ISAs.
- **Ethical issues:** Agent etiquette may require an accepted standard. Such a standard might include some, or all, of the following:
  - Agents must identify themselves.
  - They must moderate the pace and frequency of their requests to some server.
  - They must limit their searches to appropriate servers.
  - They must share information with others.
  - They must respect the authority placed on them by server operators.
  - An agent's services must be accurate and up-to-date.
- **Safety:** The agent should not destructively alter the world.
- **Tidiness:** The agent should leave the world as it found it.
- **Thrift:** The agent should limit its consumption of scarce resources.
- **Vigilance:** The agent should not allow client actions with unanticipated results.

However, such issues are not immediately critical, but will be in the medium to long terms. In the short term, we expect some basic agent-based software to be rolled out, including some basic interface agents such as mail filtering or calendar scheduling agents. More basic mobile agent services could also be provided in the short term. We can also predict comfortably that many vendors will claim that their products are agent-based even though they most certainly are not. For example, we are already hearing of terms such as *compression agents* and *system agents* when the more common terms *disk compressors* and *operating systems* would do respectively, and have done in the past.

In the medium term (3 to 5 years), some more decent agent applications probably will be rolled out for most of the classes of agents overviewed here. Perhaps, collaborative agents and integrated heterogeneous agent applications will do limited, but *real* work-flow or air traffic management or control real telecommunications networks for example, rather than just perform simulations. Useful, but limited, interface agents should be available to perform roles including the following: eager assistants, World

Wide Web guides, memory aids, and entertainment and World Wide Web filters/critics. More mobile and information agent applications and languages will soon be rolled out by vendors. One can expect reactive or hybrid agent technology to start delivering some real everyday industrial applications during this period. Furthermore, during this medium term, it can be expected that the World Wide Web will be commercialized to some degree, enabling ISAs of different classes to play a role in paying for services and performing some restricted buying and selling on our behalf, as Kasbah agents propose to do. We may also start seeing a proliferation of specialist agent conferences: agents in the aviation industry, agents in law, and so forth. The new domain of agent-based software engineering will grow from strength to strength.

In the long term (7 years and beyond), we can expect to see ISAs that *approximate* true "smartness" in that they can collaborate and learn, in addition to being autonomous in their settings. They will possess rich negotiation skills, and some may demonstrate what may be referred to, arguably, as "emotions." However, it is also at this stage society will need to confront some of the legal and ethical issues bound to follow the large-scale fielding of agent technology. In the long term too, agents will also provide yet another design approach to constructing complex pieces of software.

Think of it this way—ISAs cannot yet fly, but it certainly appears they are beginning to walk.

The following is an excerpt from the book *The Rise of Endymion* by Dan Simmons, which is set in the far distant future. It is both fascinating and somewhat chilling. In this excerpt, Aenea, a child prophet of sorts, explains the history and development of the TechnoCore, their version of ISAs:

"Once upon a time," says Aenea, "more than a thousand standard years ago, . . . the only autonomous intelligences we humans knew of were us humans. We thought then that if humankind ever devised another intelligence that it would be the result of a huge project . . . a great mass of silicon and ancient amplification, switching, and detection devices called transistors and chips and circuit boards . . . a machine with lots of networking circuits, in other words, aping—if you will pardon the expression—the human brain in form and function.

"Of course, AIs did not evolve that way. They sort of slipped into existence when we humans were looking the other way.

" . . . the earliest AIs were dumb as dirt. Or perhaps the better metaphor would be that they were as dumb as early cellular life that was in the dirt. Some of the earliest hypercritters floating in the warm medium of the datasphere—which was also evolving—were 80-byte organisms inserted into a block of RAM in a virtual computer—a computer simulated by a computer. One of the first humans to release such creatures into the datasphere ocean was name Tom Ray and he was not an AI expert or computer programmer or cyberpuke, which they called hackers then—but was a biologist, an insect collector, botanist, and bird-watcher, and someone who had spent years collecting ants in the jungle for a pre-Hegira scientist name E. O. Wilson. . . . Tom Ray created a virtual computer—a simulated computer within his real computer—for his code-sequenced creations. And then he created an actual 80-byte code-sequence creature that could reproduce, die, and evolve in his computer-within-computer.

"The 80-byte copied itself into more 80-bytes. These 80-bytes proto-AI cell-things would have quickly filled their virtual universe, . . . but Tom Ray gave each 80-byte a date tag, gave them age in other words, and programmed in an executioner that he called the Reaper. The Reaper wandered through this virtual universe and harvested old 80-byte critters and nonviable mutants.

"But evolution, as it is wont to do, tried to outsmart the Reaper. A mutant 79-byte creature proved not only to be viable, but soon out-bred and outpaced the 80-bytes. The hyper-lifes, ancestors to our Core AIs, were just born but already they were optimizing their genomes. Soon a 45-byte organism had evolved and all but eliminated the earlier artificial lifeforms. As their creator, Tom Ray found this odd. 45-bytes did not include enough code to allow for reproduction. More than that, the 45s were dying off as the 80s disappeared. He did an autopsy on one of the 45-creatures.

"It turned out that all of the 45-bytes were parasites. They borrowed needed reproductive code from the 80s to copy themselves. The 79s, it turned out, were immune to the 45-parasite. But as the 80s and 45s moved toward extinction in their co-evolutionary downward spiral, a mutant of the 45s appeared. It was a 51-byte parasite and it could prey on the vital 79s. And so it went.

"By the early twenty-first century, there was a thriving biosphere of artificial life on Old Earth, both in the quickly evolving datasphere and in the macrosphere of human life. Although the breakthroughs of DNA-computing, bubble memories, standing wave-front parallel processing, and hyper-networking were just being explored, human designers had created silicon-based entities of remarkable ingenuity. And they had created them by the billions. Microchips were in everything from chairs to cans of beans on store shelves to groundcars to artificial human body parts. The machines had grown smaller and smaller until the average human home or office was filled with tens of thousands of them. A worker's chair would recognize her as soon as she sat, bring up the file she had been working on in her crude silicon computer, chat with another chip in a coffeemaker to heat up the coffee, enable the telecommunications grid to deal with calls and faxes, interact with the main house or office computer so that the temperature was optimal, and so forth. In their stores, microchips in the cans of beans on the shelves noted their own price and price changes, ordered more of themselves when they were running short, kept track of the consumers' buying habits, and interacted with the store and the other commodities in it. This web of interaction became as complex and busy as the bubble and froth of Old Earth's organic stew in its early oceans."

It has always been true that today's science fiction is tomorrow's fact. You can expect the line to blur even further as ISA-enhanced tools become standard equipment and standard operating procedure for us all.

18-6: SOME FINAL THOUGHTS ON THE FUTURE OF DSS TECHNOLOGIES

So we went to Atari and said, "Hey, we've got this amazing thing, even built with some of your parts, and what do you think about funding us? Or we'll give it to you. We just want to do it. Pay our salary, we'll come work for you." And they said, "No." So then we went to Hewlett-Packard, and they said, "Hey, we don't need you. You haven't even made it through college yet."
                                —STEVE JOBS, FOUNDER OF APPLE COMPUTERS, INC.

We don't like their sound, and guitar music is on the way out.
                                —DECCA RECORDING COMPANY REJECTING THE BEATLES, 1962

The future of a technology-dependent activity such as decision making cannot be easily envisioned without simultaneously looking at the future of the technology upon which it depends. This final section will focus on several issues regarding the future of computing technologies and their relationship to decision support.

WHO WILL LEAD US INTO THE FUTURE?

In January 1996, a summit conference was held for top IT suppliers. The 150-plus invited attendees represented top corporate, marketing, and sales executives of such companies as IBM, Microsoft, Compaq, Intel, AT&T, Sony, and NEC.

During the conference, attendees were polled for their opinions on a variety of industry issues, using a groupware-like "instant polling" technology. The two questions yielding the most intriguing responses were the following:

1. Who do you believe will be the IT industry's most influential supplier in the year 2000?
2. Who do you believe will be the most influential supplier in 2005?

Not surprisingly, the leading response for the year 2000 was Microsoft Corporation. The turn of the century was, after all, just $3\frac{1}{2}$ years away at that point. The general consensus among the attendees was that regardless of how Microsoft responds to the countless global changes being led by the emerging Internet, it will still influence a large portion of the marketplace as a residual effect of its current market position. The most interesting outcome, however, was the consensus among the group regarding the question about 2005: Far and away, the top vote getter was "a supplier that does not yet exist."

If the response to the second question seems unexpected, it certainly shouldn't. Since the advent of the personal computer, the dynamics in the computer industry in terms of leadership have been volatile. The now ubiquitous Microsoft (arguably the most influential member of the computer industry today) was essentially nonexistent prior to the introduction of the PC, and 7 of the top 20 North American computer suppliers today did not exist before the introduction of the PC. If the Internet continues to affect the global marketplace as it has to date, the conditions are highly favorable for a major supplier displacement.

When you look closely, the responses from the summit attendees were almost clairvoyant. The results of this poll suggest that a good number of computer industry leaders clearly see the changes being brought about by the Internet and sense how vulnerable their positions potentially are in the forthcoming period of major growth and change.

THE SILICON REVOLUTION

One major driving force behind technology change, to date, has been the advancements in processor speeds and capabilities brought about by the research and development efforts of the semiconductor industry. A current state-of-the-art silicon chip smaller than the size of your thumbnail contains the equivalent complexity of a comprehensive road map of the entire United States, including every interstate, every street, and every alley. Furthermore, this same thumbnail-size chip has the capacity to route traffic on this electronic "highway system" in a trillionth of a second.

Today's microprocessors are more powerful than those made yesterday, and those available next year will undoubtedly dwarf today's capacity. The raw power of silicon technology doubles every 18 months. This observation was first made by Gordon Moore, cofounder of Intel, more than 30 years ago, and it is now known as Moore's Law. Based on this law, we can safely predict that by the year 2004 silicon chips will be in production containing more than a billion transistors. A chip of this capacity is capable of meeting the needs of 42 central office telephone switches!

In 1992, the Semiconductors Industries Association sponsored the development and publication of a "national road map" for semiconductor technology. The essence of the road map is a series of 3-year interval projections of successfully smaller and more powerful devices with each generation of memory devices approximately four times greater in density than those of the previous generation. By the year 2007, it is estimated that the typical RAM memory chip will contain 16 gigabytes of memory and the typical CPU chip will operate in excess of 1,000 gigahertz compared to today's standards of 256 megabytes and 1.4 gigahertz, respectively.

BANDWIDTH IS ALMOST FREE

Simultaneous to the advancements of silicon technology with respect to increases in storage capacity and processing power, we see vast increases in the capabilities of various communications media including glass fibers, copper wires, and wireless communication systems. Scientists at Fujitsu and elsewhere already demonstrated the ability to send data over a single strand of glass the diameter of a human hair at a speed of 1 trillion bits per second. At this speed, every word from every issue of the *New York Times*, since it was first published, could be sent to a new location in just under 1 second.

As bandwidth increases, the cost of sending information drops proportionately. Some argue that in the future communication costs will be so cheap that it won't even be cost-effective to meter them. Some future-thinking communities are already taking an aggressive stance to ensure their participation in the communications revolution. All residents of Glasgow, Kentucky, for example, have access to the Internet at speeds of 2 million bits per second for a flat rate of $11.45 per month. This service is provided by Glasgow's power company, a local municipal utility that expanded its services from providing power to also providing cable TV and broadband digital communication services. America's power companies have already installed so much fiber-optic cable that they could be the second largest provider of telecommunications should they choose to.

NETWORK POWER GROWS, TOO

Advances in the technologies of computers and bandwidth combined to feed energy into the digital hurricane: the Internet. The Internet is a network of networks—a vast, dynamic communication system built from the bottom up. All participants on this network agree on a simple set of protocols that define how data are to be formatted and routed from one place to the next. As a result of these simple rules, the Internet is capable of displaying incredibly complex behavior, including its capacity to grow without collapsing under its own weight. The Internet is currently doubling in size every year. Homes, schools, businesses, libraries, and museums are connected to the Net, and each new connection adds value to the whole. This added value was first expressed by Bob Metcalfe, inventor of the Ethernet, who observed that the power of a network increases by the square of the number of users. This statement is now known as Metcalfe's Law and it, in combination with Moore's Law, forms the foundation of the communication revolution we are now experiencing.

The impact of the World Wide Web on decision making is likely to be profound. Unlike the Internet, which is doubling in size every year, the WWW is doubling its size approximately every 90 days. In 1996, the U.S. Postal Service delivered more than 185 billion pieces of first-class mail. In that same year, the Internet handled more than 1 trillion e-mail messages. The Web has democratized the publishing and accessibility of information in ways unanticipated even a few years ago. As FCC Chairman Reed Hundt expressed, "The communication age is connected to the greatest revolution in the history of information since the invention of the printing press." Some suggest that the Industrial Revolution increased productivity fiftyfold. In the 25 years since the invention of the microprocessor, computer power increased by a factor of more than 1,000, which is the equivalent of almost one Industrial Revolution per year! Now that's progress!

DREAMS ARE BECOMING REALITIES

It has always been fashionable for technologists to look out into the future and to dream about the events of tomorrow. The world of decision making will change as rapidly as the technology and world around it changes, and, because of this relationship, we can look at the velocity of technological change and use it as a basis for envisioning what problem solving will be like in the next century. What were once dreams are now the clear realities of the future. Let's look at some of the expected technological developments that could affect decision making beyond the year 2000.

The world chess champion is now a computer. Chess endured through the years as a measure of a human's ability to reason and to strategize into the future. Although IBM publicly announced, following its limited triumph over the reigning chess champion, Gary Kasparov, that it no longer intended to pursue the development of a chess-playing computer, the near-term improvements in decision support algorithms make a computerized chess champion a reality.

By 2005, translating telephones will emerge that will allow two people anywhere on the globe to speak to each other even if they do not speak the same language. This same core technology will be used to create practical speech-to-text translators that will convert speech into visual displays. Telephones will be able to be answered by an intelligent telephone answering machine that will converse briefly with the calling party to determine the nature and priority of the call.

Within the first decade of the next century, computers will come to dominate the educational environment. Courseware will exist that will be intelligent enough to understand and correct any inaccuracies in the conceptual model of a particular student. Multimedia technologies will allow students to interact with simulations of the systems and the personalities from history they are currently studying. This same intelligent technology will be used to create human biochemical simulators that will facilitate the design and testing of advanced medicines and pharmaceuticals. And somewhere between the year 2020 and the year 2070 a computer will pass the Turing test, thus marking the dawning of human-level intelligence in a machine.[2]

18-7: CHAPTER SUMMARY

This chapter, for that matter this entire text, was intended to whet the appetite of the reader rather than satisfy it. We are no longer entering the age of information—we are in it. The management of knowledge and the decisions of tomorrow represent new horizons and the challenges that come with such adventures. The purpose of management in the next century will be refocused from productivity of the firm to productivity of the firm's knowledge. Drucker was correct in identifying knowledge as the key organizational resource of the next century. The world's organizations will compete on a playing field of knowledge competency, and the successful managers will be those who can harness the power of technology to support solutions to complex problems. The challenge is yours.

> Heavier-than-air flying machines are simply impossible.
> —LORD KELVIN, PRESIDENT, ROYAL SOCIETY, 1895

> If I had thought about it, I wouldn't have done the experiment. The literature was full of examples that said you can't do this.
> —SPENCER SILVER, 3M CORPORATION, THE DISCOVERER OF THE UNIQUE
> ADHESIVES USED ON POST-IT NOTES

---

[2]The Turing test was invented by Alan M. Turing (1912–1954) as a method to determine the degree of humanlike intelligence displayed by a computer. An interrogator is connected to one person and one machine via a terminal and, therefore, cannot see either counterpart. The interrogator's task is to determine which of the two candidates is the machine and which is the human by asking each of them questions. If the interrogator cannot make the decision within a certain time (Turing proposed 5 minutes, but the exact amount is generally considered irrelevant), the machine is declared to be intelligent.

APPENDIX A

=⟋⟍⟋⟍⟋=

DECISION STYLE INVENTORY III

DECISION STYLE INVENTORY INSTRUCTIONS

1. Use *only* the following numbers to answer each question:

    8 when the question is *most* like you.
    4 when the question is *moderately* like you.
    2 when the question is *slightly* like you.
    1 when the question is *least* like you.

2. Each of the numbers must be inserted in the box below the answers to each question.
3. You may only use the 8, 4, 2, and 1, *once* for each question.
4. For example, the numbers you might use to answer a given question could look as follows:
    8 1 4 2.
5. Notice that each number has been used only once in the answers for a given question.
6. In answering the questions, think of how you *normally* act in a situation.
7. Choose the *first* response that comes to your mind when answering the questions.
8. There is no time limit in answering questions, and there are no right or wrong answers. You can change your mind.
9. Your responses reflect how you *feel* about the responses to the questions and what you *prefer* to do, *not* what you think is the right thing to do.

	I	*II*	*III*	*IV*
1. My prime objective is to:	Have a position with status	Be the best in my field	Achieve recognition for my work	Feel secure in my job
	☐	☐	☐	☐

Source: Decision Style Inventory III and Scoring Information, adapted from Rowe, A. J. and Boulgarides, J. D. (1994). *Managerial Decision Making*, Upper Saddle River, NJ: Prentice Hall. Used by permission, © 1985. All rights reserved.

	I	*II*	*III*	*IV*
2. I enjoy jobs that:	Are technical and well defined	Have considerable variety	Allow independent action	Involve people
3. I expect people working for me to be:	Productive and fast	Highly capable	Committed and responsive	Receptive to suggestions
4. In my job, I look for:	Practical results	The best solutions	New approaches or ideas	Good working environment
5. I communicate best with others:	On a direct one-to-one basis	In writing	By having a group discussion	In a formal meeting
6. In my planning I emphasize:	Current problems	Meeting objectives	Future goals	Developing people's careers
7. When faced with solving a problem I:	Rely on proven approaches	Apply careful analysis	Look for creative approaches	Rely on my feelings
8. When using information I prefer:	Specific facts	Accurate and complete data	Broad coverage of many options	Limited data that are easily understood
9. When I am not sure about what to do I:	Rely on intuition	Search for facts	Look for a possible compromise	Wait before making a decision
10. Whenever possible I avoid:	Long debates	Incomplete work	Using numbers or formulas	Conflict with others

	I	II	III	IV
11. I am especially good at:	Remembering dates and facts	Solving difficult problems	Seeing many possibilities	Interacting with others
12. When time is important I:	Decide and act quickly	Follow plans and priorities	Refuse to be pressured	Seek guidance and support
13. In social settings I generally:	Speak with others	Think about what is being said	Observe what is going on	Listen to a conversation
14. I am good at remembering:	People's names	Places we met	People's faces	People's personalities
15. The work I do provides me:	The power to influence others	Challenging assignments	Achievement of my personal goals	Acceptance by the group
16. I work well with those who are:	Energetic and ambitious	Self-confident	Open-minded	Polite and trusting
17. When under stress I:	Become anxious	Concentrate on the problem	Become frustrated	Am forgetful
18. Others consider me:	Aggressive	Disciplined	Imaginative	Supportive
19. My decisions typically are:	Realistic and direct	Systematic or abstract	Broad and flexible	Sensitive to the needs of others
20. I dislike:	Losing control	Boring work	Following rules	Being rejected

INSTRUCTIONS FOR SCORING THE DECISION STYLE INVENTORY

1. Total the points in each of the four columns—I, II, III, IV.
2. Total the sum of these four numbers. The sum of the four columns should be 300 points. Check your addition and that you have not repeated any numbers for a given question.
3. Place your scores in the appropriate box—I, II, III, IV in the following figure.
4. Refer to Chapter 2 for a more detailed description of the four quadrant characteristics.

Analytic II	**Conceptual** III
Directive I	**Behavioral** IV

REFERENCES

Chapter 1

Alter, S. L. 1980. *Decision Support Systems: Current Practices and Continuing Challenges.* Reading, MA: Addison-Wesley.

Anthony, R. N. 1965. *Planning and Control Systems: A Framework for Analysis.* Boston: Harvard University Graduate School of Business Administration.

Donovan, J. J., and S. E. Madnick. 1977. "Institutional and Ad Hoc Decision Support Systems and Their Effective Use." MIT Working Paper No. C15R-27, Cambridge, MA.

Gorry, G. A., and M. S. Scott Morton. 1989. "A Framework for Management Information Systems." *Sloan Management Review* 13(1):49–62.

Little, J. D. 1970. "Models and Managers: The Concept of a Decision Calculus." *Management Science* 16(8):B466–85.

Silver, M. S. 1991. "Decisional Guidance for Computer-Based Decision Support." *MIS Quarterly* 15(1):105–22.

Simon, H. A. 1960. *The New Science of Management Decision.* New York: Harper & Row.

Chapter 2

Adams, J. L. 1979. *Conceptual Blockbusting: A Guide to Better Ideas,* 2d ed. Stanford, CA: Stanford Alumni Association.

Barnard, C. I. 1938. *The Functions of the Executive.* Cambridge, MA: Harvard University Press.

Beach, L. R., and T. R. Mitchell. 1978. "A Contingency Model for the Selection of Decision Strategies." *Academy of Management Review* (July):439–50.

Clemen, R. T. 1991. *Making Hard Decisions: An Introduction to Decision Analysis.* Belmont, CA: Duxbury Press.

Clough, D. J. 1984. *Decisions in Public and Private Sectors.* Upper Saddle River, NJ: Prentice Hall.

Delbecq, A. L. 1967. "The Management of Decision-Making within the Firm: Three Strategies for Three Types of Decision-Making." *Academy of Management Journal.*

Etzioni, A. 1967. "Mixed-Scanning: A 'Third' Approach to Decision Making." *Public Administration Review* 27(5):385–92.

Geoffrion, A. M., and T. J. Van Roy. 1979. "Caution: Common Sense Planning Methods Can Be Hazardous to Your Corporate Health." *Sloan Management Review* 20(4):31.

Harrison, E. F. 1995. *The Managerial Decision-Making Process.* Boston: Houghton Mifflin Co.

Katona, G. 1953. "Rational Behavior and Economic Behavior." *Psychological Review* 60:313.

Keen, P. G., and M. S. Scott Morton. 1978. *Decision Support Systems: An Organizational Perspective.* Reading, MA: Addison-Wesley.

Lindblom, C. E. 1959. "The Science of 'Muddling Through.'" *Public Administration Review* 19(Spring):113–27.

Miller, G. A. 1956. "The Magical Number Seven, Plus or Minus Two: Some Limits on Our Capability for Processing Information." *Psychology Review* 63(2):81–97.

Mintzberg, H. 1973. *The Nature of Managerial Work.* Upper Saddle River, NJ: Prentice Hall.

Myers, I. B. 1962. *Manual for the Myers-Briggs Type Indicator*. Princeton, NJ: Educational Testing Services.

Rowe, A. J., and J. D. Boulgarides. 1994. *Managerial Decision Making*. Upper Saddle River, NJ: Prentice Hall.

Saaty, R. W. 1987. "The Analytic Hierarchy Process—What It Is and How It Is Used." *Mathematical Modeling* 9(3–5):161–76.

Simon, H. A. 1960. *The New Science of Management Decision*. New York: Harper & Row.

Sprague, R. H., Jr., and E. D. Carlson. 1982. *Building Effective Decision Support Systems*. Upper Saddle River, NJ: Prentice Hall.

Thompson, J. D. 1967. *Organizations in Action*. New York: McGraw-Hill.

Tversky, A. 1972. "Elimination by Aspects: A Theory of Choice." *Psychological Review* 79:281–99.

———. 1973. "Availability: A Heuristic for Judging Frequency and Probability." *Cognitive Psychology* 5:207–32.

Tversky, A., and D. Kahneman. 1974. "Judgment under Uncertainty: Heuristics and Biases." *Science* 185:1124–31.

Zanakis, S. H., and J. R. Evans. 1981. "Heuristic Optimization: Why, When, and How to Use It." *Interfaces* 11(5):84–92.

Chapter 3

Bowers, D. G., and S. L. Seashore. 1966. "Predicting Organizational Effectiveness with Four Factor Theory of Leadership." *Administrative Science Quarterly* 11 (September):238–63.

Culnan, M. J., and B. Gutek. 1989. Why Organizations Collect and Store Information. In *Information Systems and Decision Processes*, edited by E. A. Stohr and B. R. Konsynski. Los Alamitos, CA: IEEE Computer Society Press.

Deal, T. E., and A. A. Kennedy. 1982. *Corporate Cultures*. Reading, MA: Addison-Wesley.

Gore, W. J. 1964. *Administrative Decision Making: A Heuristic Model*. New York: Wiley.

Harrison, E. F. 1995. *The Managerial Decision-Making Process*. Boston: Houghton Mifflin Co.

Mintzberg, H. 1985. "The Organization as a Political Arena." *Journal of Management Studies* 21(2):133–55.

Pascale, R. T., and A. G. Athos. 1981. *The Art of Japanese Management*. New York: Simon and Schuster.

Patz, A. E., and A. J. Rowe. 1977. *Management Control and Decision System*. New York: Wiley.

Peter, L. J., and R. Hull. 1969. *The Peter Principle*. New York: Morrow.

Peters, T. J., and R. H. Waterman, Jr. 1982. *In Search of Excellence*. New York: Harper & Row.

Robbins, S. P. 1990. *Organization Theory: Structure, Design, and Applications*, 3d ed. Upper Saddle River, NJ: Prentice Hall.

Schein, E. H. 1985. *Organizational Culture and Leadership*. San Francisco: Jossey-Bass.

Stohr, E. D., and B. R. Konsynski, eds. 1992. *Information Systems and Decision Processes*. Los Alamitos, CA: IEEE Computer Society Press.

Swanson, E. B., and R. W. Zmud. 1989. ODSS Concepts and Architecture. In *Information Systems and Decision Processes*, edited by E. A. Stohr and B. R. Konsynski. Los Alamitos, CA: IEEE Computer Society Press.

Zaleznick, A. 1970. "Power and Politics in Organizational Life." *Harvard Business Review* (May–June):101–09.

Chapter 4

Beyth-Marom, R. 1982. "How Probable Is Probable? A Numerical Translation of Verbal Probability Expressions." *Journal of Forecasting* 1:257–69.

Clemen, R. T. 1991. *Making Hard Decisions: An Introduction to Decision Analysis*. Belmont, CA: Duxbury Press.

Davis, M. W. 1988. *Applied Decision Support.* Upper Saddle River, NJ: Prentice Hall.

De Finetti, B. 1964. La Prévision: Ses Lois Logiques, Ses Sources Subjectives. Translated by H. E. Kyburg. In *Studies in Subjective Probability*, edited by H. E. Kyburg, Jr., and H. E. Smokler (New York: Wiley). First published in *Annales de l'Institut Henri Poincaré* 7 (1937):1–68.

Golub, A. L. 1997. *Decision Analysis: An Integrated Approach.* New York: Wiley.

Howard, R. A. 1988. "Decision Analysis: Practice and Promise." *Management Science* 34(6):679–96.

Howard, R. A., and J. E. Matheson. 1968. An Introduction to Decision Analysis. In *Readings on the Principles and Applications of Decision Analysis.* Stanford, CA: Decision Analysis Group, SRI International.

Savage, L. J. 1954. *The Foundations of Statistics.* New York: Wiley.

Watson, S. R., and D. M. Buede. 1987. *Decision Synthesis: The Principles and Practice of Decision Analysis.* Cambridge: Cambridge University Press.

Chapter 5

Bavelas, A. 1948. "A Mathematical Model for Group Structures." *Applied Anthropology* 7:16–30.

Coleman, D., and R. Khanna. 1995. *Groupware: Technology and Applications.* Upper Saddle River, NJ: Prentice Hall.

DeSanctis, G., and R. B. Gallupe. 1987. "A Foundation for the Study of Group Decision Support Systems." *Management Science* 33(5):589–609.

Ellis, C. A., S. J. Gibbs, and G. L. Rein. 1991. "Groupware: Some Issues and Experiences." *Communications of the ACM* 34(1):38–59.

Fellers, J. W. 1987. Skills and Techniques for Knowledge Acquisition. Indiana University Working Paper Series.

George, J. F. 1991. "The Conceptualization and Development of Organizational Decision Support Systems." *Journal of Management Information Systems* 8(3):109–25.

Gray, P. 1981. The SMU Decision Room Project. In *Transactions of the First International Conference on Decision Support Systems*, edited by D. Young and P. G. W. Keen. Providence, RI: The Institute of Management Sciences.

Hamilton, J., S. Baker, and B. Vlasic. 1996. "The New Workplace." *Business Week* 29 (April).

Harrison, E. F. 1986. *Policy, Strategy, and Managerial Action.* Boston: Houghton Mifflin Co.

———. 1995. *The Managerial Decision-Making Process.* Boston: Houghton Mifflin Co.

Holsapple, C. W. 1991. "Decision Support in Multiparticipant Decision Making." *Journal of Computer Information Systems* (Summer):37–45.

Homans, G. C. 1950. *The Human Group.* New York: Harcourt, Brace & Co.

Huber, G. P., J. S. Valacich, and L. M. Jessup. 1993. A Theory of the Effects of Group Support Systems on an Organization's Nature and Decisions. In *Group Decision Support Systems: New Perspectives*, edited by L. M. Jessup and J. S. Valacich. New York: Macmillan.

Janis, I. L. 1982. *Groupthink*, 2d ed. Boston: Houghton Mifflin Co.

Kraemer, K. F., and J. L. King. 1988. "Computer-Based Systems for Cooperative Work and Group Decision Making." *ACM Computing Surveys* 20(2):115–46.

Kunz, W., and H. Rittel. 1970. Issues as Elements of Information Systems. Working Paper No. 131. University of California–Berkeley, Center for Planning and Development Research.

Leavitt, H. 1951. "Some Effects of Certain Communication Patterns on Group Performance." *Journal of Abnormal and Social Psychology* 46.

Lindstone, H., and M. Turoff. 1975. *The Delphi Method: Technology and Applications.* Reading, MA: Addison-Wesley.

Marakas, G. M., and J. T. Wu. 1997. A Taxonomy of Multiparticipant Decision Structures. University of Maryland Working Paper Series in Information Systems.

Nunamaker, J. F., Jr., A. R. Dennis, J. S. Valacich, D. R. Vogel, and J. F. George. 1993. Group Support Systems Research: Experience from the Lab and the Field. In *Group Decision Support Systems: New Perspectives*, edited by L. Jessup and J. Valacich. New York: Macmillan.

Shull et al. 1970. *Organizational Decision Making*. City, ST.

Van de Ven, A. H., and A. L. Delbecq. 1971. "Nominal Versus Interacting Group Processes for Committee Decision Making." *Academy of Management Journal* 14:129–39.

Vogel, D. R., J. F. Nunamaker, Jr., W. B. Martz, Jr., R. Grohowski, and C. McGoff. 1989. "Electronic Meeting Systems Experience at IBM." *Journal of Management Information Systems* 6(3):25–43.

Vroom, V. H., and P. W. Yetton. 1973. Leadership Behavior on Standardized Cases. Technical Report No. 3. New Haven, CT: Yale University Press.

Chapter 6

Crockett, F. 1992. "Revitalizing Executive Information Systems." *Sloan Management Review* 38(Summer):17–29.

Dobrzeniecki, A. 1994. Executive Information Systems. IIT Research Institute White Paper Series.

Jones, J. W., and R. McLeod. 1986. "The Structure of Executive Information Systems: An Exploratory Analysis." *Decision Sciences* 17(2):220–49.

Millet, I., and C. H. Mawhinney. 1992. "Executive Information Systems—A Critical Perspective." *Information and Management* 23(1):83–93.

Peters, T., and R. H. Waterman. 1982. *In Search of Excellence*. New York: Harper & Row.

Rockart, J. F. 1979. "Chief Executives Define Their Own Data Needs." *Harvard Business Review* (March–April).

Rockart, J. F., and M. E. Treacy. 1982. "The CEO Goes On-Line." *Harvard Business Review* 60(1):82–87.

Watson, H. J., G. Houdeshel, and R. K. Rainer, Jr. 1997. *Building Executive Information Systems and Other Decision Support Applications*. New York: Wiley.

Watson, H. J., R. K. Rainer, and C. Koh. 1991. "Executive Information Systems: A Framework for Development and a Survey of Current Practices." *MIS Quarterly* 15(1):13–31.

Watson, H. J., S. Singh, and D. Holmes. 1995. "Development Practices for Executive Information Systems: Findings of a Field Study." *Decision Support Systems* 14(2):171–85.

Chapter 7

Berry, D. C., and D. E. Broadbent. 1987. "Expert Systems and the Man-Machine Interface Part Two: The User Interface." *Expert Systems* 4(1):18–28.

Gerrity, T. P., Jr. 1971. "The Design of Man-Machine Decision Systems: An Application to Portfolio Management." *Sloan Management Review* 12(2):59–75.

Hayes-Roth, F., D. A. Waterman, and D. Lenat, eds. 1983. *Building Expert Systems*. Reading, MA: Addison-Wesley.

Keen, P. G., and M. S. Scott Morton. 1978. *Decision Support Systems: An Organizational Perspective*. Reading, MA: Addison-Wesley.

Klein, M. R., and L. B. Methlie. 1995. *Knowledge-Based Decision Support Systems*, 2d ed. New York: Wiley.

Liebowitz, J., 1990. *The Dynamics of Decision Support Systems and Expert Systems*. Chicago: Dryden Press.

Minsky, M. 1975. A Framework for Representing Knowledge. In *The Psychology of Computer*

Vision, edited by P. Winston. New York: McGraw-Hill.

Rich, E., and K. Knight. 1991. *Artificial Intelligence*. New York: McGraw-Hill.

Chapter 8

Drucker, P. F. 1993. *Post-Capitalist Society*. New York: Harper Business.

Ericsson, K. A., and H. A. Simon. 1984. *Protocol Analysis: Verbal Reports as Data*. Cambridge, MA: MIT Press.

Feigenbaum, E. 1977. "The Art of Artificial Intelligence: Themes and Case Studies of Knowledge Engineering." In *Proceedings of the Fifth International Joint Conference on Artificial Intelligence*, pp. 1014–29. Cambridge, MA: MIT Press.

Gaines, B. R. 1995. The Collective Stance in Modeling Expertise in Individuals and Organizations. Knowledge Science Institute. University of Calgary. Available online from ksi.cpsc.ucalgary.ca/articles/Collective/ (accessed January 1998).

Gaines, B. R., and M. L. G. Shaw. 1995. *Knowledge Acquisition Tools Based on Personal Construct Psychology*. Knowledge Science Institute. University of Calgary. Available online from ksi.cpsc.ucalgary.ca/articles/KBS/KER/ (accessed January 1998).

Hayes-Roth, B. 1985. "A Blackboard Architecture for Control." *Artificial Intelligence* 26:251–321.

Holsapple, C. W., and A. B. Whinston. 1988. *The Information Jungle*. Homewood, IL: Dow Jones-Irwin.

Kelly, G. 1955. *The Psychology of Personal Constructs*. New York: Norton.

Kim, J., and J. F. Courtney. 1988. "A Survey of Knowledge Acquisition Techniques and Their Relevance to Managerial Problem Domains." *Decision Support Systems* 4(October):269–85.

Klein, M. R., and L. B. Methlie. 1995. *Knowledge-Based Decision Support Systems*, 2d ed. New York: Wiley.

Marakas, G. M., and J. J. Elam. 1997. "Creativity Enhancement in Problem Solving: Through Software or Process?" *Management Science* 43(8):1136–46.

Marcot, B. 1987. "Testing Your Knowledge Base." *AI Expert* (August).

Newell, A. 1982. "The Knowledge Level." *Artificial Intelligence* 18:87–127.

Petrie, C., ed. 1992. *Enterprise Integration Modeling*. Cambridge, MA: MIT Press.

van Lohuizen, C. W. W. 1986. "Knowledge Management and Policymaking." *Knowledge Creation, Diffusion, Utilization* 8(1).

Chapter 9

Brule, J. F. 1985. *Fuzzy Systems—A Tutorial*. Available online from www.austinlinks.com/Fuzzy/tutorial.html (accessed January 1998).

Dhar, V., and R. Stein. 1997. *Intelligent Decision Support Methods*. Upper Saddle River, NJ: Prentice Hall.

NIBS Pte, Ltd. 1996. *NeuroForecaster Genetica Software Package*. Available online from www.singapore.com/products/nfga (accessed November 1997).

Wayner, P. 1991. "Genetic Algorithms." *Byte* (January): 361–64.

Chapter 10

APT Data Group. 1996. *Briefing Paper: What is Metadata?* Available online from www.computerwire.com/bulletinsuk/212e_1a6.htm (accessed October 1997).

Bischoff, J., and T. Alexander. 1997. *Data Warehouse: Practical Advice from the Experts*. Upper Saddle River, NJ: Prentice Hall.

Inmon, W. H. 1992a. *Building the Data Warehouse.* New York: Wiley.

———. 1992b. "EIS and the Data Warehouse." *Database Programming and Design* (November).

Kelly, S. 1994. *Data Warehousing: The Route to Mass Customization.* New York: Wiley.

Kozar, D. 1997. The Seven Deadly Sins. In *Data Warehouse: Practical Advice from the Experts,* edited by J. Bischoff and T. Alexander. Upper Saddle River, NJ: Prentice Hall.

Chapter 11

Codd, E. F., S. B. Codd, and T. S. Clynch. 1993. "Beyond Decision Support." *Computerworld* 26 (July).

Gray, P. 1997. The New DSS: Data Warehouses, OLAP, MDD, and KDD. In *Proceedings of the Americas Conference on Information Systems,* edited by J. M. Carey, pp. 917–19. Phoenix, AZ: Association for Information Systems.

Inmon, W. H., J. D. Welch, and K. L. Glassey. 1997. *Managing the Data Warehouse.* New York: Wiley.

Chapter 12

Brynjolfsson, E., and L. M. Hitt. 1998. "Beyond the Productivity Paradox." *Communications of the ACM* 41(8):49–55.

Chapter 14

Alavi, M., and I. Weiss. 1986. "Managing the Risks Associated with End-User Computing." *Journal of MIS* (Winter).

Arinza, B. 1991. "A Contingency Model of DSS Development Methodology." *Journal of MIS* (Summer).

Blanning, R. W. 1979. "The Functions of a Decision Support System." *Information and Management* 2(September):71–96.

Courbon, J. C., J. Grajew, and J. Tolovi, Jr. 1980. "Design and Implementation of Decision Support Systems." 14.

Galletta, D. F., K. S. Hartzel, S. E. Johnson, J. L. Joseph, and S. Rustagi. 1996. "Spreadsheet Presentation and Error Detection: An Experimental Study." *Journal of MIS* 13(3):45–63.

Henderson, J. C., and R. S. Ingraham. 1982. Prototyping for DSS: A Critical Appraisal. In *Decision Support Systems,* edited by M. Ginzberg et al. New York: North-Holland.

Holsapple, C. W., S. Park, and A. B. Whinston. 1993. Framework for DSS Interface Development. In *Recent Developments in Decision Support Systems,* edited by C. Holsapple and A. Whinston. Berlin: Springer-Verlag.

Janvrin, D., and J. Morrison. 1996. Factors Influencing Risks and Outcomes in End-User Development. In *Proceedings of the Twenty-Ninth Annual HICSS Conference,* vol. 2. Los Alamitos, CA: IEEE Computer Society Press.

Lotfi, V., and C. Pegels. 1996. *Decision Support Systems for Operations Management and Management Science,* 3d ed. Homewood, IL: Irwin.

Moore, J. H., and M. G. Chang. 1983. Meta-Design Considerations in Building DSS. In *Building Decision Support Systems,* edited by J. L. Bennett. Reading, MA: Addison-Wesley.

Saxena, K. B. C. 1992. DSS Development Methodologies: A Comparative Review. In *Proceedings of the Twenty-Fifth Annual Hawaii International Conference on System Sciences.* Los Alamitos, CA: IEEE Computer Society Press.

Sprague, R. H., Jr., and E. C. Carlson. 1982. *Building Effective Decision Support Systems.* Upper Saddle River, NJ: Prentice Hall.

Walls, J., and E. Turban. 1992. "Selecting Controls for Computer-Based Information Systems." *Accounting Management Information Systems* (October).

Chapter 15

Alter, S. L. 1980. *Decision Support Systems: Current Practices and Continuing Challenges.* Reading, MA: Addison-Wesley.

Boehm, B. W., J. R. Brown, H. Kaspar, M. Lipow, G. McLeod, and M. Merritt. 1978. *Characteristics of Software Quality.* Amsterdam: North-Holland.

Davis, F. 1989. "Perceived Usefulness, Perceived Ease of Use, and User Acceptance of Information Technology." *MIS Quarterly* 13(3):319–42.

Dickson, G., and R. Powers. 1973. MIS Project Management: Myths, Opinions, and Realities. In *Information System Administration*, edited by F. W. McFarlan et al. New York: Holt, Rinehart & Winston.

Ginzberg, M. J. 1975. "A Process Approach to Management Science Implementation." Ph.D. dissertation. Massachusetts Institute of Technology.

———. 1976. "A Study of the Implementation Process." Paper presented at Implementation II: An International Conference on the Implementation of Management Science in Social Organizations, University of Pittsburgh.

Ives, B., M. H. Olson, and J. J. Baroudi. 1983. "The Measurement of User Information Satisfaction." *Communications of the ACM* 26(10):785–93.

Klein, M. R., and L. B. Methlie. 1995. *Knowledge-Based Decision Support Systems*, 2d ed. New York: Wiley.

Kolb, D. A., and A. L. Frohman. 1970. "An Organization Development Approach to Consulting." *Sloan Management Review* 12(4):51–65.

Marakas, G. M., and S. Hornik. 1996. "Passive Resistance Misuse: Overt Support and Covert Recalcitrance in IS Implementation." *European Journal of Information Systems* 5:208–19.

Meador, C. L., M. J. Guyote, and P. G. W. Keen. 1984. "Setting Priorities for DSS Development." *MIS Quarterly* 8(2).

Min, H., and S. B. Eom. 1994. "An Integrated Decision Support System for Global Logistics." *International Journal of Physical Distribution and Logistics Management* 24(1):3–23.

Schein, E. H. 1956. "The Chinese Indoctrination Program for Prisoners of War." *Psychiatry* 19:149–72.

Zand, D. E., and R. E. Sorenson. 1975. "Theory of Change and the Effective Use of Management Science." *Administrative Science Quarterly* 20(4):532–95.

Chapter 16

Ackoff, R. L., and E. Vergara, 1981. "Creativity in Problem-Solving and Planning: A Review." *European Journal of Operations Research* 7:1–13.

Amabile, T. M. 1983. *The Social Psychology of Creativity.* New York: Springer-Verlag.

Brustoloni, J. C. 1991. Autonomous Agents: Characterization and Requirements. Carnegie-Mellon Technical Report CMU-CS-91-204. Pittsburgh: Carnegie Mellon University.

Clark, R. E. 1983. "Reconsidering Research on Learning from Media." *Review of Educational Research* 53(4):445–59.

de Bono, E. 1970. *Lateral Thinking: Creativity Step by Step.* New York: Harper & Row.

Delbecq, A. L., A. H. Van de Ven, and D. H. Gustafson. 1975. *Group Techniques for Program Planning.* Glenview, IL: Scott, Foresman.

Elam, J. J., and M. Mead. 1990. "Can Software Influence Creativity?" *Information Systems Research* 1(1):1–23.

Koberg, D., and J. Bagnall. 1976. *The Universal Traveler*. Los Altos, CA: William Kaufmann.

Marakas, G. M., and J. J. Elam. 1997. "Creativity Enhancement in Problem Solving: Through Software or Process?" *Management Science* 43(8):1136–46.

Osborn, A. F. 1963. *Applied Imagination*, 3d ed. New York: Scribner.

Ripple, R. E. 1977. "Communication, Education, and Creativity." *Contemporary Educational Psychology* 2.

Rowe, A. J., and J. D. Boulgarides. 1994. *Managerial Decision Making*. Upper Saddle River, NJ: Prentice Hall.

Seiffge, I. 1974. *Probleme und Ergebnisse der Kreativitaetsforschung*. Bern: Hans Huber.

Standler, R. B. 1998. "Creativity in Science and Engineering." Available online at www.rbs0.com/create.htm (accessed September 21, 2001).

Tversky, A., and D. Kahneman. 1974. "Judgment Under Uncertainty: Heuristics and Biases." *Science* 185:1124–31.

VanGundy, A. B. *Techniques of Structured Problem Solving*, 2d ed. New York: Van Nostrand Reinhold.

Chapter 17

Brustoloni, J. C. 1991. Autonomous Agents: Characterization and Requirements. Carnegie-Mellon Technical Report CMU-CS-91-204. Pittsburgh: Carnegie Mellon University.

Franklin S., and A. Graesser. 1996. Is It an Agent, or Just a Program?: A Taxonomy for Autonomous Agents. In *Proceedings of the Third International Workshop on Agent Theories, Architectures, and Languages*. Berlin: Springer-Verlag.

Jacobs, I., J. Gunderson, and E. Hansen, eds. *W3C Candidate Recommendation*, 09-12-2001. Available online from *www.w3.org/TR/2001/CR-UAAG10-20010912/* (accessed January 16, 2002).

Janca, P. 1996. *Intelligent Agents: Technology and Application*. Norwell, MA: GiGa Information Group.

Lee, J. K. W., D. W. Cheung, and B. Kao. 1997. "Intelligent Agents for Matching Information Providers and Consumers of the World Wide Web." In *Proceedings of the Thirtieth Hawaii International Conference on Systems Sciences*. Los Alamitos, CA: IEEE Computer Society Press.

Marakas, G. M., R. D. Johnson, and J. Palmer. 2000. "A Theoretical Model of Differential Social Attributions Toward Computing Technology: When the Metaphor Becomes the Model." *International Journal of Human-Computer Studies* 52(4):719–50.

Chapter 18

Dobrzeniecki, A. 1994. *Executive Information Systems*. IIT Research Institute White Paper Series. Available online at mtiac.hq.iitri.com/MTIAC/pubs/eis/eis.txt (January 16, 2002).

Hundt, R. 1997. "The Internet: From Here to Ubiquity." *IEEE Computer* 30(10):122–24.

Kersten, G. E., and D. B. Meister. 1993. *Decision Support Systems: An Overview of Research Directions and Applications*. Available online

from www.business.carleton.ca/~gregory/papers/idrc_report_93/ (January 16, 2002).

Simmons, D. 1997. *The Rise of Endymion*. New York: Bantam Spectra.

Toffler, A. 1970. *Future Shock*. New York: Random House.

INDEX